Race, Identity, and Citizenship

Race, Identity, and Citizenship
A Reader

Edited by

**Rodolfo D. Torres
Louis F. Mirón
Jonathan Xavier Inda**

BLACKWELL
Publishers

Copyright © Blackwell Publishers Ltd 1999

First published 1999

Reprinted 2000

Blackwell Publishers Inc.
350 Main Street
Malden , Massachusetts 02148
USA

Blackwell Publishers Ltd
108 Cowley Road
Oxford OX4 1JF
 UK

Library of Congress Cataloging-in-Publication Data

Race, identity, and citizenship : a reader / edited by Rodolfo D. Torres,
Louis F. Mirón, Jonathan Xavier Inda.
        p.   cm.
  Includes bibliographical references (p.   ) and index.
  ISBN 0–631–21021—0 (alk. paper). – ISBN 0–631–21022–9 (alk. paper)
  1. Race relations. 2. Ethnic relations. 3. Group identity.
  4. Pluralism (Social Sciences) 5. Multiculturalism. 6. United States—
  Race relations. 7. United States—Ethnic realtions.
  I. Torres, Roldolfo D., 1949– . II. Mirón, Louis F. III. Inda,
  Jonathan Xavier.
  HT1521.R2354   1999
  305.8'00973—dc21   98–31141
                                                           CIP

British Library Cataloguing in Publication Data

A CIP catalogue record for this book is available from the British Library.

Typeset in 10½ on 12pt Sabon by
Grahame & Grahame Editorial, Brighton

Printed in Great Britain by TJ International Ltd, Padstow, Cornwall

This book is printed on acid-free paper

Contents

List of Contributors   viii

Acknowledgments   x

Introduction   1

PART I   MAPPING THE LANGUAGES OF RACISM   17

1   Does "Race" Matter? Transatlantic Perspectives   19
    on Racism after "Race Relations"
    Robert Miles and Rodolfo D. Torres

2   "I Know it's Not Nice, But . . . "   39
    The Changing Face of "Race"
    Colette Guillaumin

3   The Contours of Racialization: Structures,   47
    Representations and Resistance in the United States
    Stephen Small

4   Marxism, Racism, and Ethnicity   65
    John Solomos and Les Back

5   Postmodernism and the Politics of   79
    Racialized Identities
    Louis F. Mirón

PART II   CRITICAL MULTIRACIAL FEMINISMS   101

6   Theorizing Difference from Multiracial Feminism   103
    Maxine Baca Zinn and Bonnie Thornton Dill

7   Ethnicity, Gender Relations and Multiculturalism   112
    Nira Yuval-Davis

8   What's in a Name? Womanism, Black   126
    Feminism, and Beyond
    Patricia Hill Collins

PART III   FASHIONING MIXED RACE   139

       9   The Colorblind Multiracial Dilemma: 141
           Racial Categories Reconsidered
           john a. powell

      10   Multiracial Asians: Models of Ethnic Identity   158
           Maria P. P. Root

      11   Cipherspace: Latino Identity Past and Present   169
           J. Jorge Klor de Alva

PART IV   THE COLOR(S) OF WHITENESS   181

      12   Establishing the Fact of Whiteness   183
           John Hartigan, Jr.

      13   Constructions of Whiteness in European   200
           and American Anti-Racism
           Alastair Bonnett

      14   The Labor of Whiteness, the Whiteness of Labor,   219
           and the Perils of Whitewishing
           Michael Eric Dyson

      15   The Trickster's Play: Whiteness in the   225
           Subordination and Liberation Process
           Aída Hurtado

PART V   CULTURAL CITIZENSHIP, MULTICULTURALISM,   245
           AND THE STATE

      16   Citizenship   247
           Richard Delgado

      17   Cultural Citizenship, Inequality, and   253
           Multiculturalism
           Renato Rosaldo

      18   Cultural Citizenship as Subject Making: 262
           Immigrants Negotiate Racial and Cultural
           Boundaries in the United States
           Aihwa Ong

PART VI   LOCATING CLASS   295

      19   The Site of Class   297
           Edna Bonacich

      20   Between Nationality and Class   304
           Stanley Aronowitz

21   Class Racism   322
     Étienne Balibar

PART VII   GLOBALIZED FUTURES AND RACIALIZED   335
           IDENTITIES

22   Multiculturalism and Flexibility: 337
     Some New Directions in Global Capitalism
     Richard P. Appelbaum

23   Analytic Borderlands: Race, Gender and   355
     Representation in the New City
     Saskia Sassen

24   Globalization, the Racial Divide, and a   373
     New Citizenship
     Michael C. Dawson

PART VIII CRITICAL ENGAGEMENTS   387

25   Interview with Stuart Hall: Culture and Power   389
     Peter Osborne and Lynne Segal

26   Angela Y. Davis: Reflections on Race, Class, and   413
     Gender in the USA
     Lisa Lowe

Index   431

Contributors

Richard P. Appelbaum is Professor of Sociology, University of California, Santa Barbara.

Stanley Aronowitz is Professor of Sociology, Graduate Center of the City University of New York.

Maxine Baca Zinn is Professor of Sociology, Michigan State University.

Les Back is Professor of Sociology, Goldsmiths' College, University of London, London, UK.

Étienne Balibar is Professor of Philosophy, University of Paris X.

Edna Bonacich is Professor of Sociology, University of California, Riverside.

Alastair Bonnett is Professor of Human Geography, University of Newcastle upon Tyne, UK.

Angela Y. Davis is Professor of History of Consciousness, University of California, Santa Cruz.

Michael C. Dawson is Professor of Political Science, University of Chicago.

Richard Delgado is Professor of Law, University of Colorado.

Michael Eric Dyson is Visiting Professor of African-American Studies, Columbia University.

Bonnie Thorton Dill is Professor of Women's Studies, University of Maryland, College Park.

Colette Guillaumin is Head of Research at the National Centre for Scientific Research, Paris.

Stuart Hall recently retired from his position of Professor of Sociology, The Open University, London, UK.

John Hartigan, Jr. is Professor of Anthropology, Knox College, Illinois.

Patricia Hill Collins is Professor of African-American Studies, University of Cincinnati.

Aída Hurtado is Professor of Psychology, University of California, Santa Cruz.

Jonathan Xavier Inda is Professor of Chicano Studies, University of California, Santa Barbara.

J. Jorge Klor de Alva is President of the University of Phoenix.

Lisa Lowe is Professor of Comparative Literature, University of California, San Diego.

Robert Miles is Professor and Chair of Sociology, University of Glasgow, Glasgow, UK.

Louis F. Mirón is Professor of Education and Social Sciences and Chair of Department of Education, University of California, Irvine.

Aihwa Ong is Professor of Anthropology, University of California, Berkeley.

Peter Osborne is Professor of Middlesex University, London, UK.

john a. powell is Professor of Law, University of Minnesota.

Maria P. P. Root is Professor of American Ethnic Studies, University of Washington.

Renato Rosaldo is Professor of Anthropology, Stanford University.

Saskia Sassen is Professor of Sociology, University of Chicago.

Lynne Segal is a Professor at Middlesex University, London, UK.

Stephen Small is Professor of African-American Studies, University of California, Berkeley.

John Solomos is Professor of Sociology and Social Policy, University of Southampton, Southampton, UK.

Rodolfo D. Torres is Professor of Public Policy and Chicano Studies, California State University, Long Beach, and Visiting Professor of Education, University of California, Irvine.

Nira Yuval-Davis is a Professor of Gender and Ethnic Studies, University of Greenwich, London, UK.

Acknowledgments

We would like to thank Susan Rabinowitz, our acquisitions editor at Blackwell Publishers for her support; she is a fine and able editor. Also at Blackwell, we would like to thank Anthony Grahame for his editorial assistance. We are especially grateful to both Jennifer A. Schwarz and Cheryl Craft in the Department of Education, University of California, Irvine, for their research assistance and technical support. A special thank you to Ricardo Duffy for his contribution to the cover art.

The authors and publishers gratefully acknowledge the following for permission to reproduce copyright material:

1   Does "Race" Matter? Transatlantic Perspectives on Racism after "Race Relations" (originally titled Does "Race" matter? Transatlantic Perspectives on Race Relations) by Robert Miles and Rodolfo D. Torres (1996). In Vered Amit-Talai and Caroline Knowles (eds), *Re-situating Identities: The politics of race, ethnicity, and culture* (adapted from chapter 1, pp. 24–46), Ontario, Canada: Broadview Press.

2   "I know it's not nice, but . . . " The changing face of "race" by Colette Guillaumin (1995). In *Racism, Sexism, Power and Ideology*, London and New York: Routledge.

3   The Contours of Racialization: Structures, representations and resistance in the United States by Stephen Small. Previously unpublished.

4   Marxism, Racism, and Ethnicity by John Solomos and Les Back (1995). *American Behavioral Scientist*, 38 (3), 407–20. Reprinted by permission of Sage Publications, Inc., Thousand Oaks.

5   Postmodernism and the Politics of Racialized Identities by Louis F. Mirón (1996). In *The Social Construction of Urban Schooling: Situating the crisis* (adapted from chapter 4: Postmodernism and the politics of urban pedagogy, pp. 101–34), Creeskill, NJ: Hampton Press. Reprinted with permission of Hampton Press.

6   Theorizing Difference from Multiracial Feminism by Maxine Baca Zinn and Bonnie Thornton Dill (1996). *Feminist Studies*, 22 (2), 321–31.

7 Ethnicity, Gender Relations and Multiculturalism by Nira Yuval-Davis (1997). In Phina Werbner and Tariq Modood (eds), *Debating Cultural Hybridity: Multi-cultural identities and the politics of anti-racism* (pp. 193–208), London: Zed Books.

8 What's in a Name? Womanism, Black Feminism, and Beyond by Patricia Hill Collins. *The Black Scholar*, 26 (1), 9–17.

9 The Colorblind Multiracial Dilemma: Racial categories reconsidered by john a. powell (1997). *University of San Francisco Law Review*, 31 (4), 789–806.

10 Multiracial Asians: Model of ethnic identity by Maria P. P. Root (1997). *Amerasia Journal*, 23 (1), 29–41.

11 Cipherspace: Latino identity past and present by J. Jorge Klor de Alva. Previously unpublished.

12 Establishing the Fact of Whiteness by John Hartigan, Jr. (1997). Reproduced by permission of the American Anthropological Association from *American Anthropologist*, 99 (3), (September), 495–505. Not for further reproduction.

13 Constructions of Whiteness in European and American Anti-Racism by Alastair Bonnett (1997). In Phina Werbner and Tariq Modood (eds), *Debating Cultural Hybridity: Multi-cultural identities and the politics of anti-racism* (pp. 173–192), London: Zed Books.

14 The Labor of Whiteness, the Whiteness of Labor, and the Perils of Whitewishing by Michael Eric Dyson (1997). In Steven Fraser and Joshua B. Freeman (eds), *Audacious Democracy: Labor, intellectuals, and the social reconstruction of America* (pp. 164–72), Copyright © 1997. Boston: Houghton Mifflin. Co. Reprinted by permission of Houghton Mifflin Company. All rights reserved.

15 The Trickster's Play: Whiteness in the subordination and liberation process by Aída Hurtado (1996). In *The Color of Privilege: Three blasphemies on race and feminism* (adapted from chapter 4: On a reflexive theory of gender subordination), Ann Arbor: University of Michigan Press.

16 Citizenship by Richard Delgado (1997). In Juan F. Perea (ed.), *Immigrants Out! The new nativism and the anti-immigrant impulse in the United States* (pp. 318–23), New York: New York University Press.

17 Cultural Citizenship, Inequality, and Multiculturalism by Renato Rosaldo (1997). In William V. Flores and Rina Benmayor (eds), *Latino Cultural Citizenship: Claiming identity, space, and rights* (pp. 27–38), Boston: Beacon Press.

18   Cultural Citizenship as Subject Making: Immigrants negotiate racial and
     cultural boundaries in the United States by Aihwa Ong (1996). *Current
     Anthropology,* 37 (5), 737–62. Chicago: The University of Chicago Press.

19   The Site of Class (originally titled Locating Class) by Edna Bonacich (1995).
     In Gary Okihiro, Marilyn Alquizola, Dorothy Fujita Rony, and K. Scott
     Wong (eds), *Privileging Positions: The sites of Asian American studies*
     (pp. 67–74), Pullman, WA: Washington State University Press.

20   Between Nationality and Class by Stanley Aronowitz (1997). *Harvard
     Educational Review,* 67 (2) (Summer), 188–207. Copyright © 1997 by the
     President and Fellows of Harvard College. All rights reserved.

21   Class Racism by Étienne Balibar. (1988). In Montserrat Guibernau and
     John Rex (eds), *The Ethnicity Reader: Nationalism, multiculturalism and
     migration.* (pp. 318–29), Cambridge: Polity Press. Copyright © *Race,
     Nation, Class, les Identitès Ambiguîs* (Editions La Dècouverte).

22   Multiculturalism and Flexibility: Some new directions in global capitalism
     by Richard P. Appelbaum (1991). In Avery F. Gordon and Christopher
     Newfield (eds), *Mapping Multiculturalism* (pp. 297–316), Minneapolis:
     University of Minnesota Press.

23   Analytic Borderlands: Race, Gender and Representation in the New City by
     Saskia Sassen (1996). In Anthony D. King (ed.), *Re-Presenting the City:
     Ethnicity, capital and culture in the 21st-century metropolis* (pp. 183–202),
     New York: New York University Press and Macmillan Press.

24   Globalization, the Racial Divide, and a New Citizenship by Michael C.
     Dawson (1997). In Stanley B. Greenberg and Theda Skocpol (eds), *The New
     Majority: Toward a popular progressive politics* (pp. 264–78), New Haven:
     Yale University Press.

25   Interview with Stuart Hall: Culture and Power by Peter Osborne and Lynne
     Segal (1997). *Radical Philosophy,* 86 (Nov./Dec.), 24–41.

26   Angela Y. Davis: Reflections on Race, Class, and Gender in the USA by Lisa
     Lowe (1997). In Lisa Lowe and David Lloyd (eds), *The Politics of Culture
     in the Shadow of Capital* (pp. 303–23), Copyright © Durham, NC: Duke
     University Press. Reprinted with permission.

The publishers apologize for any errors or omissions in the above list and would
be grateful to be notified of any corrections that should be incorporated in the
next edition or reprint of this book.

Introduction

> The first task of social science is to deconstruct common sense categories and to set up rigorous analytic concepts in their place. Here, it appears to us that an excessively vague use of the vocabulary of "race" should be rejected, and that one should resist the extensions which banalise the evil, or remove its specificity.
>
> *Michel Wieviorka (1997)*

In recent years, race and ethnicity have been the focus of theoretical, political, and policy debates. Particular attention has focused on how best to conceptualize contemporary racism(s) and racialized relations in the context of demographic shifts, changing class formations, and new forms of global dislocations. Dramatic national and international changes, both economic and political, have created conditions that have changed the racialized discourses of contemporary societies. The changing conditions of "race relations" in the United States present immense challenges and opportunities for scholars and activists to rethink the nature of contemporary racialized inequality. With President Bill Clinton's Initiative on Race and the acrimonious debates on affirmative action, immigration, and language policy, it is more evident now than ever before that there is a need for a volume that represents critical perspectives of trends and developments in the analysis of race, racism, and ethnicity in contemporary societies.

"Race" and "ethnicity," though key concepts in sociological discourse and public debate, have remained problematic. Policy pundits, journalists, conservative and liberal academics alike all work within categories of "race" and "ethnicity" and use these concepts in public discourse as though there is unanimity regarding their analytical value. Like all other component elements of what Antonio Gramsci called common sense, much of the everyday usage is uncritical. Racialized group conflicts are similarly advanced and framed as a "race relations" problem, and presented largely in black/white terms. A prime example of this confusion is the analysis of the causes of the 1992 Los Angeles riots. In the aftermath of the riots, academics and journalists analyzed the riots as a matter of "race relations:" first "it" was a problem between blacks and whites, then between blacks and Koreans, and then between blacks and Latinos, and back to blacks and whites. The interpretation of the riots as a "race relations" problem failed to take into account the economic restructuring and the drastic shifts in demographic patterns which have created new dynamics of class and racialized ethnic relations in Los Angeles.

The analytical status of the ideas of "race" and "race relations" have been questioned for more than a decade within British academic discussions, and it is only more recently that some US scholars have begun to consider the rationale and implications of this critique. A few US writers have begun to shift from treating "race" as an explanatory construct to focusing on racism as a structure and ideology of domination and exclusion, thereby moving beyond "race relations" as black/white relations. At the heart of this volume lie several related questions. How has the notion of "race" changed over time? Should we jettison the concept of race, but continue to study racism? What is the relation between changing structural class formations and racialized inequalities? Is the black/white paradigm of race relations able to grasp the new patterns of conflict and racialized inequalities in a changing global economy? How do we understand the concept of "mixed race" in the racializing project? These issues have been hotly contested, not least by writers committed to an open and critical dialogue on "race." The contributors to this volume will focus on these issues and related themes, and thus offer critical perspectives related to the meaning and significance of racism and ethnicity in an increasingly diverse society.

Race Talk

The dominant image of the United States, both in the popular public imagination and in contemporary academic discourse, is predicated upon long established views about "race." Here "races" are fixed and given, unchanging and unchangeable. They are assigned analytical value as determinants of behavior as to how people are and what they do as members of racialized groups. Accordingly, racialized groups are perceived as discrete and homogeneous; the same now as they have always been, and their members indistinguishable from each other. This view presupposes as it reinforces the perception that civil society is balkanized and fragmented.

For example, in the fall of 1994, Richard J. Herrnstein and Charles Murray published a rather controversial book, *The Bell Curve: Intelligence and Class Structure in American Life*, in which they asserted that America was swamped with a myriad of social problems – ranging from crime, homelessness, illiteracy, poverty, teenage pregnancy, unemployment, and the breakdown of the family – which could be very strongly correlated with low intelligence. Moreover, they suggested that no level of social engineering could change this, given that intelligence, which they believed could be measured accurately by IQ tests, was determined significantly by genetics. Herrnstein and Murray concluded that since the average IQ test scores of various racial/ethnic groups differed, then their intelligence had to differ as well. Needless to say, "whites" were on the top end of the intelligence scale while "blacks" were on the bottom. The end result of such reasoning, and hence the controversy over the book, is that no matter what we do, no matter how much money we pour into education or welfare or any other social programs, racialized groups are often associated with the problems mentioned above. Racialized populations are just not capable of moving beyond their marginal social existence and they are by nature not bright enough to do so. Said otherwise, such logic naturalizes and justifies social inequality, fore-closing the possibility that social and state intervention might remedy the ills that afflict racialized populations.

What all this amounts to is the familiar practice of differentiating the human species into a number of natural and distinct "races" on the basis of their typical phenomenal characteristics, which are seen largely in biological terms, and the ranking of such groups as superior and inferior, in this case on the basis of puta-tive intelligence. And since such differences are located in a pre-social realm, that is, since they are thought to be natural, a part of nature, they are seen as immutable. This is a familiar practice because it has a conspicuous history in Western culture, developing in the wake of European exploration and coloniza-tion during the fifteenth and sixteenth centuries – when Europeans elaborated a worldview that distinguished them, as children of God or human beings, from the "others" they encountered in the New World – and eventually leading to the "scientific" systems of classification advanced during the eighteenth and nine-teenth centuries, which created seemingly immutable hierarchies based on the phenomenal and biological differences of humankind (Omi and Winant, 1994). During this latter period (1850s), one notable scheme of human classification was elaborated by Robert Knox, a Scottish anatomist, who argued, as Michael Banton notes:

> First, that variations in the constitution and behaviour of individuals were to be explained as the expression of different underlying biological types of a relatively permanent kind; second, differences between these types explained variations in the cultures of human populations; third, the distinctive nature of the types explained the superiority of Europeans in general and Aryans in particular; fourth, friction between nations and individuals of different type arose from innate characters. (1977: 47)

The upshot here is that Knox insists on the essential superiority of white Europeans, distinguishing this group from "other" groups and effectively estab-lishing a social hierarchy in such a way that physical markers come to designate the place that a group occupies in social relationships. In other words, he grounds his hierarchy on the belief that certain physical traits, such as skin color, body type, etc., are tied to attributes of behavior, intellect, and morality. As such, "race" is constructed as an essence, a natural phenomenon whose meaning is prior to and beyond the reach of human intervention. There's simply nothing that can be done to change this order; it's just the way things are, naturally.

Despite this history of appealing to nature in constructing schemes of "racial" classification, of which *The Bell Curve* is only the latest manifestation, today scientists and social scientists generally agree that "race" has no validity as a biological, natural category in the human species. These people are following in the footsteps of pioneers such as anthropologist Franz Boas, to name only one notable figure, who in the early part of the twentieth century challenged the notion of races as biologically fixed natural groupings which could be hierarchically ordered by proximity to apes (see Mukhopadhyay and Moses, 1997). One such group of adherents, the American Anthropological Association, recently produced, partly in response to *The Bell Curve*, a document that details its position on the question of "race," concluding "that human populations are not unambiguous, clearly demarcated, biologically distinct groups" (American Anthropological Association, 1997). This is not to deny the physical diversity of the human species, since individuals and populations do differ in visible characteristics such as body size and shape, facial features, hair texture, and skin color, but given that "physical traits vary independently of one another, knowing the frequencies of one trait does not predict the presence or frequencies of others" (ibid.), thus rendering "any attempt to establish lines of division among biological populations arbitrary and subjective" (ibid.). Nor is it to deny genetic variation in the human population, but regardless of how racial groups are defined, genetic data show that "there are greater differences among individuals within large geographic populations than the average differences between them." All this means that there is no biological basis for dividing groups into "races," and thus that inequalities between human groups, including hierarchies based on "natural" intelligence, are not consequences of their biological inheritance. And if they are not effects of biological inheritance, then they must be the result of something else – something like historical and contemporary social, economic, and political circumstances. We will return to such contingencies shortly, but the point for now is that "race" simply does not exist as a biological fact.

But if "race" does not exist, the fact that *The Bell Curve* was published and generated so much attention (so much, in fact, that, according to Henry Giroux (1996), the book's claims set the agenda for discussions on affirmative action, civil rights, crime, and welfare on public affairs programs such as *Larry King Live* and *Nightline*, as well as a host of other visual and print media) only goes to show that "race" nevertheless matters. In fact, it matters so much that it has become almost impossible for one to think outside of "racial" categories. In the US, for example, one cannot interact with others without automatically positioning them within the systems of racial classification that pervade our particular social field. Thus, whatever else one may be, one is always positioned as "black" or "white "or "Hispanic" or "Asian" and so on. "Race" also plays a highly visible role in national politics.

On June 14, 1997, President Bill Clinton, in a commencement address at the University of California, San Diego, noted that even as America is rapidly becoming the world's first truly multiracial society, "race" remains an issue that too often disunites our nation. He has thus proposed a plan to: (1) promote a national dialogue on race issues; (2) increase the nation's understanding of the history and future of race relations; (3) identify and create plans to calm racial tension and promote increased opportunity for all Americans; and (4) address crime and the administration of justice (One America, 1997). Through this plan, called "One America in the 21st Century: The President's Initiative on Race," the

President hopes to get to the root of the "racial tension" in America and thus develop a blueprint for improving "race relations" in the twenty-first century: the goal, in other words, "is to have a diverse, democratic community in which we respect, even celebrate our differences, while embracing the shared values that unite us" (One America, 1998). Simply put, then, "race" is everywhere, structuring our world from the level of everyday life to that of national politics. Yet, we have to ask ourselves: if "race" is so important, but does not exist, at least not as a matter of biology, then what is "it?" Is race a matter of culture? Or birth? Or is "it" a matter of both? Or neither? And if "it" is not a matter of biology, then are there any criteria for racial identity? If so, what might they be? Finally, we might ask, in a more straightforward manner, what is "race" anyway (see Fuss, 1989)?

Race: Now You See It, Now You Don't

We should state from the outset that we do not believe that "race" as such exists. There is simply no biological basis for dividing the human species into groups based on the idea that certain physical traits, such as skin color, are tied to attributes of behavior, intellect, and morality. "Race" is not a fact of nature. But "it" does exist to the extent that "race" is an integral part of a classificatory system through which a racialized social order is reproduced and maintained. The argument here is that society gives meaning to things by allotting them different places within a classificatory system; or rather, that social groups impose meaning on their world by ordering and organizing matter, often through the construction of binary oppositions such as us/them, self/other, and white/black (Hall, 1997; see also Douglas, 1966). The power of "race," then, as David Theo Goldberg has pointed out,

> has consisted in its adaptive capacity to define population groups, and by extension social agents, as self and other at various historical moments. It has thus facilitated the fixing of characterizations of inclusion and exclusion, giving an apparent specificity otherwise lacking to social relations . . . [It is] able to signify not so much in itself as by adopting and giving naturalized form to prevailing conceptions of social group formation at different times. (1992: 558)

Thus, while "race" may not be a natural category, "it" nevertheless plays a central role in the construction and rationalization of orders of difference, making group relations appear as if they were natural and unchangeable. The fundamental importance that "race" bears upon itself, then, "is not of biological but of naturalized group relations" (1992: 559); "it" gives social relations the facade of long duration, hence reducing, essentializing, and fixing difference. This is not to suggest, however, that "race" makes no reference to biology at all. In fact, "race" today, particularly in the United States, would make little sense if "it" did not have a biological referent. But, and this is a crucial point, "it" is a biological referent that is socially constructed, leaving us with a definition of "race" or "races" as "groups that are *socially* defined in a given place and time, but on the basis of *physical* attributes such as skin color, facial features, hair texture, or stature" (Van den Berghe, 1996: 1054).[1] This signifies that although "race" may have a foundation in biology since "it" carves out populations on the basis of phenomenal characteristics, most notably skin color, "it" really is just a name or concept, albeit a very powerful one, that retroactively constitutes and naturalizes the groupings to which "it" appears to refer and that "it" identifies in "its" own name. In other words, "race" does not refer to a pregiven or already constituted object, but actually constitutes the object itself, bringing together into a unity a number of elements that formerly co-existed independently of one another.[2] And since the "process of naming objects actually amounts to the very act of their constitution" (Laclau, 1989: xiv), then the meaning of "race" is fundamentally unstable and open to all sorts of rearticulations. In short, "race" is a fluid, unfixed, almost vacuous concept capable of multiple meanings. What this suggests, then, is that "race," even as "it" makes group relations appear natural, must be seen, not as a natural fact, but as a protean marker of difference that will signify distinct meanings within specific social and historical contexts.

In the United States, for instance, racial classification has historically been structured around a very rigid white/black color line, such that white is construed as a pure category, making anyone who is racially mixed non-white. Thus millions of people in the US are considered – and consider themselves – "black" even though they may be of racially mixed white/black ancestry. This reasoning follows from what Marvin Harris has called the hypo-descent or one-drop rule:

> By what ingenious computation is the genetic tracery of a million years of evolution unraveled and each man [sic] assigned his proper social box? In the United States, the mechanism employed is the rule of hypo-descent. This descent rule requires Americans to believe that anyone who is known to have had a Negro ancestor is a Negro. We admit nothing in between . . . "Hypo-descent" means affiliation with the subordinate rather than the superordinate group in order to avoid the ambiguity of intermediate identity. (Quoted in Omi and Winant, 1986: 60)

Thus the US has really never developed intermediate categories in which to place people of mixed race.[3] In contrast, Brazil has historically had less strict conceptions of race, elaborating a series of intermediate social categories, ranging from "*galego*," "*loiro*," and "*branco de terra*," which are the lighter or "whiter" designations, to "*preto*," "*moreno*," and "*pardo*," which are on the darker end of the scale. This doesn't mean, however, that Brazil is a racially egalitarian society: to be recognized as part of the lighter designations is to belong to the upper status groups. And, in contrast to both the US and Brazil, South Africa, which is known to maintain rigid hierarchies, recognizes three racial categories: black refers to any member of any aboriginal tribe of Africa; white is defined as anyone who in appearance is clearly a white person; and colored refers to a person who is not white or black. The latter group, because it is the in-between group in what is essentially a bi-polar, white/black classificatory system, is socially marginal; they are viewed with suspicion and distrust by other social groups (Scheper-Hughes, 1997). All these examples show, then, that race is, for all intents and purposes, a fluid, unfixed concept which signifies differently depending on the social and historical contexts in which "it" is articulated.

The upshot of all this is that since "race" as such does not exist, then in order for a group to become a "race," to be called a "race," "it" really has to be made or categorized into one. In other words, since race does not refer to an already constituted object, a group cannot be a race outside of the active forces that construct "it." Thus a "racial group," in order to be itself, has to undergo some kind of process that would turn "it" into itself. Following Robert Miles, we would like to call this process **racialization**, which basically refers to:

> those instances where social relations between people have been structured by the signification of human biological characteristics in such a way as to define and construct differentiated social collectivities. . . . The concept therefore refers to a process of categorization, a representational process of defining an Other (usually, but not exclusively) somatically. (1989: 75)

What "racialization" does, then, is steer us to thinking about "race" in terms of processes rather than as a natural category. In short, it calls attention to the ways in which "race" is always actively constructed, to how its referents are inherently unstable, thus making "it" open to multiple meanings.

Fixing Race

Since "race" is a concept capable of multiple significations, and consequently since the groups to which "it" refers vary in different historical and social contexts, it stands to reason that the meaning(s) of race will be highly open to contestation, so that one must attend, on the one hand, to the ways in which particular ideologies, or modes of thinking, construct racial hierarchies that justify socioeconomic inequality, and, on the other, to the ways in which such constructions are challenged and the racializing project thus rearticulated. Beginning with the one hand, we have already seen, particularly through our discussions of *The Bell Curve* and of Knox's racial classificatory system, that race matters not only because "it" is one of the common sense categories through which people and groups interpret the world around them, giving order to what would otherwise be an untidy experience, but also because "it" is a category in whose name social hierarchies are produced and maintained. What we are really talking about here, then, is what is commonly known as racism, an exclusionary and marginalizing practice that quite often works through the construction of binary oppositions such as us/them, self/other, and white/black (or white/other). These binary constructions are hardly ever neutral; there is always a dimension of power between the end points of such oppositions. Thus when we talk about binary opposition like us/them, as Jacques Derrida has emphasized, "we are not dealing with . . . peaceful coexistence . . . but rather with a violent hierarchy. One of the two terms governs the other . . . or has the upper hand" (1981: 41). Indeed, these constructions embody a logic that valorizes the first term while subordinating the second. And this is not simply a matter of semantics because such classificatory practices carry material consequence. For example, Stuart Hall, focusing on the period of plantation slavery and its aftermath in the US, points out how the discourses that sought to justify slavery, and thus the exploitation of a particular group of human beings, were structured by a series of binary oppositions:

> There is the powerful opposition between "civilization" (white) and "savagery" (black). There is the opposition between the biological or bodily characteristics of the "black" and "white" "races," polarized into their extreme opposites – each the signifiers of an absolute difference between human "types" or species. There are the rich distinctions which cluster around the supposed link, on the one hand, between the white "races" and intellectual development – refinement, learning and knowledge, a belief in reason, the presence of developed institutions, formal government and law, and a "civilized" restraint in their emotional, sexual and civil life, all of which are associated with "Culture"; and on the other hand, the link between the black "races" and whatever is instinctual – the open expression of emotion and feeling rather than intellect, a lack of "civilized refinement" in sexual and social life, a reliance on custom and ritual, and the lack of developed civil institutions, all of which are linked to "Nature." (1997: 243)

In effect, then, through such binary constructions people are classified according to a norm, setting up a symbolic boundary between the acceptable and the unacceptable, the normal and the deviant. In this particular case, the opposition is constructed in such a way that physical features, namely skin color, are linked to attributes of intellect and behavior, establishing a hierarchy of quality between white and black. The essential character of these groups are fixed eternally in nature since physical appearance is linked causally to behaviors by biological inheritance. This example of racialization, along with those of *The Bell Curve* and of Knox, is often labeled classical or traditional racism since "it" "rationalizes claims of national superiority or sociopolitical disqualification and economic exploitation of groups of individuals within a polity by attributing to them certain moral, intellectual, or social defects supposedly grounded in their "racial" endowment which, by virtue of being innate, are inevitable" (Stolcke, 1995: 7).[4] While such forms of racism that resort to crude biologisms still abound in the late twentieth century both in Europe and in the US, it is generally acknowledged that racism, which can be defined in general terms as the belief in and/or practice of excluding people on the basis of their membership in a racially defined group, has taken a new turn, toward what is often called cultural racism (Gilroy, 1990; Giroux, 1993), neo-racism (Balibar, 1991), or cultural fundamentalism (Stolcke, 1995).

This new cultural racism, rather than asserting different natural endowments of human races, notions which have generally lost credibility, emphasize differences of cultural heritage and their incommensurability. In other words, as Étienne Balibar has noted:

> It is a racism whose dominant theme is not biological heredity but the insurmountability of cultural differences, a racism which, at first sight, does not postulate the superiority of certain groups or peoples in relation to others but "only" the harmfulness of abolishing frontiers, the incompatibility of life-styles and traditions. . . . (1991: 21)

The logic here is that humanity is divided into a number of groups who are the bearers of distinct and incommensurable cultures, and whose members are prone to enter into conflict with one another since it is human nature to be xenophobic. In an ideal world, each culture would be spatially segregated from one another, each in its own little piece of earth; only with such separation could any of them flourish. In theory, then, this view does not imply the ordering of different cultures hierarchically. In fact, it appears to be quite the opposite, seemingly bent towards the recognition of the variety and equality of cultures. But what happens when a particular territory, let us say a national territory, is inhabited by a multiplicity of cultures? The theory goes as follows: in such a situation – which is not unlike the one found today in the US and throughout Europe, where, primarily as a result of immigration after World War II, different cultural groups interact with one another on a daily basis – the only result can be cultural conflict as each culture struggles to maintain its integrity. Here cultural racism assumes a set of symmetrically opposed counterconcepts (binary oppositions one might say), that of the national and the citizen on one side, and the alien, the foreigner, the stranger, and the immigrant on the other; with this latter grouping, the "other" of the nation, most often being construed:

> as a *political* threat to national identity and integrity on account of immigrants' cultural diversity because the nation-state is conceived as founded on a bounded and distinct community which mobilizes a shared sense of belonging and loyalty predicated on a common language, cultural traditions, and beliefs. (Stolcke, 1995: 8)

This "other," then, since "it" poses a threat to the nation, is relegated to the margins of society, often blamed for all the social and economic ills that befall the nation. Thus, although the new cultural racism appears to be egalitarian, "it" actually constructs a hierarchy such that the national is valued over the nonnational. The curious thing, too, is that those cultures considered incommensurable to the national culture almost always belong to people whose visible characteristics distinguish them from the majority "white" population. In other words, although the new cultural racism does not appear to exclude and marginalize populations on the basis of their biological heritage, one can not really discount the element of biology since those who belong to the incommensurable cultures are most often non-white. In either case, though, whether we are speaking of classical racism or the new cultural kind, the results of the process of racialization are the same: those who are non-white are often excluded from society. In short, the hierarchy does not really change: "white" remains on top.

The notion of racialization – the representation and definition of the Other based on the signification of human biological characteristics – is particularly useful in understanding the US discourse on non-European immigrants and natives. Until recently, the discourse on Native Americans, African-Americans, Latinos, and Asian-Americans has largely depended on a phenotypical represen-tation and evaluation, giving both color and physical features social significance. By reason of such features, these populations were perceived as bearers of diseases and as endangering European-American morals and "racial" purity, thus providing the ideological context, in part, for the enactment of past restrictive immigration laws and discriminatory policies. Even though reference to pheno-typical characteristics are absent from contemporary policy discussions, the racialization process continues to inform many group practices and individual actions. We would include as instances of racialization the "hate crimes" directed at Asian-Americans and other racialized groups; the violent attacks, vandalism, racial slurs, and hateful mail directed at immigrant institutions, churches, and individuals; and racialized code words such as "welfare queen," "Willie Horton," "illegal alien," "model minority," among others.

To understand the antipathy toward racialized groups, we suggest that this is the result of categorizing them on the basis of their physical features (skin color, mostly). Past significations of immigrants, by ascribing them with real or alleged biological or cultural characteristics, are available as part of the American culture for reinterpretation, given the existence of certain stimulus. In contemporary US society, the stimuli that led to the renewed attack on Asian immigrants can be attributed, first, to the decline of US capitalism as an economic power, particu-larly its economic position in relations to Japan. Much of the political debate in the late 1980s and early 1990s on what was wrong with the US economy focused on Japan's unfair trade practices and acquisitions of American companies, land-marks, and cultural icons. Negative imagery of Japan in the form of "Japan bashing" is articulated by both the indigenous population and the politicians, and is often reproduced through political legitimation by the state. Second, acts of violence against racialized populations, as Robert Miles and Annie Phizacklea (1981) note, can be understood as attempts to define what is the local imagined community (see also Anderson, 1991). The local American imagined community, a community based on the ethos of biblical foundation, republicanism, and indi-vidualism, is unable to regard those who express different values as part of the same community. This view of anti-immigrant antipathy is also echoed by soci-ologist Susan Smith, who, in her examination of working-class youth, suggests that anti-immigrant behaviors are attempts "to preserve both national exclusivity and neighborhood segregation" (1989: 159).

Given these insights drawn from the works of Miles, Phizacklea, and Smith, the bigotry and violence against racialized groups should be seen in the larger economic and political contexts. The authors attribute political and economic forces as having created and sustained racialized violence.

These acts cannot be explained solely as the product of spontaneous violence perpetrated by psychologically aberrant gangs of white youths. The understandings of these multiple causes have enormous implications for directing effective policies designed to address and prevent racist violence against immigrants. New research needs to address the increased use of the signification of "racial" and cultural characteristics in political campaigns and the concurrent increase of intolerance against racialized groups.

Contesting Race

So much for the ways in which particular ideologies construct racialized hierarchies that justify the marginalization of certain populations. As to the ways in which such naturalizing constructions are challenged and the racializing project thus rearticulated. That is the purpose of the essays we have brought together in this reader. Given the perspective developed in this introduction, that is, given that we view race and ethnicity in terms of social and cultural processes and not as natural categories, our primary goal in this volume is to put forth a collection of articles that not only illustrates but also challenges some of the different ways in which race and ethnicity have historically been constructed. In other words, since race and ethnicity, in our opinion, do not refer to already constituted objects, we have brought together essays that offer different takes on and critiques of the fashioning of such objects; takes and critiques that not only come from a variety of disciplines – ranging from philosophy and political economy to sociology, anthropology, and history – but that also articulate race and ethnicity with a host of other socially significant processes, in particular those of citizenship, class, gender, identity politics, and globalization, to name only a few. Taken as a whole, then, these articles, drawing on a diversity of theoretical perspectives, call attention to the manners in which race and ethnicity are always actively constructed – and constructed at the intersection of a myriad of social processes. With this in mind, the book is organized into several parts, each of which addresses a particular theme that we have identified as representative of some of the most important topics related to the question of race and ethnicity.

Part I, "Mapping the Languages of Racism," sets the context for the rest of the volume. It is the section most explicitly concerned with examining the historicity of "race" as a category of social classification. It is also the section most directly preoccupied with critiquing the various ways in which the idea of race has been employed in Western culture, specifically as "it" has been used to marginalize and legitimate the exploitation of certain populations. The articles in this part thus raise a number of basic questions: What is race? Does race matter? Does "it" even exist? What is the historicity of the notion of race? How do racialized barriers constrain people's lives? Can racialized populations resist the obstacles which confront them? How have debates about race and ethnicity been influenced in one way or another by Marxist and neo-Marxist scholarship and research? How does postmodern social theory help us to reframe notions of racial and ethnic identity? In what ways do notions of race intersect with those of ethnicity?

Part II, "Critical Multiracial Feminisms," situates the discussion of race within the conceptual framework of multiracial feminism, a perspective that aims to transcend the mere recognition of diversity and heterogeneity among women to examine structures of domination, specifically those structures that situate genders differently on the basis of race. The chapters in this section, despite their varied concerns and multiple intellectual positionings, share an emphasis on "race" as a primary force in understanding the social construction of gender. It is thus the importance of race, its centrality, and the battles against racial subjection that unite the distinct feminist perspectives we bring together here. These essays address such questions as: What is multiracial feminism? What are its distinguishing features? In what ways do gender relations affect and are affected by ethnicity, culture, racism and anti-racism? How does gender fit in with other strategies of negotiating difference such as multiculturalism, identity politics and coalition politics? How does one ensure group unity while recognizing the tremendous heterogeneity that operates within the boundaries of terms such as "black women?" What are some of the implications of using different names, such as "womanism" and "black feminism," to capture a black women's standpoint?

Part III, "Fashioning Mixed Race," considers some of the ways we think about racial categories, in particular, racial categories of mixture. Thus one of the primary purposes of the articles in this section is to locate the concept of "mixed race" in the racialized project, focusing on how current transformations in the body politic are being marked by reconfigured "racial" categories. They also interrogate both the possibilities and limits of mixed-race formation, drawing attention to how everyone is, in some sense, always already mixed. Through such inquiries, the papers raise the following questions: How do we understand the concept of "mixed race" in the racializing project? How might we re-examine racial categories if we are informed by the insight of race as a social construction and an anti-racist project? In what ways do multiracial Asian-Americans challenge current definitions and assumptions about culture and ethnicity in relationship to race? How has the notion of *mestizaje*, as a category of mixture, functioned in Latin America and among Latinos in the US? How does *mestizaje* function as both a dangerous site and a wellspring of creativity?

Part IV, "The Color(s) of Whiteness," examines how different racial projects struggle to define and redefine the meanings of race and racial identities, specifically the meanings of whiteness and white identities. The articles gathered here begin from the premise that it is not possible to assume a normative whiteness, one whose invisibility and relatively monolithic makeup signal immunity from political or cultural challenge, so that one must really deal with a variety of "whitenesses." As such, these essays explore the racial politics and culture in the United States and Europe as they shape the multiple identities and statuses of whites. They address such questions as: How is whiteness, as an analytical object, being established as a powerful means of critiquing the reproduction and maintenance of systems of racial inequality? How does whiteness as an analytical concept bring to light how the unmarked and normative position of whites is maintained by positing race as a category of difference? What is the significance of whiteness as a social construction in the anti-racist project? What are the practical and theoretical implications of anti-essentialist readings of whiteness? How is whiteness – which has reflexively, if unconsciously, been defined in universal terms – composed of particular identities? How do these particular identities fit into contemporary debates about the labor movement? How do we integrate white privilege in the analysis of domination and subordination?

Part V, "Cultural Citizenship, Multiculturalism, and the State," explores the notion of citizenship, which since the eighteenth century has been one of the defining marks of modernity, functioning to establish the meaning of full membership in society. Thus what it means to be a member of society in many parts of the world has come to be understood, to a large degree, in terms of what it means to be a right-bearing citizen of a territorial nation-state, with the state determining the boundaries of that membership, specifying who does and does not belong. This means that in order for there to be citizens there must be non-citizens and, therefore, that the citizenship project works both through inclusion and exclusion, often creating substantial barriers for those who wish to be included. How, then, has citizenship historically been defined? How has it operated as an exclusionary practice? How do contemporary nativist movements wish to restrict citizenship? Would it be helpful to view citizenship not just as a process of being made but also as one of self-making in relation to nation-states and transnational processes? How can one be a full citizen and remain culturally different from mainstream society? What would citizenship look like if we viewed it from the position of the socially and culturally marginalized?

Part VI, "Locating Class," stresses the importance of bringing class into the picture, highlighting it as one of the significant social positions that intersects with race and ethnicity. For too often, in contemporary discourses, class is paid scant attention, thus relegating this crucial category to the margins. For instance, both feminism and multiculturalism, in many cases, have placed so much emphasis on the politics of identity – on differences based on race, ethnicity, and gender – that they often pay cursory attention to class, and hence to the effects of material systems of domination on racialized subjects. Given this scenario, the articles in this section explore such questions as: How does class intersect with race and ethnicity? What happens when we treat class not as an identity but as a system of economic power and domination? How can property relations be analyzed in conjunction with concerns over gender and race? What happens to the American ideology of equal opportunity when one uses a class-based analysis nested within ethnicity? What is happening to educational opportunities for the poor, the working class, and racial minorities? Can one say that a social class, by its situation and its ideology, is predisposed to racist attitudes and behavior?

Part VII, "Globalized Futures and Racialized Identities," connects the discussion of race and ethnicity to recent changes in national and political economy.

The section brings diverse expertise to bear on concrete questions of the relation of race and ethnicity to globalization, to those processes, operating on a global scale, which cut across national boundaries, integrating and connecting communities and organizations in new space-time combinations, making the world in reality and in experience more interconnected. How do Marx's views on globalization help to investigate the emergence of new transnational forms of labor exploitation? How has global capitalism shaped the feminization of labor worldwide, and the ethnicizing of labor on the home front? How does one address the multiple presences and articulations of race and gender in the political economy and their multiple absences in the dominant representations of that economy? In what ways are cities strategic to economic globalization? How has the globalization of the American economy spurred new political conflicts and alliances, many of which are profoundly racialized? Does globalization make inequality worse? How is globalization of the American economy remaking the racial and ethnic map of the United States?

Finally, part VIII, "Critical Engagements," brings together interviews with two of the leading theorists of race on the contemporary scene: Stuart Hall and Angela Davis. These interviews deal with a number of questions pertinent to the entire volume and thus serve to complement nicely the ideas put forth by many of the other writers gathered here: How do we move away from the essentialism debate towards a new kind of cultural positionality, a different logic of difference? Can the notion of diaspora offer a new theoretical model for cultural identity? How do notions of diaspora relate to multiculturalism? How has the conjunction of race, class, and gender shifted in our contemporary period? Has the anti-racist critique changed white feminism? How does one articulate women of color as a political project?

Overall, then, the essays in this volume explore the contradictory and powerful meanings of the concepts of "race" and racism(s). Above all, they call attention to the various manners in which race and ethnicity are always actively constituted at the crossroads of a myriad of social processes. They powerfully reject the near universal theoretical tendency to naturalize the epiphenomena of race. Although at times powerfully arguing against the analytic usefulness of the category of race, the authors agree that racism, in its varying institutional, cultural, environmental, and economic forms exerts a lasting influence over individual behavior, public policies, and white hegemony. What counts in the following essays is not the debates over the existence of race *per se* but rather the existential qualities of racism(s) throughout civil society, the political sphere, and in everyday lived experience.

Notes

1 An ethnic group, by contrast, as van den Berghe notes, "is also socially defined, but on the basis of cultural attributes such as language, religion, lifestyle, traditions, or costume. Empirically, some groups may be defined both physically and culturally, and

thus be both ethnic and racial groups. So, while the conceptual distinction is clear in theory, the two categories sometimes overlap in subtle and complicated ways" (1996: 1054–5). Our primary interest here is on what may be called racialized ethnic groups.
2 For example, if we look at the designations "black" and "colored," which are marks of racial difference, they mean very different things in the distinct contexts of England and the Caribbean. In the English system, "organized around a binary dichotomy which reflects the colonizing order of "white/not-white," the terms black and colored are more or less synonymous," bringing together peoples whose origins lie in such diverse places as Africa, India, and the West Indies, "whereas in the Caribbean system, where race is organized in an ascending spectrum of classifications, black and colored denote different points on the scale rising toward the ultimate term, white," and it covers only people of African descent (Lowe, 1991: 26).
3 We say "never really developed" because around the turn of the last century the US census did make an effort to count mulattos, quadroon and octoroons, which were meaningful categories at the time. And, more recently, in trying to figure out the thorny question of race for its population count in the year 2000, the US Census Bureau has considered developing a mixed-race or multi-racial category. There is, however, a lot of resistance to the creation of such a category, much of it coming from African-American leaders, who fear that a "Mixed Race" category will dilute the cultural identity and political power of their community.
4 In talking about racism in terms of racialization, we do not mean to imply that racialization necessarily implies racism. Racialization simply refers, quoting Miles again, "to a process of categorization, a representational process of defining an Other (usually, but not exclusively) somatically" (1989: 75). Racism is a specific form of racialization whereby those groups of classified races are hierarchically organized, thus legitimating the exploitation of one group by another.

References

American Anthropological Association. (1997). Draft Official Statement on "Race." http://www.ameranthassn.org/racepp.htm (Jan. 4, 1997).

Anderson, B. (1991). *Imagined Communities: Reflections on the origin and spread of nationalism* (rev. edn). London: Verso.

Balibar, É. (1991). Is there a neo-racism? In Étienne Balibar and Immanuel Wallerstein (eds), *Race, Nation, Class: Ambiguous identities*. London and New York: Verso.

Banton, M. (1977). *The Idea of Race*. Cambridge, MA: Tavistock Publications.

Derrida, J. (1981). *Positions*. Chicago: University of Chicago Press.

Douglas, M. (1966). *Purity and Danger: An analysis of the concepts of pollution and taboo*. London and New York: Routledge.

Fuss, D. (1989). *Essentially Speaking: Feminism, nature and difference*. New York: Routledge.

Gilroy, P. (1990). One nation under a groove: The cultural politics of "race" and racism in Britain. In David Theo Goldberg (ed.), *Anatomy of Racism*. Minneapolis and London: University of Minnesota Press.

Giroux, H. (1993). Living dangerously: Identity politics and the new cultural racism: Towards a critical pedagogy of representation. *Cultural Studies*, 7 (1), 1–27.

Giroux, H. (1996). Race talk and the bell curve debate: The crisis of democratic vision. *Cultural Critique*, 34, 5–26.

Goldberg, D. T. (1992). The semantics of race. *Ethnic and Racial Studies*, 15 (4), 543–69.

Hall, S. (1997). The spectacle of the "other." In Stuart Hall (ed.), *Representation: Cultural representations and signifying practices*. London: Sage Publications.

Herrnstein, R. J. and Murray, C. (1994). The Bell Curve: Intelligence and class structure in American life. New York: Free Press.

Laclau, E. (1989). Preface. In *The Sublime Object of Ideology*. Slavoj Žižek (ed.), London and New York: Verso.

Lowe, L. (1991). *Critical Terrains: French and British Orientalisms*. Ithaca and London: Cornell University Press.

Miles, R. and Phizacklea, A. (1981). Racism and Capitalist Decline. In Michael Harloe (ed.), *New Perspectives in Urban Change and Conflict*. London: Heinemann Educational Books.

Miles, R. (1989). *Racism*. London: Routledge.

Mukhopadhyay, C. C. and Moses, Y. T. (1997). Reestablishing "race" in anthropological discourse. *American Anthropologist*, 99 (3), 517–33.

Omi, M. and Winant, H. (1986). *Racial Formation in the United States: From the 1960s to the 1980s*. New York and London: Routledge.

Omi, M. and Winant, H. (1994). *Racial Formation in the United States: From the 1960s to the 1990s* (2nd edn). New York and London: Routledge.

One America. The advisory board: The President's initiative on race. http://www.whitehouse.gov/Initiatives/OneAmerica/advisory-plain.html (Dec. 14, 1997).

One America. Initiative overview. http://www.whitehouse.gov/Initiatives/OneAmerica/overview-plain.html (Mar. 17, 1998).

Scheper-Hughes, N. Mixed feelings: The recovery of spoiled identities in the new South Africa. http://www.nhc.rtp.nc.us:8080/conlect/hongkong/scheper.htm (Dec. 17, 1997).

Smith, S. (1989). *The Politics of "Race" and Residence*. Cambridge, MA: Polity Press.

Stolcke, V. (1995). Talking culture: New boundaries, new rhetorics of exclusion in Europe. *Current Anthropology*, 36 (1), 1–24.

Van den Berghe, P. L. (1996). Racism. In David Levinson and Melvin Ember (eds), *Encyclopedia of Cultural Anthropology* (vol. 3). New York: Henry Holt and Company.

Wieviorka, M. (1997). Is it so difficult to be an anti-racist? In Pnina Werbner and Tariq Modood (ed.), *Debating Cultural Hybridity: Multi-cultural identities and the politics of anti-racism*. London and New Jersey: Zed Books.

Part I

Mapping the Languages of Racism

1

Does "Race" Matter? Transatlantic Perspectives on Racism after "Race Relations"

Robert Miles and Rodolfo D. Torres

The discourse promoting resistance to racism must not prompt identification with and in terms of categories fundamental to the discourse of oppression. Resistance must break not only with *practices* of oppression, although its first task is to do that. Resistance must oppose also the *language* of oppression, including the categories in terms of which the oppressor (or racist) represents the forms in which resistance is expressed.

D. T. Goldberg (1990: 313–14)

Introduction

In April 1993, one year after the Los Angeles civil unrest, a major US publisher published a book with the creatively ambiguous title *Race Matters* by the distinguished scholar Cornel West. The back cover of the slightly revised edition published the following year categorized it as a contribution to both African-American Studies and Current Affairs. The latter was confirmed by the publisher's strategy of marketing the book as a "trade" rather than as an "academic" title: this was a book for the "American public" to read. And the American public was assured that they were reading a quality product when they were told that its author had "built a reputation as one of the most eloquent voices in America's racial debate."

Some two years later, the *Los Angeles Times* published an article by its science writer under the headline "Scientists Say Race Has No Biological Basis." The opening paragraph ran as follows:

Researchers adept at analysing the genetic threads of human diversity said Sunday that the concept of race – the source of abiding cultural and political divisions in American society – simply has no basis in fundamental human biology. Scientists should abandon it.

And, on the same day (February 20, 1995), the *Chronicle of Higher Education* reproduced the substance of these claims in an article under the title " A Growing Number of Scientists Reject the Concept of Race." Both publications were reporting on the proceedings of the American Association for the Advancement of Science in Atlanta.

If the notion of "race" simply has no basis in "fundamental human biology," how are we to evaluate Professor West's assertion that "Race Matters?" If "race" matters, then surely "races" must exist! But if there are no "races," then "race" cannot matter. These two contributions to public political debate seem to reveal a contradiction. Yet, within the specific arena of academic debate, there is a well-rehearsed attempt to dissolve the contradiction which runs as follows. It is acknowledged that, earlier this century, the biological and genetic sciences established conclusively in the light of empirical evidence that the attempt to establish the existence of different types or "races" of human being by scientific procedures had failed. The idea that the human species consists of a number of distinct "races," each exhibiting a set of discrete physical and cultural charac-teristics is therefore false, mistaken. The interventions reported as having been made in Atlanta in February 1995 only repeat what some scientists have been arguing since the 1930s. Yet the fact that scientists have to continue to assert these claims demonstrates that the contrary is still widely believed and articulated in public discussion.

Because this scientific knowledge has not yet been comprehensively under-stood by "the general public" (which not only persists in believing in the existence of "races" as biologically discrete entities but also acts in ways con-sistent with such a belief), it is argued that social scientists must employ a *concept* of "race" to describe and analyse these beliefs, and the discrimination and exclusion that are premised on this kind of classification. In other words, while social scientists know that there are no "races," they also know that things believed to exist (in this case "races") have a real existence for those who believe in them and actions consistent with the belief have real social consequences. In sum, because people believe that "races" exist (i.e. because they utilize the *idea* of "race" to comprehend their social world), social scientists need a *concept* of "race."

Or do they? This chapter will explore the reasons why this question needs to be asked. It will also answer it by suggesting that social scientists do not need to, and indeed should not, transform the *idea* of "race" into an analytical category and use "race" as a *concept* in order to claim that individual and collective behavior is determined or motivated by a really-existing phenomenon labelled "race." Preeminent amongst the reasons for such an assertion is that the arenas of academic and political discourse cannot be clinically separated. Hence, Professor West, in seeking to use his status as a leading African-American scholar to make a political intervention in Current Affairs by arguing that "Race Matters" is likely to legitimate and reinforce the widespread public belief that "races" exist irrespective of his views on this issue. For if this belief in the exis-tence of "races" was not widespread, there would be no news value in publishing an article in a leading daily US newspaper that claims that "Race Has No Biological Basis."

Criticizing "Race" as an Analytical Category

We begin this exploration by crossing the Atlantic in order to consider the issue as it has been discussed in Britain since the early 1950s. As we shall see, the development of the British discussion has in fact been influenced substantially by the preconceptions and language employed in the US: the use of "race" as an analytical category in the social sciences is a transatlantic phenomenon.

It is now difficult to conceive, but forty years ago no one would have suggested that "Race Matters" in Britain. The idea of "race" was employed in public and political discussion, but largely in order to discuss "the colonies": the "race problem" was spatially located beyond British shores in the British Empire and especially in certain colonies, notably South Africa. It is relevant to add that this too had not always been so. During the nineteenth and early twentieth centuries, it was widely believed that the population of Britain was composed of a number of different "races" (e.g. the Irish were identified as being "of the Celtic race") and, moreover, migration to Britain from central and eastern Europe in the late nineteenth century was interpreted using the language of "race" to signify the Jewish refugees fleeing persecution (e.g. Barkan, 1992: 15–65). But, as the situation in the port city of Liverpool after World War I suggested (e.g. Barkan, 1992: 57–65), the language of "race" used to refer to the interior of Britain was to became tied exclusively to differences in skin color in the second-half of the twentieth century. What, then, was the "race" problem that existed beyond the shores of Britain?

Briefly expressed, the problem was that, or so it was thought, the colonies were spatial sites where members of different "races" (Caucasian, white, African, Hindu, Mongoloid, Celts: the language to name these supposed "races" varied enormously) met and where their "natures" (to civilize, to fight, to be lazy, to progress, to drink, to engage in sexual perversions etc.) interacted, often with tragic consequences. This language of "race" was usually anchored in the signification of certain forms of somatic difference (skin color, facial characteristics, body shape and size, eye color, skull shape) which were interpreted as the physical marks which accompanied, and which in some unexplained way determined, the "nature" of those so marked. In this way, the social relations of British colonialism were explained as being "rooted" simultaneously in the biology of the human body and in the cultural attributes determined by "nature."

But the "race" problem was not to remain isolated from British shores, to be contained there by a combination of civilization and violence. All Her Majesty's subjects had the right of residence in the Motherland, and increasing numbers of them chose to exercise that right as the decade of the 1950s progressed. Members of "colored races," from the Caribbean and the Indian subcontinent in particular, migrated to Britain largely to fill vacancies in the labor market but against the will of successive governments (Labour and Conservative) who feared that they carried in their cheap suitcases not only their few clothes and personal possessions but also the "race problem" (e.g. Joshi and Carter, 1984; Solomos, 1989; Layton-Henry, 1992). By the late 1950s, it was widely argued that, as a result of "colored immigration," Britain had imported a "race" problem: prior to this migration, so it was believed, Britain's population was "racially homogeneous," a claim that neatly dispensed with not only earlier racialized classifications of both migrants and the population of the British Isles but also the history of interior racisms (Miles, 1993: 80–104).

The political and public response to immigration from the Caribbean and the Indian subcontinent is now a well-known story (e.g. Solomos, 1989; Layton-Henry, 1992), although there are a number of important byways still to be explored. What is of more interest here is the academic response. A small number of social scientists (particularly sociologists and anthropologists) wrote about these migrations and their social consequences using the language of everyday life: *Dark Strangers* and the *The Colour Problem* were the titles of two books that achieved a certain prominence during the 1950s and their authors subsequently pursued distinguished academic careers. Considered from the point of view of the 1990s, these titles now seem a little unfortunate, and perhaps even a part of the problem insofar as they employ language that seems to echo and legitimate racist discourses of the time.

But can the same be said for two other books that became classic texts within the social sciences: Michael Banton's *Race Relations* (1967) and John Rex's *Race Relations in Sociological Theory* (1970). Both were published in the following decade and were widely interpreted as offering different theoretical and political interpretations of the consequences of the migration to, and settlement in, Britain of British subjects and citizens from the Caribbean and the Indian subcontinent. And indeed they did offer very different analyses. Notably, Rex sought to re-interpret the concept of racism to ensure that it could encompass the then contemporary political discourses about immigration which avoided any direct references to an alleged hierarchy of "races" while at the same time referring to or implying the existence of different "races." Banton interpreted this shift in discourse as evidence of a decline in racism, a conclusion that was to lead him to eventually reject the concept of racism entirely (1987).

But what is more remarkable is that, despite their very different philosophical and theoretical backgrounds and conclusions, they had something in common. Both Banton and Rex mirrored the language of everyday life, incorporated it into academic discourse and thereby legitimated it. They agreed that Britain (which they both analyzed comparatively with reference to the US and South Africa) had a "race relations" problem and Rex in particular wished to conceptualize this problem theoretically in the discipline of sociology. In so doing, both premised their arguments on the understanding that scientific knowledge proves that "races" do not exist in the sense widely understood in everyday common sense discourse: if "race" was a problem, it was a social and not a biological problem, a problem rooted in part at least in the continued popular belief in the existence of "races." Indeed, John Rex had been one of the members of one of the team of experts recruited by UNESCO to discredit officially the continuing exploitation of nineteenth-century scientific knowledge about "race" by certain political groups and to educate public opinion by making widely known the more recent conclusions of biological and genetic scientists (Montagu, 1972).

The concept of "race relations" seemed to have impeccable credentials, unlike the language of *Dark Strangers* for example. This is in part because the notion was borrowed from the early sociology of the "Chicago School" in the US which, amongst other things, was interested in the consequences of the early-twentieth-century migration from the southern to the northern states of "Negroes" fleeing poverty (and much else) in search of wage labor alongside the continuing large-scale migration from Europe to the US. As a result of the former migration, "Negro" and "white races" entered, so it was conceptualized, into conflicting social relations in the burgeoning industrial urban areas of the northern states and sociologists had named a new field of study. "Colored migration" to British cities after 1945 provided an opportunity for sociologists to import this field of study into Britain: Britain too now had a "race relations" problem.

Moreover, for Rex at least, "race relations situations" were characterized by definition by the presence of a racist ideology. Hence, the struggle against colonialism could now be pursued within the Mother Country "herself": by intervening in the new, domestic "race relations" problem on the side of the colonized victims of racism, one could position oneself against the British state now busily seeking a solution to that problem by the introduction of immigration controls intended specifically to prevent "colored" British subjects from entering Britain. Such was the rush to be on the side of the angels that few, if any, wondered about what the angels looked like and even whether there was any validity in the very concept of angel.

There was a further import from the US that had a substantial impact on the everyday and academic discourses of "race relations" in the late 1960s and early 1970s in Britain: the struggle for Civil Rights and against racism on the part of "the blacks" in the US (the notion of "Negro" was now past its shelf life and, like "colored" before it, it had been ejected into the wastepaper basket of politically unacceptable language) had the effect of mobilizing not only many "blacks" in Britain but also many "whites" politically inclined towards one or other of several competing versions of socialist transformation. And, if radical "blacks" were busy "seizing the time" in the names of anti-racism and "black autonomy," there was little political or academic space within which radically-inclined "white" social scientists could wonder about the legitimacy and the consequences of seizing the language of "race" to do battle against racism. For it was specifically in the name of "race" that "black" people were resisting their long history of colonial oppression: indeed, in some versions of this vision of liberation, contemporary "blacks" were the direct descendants and inheritors of the African "race" which had been deceived and disinherited by the "white devils" many centuries ago. In this "race war," the "white race" was soon to face the Day of Judgment.

Possession of a common language and associated historical traditions can blind as well as illuminate. It is especially significant that both the Left and the Right in Britain looked across the Atlantic when seeking to analyze and to offer forecasts about the outcome of the "race relations" problem that both agreed existed within Britain. The infamous speeches on immigration made by the MP Enoch Powell in the late 1960s and 1970s contained a great deal of vivid imagery refracting the then contemporary events in cities in the US and framing them as prophecies of what was inevitably going to happen in due course in English cities if the "alien wedge" was not quickly "repatriated." While at the same time, the Left drew political inspiration from the "black" struggle against racism and sought to incorporate aspects of its rhetoric, style and politics. Hence, while there was disagreement about the identity of the heroes and the villains of "race relations" in the US, there was a fundamental agreement that "race relations" in the US provided a framework within which to assess the course of "race relations" in Britain. Even legislation intended to regulate "race relations" and to make racialized discrimination illegal refracted the "American experience."

As a result, the academic response to the "race relations" problem in Britain was largely isolated from the situations elsewhere in Europe, particularly in northwest Europe which was experiencing a quantitatively much more substantial migration than that taking place in Britain, and from academic and political writing about those situations. Two features of those situations are pertinent to the argument here.

First, the nation states of northwest Europe had recently experienced either fascist rule or fascist occupation and therefore the direct consequences of the so-called "final solution to the Jewish question" which sought to eliminate the "Jewish race." Hence, the collective historical memory of most of the major cities of northwest Europe was shaped by the genocide effected against the Jews and legitimated in the name of "race," even if that historical memory was now the focus of denial or repression. Second, this experience left the collective memory especially susceptible to the activities of UNESCO and others seeking to discredit the idea of "race" as a valid and meaningful descriptor. Hence, the temporal and spatial proximity of the Holocaust rendered its legitimating racism (a racism in which the idea of "race" was explicit and central) an immediate reality: in this context, few people were willing to make themselves vulnerable to the charge of racism, with the result that suppressing the idea of "race," at least in the official and formal arenas of public life, became a political imperative.

The political and academic culture of mainland northwest Europe has therefore been open to two developments which distinguish it from that existing in the islands that lie to the north of the coast of France. First, in any debate about the scope and validity of the concept of racism, the instance of the Jewish experience of racism is much more likely to be discussed, and even to be prioritized over any other. Second, the idea of "race" itself became highly politically sensitive. Its very use as a descriptor is more likely to be interpreted in itself as evidence of racist beliefs and, as a result, the idea is rarely employed in everyday political and academic discussion, at least not in connection with domestic social relations.

However, in Britain, given the combination of the colonial migration and the multiple ideological exchanges with the US, there were far fewer constraints on the everyday use of the idea of "race" and on a redefinition of the concept of racism. As a result, the latter came to refer exclusively to an ideology held by "white" people about "black" people which was rooted in capitalist expansion beyond Europe and colonial exploitation.

Having recognized the relative distinctiveness of the political and academic space in northwest Europe and then having occupied that space, one can view those social relations defined in Britain and the US as "race relations" from another point of view. For there is no public or academic reference to the existence of "race relations" in contemporary France or Germany. It then becomes possible to pose questions that seem not to be posed from within these intimately interlinked social and historical contexts. What kinds of social relations are signified as "race relations?" Why is the idea of "race" employed in everyday life to refer to only certain groups of people and only certain social situations? And why do social scientists unquestioningly import everyday meanings into their reasoning and theoretical frameworks in defining "race" and "race relations" as a particular field of study? As a result, what does it mean for an academic to claim, for example, that "race" is a factor in determining the structure of social inequality? Or that "race" and gender are interlinked forms of oppression? What is intended and what might be the consequences of asserting, as an academic, that "race matters?"

These are the kinds of question that one of the current authors has been posing for nearly fifteen years (e.g. Miles, 1982; 1984; 1989), influenced in part by the important writing of the French theorist Guillaumin (1972; 1995). The answers to these questions lead to the conclusion that one should follow the example of biological and genetic scientists and refuse to attribute analytical status to the *idea* of "race" within the social sciences, and thereby refuse to use it as a descriptive and explanatory *concept*. The reasoning can be summarized as follows (cf. Miles, 1982: 22–43; 1993: 47–9).

First, the idea of "race" is used to effect a reification within sociological analysis insofar as the outcome of an often complex social process is explained as the consequence of something named "race" rather than of the social process itself. Consider the recent publication of *The Bell Curve* (1994) by Richard J. Hernstein and Charles Murray and the authors' common assertion that "race" determines academic performance and life chances. The assertion can be supported with statistical evidence which demonstrates that, in comparison with "black people," "white people" are more likely to achieve top grades in school and to enter the leading universities in the US. The determining processes are extremely complex, including amongst other things parental class position, and active and passive racialized stereotyping and exclusion in the classroom and beyond. The effects of these processes are all mediated via a prior racialized categorization into a "white/black" dichotomy which is employed in everyday social relations. Hence, it is not "race" that determines academic performance: rather, academic performance is determined by an interplay of social processes, one of which is premised on the articulation of racism to effect and legitimate exclusion. Indeed, given the nineteenth-century meanings of "race," this form of reification invites the possibility of explaining academic performance as the outcome of some quality within the body of those racialized as "black."

Second, when academics who choose to write about "race relations" seek to speak to a wider audience (an activity which we believe to be fully justified) or when their writings are utilized by non-academics, their use unwittingly legitimates and reinforces everyday beliefs that the human species is constituted by a number of different "races," each of which is characterized by a particular combination of real or imagined physical features or marks and cultural practices. When Professor West seeks to persuade the "American public" that "Race Matters," there is no doubt that he himself does not believe in the existence of biologically defined "races," but he cannot control the meanings attributed to his claim on the part of those who identify differences in skin color, for example, as marks designating the existence of "blacks" and "whites" as discrete "races." Unintentionally, his writing may then come to serve as a legitimation not only of a belief in the existence of "race" as a biological phenomenon but also of racism itself. He could avoid this outcome by breaking with the "race relations" paradigm.

Third, as a result of reification and the interplay between academic and common sense discourses, the use of "race" as an analytical concept can incorporate into the discourse of anti-racism a notion which has been central to the evolution of racism. As a result, anti-racist activities then promote the idea that "races" really exist as biological categories of people. Thus, while challenging the legitimation of unequal treatment and stereotyping implicit and explicit in racism, the reproduction within anti-racist campaigns of the idea that there are real biological differences creating groups of human beings sustains in the public consciousness a notion which constitutes an ideological precondition for stereotyping and unequal treatment. In other words, use of the idea of "race" as a concept sustains one of the conditions for the reproduction of racism within the discourse and practice of anti-racism.

For these reasons, the idea of "race" should not be employed as an analytical category within the social sciences. It follows that the object of study should not be described as "race relations." Hence, we reject the "race relations" problematic as the locus for the analysis of racism. But we do not reject the concept of racism. Rather, we critique the "race relations" problematic in order to retain a concept of racism which is formulated in such a way as to recognize the existence of a plurality of historically-specific racisms, not all of which employ explicitly the idea of "race." In contrast, the "race relations" paradigm refers exclusively to either "black/white" social relations or social relations between "people of color" and "white people," with the result that there is only one racism, the racism of "whites" which has as its object and victim "people of color" (e.g. Essed, 1991). Moreover, as is increasingly recognized in the academic literature of the past decade, many recent and contemporary discourses which eschew use of the idea of "race" nevertheless advance notions that were previously a referent of the "idea" of "race." We can only comprehend contemporary discourses that dispense with the explicit use of the idea of "race" and those discourses which naturalize and inferiorize "white" populations if we rescue the concept of racism from the simultaneous inflation and narrowing of its meaning by the intersection of the academic and political debate that has taken place in Britain and the US since the end of World War II.

Reflections on the Racialization of the US by the American Academy

When one views the contemporary academic debate about racism in the US both from this analytical position and from Europe, one is struck by the following things. First, when compared with the mid- and late 1960s, it is now an extremely contested debate, a debate in which many voices are heard arguing different positions. On the one hand, writers such as Wellman (1993) continue to assert that racism remains the primary determinant of social inequality in the US while, on the other, writers such as Wilson (1987) claim that the influence of racism has declined substantially, to the point where it cannot be considered to be a significant influence on current structures of inequality. Between these two positions, one finds writers such as West who assert that the continuing impact of racism has to be assessed in terms of its relationship with the effects of class, sexism and homophobia (e.g. 1994: 44). Moreover, it is a debate in which the voices of "Afrocentrists" (e.g. Karenga, 1993), "black feminists" (e.g. hooks, 1990; Guy-Sheftall, 1995) and "critical race theorists" (Delgado, 1995; Wing, 1997) have become extremely influential over the last decade, while at the same time a "black" conservative intellectual tradition has emerged and attracted increasing attention (e.g. Sowell, 1994; Faryna, Stetson, and Conti, 1997).

Second, it remains a debate in which it is either largely taken for granted or explicitly argued that the concept of racism refers to an ideology and (in some cases) a set of practices, of which "black" people are the exclusive victim: racism refers to what "white" people think about and do to "black" people. While the concept of institutional racism goes further by eschewing any reference to human intentionality, it retains the "white/black" dichotomy in order to identify beneficiary and victim. Thus the scope of the concept of racism is very narrowly defined: the centrality of the "white/black" dichotomy denies the possibility by definition that any group other than "white" people can articulate, practice or benefit from racism and suggests that only "black people" can be the object or victim of racism.

Some of West's writing illustrates this difficulty. He clearly distinguishes himself from those he describes as black nationalists when he argues that their obsession with white racism obstructs the development of the political alliances that are essential to effecting social changes that will alleviate the suffering of black people in the US and that white racism alone cannot explain the socio-economic position of the majority of black Americans (1994: 82, 98–9). Moreover, he goes so far as to suggest that certain black nationalist accounts "simply mirror the white supremacist ideals we are opposing" (1994: 99). Yet, he seems reluctant to identify any form of racism other than white racism. In his carefully considered discussion of what he describes as "Black-Jewish relations," he employs a distinction between black anti-Semitism and Jewish anti-black racism (1994: 104; see also Lerner and West, 1995: 135–56) which suggests that these are qualitatively different phenomena: Jews can articulate racism while African-Americans can express anti-Semitism. This interpretation is reinforced by his assertion that black anti-Semitism is a form of "xenophobia from below" which has a different institutional power when compared with "those racisms that afflict their victims from above" (1994: 109–10); even though he claims that both merit moral condemnation.

A similar distinction is implicit in the recent writing of Blauner who, partly in response to the arguments of one of the current authors, has revised his position significantly since the 1960s. Blauner returns to the common distinction between "race" and ethnicity, arguing that the "peculiarly modern division of the world into a discrete number of hierarchically ranked races is a historic product of Western colonialism" (1992: 61). This he argues is a very different process from that associated with ethnicity. Hence, Blauner refrains from analysing the ideologies employed to justify the exclusion of Italians and Jews in the US in the 1920s as racism: these populations are described as "white ethnics" who were "viewed racially" (1992: 64). Concerning the period of fascism in Germany, Blauner refers to genocide "where racial imagery was obviously intensified" (1992: 64), but presumably the imagery could never be intensified to the point of warranting description as racism because the Jews were not "black." Yet, as we shall see shortly in the case of the writing of West, Blauner comes very close to breaking with the "race relations" problematic when he argues (1992: 61):

> Much of the popular discourse about race in America today goes awry because ethnic realities get lost under the racial umbrella. The positive meanings and potential of ethnicity are overlooked, even overrun, by the more inflammatory meanings of race.

Third, it is a debate which is firmly grounded in the specific realities of the history and contemporary social structure of the US, or rather a particular interpretation of those particular realities. It is perhaps not surprising therefore that scholars of racism in the US have shown so little interest in undertaking comparative research. There are important exceptions. Some comparative work has been undertaken which compares the US with South Africa (e.g. Van den Berghe 1978; Fredrickson 1981; 1995; 1997; for a recent study, see Marx, 1998), and a comparison between the US and England achieved some prominence some twenty years ago (Katznelson, 1976; for a recent analysis, see Small, 1994). More recently, the "neo-conservative" Sowell (1994) has chosen a comparative international arena to demonstrate what he sees as the explanatory power of his thesis; although it is arguable whether this constitutes a contribution to the sociology of racism. But the vast bulk of work by scholars in the US on racism focuses on the US itself.

The fact that this is so may perhaps be explained as the outcome of a benign ethnocentrism. But one also wonders whether it is not also a function of the limited scope of a theory of racism that is closely tied to the "race relations" paradigm by means of racialized dualism which bifurcates the US into "blacks" and "whites." The corollary is that racism is considered to be exclusively a condition or effect of a society structured by a racialized dualism. Such a theoretical position has limited potential to be used to analyze social formations where there is no "black" presence.

Yet, there is evidence of an increasingly conscious unease with this "race relations" paradigm and the "black/white" dichotomy. For example, as we have already noted, West argues in a recent book that "race matters" (1994: 155–6):

> Race is the most explosive issue in American life precisely because it forces us to confront the tragic facts of poverty and paranoia, despair and distrust.

But he also argues that it is necessary to formulate new frameworks and languages in order to comprehend the current crisis in the US and to identify solutions to it (1994: 11). Indeed, he asserts that it is imperative to move beyond the narrow framework of "dominant liberal and conservative views of race in America," views which are formulated with a "worn-out vocabulary" (1994: 4). But it seems that West does not accept that the idea of "race" itself is an example of this exhausted language for he employs it throughout with even a momentary hesitation, despite his belief that the manner in which "we set up the terms for discussing racial issues shapes our perception and response to these issues" (1994: 6). Later in the book, he seems to be on the verge of following through the logic of this argument to its ultimate conclusion when he argues that the Clarence Thomas/Anita Hill hearings demonstrate that "the very framework of racial reasoning" needs to be called into question in order to reinterpret the black freedom struggle not as an issue of "skin pigmentation and racial phenotype" but, instead, as an issue of ethics and politics (1994: 38). And yet West does not follow through the logic of this argument to the point where it is acknowledged that there cannot be a place for the use of the idea of "race" as an analytical concept in the social sciences.

But there is a transatlantic trade in theories of racism and this is now two-way. Some scholars in the US have taken note of debates and arguments generated in Europe, including those contributions which question some of the key assumptions that characterize the debate. Some of these writers have also acknowledged and responded to the criticisms of one of the authors of this paper of the use of the idea of "race" as an analytical concept and of the way in which the concept of racism has been inflated (Miles, 1982; 1989; 1993). Recent contributions by Wellman (1993), Blauner (1992), Omi and Winant (1993; 1994) and Goldberg (1993) all refer to and comment on these arguments, with varying degrees of enthusiasm. Interestingly, they all seem to ignore the writing of Lieberman and his associates (e.g. Lieberman, 1968; Reynolds, 1992) in the US who argue for a position which overlaps in important respects with that outlined here.

Goldberg offers perhaps the most complex and thoughtful response in the course of a wide-ranging and, in part, philosophically inspired analysis of contemporary racisms and of the conceptual language required to analyze these racisms. His important analysis requires a more extended evaluation than is possible in the limited space available here. We have chosen to focus instead on the work of Omi and Winant. This is in part because their writing has already had considerable influence in both the US and in Britain, partly because of the way in which some of their key concepts have parallels in the equally influential work of Gilroy (1987). And this influence is deserved.

There is much to learn from their theoretical and conceptual innovations. We prefer to employ a concept of racialized formation (rather than racial formation), but we agree that racialized categories are socially created, transformed and destroyed through historical time (1994: 55). We too recognize that it is essential to differentiate between "race" (although we do not use "race" as a *concept* but rather we capture its use in everyday life by referring to the *idea* of "race") and the concept of racism, a distinction that allows us to make a further distinction between racialization and racism (although Omi and Winant refer to this as a distinction between racial awareness and racial essentialism) (compare Omi and Winant, 1994: 71 with Miles, 1989: 73–84). And we also agree that it is essential to retain the concept of racism (Wellman is simply mistaken when he claims that Miles argues that racism is not a useful concept, 1993: 3), to identify a multiplicity of historically specific racisms, with the consequence that there is "nothing inherently white about racism" (Omi and Winant, 1994: 72; see also 1994: 73, and compare with Miles, 1989: 57–60; 1993).

It is important to highlight these areas of agreement prior to considering Omi and Winant's defence of the use of the idea of "race" as an analytical concept in the social sciences in order to indicate both the innovations that they have stimulated within the discussion about racism in the US and their failure to pursue the logic of these innovations to their ultimate conclusion. Partly as a result of their emphasis upon the way in which the idea of "race" has been socially constructed and reconstructed, there is now a debate within the literature in the US about the theoretical and analytical status of the idea of "race." Other scholars in the US have made important contributions to the development of this debate, notably Lieberman (1968), Fields (1990), Roediger (1994), and most recently Appiah (1996). Fields' work is especially relevant in this context because it reaches a conclusion that accords closely with that articulated by one of the current authors (see Miles, 1982; 1993: 27–52). Omi and Winant have criticized Fields' conclusions in the course of defending their continued use of "race" as an analytical concept and it is therefore relevant to reflect upon the arguments and evidence that they have employed. Omi and Winant offer two criticisms of the position that the idea of "race" should be analyzed exclusively as a social or ideological construct (1993: 5). First, they suggest that it fails to recognize the social consequences of the longevity of the concept of "race." Second, they claim that, as a result of this longevity, "race is an almost indissoluble part of our identities," a fact that is not recognized by those who argue that "race" is an ideological construct. They are mistaken on both counts. The writing of Miles highlights the historical evolution of the meanings attributed to the idea of "race" and, for example in his discussions of colonialism and of the articulation between racism and nationalism, stresses the way in which the idea of belonging to the "white race" was central to the construction of the identity of the British bourgeoisie and working class (1982; 1993). Indeed, these claims can be refuted simply by citing a quotation from Fields that Omi and Winant themselves reproduce (1993: 5).

Fields writes (1990: 118):

> Nothing handed down from the past could keep race alive if we did not constantly reinvent and re-ritualise it to fit our own terrain. If race lives on today, it can do so only because we continue to create and re-create it in our social life, continue to verify it, and thus continue to need a social vocabulary that will allow us to make sense, not of what our ancestors did then, but of what we choose to do now.

Thus, Fields certainly does not deny that, in the contemporary world, people use the idea of "race" to classify themselves and others into social collectivities and act in ways consistent with such a belief, actions which collectively produce structured exclusion. And, hence, Omi and Winant's critique is shown to be vacuous. Fields' key objective is to critique the way in which historians invoke the idea of "race" to construct explanations for events and processes in the past, and her critique applies equally to the work of sociologists such as Omi and Winant who have reinvented and re-ritualized the idea of "race" to fit their own terrain within the academy (which is after all only one more arena of social life).

Let us examine how Omi and Winant reinvent and thereby reify the idea of "race" in the course of their sociological analysis. Consider the following claim: "One of the first things we notice about people when we meet them (along with their sex) is their race" (1994: 59). Elsewhere, they argue that "To be raceless is akin to being genderless. Indeed, when one cannot identify another's race, a microsociological 'crisis of interpretation' results . . . " (1993: 5). How are we to interpret this assertion? While they also claim that "race is . . . a socially constructed way of differentiating human beings" (1994: 65), the former assertion is at the very least open to interpretation as suggesting that "race" is an objective quality inherent in a person's being, that every human being is a member of a "race," and that such membership is inscribed in a person's visible appearance. It is in the interstices of such ambiguity that the idea of "race" as a biological fact does not just "live on" but is actively recreated by social scientists in the course of their academic practice.

This argument sometimes stimulates incomprehension on the part of scholars in the US who echo arguments employed in some critiques of this position in Britain. Thus, it is often said: "How can you deny analytical status to the idea of race and ultimately the existence of race when blacks and whites are so obviously different and when all the evidence demonstrates that their life chances differ too?" In responding to this question, it is necessary first to problematize what it takes for granted, specifically that the "black/white" division is obvious. The quality of *obviousness* is not inherent in a phenomenon, but is the outcome of a social process in the course of which meaning is attributed to the phenomena in a particular historical and social context. The meaning is learnt by those who are its subject and object. They therefore learn to habitually recognize it, and perhaps to pass on this signification and knowledge to others, with the result that the quality of obviousness attributed to the phenomenon is reproduced through historical time and social space.

Skin color is one such phenomenon. Its visibility is not inherent in its existence but is a product of signification: human beings identify skin color to *mark* or symbolize other phenomena in a historical context in which other significations occur. When human practices include and exclude people in the light of the signi-fication of skin color, collective identities are produced and social inequalities are structured. It is for this reason that historical studies of the meanings attributed to skin color in different historical contexts and through time are of considerable importance. And it is in relation to such studies that one can inquire into the continuities and discontinuities with contemporary processes of signification which sustain the obviousness of skin color as a social *mark*. Historically and contemporarily, differences in skin color have been and are signified as a mark which suggests the existence of different "races." *But people do not see "race": rather, they observe certain combinations of real and sometimes imagined somatic and cultural characteristics, to which they attribute meaning with the idea of "race."* A difference of skin color is not essential to the process of marking: other somatic features can be and are signified in order to racialize. Indeed, in some historical circumstances, the absence of somatic difference has been central to the powerful impact of racism: the racialized "enemy within" may be identi-fied as a threatening presence even more effectively if the group is not "obviously different" because "they" can then be imagined to be everywhere.

Omi and Winant reify this social process and reach the conclusion that all human beings belong to a "race" because they seek to construct their analytical *concepts* to reproduce directly the common sense ideologies of the everyday world. Because the idea of "race" continues to be widely used in everyday life in the US (and Britain) to classify human beings and to interpret their behavior, then Omi and Winant believe that social scientists should employ a *concept* of race. This assumption is the source of our disagreement with them. We believe that one of the contemporary challenges in the analysis of racisms is to develop a conceptual vocabulary that explicitly acknowledges that people use the *idea* of "race" in the everyday world while resisting the use of the idea of "race" as an analytical *concept* when social scientists analyze the discourses and practices of the everyday world. It is not the *concept* of "race" that "continues to play a fundamental role in structuring and representing the social world" (Omi and Winant, 1994: 55) but rather the *idea* of "race." The task of social scientists is to develop a theoretical framework for the analysis of this process of structuring and representing which breaks completely with the reified language of biological essentialism. Hence, we object fundamentally to Omi and Winant's project of developing a critical theory of the *concept* of "race" (1993: 6–9) because we also recognize the importance of historical context and contingency in the framing of racialized categories and the social construction of racialized experiences (cf. Omi and Winant, 1993: 6): we believe that historical context requires us to criticize all concepts of "race" and this can be done by means of a concept of racialization (Miles, 1989: 73–7). Omi and Winant's defence of the concept of "race" is a classic example of the way in which the academy in the US continues to racialize the world.

Furthermore, the concept of racialization employed by Omi and Winant is not fully developed and is not used in a sustained analytical manner. This is because it is grounded in a "race relations" sociology, a sociology that reifies the notion of "race" and thereby implies the existence of "racial groups" as biological categories. Additionally, they fail to take account of the interplay between the social relations of production and the racialization process. The authors of this paper argue that the process of racialization takes place and has its effects in the context of class and production relations and that the idea of "race" may indeed not even be explicitly articulated in this process (see Miles, 1989; 1993).

Bringing Class Back In

The collapse of the communist project in central and eastern Europe, in conjunction with the fashionable predominance of post-modern theory, has, of course, resulted in a "retreat from class" in sociological analysis over the past decade or so (e.g. Wood 1986, 1995). To reassert the importance of class and production relations in relation to the process of racialization will therefore be viewed as an attempt to return to an outdated theoretical paradigm. But Marxist theory has always been a site of conflicting and competing readings of Marx: the Stalinist project certainly died with the collapse of communism, but other readings of Marx, other traditions of Marxist theory, can offer an explanation for what happened in central and eastern Europe in the late 1980s and the early 1990s. Moreover, much of the language and subject matter of postmodern theory presumes an explanation for the increasing importance of contingency, ambiguous and plural identites, the dissolution of the nation-state and that complex of social transformations summarized in the concept of globalization. We are not intending to be simply mischievous by suggesting that there are several useful insights into these very processes in that classic rallying cry to class struggle, *The Communist Manifesto*. More detailed investigations by contemporary analysts working within the tradition of political economy testify to the continuing vigor and power of this tradition of analysis (e.g. Balibar and Wallerstein, 1991).

The necessary re-evaluation of the nature of class analysis in the light of, for example, feminist theory amongst other critical interventions cannot be the substance of this paper (see, for example, Balibar, 1995). But it is important to draw attention to the continuing importance of class analysis to the analysis of the racialization process. The gendered subjects and objects of the racialization process continue to be differentially located in the structures of capitalist relations of production. For example, however one interprets the concept of the reserve army of labor, there is no doubt that very large numbers of people in Europe and North America fail to find a long term position in the labor market: racialized cultural minorities are widely over-represented amongst those in position. And an interrelationship between international migration and exclusionary processes helps to ensure that the ranks of the small entrepreneur include racialized minorities who sustain a complex of financial and cultural ties with their country of origin. These are but two simple examples of the interplay between racialization and class. Both are in turn related to the continuing dispossession of small-scale, independent rural producers in what used to be called the Third World and to the continuing competitive search for the most profitable location for the production of commodities and services by the very large units of capital which are able to treat the slowly dissolving political network of nation-states as alternative locations for their activities.

Conclusion

West begins his first essay in his book *Race Matters* with a reference to the Los Angeles riots of April 1992. He denies that they were either a "race riot or a class rebellion." Rather, he continues:

> this monumental upheaval was a multi-racial, trans-class, and largely male display of social rage . . . Of those arrested, only 36 percent were black, more than a third had full-time jobs, and most claimed to shun political affiliation. What we witnessed in Los Angeles was the consequence of a lethal linkage of economic decline, cultural decay, and political lethargy in American life. Race was the visible catalyst, not the underlying cause. (1994: 3–4)

And he concludes by claiming that the meaning of the riots is obscured because we are trapped by the narrow framework imposed by the dominant views of "race" in the US.

The *Los Angeles Times* Opinion Editor, Jack Miles, rendered a different version of the narrow framework of the "black/white" dichotomy. In an essay in the October 1992 issue of *The Atlantic Monthly* titled "Blacks vs Browns," Miles suggested that Latinos were taking jobs that the nation, by dint of the historic crimes committed against them, owed to African-Americans. He blamed Latinos for the poverty in African-American communities – a gross misattribution of responsibility – while reinforcing "race" as a relevant analytical and social category. His confusion was revealing: the "two societies, one black, one white – separate and unequal" dichotomy articulated by de Tocqueville and made famous by the 1968 report of the National Advisory Commission on Civil Disorders cannot provide an analytical framework to deconstruct the post-Fordist racialized social relations of the 1990s.

The meaning of West's argument is constructed by what is not said as much as what is. There is a silence about the definition of "race riot": what would have had to have happened for the events to be classified as a matter of "race?" Presumably, the events of April 1992 would have been a "race riot" if the principal actors had been "blacks" and "whites." Hence, West refers to "race" only as the visible catalyst: Rodney King was "obviously black" and the police officers who arrested him were "obviously white." But the riots themselves did not fit the "race relations" paradigm because the rioters and those who became the victims of the riot were not exclusively "blacks" and "whites." Indeed, as the media were framing the events of April 1992 in "black/white" terms in the great melodrama of "race relations," the first image across the airwaves was of men atop a car waving the Mexican flag! Thus, "Hispanic" may signify presumptively as "white" in the social dynamics that rest on a system of neat racialized categories, but this has little to do with the popular understanding and experience of Latinos. We believe that the analytical task is therefore to explain the complex nature of the structural changes associated with the emergence of the post-Fordist socio-economic landscape and the reconfigured racialized social relations in Los Angeles specifically and in the US and beyond more generally (see Valle and Torres, 1998).

As a simple measure of these reconfigured social relations, consider the following. Perhaps half of the businesses looted or burned during the LA riots were owned by Korean-Americans and another third or so were owned by Mexican-Americans/Latinos and Cuban-Americans. Those engaged in the looting and burning certainly included African-Americans, but poor, recent and often undocumented immigrants and refugees from Mexico and Central America were equally prominent. Of those arrested, 51 percent were Latinos and 36 percent were African-Americans. And, of those who died in the civil unrest, about half were African-Americans and about a third were Latinos. All this is only surprising if one begins with the assumption that the events were or could have been "race riots" in the sense that became hegemonic in the 1960s. Such an assumption is problematic for two reasons.

First, academics, media reporters and politicians "conspired" to use the vocabulary of "race" to make sense of the Los Angeles riots because it is a central component of everyday common sense discourse in the US. And, when it became overwhelmingly apparent that it was not a "black/white" riot, the language of "race" was nevertheless unthinkingly retained by means of a switch to the use of the notion of "multi-racial" in order to encompass the diversity of historical and cultural origins of the participants and victims. Thus, while the "race relations" paradigm was dealt a serious blow by the reality of riots, the vocabulary of "race" was retained. But, and here we find the source of West's unease, the idea of "race" is so firmly embedded in common sense that it cannot easily encompass a reference to "Koreans" or "Hispanics" or "Latinos" for these are neither "black" nor "white." It is thus not surprising that pundits and scholars such as West stumble over "racial" ambiguity. The clash of racialized language with a changing political economy presents challenges for scholars and activists alike.

Second, if one had begun with an analysis grounded simultaneously in history and political economy rather than with the supremely ideological notion of "race relations," one would have quickly concluded that the actors in any riot in central Los Angeles would probably be *ethnically* diverse. Large-scale inward migration from Mexico and Central America and from south-east Asia into California has coincided with a restructuring of the California economy, the loss of major manufacturing jobs and large-scale internal migration within the urban sprawl of "greater" Los Angeles, with the consequence that the spatial, ethnic and class structure that underlay the Watts riots of 1965 had been transformed into a much more complex set of relationships. The most general conditions were structural in nature, and thus the decline and shift in the manufacturing base in Los Angeles was not unique but represented a shift in the mode of capital accumulation worldwide (Fordist to Flexible).

In order to analyze those relationships, there is no need to employ a concept of "race": indeed, its retention is a significant hindrance. But it is necessary to draw upon the insights consequent upon the creation of the concept of *racisms*. The complex relationships of exploitation and resistance, grounded in differences of class, gender and ethnicity, give rise to a multiplicity of ideological constructions of the racialized Other. For, while the idea of "race" does not matter outside the process of racialization to which academics are active contributors, the racisms articulated in Los Angeles and elsewhere to naturalize, inferiorize, exclude and sustain privilege and growing class inequality certainly do matter.

Acknowledgment

We wish to express thanks to David Theo Goldberg and David Gullette for their helpful comments on an earlier version of this work. Rodolfo Torres would like to acknowledge Antonia Darder and Victor Valle for their continued support. This is a slightly revised version of the original essay published in *Re-Situating Identities: The Politics of Race, Ethnicity, and Culture*, edited by Vered Amit-Talai and Caroline Knowles.

References

Appiah, K. A. (1996). Race, Culture, Identity: Misunderstood Connections. In K.A. Appiah and A. Gutmann, *Color Conscious: The Political Morality of Race*. Princeton: Princeton University Press.
Balibar, E. (1995). *The Philosophy of Marx*. London: Verso.

Balibar, E. and Wallerstein, I. (1991). *Race, Nation, Class: Ambiguous Identities*. London: Verso.

Banton, M. (1967). *Race Relations*. London: Tavistock.

Banton, M. (1987). *Racial Theories*. Cambridge: Cambridge University Press.

Barkan, E. (1992). *The Retreat of Scientific Racism: Changing Concepts of Race in Britain and the United States between the Wars*. Cambridge: Cambridge University Press.

Blauner, B. (1992). Talking Past Each Other: Black and White Languages of Race. *The American Prospect*, 10, 55–64.

Delgado, R. (1995). *Critical Race Theory: The Cutting Edge*. Philadelphia: Temple University Press.

Essed, P. (1991). *Understanding Everyday Racism: An Interdisciplinary Theory*. Newbury Park: Sage.

Faryna, S., Stetson, B., and Conti, J. (1997). *Black and Right: The Bold New Voice of Black Conservatives in America*. Westport: Praeger.

Fields, B. J. (1990). Slavery, Race and Ideology in the United States of America. *New Left Review*, 181, 95–118.

Fredrickson, G. M. (1981). *White Supremacy*. New York: Oxford University Press.

Fredrickson, G. M. (1995) *Black Liberation: A Comparative History of Black Ideologies in the United States and South Africa*. New York: Oxford.

Fredrickson, G. M. (1997). *The Comparative Imagination: On the History of Racism, Nationalism, and Social Movements*. Berkeley: University of California Press.

Gilroy, P. (1987). *"There Ain't No Black in the Union Jack": The Cultural Politics of Race and Nation*. London: Hutchinson.

Goldberg, D. T. (1990). The Social Formation of Racist Discourse. In D. T. Goldberg (ed.), *Anatomy of Racism*. Minneapolis: University of Minnesota Press.

Goldberg, D. T. (1993). *Racist Culture: Philosophy and the Politics of Meaning*. Oxford: Blackwell.

Guillaumin, C. (1972). *L'Ideologie Raciste*. Paris: Mouton.

Guillaumin, C. (1995). *Racism, Sexism, Power and Ideology*. London: Routledge.

Guy-Sheftall, B. (1995). *Words of Fire: An Anthology of African American Feminist Thought*. New York: The New Press.

hooks, B. (1990). *Yearning: Race, Gender and Cultural Politics*. Boston: South End Press.

Joshi, S. and Carter, B. (1984). The Role of Labour in the Creation of a Racist Britain. *Race and Class*, 25(3), 53–70.

Karenga, M. (1993). *Introduction to Black Studies*. Los Angeles: University of Sankore Press.

Katznelson, I. (1976). *Black Men, White Cities*. Chicago: University of Chicago Press.

Layton-Henry, Z. (1992). *The Politics of Immigration*. Oxford: Blackwell.

Lerner, M. and West, C. (1995). *Jews and Blacks: Let the Healing Begin*. New York: G. P. Putnam's Sons.

Lieberman, L. (1968). The Debate Over Race: A Study in the Sociology of Knowledge. *Phylon*, 39, 127–41.

Marx, A. W. (1998). *Making Race and Nation: A Comparison of South Africa, the United States, and Brazil*. Cambridge: Cambridge University Press.

Miles, R. (1982). *Racism and Migrant Labour: A Critical Text*. London: Routledge and Kegan Paul.

Miles, R. (1984) Marxism versus the Sociology of Race Relations. *Ethnic and Racial Studies*, 7(2), 217–37.

Miles, R. (1989). *Racism*. London: Routedge.

Miles, R. (1993). *Racism After "Race Relations."* London: Routledge.

Montagu, A. (1972). *Statement on Race*. London: Oxford University Press.

Omi, M. and Winant, M. (1993). On the Theoretical Status of the Concept of Race. In C. McCarthy and W. Crichlow (eds), *Race, Identity and Representation*. New York: Routledge.

Omi, M. and Winant, M. (1994). *Racial Formation in the United States: From the 1960s to the 1990s* (2nd edn). New York: Routledge.

Rex, J. (1970). *Race Relations in Sociological Theory*. London: Weidenfeld and Nicolson.

Reynolds, L. T. (1992). A Retrospective on "Race": the Career of a Concept. *Sociological Focus*, 25(1), 1–14.

Roediger, D. (1994). *Towards the Abolition of Whiteness: Essays on Race, Politics and Working Class History*. London: Verso.

Small, S. (1994). *Racialised Barriers: The Black Experience in the United States and England in the 1980s*. London: Routledge.

Solomos, J. (1989). *Race and Racism in Contemporary Britain*. London: Macmillan.

Sowell, T. (1994). *Race and Culture: A World View*. New York: Basic Books.

Valle, V. and Torres, R. (1998). Latinos in a "Post-industrial" Disorder: Politics in a Changing City. In A. Darder and R. Torres (eds), *The Latino Studies Reader: Culture, Economy, and Society*. Oxford: Blackwell Publishers.

Van den Berghe, P. L. (1978). *Race and Racism: A Comparative Perspective*. New York: John Wiley and Sons.

Wellman, D. (1993). *Portraits of White Racism* (2nd edn). Cambridge: Cambridge University Press.

West, C. (1994). *Race Matters*. New York: Vintage Books.

Wilson, W. J. (1987). *The Truly Disadvantaged*. Chicago: University of Chicago Press.

Wing, A. K. (1997). *Critical Race Feminism: A Reader*. New York: New York University Press.

Wood, E. M. (1986). *The Retreat from Class: A New 'True' Socialism*. London: Verso.

Wood, E. M. (1995). *Democracy Against Capitalism: Renewing Historical Materialism*. Cambridge: Cambridge University Press.

2

"I Know it's Not Nice, But . . ." The Changing Face of "Race"

Colette Guillaumin

The idea of race is one of the most contradictory and violent in our world today. Having been for so many years, probably more than a century, a sort of first truth, something so obvious that no one ever thought to call it into question (in much the same way as sex today), it has become over the last few decades an explosive topic. As something which was part of, and exploited by, a world becoming increasingly efficient technologically, and more and more centralized, race became transformed in the middle of the present century into a means for states to achieve their goals of domination, exploitation and extermination. This is a matter of simple fact.

Race is Not a Neutral Idea

No, the term "race" is not just one banal, harmless designator among others. Nor is it a "given," a word which in itself is neutral and can be used socially in a way which is either "good" or "bad," indifferent or pernicious, according to the circumstances. The notion of categorizing humankind into closed, anatomical and physiological entities is a strange one, and it seems astonishing that as it grew and became more complex it was not greeted with greater suspicion. At a time when the whole idea of "race" was becoming socially accepted (essentially around the beginning of the nineteenth century), de Tocqueville was virtually alone in sensing that there was something shameful underlying its use. No doubt the same thing was seen by other, less famous people whose voices were not so widely heard, but among the notable intellectuals and politicians of the day, precious few showed any reticence.

At the very time when the idea of race was acquiring such social importance, during the first half of the nineteenth century, the anthropologist Franz Boas was already aware of the unreliability of anatomical measurements, which varied from one generation to the next according to living conditions, so that the shape of the bones in our skull was influenced by that most vulgar of commodities, the food we ate. . . . Today we know perfectly well (as we probably always did, but what we know and what we are prepared to acknowledge are not always the same thing . . .) that any physical characteristic whatsoever can be made into a "discriminator" in some socially or politically motivated system of classification (by opposition to a disinterested, scientific one). The choice of somatic criteria is symbolic of the intentions of the classifiers, and nothing more. The Nazis deciding who was (and was not) a Jew, as they put it more than once (when offering Fritz Lang an important role in the cinema industry of the Third Reich, for instance), or the government of the Republic of South Africa classifying Chinese people as belonging to one race and Japanese to another, are sufficient illustration that these things are a matter of politics rather than objective reality, and that the users of such distinctions are well aware of the fact.

"Race Does Not Exist"

What is the position today? For about the last ten years we have clearly been at a crucial stage in the development of the notion of race. A number of voices have been raised claiming that "race" does not exist. They are not very numerous, but their importance is considerable. While the meaning of the term has been constantly changing since its emergence, this is the first time any attempt has been made to destroy the very concept itself, which is extremely important. It is certainly crucial in that it marks a break with one of the most untouchable sacred cows of our time, but it becomes even more so when we look at the real significance of this attempted rejection. A number of researchers are currently working to ensure that "race" is shelved away among other notions which, in the history of science (and natural science in particular), belong firmly to the past. This tendency developed progressively through the period 1965–75, beginning with the questioning of the idea on theoretical and conceptual grounds. The physical anthropologist Jean Hiernaux remarked at the time: "Race is not a fact, but a concept."[1] This apparently simple observation in fact represents a turning-point. It acts as a logical introduction to the statement made by the haemo-typologist Jacques Ruffié in his inaugural lecture at the Collège de France in December 1972:

> In our part of the world, in most Latin countries, physical anthropology has grad-
> ually become separated from the sociology of culture . . . Now, in man, there is no
> such thing as race. That is why, despite numerous and rigorous studies, nobody has
> ever been able to agree on how humanity should be divided up into races.

This position and its variants underlie the critique of race advanced by population geneticists as well as by physical anthropologists in the strict sense of the
term.
    How is it that the scientific community should have arrived at a position so
startlingly opposed to the common-sense view of our age?

What we today call a race was not, contrary to widespread opinion, something self-evident to people of earlier centuries. While there may be arguments among historians, sociologists and researchers in all the other disciplines that are concerned with the role of race in society about the precise historical moment when the notion emerged in the form in which we know it today, when both the term and the idea were born, there is no debate about the thing itself.

The word "race" (which came into French only relatively recently, in the sixteenth century) originally had a very precise sense: it meant "family" or, more accurately, "family relationship." Moreover, it was only ever applied to important dynasties (the race of the Bourbons, the race of David, etc.). In no way was it applied at that time to large groups of people with no legal link of kinship between them. From referring to legally circumscribed, noble families, it shifted to being applied to much wider groups, the attribution to whom of some common physical trait served as a pretext for designating them as a single entity, now called a "race." This shift from surname to skin color is a considerable one: from narrow legal link binding family groups together, to complete geographical dispersion, the term underwent a semantic journey of extraordinary proportions. However, it took a long time, and a major change in our ways of thinking, before "race" became applied to groups of people lumped together according to some common physical characteristic, rather than just a shared surname.

The evolution of the term then went through another important stage. During the first half of the nineteenth century, other, quite different characteristics began to be slipped in alongside the physical (or supposedly physical) common denominators of human groups: these were social, or cultural traits. Philological research had identified specific groupings (Indo-European languages, Semitic languages, etc.) among the language-forms then known, and these were quickly absorbed into the systems of somatic classification which were then sweeping all before them. It was a short step from there to suggesting the existence of Indo-European and Semitic races. We all know what that led to a century later.

But What Actually is "Race?"

The concept of "race" was formed at a historically determined (or determinable) period, as the result of an oscillation between meanings generated from diverse sources, and the combining of several different types of classification (legal, anatomical, linguistic . . .). Heterogeneous lines of thought came to be fused in the single claim that human groups were differential by nature, and that there was a natural line of separation between them. This has now become the *de facto* everyday meaning of the term "race." But, however irritating it might be to go on repeating it, we should never forget that "race" is not a spontaneously given product of perception and experience. It is an idea built up (and slowly, at that) from elements which might equally well be physical traits as social customs, linguistic peculiarities as legal institutions, lumped together and homogenized according to the precept that they must ultimately all be biological phenomena.

This idea carries a great deal of weight in a society obsessed with the sanctity of "Science," which has been invested with the power not only to unveil and understand natural phenomena, but to establish what actually constitutes those phenomena themselves.

Jacques Ruffié's assertion that no such physical category exists within humanity certainly marked a turning-point. At the same time, though, it fell within a critical tradition which was not new, but had been expressed quite differently in the middle of the present century.

This was the period when race, which had originally been a purely descriptive notion, became transformed into a legal one. From being an "idea" it was turned into a concrete social fact. The scientific community in the 1930s, particularly people working in the social sciences, made strenuous efforts to oppose this and to defuse the legalization of the notion of race which the Nazi regime was bringing about. They proclaimed the complete inadequacy of such a "purely physical" notion to account for, describe and influence those aspects of human life which were dependent on society and culture, although they did not challenge its relevance to the physical domain. Many different stands were taken at that time. In December 1938, for instance, the American Psychological Association declared that:

> In the experiments which psychologists have made upon different peoples, no characteristic, inherent psychological differences which fundamentally distinguish so-called "races" have been disclosed. [. . .] There is no evidence for the existence of an inborn Jewish or German or Italian mentality. [. . .] The Nazi theory that people must be related by blood in order to participate in the same cultural or intellectual heritage has absolutely no support from scientific findings.

But these warnings could never be more than symbolic, since the legal and political systems which exploited the notion of race were already in place.

So a critical attempt was made to break the syncretic link between physical and socio-cultural traits which had been forged and developed over the preceding centuries. But it did not call the notion itself into question. It was a statement of principle as well as a moral protest. Both are necessary, but not sufficient. The idea of race was left very solidly in place, and in the end went absolutely unquestioned as such. There had been an attempt to limit the damage, it had failed, and in 1945 the state of South Africa in its turn adopted legal categories of race.

These stands were to influence various declarations of the international organizations throughout the 1950s. Their concern was still the same: to demonstrate that the material, physical fact of "race" (which still went unchallenged except by the occasional isolated researcher) was quite separate from social or psychological characteristics. The intention was to show that race, still assumed to exist in itself, had no connection with or influence over the way in which human beings behaved.

The UNESCO "Statement on the Nature of Race and Race Differences" of 1951 provides a good illustration of this position:

Since race, as a word, has become coloured by its misuse in connexion with national linguistic and religious differences, and by its deliberate abuse by racialists, we tried to find a new word to express the same meaning of a biologically differentiated group. On this we did not succeed, but agreed to reserve race as the word to be used for anthropological classification of groups showing definite combinations of physical (including physiological) traits in characteristic proportions. [. . .] National, religious, geographical, linguistic and cultural groups do not necessarily coincide with racial groups; and the cultural traits of such groups have no demonstrated connexion with racial traits. Americans are not a race, nor are Frenchmen, nor Germans; nor *ipso facto* is any other national group. Moslems and Jews are no more races than are Roman Catholics and Protestants; nor are people who live in Iceland or Britain or India, or who speak English or any other language, or who are culturally Turkish or Chinese and the like, thereby describable as races. The use of the term "race" in speaking of such groups may be a serious error, but it is one which is habitually committed.[2]

Talking About "Difference"

Looking back on this from our position today, we are struck by the pathetic aspect of a protest so resolute and yet so far removed from a reality of repression and violence. It is also striking to see that we are forgetting here – and when I say "we," I mean all of us who work in the human sciences and are reduced to exasperation and despair by this notion so difficult to tie down – that the idea of race did not belong exclusively to the natural sciences, either historically, or socially, or ideologically. Despite that, however, the idea was challenged as if it did. Moreover, as if that were the only way in which race could, and should, be envisaged.

And yet, while it had become a geographical classification in the work of Linné, and was extrapolated into linguistics in the first half of the nineteenth century during the triumph of philology, race was also a subject for debate in the streets, in political quarters, in the salons, where it came to represent what was "peculiar" about each human group. It was the equivalent of our "difference," and that is certainly how it was understood. A case in point was Balzac, the first major novelist to make extensive use of the idea. The current vogue notion of difference is so ambiguous that it is often defended just as much by traditional racists as by anti-racists, whilst even the victims of racism themselves invoke it as something they wish to cultivate. This is because difference has come to inherit all the connotations relating to the specificity of human groups which in the old days were carried by the notion of race. It is true that the idea of difference is an attempt to get away from the imperative of physical naturality imposed by race, and in that sense its aim is certainly to break down the rigidity of the racist system of thought. But at the same time it attracts those who persist in thinking in racist terms, but no longer dare use the word "race." When, for reasons of censorship, political prudence or simply cynicism, these people choose "difference" instead of "race," they know that they will still be understood as saying something about the "natural" specificity of human groups. For it is impossible to destroy the deeper strata of a system of thought simply by taking away a particular element; its configuration needs to be modified by adding some new trait.

So, the social sciences forgot the circumstances in which the idea of race came into existence and developed, and failed to take account of the fact that the great theorists of race were from their own camp, rather than from the natural sciences. Gobineau was not a scientist, nor were Vacher de Lapouge and, later, Chamberlain and Rosenberg, and so on.

Today, a few people in the human-related sciences are awakening from this lethargy and trying to reject a notion whose origin is clearly to be sought in socio-intellectual modes of thought which have nothing to do with experimental scientific practice. But this awakening has come as a surprise for the social sciences, which thought that they had discreetly disposed of a category for which they were largely responsible by pushing it off into the domain of the natural sciences. If the responsibility is indeed theirs, it is less because they had a part in the invention of "race" than because they are the very disciplines on which the study of the phenomenon depends: as a social trait, it falls within their sphere of understanding and analysis. Sociologists, historians and epistemologists were perhaps unwilling to see that this hot potato was their problem, but that is certainly the case. And the natural sciences keep reminding them of it by denying that race has anything to do with them.

What is the Position of "Race" Today?

We now find ourselves at a stage where the pertinence of the notion of race in the natural sciences of man is being refuted on grounds of scientific reason and intellectual honesty (not to mention logic and common sense). This is quite an event, something new in these fields of research. As we have seen, however, it is not an isolated move, for race has been analyzed and challenged by other disciplines for some decades now. But this stand is unlikely to achieve its desired aim of eliminating the idea that human beings are "naturally" different, and that the great divides in society (national, religious, political, etc.) reflect "natural" differences. For negations are not recognized as such by our unconscious mental processes. From this point of view, a fact affirmed and a fact denied exist to exactly the same degree, and remain equally present in our affective and intellectual associative networks. Just talking about race means that it will always be there in residue. "Race" is about the least conceptional, cold and abstract of notions, so it appeals from the start to the unconscious side of the mechanisms we have for acquiring knowledge and relating to other human beings. The ideologues of racism have always been well aware of this, which is why they are still peddling their views today.

In other words, simply showing that a category of this type has no scientific basis is insufficient to remove it from the mental universe not simply of the majority of people, but even of those who are intellectually convinced that it does not exist as a "natural" reality. It is a necessary operation, but not a sufficient one.

The human sciences began by saying: "race" is a matter for the natural sciences, it is none of our business, it has no influence on cultural and social phenomena, and so on. Today, the natural sciences are replying: "race" does not exist, it is not a pertinent criterion of classification. Each of these two propositions is partially true, but they hide a third which comes much closer to fitting the real facts. And if ever one revolution or one proposition could conceal another, this is certainly a case in point. Whether race is or is not "a fact of nature," whether it is or is not a "mental reality," it is today, in the twentieth century, a legal, political and historical reality which plays a real and constraining role in a number of societies.

(a) That is why any appeal to race (even under the pretext of a love of different cultures, or the search for "roots," etc.) is a political move which can never be neutral, given the facts. For it is a question of facts, and not one of intentions or opinions, as some people would once again have us believe.
(b) That is why simply rejecting the notion of race is not enough. Denying its existence as an empirically valid category, as the human, social and, ultimately, natural sciences are trying to do, can never, however correct the intention, take away that category's reality within society or the state, or change the fact that while it may not be valid empirically, it certainly exerts an empirical effect. To claim that a notion which is present in a society's vocabulary, i.e. in both its way of organizing the world and in its political and human history, can be negated in this way is a paradoxical position, because that which is negated has de facto existence. It is perhaps also an attempt to take away the horror of that reality, its unbearable brutality: it is impossible that something of that kind should exist. Precisely because its existence is unbearable.

However, while the reality of "race" is indeed neither natural and biological, nor psychological (some innate tendency of the human mind to designate the other as a natural entity), it does nevertheless exist. It is not possible to argue that a category which organizes whole states (the Third Reich, the Republic of South Africa, etc.), and which is incorporated into the law, does not exist. It is not possible to claim that the category which is the direct cause, the primary means, of the murder of millions of human beings does not exist.

But the slow path to intellectual understanding traced by successive and cumulative attempts to elucidate the concept shows that race is a social category of exclusion and murder. Its real nature has gradually been unmasked. The process has not been a simple one, for it is hard not to believe that "race does not exist" when the idea that it is a "natural" category has been proved false (as indeed it is), while at the same time that idea was all that was left after the patient critique undertaken by the social sciences. And when, above all, that celebrated "natural" definition was the very same one which "legitimized" the legal inscription of "race" in racist regimes.

Yet the legal inscription of race and the practices that accompany it certainly do exist. And they are precisely the reality of race. Race does not exist. But it does kill people. It also continues to provide the backbone of some ferocious systems of domination. And in France today it is rearing its ugly head once again. Not in the shameful margins of our society, but behind the honourable mask of "opinion" and "ideas." Let us be clear about this. The idea, the notion of race is a technical means, a machine, for committing murder. And its effectiveness is not in doubt. It is a way of rationalizing and organizing by murderous violence the domination of powerful social groups over other groups reduced to powerlessness. Unless anyone is prepared to claim that, since race does not exist, nobody is or can ever have been repressed or killed because of their race. And nobody can make that claim, because millions of human beings have died as a result of their race, and millions of others are now dominated, excluded and repressed for the same reason.

No, race does not exist. And yet it does. Not in the way that people think; but it remains the most tangible, real and brutal of realities.

Notes

1   See J. Hiernaux, "De l'individu à la population: l'anthropobiologie," in *La Science face au racisme* (re-edition of the first issue of *Le Genre humain*), Brussels, Editions Compexe, 1986.
2   In A. Montague (ed.), *Statement on Race*. Oxford: Oxford University Press, 1972 (3rd edn), pp. 139–47 (p. 141; p. 143).

3

The Contours of Racialization: Structures, Representations and Resistance in the United States

Stephen Small

Introduction

This work examines patterns of "race relations" in the United States of America in the 1980s and 1990s, with a particular focus on the experiences of African-Americans. It considers some key facts of "race relations," a number of key incidents which reflect these broader facts, as well as the responses of African-Americans to them. I suggest that "race" and "racism" continue to play a decisive role in black people's lives, but that, due to the intricate relationships between "racism," and economic and political power, a new conceptual framework is needed to provide a better understanding of how this unfolds. A framework of "racialization" is introduced, in which the concepts of "racialized barriers" and "racialized" hostility (including "racialized" structures, images, ideologies and identities) are defined and examined. Each of these terms are defined and examples of them provided. I argue that while we cannot reduce the problems which blacks face to economics and politics alone, nor can we focus exclusively on "racism." A better approach is one which considers "racialized" hostility alongside a broad array of economic and political factors.

Terms and Concepts

Words like "race relations," "race," "racial," "racism," and "racist" have been put in quotation marks to highlight the fact that although these words are commonly used, the precise meanings and significance of them is deeply contested. For example, do "races" exist as distinct biological groups? Or do they simply reflect the social definitions and constructions of different groups? If we call a relationship "racial," does that mean it was determined by "race?" Or that ideas and beliefs about "race" are simply aspect of that? Is there one "racism" or several different "racisms?" If we can identify "racism" does that mean we can identify "non-racism?" Can we distinguish the content of "racism," from the intentions of "racists" and from the outcomes or consequences of "racism?" And does the term "race relations" mean that relationships between blacks and whites are relationships between biological distinctive "races?"

In recent decades social scientists have questioned the language and concepts used to analyze what was previously called "race relations" (Banton, 1977; Miles, 1982; 1989; Winant, 1994). I have been a critic of this language (Small, 1989; 1991; 1993; 1994b). Along with these authors, I believe that these concepts, and the assumptions underlying them, create more problems than they solve. The words "race," and "racial" suggest the existence of discrete biological "races," and imply that anything which is "racial" results primarily from this fact. For example, the idea of "racial conflict" suggests conflict results mainly from contact between "races" in and of themselves, rather than because of other factors, such as economics and political competition. But the vast majority of scientists, genetic and social, agree that discrete biological "races" do not exist, and that biological distinctiveness bears little relationship to the "racial" identities of communities scattered across the world today (Banton, 1977). In addition, Williams has argued that the origin of slavery had to do primarily with economics – "it had to do not with the color of the laborer, but the cheapness of the labor" (Williams, 1944: 19); and that because slavery became overwhelmingly identified with Africans, "a racial twist has thereby been given to what is basically an economic phenomenon" (Williams, 1944: 7).

The words "racism," and "racist" suggest that there is one type of "racism" and that individuals are either "racist" (say like the Ku Klux Klan) or "non-racist." The reality is far more complex. For example, we cannot say a person who opposes Affirmative Action, or who is in favour of tighter immigration control is "racist" (because this opposition may be motivated by a wide variety of factors, for example, a genuine belief in treating all individuals equally without regard to ethnicity or "race.") Nor can we say that a person who expresses support for "color blind" policies is "non-racist." For example, in 1988 President Bush openly supported "color blind" policies and said he did not want "race" to enter into his campaign, yet he condoned the use of negative stereotypes of black crime in strengthening his political campaigns (Small, 1994b: 89). The intentions people hold, and what they do can be markedly different from what they say they will do. As we will see in the following sections, attitudes and ideologies that might be called "racist" can take different forms and be motivated by many different factors.

Because it owes its origin to mistaken assumptions from the past, the language of "race relations" fails to acknowledge these kinds of complexities, and often leads to an oversimplified focus on "race" while ignoring the complexities of economics, political and social power, and the consequences of the routine operation of key institutions in contemporary life. This is a language that we cannot afford to employ if we wish to understand such complexities, or bring about change.

I believe a better approach is provided by working within the "racialization" problematic or framework. This framework is a set of assumptions and key concepts which explore the multiple factors that shape what has previously been called "race relations." Some of these factors entail explicit reference to "race," for example, beliefs about the existence of "races," prejudice, and discrimination based on such beliefs. But other factors – such as competition for economic and political resources (education, jobs, housing, elected office) – may seem to have no racialized referent. The "racialization" problematic enables us to draw out the relationship between these seemingly unrelated variables, and, importantly, to begin to assess the significance of each of them. In sum, analysts working within the "racialization" problematic are able to ask the question: "If 'race relations' are not the relationship between biologically different 'races,' then what are they?" This turns our attention to economics, politics, power; and to the ways in which structures, images and ideologies operate to sustain inequality and injustice.

The key concept within the "racialization" problematic is the process of "racialization" which refers primarily to a historically specific ideological process, and the structures that accompanied this process (Omi and Winant, 1994; Small, 1994b). It refers to the ways in which diverse ethnic groups from Europe and Africa came to be defined as the white "race" and the black "race" in the colonization and conquest of the Americas (Banton, 1977; Miles, 1982). It also refers to the institutional arrangements which accompanied these processes: the legal system (in slavery, and Jim Crow segregation), the economic system (the plantation economy, and the distribution of jobs), as well as housing (with blacks confined to the ghetto). The laws and policies introduced to end segregation, for example, Civil Rights legislation, voting rights laws, and Affirmative Action, continue processes of "racialization" though their goals are clearly in a different direction.

Rather than "race" and "racial" I prefer the concept of "racialized groups." As well as moving away from the notion that blacks and whites are biologically discrete groups, it emphasizes how definitions of who is white and who is black vary from context to context. Rather than conceptualizing "racism" or "racists" and "non-racists" I find it more useful to examine the intentions, content and outcomes of ideologies and actions, and how they impact upon groups defined by "race" in different ways. In this way, interactions between groups that are defined as "races" are conceptualized as "racialized relations." It is assumed that ideas and beliefs about "race," both at present and in the past, have shaped these relationships, and that other factors, such as economics, class, and gender are central. But there is no presumption that "racism" is the primary or most important variable. The concrete examples elaborated below demonstrate that this is not simply a matter of changing the words, or playing semantics; but rather a matter of challenging the assumptions, and of improving the analysis by identifying as central a number of variables that are often ignored, neglected or obscured.

The concepts of "racialized" barriers and hostility (including structures, images and ideologies) emphasizes the systemic and sustained obstacles to black aspirations. They refer to the activities of key institutions, and the actions of those who work in them, which result in the exclusion or victimization of African-Americans. It is important to note that "hostility" is not used in its usual sense of explicit and direct violent or aggressive action, but rather to mean "attitudes and actions where the intentions and/or outcomes are detrimental to black people" (Small, 1994b: 210, fn 6).

Finally, "racialized" identities refers to how groups and individuals embrace the idea of "race" and difference, in their efforts to compete and succeed. Developing organizations around a common and shared experience – a black identity – is a primary example of this, particularly for African-Americans who have sustained resistance to hostility, discrimination and exclusion of various kinds (T'Shaka, 1990).

Inequality and Institutional Practices

"Racialized" structures are the institutional pillars of society. They are the routine, recurrent and organized features of contemporary life. The idea of "racialized" structures has two key components. First, it refers to the distribution of valuable resources such as political power, employment, education and housing. Primarily this aspect involves who owns what, works and lives where, and has good health. Secondly, it refers to the normal, recurrent and routinized procedures of institutions that shape and constrain our daily lives, from politics (voting and political representatives), economics (businesses, employment), education (universities, schools), health (hospitals) and other spheres of social life (family, media, music, sport). These behaviors and actions sustain the distribution of resources. The practices of key institutions in the contemporary United States shape and determine who succeeds and who fails, who is rewarded and who is punished.

"Racialized" inequality is revealed in differences in the share of, and access to, valued resources. It is captured in the notion of a "Color Line," that is, of material disparities between blacks and whites (Small, 1994b: 15). What it means is that, on the basis of all the key indicators, blacks are at a disadvantage compared to whites. A recent study of black and white wealth argued that "materially, whites and blacks constitute two nations, . . . two middle classes" (Oliver and Shapiro, 1995: 7). Whites have far more wealth than blacks, and rich whites have far more wealth than rich blacks. When compared with the richest blacks, the richest whites "controlled four times as much wealth as blacks with the same degrees" (Oliver and Shapiro, 1995: 8). While middle class blacks earn only 70 cents for every dollar earned by middle class whites (Oliver and Shapiro, 1995: 7). Not only do whites benefit from better earnings but they also benefit from a tax system that affects them less adversely. Whites benefit from low taxes on capital gains, from real estate taxes and from the tax deduction for home mortgages (Oliver and Shapiro, 1995: 43). Wealth is important not only because it reveals the greatest disparities, but also because wealth "captures the historical legacy of low wages, personal and organizational discrimination and institutionalized racism" (Oliver and Shapiro, 1995: 5). It is testimony to the fact that we cannot begin to analyze the present without some consideration of how it was shaped by the past.

For blacks as a whole, income is almost 60 percent that of whites, but this understates the disparities; the median net worth of black households (that is, total assets less liabilities) was only about one-tenth that of whites in 1989 (O'Hare et al., 1991: 30); the median annual income for black families amounted to $20,200 while for white families it was substantially higher (ibid.: 27). Similar disparities can be found in patterns of employment. White men are still twice as likely as their black counterparts to work in administration, management, or a profession (O'Hare et al., 1991: 25).

Residential segregation remains pervasive. Blacks and whites are to be found in different neighborhoods, regardless of their levels of earnings, or occupations (O'Hare et al., 1991: 9). Furthermore, the proportion of blacks residing in high-poverty areas (defined as census tracts with at least 20 percent of the residents in poverty) increased by almost 20 percent during the 1980s (O'Hare et al., 1991: 9). The pattern of segregation is so entrenched and severe that it has led two authors to call it "American Apartheid" (Massey and Denton, 1993). The picture is the same in education and health and in experiences with the criminal justice system. White students are twice as likely as blacks to graduate from college, while around 20 percent of whites earn a degree, as compared with 11 percent of blacks (O'Hare et al., 1991: 22). Young black people experience more health problems and have more conflicts with the criminal justice system.

The "racialized" structure of inequality reflects not just disparities between blacks and whites, but also within the black population. Educational, occu-pational and economic mobility of some blacks has continued, alongside the continued entrenchment of the majority in poverty or in low paid, dead-end and part time jobs. This stratification has pronounced gender dimensions. Black married couples are the most economically successful families, while so-called "female-headed" families experience the most economic hardship. Black families comprised of married couples, and in which the head of the household is 25 to 44 years old and a college graduate, have median incomes of $54,400; that is 93 percent of whites medium income of $58,800 (O'Hare et al., 1991: 28). At the same time, 26 percent of black families revealed incomes below $10,000 (O'Hare et al., 1991: 27). Women are more likely to earn less, to find themselves in part-time jobs (most often without health benefits), and to be in poverty, especially if they head families with children. The median income of black female-headed households is less than $12,000, compared with nearly $19,000 for white female-headed households (O'Hare et al., 1991: 28).

On the whole, then, blacks are at considerable disadvantage compared to whites, and face problems of "racialized" hostility which whites do not face. But black efforts to survive and succeed have produced varied results. While the majority of institutions are still dominated by whites, blacks, in small number, can still be found among executives and managers, and there are black businesses which control limited but significant resources. This is particularly important in cities such as New York, Washington, D.C., Detroit, Chicago, and Los Angeles, where blacks are either a majority, or a very substantial proportion of the residents. Blacks can be found working in, managing, even controlling television and film media (such as black Entertainment Television, films like "Devil in a Blue Dress" and "Waiting to Exhale") print media (such as *Ebony, Jet*, and an array of black newspapers), music videos (Rose, 1994). The significance of this presence is important when we seek to understand the dominant images and representations of black people in American society. This is discussed in the following section.

"Racialized" discrimination is widespread, and continues to constrain the aspirations of black people, at all class positions, and both genders. This includes violence, attacks, exclusion and (verbal) abuse. A 1991 study of 6.4 million applications for home mortgages, carried out by the Federal Reserve found that banks "rejected black applicants twice as often as whites nationwide" (Oliver and Shapiro, 1995: 19). "Blacks who do qualify, moreover, pay higher interest rates on home mortgages than whites" (Oliver and Shapiro, 1995: 8). This was true regardless of financial status because the same study also suggested "The poorest white applicant . . . was more likely to get a mortgage loan approved than a black in the highest income bracket" (Oliver and Shapiro, 1995: 19–20). The authors concluded that "discrimination follows blacks no matter where they want to live and no matter how much they earn" (Oliver and Shapiro, 1995: 20). Discrimination within the real estate industry – via subsidies to those who live in the suburbs, mainly whites, and penalization of those who seek inner city housing, mainly blacks – has long historical precedent (Massey and Denton, 1993).

This hostility is also reflected in a number of internationally covered incidents, such as the Stuart case in Boston, the Rodney King beating, and the riots that followed the court case, the implementation of Proposition 187 in California in 1994, mobilization around the so-called "Civil Rights Initiative" (which calls for the abolition of Affirmative Action), as well as in attitudes towards the O. J. Simpson case, and the Million Man March (Small, 1994b; Feagin and Vera, 1995; *Time*, October 1995).

Another element of "racialized" structures that must be considered is the increased importance of other ethnic groups, and their salience in the political arena (Jennings, 1994). Minorities like Asians and Latinos have grown dramatically in number and economic and political significance – particularly at the regional level as in the south western states – and their presence has made analysis of "racialized" and ethnic inequality that much more complex (Chang and Leong, 1994). These groups face extensive hostility, exclusion and victimization of various kinds. They are important because blacks alone can no longer set the political agenda, are more often outnumbered, demographically and in terms of resources, and because there is often competition between blacks and other groups for the same resources (Jennings, 1994; Small, 1994b).

Finally, it is important to recognize the international context as a decisive factor in the unfolding of these processes. Dramatic international changes – from transnational corporations and global competition, the massive innovations in computer technology and communications, and military involvement in the Gulf war, Somalia, Haiti and Bosnia; from the disintegration of the Soviet Union to the unification of Germany; and, of course, the European Union (Small, 1994b; Lusane, 1994; Oliver and Shapiro, 1995); and international terrorism. This context shapes the attitudes of government, business executives and the policies and strategies that they decide appropriate for domestic policies of education, employment, welfare and policing. It is fear of global competition – especially from Japan and the European Union – which has encouraged a preoccupation with the Budget Deficit, changing policies of education and skill training, a restructuring of employment, and a strengthening of resolve to reduce expenditure on welfare in general, Affirmative Action in particular. These are patterns exemplified elsewhere in the world, particularly Europe (Wrench and Solomos, 1993). In a world of increasing interdependence and competition – and a dizzying array of factors that shape "racialized" and ethnic relations – international factors can only become more important (Rattansi and Westwood, 1994; Winant, 1994).

Screening the Images

The images of black people which are prevalent in US society are a central factor in shaping relations between blacks and whites, and in shaping relations within the black community, because they influence the attitudes, expectations and responses of the various communities. By images and representations I mean the roles in which blacks are found in television, film, and print media (newspapers, magazines, books). These images are also important because they do not reflect the general experience of black people – they abbreviate it, encapsulate it, and in doing so distort it. Though they appear to present a range of roles such images are overwhelmingly narrow, unrepresentative and stereotypical. This means that given the dramatic patterns of residential segregation then most whites get their views and beliefs about blacks not from personal experience but from the media. One reason that the O. J. Simpson trial was so important, is that it provided a channel through which whites and blacks interacted, and disagreed so vehemently.

A dominant set of images concerns black success: in sport, music, and television, and to a lesser extent in politics and business. Shows like the Cosby show, Arsenio Hall, Oprah Winfrey, outstanding athletes (Michael Jordan, Jerry Rice), entertainers such as Whitney Houston, film stars like Denzil Washington, Wesley Snipes and Angela Bassett, highly visible black newsreaders like Bryant Gumbel and Bernard Shaw all lead to an impression that African-Americans have achieved equality. But the facts contradict this image. These images do not reflect the experiences of the vast majority of African-Americans, and most

African-Americans are either excluded from these industries, or occupy sub-ordinate and powerless roles (Rose, 1994; Guerrero, 1993; Omi, 1989). A second set of images concerns black failure: reluctance and laziness around work, and welfare dependency, especially welfare mothers (Small, 1994b; Glenn, 1994). Black men presented as unwilling to work, and dependent on the mothers of their children, the mothers themselves dependent on the largesse of government hand-outs (Jewell, 1988).

A third set of images is of black crime. In the United States crime is pervasive – there is not a social class or "racialized" group which is free from crime. Yet, if one reviews stories on crime in the media, one could not be blamed for believing most crime is committed by blacks. In fact, most crime is committed by whites, and the crime which costs society the most is committed by middle-class whites – that is, corporate crime, laxity in health and safety provisions, tax evasion (Mokhiber, 1988; Simon and Eitzen, 1993). Media images distort this picture. However, these images, while biassed, are not entirely inaccurate – that is because though they are less likely to commit certain crimes, blacks are more likely to be arrested. For example, the US government estimates that 15–20 percent of drug users in the United States are black. Yet in certain regions, blacks are over-whelmingly arrested for drug crimes – in New York in 1989, 92 percent of those arrested were African-American or Latino (Duster, 1995: 22). Not only that but punishments vary tremendously; possession with intent to distribute five grams of cocaine brings "a variable sentence of 10 to 37 months" while possession with intent to distribute five grams of crack "brings a mandatory minimum five-year sentence" (Duster, 1995: 23).

A final image is that of reverse racism: the excesses of Affirmative Action, of white "victims" of "reverse discrimination" being kept out of jobs and education, of the financial burden of "race specific" policies, of incompetent blacks and other minorities being admitted to jobs and colleges, and of black "racists." These images are pervasive in debates on higher education, on unemployment and the Budget Deficit. And of course, of the unfairness of the O. J. Simpson decision, and the largely black jury that proclaimed it. The ideologies and activities of Minister Louis Farrakhan of the Nation of Islam figures prominently here – as a fanatic, anti-Semite and hater of whites, fomenting "racial" dissent, and damaging "race relations."

Related to these images is the fact that so called "Black Conservatives" have been given substantial time of television to argue that people like Jesse Jackson, and organizations like the NAACP, are antiquated and out of touch with the majority of the black community. People like Shelby Steele, and Thomas Sowell, both academics and Alan Keyes, candidate for the Republican nomination for president for 1996, join in the chorus against Affirmative Action, insisting, contrary to the evidence, that "racialized" discrimination has ended, or is less relevant to the black experience, and that black laziness, dependence and a culture of poverty is to blame for continuing inequality (Boston, 1988; Small, 1994b: 90). The fact is that these individuals represent a tiny and unrepresen-tative section of the black community. And it is no joke that one finds so many of the television shows about black people to be situation comedies, many of them involving professional comedians and/or rap artists. "The Fresh Prince of Bel Air," "Family Affairs," "Martin," "Roc," and others. Collectively this contributes to the impression that black people are comedians and their lives, experiences and attitudes are not to be taken seriously. Where are the images of "racialized" hostility and exclusion? Of black resilience and strength, of moral courage and stamina, against all the odds? They are there, to be sure, but sandwiched infrequently and irreverently between this larger picture of sloth, undeserved privilege and hatred.

The overall impact of such stereotypical images is more difficult to ascertain. Guerrero has argued that:

> The representation of black people on the commercial screen has amounted to one grand, multifaceted illusion. For blacks have been subordinated, marginalized, positioned, and devalued in every possible manner to glorify and relentlessly hold in place the white-dominated symbolic order and racial hierarchy of American society. (1993: 2)

Wong has studied images of people of color in some of the most important, widely seen and successful films of the 1980s, such as "Driving Miss Daisy," "Clara's Heart," and "The Hand that Rocks the Cradle" (Wong, 1994). She demonstrates the blacks in particular, and people of color generally, are cast in roles as caregivers, nurturers, looking after, assisting, helping white families. She suggests that there is a common underlying purpose in such images – they serve "to allay racial anxieties; those who fear the erosion of their dominance and the vengeance of the oppressed can exorcise their dread in displaced forms" (Wong, 1994: 69). They also create an "illusion of equality and reciprocity with the caregiver" (Wong, 1994: 69). In the 1990s many films continue to fulfill a similar function.

Masking and Unmasking Ideologies

The notion of "racialized" ideologies refers to the systematic statements and elaborations about the way in which society is organized, or ought to be organized, if it is to function well. Statements about "free market principles," about the appropriate size of government, about individualism and family values and morality, all exemplify the dominant ideologies of capitalist societies such as the United States.

These ideologies shape our lives. Ideologies that make explicit reference to "race" are the most obvious examples of "racialized" ideologies; closely followed by those in which it is clear that "race" is indirectly referred to, or implied. But all ideologies are "racialized" in that they have differential consequences for populations called black and white.

Among these ideologies are statements about fairness, equal opportunities and "racism." It used to be useful to talk about "racist" and "non-racist" ideologies, in a context in which the expression of "racist" sentiment by those with power was accepted, expected or condoned, especially prior to the 1960s (Wilson, 1978). But this is no longer the context – the successes of the Civil Rights Movement has made such actions unacceptable. Those who harbor hostility to black people, especially those who have power, are less likely to use overt, explicit language to express this anger (Omi and Winant, 1994: ch. 6). But many statements which lack explicit reference to ideas and beliefs about "race," continue to be made, in which it is possible to identify hostility to blacks. They are more likely to be covert and indirect, argue Omi and Winant, to rearticulate "racism" by using "codewords" and double entendres (Omi and Winant, 1994: 123). This makes it more difficult to identify so-called "racists."

Furthermore, there are many ideologies in which no "racial" content is found, or where open opposition to "racism" is expressed – as in the demand for "color blind" policies – but which nevertheless can have major adverse consequences for black people. The idea that all applicants to college should be treated "equally," that there should be no Affirmative Action, despite the fact that blacks have faced, and continue to face extensive discrimination and inequality, is one example.

In this context – and I believe this is the main context of the 1990s – the argument presented here is that it is not useful to approach ideologies by asking whether they are "racist" or "non-racist." It is more useful to acknowledge the varied ideologies, and to examine them for their "racialized" intentions, content and consequences. In other words, it is more useful to consider all ideologies in terms of the intentions of those promoting them, the content of the ideologies, and the outcomes they have or are likely to have, for different "racialized" groups. When we consider the content of ideologies I suggest that we should analyze those with explicit "racialized" reference, those with coded "racialized" reference, and those without any "racialized" reference but in which we can identify hostile intentions of those advocating them, or adverse consequences of the ideology for blacks. This approach builds upon the innovative analytical on the changing nature of "racism" in the 1980s, carried out by Omi and Winant (1994). Let's consider some concrete examples.

One example of a straightforward expression of a "racialized" ideology is when extremist groups like the Ku Klux Klan, or the White American Resistance (WAR) make openly hostile statements about blacks. Engaging a different rhetoric in mainstream politics provides a different kind of example, as when President Bush and Vice-President Quayle explained the 1992 riots in Los Angeles as an outcome of liberal policies (which had somehow favored minorities) (Lusane, 1994). Similarly, Pat Buchanan, a leading Republican who previously worked for Nixon and Reagan, offers a related example. He claims to be in favor of equal opportunities but advocates policies that oppose black and Latino lives and interests generally by implying that all Mexican immigrants are undocumented. Closely related are arguments that policies around welfare, crime, and Affirmative Action favor blacks and minorities, while harming whites.

We can also examine ideologies with coded "racialized" reference, which entail what Omi and Winant call the "rearticulation" of "racism," that is, the rearrangement of ideas and assumptions about policies, such that although no reference is made to "race," the words themselves are heavily saturated with such meanings and interests (Omi and Winant, 1994). When politicians highlight crime in the "inner city," the burden on the welfare state, "reverse racism," when they say anti-discrimination policies are "un-American," these are understood to have "racialized" reference. They are understood to be promoting policies believed to benefit whites, while penalizing blacks. For example, when advocates proposed the so-called "Civil Rights Initiative" currently under consideration in California, their goal was, and is, to abolish "race" specific policies, and their argument is based on a notion that blacks, and other minorities, get undeserved and unnecessary preferential treatment while the white majority faces "reverse racism" as a consequence.

There are also ideologies without any "racialized" reference, but in which we can identify hostile intentions of those advocating them, or adverse consequences of the ideology for blacks. For example, when a local bus company in Richmond, California wanted to abandon several bus routes as unprofitable and inconvenient, it was clear that it was motivated by a desire to prevent young black shoppers – the group most dependent on the bus service – from frequenting the shopping mall. Similarly a decision to produce a list of young black men barred from shopping in their stores, by a group of store owners in a shopping mall in Georgia had clear "racialized" intention, though the owners vehemently denied so.

Finally, one step further removed are those policies which openly claim to be "anti-racist" – for example, "color-blind" policies, even "free market" polices. These are presented as impartial, unbiassed, even "anti-racist," because they treat everyone equally, regardless of color, nationality, "racialized" identity. But to treat all equally, while denying the very real evidence of "racialized" discrimination at present, and in the past, is to effectively treat them unequally. The significance is to be found not in the content but in the outcomes they have or are likely to have, for different "racialized" constituencies. It is widely agreed that the decision to abolish Affirmative Action at the University of California – although proclaimed in the interests of fairness and equality – will have substantial adverse impact on the likelihood of blacks entering and graduating from the university.

Resisting the Onslaught

Despite the many obstacles which confront them, black people continue to resist in various ways. This resistance entails collective and individual strategies, physical and ideological strategies, many of which are articulated around the organizations and institutions of the black community, and the cultural patterns prevalent in it. Activism and leadership have always been present in this opposition to injustice, and black women have been central to all these activities, as well as developing a distinctive tradition of their own. The various forms of resistance present in the contemporary United States reflect traditions of resistance and resilience by Africans and African-Americans to European conquest and colonization (Marable, 1992; Small and Walvin, 1994).

It used to be possible to classify the goals and strategies of African-Americans in the simple notions of integration and/or separatism; but today the range and diversity of goals and strategies defies such a framework. Blacks have various goals, and employ various strategies; among the goals are integration and incorporation in the present system, primarily focusing on overcoming the starkest feature of discrimination and injustice; others seek fundamental change in the current system; still others see the way forward in developing distinctive black institutions and communities (T'Shaka, 1990). The strategies vary – some see broad alliances with other people of color, and with whites, as in the Rainbow coalition strategy of Jesse Jackson (Collins, 1986; Lusane, 1994); others call for the consolidation and expansion of black organizations, the resuscitation of them, and the regeneration of self-reliance and self-dependence. A strategy best exemplified in the work of Louis Farrakhan's Nation of Islam, but certainly one widely endorsed by a diverse array of black organizations – such as Baptist and Methodist Churches, educational and community organizations – which may be at odds with the tactics and spirit of Farrakhan.

Many African-Americans seek to work within the system. Like the majority of Americans they seek success in education, employment and in political representation and participation. Socialized in the United States, they seek the goals and rewards promised to all Americans – good education, secure well-paying employment and a home. Some seek to achieve these though the ethos of a "color-blind" meritocracy, down-playing "race," and trying to swim or sink on merit and hard work alone. Others use the few measures currently available to them via Affirmative Action.

Community organizing is central to the strategies embraced by African-Americans. In cities across the nation, community groups, institutions and cooperative societies daily plan their assault on inequality and injustice. In education, health and welfare, the criminal justice system and housing, these groups fight poor schooling and health facilities, inadequate finances and homelessness. This community organizing is tied into a national network of organizations – like the Children's Defense League, the National Association for the Advancement of Colored People, the Urban League and others. Needless to say, black churches – Baptist, Methodist and African Episcopalian, and the Nation of Islam – are key. Frequently, local community organizing assumes new proportions – the Million Man March in Washington, D.C. in October 1995, is only one in a long history of marches that epitomizes the centrality of mass mobilization in African-American protest. The backbone of such organizing is, of course, black families. In light of the many obstacles which black families face it is a surprise that much more devastation has not be caused. Too many analysts have focused on damage and destruction; far too few on the resourcefulness and resilience of black families argues Billingsley (1992).

Black theorists and analysts have developed an array of literature which systematically analyzes the problems confronting black people, and offers ways of moving beyond them. These analysts offer insights, counter-explanations and evidence to challenge dominant views. They articulate and elaborate philosophies which challenge the crude and simplistic images of free-market competition, individualism and "color-blindness" that bombard black communities, suggesting alternative goals and strategies – from multi-culturalism to nationalism and "racialized" identities (T'Shaka, 1990; Hine, 1995; Lusane, 1994). Black women have been central here, among them, Barbara Christian, Angela Davis, June Jordan and bell hooks. And collections of writings and analyses by black women – which highlight the concerns and priorities of black women – continue to be produced (Hine, 1995; Guy-Sheftall, 1995).

Similarly, in film blacks have worked to produce counter images to the simplistic and stereotypical ones which flow from Hollywood and the main television networks (Diawara, 1993). Spike Lee's "Crooklyn," John Singleton's "Higher Learning," Mosley's "Devil in a Blue Dress," Haile Gerima's "Sankofa," Julie Dash's "Daughters of the Dust," all reflect the values and priorities of black life, and its many links across the world. Though they do not have the extensive distribution of Hollywood, they offer concrete alternative renditions of family, community and identity among African-Americans.

It is clear that activism and leadership have been central planks of these strategies, at the level of both formal and community politics. Lusane has suggested that there are five tiers of black leadership in contemporary America (1994: 29–31). He identifies national umbrella organizations such as the Black Leadership Forum; at the federal level, the Congressional Black Caucus; organizations of black elected officials, including the National Conference of Black Mayors; the systematic efforts of Churches like the National Baptist Convention; and local leaders such as city elected officials, civil rights organizations and radical groups. Collectively such groups form a redoubtable challenge to injustice.

Black women have been, and remain, central to all these traditions of resistance; in fact in the activities just described they have often been in the majority. But their contribution has also differed, their modes of organization differed, because of the additional problems they have faced (Guy-Sheftall, 1995; Hine, 1995). While black men have faced "racialized" and class hostility; and white women have faced sexism and class hostility, black women have also faced sexism, much of it coming from black men, and racism, much of it from white women (Glenn, 1994). In this way black women have occupied a unique intersection of hostilities, and have had to develop strategies accordingly. The attempt to exclude women from the Million Man March is reflective of this.

Patricia Hill Collins suggests that black women's involvement in struggle has been primarily mobilized around group survival and institutional transformation (Collins, 1991). Their priorities have grown out of their awareness that they occupy a unique location in American society, at the intersection of "racism," sexism and class hostility, one in which they face problems which white women in general do not face – including physical survival, powerlessness and identity – as well as facing the problems white women face, but to greater degree (for example, sexual objectification, discrimination, failure to provide support for child care) (Collins, 1994). Black women have struggled to ensure their own physical survival, and that of their children; to change institutions like schools, hospitals, and the workplace; and to create a sense of self and collective identity which can withstand the array of negative images which pervade American institutions (Christian, 1994).

Conclusion

Patterns of "racialized" relations in the United States are more complex than ever before. The links between "racialized" hostility, economics and politics have never been so intricate; nor has the relationship between structures, images and ideologies; the tactics of those hostile to the African-American presence have taken a greater range of forms; the African-American population manifests greater stratification than ever before; while national and international factors shape one another in ways previously absent. "Racialized" processes are more intricate and illusive, yet the old atrocities and entrenched inequalities persist. This makes it more difficult to analyze, and it requires clearer grasp of the facts, clearer conceptual framework for analysis and clear understanding of theories.

In light of these developments, this work has suggested that analysis of "racialized" images and ideologies, should not be divorced from the realities of "racialized" structures, involving resource allocation, ownership and control; nor from the mobilization around "racialized" group membership and identities. It becomes clear that the best understanding of "racialized" processes will derive from an examination of the multiple factors involved. An exclusive focus on the distribution of resources alone, or on how images and ideologies are articulated alone, risks losing sight of how each set of forces has an impact on the other.

"Racialized" structures shape many images and ideologies. Poverty causes material hardship, and in a society in which a premium is put on material possessions, African-Americans are led to doubt their own self-worth, as humans. For example, ownership and control of media institutions shapes how certain images prevail, and others are ignored, neglected, or discarded. Control of government institutions affects the policies that prevail, just as control of businesses hinders or helps opportunities. These same institutions are positioned so as to restrict or expand the incidence of "racialized" discrimination. In the black community, the never-employed, the unemployed, the unskilled and the skilled continue to face hostility. And the black middle class – the group that is supposed to demonstrate that meritocracy rules supreme – are sick and tired of being subjected to second class treatment; professors being treated as if they are students; air pilots as if they are attendants. Had these incidents been isolated and infrequent, one might look upon them with alacrity – but they are systemic, routine and endemic (Benjamin, 1991).

Similarly, "racialized" images and ideologies shape structure; black people continue to be subjected to the most pernicious degradation and vilification of color and culture in images disseminated by politicians, press, television, literature and popular culture so that white people despise black people, and even black people can despise one another. The psychological consequences are immense (Akbar, 1984). Ideologies of "color-blindness" create the appearance of equality and fairness, while hiding practices of discrimination. The case of the Stuart family in Boston – in which a young middle-class white man shot his pregnant fiancée, and blamed it on a black man – exemplifies these problems. The image of black criminality, so common in the United States, led the Boston police to believe this man's story, to harass the entire black community in Boston, and arrest an innocent man (Feagin and Vera, 1995). A similar event happened in New York city when a white couple from Canada murdered their child in Central Park and then told police that a black man kidnapped him.

One outcome of these "racialized" practices is that whites have an understanding of the experiences and treatment of black people that is largely at variance with the understandings expressed by blacks. Whites regard "racialized" discrimination as minimal and irrelevant, and consider Affirmative Action unjust; most blacks see discrimination is a major reason for the problems they continue to face, and believe Affirmative Action, or similar policies, are indispensable for progress (Small, 1994b). This divergence in views was reflected in the O. J. Simpson decision, in which whites overwhelmingly believed he was guilty, and the jury biassed; while the majority of blacks felt he was innocent, and the jury impartial.

It may be of no comfort to acknowledge the pervasiveness of "racialized" structures, images and ideologies in the United States today, or for that matter, in the contemporary world. But we do an injustice to ignore their ubiquity. Only by acknowledging both the crude and the subtle workings of these processes can we begin to understand the complexities under way, and begin the more difficult task of arresting, containing and reversing their effects.

References

Akbar, Na'im. *Chains and Images of Psychological Slavery*. Jersey City: New Mind Productions, 1984.

Banton, Michael P. *The Idea of Race*. London: Tavistock, 1977.

Benjamin, Lois. *The Black Elite. Facing the Color Line in the Twilight of the Twentieth Century*. Chicago: Nelson Hall Publishers, 1991.

Billingsley, Andrew. *Climbing Jacob's Ladders. The Enduring Legacy of African-American Families*. New York and London: Simon and Schuster, 1992.

Boston, Thomas. *Race, Class and Conservatism*. London: Unwin Hyman, 1988.

Chang, Edward T and Russell C. Leong (eds). *Los Angeles Struggles Toward Multiethnic*

Community. Asian American, African American and Latino Perspectives. Seattle and London: University of Washington Press, 1994.

Christian, Barbara. An Angle of Seeing: Motherhood in Buchi Emecheta's Joys of Motherhood and Alice Walker's Meridian. In Evelyn Nakano Glenn, Grace Change and Linda Rennie Forcey (eds), *Mothering. Ideology, Experience, and Agency.* New York and London: Routledge, 1994, pp. 95–120.

Collins, Patricia Hill. Shifting the Center: Race, Class, and Feminist Theorizing about Motherhood. In Evelyn Nakano Glenn, Grace Change and Linda Rennie Forcey (eds), *Mothering. Ideology, Experience, and Agency.* New York and London: Routledge, 1994, pp. 45–65.

Collins, Patricia Hill. *Black Feminist Thought. Knowledge, Consciousness, and the Politics of Empowerment.* New York and London: Routledge, 1991.

Collins, Sheila D. *The Rainbow Challenge. The Jackson Campaign and the Future of US Politics.* New York: Monthly Review Press, 1986.

Diawara, Manthia (ed.). *Black American Cinema.* New York and London: Routledge, 1993.

Duster, Troy. The New Crisis of Legitimacy in Controls, Prisons and Legal Structures, *The American Sociologist,* Spring, 1995, pp. 20–9.

Feagin, Joe R. and Hernan Vera. *White Racism. The Basics.* New York and London: Routledge, 1995.

Glenn, Evelyn Nakano, Grace Chang and Linda Rennie Forcey. *Mothering. Ideology, Experience, and Agency.* New York and London: Routledge, 1994.

Guerrero, Ed. *Framing Blackness. The African American Image in Film,* Temple University Press, Philadelphia, 1993.

Guy-Sheftall, Beverly. *Words of Fire. An Anthology of African-American Feminist Thought.* New York: The New Press, 1995.

Hacker, Andrew. *Two Nations. Black and White, Separate, Hostile and Unequal.* New York: Charles Scribner's Sons, 1992.

Hine, Darlene Clark, Wilma King and Linda Reed. *"We Specialize in the Wholly Impossible." A Reader in Black Women's History.* New York: Carlson Publishing, Inc., 1995.

Jennings, James (ed.). *Blacks, Latinos, and Asians in Urban America. Status and Prospects for Politics and Activism.* Westport, CT and London: Praeger, 1994.

Jewell, K. Sue. *Survival of the Black Family. The Institutional Impact of US Social Policy.* New York, Westport, CT and London: Praeger, 1988.

Landry, Bart. *The New Black Middle Class.* Los Angeles and London: University of California Press, Berkeley, 1987.

Lusane, Clarence. *African Americans at the Crossroads. The Restructuring of Black Leadership and the 1992 Elections.* Boston: South End Press, 1994.

Massey, Douglas S. and Nancy A. Denton. *American Apartheid. Segregation and the Making of the Underclass.* Cambridge, MA and London: Harvard University Press, 1993.

Marable, Manning. *Beyond Black and White.* London and New York: Verso, 1995.

Marable, Manning. *The Crisis of Color and Democracy. Essays on Race, Class and Power.* Maine: Common Courage Press, 1992.

Miles Robert. *Racism and Migrant Labour.* London: Routledge and Kegan Paul, 1982.

Miles, Robert. *Racism.* London and New York: Routledge, 1989.

Mokhiber, Russell. *Corporate Crime and Violence. Big Business Power and the Abuse of the Public Trust.* San Francisco: Sierra Club Books, 1988.

Morrison, Toni (ed.). *Race-ing Justice, En-Gendering Power. Essays on Anita Hill, Clarence Thomas and the Construction of Social Reality.* London: Chatto and Windus, 1993.

Oliver, Melvin L. and Thomas M. Shapiro. *Black Wealth, White Wealth. A New Perspective on Racial Inequality.* New York and London: Routledge, 1995.

O'Hare, William P., Kelvin M. Pollard, Taynia L. Mann, and Mary M. Kent. *African Americans in the 1990s.* Population Reference Bureau, vol. 46, no. 1, July 1991.

Omi, Michael. In Living Color: Race and American Culture. In Ian Angus and Sut Jhally (eds), *Cultural Politics in Contemporary America.* New York and London: Routledge, 1989, pp. 111–22.

Omi, Michael, and Howard Winant. *Racial Formation in the United States. From the 1960s to the 1980s* (2nd edn). London and New York: Routledge and Kegan Paul, 1994.

Rattansi, Ali and Sallie Westwood. *Racism, Modernity and Identity on the Western Front.* Polity, 1994.

Rose, Tricia. *Black Noise. Rap Music and Black Culture in Contemporary America.* Hanover and London: Weysleyan University Press, 1994.

Simon, David R. and D. Stanley Eitzen. *Elite Deviance* (4th edn). Boston: Allyn and Bacon, 1993.

Small, Stephen. Concepts and Terminology in Representations of the Atlantic Slave Trade, *Museum Ethnographers Journal*, December 1994a, pp. 1–14.

Small, Stephen. *Racialised Barriers: The Black Experience in the United States and England.* New York and London: Routledge, September 1994b.

Small, Stephen. Unravelling Racialised Relations in the United States of America and the United States of Europe. In John Wrench and John Solomos (eds), *Racism and Migration in Europe.* Oxford and New York: Berg Publishers Inc., 1993.

Small, Stephen. Racialised Relations in Liverpool: A Contemporary Anomaly. *New Community*, vol. 11, no. 4, pp. 511–37, 1991.

Small, Stephen. Racial Differentiation in the Slave Era: A Comparative Analysis of People of "Mixed-Race" in Jamaica and Georgia. Unpublished Ph.D. dissertation, University of California, Berkeley, 1989.

Small, Stephen and James Walvin. African Resistance to Enslavement. In Tony Tibbles (ed.), *Transatlantic Slavery. Against Human Dignity.* Merseyside Maritime Museum, September 1994, pp. 42–9.

Thiong'o, Nugugi Wa. *Moving the Centre. The Struggle for Cultural Freedoms.* London: James Currey, 1993.

Time, October 30, 1995.

T'Shaka, Oba. *The Art of Leadership. Volume 1*, Richmond, CA: Pan Afrikan Publications, 1990.

Turner, Patricia. *Ceramic Uncles and Celluloise Mammies.* London and New York: Routledge, 1994.

Walvin, James. *Black and White: The Negro and English Society 1555–1945.* London: Allen Lane, 1973.

Williams, Eric. *Capitalism and Slavery.* London: André Deutsch, 1944.

Wilson, William Julius. *The Declining Significance of Race: Blacks and Changing American Institutions.* Chicago: University of Chicago Press, 1978.

Winant, Howard. *Racial Conditions. Politics, Theory, Comparisons.* Minneapolis and London: University of Minnesota Press, 1994.

Wong, Sau-ling C. Diverted Mothering: Representations of Caregivers of Color in the Age of "multiculturalism." In Evelyn Nakano Glenn, Grace Chang and Linda Rennie Forcey (eds), *Mothering. Ideology, Experience, and Agency*. New York and London: Routledge, 1994. pp. 67–91.

Wrench, John and John Solomos. *Racism and Migration in Europe*. Oxford and New York: Berg Publishers, 1993.

4

Marxism, Racism, and Ethnicity

John Solomos and Les Back

Contemporary debates about race and ethnicity have been influenced in one way or another by Marxist and neo-Marxist scholarship and research. This is clear from both recent theoretical texts on the subject and from empirical and historical studies in a number of societies. Indeed, it can be argued that an engagement with Marxism has been at the heart of many of the most original contributions to recent debates in this field. It is therefore appropriate that, even at a time when Marxist scholarship is perhaps in relative decline and Marxism as a political ideology seems discredited, an attempt is made to reassess its contribution to our understanding of racial and ethnic relations in contemporary societies. This is what this article tries to do, at least in a partial sense, by taking a critical look at Marxist-influenced scholarship in this field.

The first part of the article looks at the development of a Marxist approach to racism and ethnicity. This includes an attempt to define the key questions with which Marxists have been concerned during recent years. The emergence of new critical perspectives from within the Marxist paradigm is then explored by reference to some of the main texts produced over the past decade or so. The concluding part of the article looks at the attempts to develop a post-Marxist analysis that takes account of the limitations of existing accounts of the dynamics of racial and ethnic relations.

From Classical to Neo-Marxism

The works of Marx and Engels contain a number of scattered references to the pertinence of racial and ethnic relations in particular societies – for example, the references to race as an economic factor in the slavery of the United States and the position of Irish migrant workers in Britain. But they contain little historical or theoretical reflection on the role of such processes in the development of capitalist social relations as a whole. Perhaps even more damaging, a number of critics have argued that several statements on race by Marx and Engels reveal traces of the dominant racial stereotypes of their time and an uncritical usage of common sense racist imagery. Additionally, a number of critics of Marxism have argued that the reliance by Marxists on the concept of class has precluded them from analyzing racial and ethnic phenomena in their own right, short of subsuming them under wider social relations or treating them as a kind of super-structural phenomenon (Solomos, 1986).

This kind of criticism has been a recurrent theme in both sociological and historical writing on this subject over the years. Yet it is clear from writings in the United States, Great Britain, and other societies that Marxism has provided an important source of theoretical influence in research on race and ethnicity. This can be seen in the number of important theoretical studies that have been produced by Marxist writers. There is also by now a sizable number of histori-cal studies that have been produced from within the Marxist paradigm. What seems clear is that Marxist discussion of race and racism is searching for a new agenda for the analysis of the dynamics of racial categorization, and there are some encouraging signs of development and renewal.

What of the themes that have helped to define a specifically Marxist approach to the study of racism and ethnicity? Although it is not easy to state categorically what the main concerns of all Marxist approaches to this subject have been, it is clear that a number of themes have been emphasized in recent Marxist scholar-ship. For example, the role of political institutions has provided a major area of research for those scholars who have attempted to use a Marxist perspective. A number of studies have focused specifically on the role of the state as a site for the reproduction of racially structured situations. Drawing partly on recent Marxist debates on the nature of the capitalist state, a number of studies have analyzed the interplay between politics and racism in specific historical settings. Studies of the role of state institutions in maintaining racialized structures in a number of societies, particularly the United States and South Africa, have high-lighted the importance of the political context of racism. This has raised important questions and problems: What is the precise role of the state in the reproduction of racially structured social relations? How far can the state be transformed into an instrument of anti-racist political actions? These and other questions are currently being explored and debated.

Important contributions are being made to this debate from a number of countries, which are helping to fashion new perspectives on the role of the state in maintaining racial domination. A good example of such research is the numerous studies of the South African state and its role in institutionalizing the apartheid system during the period since 1948. These studies have shown that the role of state and legal institutions was a central part of the processes leading to the establishment of apartheid and its maintenance. They have also suggested that there is a need to include the state as a key actor in the study of racism in different national and political contexts.

Another important theme has been the role of racism as a source of division within the working class. This theme was central to the work of early Marxist writers such as Oliver Cox (1948). It has once again become central to contem-porary debates about racism and class formation. In a number of studies about the role of racism and ethnicity in Western Europe and the United States, this question has been investigated from both a theoretical and a historical perspective. Stephen Castles and Mark Miller (1993) have recently looked at the complex ways in which class, race, and ethnicity have interacted in particular historical contexts to create distinct strata within the working class.

This concern with the state and politics has been evident in studies about the United States and Europe as well. A key concern of a number of recent US studies has been the interrelationship between relations of politics, power, and racism. As Michael Omi and Howard Winant (1986) argue in *Racial Formation in the United States*, one of the most salient features of racial relations in contemporary societies is the role of political and legal relations in defining the existence of racial categories and defining the social meanings of notions such as racial inequality, racism, and ethnicity.

This theme has been taken up in studies of the situation of black and other ethnic minorities in Europe during recent years. Such studies have looked particularly at the processes by which minority communities and migrant workers are often excluded from equal access to the political institutions and are denied basic social and economic rights. It is interesting to note in this context that in countries such as Germany and France, a key point in recent political conflicts has been the question of whether migrant workers should be given greater political rights.

A final aspect of recent debates about the pertinence of Marxism to the analysis of race and racism is the question of whether there is an intrinsic Eurocentric bias in the core of Marxist theory. This is a theme that has been taken up during recent years by a number of critics of Marxism and by others who profess to be sympathetic to the Marxist tradition. Perhaps the most important statement of this position is Cedric Robinson's (1983) *Black Marxism*, which argues forcefully that Marxism is inextricably tied to Western European philosophical traditions that cannot easily incorporate the experience of racism and ethnic divisions. This and other studies seem certain to raise questions that will play a part in Marxist discussions for some time to come.

Critical Perspectives on Marxism and Racism

The 1970s and 1980s were an important period in the emergence of a Marxist approach to race and ethnicity. This period saw the emergence of a number of substantial criticisms of the research agenda on race relations, written largely from a neo-Marxist perspective. Such criticisms were influenced both by theoretical and political considerations, and they helped to stimulate new areas of debate. One of the most ambitious attempts to provide a theoretical foundation for a Marxist framework can be found in the work of Robert Miles. The starting point of Miles's critique was his opposition to the existence of a sociology of race and his view that the object of analysis should be racism, which he viewed as integral to the process of capital accumulation (Miles, 1982; 1986).

The work of Miles represents the most worked-out attempt to develop a Marxist analysis of racism as a social and historical phenomenon. His writings reflect a deep concern with overcoming the potentially divisive impact of racism on class organization and radical political action. His analysis was first articulated in 1982 in *Racism and Migrant Labour* and is perhaps the most sustained attempt to include the study of racism within the mainstream of Marxist social theory. His empirical research has focused specifically on the situation in Britain and in the rest of Western Europe and has looked at the role of political, class, and ideological relationships in shaping our understandings of racial conflict and change in these societies.

For Miles, the idea of race refers to a human construct, an ideology with regulatory power within society. Analytically, race constitutes a paper tiger (Miles, 1988), which may be a common term of reference within everyday discourse but which presents a serious theoretical problem. It is here that Miles diverges from what he sees as the race relations problematic. Miles (1982: 42) is concerned with the analytical and objective status of race as a basis of action. Race is thus an ideological effect, a mask that hides real economic relationships (Miles, 1984). Thus the forms of class consciousness that are legitimate for Miles must ultimately be reduced to economic relations that are hidden within the regulatory process of racialization.

It is within this context that the concepts of racial categorization and racialization have been used to refer to what Miles calls "those instances where social relations between people have been structured by the signification of human biological characteristics in such a way as to define and construct differentiated social collectivities" (Miles, 1989b: 75). A number of writers have attempted to use these concepts to analyze the processes by which the term race has been socially and politically constructed in specific historical, political, and institutional contexts.

Good examples of such studies include attempts to critically analyze the role of race relations legislation, the emergence of black minority representation in political institutions, and the development of public policies dealing with specific aspects of racial inequality in areas such as employment and housing. The premise of such studies is that the processes by which race is given particular meanings are variable across and within national boundaries and are shaped by political, legal, and socioeconomic environments. Comparative studies of immigration policies in Europe have shown, for example, that the construction of legislation to control the arrival of specific groups of migrants was often the subject of intense political and ideological controversy.

For Miles, the process of racialization is interrelated with the conditions of migrant laborers. Its effects are the result of the contradiction between "on the one hand the need of the capitalist world economy for the mobility of human beings, and on the other, the drawing of territorial boundaries and the construction of citizenship as a legal category which sets boundaries for human mobility" (Miles, 1988: 438). Within the British setting, this ideological work conducted primarily by the state acts as a means of crisis management and results in racializing fragments of the working class. Race politics are thus confined to the forces of regulation. For Miles, the construction of political identities that use racial consciousness play no part in the development of a progressive politics.

Miles raises some fundamental questions about the nature of political action within communities of migrant labor. The most important of these is the degree to which black and minority politics are really distillations of class conflict. If this is true, then any movements away from class-based political action (i.e. movements toward any notions of black community politics) are doomed to failure (Miles, 1988; 1989b). If one takes this argument further, class-based political action is ultimately in opposition to any sort of sustained political organization around a notion of race. For Miles, the politics of race is narrowly confined to the struggle against racism. This is neatly captured in the way he uses Hall's (1980: 341) statement on the relationship between class and race. He concludes that it is not race but racism that can be the modality in which class is lived and fought through (Miles, 1988: 447).

Miles' (1989b) insistence that racial differentiations are always created in the context of class differentiation is a core feature of his critique of the sociology of race relations. However, his position could be said to result in a kind of class reductionism that ultimately limits the scope of theoretical work on conceptualizing racism and racialized social relations. For example, in some contexts, class exploitation may be incidental to the construction of situations of racial dominance (Goldberg, 1992). However, the greatest contribution that Miles makes is his insistence that races are created within the context of political and social regulation. Thus race is above all a political construct. It is within this context that the concepts of racial categorization and racialization have been used to refer to what Miles (1989b) refers to as instances in which social relations between people are structured by the signification of human biological characteristics in a manner that defines and constructs differentiated social collectivities. His work constitutes an attempt to reclaim the study of racism from an apoliticized sociological framework and locate it squarely in a Marxist theorization of social conflict.

Another influential critique of the sociology of race during the early 1980s emanated from the Centre for Contemporary Cultural Studies (CCCS) in Birmingham, England. The work of the CCCS Race and Politics Group during this period was particularly concerned with the changing nature of the politics of race during the 1970s and the development of new forms of racial ideology. The theoretical approach of the CCCS group was influenced by the work of Stuart Hall (1980) in particular. The CCCS group was critical of the arguments both of the sociologists of race and of Miles.

The work of the CCCS group resulted in the publication of *The Empire Strikes Back* (CCCS, 1982). This volume attracted widespread attention at the time and still remains a point of reference in current debates. Two of the contributors to this volume have subsequently attempted to develop substantive studies derived from it (Gilroy, 1987; Solomos, 1988; 1989). A major concern of the CCCS group was the need to analyze the complex processes by which race is constructed as a social and political relation. The CCCS group emphasized that the race concept is not simply confined as a process of regulation operated by the state but that the meaning of race as a social construction is contested and fought over. In this sense, the CCCS group viewed race as an open political construction whereby the political meaning of terms such as black are fought over. Collective identities spoken through race, community, and locality are, for all their spontaneity, powerful means to coordinate action and create solidarity (Gilroy, 1987).

Within this model of political action, a multiplicity of political identities can be held. An inclusive notion of black identity can prevail and, at the same time, allow heterogeneity of national and cultural origins within this constituency (Gilroy, 1987: 236). Gilroy, for example, argues that the crucial question here is the extent to which notions of race can be reforged into a political color of opposition. He holds little hope that this process can be developed within the arena of representative democracy. Instead, he views pressure group strategies, which have evolved out of community struggles that use a specifically black political vernacular, as the way forward. Gilroy argues for a radical revision of class analysis in metropolitan contexts. He suggests that political identities that are spoken through race can be characterized as social movements that are relatively autonomous from class relations.

It should also be noted that *The Empire Strikes Back* was one of the first books on race relations in Britain to look in any depth at the question of gender and the role of sexism in the context of racialized relations. The contributions of Hazel Carby and Pratibha Parmar to this volume provide a point of reference and debate about the interplay among race, class, and gender during the 1980s. They also highlight the relevance of looking at this dimension of racial relations in a context where the bulk of research remained gender blind.

In exploring these issues, *The Empire Strikes Back* acted as a catalyst to a politicization of debates about the role of research in relation to race relations. In a sense, the political struggles that were occurring within black communities during the 1980s were being echoed in the context of the production of knowledge about racism. The sociology of race relations stood accused of being implicitly conservative and unable to articulate the theorization of racism with the nature of a class divided and structural inequalities in power. On the other hand, the sociologists of race and ethnic relations were also criticized for letting their theoretical imaginations be colored by an implicit Eurocentrism. The result was that the sociological literature demonstrated an inability to record the experiences of the black people in Britain in a sympathetic way (Lawrence, 1981). These challenges marked an attempt to articulate the theoretical debates about how to understand racism with the political urgencies of economic crisis and the ideological challenge of the conservative new right. The point we want to emphasize here is that this debate needs to be situated within the political conjuncture of the early 1980s. It is quite clear that the preoccupation with prioritizing the analysis of racism was linked to a concern to fix the theoretical debate on questions of power and inequality. However, in making the conceptualization of racism a priority, these critiques failed to develop a theoretical framework for an elaborated analysis of wider social and cultural processes. It is this issue that has become one of the central theoretical questions of recent years.

Conceptualizing Contemporary Racisms

The debates of the early 1980s continue to influence research agendas. However, a number of recent developments have meant that the neo-Marxist critiques of the early 1980s have not been able to cope with the complexities of theorizing racism during the 1990s. The first of these is the crisis within Marxism itself. In this context, some have called for a radical revision of class analysis (Anthias, 1992; Castells, 1983; Gilroy, 1987) to incorporate political movements that mobilize around forms of identity other than class. Others have suggested a need to move away from Marxism as a framework of analysis and have taken on some of the concerns of poststructuralism and postmodernism (Gates, 1986; Goldberg, 1990).

One of the results of this shift is the growing concern with the status of cultural forms and a return to an analysis of the nature of ethnicity in metropolitan settings. The political naïveté of the early work on ethnicity meant that, for much of the 1980s, the analysis of cultural processes and forms was rejected in favor of a focus on the politics of racism. The rejection of "culture" was tied to the notion that the culturalist perspective of the 1970s did little more than blame the victims of racism (Lawrence, 1982). However, the question of cultural production and the politics of identity is fast becoming an important area of contemporary debate. New perspectives are being developed that examine the ways in which cultural forms are being made and remade producing complex social phenomena (Hewitt, 1991). These new syncretic cultures are being plotted within the global networks of the African and South Asian diaspora (Bhachu, 1991; Gilroy, 1987).

The process of reclaiming culture in critical debate has simultaneously involved a re-examination of how racism is conceptualized. These contributions engage in one way or another with the arguments of poststructuralism and postmodernism, and they point to the need to avoid uniform and homogeneous conceptualizations of racism. Although not yet part of the agenda of mainstream research on race relations, a range of studies of racialized discourses in the mass media, literature, art, and other cultural forms has begun to be produced. Reacting against what they see as the lack of an account of cultural forms of racial discourse, a number of writers have sought to develop a more rounded picture of contemporary racial imagery by looking at the role of literature, the popular media, and other cultural forms in representing changing images of race and ethnicity.

As David Goldberg has pointed out, "the presumption of a single monolithic racism is being displaced by a mapping of the multifarious historical formulations of racisms" (1990: xiii). In this context, it is perhaps not surprising that a key concern of many recent texts in this field is to explore the interconnections between race and nationhood, patriotism, and nationalism rather than analyze ideas about biological inferiority. The ascendancy of the political right in Britain during the 1980s prompted commentators to identify a new period in the history of English racism. The "new racism," or what Fanon (1967) referred to as "cultural racism," has its origins in the social and political crisis afflicting

Britain (Barker, 1981; Gilroy, 1990). Its focus is the defense of the mythic "British/English way of life" in the face of attack from enemies outside ("Argies," "Frogs," "Krauts," "Iraqis") and within ("black communities," "Muslim funda-mentalists"). Paul Gilroy (1987: 55–6) points to an alarming consequence of new racism in which blackness and Englishness are reproduced as mutually exclusive categories.

The new cultural racism points to the urgency of comprehending racism and notions of race as changing and historically situated. As Goldberg (1992) has pointed out, it is necessary to define race conceptually by looking at what this term signifies at different times – thus the question of whether race is an on-tologically valid concept or otherwise is sidestepped in favor of an interrogation of the ideological quality of racialized subjectivities. The writing on new racism shows how contemporary manifestations of race are coded in a language that aims to circumvent accusations of racism. In the case of new racism, race is coded as culture. However, the central feature of these processes is that the qualities of social groups are fixed, made natural, and confined within a pseudo-biologically defined culturalism (Barker, 1981). What is clear from these writings is that a range of discourses on social differentiation may have a metonymic relationship to racism. The semantics of race are produced by a complex set of interdiscursive processes in which the language of culture and nation invokes a hidden racial narrative. The defining feature of this process is the way in which it naturalizes social formations in terms of a racial/cultural logic of belonging.

The politics of race and racism has undergone numerous transformations during recent decades. Debates about the ontological status of race, the object of investigation, and the agenda for research in this field are partly the result of these transformations. Whereas some authors writing in the tradition of race and ethnic relations studies have been careful to separate the research process from political action, such a separation is in some ways impossible and even un-desirable. This is why the political agendas involved in conceptualizing racism need to be made explicit.

It is perhaps because analytical debates necessarily involve political disputes that no one theoretical perspective is dominant at the present time. Indeed, much of the mainstream research in this field is not theoretically informed in any substantial way. There is a need for greater theoretical clarity on key concepts and a broadening of the research agenda to cover issues that have been neglected, such as the politics of culture and identity. In this sense, Michael Banton (1991) may well be right in his contention that different theoretical paradigms may be able to contribute their own distinctive accounts of the processes that involve the attribution of specific meanings to racial situations. However, the point that Banton misses is that the various paradigms that are adopted within this area of research contain an implicit or explicit political position *vis-à-vis* the politics knowledge production. In this case, it is not a matter of choosing appropriate analytical tools from some diverse theoretical bag, but rather it is necessary to situate these paradigms in relation to each other and political debates over what could or should be the focus of analysis.

The question of how to conceptualize racism is not purely an academic matter; it is connected with a wider political culture in any given historical conjuncture. Our own awareness that this is the case has been heightened by our current research into local politics and racism in Birmingham and the dilemmas we face with regard to the relationship between research and political interventions (Back and Solomos, 1993). One of the starting points of this research is that race is foremost a political construct. As a result, racialized assertions need to be located within processes of social regulation and identity formation. In the course of our research, however, it has become clear that racism manifests itself in plural and complex forms. In this situation, the logic of racism needs to be appraised in what we call metonymic elaborations. This means that racisms may be expressed through a variety of coded signifiers. We have already discussed one such elaboration (i.e. the coding of race as culture). Contemporary racisms have evolved and adapted to new circumstances. The crucial property of these elaborations is that they can produce a racist effect while denying that this effect is the result of racism. For example, the new racisms of the 1980s are coded within a cultural logic. As a result, the champions of this racism can claim that they are protecting their way of life and that the issue of color or phenotype is irrelevant.

In this context, unitary or simplistic definitions of racism become hard to sustain. However, it seems clear that contemporary racisms share some central features. They attempt to fix human social groups in terms of natural properties of belonging within particular political and geographical contexts. The assertion that racialized subjects do not belong within, say, British society is then associated with social and cultural characteristics designated to them within the logic of particular racisms.

In this context, the meanings of race and racism need to be located within particular fields of discourse and articulated to the social relations found within that context. It is then necessary to see what kinds of racialized identities are being formed within these contexts. We are suggesting a position that builds into any analysis a rigorous scrutiny of racialized definitions, whether they are operated by the local state or by the range of political mobilizations that are occurring around racial and ethnic identities within black communities. This approach seeks to decipher the meanings of racialized identities without attempting to prioritize one classification as more legitimate than another.

We are suggesting a model for conceptualizing racisms that is (a) sensitive to local and contextual manifestations of racist discourse and (b) able to connect local manifestations with wider or national public discourses. The theoretical work on racism has produced accounts of racism that derive contemporary forms of racism from public political discourse. This evidence is then used to generalize about broad trends within British society. We are suggesting that there is a need to situate racisms within particular settings and then move toward a more general account of their wider significance.

One of the weaknesses of the literature that examines media and political discourses is that it has not attempted to look at how these ideological forms manifest themselves at the local level within specific communities. The question remains: How pervasive is the new racism? Or, How do these national discourses relate to the particularities of a specific social context? Gilroy, for example, alludes to a new kind of cultural politics that defines new racism and develops a political and cultural aesthetic that is both black and English. Hall (1988: 30), returning to the flag metaphor, refers to a shift in his own thinking: "Fifteen years ago we didn't care, or at least I didn't care, whether there was any black in the Union Jack. Now not only do we care but we must."

A series of empirical studies has shown evidence that significant dialogues are taking place within multiethnic communities of working-class youth (Hewitt, 1986; Jones, 1988). In the encounter between black young people and their white inner-city peers, "black culture has become a class culture . . . as two generations of whites have appropriated it, discovered its seductive forms of meaning for their own" (Gilroy, 1990: 273). The result is that it is impossible to speak of black culture in Britain separately from the culture of Britain as a whole. These processes have important implications for developing an analysis of racism that is socially, politically, and even geographically situated. The local context has important effects resulting in complex outcomes in which particular racisms may be muted whereas others flourish (Back, 1993).

Another focus within the emerging literature on the cultural politics of racism has been the social construction of race and difference in literature and the cinema. This has been a neglected area of research but, during recent years, this has been remedied by the publication of a number of important studies of race, culture, and identity. Originating largely from the United States, such studies have looked at a number of areas including literature, the cinema, and other popular cultural forms. They have sought to show that within contemporary societies our understandings of race, and the articulation of racist ideologies, cannot be reduced to economic, political, or class relations.

This type of approach is in fact more evident outside sociology. During recent years, the work of literary and cultural theorists in the United States and Britain has begun to explore seriously the question of race and racism and has led to a flowering of studies that use the debates around poststructuralism and post-modernism as a way of approaching the complex forms of racialized identities in colonial and postcolonial societies (Gates, 1986; 1988; Goldberg, 1990).

There has also been a growth of interest in historical research on the origins of ideas about race and in the dynamics of race, class, and gender during the colonial period (Ware, 1992). This has been reflected in important and valuable accounts of the changing usage of racial symbols during the past few centuries and in accounts of the experiences of colonialism and their impact on our understandings of race and culture. The work of Gayatri Spivak (1987) has helped to highlight, for example, the complex processes of racial and gender identification experienced by the colonized during the colonial and postcolonial periods. Other studies have sought to show that the oppressed themselves have produced their own discourses about race and identity in the context of their own experiences of domination and exclusion (Bhabha, 1990; Young, 1990).

Equally, it has also become clear that there is a need to shed the narrow confines of the race relations problematic and develop a more sophisticated analysis of the impact of various racisms on the white majority. An embryonic literature exists on the politics of whiteness that is attempting to develop such a focus of inquiry. However, there are immediate difficulties with this endeavor, as Richard Dyer has shown in his discussion of film representations. Dyer contends that white ethnicity in the cinema is implicitly present but explicitly absent and, as a result, it has "an everything and nothing quality" (1988: 44–6). In these representations, whiteness is equated with normality and, as such, it is not in need of definition. Thus "being normal" is colonized by the idea of "being white." From a different perspective, bell hooks has graphically discussed the terrorizing effect that whiteness has on the black imagination. Writing on her experience of growing up as a black woman in the American South, she comments, "Whiteness in the black imagination is often a representation of terror" (hooks, 1992: 342). Clearly, there is a need for a research agenda that looks at the way white subjectivities are racialized and how whiteness is manifested in discourse, communication, and culture.

This turn within critical writing has important implications. One of the fundamental criticisms of the sociology of race and ethnic relations is that it has too often focused on the victims rather than the perpetrators of racism. Prioritizing whiteness as an area of critical endeavor has the potential to disrupt the sociological common sense that equates the discussion of racism with the empirical scrutiny of black communities.

Hall has pointed out the urgency of deconstructing the meanings of whiteness, not just for countering racism but also for the well-being of the African and Asian diaspora living in Britain:

> I think for black people who live in Britain this question of finding some way in which the white British can learn to live with us and the rest of the world is almost as important as discovering our own identity. I think they are in more trouble than we are. So we, in a curious way, have to rescue them from themselves – from their own past. We have to allow them to see that England is a quite interesting place with quite an interesting history that has bossed us around for 300 years [but] that is finished. Who are they now? (BBC Radio, 1989)

There is already an emerging literature that is trying to answer the rhetorical question Hall has asked (Back, 1993; Jones, 1988). However, the connection between race and nation may well be eclipsed during the 1990s by the specter of an integrated and racialized Europe.

Theoretically, comprehending whiteness is certainly an important intellectual project. However, there are a number of possible shortcomings. In the hurry to shift the critical gaze, there is always a danger of suspending reflection on the analytical terms of this project. Like many of the debates on the ontological status of culture, there is a danger of reifying whiteness and reinforcing a unitary idea of race. To avoid this, it is crucial to locate any discussion of whiteness in a particular empirical and historical context. Equally, one must insist that whiteness is a political definition that regulates the consent of white subjects within the context of white supremacy. Additionally, any discussion of whiteness must incorporate an appreciation of how gendered processes are inextricably articulated with the semantics of race (Back, 1993; Ware, 1992). We are arguing that interrogating whiteness as a form of identity and a political discourse must (a) focus on decolonizing the definition of "normal" and (b) simultaneously prohibit the reification of whiteness as a social identity.

In summary, we are suggesting that the theoretical engagements of the early 1980s cannot adequately conceptualize racism during the 1990s. The political struggles that underscored these debates have moved on. In many ways, the turn toward the conceptualization of culturally defined racisms and the politics of identity has been led by the political events of the late 1980s. In particular, the continuing hegemony of the conservative right in Britain has challenged theorists to reappraise the usefulness of Marxist orthodoxy. This is perhaps best exemplified by the debate over the New Times thesis (see Hall and Jacques, 1989; Sivanandan, 1990), which suggests that a range of sites for social antagonism and resistance exists within contemporary Britain that cannot be conceptualized within a conventional class analysis. Equally, in the context of the complex forms of identity politics, the semantics of race cannot be confined to the politics of regulation (Miles, 1989a). The controversy over the publication of Salman Rushdie's book, *The Satanic Verses*, has provided a warning that the politics of culture cannot be appreciated within the conceptual language of the 1980s.

Questions of cultural production and change must be integrated within a contemporary conceptualization of racism. Thus we are suggesting that these theoretical debates need to be contextualized within a shifting political context. The certainties of the critique of the race relations problematic are no longer tenable. What seems to characterize the contemporary period is, on the one hand, a complex spectrum of racisms and, on the other hand, the fragmentation of the definition of blackness as a political identity in favor of a resurgence of ethnicism and cultural differentiation. At the same time, and perhaps paradoxically, new cultures and ethnicities are emerging in the context of dialogue and producing a kaleidoscope of cultural syncretisms. There may well be contradictory trends emerging, but neither the race relations problematic of the 1970s nor the racism problematic of the 1980s is equipped to deal with the contemporary situation.

Conclusion

In summary, we are suggesting that Marxist scholarship on racism and ethnicity has made a valuable contribution to our knowledge of racial and ethnic relations during recent years. But it is important to bear in mind that, like all other major theoretical paradigms, Marxism has not provided an answer to all the theoretical and empirical conundrums that we face. The analysis of contemporary racisms needs to be situated within particular discursive contexts. Racism cannot be reduced to class relations, but neither can it be seen as completely autonomous from wider social relations such as gender and sexuality. It is clear that the 1990s will pose serious questions with regard to the way racism is conceptualized. In this context, the orthodoxies of the past 10 years may prove inappropriate when attempting to meet these challenges.

From this perspective, it is important to maintain an openness in theoretical and research agendas on racism and ethnicity. The experience of the past decade would seem to point to the need to see the Marxist contribution to these agendas as by no means fixed and unchanging. The challenge over the next period for those scholars influenced by the Marxist tradition will be to show the relevance of their theoretical and historical insights to the analysis of contemporary forms of racial and ethnic relationships.

References

Anthias, F. (1992). Connecting "race," and ethnic phenomena. *Sociology*, 26, 421–38.

Back, L. (1993). Race, identity and nation within an adolescent community in South London. *New Community*, 19, 217–33.

Back, L. (1993). Cultures of racism, rituals of masculinity: Mutual crossings of racism and gender. In N. Lindisfarne and A. Cornwall (eds), *The Meanings of Masculinity*. London: Routledge.

Back, L. and Solomos, J. (1993). Doing research, writing politics: The dilemmas of political intervention in research on racism. *Economy and Society*, 22, 178–99.

Banton, M. (1991): The race relations problematic. *British Journal of Sociology*, 42, 115–30.

Barker, M. (1981). *The New Racism*. London: Junction Books.

BBC Radio (1989, April 4). *After Dread and Anger*.

Bhabha, H. K. (1990). Interrogating identity: The postcolonial prerogative. In D. T. Goldberg (ed.), *Anatomy of Racism* (pp. 183–209). Minneapolis: University of Minnesota Press.

Bhachu (1991). Culture, ethnicity and class amongst Punjabi Sikh women in 1990's Britain. *New Community*, 17, 401–12.

Castells, M. (1983). *The City and the Grassroots*. London: Edward Arnold.

Castles, S. and Miller, M. (1993). *The Age of Migration*. Basingstoke: Macmillan.

Centre for Contemporary Cultural Studies (1982). *The Empire Strikes Back*. London: Hutchinson.

Cox, O. C. (1948). *Caste, Class and Race*. New York: Monthly Review.

Dyer, R. (1988). White. *Screen*, 29 (4), 44–5.

Fanon, F. (1967). *Towards the African Revolution*. New York: Monthly Review.

Gates, H. L., Jr. (ed.). (1986). *"Race," Writing and Difference*. Chicago: University of Chicago Press.

Gates, H. L., Jr. (1988). *The Signifying Monkey*. New York: Oxford University Press.

Gilroy, P. (1987). *There ain't no Black in the Union Jack*. London: Hutchinson.

Gilroy, P. (1990). One nation under a groove: The cultural politics of "race" and racism in Britain. In D. T. Goldberg (ed.), *Anatomy of Racism* (pp. 263–82). Minneapolis: University of Minnesota Press.

Goldberg, D. T. (ed.). (1990). *Anatomy of Racism*. Minneapolis: University of Minnesota Press.

Goldberg, D. T. (1992). The semantics of race. *Ethnic and Racial Studies*, 15, 543–69.

Hall, S. (1980). Race articulation and societies structured in dominance. In UNESCO, *Sociological Theories: Race and Colonialism* (pp. 305–45). Paris: UNESCO.

Hall, S. (1988). New ethnicities. In K. Mercer (ed.), *Black film/British Cinema ICA documents* (no. 7). London: British Film Institute.

Hall, S. and Jacques, M. (1989). *New Times: The changing face of politics in the 1990s*. London: Lawrence and Wishart.

Hewitt R. (1986). *White Talk Black Talk: Inter-racial friendship and communication amongst adolescents*. Cambridge: Cambridge University Press.

Hewitt, R. (1991, June). *Language, Youth and the Destabilisation of Ethnicity*. Paper presented at the Conference on Ethnicity in Youth Culture: Interdisciplinary Perspectives, Fittjagard, Botkyrka, Sweden.

hooks, b. (1992). Representing whiteness in the black imagination. In L. Grossberg, C. Nelson, and P. Treichler (eds), *Cultural Studies* (pp. 338–46). London: Routledge.

Jones, S. (1988). *Black Culture, White Youth: The reggae tradition from JA to UK*. Basingstoke: Macmillan.

Lawrence, E. (1981). White sociology, black struggle. *Multi-Racial Education*, 9, 3–17.

Lawrence, E. (1982). In the abundance of water the fool is thirsty: sociology and black "pathology." In CCCS, *The Empire Strikes Back* (pp. 95–142). London: Hutchinson.

Miles, R. (1982). *Racism and Migrant Labour*. London: George Allen and Unwin.

Miles, R. (1984). Marxism versus the "sociology of race relation?" *Ethnic and Racial Studies*, 7, 217–37.

Miles, R. (1986). Labour migration, racism and capital accumulation in Western Europe. *Capital and Class*, 28, 49–86.

Miles, R. (1988). Racism, Marxism and British politics. *Economy and Society*, 17, 428–60.

Miles, R. (1989a, April). *From Where we have Come to Where we are Going: Reflections on racism and British politics, 1945–2000*. Paper presented at the annual conference of the Political Studies Association, University of Warwick.

Miles, R. (1989b). *Racism*. London: Routledge.

Omi, M. and Winant, H. (1986). *Racial Formation in the United States*. New York: Routledge and Kegan Paul.

Robinson, C. (1983). *Black Marxism: The Making of the Black Radical Tradition*. London: Zed.

Sivanandan, A. (1990). All that melts into air is solid: The hokum of New Times. *Race and Class*, 31(3), 1–30.

Solomos, J. (1986). Varieties of Marxist conceptions of "race," class and the state: A critical analysis. In J. Rex and D. Mason (eds), *Theories of Race and Ethnic Relations* (pp. 84–109). Cambridge: Cambridge University Press.

Solomos, J. (1988). *Black Youth, Racism and the State*. Cambridge: Cambridge University Press.

Solomos, J. (1989). *Race and Racism in Contemporary Britain*. Basingstoke: Macmillan.

Spivak, G. C. (1987). *In Other Worlds*. London: Methuen.

Ware, V. (1992). *Beyond the Pale: White Women, Racism and History*. London: Verso.

Young, R. (1990). *White Mythologies: Writing History and the West*. London: Routledge.

5

Postmodernism and the Politics of Racialized Identities

Louis F. Mirón

Recasting the politics of ethnic identity

Toward a notion of collective identity

Students' lived culture is fertile soil for the fomenting of identity politics over the struggle of who students are in the classroom. As the composition of student demographics undergoes rapid change in many large urban school districts, owing to the infusion of new ethnic groups, students' personal identities become problematic. Indeed, the urban classroom is transformed into a site of the formation of collective (social) identity. The classroom becomes the terrain of "identity politics" (see Grossberg, 1993; see also Aronowitz, 1994). For example, immigrant groups and students of multiple ethnic origins (e.g., Chicanos) collide with mainstream US culture (Spindler and Spindler, 1994), spawning the formation of the "subaltern identity" (see Grossberg, 1993). The formation of subaltern identities is a dialectical process that both derives from minority students' subordinate positions as well as student culture (see Lauria, Mirón, and Dashner, 1994).

Researchers in bilingual/bicultural education (Baca and Cervantes, 1989; Fishman, 1976; Paulston, 1980) as well as English-as-a-second-language (Cummins, 1993) have well understood the phenomena of cultural and linguistic "switching." Shifting from native language (L1) to English (L2) or between dialects for students whose native language is English reveals a capacity for students to shift not only codes of language (sometimes within the same class period), but such cultural dexterity, in which language plays a significant role, signals a capacity to switch identities. This shifting is part of students' coping strategies when their "enduring" self is threatened (Spindler and Spindler, 1994). This capacity is theoretically heightened when identity is viewed as relational and in the process of formation (Smith, 1992).

Students resist their representations as disadvantaged minorities when viewed through the conceptual eyes of the dominant culture. When thrust into elite schools, as Herr and Anderson's (1993) research illuminates, token ethnic minority students often cast off old identities at school, only to reassume them at home or in the neighborhood. It is clear that students assume a variety of identities in school, but the site of cultural and identity politics extends far beyond the inner-city school (see Bondi, 1993). As students gain a sense of their own ethnic heritage, thereby becoming an active participant in their individual and collective identity formation, knowledge and awareness of *others'* ethnicity renegotiates their entry into the terrain of identity politics. Biesta (1994) calls this transition in pedagogical relations the development of "practical intersubjectivity."

I argue here using the previous analysis of ethnic identity that dominant power relations embedded in racial formations have largely prevented blacks from making affirmative gains in cultural/identity politics. Moreover, the governing psychologically based definition of ethnic identity as a component of self-concept has reproduced modernist assumptions of a unitary, autonomous self.

Modernist theorists conceptualized identity in purely psychological terms. Ethnicity was also atomized within the free, unitary self as "an individual's membership in a group sharing a common ancestral heritage" (Buriel and Cardoza, 1993: 197). However, we must be cautious about the postmodern possibilities of forging a new politics of ethnic identity in city schools. Such social realities as the concept of individual, autonomous identity do not disappear simply because radical theorists, bent on achieving a deepening experience of democracy, declare the onset of a postmodern age. However, ideologies (and public policies) *do* change. The postmodern argument is that "discourse shapes the world." I agree with this contention and suggest that the place to begin forging a new cultural politics of ethnic identity is with new language and new ideas. The first of these is the concept of identity as process.

Ethnic identity as social process

Ethnic identity is not a commodity that is formed naturally as a by-product of descent, culture, and genetic transmission. Rather, like other social realities, ethnic identity is socially constructed and reformed owing to historical conditions (Smith, 1992). Ethnic identity is, itself, part and parcel of a *social formation,* a process that is not fixed in time and that can change over time. In the present context of city schooling in particular, the reconstitution of demographics with a majority ethnic population in major US cities potentially marks a period of the development of new ethnic identities. Schools can make use of the new social space of ethnic identity and strategically shape a sense of their individual and collective self. Doing so assists students in what Philip Wexler believes is their most important labor – identity work. He asserts that:

> Students work in school. Their most central activity is the work of "becoming somebody." To become somebody means to establish a credible identity in the specific context of school work conditions and exigencies. The most salient of these con-

ditions are: organizational ideals and demands; and specific cultural channels of peer-defined status. (quoted in Herr and Anderson, 1993: 16)

Although Wexler focuses on a social class analysis of public schooling, he does make note of the "cultural channels," which I assert circulate both inside and outside of school. It is the site of cultural politics in the city school, the arena in which the contests for unitary versus collective identity formation is waged, where this important part of student's work can be nurtured.

The central point about understanding ethnic identity as *social process* is that the process is *relational*. That is, there is no personal ethnic identity apart from a relationship to other (ethnic and nonethnic) identities (see Hall, 1991). Furthermore, the processes of identity formation within the social context of ethnicity (defined here as discursive practice of one's own and others' collective ethnic identities) is inseparable from the broader social relations of power and material and ideological structures.

Without the discourse into other ethnic groups, there can be no consciousness of ethnicity as a *collective* lived cultural experience for students in inner-city schools. More to the point: If African-American students, historically predefined by racial categories, are unaware of the cultural legacies of theirs and other ethnic groups (e.g., Latinos), then they may continue to view themselves as "blacks." The rapidly changing demographics in city schools thus presents both new cultural opportunities to forge identity politics and institutional barriers (racial and social) to realizing such a new praxis in the hopes of further democratizing public schooling (see Giroux, 1993; see also Britzman, 1993). The problematic issue is the processes by which both teachers and students can develop the capacity to engage in discursive practices such as communicative action.

Embracing ethnicity

A postmodern politics of ethnic identity embraces consciousness of other groups. It also calls for social action through a constant reflexive monitoring of the intentions, motivations, and reasons that propel groups into action (Giddens, 1984). The process of collective ethnic identity formation moves substantially beyond the notions of the autonomous modern self to embrace the recognition of *ethnicity* as a contested cultural terrain whose borders city schools can redraw. This reboundarying assumes considerable degree of conflict over values and the shared sense of common purpose (Ball, 1987; Olsen, 1994). Within this framework, conflict is elevated to a normative status.

The current popular movement to incorporate multicultural curricula and cultural diversity in urban school districts rests on the conservative assumption of what Kobena Mercer calls "imaginary unities" (cited in Giroux, 1993: 310). The goal of most multicultural curricula and cultural diversity initiatives is to celebrate difference under the banner of cultural harmony (see West, 1993a). There is no politics of identity and difference within this scenario, no "contested cultural terrain" that the schools, through struggle, confidently embrace. By denying cultural conflict, these school reform initiatives unintentionally deny ethnic minority students the opportunity to draw on collective identities within the sociality of ethnicity.

Borrowing on Giroux's notion of border pedagogy, I explore the implications of the deliberate politicizing (through cultural conflict) by schools and other institutions for the formation of ethnic identity for students. The purposeful use of conflict resolution techniques moves beyond the utilitarian notions of fostering individual identity by improving students' self-concept and self-esteem. The concern here is with the building of *collective* identity, therefore restoring a sense of community, springing from a respect for difference that does not relegate the culture of ethnic minorities to the status of the "other" (Fordham, 1993; hooks, 1993; Ogbu, 1988).

The entrenched social reality is that ethnicity is experienced primarily by white individuals and groups. In cities such as New Orleans, Atlanta, Detroit, and other heavily populated black urban centers, black students are shaped primarily by race, with class and gender categories playing important intersecting roles. For example, low-income black male youths who live in public housing developments live their lives in racial fear: fear of crime from other black youths, and fear of harassment and intimidation from white citizens and police officers. Before postmodern social analysis can inform political practice, the constitution of subjectivity at the intersection of race, class, and gender in the context of inner-city schools must be firmly confronted.

Let me be more specific. The dynamics of racial formation have shaped the constitution of subjectivity for racial/ethnic minorities by the essential trait of skin color: the darker the skin, the greater the subordination (see McCarthy and Crichlow, 1993). I have more to say about the implications for the altering of practice to realize this theoretic ideal of the confrontation by whites of the social construction of human subjectivity through racial, ethnic, gender, and class categories of identity (Foster, 1993; West, 1993a) toward the conclusion of this paper.

Given the pervasiveness of race in the formation of individual identity for blacks and other racial minorities, ethnicity must be not only imagined but deliberately fostered in the inner-city classroom. Inside the school as sites, and increasingly outside of the school building, of cultural production and contestation, it is possible to take seriously the insight that "the real is not a pregiven state that reproduces itself by means of the political but rather is political production itself" (Delany, quoted in Britzman, 1993: 25).

Embracing ethnicity, then, means two concrete things. One is to imagine how ethnic identities were constructed for particular groups of people, for example, blacks, Hispanics, and whites, in a local social formation and, second, to *critically reimagine* how such ethnic identities can be redefined as embracing the praxis of drawing from collective ethnic identities in the new social space of the city. Only through a recasting of the politics of ethnic identity as a form of the cultural politics of the school and of the classroom is this conceivable within the dominant paradigm of modernism. The postmodern cultural imagination can become real only through a genuine debate and appraisal of the modern social structures of race, social class, and ideology.

From ethnicity to new political subjects

A relational definition of ethnic identity not only focuses conceptual attention on ethnic identity as social process, but it also sheds light on the constitution of new political subjects (roles). The binary categories of the project of the Enlightenment – structure versus agency, the individual's recognition of universal reason versus the awareness of collective political actors and their material self-interest – potentially erode. Ultimately, whether employing Marxist or liberal theories of the political subject, this bifurcation of subjectivity "offers a reductionist view of the relationship between consciousness, agency, and social change" (Smith, 1992: 500). The implication for urban schooling is that educational (social) change in inner-city schools derives from students' total experience of their own ethnic identities, their discursive consciousness of ethnicity (Giddens, 1984) in relation to their own group, and their awareness of differences within other ethnic groups. Put simply, in the new global context of city schooling, students can mobilize for democratic educational change to the extent that they give equal value to erasing injustices and inequality for all ethnic groups in the multiethnic urban school.

In the idiosyncratic vernacular of postmodern social analysis, the political subject is *decentered*. This means that in an age of multiple identities, there are no clear roles that political subjects may assume in their quest for the deepening of democracy. Classroom teachers, for example, both labor under oppressive conditions of state regulation and may join with parents under the ideological space of empowerment in the struggle to make public schooling in the city more responsive to, and more reflective, of local community needs and values. Also, students under a more democratic educational system may pressure school boards, principals, and central office administrators for greater control over the curriculum and their own learning. There are both prospects and limitations of discursive practices in contemporary school reform to use power to pursue moral ends (Mirón, 1991; Mirón and Elliott, 1994). These ends derive from the shared values of local communities and the conflict over values embedded in the practice of radical democracy in urban public schooling.

The point for the radical democratization of city schooling, then, is that classroom teachers, with their ethnic minority students (see Biesta, 1994), must jointly enter the discourse of the politics of education as new political subjects. Exercising their power morally to authorize and create deep democratic space for their students in their own classrooms (see Giroux, 1993), classroom teachers can engage students in the cultural politics over the struggle for collective ethnic identity and difference. By extension, students potentially reconstitute themselves as political/learning subjects, capable of questioning, resisting, and transforming dominating forms of discourse such as national curriculum goals.

It is vitally important, therefore, for both the theory and practice of the constitution of new political subjectivity in inner-city schools to hold foremost the idea of the school and classroom as a site of cultural/identity politics. Historically, classroom teachers and other education professionals at the school site viewed the curriculum as depoliticized texts (see Pinar and Bowers, 1992). Indeed, because of the manipulative ideologies that divorced education from politics, classroom teachers engaged in procedural democracy (election of school board candidates and, in the classroom, equal treatment for all racial groups) mainly through the auspices of the teachers' unions, and then only begrudgingly. The idea that their own sites of practice may also be considered (and valued) as political is a foreign idea to most classroom teachers. Postmodern social analysis, however, offers the possibility that classroom teachers, like Socrates, may become teachers of the body politics as well. Practicing their craft as transformative intellectuals (Foster, 1986; Giroux, 1983), classroom teachers (and other caring professionals; see Goldner, 1993; Noddings, 1984, 1994) may engage their students to undo racism, deconstruct the ethnocentrism of Western Civilization, and embrace the feminist agenda of liberation for all from the terrors of patriarchy. Following the postmodern social analysis of Henry Giroux, I explore the underlying values and philosophical tenets of this view of radical democracy in the praxis of the urban classroom in the next section.

A Theory of Urban Pedagogy

In *Border Crossings: Cultural Workers and the Politics of Education* (1993) Henry Giroux proposes a theory of pedagogy to realize the ideal of deep, radical democracy in the school and other public spheres. I stress here that my reliance on Giroux's metaphor of *border crossings* and his development of *border pedagogy* as a postmodern praxis for the deepening of democracy in the urban public school classroom is based on the richness and intensity of the writing. It is my belief that Giroux's work is in dual need of empirical evidence and critique. I intend to make his writing more accessible to practitioners and theorists in urban education. Giroux's capacity to develop a theoretical project and vision that entertains an idea about what democracy can mean in the public school classroom is, in my judgment, rare in radical scholarship and in dire need of appropriation in the context of city schooling. All too often, the discourse of crisis surrounding the social context of public education in the city has wrongly focused educators' attention away from the problems and prospects of the social production of knowledge to the virtually impossible task of providing technological panaceas to fix schools and students.

Situating power/knowledge in city classrooms

Giroux is careful to credit radical, critical scholarship of the 1980s and 1990s. He does not stop there, however. Giroux extends the influence of critical theory to propose counter-hegemonic strategies to the conservative Reagan and Bush administrations. Cast mainly in functionalist categories, much critical scholarship of the 1970s and 1980s broke the mythological split between public schooling and inequality; poor quality schools, as Bowles and Gintis argued in *Schooling and Capitalist America* (1976), "produced passive workers who would adjust to the imperatives of the capitalist order" (quoted in Giroux, 1993: 151). This understanding contrasted markedly with the hegemonic ideology of public schooling as fostering upward economic and social mobility for the masses of poor and minority students. However, Giroux argues that much of the radical, critical scholarship "exhausted itself in its ability to take up power *dialectically* [productively] or to consider what schools could do to apply power productively" (1993: 151, emphasis added; see also Foster, 1986; 1989; Mirón and Elliott, 1994). Following Foucault (1977), I assert that power is everywhere and is inextricably tied to knowledge. Students can exercise power, and the move by principals and teachers to embrace their voices builds on what I term the "moral exercise of power" (Mirón and Elliott, 1994). Pervasive throughout students' lived cultural experience in inner-city classrooms is the use of power to resist representations by the dominant culture and to forge an identity politics in the struggle over their personal and collective identities.

In the context of public education in city schools, I argued in the previous section that classroom teachers could, as transformative intellectuals, foster students' new ethnic identity and awareness of others' ethnicity. In turn, this knowledge would create new political student subjects who would act on Mouffe's concept of democratic equivalence by resisting racism, sexism, homophobia, and ethnocentrism in their schools and local communities. Giroux's concept of border pedagogy embraces the notion that classroom teachers' use of power can both oppress and liberate students. In the increasingly ethnic majority urban school districts across the country, schools as sites of cultural/identity politics can foster the possibility of multiple student identities, wherein schools can celebrate difference while searching for community. More concretely, Giroux argues that a new postmodern cultural politics in the classroom should move "beyond identifying [specific] interests . . . to ask how these interests function. How do they produce particular ways of life?" (1993: 153).

Understanding, through pedagogy, how students construct meaning rather than simply how students receive it through reified knowledge (Everhart, 1983) is central to linking power and knowledge in the classroom. Although it is certainly true that racism pervades inner-city schools, classrooms, and local communities, many black and white students resist racism as well. At the University of New Orleans, faculty in the Department of Curriculum and Instruction are searching for ways to incorporate *A World of Difference*, an antibias curriculum project of the Anti Defamation League, a national Jewish organization dedicated to fighting prejudice and racism against all oppressed people.

By incorporating curricula that lay bare the colonizing legacies of western Europe, Giroux (1993) argues that educators and other cultural workers can take "seriously the identities of subordinate cultures" (p. 154). Schooling for ethnic minorities in city schools can then assume a counter-hegemonic role as a site of cultural politics. I extend Giroux's case and argue that *only* to the extent that public school teachers in the city are fully capable of understanding how students construct meaning can schools in the city be transformed from technical arenas of instruction to sites for cultural praxis and liberation.

In this regard, Giroux makes the following specific points: First, there exists material structures that constrain the production of meaning and knowledge in the classroom. Textbook companies, school-business partnerships, state government, courses in free enterprise, all limit the discourses on students' construction of meaning. In the context of the crisis in urban schooling, these material and companion ideological strategies of the Entrepreneurial Coalition (see Mirón, 1996) are especially problematic, as meaning can be subsumed under the experience of individual student choice. Institutionalizing the latter under the discourses of the Entrepreneurial Coalition, obviously, would make the possibilities for culturally based politics in city schools and classrooms problematic indeed.

Second is the issue of the production of texts. Giroux is concerned with the processes through which the production of educational texts in the wider society both shape and provide spaces for the construction of meaning in the classroom (see De Vaney, 1994). Texts in their various forms provide powerful discourses that produce the ideologies that students carry with them in schools. As students engage in the dialectical process of receiving and creating meaning through their lived cultural experiences, such ideologies (like competition, individualism, or diversity) help locate their social position in history and equip them with power (conceived as self-knowledge) to modify these positions through new discourses.

The third point concerns the possibilities of communities. A theory of border pedagogy in the urban context necessitates that classroom teachers take students out into local communities to examine how cultural articulations (see Smith, 1992) and local ideologies "accumulate historical weight" for students (Giroux, 1993: 154). In addition to the ideologies that students carry with them into their schools and classrooms, also of vital interest to Giroux are the processes whereby historical, social, and political conditions foster lived experience for students initially. Racism, for example, in the inner city vastly determines the social identities of students from racially defined categories, for example, blacks and Native Americans. Precisely pinpointing how racism helps constitute human subjectivity for students in segregated school decades following *Brown v. Board of Education Topeka, Kansas* is prerequisite for the construction of meaning in the cities' multiethnic/multicultural classrooms throughout America.

Embracing the value of radical democracy in city public schools

The current decentralization of large urban school districts in the form of school-based management and choice is unlikely to lead to democratic practices in the classroom. Giroux argues that schools should be conceived as democratic public spheres. Conservative ideological movements have successfully exploited the crisis of authority in American society and called for the redefinition of government. In public education, the concept of public schools is equated with *government-sponsored schools*. Hence, the negative characteristics associated with a bloated governmental bureaucracy – inefficiency, riddled with patronage and corruption, and organizationally driven, rather than client oriented – are pinned on public schools, not altogether wrongly.

Giroux's dream is to radically redefine the public sphere in education by making explicit the institutional and cultural links between schooling and the reconstruction of public life. This is one of many border crossings: he implores teachers and other cultural workers to take up the courage to fulfill the goal of the deepening of democracy in the broader society, the foremost ideal of critical pedagogy (see McLaren, 1994). Teachers and administrators are presently located vast social distances from the cultural and epistemological border that Giroux wishes to traverse. The conditions of widespread poverty, single-parent families, chronically underfunded schools, and a historically unresponsive professional bureaucracy bent on maintaining the contours of the one best system (see Tyack, 1974) make for a social context that makes incremental reform difficult (see Mirón and St. John, 1994) and deep democracy nearly impossible to attain.

Radical democratic practice in the urban classroom is nearly impossible, simply because there is no value of democracy undergirding professional activity, neither in the discourse of reform nor the politics of organizational maintenance (see Schlechty, 1990). This pessimism is predicated on the modernist assumption that educators will find neither the will nor the courage to take seriously Giroux's admonition that "schools and teachers need to gain a vision of why they're doing what they're doing" and to place "the notion of authority" within "an ethical and political referent" (1993: 154). However, the opening of the new politics of community allows for the possibility that even beleaguered inner-city schools can engage in the cultural struggle for democracy in the classroom. Whether the intensity of this engagement is radically or incrementally designed is an empirical question.

Educators in the city cannot be expected to muster the courage to take up this struggle alone. Based on the common principles of difference, equality, justice, and personal and community freedom, educators can join forces with artists and other cultural workers, such as those in the KOS (Kids of Survival) project in the Bronx. In this manner political coalitions based on Mouffe's (1988) concept of democratic equivalence can be established with the intent "to reclaim progressive notions of the *public* in public schooling so that education can become a real public service just as one might say that the arts need to be taken up pedagogically in the same ways" (Giroux, 1993: 155, emphasis in original). It goes without saying that no government mandate such as school choice can further the goal of deepening democracy in public schools.

The theory of border pedagogy makes imperative the centrality of language in equipping classroom teachers and others with the vocabulary to redraw the boundaries of the public schools. Classroom teachers can then engage in communicative action (Habermas, 1970) to insert a critical concept of democracy. In this sense, Giroux argues that discourse is the praxis of border pedagogy. Finding the appropriate methods and techniques to teach students in the inner city the effects of racism is not only misplaced. Worse, such technism undermines the global project of formulating a critical educational vision and imagination. By focusing on the discourses of methodology, the language of classroom teachers becomes depoliticized. Negotiating the transition from instructional technicians to cultural pedagogical workers implies redefining teachers' roles as public intellectuals (see J. Anderson, 1993; Foster, 1986). In the context of the city, wherein a decidedly anti-intellectual milieu prevails, this means that school business partners must come to realize the value of a redefined teacher role. As I discuss at the conclusion of this chapter, this is not easy.

Authorizing student voices

As critics of critical pedagogy and postmodernism have argued, the unequal power relations between teachers and students in the classroom may work to disempower, rather than morally empower, students (see Ellsworth, 1989). In inner-city schools the increasing public health hazard of violence and the absence of a strong democratic tradition makes for the potential abuse of power by police, teachers, and school administrators (see Troyna and Hatcher, 1991; see also Curcio and First, 1993). Giroux, however, distinguishes between authoritarianism and authority. Educators cannot disavow authority relations in the classroom; to do so would be immoral. The concept of authoritarianism in the classroom derives from the banking notion of education that Paulo Freire first criticized (see also Illich, 1971). That is, this view assumes that teachers simply transmit knowledge from one authoritative source (teachers or textbooks) to a passive, unreflective student. As Biesta (1994) theorizes, this pedagogy wrongly assumes an asymmetrical relationship between teacher and learner.

The multiplicity of identities and subjectivities embedded within the paradigm of postmodernism creates intellectual room for *student* production of knowledge. Within this framework teachers can instill in their classrooms the conditions wherein students can engage in both the critique and production of knowledge. For example, students in distressed neighborhoods in the city can make use of oral histories to interrogate how the ideologies of economic growth helped legitimize the dislocation and removal of poor black families during the construction of interstate highways. By exercising authority, not romantically denying its institutional presence, teachers can overcome Bakhtin's warning that institutions function to silence certain voices "before they even become vocalized in the public domain" (in Herr and Anderson, 1993: 13). Schools can affirmatively engage in the student production of knowledge. Their historical role of transmitting and distributing the knowledge and values of other cultures can (and should) be overcome.

Giroux is quick to point out that it is not enough to uncritically give voice to student experiences. The critical reflection of students' own lived cultural experiences is potentially a powerful tool for the forging of a border pedagogy in the city. The concrete interrogation of the processes by which hegemonic ideologies and socially constructed realities such as racial and ethnic identities shape their understanding of their histories is a marker that begins the process of border crossing. What I mean to say is that student empowerment through the cultural struggle to find voice in the classroom should not focus on the sometimes cathartic process of storytelling (although this could indeed be cathartic for some oppressed students); rather, the politics of finding voice in the classroom is not separate from the politics of difference: Both struggles are inherently *social* and *political*. They are designed primarily with the long-term aim of critical pedagogy of the deepening of democratic practice in the wider society. In the short run, these sites of cultural politics are meant to achieve student understanding of how social relations are constituted so that they can be ultimately transformed via resistance and the mediations of student culture. Such lofty goals must, of course, be built out of a theory of pedagogy and new political communities that seek to unify while embracing and celebrating difference.

Border Pedagogy and the Politics of Difference

My overriding purpose is to examine the crisis in urban schooling by situating it at the nexus of the global economy and the new social space of urban ethnicity. Conceptualizing the postmodern category of difference is paramount. In particular, developing a theory of urban pedagogy that helps teachers and students deconstruct the social determinants of race and ethnicity in city schooling marks a border crossing from the schools as transmitters of knowledge to schools as active producers of knowledge for the mutual benefits of students and local communities. Breaking down the barriers of *artificial* (socially constructed) difference, then, enables the cultural politics of genuine difference based on achieving the principles of justice, freedom, and equality for students occupying varying historical locations to commence. Giroux organized his understanding of the concept of difference into the categories of conservative, liberal, and radical.

Difference as social deviance

As Giroux observes, conservative ideological forces such as the New Right have invoked the notion of difference to justify social relations of racism, male dominance, and classism. Invoking the supposed natural laws of science and culture, New Right groups have justified these unequal power relations by equating the category of difference with the idea of deviance.

The effect of this conceptualization of difference is well illustrated with the history of bilingual education in this country. Prior to the enactment of bilingual education, speakers of languages other than English were prohibited from receiving instruction in their native tongues because foreign languages were viewed as linguistic handicaps in the United States (see Fishman, 1976). I hasten to point out that even within the broad social context of the global economy, calls for English-only legislation are not abating. There seems to be an even greater reluctance on behalf of classroom teachers in inner-city schools to build on the rich oral language traditions of African-American students as a pedagogical bridge to acquiring standard English. Although temporarily ignoring the ethnocentric bias of conventional curricula in underfunded inner-city classrooms, I simply point out how material and ideological structures greatly constrain the opportunities for teachers to employ alternate views of difference with their multiethnic student clientele.

The liberal ambivalence with race

Liberals are ambivalent in their attitudes on race. An ideologically palatable position holds that tolerance for racial differences should co-exist within a framework of cultural diversity. Under that vague conceptual umbrella, liberals place the construct of race in a generic, universal category of diversity as one example of endless possibilities within the varied cultures in the United States. Giroux agrees with Rothenberg's argument that a major difficulty with this perspective is that, by refusing to ascribe any independent status to the category of race as a central factor in the construction of the social formation in this country "it redefines race in a way that denies the history of racism in the United States and, thus, denies white responsibility for the present and past oppression and exploitation of people of color" (cited in Giroux, 1993: 171; see also West, 1993b). The modernist's unproven assumption of the natural progressive movement of history, as witnessed by a societal denial of the viscousness of racism under the rubric of an unspecified difference, undergirds liberal ideology and unintentionally reproduces unequal power relations hidden in race (see Giddens, 1984). The implication for city schools is ironic. By celebrating cultural diversity, for example, through specifically designated African-American awareness weeks, I argue that both whites and blacks are attributed responsibility for the pernicious effects of race on poor blacks, Hispanics, Asians, and Native Americans.

Giroux asserts that the liberal ambivalence with racism is also evident in the widespread attempts at cultural assimilation. By treating racial inequality in culturally deficit terms, students' lived cultural experiences of history and language get relegated to the invisible category of the *other*. I contend that no cultural narratives can be produced within a model of race that views blacks and other minorities as having cultural deficits because they were not able to fully integrate their culture into the dominant US culture as white European immigrant groups seemingly accomplished. The ironic realization is that the ideology of assimilation continues as educators and other professionals continue to plead that education can lead the way out of poverty (Frazier, 1993).

Radical conceptions of difference

A critical postmodern analysis of racial and other categories of difference points to the multilayered and fractured construction of individual identities. As I have illustrated, ethnic identity is socially constructed and can be reformed in discourse and political struggle. Racial identities, too, are unstable and have shifted according to the drifts of political winds. Once defined by the US Census Bureau by race, Hispanics are now identified by ethnic categories as Central American, Mexican-American, Cuban, and the like.

Giroux takes issue with the radical, postmodern notion that identities are shaped in discourse through language use and the content of what students are allowed to voice in the classroom. By stressing the indeterminacy of the self, Giroux argues that little space is available for human agency. In my judgment this conclusion on agency is wrong. He observes: "In effect subjectivity becomes an effect of language, and human agency disappears into the discredited terrain of human will" (p. 172). I agree with the position taken by Anthony Giddens (1982; 1984) that social theory must always leave theoretic space for human agency. My concern here is to show how social context and discursive practices in urban schooling construct individual and collective identities. I assert that discursive practices such as schooling both shape and allow space for agency.

In the social context of urban schooling, it is clear that much pedagogical practice rests on the assumption that ethnic dialects interfere in the goal of assimilation for minority students. Many students of multiple cultural backgrounds, for example, immigrants and Mexican-American students in border towns and states, are therefore silenced or forced to make a choice of survival, rejecting one of their multiple identities (the ethnic one) in favor of assimilation. Clearly, individual identities are woven in discourse, privileging specific use of language and silencing other uses. Herr and Anderson's oral history of Victor, the first Hispanic admitted into a private, affluent high school in a southwest city is telling:

> I really don't see myself as a Hispanic person. We were talking about this in the car this morning with Ariel and he said that when you go to this school it's like going to Candyland . . . You know, hypothetically speaking there's no drugs, there isn't any alcohol . . . It's Candyland . . . You go and you're sheltered . . . I really don't label myself as the typical Hispanic person; I kind of label myself as the typical Anglo Hispanic person . . . l kind of look at myself as kind of an Anglo person in some ways. The way I speak sometimes, I really don't have a strong accent and black people have some strong accents, you know the way they pronounce the words and Vietnamese and Asian people and all that – you know I really don't, if you look at it, I'm Hispanic, you know my blood, my color, my background, but right now I'm turning into an Anglo. (1993: 14)

Giroux makes the same criticism of certain postmodern conceptions of the differences within social groups as he levies against the disappearance of a theory of human agency. In particular, he controversially attacks a strand of feminist discourse for its version of identity politics because of its often unstated assumption that one's social location (i.e. gender) determines political stance and ideologies. This unreflective embrace of "the authority of experience" ignores the way that personal identity is often taken up in multilayered and contradictory fashion. Because personal identity is potentially always shifting, Giroux argues that it cannot be an unproblematic basis of political practice. A relatively straightforward example is the divisions within the Latin community in Miami, in which Cubans are often ideologically pitted against Central Americans from countries like El Salvador and Nicaragua as well as the Caribbean immigrants from Haiti and elsewhere. In these instances, one's shared cultural background does not universally determine a political position *vis-à-vis* US imperialism.

Antibias Pedagogy as Cultural Politics

The foregoing review of both traditional and radical conceptions of difference makes clear that Giroux views significant social struggles such as resisting racism as part of the broader politics of the deepening of democratic practices. For if a hierarchy of oppression exists in progressive social movements, one that privileges dominant relations of any kind (whether of race, gender, or class categories), the hopes for forging a common purpose in education and other cultural spheres remain dim. Giroux relentlessly calls for a mode of resistance that keeps foremost in mind the philosophical principles of freedom, equality, and justice. Forging an antibias pedagogy, then, in the inner city and in other urban contexts characterized by the divisiveness of racial, political, and ethnic cleavages poses a genuine test of the Utopian dream of a radical democracy.

Giroux continues to insist that forging the deepening of democracy must begin with a radical pedagogical practice. After all, racism, like other forms of social biases, are both taught and learned. Within this perspective, pedagogy is not separate from politics; indeed, it constitutes a form of cultural politics within the schools and inside of the classrooms. By insisting that teachers especially reject all forms of totalizing narratives under the guise of universal reason, it is conceivable that public school educators can join with other public servants such as artists and activists within the academy to forge a "wider struggle for democratic public life and critical citizenship" (Giroux, 1991: 245). In the remainder of this paper I map out how an antibias pedagogy might wield potential for achieving the radical goals of critical pedagogy. I continually emphasize the situatedness of urban education, schools caught up in the midst of extremely complex circumstances and harsh material life. Many students in the inner city, large percentages of whom live below the poverty line, confront dangers on walks to and from school, and generally face the pernicious effects of racism every day of their lives.

These unintended consequences of social reproduction (see Giddens, 1984) are institutionalized in the discursive practices of schools, despite decades of legislation and affirmative action programs.

First, a critical literacy must be formed that places at the center of social analysis the unequal power relations that systematically work against people of color. In this way, illiteracy among racial/ethnic minorities is not viewed as a technical problem of a lack of reading and writing skills, but rather works to sustain high levels of poverty among poor blacks, Hispanics, and Native Americans. Paulo Freire recognized this phenomena early on in his attempts to teach peasants critical literacy in Brazil using the process of conscientization and the construction of generative themes. Grounding literacy pedagogy in the circumstances of oppression constructed meaning for the poor in Brazil, linking the formal learning of language with resistance to bias and oppression. As Freire (1973) well describes in *Pedagogy of the Oppressed,* Brazilian peasants saw relevance and value in literacy skills, in part out of their collaboration with their adult teachers, and in part out of the common struggle against poverty.

In the same manner, critical literacy and antibias pedagogy can be coupled by the reading of various texts (books, print media, advertising) that both create conditions for the reproduction of racial inequality and offer students the opportunity to move beyond racism by writing their own texts. Giroux offers the example of black students conducting oral histories to examine which voices are silent and which are privileged in conventional history books.

Such a critical literacy in the context of city schooling can reconfigure the concept of ethnicity as a means for students and teachers to exercise power through the cultural politics of the school. The construction of new subject identities (political roles; see Mouzelis, 1992) within a multiethnic milieu redefines the negative labeling of race as a means to maintain white, middle-class hegemony. Blacks can become collective political agents. They may form alliances with other ethnic-racial groups to struggle against undemocratic schools.

Second, an antibias pedagogy as part of a theory of urban pedagogy must be more than a postmodern exercise in deconstruction. Both teachers and students of color need to understand in their bodies and souls – not only in their head – how racial "narratives are taken up as part of an investment of feeling, pleasure, and desire" (Giroux, 1991: 249). For it is certainly true, despite contemporary racial political rhetoric, that some racial social groups benefit from the discourse of racism. For example, when well-financed corporate political action committees line up to offer financial support for black school board candidates or mayoral prospects for the expressed purpose of controlling public policies (see Mirón and Brooks, 1993), the jobs and material rewards that these officials ultimately dole out to loyal constituents may ultimately sustain white, corporate hegemony in urban schooling. In short, an anti-racist pedagogy must begin with the discomforting realization that, perhaps unwittingly, racial identities for blacks and other people of color are difficult to shed. Ironically, there is sometimes both satisfaction and grief in the lived cultural experiences of racism.

Finally, embracing a broader cultural politics of democratic practice in the urban classroom, antibias pedagogy gives voice to racial minorities that extends beyond individual accounts of racism. It is equally important to weave individual narrative accounts within the relational properties of racism. Clearly, racism as hegemonic ideology serves the material interests of specific groups (e.g., white, middle-class male professionals) and therefore works against democratic principles of equity, justice, and fairness. Classroom teachers in the city, of all racial groups, must attend to how they might unintentionally subscribe to racist ideologies and practices. Only then can they begin to view the issue as rooted in a culture that reproduces the *structural* causes of racism as they decry individual transgressions of the oppression of racial-ethnic minorities (Giroux, 1991).

I offer the following illustration drawn from my own teaching to underscore both the complexities and the passions involved in formulating an antibias pedagogy. In 1989, I asked white and black students at Loyola University of New Orleans to investigate whether specific institutional practices within the social relations of fraternity and sorority life reproduced racial segregation on the campus.

I taught an undergraduate elective course entitled *Culture and Learning* to a class of 40 students, of whom approximately 10 were black and 30 white. I assigned them the task of investigating why there existed separate black and white sororities and fraternities on campus. Did selection or recruitment practices formally or informally prohibit black or white students from joining these institutions? Did the university bylaws governing the charters of student organizations encourage the formation of distinctly racial social groups?

I learned that the formal policies and procedures of the university and student-run organizations did not prohibit black students from joining white social organizations, nor white students from joining black social organizations. Indeed, the universal finding of all of the research groups I had helped the students to organize was that racially organized fraternities and sororities were the result of freedom of choice of the students themselves. Indeed, there was black representation on the Panhellenic Council, the university governing board of fraternity and sorority life. However, black students ran their own organizations and, with a few exceptions, white organizations had exclusive white membership (I recall an instance or two in which a white fraternity had a black student in its membership).

When I opened the final class meeting to discussion as to why the university would allow students to form separate social organizations for whites and blacks, given the long history of advocacy for civil and human rights, the answer I received was that "both whites and blacks wanted it that way." Shockingly, I learned from my mostly middle-class black students that, as a social group, they distanced themselves from low-income blacks in the inner-city neighborhoods and public housing developments in New Orleans. "Those students aren't 'black'" they informed the white students (and myself) in the class. I believe that the substantive point that the middle-class African-American students were trying to make to the white students enrolled in *Culture and Learning* was that the black fraternity and sorority members were proud of their organizations. What had become the black stereotype in New Orleans, as in many cities, was black identity as the deviant underclass. For black students in my class, then, being black at Loyola University meant being a member of the middle class, just as middle class as the white students. I am reminded of Herr and Anderson's oral history of Victor (cited earlier) who really did not see himself as Hispanic.

Had I explored the boundaries of racism in the context of the university, indeed had I crossed the cultural border of voluntary racist practices, I would have encouraged both black and white students to examine not only the accommodating culture of racism within social life at the university. I would also have tried to open a dialogue to examine how race, identity, class, and gender categories shaped racial identity for both middle-class black students at Loyola University in New Orleans and lower socioeconomic black groups. In hindsight, I would have pointed out that, in both cases, racial identities are *socially constructed* by white, middle-class experience. The white students in my class, however, remained virtually free of racial identification. That is, whereas black middle-class students were quick to inform their white classmates that poor blacks living in public housing were not really black, the practice of holding up black social organizations as models of middle-class student life – capable of competing with white organizations – was unintentionally reproduced. The modernist conception of racial identity pervades the constitution of subjectivity in the pedagogical illustration I cited.

From my recollection of the class discussion of seven years ago, the cultural category of ethnicity was not part of the discourse. Indeed, when I look back over it from a postmodern perspective, my organizing of the research project, and subsequent class discussions, unconsciously took up the social construction of race – exclusively for black students. Owing to my genuine concern with the incongruence between liberal ideologies of the Jesuits and the clear social segregation of student life by race, I set out to explore the causes of racial segregation. Ironically, the class discussions focused on the relationships between culture and learning; yet I raised no questions of black or white ethnic culture. Nor did my students ask any questions about ethnicity. Anecdotally, it seemed that all social celebrations of black student life were defined in race and class terms. The contribution of African-American culture to the vitality of the social organizations, the university, and to the larger New Orleans community was conspicuously absent.

The Boundaries of the Urban School

This brief account of my introduction to antibias pedagogy highlights the difficulty of border crossing in any concrete pedagogical situation. This difficulty holds special relevance when the cultural and pedagogical borders literally fence in an inner-city school, thus making real the construct of social isolation (see Garvin, 1994; Wilson, 1987). Giroux is correct in his observation that educators must deliberately create alliances with other cultural workers if the goal of the deepening of democracy is to begin to take root in the city classroom. Schools situated in the inner city have historically been undemocratic places. Research and intervention in the implementation of the Accelerated Schools Process (ASP) in urban school districts (see Mirón and St. John, 1994; St. John et al., 1992) found that the traditions within some predominantly lower socioeconomic African-American populated schools often relied on corporal punishment and verbal abuse of black students to enforce formal and informal school discipline policies. Such a blatant coercive climate of disciplinary power (Foucault, 1977) in some of the poor African-American school communities does not bode well for antibias pedagogy or critical pedagogy of any form.

When schools were better funded and national policies were more favorable to the alleviation of human suffering in the urban ghettoes, the larger struggle for civil rights helped teachers share a common vision and purpose. However, the present social and economic conditions in these schools make fighting crime the prime concern. It will be difficult to wage the struggle for the deepening of democracy in public schools in which metal detectors, safety, and drug trafficking are daily obsessions with parents, administrators, and the general public. It is not an exaggeration to state that, in many schools in the inner city (and increasingly even in rural and some suburban school districts), the high school campus resembles a modern police state. Under these social conditions, it is perhaps unrealistic to expect teachers and students alone to concern themselves with the crisis of democracy. It may come to pass that the place to begin this ambitious undertaking is outside of the formal boundaries of the urban school.

Eventually, the institution of public schooling may have to be reconfigured in the inner city (see Mirón, 1995). The circumstances of economic and social hardship may pose too difficult a set of institutional barriers to redirect pedagogical practice to a cultural politics. I suggest that we borrow images and metaphors from the performing arts. Around the country students are linking up with arts programs as a means of forging personal and ethnic identity (see Ball and Heath, 1993). As I have argued, the place to begin in the context of the changing demographics of city schools is with students' sense of their own ethnic identity and the collective celebration of difference through an appreciation of the multiple possibilities of forging ethnic and social identities. I propose a reconceptualized vision of urban schooling following the analysis of student narratives of their awareness of their and others' ethnicity, which schools can deliberately foster or institutionally hinder.

I seek to let the voices of ethnic minority students in city schools speak for themselves. Although I do not believe in removing one's moral politics from the representation of students' lived experiences and personal/social identities, my aim is to use the medium of student voices and qualitative research to both combat the school's historical silencing of student narratives and to temper my own passion for affirmative ethnicity (see Paulston, 1980). What I hope to achieve in these student narratives is a concrete portrait of student culture, in particular, of how students' understanding of their own lived experiences in the school and classroom is part and parcel of what Wexler (1988, cited in Herr and Anderson, 1993) characterizes as identity work. I partially establish that there exists in the school (conceptualized as a social organization) a hidden cultural politics that fosters an accommodation (Everhart, 1983; see also Gilligan, 1993) of student ethnic identity to the dominant culture of the school and wider society. At the same time student culture resists this tendency to accommodate.

References

Anderson, J. (1993). The public intellectual. *The New Yorker*, pp. 39–48.

Aronowitz, S. (1994). The situation of the left in the United States. *Socialist Review*, 23 (3), 48–55.

Baca, L. and Cervantes, H. (1989). *The Bilingual Special Education Interface*. Columbus, OH: Merill Hill.

Ball, A. and Heath, S. (1993). Dances of Identity: Finding an ethnic self in the arts. In S. Heath and M. McLaughlin (eds), *Identity and Inner-City Youth: Beyond ethnicity and gender* (pp. 69–94). New York: Teachers College Press.

Ball, S. (1987). *The Micropolitics of the School: Towards a theory of school organization*. London: Methuen.

Biesta, G. (1994). Education as Practical Intersubjectivity: Towards a critical-pragmatic understanding of education. *Educational Theory*, 44 (3), 299–319.

Bondi, L. (1993). *Place and the Politics of Identity* (pp. 84–102). New York: Routledge.

Bowles, S. and Gintis, H. (1976). *Schooling and Capitalist America: Educational reform and the contradictions of economic life*. London: Routledge and Kegan Paul.

Britzman, D. (1993). The Ordeal of Knowledge: Rethinking the possibilities of multicultural education. *The Review of Education*, 15, 123–35.

Buriel, R. and Cardoza, D. (1993). Mexican American Ethnic Labeling: An intrafamilial and intergenerational analysis. In M. Bernal and G. Knight (eds), *Ethnic Identity: Formation and transmission among Hispanics and other minorities* (pp. 197–209). Albany: State University of New York Press.

Cummins, J. (1993). Empowering Minority Students: A framework for intervention. In M. Fine and L. Weis (eds), *Beyond Silenced Voices: Class, race, and gender in United States schools* (pp. 101–9). Buffalo, NY: State University of New York Press.

Curcio, J. and First, P. (1993). *Violence in the Schools: How to proactively prevent and defuse it*. Newbury Park, CA: Corwin.

Davis, B. and McCaul, E. (1991). *The Emerging Crisis: Current and projected status of children in the United States*. Orono, ME: Institute for the Study of At-Risk Students.

De Vaney, A. (ed.). (1994). *Watching Channel One: The convergence of students, technology and private business*. Albany: State University of New York Press.

Ellsworth, E. (1989). Why doesn't this feel empowering? Working through the repressive myths of critical pedagogy. *Harvard Educational Review*, 59 (3), 297–324.

Everhart, R. (1983). *Reading, Writing and Resistance*. New York: Routledge.

Fishman, J. (1976). *Bilingual education: an international sociological perspective*. Rowley, MA: Newbury House.

Fordham, S. (1993). Those loud black girls: (black) women, silence, and gender "passing" in the academy. *Anthropology and Education Quarterly*, 24 (1), 3–32.

Foster, M. (1993). Resisting Racism: Personal testimonies of African-American teachers. In L. Weis and M. Fine (eds), *Class, Race, and Gender in United States Schools* (pp. 273–88). Albany: State University of New York Press.

Foster, W. (1986). *Paradigms and Promises: New approaches to educational administration*. Buffalo, NY: Prometheus Books.

Foster, W. (1989, April). *School Leaders as Transformative Intellectuals: A theoretical argument*. Paper presented at the conference of the American Educational Research Association. San Francisco.

Foucault, M. (1977). *Discipline and Punish: The birth of the prison*. New York: Pantheon Books.

Frazier, L. (1993, October 6). Education matters. *Times-Picayune*: B1.

Freire: (1973). *Pedagogy of the Oppressed*. New York: Seasbury Press.

Garvin, J. (1994). *Public Housing and Social Isolation in New Orleans: A case study*. Unpublished dissertation, University of New Orleans.

Giddens, A. (1982). *Profiles and Critiques in Social Theory*. Berkeley: University of California Press.

Giddens, A. (1984). *The Constitution of Society*. Berkeley: University of California Press.

Gilligan, C. (1993). Joining the Resistance: Psychology, politics, girls, and women. In L. Weis and M. Fine (eds), *Beyond Silenced Voices: Class, race, and gender in United States schools* (pp. 143–69). Albany: State University of New York Press.

Giroux, H. (1983). *Theory and Resistance in Education*. South Hadley, MA: Bergin and Garvey.

Giroux, H. (ed.). (1991). *Post Modernism, Feminism, and Cultural Politics: Redrawing educational boundaries*. Albany: State University of New York Press.

Giroux, H. (1993). *Border Crossings: Cultural workers and the politics of education*. New York: Routledge and Kegan Paul.

Goldner, V. (1993). Power and Hierarchy: Let's talk about it. *Family Practice*, 32, 157–62.

Grossberg, L. (1993). Cultural studies and/or new worlds. In C. McCarthy and W. Crichlow (eds), *Race, Identity, and Representation in Education* (pp. 89–105). New York: Routledge.

Habermas, J. (1970). Toward a theory of communicative competence. *Inquiry*, 13, 205–18.

Hall, S. (1991). Ethnicity, identity and difference. *Radical America*, 13 (4), 10–16.

Hannaway, J. and Carnoy, M. (eds). (1993). *Decentralization and School Improvement: Can we fulfill the promise?* San Francisco, CA: Jossey-Bass.

Herr, K. and Anderson, G. (1993). Oral History for Student Empowerment: Capturing students' inner voices. *Qualitative Studies in Education* (no. 41230).

hooks, b. (1993). *Sisters of the Yam: Black women and self-recovery*. Boston: South End Press.

Illich, I. (1971). *Deschooling Society*. New York: Harrow Books.

Lauria, M., Mirón, L. and Dashner, D. (1994). *Student Resistance to the Entrepreneurial Coalition's Drive for Ideological Hegemony in Public Schooling* (no. 28). New Orleans: University of New Orleans, College of Urban and Public Affairs.

McCarthy, C. and Crichlow, W. (eds). (1993). *Race, Identity, and Representation in Education*. New York: Routledge.

McLaren, P. (1994). *Life in Schools: An Introduction to critical pedagogy in the foundations of education* (2nd edn). New York: Longman.

Mirón, L. F. (1991, Fall). The dialectics of school leadership: Post structural implications. *Organizational Theory Dialogue*, 1–5.

Mirón, L. F. (1995). Pushing the boundaries of urban school reform: Linking student outcomes to community development. *Journal of a Just and Caring Education*, 1 (1), 98–114.

Mirón, L. F. (1996). *The Social Construction of Urban Schooling: Situating the crisis*. Cresskill, NJ: Hampton Press.

Mirón, L. F. and Brooks, C. (1993). Great Expectations: A critic analysis of the lessons of a grassroots movement to reform an urban school board. *The International Journal of School Reform*, 2 (3), 242–8.

Mirón, L. F. and Elliott, R. (1994). Moral leadership in a post structural era. In S. Maxcy (ed.), *Postmodern School Leadership: Meeting the crisis in educational administration*. Westport CT: Praeger.

Mirón, L. F. and St. John, E. (1994). *The Urban Context and the Meaning of School Reform* (no. 7. DURPS Working Paper Series). University of New Orleans College of Urban and Public Affairs.

Mouffe, C. (1988). Radical democracy: Modern or postmodern? In A. Ross (ed.), *Universal Abandon?: The politics of post modernism* (pp. 31–45). Minneapolis: University of Minnesota Press.

Mouzelis, N. (1992). Marxism or post-Marxism? *New Left Review*, 3 (167), 107–23.

Noddings, N. (1984). *Caring: A feminine approach to ethics and moral education*. Berkeley: University of California Press.

Noddings, N. (1994). *Towards an Ethics of Care in the Schools*. New York: Teachers College Press.

Ogbu, J. (1988). Class stratification, racial stratification, and schooling. In L. Weis (ed.), *Class, Race, and Gender in American Education* (pp. 46–71). Albany: State University Press of New York.

Olsen, L. (1994). *The Road Not Taken: Implementing a community specific multi-cultural curriculum*. Unpublished dissertation.

Paulston, C. (1980). *Bilingual Education: Theories and issue*. Rowley, MA: Newbury House.

Pinar, W. F. and Bowers, C. A. (1992). Politics of curriculum: origins, controversies and significance of critical perspectives. *Review of Research in Education*, 18, 163–91.

Schlechty, P. (1990). *Schools for the 21st Century: Leadership imperatives for educational reform*. San Francisco: Jossey Bass.

Smith, M. P. (1992). Post modernism, urban ethnography, and the new social space of ethnic identity. *Theory and Society*, 21 (4), 493–531.

Spindler, G. and Spindler, L. (1994). *Pathways to Cultural Awareness: Cultural therapy with teachers and students*. Thousand Oaks, CA: Corwin.

St. John, E., Mirón, L. and Davidson, B. (1992). Teacher inquiry and school transformation: An examination of exemplary schools. *Louisiana Social Studies Journal*, 24 (1), 9–16.

Troyna, B. and Hatcher, R. (1991). Racist incidents in schools: A framework for analysis. *Journal of Educational Policy*, 6 (1), 17–31.

Tyack, D. (1974). *The One Best System*. Cambridge, MA: Harvard University Press.

West, C. (1993a). *Keeping Faith: Philosophy and race in America*. New York: Routledge.

West, C. (1993b). The new cultural politics of difference. In W. Crichlow and C.

McCarthy (eds), *Race, Identity and Representation in Education* (pp. 11–24). New York: Routledge.

Wexler, P. (1988). Symbolic economy of identity and denial of labor: Studies in high school number one. In L. Weis (ed.), *Class, Race, and Gender in American Education* (pp. 302–11). Albany: State University of New York.

Wilson, W. (1987). *The Truly Disadvantaged: The inner city, the underclass, and public policy*. Chicago, IL: The University of Chicago Press.

Part II

Critical Multiracial Feminisms

6

Theorizing Difference from Multiracial Feminism

Maxine Baca Zinn and Bonnie Thornton Dill

Women of color have long challenged the hegemony of feminisms constructed primarily around the lives of white middle-class women. Since the late 1960s, US women of color have taken issue with unitary theories of gender. Our critiques grew out of the widespread concern about the exclusion of women of color from feminist scholarship and the misinterpretation of our experiences,[1] and ultimately "out of the very discourses, denying, permitting, and producing difference."[2] Speaking simultaneously from "within and against" *both* women's liberation *and* anti-racist movements, we have insisted on the need to challenge systems of domination,[3] not merely as gendered subjects but as women whose lives are affected by our location in multiple hierarchies.

Recently, and largely in response to these challenges, work that links gender to other forms of domination is increasing. In this article, we examine this connection further as well as the ways in which difference and diversity infuse contemporary feminist studies. Our analysis draws on a conceptual framework that we refer to as "multiracial feminism."[4] This perspective is an attempt to go beyond a mere recognition of diversity and difference among women to examine structures of domination, specifically the importance of race in understanding the social construction of gender. Despite the varied concerns and multiple intellectual stances which characterize the feminisms of women of color, they share an emphasis on race as a primary force situating genders differently. It is the centrality of race, of institutionalized racism, and of struggles against racial oppression that link the various feminist perspectives within this framework. Together, they demonstrate that racial meanings offer new theoretical directions for feminist thought.

Tensions in Contemporary Difference Feminism

Objections to the false universalism embedded in the concept "woman" emerged within other discourses as well as those of women of color.[5] Lesbian feminists and postmodern feminists put forth their own versions of what Susan Bordo has called "gender skepticism."[6]

Many thinkers within mainstream feminism have responded to these critiques with efforts to contextualize gender. The search for women's "universal" or "essential" characteristics is being abandoned. By examining gender in the context of other social divisions and perspectives, difference has gradually become important – even problematizing the universal categories of "women" and "men." Sandra Harding expresses the shift best in her claim that "there are no gender relations *per se*, but only gender relations as constructed by and between classes, races, and cultures."[7]

Many feminists now contend that difference occupies center stage as *the* project of women studies today.[8] According to one scholar, "difference has replaced equality as the central concern of feminist theory."[9] Many have welcomed the change, hailing it as a major revitalizing force in US feminist theory.[10] But if *some* priorities within mainstream feminist thought have been refocused by attention to difference, there remains an "uneasy alliance"[11] between women of color and other feminists.

If difference has helped revitalize academic feminisms, it has also "upset the apple cart" and introduced new conflicts into feminist studies.[12] For example, in a recent and widely discussed essay, Jane Rowland Martin argues that the current preoccupation with difference is leading feminism into dangerous traps. She fears that in giving privileged status to a predetermined set of analytic categories (race, ethnicity, and class), "we affirm the existence of nothing but difference." She asks, "How do we know that for us, difference does not turn on being fat, or religious, or in an abusive relationship?"[13]

We, too, see pitfalls in some strands of the difference project. However, our perspectives take their bearings from social relations. Race and class differences are crucial, we argue, not as individual characteristics (such as being fat) but insofar as they are primary organizing principles of a society which locates and positions groups within that society's opportunity structures.

Despite the much-heralded diversity trend within feminist studies, difference is often reduced to mere pluralism: a "live and let live" approach where principles of relativism generate a long list of diversities which begin with gender, class, and race and continue through a range of social structural as well as personal characteristics.[14] Another disturbing pattern, which bell hooks refers to as "the commodification of difference," is the representation of diversity as a form of exotica, "a spice, seasoning that livens up the dull dish that is mainstream white culture."[15] The major limitation of these approaches is the failure to attend to the power relations that accompany difference. Moreover, these approaches ignore the inequalities that cause some characteristics to be seen as "normal" while others are seen as "different" and thus, deviant.

Maria C. Lugones expresses irritation at those feminists who see only the *problem* of difference without recognizing *difference*.[16] Increasingly, we find that difference *is* recognized. But this in no way means that difference occupies a "privileged" theoretical status. Instead of using difference to rethink the category of women, difference is often a euphemism for women who differ from the traditional norm. Even in purporting to accept difference, feminist pluralism often creates a social reality that reverts to universalizing women:

> So much feminist scholarship assumes that when we cut through all of the diversity among women created by differences of racial classification, ethnicity, social class, and sexual orientation, a "universal truth" concerning women and gender lies buried underneath. But if we can face the scary possibility that no such certainty exists and that persisting in such a search will always distort or omit someone's experiences, with what do we replace this old way of thinking? Gender differences and gender politics begin to look very different if there is no essential woman at the core.[17]

What is Multiracial Feminism?

A new set of feminist theories have emerged from the challenges put forth by women of color. Multiracial feminism is an evolving body of theory and practice informed by wide-ranging intellectual traditions. This framework does not offer a singular or unified feminism but a body of knowledge situating women and men in multiple systems of domination. US multiracial feminism encompasses several emergent perspectives developed primarily by women of color: African-Americans, Latinos, Asian-Americans, and Native Americans, women whose analyses are shaped by their unique perspectives as "outsiders within" – marginal intellectuals whose social locations provide them with a particular perspective on self and society.[18] Although US women of color represent many races and ethnic backgrounds – with different histories and cultures – our feminisms cohere in their treatment of race as a basic social division, a structure of power, a focus of political struggle, and hence a fundamental force in shaping women's and men's lives.

This evolving intellectual and political perspective uses several controversial terms. While we adopt the label "multiracial," other terms have been used to describe this broad framework. For example, Chela Sandoval refers to "US Third World feminisms," [19] while other scholars refer to "indigenous feminisms." In their theory text-reader, Alison M. Jagger and Paula S. Rothenberg adopt the label "multicultural feminism." [20]

We use "multiracial" rather than "multicultural" as a way of underscoring race as a power system that interacts with other structured inequalities to shape genders. Within the US context, race, and the system of meanings and ideologies which accompany it, is a fundamental organizing principle of social relationships.[21] Race affects all women and men, although in different ways. Even cultural and group differences among women are produced through interaction within a racially stratified social order. Therefore, although we do not discount the importance of culture, we caution that cultural analytic frameworks that ignore race tend to view women's differences as the product of group-specific values and practices that often result in the marginalization of cultural groups which are then perceived as exotic expressions of a normative center. Our focus on race stresses the social construction of differently situated social groups and their varying degrees of advantage and power. Additionally, this emphasis on race takes on increasing political importance in an era where discourse about race is governed by color-evasive language[22] and a preference for individual rather than group remedies for social inequalities. Our analyses insist upon the primary and pervasive nature of race in contemporary US society while at the same time acknowledging how race both shapes and is shaped by a variety of other social relations.

In the social sciences, multiracial feminism grew out of socialist feminist thinking. Theories about how political economic forces shape women's lives were influential as we began to uncover the social causes of racial ethnic women's subordination. But socialist feminism's concept of capitalist patriarchy, with its focus on women's unpaid (reproductive) labor in the home failed to address racial differences in the organization of reproductive labor. As feminists of color have argued, "reproductive labor has divided along racial as well as gender lines, and the specific characteristics have varied regionally and changed over time as capitalism has reorganized." [23] Despite the limitations of socialist feminism, this body of literature has been especially useful in pursuing questions about the inter-connections among systems of domination.[24]

Race and ethnic studies was the other major social scientific source of multiracial feminism. It provided a basis for comparative analyses of groups that are socially and legally subordinated and remain culturally distinct within US society. This includes the systematic discrimination of socially constructed racial groups and their distinctive cultural arrangements. Historically, the categories of African-American, Latino, Asian-American, and Native American were constructed as both racially and culturally distinct. Each group has a distinctive culture, shares a common heritage, and has developed a common identity within a larger society that subordinates them.[25]

We recognize, of course, certain problems inherent in an uncritical use of the multiracial label. First, the perspective can be hampered by a biracial model in which only African-Americans and whites are seen as racial categories and all other groups are viewed through the prism of cultural differences. Latinos and Asians have always occupied distinctive places within the racial hierarchy, and current shifts in the composition of the US population are racializing these groups anew.[26]

A second problem lies in treating multiracial feminism as a single analytical framework, and its principle architects, women of color, as an undifferentiated category. The concepts "multiracial feminism," "racial ethnic women," and "women of color" "homogenize quite different experiences and can falsely universalize experiences across race, ethnicity, sexual orientation, and age." [27] The feminisms created by women of color exhibit a plurality of intellectual and political positions. We speak in many voices, with inconsistencies that are born of our different social locations. Multiracial feminism embodies this plurality and richness. Our intent is not to falsely universalize women of color. Nor do we wish to promote a new racial essentialism in place of the old gender essentialism. Instead, we use these concepts to examine the structures and experiences produced by intersecting forms of race and gender.

It is also essential to acknowledge that race is a shifting and contested category whose meanings construct definitions of all aspects of social life.[28] In the United States it helped define citizenship by excluding everyone who was not a white, male property owner. It defined labor as slave or free, coolie or contract, and family as available only to those men whose marriages were recognized or whose wives could emigrate with them. Additionally, racial meanings are contested both within groups and between them.[29]

Although definitions of race are at once historically and geographically specific, they are also transnational, encompassing diasporic groups and crossing traditional geographic boundaries. Thus, while US multiracial feminism calls attention to the fundamental importance of race, it must also locate the meaning of race within specific national traditions.

The Distinguishing Features of Multiracial Feminism

By attending to these problems, multiracial feminism offers a set of analytic premises for thinking about and theorizing gender. The following themes distinguish this branch of feminist inquiry.

First, multiracial feminism asserts that gender is constructed by a range of interlocking inequalities, what Patricia Hill Collins calls a "matrix of domination." [30] The idea of a matrix is that several fundamental systems work with and through each other. People experience race, class, gender, and sexuality differently depending upon their social location in the structures of race, class, gender, and sexuality. For example, people of the same race will experience race differently depending upon their location in the class structure as working class, professional managerial class, or unemployed; in the gender structure as female or male; and in structures of sexuality as heterosexual, homosexual, or bisexual.

Multiracial feminism also examines the simultaneity of systems in shaping women's experience and identity. Race, class, gender, and sexuality are not reducible to individual attributes to be measured and assessed for their separate contribution in explaining given social outcomes, an approach that Elizabeth Spelman calls "popbead metaphysics," where a woman's identity consists of the sum of parts neatly divisible from one another.[31] The matrix of domination seeks to account for the multiple ways that women experience themselves as gendered, raced, classed, and sexualized.

Second, multiracial feminism emphasizes the intersectional nature of hierarchies at all levels of social life. Class, race, gender, and sexuality are components of both social structure and social interaction. Women and men are differently embedded in locations created by these cross-cutting hierarchies. As a result, women and men throughout the social order experience different forms of privilege and subordination, depending on their race, class, gender, and sexuality. In other words, intersecting forms of domination produce *both* oppression *and* opportunity. At the same time that structures of race, class, and gender create disadvantages for women of color, they provide unacknowledged benefits for those who are at the top of these hierarchies – whites, members of the upper classes, and males. Therefore, multiracial feminism applies not only to racial ethnic women but also to women and men of all races, classes, and genders.

Third, multiracial feminism highlights the relational nature of dominance and subordination. Power is the cornerstone of women's differences.[32] This means that women's differences are *connected* in systematic ways.[33] Race is a vital element in the pattern of relations among minority and white women. As Linda Gordon argues, the very meanings of being a white woman in the United States have been affected by the existence of subordinated women of color: "They intersect in conflict and in occasional cooperation, but always in mutual influence."[34]

Fourth, multiracial feminism explores the interplay of social structure and women's agency. Within the constraints of race, class, and gender oppression, women create viable lives for themselves, their families, and their communities. Women of color have resisted and often undermined the forces of power that control them. From acts of quiet dignity and steadfast determination to involvement in revolt and rebellion, women struggle to shape their own lives. Racial oppression has been a common focus of the "dynamic of oppositional agency" of women of color. As Chandra Talpade Mohanty points out, it is the nature and organization of women's opposition which mediates and differentiates the impact of structures of domination.[35]

Fifth, multiracial feminism encompasses wide-ranging methodological approaches, and like other branches of feminist thought, relies on varied theoretical tools as well. Ruth Frankenberg and Lata Mani identify three guiding principles of inclusive feminist inquiry: "building complex analyses, avoiding erasure, specifying location."[36] In the last decade, the opening up of academic feminism has focused attention on social location in the production of knowledge. Most basically, research by and about marginalized women has destabilized what used to be considered as universal categories of gender. Marginalized locations are well suited for grasping social relations that remained obscure from more privileged vantage points. Lived experience, in other words, creates alternative ways of understanding the social world and the experience of different groups of women within it. Racially informed standpoint epistemologies have provided new topics, fresh questions, and new understandings of women and men. Women of color have, as Norma Alarcón argues, asserted themselves as subjects, using their voices to challenge dominant conceptions of truth.[37]

Sixth, multiracial feminism brings together understandings drawn from the lived experiences of diverse and continuously changing groups of women. Among Asian-Americans, Native Americans, Latinos, and blacks are many different national cultural and ethnic groups. Each one is engaged in the process of testing, refining, and reshaping these broader categories in its own image. Such internal differences heighten awareness of and sensitivity to both commonalities and differences, serving as a constant reminder of the importance of comparative study and maintaining a creative tension between diversity and universalization.

Difference and Transformation

Efforts to make women's studies less partial and less distorted have produced important changes in academic feminism. Inclusive thinking has provided a way to build multiplicity and difference into our analyses. This has led to the discovery that race matters for everyone. White women, too, must be reconceptualized as a category that is multiply defined by race, class, and other differences. As Ruth Frankenberg demonstrates in a study of whiteness among contemporary women, all kinds of social relations, even those that appear neutral, are, in fact, racialized. Frankenberg further complicates the very notion of a unified white identity by introducing issues of Jewish identity.[38] Therefore, the lives of women of color cannot be seen as a *variation* on a more general model of white American womanhood. The model of womanhood that feminist social science once held as "universal" is also a product of race and class.

When we analyze the power relations constituting all social arrangements and shaping women's lives in distinctive ways, we can begin to grapple with core feminist issues about how genders are socially constructed and constructed differently. Women's difference is built into our study of gender. Yet this perspective is quite far removed from the atheoretical pluralism implied in much contemporary thinking about gender.

Multiracial feminism, in our view, focuses not just on differences but also on the way in which differences and domination intersect and are historically and socially constituted. It challenges feminist scholars to go beyond the mere recognition and inclusion of difference to reshape the basic concepts and theories of our disciplines. By attending to women's social location based on race, class, and gender, multiracial feminism seeks to clarify the structural sources of diversity. Ultimately, multiracial feminism forces us to see privilege and subordination as interrelated and to pose such questions as: How do the existences and experiences of all people – women and men, different racial-ethnic groups, and different classes – shape the experiences of each other? How are those relationships defined and enforced through social institutions that are the primary sites for negotiating power within society? How do these differences contribute to the construction of both individual and group identity? Once we acknowledge that all women are affected by the racial order of society, then it becomes clear that the insights of multiracial feminism provide an analytical framework, not solely for understanding the experiences of women of color but for understanding *all* women, and men, as well.

Notes

1   Maxine Baca Zinn, Lynn Weber Cannon, Elizabeth Higginbotham, and Bonnie Thornton Dill, "The Costs of Exclusionary Practices in Women's Studies," *Signs* 11 (winter 1986): 290–303.
2   Chela Sandoval, "US Third World Feminism: The Theory and Method of Oppositional Consciousness in the Postmodern World," *Genders* (spring 1991): 1–24.
3   Ruth Frankenberg and Lata Mani, "Cross Currents, Crosstalk: Race, 'Postcoloniality,' and the Politics of Location," *Cultural Studies* 7 (May 1993): 292–310.
4   We use the term "multiracial feminism" to convey the multiplicity of racial groups and feminist perspectives.
5   A growing body of work on difference in feminist thought now exists. Although we cannot cite all the current work, the following are representative: Michèle Barrett, "The Concept of Difference," *Feminist Review* 26 (July 1987): 29–42; Christina Crosby, "Dealing with Difference," in *Feminists Theorize the Political*, ed. Judith Butler and Joan W. Scott (New York: Routledge, 1992), 130–43; Elizabeth Fox-Genovese, "Difference, Diversity, and Divisions in an Agenda for the Women's Movement," in *Color, Class, and Country: Experiences of Gender*, ed. Gay Young and Bette J. Dickerson (London: Zed Books, 1994), 232–48; Nancy A. Hewitt, "Compounding Differences," *Feminist Studies* 18 (summer 1992): 313–26; Maria C. Lugones, "On the Logic of Feminist Pluralism," in *Feminist Ethics*, ed. Claudia Card (Lawrence: University of Kansas Press, 1991), 35–44; Rita S. Gallin and Anne Ferguson, "The Plurality of Feminism: Rethinking 'Difference,'" in *The Woman and International Development Annual* (Boulder: Westview Press, 1993), 3: 1–16; and Linda Gordon, "On Difference," *Genders* 10 (spring 1991): 91–111.
6   Susan Bordo, "Feminism, Postmodernism, and Gender Skepticism," in *Feminism/Postmodernism*, ed. Linda J. Nicholson (London: Routledge, 1990), 133–56.
7   Sandra G. Harding, *Whose Science? Whose Knowledge? Thinking from Women's Lives* (Ithaca: Cornell University Press, 1991), 179.
8   Crosby, *Feminists Theorize the Political*, 131.
9   Fox-Genovese, *Color, Class, and Country*, 232.
10 Faye Ginsberg and Anna Lowenhaupt Tsing, *Introduction to Uncertain Terms, Negotiating Gender in American Culture*, ed. Faye Ginsberg and Anna Lowenhaupt Tsing (Boston: Beacon Press, 1990), 3.
11 Sandoval, "US Third World Feminism," 2.
12 Sandra Morgan, "Making Connections: Socialist-Feminist Challenges to Marxist Scholarship," in *Women and a New Academy: Gender and Cultural Contexts*, ed. Jean F. O'Barr (Madison: University of Wisconsin Press, 1989), 149.
13 Jane Rowland Martin, "Methodological Essentialism, False Difference, and Other Dangerous Traps," *Signs* 19 (spring 1994): 647.
14 Barrett, "The Concept of Difference," 32.
15 bell hooks, *Black Looks: Race and Representation* (Boston: South End Press 1992), 21.
16 Lugones, *Feminist Ethics*, 35–44.
17 Patricia Hill Collins, Foreword to *Women of Color in US Society*, ed. Maxine Baca Zinn and Bonnie Thornton Dill (Philadelphia: Temple University Press, 1994), xv.

18 Patricia Hill Collins, "Learning from the Outsider Within: The Sociological Significance of Black Feminist Thought," *Social Problems* 33 (December 1986): 514–32.

19 Sandoval, "US Third World Feminism," 1.

20 Alison M. Jagger and Paula S. Rothenberg, *Feminist Frameworks: alternative Theoretical Accounts of the Relations between Women and Men*, 3rd edn (New York: McGraw-Hill, 1993).

21 Michael Omi and Howard Winant, *Racial Formation in the United States: From the 1960s to the 1980s*, 2nd edn (New York: Routledge, 1994).

22 Ruth Frankenberg, *The Social Construction of Whiteness: White Women, Race Matters* (Minneapolis: University of Minnesota Press, 1993).

23 Evelyn Nakano Glenn, "From Servitude to Service Work: Historical Continuities in the Racial Division of Paid Reproductive Labor," *Signs* 18 (autumn 1992): 3. See also Bonnie Thornton Dill, "Our Mothers' Grief: Racial-Ethnic Women and the Maintenance of Families," *Journal of Family History* 13, no. 4 (1988): 415–31.

24 Morgan, *Women and a New Academy*, 146.

25 Maxine Baca Zinn and Bonnie Thornton Dill, "Difference and Domination," in *Women of Color in US Society*, 11–12.

26 See Omi and Winant, *Racial Formation in the United States*, 53–76, for a discussion of racial formation.

27 Margaret L. Andersen and Patricia Hill Collins, *Race, Class, and Gender: An Anthology* (Belmont, CA: Wadsworth, 1992), xvi.

28 Omi and Winant, *Racial Formation in the United States*.

29 Nazli Kibria, "Migration and Vietnamese American Women: Remaking Ethnicity," in *Women of Color in US Society*, 247–61.

30 Patricia Hill Collins, *Black Feminist Thought: Knowledge, Consciousness, and the Politics of Empowerment* (Boston: Unwin Hyman, 1990).

31 Elizabeth Spelman, *Inessential Women: Problems of Exclusion in Feminist Thought* (Boston: Beacon Press, 1988), 136.

32 Several discussions of difference make this point. See Baca Zinn and Dill, *Women of Color in US Society*, 10; Gordon, "On Difference," 106; and Lynn Weber, in the "Symposium on West and Fenstermaker's 'Doing Difference,'" *Gender and Society*, 9 (August 1995): 515–19.

33 Evelyn Nakano Glenn, "From Servitude to Service Work," 10.

34 Gordon, "On Difference," 106.

35 Chandra Talpade Mohanty, "Cartographies of Struggle: Third World Women and the Politics of Feminism," in *Third World Women and the Politics of Feminism*, ed. Chandra Talpade Mohanty, Ann Russo, and Lourdes Torres (Bloomington: Indiana University Press, 1991), 13.

36 Frankenberg and Mani, "Cross Currents, Crosstalk," 306.

37 Norma Alarcón, "The Theoretical-Subject(s) of *This Bridge Called My Back* and Anglo-American Feminism," in *Making Face, Making Soul, Haciendo Caras: Creative and Critical Perspectives by Women of Color*, ed. Gloria Anzaldúa (San Francisco: Aunt Lute, 1990), 356.

38 Frankenberg, *The Social Construction of Whiteness*. See also Evelyn Torton Beck, "The Politics of Jewish Invisibility," *NWSA Journal* (fall 1988): 93–102.

7

Ethnicity, Gender Relations and Multiculturalism

Nira Yuval-Davis

In this chapter I examine critically some of the ways in which gender relations affect and are affected by ethnicity, culture, racism and anti-racism, and how these relate to strategies of negotiating difference such as multiculturalism, identity politics and coalition politics. In conclusion I argue for a "transversal politics," a model of political work thus named by Italian feminists which reflects anti-racist feminist analysis and practice in recent years in several different countries. Before engaging more deeply with the substantive issues and theoretical arguments, however, several conceptual definitions central to my argument are called for.

Racist Discourse, Ethnic Projects and Cultural Resources

Racist discourse is defined (following Anthias and Yuval-Davis, 1984; 1992; Yuval-Davis, 1991; 1992a) as involving the use of ethnic categorizations (which might be constructed around biological, cultural, religious, linguistic or territorially based boundaries) as signifiers of a fixed, deterministic genealogical difference of "the Other." This "Otherness" serves as a basis for legitimizing exclusion and/or subordination and/or exploitation of the members of the collectivity thus labelled.

Ethnicity relates to the politics of collectivity boundaries, dividing the world into "us" and "them" around, usually, myths of common origin and/or common destiny, and engaging in constant processes of struggle and negotiation. These are aimed, from specific positionings within the collectivities, at promoting the collectivity or perpetuating its advantages by means of access to state and civil society powers. Ethnicity, according to this definition, is, therefore, primarily a political process which constructs the collectivity and "its interest" – not only as a result of the general positioning of the collectivity in relation to other collectivities, but also as a result of the specific relations of those engaged in "ethnic politics" with others within that collectivity (Yuval-Davis, 1994).

Gender, class, political and other differences play a central role in the construction of specific ethnic politics, and different ethnic projects of the same collectivity can be engaged in intense competitive struggles for hegemonic positions. Some of these projects can involve different constructions of the actual boundaries of the collectivity – as, for example, has been the case in the debate about the boundaries of the "black" community in Britain (Sivanandan, 1982; Modood, 1988; Brah, 1991). Ethnicity is not specific to oppressed and minority groupings. On the contrary, one of the measures of the success of hegemonic ethnicities is the extent to which they succeed in "naturalizing" their ideologies and practices to their own advantage.

Ethnic projects mobilize all available relevant resources for their promotion. Some of these resources are political, others are economic, and yet others are cultural – relating to customs, language, religion, and so on. Class, gender, political and personal differences mean that people positioned differently within the collectivity could sometimes, while pursuing specific ethnic projects, use the same cultural resources for promoting opposed political goals (for example, using various Qur'an surahs to justify pro- and anti-legal abortion politics, as was the case in Egypt, or using rock music to mobilize people for and against the Extreme Right in Britain). At other times, different cultural resources are used to legitimize competing ethnic projects of the collectivity – for example, the Bundists used Yiddish as "the" Jewish language – in an ethnic-national project whose boundaries were East European Jewry, while the Zionists (re)invented modern Hebrew (until then used mostly for religious purposes) in order to include in their project Jews from all over the world. Similarly, the same people can be constructed in different ethnicist-racist political projects in Britain as "Paki," "black," "Asians," or "Muslim fundamentalists."

Given this multivocality of ethnic emblems and resources, it is clear why ethnicity cannot be reduced to culture, and why "culture" cannot be seen as a fixed, essentialist category. As Gill Bottomley proposes when she discusses the relationship between ethnicity and culture: "Categories and ways of knowing . . . are constructed within relations of power and maintained, reproduced and resisted in specific and sometimes contradictory ways" (Bottomley, 1991: 305). More specifically, she claims:

> "Culture," in the sense of ideas, beliefs and practices that delineate particular ways of being in the world, also generate conscious and unconscious forms of resistance – to homogenization, to devaluation, to marginalizing by those who fear difference. (Bottomley, 1991: 12)

Women and Culture

The insight above is extremely important when we come to look at the contradictory relation between women and culture. Women, who are usually marginalized by hegemonic ethnic projects, often find ways of resistance – "patriarchal bargaining" is how Deniz Kandiyoti (1988) describes these survival strategies of women within the constraints of specific social situations. As the women from Women Against Fundamentalism called out when they counter-demonstrated against the anti-Rushdie Islamist demonstration in London in 1989: "Our tradition – resistance, not submission!" On the other hand, the compliant behavior of women can fulfill crucial roles in hegemonic ethnic projects. Collectivities are composed, as a general rule, of family units. A central link between the place of women as national reproducers and women's sub-jugation can be found in the different regulations – customary, religious or legal – which determine the family units within the boundaries of the collectivity and how they come into existence (marriage), or reach their end (divorce and widow-hood). Women need not only to bear, biologically, children for the collectivity, but also to reproduce it culturally. The question of which children are considered legitimate members of the family and/or the collectivity plays a crucial role in this.

However, there are several other dimensions to the roles women play in the cultural construction of collectivities. The mythical unity of ethnic "imagined communities," which divides the world between "us" and "them," is culturally maintained and ideologically reproduced by a whole system of diacritical emblems, which Armstrong (1982) calls symbolic "border guards." These "border guards" can identify people as members or non-members of a specific collectivity. They are closely linked to specific cultural codes, styles of dress and public conduct, as well as to more elaborate bodies of customs, literary and artistic modes of creativity and, of course, language. Symbols of gender play a particularly significant role in this articulation of difference.

Just outside Cyprus airport there is a big poster of a mother mourning her child – Greek Cyprus mourning and commemorating the Turkish invasion. In France, it was *La Patrie*, a figure of a woman giving birth, that personified the revolution; in Ireland, Mother Ireland; in Russia Mother Russia; and in India, Mother India. Women often come to symbolize the national collectiv-ity, its roots, its spirit, its national project (Yuval-Davis and Anthias, 1989; Yuval-Davis, 1993). Moreover, women often symbolize national and collective "honor." Shaving the heads of women who "dare" to fraternize – or even to fall in love – with "the enemy" is but one expression of this. In a television programme on Dutch television in February 1994, a young Palestinian man boasted proudly that he had killed his female cousin (who was married and a mother of two) because she had co-operated with the Israelis, and thus brought dishonor on the family. Forced veiling or insistence on particular styles of dress and behavior are milder forms of the same construction of women. Women's distinctive ways of dressing and behaving very often – especially in minority situations – come to symbolize the group's cultural identity and its boundaries.

Because of this construction of womanhood as epitomizing the collectivity, systematic rapes have become part of warfare, as in Bosnia. In the Geneva Convention, rape is still defined (although women's human rights' organizations have been campaigning against this) not as a war crime or a form of torture, but as a "crime against honor." And it is not the woman's honor that is being referred to, but that of her family and her collectivity. Making videos of such rapes in order to screen them on Serbian television and other TV stations has been the ultimate grotesquery associated with this practice.

The other side of this coin is that wars are declared and fought for the sake of "womenandchildren" (as one word, in Cynthia Enloe's usage; see Enloe, 1990). Protecting the honor and welfare of the collectivity's women and children – who, traditionally, are left at the rear while the men fight on the battlefront – is the most common justification for men's obligation to fight and kill – and *be* killed. (The recent incorporation of women into the militaries might, however, help to shift the traditional grounds of legitimation of organized violence somewhat [see Yuval-Davis, 1992c; 1997: ch. 5]).

Women, however, are not only accorded the task of symbolizing their nation or ethnic collectivity; they are often also usually expected to reproduce it culturally. As Floya Anthias and I have written (Anthias and Yuval-Davis, 1984; Yuval-Davis and Anthias, 1989), women are often the ones chosen to be the inter-generational transmitters of cultural traditions, customs, songs, cuisine, and, of course, the mother tongue *(sic!)*. This is especially true in minority situations in which the school and the public sphere present different hegemonic cultural models to that of the home. Often, wives of immigrants are at least partially excluded from the public sphere because of legal restrictions, a lack of work opportunities or linguistic inadequacies, while at the same time they are expected to remain the primary bearers of a distinctive "home" culture. This is one of the main reasons that stronger social control is likely to be exercised on girls than on boys, especially among the children of immigrants. The importance of women's culturally "appropriate behavior" can gain special significance in "multicultural societies."

Multiculturalism

Trinh Minh-ha has commented (1989: 89–90) that there are two kinds of social and cultural differences: those which threaten and those which do not. Multiculturalism is aimed at nourishing and perpetuating the kind of differences which do not. As Andrew Jakubowicz concluded in relation to the Australian policies of multiculturalism:

> Multi-culturalism gives the ethnic communities the task to retain and cultivate with government help their different cultures, but does not concern itself with struggles against discriminatory policies as they affect individuals or classes of people. (1984: 42)

Carl-Ulrik Schierup (1995) has claimed that multiculturalism is an ideological base for transatlantic alignment aimed at the transformation of the welfare state. This alignment aspires to be the hegemonic credo in the contemporary era of postmodern modernity. He argues, however, that the paradoxes and dilemmas of existing multiculturalisms confront its ideological framework with similar problems to the ones that "real socialisms" present to "Socialism."

Multiculturalist policies have been developed in Britain in order to accommodate the settlement of immigrants and refugees from its ex-colonial countries, and have broadly followed forms of legislations and political projects which were developed for this purpose in the US, as well as other ex-imperial settler societies such as Canada and Australia. In all these states there is a continuous debate about the limits of multiculturalism between those who want a continued construction of the national collectivity as homogeneous and assimilatory, and those who have been calling for the institutionalization of ethnic pluralism and the preservation of the ethnic minorities' cultures of origin as legitimate parts of the national project. A controversial related question is the extent to which the conservation of collective identities and cultures is important in itself, or only because of the collective will that promotes this preservation, and whether projects aimed at the conservation of cultures can avoid the reification and essentialization of these cultures. As Floya Anthias has put it:

> Debates on cultural diversity confuse culture and ethnicity. . . . Is it the boundaries that should be kept or the cultural artifacts that act as their barbed wire? However, the question is not just about homogeneity, but also about western cultural hegemony. (1993: 9)

In Australia, for instance, the call of those who have objected to multiculturalism has been for an "Anglomorphic society," even if the members of the Australian national collectivity are not of Anglo-Celtic origin, as this quotation from Knopfelmacher (1984; see also Yuval-Davis, 1991: 14) demonstrates: "With anglomorphy firmly established in Australia and stable as a rock, the 'British' character of the country is independent of the 'race' of the immigrants." In the US, the ideological target has been the American "melting-pot," but those who object to multiculturalism in the American context emphasize the primacy of its European cultural heritage: "Would anyone seriously argue that teachers should conceal the European origins of American civilisation?" (Schlesinger, 1992: 122). Collective cultural identity rather than the ethnic origin and color of collectivity members seems to be the crucial factor in these constructions.

It would be a mistake, however, to suppose that those who advocate multiculturalism assume a civil and political society in which all cultural identities would have the same legitimacy. In Australia, for instance, the government's document on multiculturalism emphasizes "the limits of multi-culturalism" (Office of Multicultural Affairs, 1989), and in all states in which multiculturalism is an official policy there are cultural customs (such as polygamy, using drugs, etc.) which are considered illegal as well as illegitimate, giving priority to cultural traditions of the hegemonic majority. Moreover, in multiculturalist policies the naturalization of a Western hegemonic culture continues, while the minority cultures become reified and differentiated from what is regarded by the majority as normative human behavior.

John Rex describes multiculturalism as an enhanced form of the welfare state in which "the recognition of cultural diversity actually enriches and strengthens democracy" (1995: 31). This happens for three basic reasons: because the values of specific cultures might be intrinsically of value, and might enrich society; because the social organization of minority communities provides them with emotional support; and because it also provides them with more effective means of getting further resources and defending their collective rights. The question arises, however, concerning the nature of these collective rights, and what specific provisions the state needs to make towards individuals and collectivities in its heterogeneous population. Jayasuriya has pointed out that two separate issues are involved here: "One is the centrality of needs in the collective provision of welfare and the other is the difficult question of boundaries of need in claiming for one's right" (1990: 23).

The most problematic aspects of these questions become apparent when the provision relates not to differential treatment in terms of access to employment or welfare but to what has been defined as the different cultural needs of different ethnicities. These can vary from the provision of interpreters to the provision of funds to religious organizations. In the most extreme cases – as in the debates around Aboriginals, on the one hand, and Muslim minorities following the Rushdie affair, on the other – there have been claims for enabling the minorities to operate according to their own customary and religious legal systems. While the counter-arguments have ranged from the fact that this would imply a *de facto* apartheid system to arguments about social unity and political hegemony, those who support these claims have seen them as a natural extension of the minorities' social and political rights. This raises the question of how one defines the boundaries of citizens' rights. Jayasuriya (1990) distinguishes between needs – which are essential, and therefore require satisfaction by the state – and wants, which fall outside the public sector and are to be satisfied within the private domain in a voluntary way.

The differentiation between public and private domains plays a central role in delineating boundaries of citizenship in the literature, although not enough attention is being given to the fact that the public domain contains both the state domain and the domain of civil society. Turner (1990), for instance, has anchored his typology of citizenship in the extent to which the state enters or abstains from entering the private domain. As the examples above show, however, the dichotomous construction of private/public spheres is culturally specific, as well as gender-specific in itself (Yuval-Davis, 1991; 1992b; 1997). The whole debate on multiculturalism stumbles on the fact that the boundaries of difference, as well as the boundaries of social rights, are determined by specific hegemonic – perhaps universalistic, but definitely not universal – discourses. And as we saw above, universalist discourses which do not take into account the differential positionings of those to whom they refer often cover up racist (and I would add sexist, classist, ageist, disablist, etc.) constructions.

One of the primary examples for a multiculturalist perspective which reifies and homogenizes specific cultures is the book published in 1993 by UNESCO called *The Multi-Cultural Planet* (Laszlo, 1993), in which the world is divided into culturally homogeneous regions, such as "the European culture" (but also "the Russian and East European culture," "the North American culture," "the Latin-American," "the Arab," "the African," etc.), among which dialogues and openness should be developed.

Although multiculturalism is generally hailed by its promoters as a major anti-racist strategy, it has been criticized from the Left for ignoring questions of power relations, accepting as representatives of minorities people in class and power positions very different from those of the majority members of that community, and being divisive by emphasizing the differential cultures of members of the ethnic minorities, rather than what unites them with other blacks who share with them similar predicaments of racism, subordination and economic exploitation (Bourne and Sivanandan, 1980; Mullard, 1980). Other critiques from the Left have been directed against both the "multiculturalist" and "anti-racist" positions (Rattansi, 1992; Sahgal and Yuval-Davis, 1992).

These critiques have pointed out that in both approaches there is the inherent assumption that all members of a specific cultural collectivity are equally committed to that culture. They tend to construct the members of minority collectivities as basically homogeneous, speaking with a unified cultural or racial voice. These voices are constructed so as to make them as distinct as possible (within the boundaries of multiculturalism) from the majority culture, so as to make them "different." Thus, within multiculturalism, the more traditional and distanced from the majority culture the voice of the "community representatives" is, the more "authentic" it would be perceived to be within such a construction. Within "anti-racism," a similar perspective also prevailed. The voice of the "black" (of the all-encompassing binary division black/white) has often been constructed as that of the macho liberatory hero, rejecting all which might be associated with white Eurocentric culture.

Such constructions do not allow space for internal power conflicts and interest differences within the minority collectivity: conflicts along the lines of class and gender as well as, for instance, politics and culture. Moreover, they tend to assume collectivity boundaries which are fixed, static, ahistorical and essentialist, with no space for growth and change. When such a perspective becomes translated into social policy, "authenticity" can become an important political tool with which economic and other resources can be claimed from the state on the grounds of being "the" representative of "the community" (Cain and Yuval-Davis, 1990). As Yeatman observes:

> It becomes clear that the liberal conception of the group requires the group to assume an authoritarian character: there has to be a headship of the group which represents its homogeneity of purpose by speaking with the one, authoritative voice. For this to occur, the politics of voice and representation latent within the hetero-geneity of perspectives and interests must be suppressed. (Yeatman, 1992: 4)

This liberal construction of group voice, therefore, can inadvertently collude with authoritarian fundamentalist leaders who claim to represent the true "essence" of their collectivity's culture and religion, and have high on their agenda the control of women and their behavior.

Multiculturalism, therefore, can often have very detrimental effects on women in particular, as "different" cultural traditions are often defined in terms of culturally specific gender relations, and the control of women's behavior (in which women themselves, especially older women, also participate and collude) is often used to reproduce ethnic boundaries. An example of such a collusion, for instance, is the case in which the judge refused a request for asylum to an Iranian woman who had had to escape from Iran after refusing to veil because "this is your culture" (case recounted by the solicitor Jacqui Bhabha). Another is the placement of a young Muslim girl, who had fled her parents' home because of their restrictive control of her behavior, in another Muslim home, even more pious, against her wishes and the advocacy of the Asian Women's Refuge (case recounted by Southall Black Sisters).

A contradictory multiculturalist practice is described by Jeannie Martin (1991): the practices of "ethnic families" are weighted against a "good society" model, which becomes identical with some unspecified Anglo-family norm, "on behalf of ethnic women," focusing on "atavistic practices such as clitoridectomy, child marriages, etc.," as the "limits of multicultural diversity." Martin describes this approach as typical of the "ethnicists" among the multiculturalist theorists in Australia, and points out that what motivates them is not a real concern for women – because the ethnicists assume that women's subordination is part of the natural order of things in which the family is at the forefront. Rather, this is a device for establishing ranking among men of diverse backgrounds, based on the degree of their deviation from the Anglo-model – constructed as the ideal, positive model.

An alternative dynamic model of cultural pluralism to the multiculturalist ones has been developed by Homi Bhabha (1990; 1994a; 1994b). Abolishing the division of space/time and structure/process, and emphasizing the constantly changing and contested nature of the constructed boundaries of the national "imagined community," and of the narratives which constitute its collective cultural discourses, Bhabha notes the emerging counter-narratives from the nation's margins – by those national and cultural "hybrids" who have lived, because of migration or exile, in more than one culture. Such "hybrids" both evoke and erase the "totalizing boundaries" of their adoptive nation. Such counter-narratives do not, of course, have to come from immigrant minorities. The growing voice of Indigenous People, for example, is an instance of a counter-narrative which is heard from within. So too, of course, counter-narratives about the boundaries of "the nation" have disintegrated the former Yugoslav and Soviet nations; and while not being as radical in other national communities, the construction of the nation and its boundaries are a matter of constant debate everywhere. It is important to note in this context what Homi Bhabha fails to consider: that "counter-narratives," even if they are radical in their form, do not necessarily have to be progressive in their message. As Anna Lowenhaupt Tsing (1993: 9) claims, such counter-narratives have to be situated "within wider negotiations of meaning and power at the same time as recognizing local stakes and specificities."

Another danger in Bhabha's approach is that it may interpolate essentialism through the back door – that the old "multiculturalist" essentialist and homogenizing constructions of collectivities are attributed to the homogeneous collectivities from which the "hybrids" have emerged, thus replacing the mythical image of society as a "melting-pot" with the mythical image of society as a "mixed salad." Characteristic of such a position has been, for example, the description by Trinh Minh-ha of herself, in a recent conference on Racisms and Feminisms in Vienna (October 1994), as standing "on the margin, resisting both the majority culture and that of her own group."

It is against this construction of essentialist fixed constructions of cultures, nations and their boundaries, and the reduction of ethnicity to "culture," that transversal politics have been developed.

Feminism, Multiculturalism, and Identity Politics

The feminist version of "multiculturalism" developed as a form of "identity politics" which replaced earlier feminist constructions of womanhood, informed primarily by the hegemonic experiences of white, middle-class Western women. Despite the politically important introduction of the differentiation between sex and gender – the former described as a fixed biological category, the latter as a variable cultural one – the feminist technique of "consciousness-raising" assumes, as a basis for political action, a *de facto* fixed reality of women's oppression that has to be discovered and then changed, rather than a reality which is being created and re-created through practice and discourse. Moreover, it is assumed that this reality of women's oppression is shared by all women, who are perceived to constitute a basically homogeneous social grouping sharing the same interests. Women's individual identities have come to be equated with women's collective identity, whereas differences, rather than being acknowledged, have been interpreted by those holding the hegemonic power within the movement as mainly reflections of different "stages" of "raised consciousness."

Although the fallacy of this position has been acknowledged to a large extent by many activists and scholars in the various women's movements in recent years, the solution has often been to develop essentialist notions of difference such as, for example, between black and white women, middle-class and working-class women, or Northern and Southern women. Within each of these idealized groups, the assumptions about "discovered" homogeneous reality usually continue to operate. "Identity politics" tend not only to homogenize and naturalize social categories and groupings, but also to deny shifting boundaries of identities and internal power differences and conflicts of interest. On the other hand, as Daiva Stasiulis and I have pointed out (1995), there are also serious problems with the analyses of many postmodernist feminists who have developed alternative non-essentialist deconstructionist approachs to grapple with the notion of "difference" (e.g., Gunew and Yeatman, 1993; Larner, 1993; Nicholson, 1990;Young, 1990). By using terms such as "contingent identities" and "hyphenated feminisms," they virtually dispense with notions of asymmetrical and systemic power relations (Fuss, 1989; Stasiulis, 1990: 294; Yuval-Davis, 1991; 1994).

It is important to emphasize that postmodernist deconstructionist approaches are not necessarily immune to *de facto* essentialist constructions, as Paul Gilroy (1994) has pointed out. These often occur when notions of "strategic essentialism" of the Gayatri Spivak variety are evoked: while it is acknowledged that such categories involve "arbitrary closures" for the sake of political mobilization, these categories become reified via social movements and state policy practices.

Rejecting such reified constructions of categories does not negate the primary importance that considerations of individual and collective positionings, power relations both within and in relation to other collectivities, and the cultural, political and economic resources which they carry, should have in the construction of any political alliances.

Transversal Politics

Transversal politics are based on dialogue that takes into account the different positionings of women, or people in general, but does not grant any of them *a priori* privileged access to the "truth." In "transversal politics," perceived unity and homogeneity are replaced by dialogues that give recognition to the specific positionings of those who participate in them, as well as to the "unfinished knowledge" (to use Patricia Hill Collins' term [1990]) that each such situated positioning can offer.

Central to transversal politics are the processes which the Italian feminists from Bologna's Women's Resource Centre have called "rooting" and "shifting." The idea is that each participant in the dialogue brings with her the rooting in her own grouping and identity, but tries at the same time to shift in order to put herself in a situation of exchange with women who have different groupings and identities.

Transversal politics are not just coalitions of "identity politics" groups which assume that all members of such groups are equally positioned and culturally, socially and politically homogeneous. Gender, class, race, ethnicity, location, sexuality, stage in the life cycle, ability, and all other dimensions of specific positionings are taken into consideration, as well as the particular value systems and political agendas of the participants in the exchange.

In another place (Yuval-Davis, 1994) I have explored in detail a variety of approaches to coalition politics, and brought two very different examples of transversal politics. The first example is that of the London-based group Women Against Fundamentalism (WAF). WAF includes women from a variety of religious and ethnic origins (Christians, Jews, Muslims, Sikhs, Hindus, etc.). Many of the members also belong to other campaigning organizations, often with a more specific ethnic affiliation: Southall Black Sisters (SBS), the Jewish Socialist Group, and the Irish Abortion Support Group. However, except for SBS – which had an organizational and ideological initiatory role in establishing WAF – women come there as individuals rather than as representatives of any group or ethnic category. On the other hand, there is no attempt to "assimilate" the women who come from the different backgrounds. Differences in ethnicity and point of view – and the resulting different agendas – are recognized and respected. But what is celebrated is the common political stance of WAF members, as advocating "the Third Way" against fundamentalism and against racism. At the same time, WAF campaigns on, for instance, state religious education, or women's reproductive rights, have been informed by the differential experiences of the group's women, given their different positionings and backgrounds. Inderpal Grewal and Caren Kaplan (1994) describe the Asian Women's Shelter group in San Francisco as having very similar political dynamics in its work to those of WAF.

The other example of transversal politics in action is described in my article, "Women, Ethnicity and Empowerment" (1994). It refers to a meeting that took place in Bologna in 1992 between Italian, Israeli and Palestinian feminists. Although since the 1980s there had been many dialogue groups which had brought Israelis and Palestinians together, such meetings very often seemed to bear some of the worst characteristics of identity politics – participants perceived one another as "representatives" of their national collectivities, thus forming an internally homogeneous delegation. These meetings frequently deteriorated into mutual collective guilt invocations that only helped to reify national boundaries. The aim of the Italian feminists who invited both the Israeli and the Palestinian women to participate in the meeting (as well as Algerian, black British feminists and myself as outside supporters) was to break out of this pattern, and – given the responses of many of the participants afterwards – they largely succeeded.

The boundaries of the different national groupings at the meeting were determined not by an essentialist notion of difference but by a concrete and material political reality. The Israeli group, for instance, included both Jewish and Palestinian women citizens of Israel. Also, the women involved in the different groups were not perceived simplistically as representatives of their groupings. While their different positionings and backgrounds were recognized and respected – including the differential power relations inherent in their corresponding affiliations as members of Occupier and Occupied collectivities – all the women who were sought and invited to participate in the dialogue were committed to refusing "to participate unconsciously in the reproduction of existing power relations," and "to finding a fair solution to the conflict" (Italian letter of invitation, December 1990). The Italian feminists who organized the meetings between the Palestinian and Israeli women also later supported similar dialogues developed between Serbian, Croatian and Bosnian women in the former Yugoslavia, under the umbrella name Women in Black.

Two things are vital in developing the transversal perspective: first, that the process of shifting should not involve self-decentering, that is, losing one's own rooting and set of values. As Elsa Barkley Brown has pointed out: "one has no need to 'decentre' anyone in order to centre someone else; one has only to constantly pivot the centre" (1989: 922). It is vital in any form of coalition and solidarity politics to keep one's own perspective on things while empathizing and respecting others. In multiculturalist types of solidarity politics there can be a risk of uncritical solidarity. This was very prevalent, for instance, in the politics of some sections of the Left with regard to the Iranian revolution or the Rushdie affair. They regarded it as "imperialist" and "racist" for the West to intervene in "internal community matters." Women are often the victims of such a perspective, which allows the so-called (male) representatives and leaders of "the community" to determine policies that ultimately concern women, their well-being and their physical safety.

Secondly – and following from this first point – the process of shifting should not homogenize the "other." Just as there are diverse positions and points of view among people who are similarly rooted, so there are among the members of the other group. The transversal coming together should not be with the members of the other group *en bloc*, but with those who, in their different rooting, share compatible values and goals to one's own. Transversal politics do not assume that the dialogue lacks boundaries, and that each conflict of interest is reconcilable. However, the boundaries of such a dialogue are determined by the message rather than the messenger. The struggle against oppression and discrimination might (and mostly does) have a specific categorical focus, but is never confined just to that category, which can thus avoid reification.

A word of caution, however, is required here. A transversal politics is not always possible, as the conflicting interests of people who are situated in specific positionings are not always reconcilable. When solidarity is possible, however, it is important that it is based on transversal principles.

References

Anthias, Floya (1993) "Rethinking Categories and Struggles: Racism, Anti-racisms and Multiculturalism." Paper delivered at the European workshop on Racism and Anti-Racist Movements, University of Greenwich, September 1993.

Anthias, Floya and Nira Yuval-Davis (1984) "Contextualising Feminism: Ethnic, Gender and Class Divisions." *Feminist Review*, 15: 62–75.

Anthias, Floya and Nira Yuval-Davis (1992) *Racialised Boundaries: Race, Nation, Gender, Color and Class and the Anti-Racist Struggle*. London: Routledge.

Armstrong, J. (1982) *Nations Before Nationalism*. Chapel Hill, NC: University of North Carolina Press.

Balibar, Étienne (1992) "Paradoxes of Universality," in David Goldberg (ed.), *Anatomy of Racism*. Minneapolis, MN: University of Minnesota Press.

Barkley Brown, Elsa (1989) "African-American Women's Quilting: A Framework for

Conceptualising and Teaching African-American Women's History." *Signs,* 14, 4: 921–9.

Bhabha, Homi (ed.) (1990) *Nation and Narration.* London: Routledge.

Bhabha, Homi (1994a) *The Location of Culture.* London: Routledge.

Bhabha, Homi (1994b) "Subaltern Secularism." *Women Against Fundamentalism Journal,* 6.

Bhabha, Jacqui (1994) Personal legal notes.

Bottomley, Gill (1991) "Culture, Ethnicity and the Politics/Poetics of Representation." *Diaspora,* 3: 303–20.

Bourne, Jenny and A. Sivanandan (1980) "Cheerleaders and Ombudsmen: The Sociology of Race Relations in Britain." *Race and Class,* 21, 4.

Brah, Avtar (1991) "Difference, Diversity, Differentiation." *International Review of Sociology,* New Series 2: 53–72.

Cain, Harriet and Nira Yuval-Davis (1990) "'The Equal Opportunities Community' and the Anti-Racist Struggle." *Critical Social Policy,* Autumn.

Enloe, Cynthia (1990) ""Womenandchildren": Making Feminist Sense of the Persian Gulf Crisis. *The Village Voice,* 25 September.

Fuss, Diana (1989) *Essentially Speaking: Feminism, Nature and Difference.* New York: Routledge.

Gilroy, Paul (1994) *The Black Atlantic: Modernity and Double Consciousness.* London: Verso.

Grewal, Inderpal and Caren Kaplan (1994) "Introduction: Transnational Feminist Practices and Questions of Postmodernity," in I. Grewal and C. Kaplan (eds), *Scattered Hegemonies.* Minneapolis, MN: University of Minnesota Press: 1–35.

Gunew, Sneja and Anna Yeatman (eds) (1993) *Feminism and the Politics of Difference.* St. Leonards, NSW: Allen and Unwin.

Hill Collins, Patricia (1990) *Black Feminist Thought: Knowledge, Consciousness and the Politics of Empowerment.* Boston, MA: Unwin Hyman.

Jakubowicz, Andrew (1984) "State and Ethnicity: Multiculturalism as an Ideology." *Australia and New Zealand Journal of Sociology,* 17, 3.

Jayasuriya, L. (1990) "Multiculturalism, Citizenship and Welfare: New Directions for the 1990s." Paper delivered at the 50th Anniversary Lecture Series, Department of Social Work and Social Policy, University of Sydney.

Kandiyoti, Deniz (1988) "Bargaining with Patriarchy." *Gender and Society,* 2, 3.

Knopfelmacher, Prof. (1984) "Anglomorphism in Australia." *The Age,* 31 May, Melbourne.

Larner, Wendy (1993) "Changing Contexts: Globalisation, Migration and Feminism in New Zealand," in S. Gunew and A. Yeatman (eds), *Feminism and the Politics of Difference.* Sydney: Allen and Unwin.

Laszlo, Ervin (ed. for UNESCO) (1993) *The Multi-Cultural Planet.* Oxford: One World.

Martin, Jeannie (1991) "Multiculturalism and Feminism," in G. Bottomley, M. de Lepervanche and J. Martin (eds), *Intersexions.* Sydney: Allen and Unwin: 110–31.

Minh-ha, Trinh T. (1989) *Woman, Native, Other.* Bloomington, IN: Indiana University Press.

Modood, Tariq (1988) "'Black,' Racial Equality and Asian Identity." *New Community,* 14, 3: 397–404.

Mullard, Chris (1980) *Racism in Society and School.* London: Institute of Education, University of London.

Nicholson, Linda J. (ed.) (1990) *Feminism/Modernism.* New York: Routledge.

Office of Multicultural Affairs (1989) *National Agenda for a Multicultural Australia.* Canberra: AGPS.

Rattansi, Ali (1992) "Changing the Subject? Racism, Culture and Education," in J. Donald and A. Rattansi (eds), *"Race," Culture and Difference.* London: Sage.

Rex, John (1995) "Ethnic Identity and the Nation State: The Political Sociology of Multi-Cultural Societies." *Social Identities,* 1, 1: 21–41.

Sahgal, Gita and Nira Yuval-Davis (eds) (1992) *Refusing Holy Orders: Women and Fundamentalism in Britain.* London: Virago.

Schlesinger, Arthur M., Jr. (1992) *The Disuniting of America: Reflections on a Multicultural Society.* New York: W. W. Norton.

Sivanandan, A. (1982) *A Different Hunger.* London: Pluto Press.

Schierup, Carl-Ulrik (1995) "Multi-culturalism and Universalism in the US and EU Europe." Paper delivered at the *Nationalism and Ethnicity* workshop, Bern, 2–4 March.

Stasiulis, Daiva K. (1990) "Theorising Connections: Race, Ethnicity, Gender and Class," in P. Li (ed.), *Race and Ethnic Relations in Canada.* Toronto: Oxford University Press.

Stasiulis, Daiva and Nira Yuval-Davis (eds) (1995) *Unsettling Settler Societies: Articulations of Gender, Ethnicity, Race and Class.* London: Sage.

Tsing, Anna Lowenhaupt (1993) *In the Realm of the Diamond Queen.* Princeton, NJ: Princeton University Press.

Turner, Bryan (1990) "Outline of a Theory of Citizenship." *Sociology,* 24, 2.

Yeatman, Anna (1992) "Minorities and the Politics of difference." *Political Theory Newsletter,* 4, 1: 1–11.

Young, Iris Marion (1990) *Justice and the Politics of Difference.* Princeton, NJ: Princeton University Press.

Yuval-Davis, Nira (1991) "Ethnic/Racial and Gender divisions and the Nation in Britain and Australia," in Richard Nile (ed.), *Immigration and the Politics of Ethnicity and Race in Australia and Britain.* London: Institute of Commonwealth Studies: 14–26.

Yuval-Davis, Nira (1992a) "Zionism, Anti-Zionism and the Construction of Contemporary 'Jewishness.'" *Review of Middle East Studies,* 5: 84–109.

Yuval-Davis, Nira (1992b) "Secularism, Judaism and the Zionist Dilemma." *WAF: Journal of Women Against Fundamentalism,* 3: 8–10.

Yuval-Davis, Nira (1992c) "The Gendered Gulf War: Women's Citizenship and Modern Warfare," in H. Bresheeth and N. Yuval-Davis (eds), *The Gulf War and the New World Order.* London: Zed Books: 219–25.

Yuval-Davis, Nira (1993) "Gender and Nation." *Ethnic and Racial Studies,* 16, 4: 621–32.

Yuval-Davis, Nira (1994) "Women, Ethnicity and Empowerment." Special issue on "Shifting Identities, Shifting Racisms," in K. Bhavnani and A. Phoenix (eds), *Feminism and Psychology,* 4, 1: 179–98.

Yuval-Davis, Nira (1997) *Gender and Nation.* London: Sage.

Yuval-Davis, Nira and Floya Anthias (eds) (1989) *Woman – Nation – State.* London: Macmillan.

8

What's in a Name? Womanism, Black Feminism, and Beyond

Patricia Hill Collins

Black women are at a decision point that in many ways mirrors that faced by African-Americans as a collectivity. Building on the pathbreaking works by Toni Cade Bambara, Ntozake Shange, Angela Davis, Toni Morrison, June Jordan, Alice Walker, Audre Lorde and other black women who "broke silence" in the 1970s, African-American women in the 1980s and 1990s developed a "voice," a self-defined, collective black women's standpoint about black womanhood (Collins, 1990). Moreover, black women used this standpoint to "talk back" concerning black women's representation in dominant discourses (hooks, 1989). As a result of this struggle, African-American women's ideas and experiences have achieved a visibility unthinkable in the past.

But African-American women now stand at a different historical moment. Black women appear to have a voice, and with this new-found voice comes a new series of concerns. For example, we must be attentive to the seductive absorption of black women's voices in classrooms of higher education where black women's texts are still much more welcomed than black women themselves. Giving the illusion of change, this strategy of symbolic inclusion masks how the everyday institutional policies and arrangements that suppress and exclude African-Americans as a collectivity remain virtually untouched (Carby, 1992; Du Cille, 1994). Similarly, capitalist market relations that transformed black women's writing into a hot commodity threaten to strip their works of their critical edge. Initially, entering public space via books, movies, and print media proved in-vigorating. But in increasingly competitive global markets where anything that sells will be sold regardless of the consequences, black women's "voices" now flood the market. Like other commodities exchanged in capitalist markets, surplus cheapens value, and the fad of today becomes the nostalgic memory of tomorrow.

While a public voice initially proved dangerous, black women's coming to voice ironically fostered the emergence of a new challenge. The new public safe space provided by black women's success allowed longstanding differences among black women structured along axes of sexuality, social class, nationality, religion, and region to emerge. At this point, whether African-American women can fashion a singular "voice" about the black *woman's* position remains less an issue than how black women's voices collectively construct, affirm, and maintain a dynamic black *women's* self-defined standpoint. Given the increasingly troublesome political context affecting black women as a group (Massey and Denton, 1993; Squires, 1994), such solidarity is essential. Thus, ensuring group unity while recognizing the tremendous heterogeneity that operates within the boundaries of the term "black women" comprises one fundamental challenge now confronting African-American women.

Current debates about whether black women's standpoint should be named "womanism" or "black feminism" reflect this basic challenge of accommodating diversity among black women. In her acclaimed volume of essays, *In Search of Our Mothers' Gardens,* Alice Walker introduced four meanings of the term "womanist." According to Walker's first definition, a "womanist" was "a black feminist or feminist of color (1983: xi). Thus, on some basic level, Walker herself uses the two terms as being virtually interchangeable. Like Walker, many African-American women see little difference between the two since both support a common agenda of black women's self-definition and self-determination. As Barbara Omolade points out, "black feminism is sometimes referred to as Womanism because both are concerned with struggles against sexism and racism by black women who are themselves part of the black community's efforts to achieve equity, and liberty" (Omolade, 1994: xx).

But despite similar beliefs expressed by African-American women who define themselves as black feminists, as womanists, as both, or, in some cases, as neither, increasing attention seems devoted to delineating the differences, if any, between groups naming themselves as "womanists" or "black feminists." The *name* given to black women's collective standpoint seems to matter, but why?

In this paper, I explore some of the theoretical implications of using the terms "womanism" and "black feminism" to name a black women's standpoint. My purpose is not to classify either the works of black women or African-American women themselves into one category or the other. Rather, I aim to examine how the effort to categorize obscures more basic challenges that confront African-American women as a group.

Womanism

Alice Walker's multiple definitions of the term "womanism" in *In Search of Our Mothers' Gardens,* shed light on the issue of why many African-American women prefer the term womanism to black feminism. Walker offers two contradictory meanings of "womanism." On the one hand, Walker clearly sees womanism as rooted in black women's concrete history in racial and gender oppression. Taking the term from the Southern black folk expression of mothers to female children "you acting womanish," Walker suggests that black women's concrete history fosters a womanist worldview accessible primarily and perhaps exclusively to black women. "Womanish" girls acted in outrageous, courageous, and willful ways, attributes that freed them from the conventions long limiting white women. Womanish girls wanted to know more and in greater depth than what was considered good for them. They were responsible, in charge, and serious.

Despite her disclaimer that womanists are "traditionally universalist," a philosophy invoked by her metaphor of the garden where room exists for all flowers to bloom equally and differently, Walker simultaneously implies that black women are somehow superior to white women because of this black folk tradition. Defining womanish as the opposite of "frivolous, irresponsible, not serious," and girlish, Walker constructs black women's experiences in opposition to those of white women. This meaning of womanism sees it as being different from and superior to feminism, a difference allegedly stemming from black and white women's different histories with American racism. Walker's much cited phrase, "womanist is to feminist as purple to lavender" (1983: xii) clearly seems designed to set up this type of comparison – black women are "womanist" while white women remain merely "feminist."

This usage sits squarely in black nationalist traditions premised on the belief that blacks and whites cannot function as equals while inhabiting the same territory or participating in the same social institutions (Pinkney, 1976; Van Deburg, 1992). Since black nationalist philosophy posits that white people as a group have a vested interest in continuing a system of white supremacy, it typically sees little use for black integration or assimilation into a system predicated on black subjugation. Black nationalist approaches also support a black moral superiority over whites because of black suffering.

Walker's use of the term womanism promises black women who both operate within these black nationalist assumptions and who simultaneously see the need to address "feminist" issues within African-American communities partial reconciliation of these two seemingly incompatible philosophies. Womanism offers a distance from the "enemy," in this case, whites generally and white women in particular, yet still raises the issue of gender. Due to its endorsement of racial separatism, this interpretation of womanism offers a vocabulary for addressing gender issues within African-American communities without challenging the racially segregated terrain that characterizes American social institutions.

This use of womanism sidesteps an issue central to many white feminists, namely, finding ways to foster interracial cooperation among women. African-American women embracing black nationalist philosophies typically express little interest in working with white women – in fact, white women are defined as part of the problem. Moreover, womanism appears to provide an avenue to foster stronger relationships between black women and black men, another very important issue for African-American women regardless of political perspective. Again, Walker's definition provides guidance where she notes that womanists are "committed to survival and wholeness of entire people, male *and* female" (1983: xi). Many black women view feminism as a movement that at best, is exclusively for women and, at worst, dedicated to attacking or eliminating men. Sherley Williams takes this view when she notes that in contrast to feminism, "womanist inquiry . . . assumes that it can talk both effectively and productively about men" (1990: 70). Womanism seemingly supplies a way for black women to address gender oppression without attacking black men.

Walker also presents a visionary meaning for womanism. As part of her second definition, Walker has a black girl pose the question "Mama, why are we brown, pink, and yellow, and our cousins are white, beige, and black?" (1983: xi). The response of "the colored race is just like a flower garden, with every color flower represented," both criticizes colorism within African-American communities and broadens the notion of humanity to make all people people of color. Reading this passage as a metaphor, womanism thus furnishes a vision where the women and men of different colors coexist like flowers in a garden yet retain their cultural distinctiveness and integrity.

This meaning of womanism seems rooted in another major political tradition within African-American politics, namely, a pluralist version of black empowerment (Van Deburg, 1992). Pluralism views society as being composed of various ethnic and interest groups, all of whom compete for goods and services. Equity lies in providing equal opportunities, rights, and respect to all groups. By retaining black cultural distinctiveness and integrity, pluralism offers a modified version of racial integration premised not on individual assimilation but on group integration. Clearly rejecting what they perceive as being the limited vision of feminism projected by North American white women, many black women theorists have been attracted to this joining of pluralism and racial integration in this interpretation of Walker's "womanism." For example, black feminist theologian Katie Geneva Cannon's (1988) work, *Black Womanist Ethics,* invokes this sense of the visionary content of womanism. As an ethical system, womanism is always in the making – it is not a closed fixed system of ideas but one that continually evolves through its rejection of all forms of oppression and commitment to social justice.

Walker's definition thus manages to invoke three important yet contradictory philosophies that frame black social and political thought, namely, black nationalism via her claims of black women's moral and epistemological superiority via suffering under racial and gender oppression, pluralism via the cultural integrity provided by the metaphor of the garden, and integration/assimilation via her claims that black women are "traditionally universalist" (Van Deburg, 1992). Just as black nationalism and racial integration coexist in uneasy partnership, with pluralism occupying the contested terrain between the two, Walker's definitions of womanism demonstrate comparable contradictions. By both grounding womanism in the concrete experiences of African-American women and generalizing about the potential for realizing a humanist vision of community via the experiences of African-American women, Walker depicts the potential for oppressed people to possess a moral vision and standpoint on society that grows from their situation of oppression. This standpoint also emerges as an incipient foundation for a more humanistic, just society. Overall, these uses of Walker's term "womanism" creates conceptual space that reflects bona fide philosophical differences that exist among African-American women.[1]

One particularly significant feature of black women's use of womanism concerns the part of Walker's definition that remains neglected. A more troublesome line for those self-defining as womanist precedes the often cited passage, "committed to survival and wholeness of entire people, male *and* female" (1983: xi). Just before Walker offers the admonition that womanists, by definition, are committed to wholeness, she states that a womanist is also "a woman who loves other women, sexually and/or non-sexually" (1983: xi). The relative silence of womanists on this dimension of womanism speaks to black women's continued ambivalence in dealing with the links between race, gender and sexuality, in this case, the "taboo" sexuality of lesbianism. In her essay "The Truth That Never Hurts: Black Lesbians in Fiction in the 1980s," black feminist critic Barbara Smith (1990) points out that African-American women have yet to come to terms with homophobia in African-American communities. Smith applauds the growth of black women's fiction in the 1980s, but also observes that within black feminist intellectual production, black lesbians continue to be ignored. Despite the fact that some of the most prominent and powerful black women thinkers claimed by both womanists and black feminists were and are lesbians, this precept often remains unacknowledged in the work of African-American writers. In the same way that many people read the Bible, carefully selecting the parts that agree with their worldview and rejecting the rest, selective readings of Walker's womanism produce comparable results.

Another significant feature of black women's multiple uses of womanism concerns the potential for a slippage between the real and the ideal. To me, there is a distinction between describing black women's historical responses to racial and gender oppression as being womanist, and using womanism as a visionary term delineating an ethical or ideal vision of humanity for all people. Identifying the liberatory *potential* within black women's communities that emerges from concrete, historical experiences remains quite different from claiming that black women have already *arrived* at this ideal, "womanist" endpoint. Refusing to distinguish carefully between these two meanings of womanism thus collapses the historically real and the future ideal into one privileged position for African-American women in the present. Taking this position is reminiscent of the response of some black women to the admittedly narrow feminist agenda forwarded by white women in the early 1970s. Those black women proclaimed that they were already "liberated" while in actuality, this was far from the truth.

Black Feminism

African-American Women who use the term black feminism also attach varying interpretations to this term. As black feminist theorist and activist Pearl Cleage defines it, feminism is "the belief that women are full human beings capable of participation and leadership in the full range of human activities – intellectual, political, social, sexual, spiritual and economic" (1993: 28). In its broadest sense, feminism constitutes both an ideology and a global political movement that confronts sexism, a social relationship in which males as a group have authority over females as a group.

Globally, a feminist agenda encompasses several major areas. First and foremost, the economic status of women and issues associated with women's global poverty, such as educational opportunities, industrial development, environmental racism, employment policies, prostitution, and inheritance laws concerning property, constitute a fundamental global women's issue. Political rights for women, such as gaining the vote, rights of assembly, traveling in public, officeholding, the rights of political prisoners, and basic human rights violations against women such as rape and torture constitute a second area of concern. A third area of global concern consists of marital and family issues such as marriage and divorce laws, child custody policies, and domestic labor. Women's health and survival issues, such as reproductive rights, pregnancy, sexuality, and AIDS constitute another area of global feminist concern. This broad global feminist agenda finds varying expressions in different regions of the world and among diverse populations.

Using the term "black feminism" positions African-American women to examine how the particular constellation of issues affecting black women in the United States are part of issues of women's emancipation struggles globally (Davis, 1989; James and Busia, 1994). In the context of feminism as a global political movement for women's rights and emancipation, the patterns of feminist knowledge and politics that African-American women encounter in the United States represent but a narrow segment refracted through the dichotomous racial politics of white supremacy in the United States. Because the media in the United States portrays feminism as a for-whites-only movement, and because many white women have accepted this view of American apartheid that leads to segregated institutions of all types, including feminist organizations, feminism is often viewed by both black and whites as the cultural property of white women (Caraway, 1991).

Despite their media erasure, many African-American women have long struggled against this exclusionary feminism and have long participated in what appear to be for-whites-only feminist activity. In some cases, some black women have long directly challenged the racism within feminist organizations controlled by white women. Sojourner Truth's often cited phrase "ain't I a woman" typifies this long-standing tradition (Joseph, 1990). At other times, even though black women's participation in feminist organizations remains largely invisible, for example, Pauli Murray's lack of recognition as a founding member of NOW, black women participated in feminist organizations in positions of leadership. In still other cases, black women combine allegedly divergent political agendas. For example, Pearl Cleage observes that black feminist politics and black nationalist politics need not be contradictory. She notes, "I don't think you can be a true black

Nationalist, dedicated to the freedom of black people without being a feminist, black *people* being made up of both men and *women,* after all, and feminism being nothing more or less than a belief in the political, social and legal equality of women" (1994: 180).

Using the term "black feminism" disrupts the racism inherent in presenting feminism as a for-whites-only ideology and political movement. Inserting the adjective "black" challenges the assumed whiteness of feminism and disrupts the false universal of this term for both white and black women. Since many white women think that black women lack feminist consciousness, the term "black feminist" both highlights the contradictions underlying the assumed whiteness of feminism and serves to remind white women that they comprise neither the only nor the normative "feminists." The term "black feminism" also makes many African-American women uncomfortable because it challenges black women to confront their own views on sexism and women's oppression. Because the majority of African-American women encounter their own experiences re-packaged in racist school curricula and media, even though they may support the very ideas on which feminism rests, large numbers of African-American women reject the term "feminism" because of what they perceive as its association with whiteness: Many see feminism as operating exclusively within the terms white and American and perceive its opposite as being black and American. When given these two narrow and false choices, black women routinely choose "race" and let the lesser question of "gender" go. In this situation, those black women who identify with feminism must be recoded as being either non-black or less authentically black. The term "black feminist" also disrupts a longstanding and largely unquestioned reliance on black racial solidarity as a deep tap root in black political philosophies, especially black nationalist and cultural pluralist frameworks (Dyson, 1993). Using family rhetoric that views black family, community, race and nation as a series of nested boxes, each gaining meaning from the other, certain rules apply to all levels of this "family" organization. Just as families have internal naturalized hierarchies that give, for example, older siblings authority over younger ones or males over females, groups defining themselves as racial-families invoke similar rules (Collins, forthcoming). Within African-American communities, one such rule is that black women will support black men, no matter what, an unwritten family rule that was manipulated quite successfully during the Clarence Thomas confirmation hearings. Even if Anita Hill was harassed by Clarence Thomas, many proclaimed in barber shops and beauty parlors, she should have kept her mouth shut and not "aired dirty laundry." Even though Thomas recast the life of his own sister through the framework of an unworthy welfare queen, in deference to rules of racial solidarity, black women should have kept our collective mouths shut. By counseling black women not to remain silent in the face of abuse, whoever does it, black feminism comes into conflict with codes of silence such as these.

Several difficulties accompany the use of the term "black feminism." One involves the problem of balancing the genuine concerns of black women against continual pressures to absorb and recast such interests within white feminist frameworks. For example, ensuring political rights and economic development via collective action to change social institutions remains a strong focal point in the feminism of African-American women and women of color. Yet the emphasis on themes such as personal identity, understanding "difference," deconstructing women's multiple selves, and the simplistic model of the political expressed through the slogan the "personal is political," that currently permeate North American white women's feminism in the academy can work to sap black feminism of its critical edge. Efforts of contemporary black women thinkers to explicate a long-standing black women's intellectual tradition bearing the label "black feminism" can attract the attention of white women armed with a different feminist agenda. Issues raised by black women not seen as explicitly "feminist" ones, primarily issues that affect only women, receive much less sanction. In a sense, the constant drumbeat of having to support white women in their efforts to foster an anti-racist feminism that allows black women access to the global network of women's activism diverts black women's energy away from addressing social issues facing African-American communities. Because black feminism appears to be so well-received by white women, in the context of dichotomous racial politics of the United States, some black women quite rightfully suspect its motives.

Another challenge facing black feminism concerns the direct conflict between black feminism and selected elements of black religious traditions. For example, the visibility of white lesbians within North American feminism overall comes into direct conflict with many black women's articles of faith that homosexuality is a sin. While individual African-American women may be accepting of gays, lesbians and bisexuals as individuals, especially if such individuals are African-American, black women as a collectivity have simultaneously distanced themselves from social movements perceived as requiring acceptance of homosexuality. As one young black woman queried, "why do I have to accept lesbianism in order to support black feminism?" The association of feminism with lesbianism remains a problematic one for black women. Reducing black lesbians to their sexuality, one that chooses women over men, reconfigures black lesbians as enemies of black men. This reduction not only constitutes a serious misreading of black lesbianism – black lesbians have fathers, brothers, and sons of their own and are embedded in a series of relationships as complex as their heterosexual brothers and sisters – it simultaneously diverts attention away from more important issues (Lorde, 1984). Who ultimately benefits when the presence of black lesbians in any black social movement leads to its rejection by African-Americans?

The theme of lesbianism and its association with feminism in the minds of many African-Americans also overlaps with another concern of many African-American women, namely their commitment to African-American men. Another challenge confronting black feminism concerns its perceived separatism – many African-Americans define black feminism as being exclusively for black women only and rejecting black men. In explaining her preference for "womanism,"

Sherley Ann Williams notes, "one of the most disturbing aspects of current black feminist criticism (is) its separatism – its tendency to see not only a *distinct* black female culture but to see that culture as a separate cultural form having more in common with white female experience than with the facticity of African-American life" (1990: 70). This is a valid criticism of black feminism, one that in my mind, must be addressed if the major ideas of black feminism expect to avoid the danger of becoming increasingly separated from African-American women's experiences and interests. But it also speaks to the larger issue of the continuing difficulty of positioning black feminism between black nationalism and North American white feminism. In effect, black feminism must come to terms with a white feminist agenda incapable of seeing its own racism as well as a black nationalist one resistant to grappling with its own sexism (White, 1990). Finding a place that accommodates these seemingly contradictory agendas remains elusive (Christian, 1989).

Beyond Naming

African-American women's efforts to distinguish between womanism and black feminism illustrates how black women's placement in hierarchical power relations fosters different yet related allegiances to a black women's self-defined standpoint. While the surface differences distinguishing African-American women who embrace womanism and black feminism appear to be minimal, black women's varying locations in neighborhoods, schools, and labor markets generate comparably diverse views on the strategies black women feel will ultimately lead to black women's self-determination. In a sense, while womanism's affiliation with black nationalism both taps a historic philosophy and a set of social institutions organized around the centrality of racial solidarity for black survival, this position can work to isolate womanism from global women's issues. At the same time, while black feminism's connections to existing women's struggles both domestically and globally fosters a clearer political agenda regarding gender, its putative affiliation with whiteness fosters its rejection by the very constituency it aims to serve.

No term currently exists that adequately represents the substance of what diverse groups of black women alternately call "womanism" and "black feminism." Perhaps the time has come to go beyond naming by applying main ideas contributed by both womanists and black feminists to the over-arching issue of analyzing the centrality of gender in shaping a range of relationships within African-American communities. Such an examination might encompass several dimensions.

First, it is important to keep in mind that the womanist/black feminist debate occurs primarily among relatively privileged black women. Womanism and black feminism would both benefit by examining the increasing mismatch between what privileged black women, especially those in the academy, identify as important themes and what the large numbers of African-American women who stand outside of higher education might deem worthy of attention. While these African-American women physically resemble one another and may even occupy the same space, their worlds remain decidedly different. One might ask how closely the thematic content of newly emerging black women's voices in the academy speak for and speak to the masses of African-American women still denied literacy. Black women academics explore intriguing issues of centers and margins and work to deconstruct black female identity while large numbers of black women remain trapped in neighborhoods organized around old centers of racial apartheid. Talk of centers and margins, even the process of coming to voice itself, that does not simultaneously address issues of power leaves masses of black women doing the dry cleaning, cooking the fast food, and dusting the computer of the sister who has just written the newest theoretical treatise on black women.

Second, shifting the emphasis from black women's oppression to how institutionalized racism operates in gender-specific ways should provide a clearer perspective on how gender oppression works in tandem with racial oppression for both black women and men. This shift potentially opens up new political choices for African-Americans as a group. Just as feminism does not automatically reside in female bodies, sexism does not reside in male ones. It may be time to separate political philosophies such as black nationalism, Afrocentrism, and feminism, from the socially constructed categories of individuals created by historical relations of racism and sexism. Black men cannot have black women's experiences but they can support African-American women by advocating anti-racist and anti-sexist philosophies in their intellectual and political work (see, e.g., Marable, 1983; Hooks and West, 1991; and Awkward, 1995). Focusing on gender as a structure of power that works with race should provide the much needed space for dialogues among black women, among black men, and between black women and men.

This approach promises to benefit the black community as a collectivity because it models sensitivity to the heterogeneity concerning not only gender, but class, nationality, sexuality, and age currently operating within the term "black community." Thus, the womanism/black feminism debate also provides an excellent opportunity to model a process of building community via heterogeneity and not sameness. For African-American women, breathing life into Alice Walker's seemingly contradictory meanings of "womanist" and "black feminist" means engaging in the difficult task of working through the diverse ways that black women have been affected by interlocking systems of oppression. Some black women will have to grapple with how internalized oppression has affected them because they are poor while others must come to terms with the internalized privilege accompanying their middle and upper-class status. Other black women must grapple with the internalized privileges that accrue to them because they engage in heterosexual behaviors or how American citizenship provides them rights denied to women elsewhere in the diaspora. Working through the interconnected nature of multiple systems of oppression and potential ways that such intersectionality might foster resistance becomes significant in moving quite diverse African-American women forward toward Walker's visionary term "womanism." A commitment to social justice and participatory democracy provide some fundamental ground rules for black women and men concerning how to relate across differences.

Finally, despite the promise of this approach, it is important to consider the limitations of womanism, black feminism, and all other putatively progressive philosophies. Whether labeled "womanism," "black feminism," or something else, African-American women could not possibly possess a superior vision of what community would look like, how justice might feel, and the like. This presupposes that such a perspective is arrived at without conflict, intellectual rigor, and political struggle. While black women's particular location provides a distinctive angle of vision on oppression, this perspective comprises neither a privileged nor a complete standpoint. In this sense, grappling with the ideas of heterogeneity within black women's communities and hammering out a self-defined, black women's standpoint leads the way for other groups wishing to follow a similar path. As for black women, we can lead the way or we can follow behind. Things will continue to move on regardless of our choice.

Note

1 For a detailed treatment of Alice Walker's and other black feminist writers, connection to black nationalist politics, see Dubey (1994).

References

Awkward, Michael. 1995. *Negotiating Differences: Race, Gender, and the Politics of Positionality*. Chicago: University of Chicago Press.

Cannon, Katie G. 1988. *Black Womanist Ethics*. Atlanta: Scholars Press.

Caraway, Nancie. 1991. *Segregated Sisterhood: Racism and the Politics of American Feminism*. Knoxville: University of Tennessee Press.

Carby, Hazel. 1992. "The Multicultural Wars." Pp. 187–99 in *Black Popular Culture*, edited by Michele Wallace and Gina Dent. Seattle: Bay Press.

Christian, Barbara. 1989. "But Who Do You Really Belong To – Black Studies or Women's Studies?" *Women's Studies*, 17, 1–2: 17–23.

Cleage, Pearl. 1993. *Deals With the Devil and Other Reasons to Riot*. New York: Ballantine Books.

Collins, Patricia Hill. 1990. *Black Feminist Thought Knowledge, Consciousness, and the Politics of Empowerment*. New York: Routledge, Chapman and Hall.

Collins, Patricia Hill. Forthcoming. "Intersections of Race, Class, Gender, and Nation: Some Implications for Black Family Studies." *Journal of Comparative Family Studies*.

Davis, Angela. 1989. *Women, Culture, and Politics*. New York: Random House.

Dubey, Madhu. 1994. *Black Women Novelists and the Nationalist Aesthetic*. Bloomington: Indiana University Press.

DuCille, Ann. 1994. "The Occult of True Black Womanhood: Critical Demeanor and Black Feminist Studies." *Signs*, 19 (3): 591–629.

Dyson, Michael. 1993. *Reflecting Black: African-American Cultural Criticism*. Minneapolis: University of Minnesota Press.

hooks, bell. 1989. *Talking Back: Thinking Feminist, Thinking Black*. Boston: South End Press.

hooks, bell and Cornel West. 1991. *Breaking Bread: Insurgent Black Intellectual Life*. Boston: South End Press.

James, Stanlie, and Abena Busia, eds. 1994. *Theorizing Black Feminisms*. New York: Routledge.

Jordan, June. 1992. *Technical Difficulties: African-American Notes on the State of the Union*. New York: Pantheon Books.

Joseph, Gloria I. 1990. "Sojourner Truth: Archetypal Black Feminist." Pp. 35–47 in *Wild Women of the Whirlwind*, edited by Joanne Braxton and Andree Nicola McLaughlin. New Brunswick: Rutgers University Press.

Lorde, Audre. 1984. *Sister Outsider*. Trumansburg, NY: The Crossing Press.

Marable, Manning. 1983. "Grounding with My Sisters: Patriarchy and the Exploitation of Black Women." Pp. 69–104 in *How Capitalism Underdeveloped Black America*. Boston: South End Press.

Massey, Douglas S. and Nancy A. Denton. 1993. *American Apartheid: Segregation and the Making of the Underclass*. Cambridge MA: Harvard University Press.

Omolade, Barbara. 1994. *The Rising Song of African American Women*. New York: Routledge.

Pinkney, Alphonso. 1976. *Red, Black, and Green: Black Nationalism in the United States*. London: Cambridge University Press.

Smith, Barbara. 1990. "The Truth That Never Hurts: Black Lesbians in Fiction in the 1980s." Pp. 213–45 in *Wild Women in the Whirlwind*, edited by Joanne Braxton and Andree Nicola McLaughlin. New Brunswick: Rutgers University Press.

Squires, Gregory D. 1994. *Capital and Communities in Black and White: The Intersections of Race, Class, and Uneven Development*. Albany: SUNY Press.

Van Deburg, William L. 1992. *New Day in Babylon: The Black Power Movement and American Culture, 1965–1975*. Chicago: University, of Chicago Press.

Walker, Alice. 1983. *In Search of Our Mothers' Gardens*. New York: Harcourt, Brace Jovanovich.

White, E. Frances. 1990. "Africa on My Mind: Gender, Counter Discourse and African-American Nationalism." *Journal of Women's History*, 2, 1 (Spring): 73–97.

Williams, Sherley Ann. 1990. "Some Implications of Womanist Theory." Pp. 68–75 in *Reading Black, Reading Feminist: A Critical Anthology*, edited by Henry Louis Gates. New York: Meridian.

Part III

Fashioning Mixed Race

9

The Colorblind Multiracial Dilemma: Racial Categories Reconsidered

john a. powell

This chapter will briefly touch on some of the ways we think about race and, more particularly, racial categories. Despite our obsession with race – which sometimes takes the form of race aversion – our national discourse is disturbingly confused, charged, and often unproductive. Our language often seems wooden and rehearsed, and the way that we discuss race is frequently in conflict with our stated ideals.[1] I focus on racial categories not just because of their general interest and importance, but because Trina Grillo was very interested in them – both professionally and experientially.[2] The concept of race is hotly contested and deconstructed in literature, law, and politics. Currently, there are several competing theories about race and its meaning and application in the United States. I will focus on two sets of claims about racial categories. I will explore the limitations of these positions and posit some alternative ways to think about racial categories.

The two positions on which I will focus seem to point in opposite directions.[3] The first, the colorblind position, calls for the end of racial categories. The second, the multiracial position, calls for the proliferation of racial categories, with particular attention to expanding multiracial categories.

I Colorblind Position

The political history of the colorblind position is more closely associated with traditional liberalism dating from the 1960s.[4] Recently, however, this position has been appropriated by the new right and recast in ways that are often at odds with the traditional liberal position.[5] This raceless position is partly rooted in the view that race is a social construct and not a scientific or biological fact.[6] The proponents of this position argue that since we have learned that race is an illusion, rather than a scientific fact, we should drop racial categories altogether. The minor differences in appearance are irrelevant, and only those who are either racist or badly misinformed would insist that we continue to utilize these pernicious categories.[7]

While the currency of these ideals is popular behind the obscure walls of academia, they have also found a voice in law and politics. Much of the conservative rhetoric about colorblindness rests heavily on the insight that the practice of recognizing racial categories is rooted in discredited biology and gene theory.[8] The sooner we remove race from law and politics the better. The proponents of this position argue that we will only solve the race problem by eliminating all racial categories. Race is seen as a bad repetitive illusion, or as a trope.

The Supreme Court has used this reasoning to attack the validity of race conscious programs such as affirmative action, set asides, and redistribution in voting.[9] In the larger political sphere, there has been public musing for months about dropping race as a category from the next census.[10]

Conceptual position

The new right's colorblind assertion is both a conceptual and a pragmatic position. The conceptual position claims that because race does not have a substantial scientific basis, it is not only an illusion but a problematic illusion. This assertion is based on the assumption that that which cannot be grounded on an objective scientific foundation is not real. This claim, however, suffers from a serious conceptual flaw.[11] While the claim that race is an illusion draws on the work of late- and post-modernists – particularly the work of Omi and Winant, which purports that race is socially constructed – the conclusion that race is not real does not comport with the deeper implication of this insight. Omi and Winant, for example, do not support the position that race can or simply should be dropped. Omi, citing the *Journal of Black Higher Education* with approval, notes that while race may not be a scientific reality, it is a social fact.[12]

While the insight that race is socially constructed is based in part on post-modernist teaching, this assertion alone distorts both the late- and post-modern positions. This colorblind position attempts to apply the late- and post-modernist insight of constructivism, but it wishes to limit this understanding to race. And there lies the error. The constructionist position is that all reality, including all concepts, are socially constructed.[13] This does not mean that this socially constructed world is an illusion, but that it is not pregiven.[14] Indeed, to claim that the socially constructed world is an illusion suggests that there is a more real world behind the illusion. But this belief that the real world is separate from us and our perceptions of it is denied by late- and post-modernists. It is not simply that the real world is unavailable to us and we misunderstand what is real, but instead it is our perceptions and categories that both represent and participate in the constitution of the world.[15]

Two examples might be useful to help clarify this claim. The first example is the self. While few would claim that the self is simply an illusion, or that the concept of the self should be discarded, post-modernism asserts that the self, like race, is also socially constructed.[16] While the social construction of the self points to an illusion or error, it is not correct to suggest that the self does not exist, but that only the unconstituted and disembodied self that forms the bases of much of liberal thinking does not exist.[17]

The second example comes from my experience as a first year student in college. As young college students, we often flexed and stretched our intellectual muscle with discussions of the existence or non-existence of God. As our first year drew to a close, we moved toward a greater consensus and conviction that God did not exist or was dead. As we collectively announced our conclusion, one of the students pointed out a significant error in our examination. She noted that at best, what we had achieved were strong arguments against the existence of the Judeo-Christian representation of God. Our interrogation had been so limited that it was silent on other possible representations of God.

Similarly, those who would abandon race because the biological or genetic foundation for race proves to be inadequate, fail to engage seriously other possible ways of understanding race.[18] Even the position that race is socially constructed instead of biologically based underestimates the force of the postmodernist claim that everything is socially constructed. Not only are race and the self socially constructed, but biology and science are as well.[19] This does not mean that all claims are either arbitrary or illusory, but that the way we think of reality as being simply represented by our senses, instead of interactive with our senses and language, is illusionary.

Pragmatic position

The second colorblind position is pragmatic and political. This position errs in assuming that the major race problem in our society is race itself, rather than racism. Many of the proponents of moving to a raceless, colorblind society argue that the categories of race are both irrelevant and politically and racially divisive.[20] Many have appropriated the language of Dr. King and the civil rights movement to give force to the call for colorblindness.[21] The language used by the new right of a raceless, colorblind society is viewed by some not simply as an error, but as a strategy or racial project to maintain white supremacy and racial hierarchy.[22] Whether it is intentional or an error, powerful evidence suggests that the colorblind, race-aversive language adopted by the new right has the effect of shoring up racial hierarchy, while masking both the subordination of the racial minority and the enjoyment of white privilege.[23] Indeed, in many respects the focus on race or racelessness not only masks racism but also actively supports it. This move is what Patricia Williams calls racism in drag.[24] The racial project of the new right can be viewed as maintaining the racial order without specific reference to race.[25]

If one is to examine the current racial project pragmatically, one must ask how the project impacts the complimentary goals of ending racial hierarchy and moving to racial justice.

II   Multiracial Position

While the race evasive stance of the new right has misappropriated the significance of race as socially constructed, the error of the multiracial movement is its failure to embrace the socially constructed nature of race altogether. The multiracial movement has become increasingly vocal as the number of "biracial" marriages and children increase.[26] The concern expressed by such groups as Project RACE (Reclassify All Children Equally) is that the current recognized racial categories do not account for the identity or experience of multiracial people.[27]

The multiracial position appropriately points out the inconsistency and incoherence of our current racial categories.[28] There is not only a problem between how the government classifies groups racially versus common use of racial categories, but there are also inconsistencies within the official US government classification itself. The current government classification is pursuant to Statistical Directive No. 15 (Directive 15), implemented by the US Office of Management and Budget (OMB).[29] The categories employed in Directive 15 are now used by all federal and state agencies that keep statistics on race. But these categories exhibit a number of inconsistencies. Michael Omi points to the incoherence of the present system of government categories:

> An investigation of Directive 15 classifications reveals significant problems in their construction and meaning. While most of the categories rely on a concept of "original peoples," only one of the definitions is specifically racial, only one is cultural and only one relies on a notion of affiliation or community recognition.[30]

There are few comparable criteria deployed across the categories. For example, Directive 15 defines a black person as one having her or his "origins in any of the black racial groups of Africa," [31] but it does not define a white person with reference to the white racial groups of Europe, North Africa, or the Middle East. Indeed *"Black" is the only category which is defined with an explicit racial designator* – one which is quite problematic. What we might ask is what are the "black racial groups of Africa?"[32] It's a small wonder that we think race means black.

Hispanics are not considered and classified as a race but as an ethnic group. The Hispanic category is, in fact, the only ethnicity that the state is interested in explicitly identifying and classifying. The category is defined through cultural designators: a person of "Mexican, Puerto Rican, Cuban, Central or South American or other Spanish culture or origin."[33] In this definition, Hispanics can be of any race.

The category of "American Indian or Alaskan Native" reveals another intriguing definitional issue. Individuals who are considered part of this category must not only have their origins in any of the original peoples of North America, but also must maintain "cultural identification" through "tribal" affiliations.[34]

The problems are not limited to inconsistencies. Some groups are left out of the classification altogether.[35] Indeed, one of the problems asserted by multiracial advocates is that they are either left out or forced to improperly identify them-selves.[36] While this may be right, it is not entirely clear how, as I will try to demonstrate shortly.

The question of how to categorize and think about multiracial groups was of serious concern to Trina.[37] She experienced the difficulty and pain of being multiracial in a society where identity is organized around very limited concepts of race. She experienced being excluded and miscategorized. Yet, she continued to question the wisdom of adopting multiracial categories. She expressed concern that many of the advocates of multiracial categories were white mothers that were particularly interested in distancing their multiracial children from the societal injury of being black in America.[38]

Trina never resolved this issue of whether there should be new multiracial cat-egories. But with her subtle and nuanced thinking, she raised many of the questions that are important to consider in embracing these complicated issues. Despite her personal pain with using the existing racial categories, she insisted on investigating this issue at the personal, historical, and political level. She raised the question of how existing categories, and particularly the black category, could be reconceptualized to make a home for the offspring of black and white parents.[39] If this reconceptualization project did not succeed, these children would have to find another home. But she was also disturbed that the call for a new multiracial category from white mothers might be another form of colorism with a strong, anti-black subtext.[40] And finally she was aware that a new multi-racial category might both weaken the black community's political position and strengthen the dominance of whites.[41] Trina was concerned that if white supremacy is not addressed, the move toward multiracial categories could easily lead to a more entrenched pigmentocracy similar to what exists in many Latin-American countries.[42]

Trina's position was not that new multiracial categories necessarily entailed anti-black sentiments. She understood the need for family and cultural identifi-cation. Her concern was not the categorical problem; rather, she focused on the political and theoretical implications of new racial categories based on the foundation for such categories and the political context in which this project is taking place.

Without trying to defend our current problematic typology, I embrace many of Trina's concerns. I will attempt to sketch out in slightly more detail how these concerns play out in the multiracial movement. I will do so by briefly examining some of the descriptive and political issues raised by the call for a new set of multiracial categories.[43] The descriptive position's call for new categories is based on the premise that multiracial subjects simply are not accurately described by the existing categories. The multiracial advocates, like the conservative color-blind advocates, make a political and pragmatic claim. They maintain that an increase in multiracial categories will weaken racial hierarchy.[44]

There are at least two versions of the multiracial descriptive claim. One is that multiracial people are of mixed blood or mixed genetic material.[45] The other is that multiracial people are people with parents of different recognizable races.

On examination, both of these positions are problematic. The first position is most blatantly tied to the racist science of the last century. It suggests that a person that is part black blood and part white blood is not adequately or accurately described as black. But this clearly rests on the discredited biological model. To sustain this position, one would have to show not only that blood lines or genes are the appropriate foundations upon which to classify races, but that they are clear as well. Stated more strongly, pure blood would define the different racial categories. But this simply cannot be shown. The attack on the biological model not only demonstrates that the supposed racial difference cannot be sustained based on blood and genetics,[46] but that the majority of white Americans have African blood and the majority of blacks have white blood and a substantial number have Indian blood.[47] Based on the *hypodescent rule*,[48] most white Americans are African-American.[49] Based on the multiracial premise, most Americans are multiracial or mixed. But this does not seem to be the conclusion toward which the multiracial movement is drawn. Indeed this conclusion undermines the implicit position that mixed-race people have a different experience and need their own category. The point then is not that we are all genetically mixed, we are, but that this is largely irrelevant for creating racial categories.

Many of the proponents of new multiracial categories are politically left of center and would reject the overt racism of nineteenth-century biology. Yet, a number of the assumptions adopted by these advocates end up unwittingly relying on this same discredited science. One of the main assertions of this science was that race and racial categories were based on blood or gene.[50] In terms of the black/white distinction one extreme version of this was the assertion that white was pure and, therefore, would be contaminated by one drop of black blood. This is also known as the hypodescent rule. The history of this rule which categorizes anyone with black ancestry as black, emerged from our racist history and a desire to maintain white purity.[51] This nineteenth-century science, which was used to both classify races and explain racial difference based on blood and genetics, has been discredited.[52] Below I will argue that many of the more salient justifications advanced by multiracial advocates rely on a version of this discredited racist science.[53]

Some multiracial advocates have anticipated this problem of relying on blood or genes. They suggest that instead we label a person multiracial if their parents are of different recognized races.[54] But if this is the designation, how do we categorize the offspring of a multiracial and monoracial union?[55] If we say that the offspring continues to be multiracial, then we are back to the problem that virtually everyone is multiracial. If we say that the person is the race of the uniracial parent, then we reproduce the problem of forcing the offspring to deny part of her heritage. Despite this difficulty, there is a strong appeal for the offspring being able to claim all the aspects of her parents. But it is not clear that this issue should be resolved based on blood. If we categorize children so that they may claim their parents' heritage, how should we categorize a black child who is raised by white parents in a culturally white environment? Of course, a totally different way of thinking about this is to suggest that the white parent that has children with a black person could be able to cross over and no longer be white. Black could be reconceptualized, once we drop the blood issue, to allow for this move.[56] One might assert that it is the responsibility of society – not heritage – that controls, but this would not be acceptable for the multiracial project.

Another position often advanced by multiracial advocates is that people should be able to define themselves.[57] While this has a great deal of intuitive value, it is probably not workable or desirable. Much of the appeal of this position stems from our ideology of individualism.[58] In our dominant discourse, we embrace the rhetoric that each person is an individual. While this is a truism in what it says, it is false in what it implies. We all may be individuals, but none of us are just individuals.[59] Given the normative structure of whiteness in the United States, the claim of individualism is often a thinly veiled effort to claim the privileges of whiteness. This position again suffers from the failure to embrace the significance of race and identity as socially constructed.[60] This does not mean that we cannot or do not participate in the constitution of our identity. But it is a false claim and a flawed hope that we can define who we are in isolation.

III   Political Project

While the new right claims that the elimination of racial categories will end racism, multiracial advocates assert that an increase in the number of racial categories will soften, if not completely destabilize, the existing racial hierarchy. The proponents of multiracialism cite the history of anti-miscegenation laws to support their position. Anti-miscegenation laws were used to protect the apparent purity of the white race. States were concerned that race mixing especially between whites and blacks would contaminate this white purity.[61] While the law spent a great deal of effort to define the racial "other," whites are largely defined in opposition to the racial other and as pure.[62] Anti-miscegenation laws, along with the arrangement of the child being the race of the mother, allowed the slave master to produce offspring with his black slaves, thereby enhancing his slave interest in the biracial offspring, and maintaining whiteness as an exclusive club. There are other ways of thinking about these issues that might reinforce what we think about racial categories.

After the emancipation formally freed the slaves, the laws that regulated black/white relations expanded to continue dominance outside of the slave state. Since it was no longer necessary for a slaveholder to classify all the children of slave mothers as slaves, for a brief period, there were many more racial categories. In addition to the black and white categories of today, the 1890 census included Chinese, Japanese, Indian, Mulatto, Quadroon, and Octoroon.[63] Only those with at least three-fourths black blood were classified as black, while those having had at least one drop of black blood but no more than one-eighth were classified as Octoroon.[64] Therefore, whites were still defined as pure and enjoyed different benefits that were attached to being white than any of the mixed races.[65] But a person half white and half black was neither black nor white.[66]

The use of multiracial categories did little to destabilize the white hierarchy. It refined the calibration, but white racial purity remained the prerequisite to being classified as white and obtaining the privileges attendant to that classification. Although every law student knows of *Plessy v. Ferguson,* few realize that under the 1890 census, Homer Plessy was not black but an Octoroon. It is also important to note that *Plessy* did not challenge the right of Louisiana to separate blacks and whites, but instead argued that as an Octoroon, he was entitled to the same rights and privileges as whites.[67] Indeed, one of the objections raised by Plessy was that the Louisiana statute in question took away his property interest in his whiteness by classifying him as colored.[68] The court denied Plessy relief. Even if it had granted him relief, it is not clear how this would have benefited those classified as black instead of Octoroon. But it is not possible to understand Plessy or to understand how race operates in our society without understanding what Homer Plessy knew: that whiteness was a ticket to psychological and economic privilege.[69]

Some advocates of multiracialism cite Latin America generally, and Brazil in particular, as examples of how multiracial categories have been used to soften the harshness of US-style racism.[70] Brazil did not enact the formal anti-miscegenation laws prevalent in the United States,[71] even though Brazil has many more racial categories than the United States.[72] Brazil has often been regarded as an example of a multiracially open and tolerant society. However, recent scholarly work points to pigmentocracies in Brazil and other Latin-American countries, in addition to strong anti-black sentiments.[73] A closer examination of these multiracial systems suggests that they leave the extreme poles of whiteness and blackness undisturbed. It also cautions against multiracial backing into the position of Homer Plessy. The current situation in Brazil and our own history demonstrate that an increase in racial categories does not necessitate a movement toward racial justice.[74]

Of course in order to avoid the error discussed above about the existence of God, I must concede that even if my argument is right, there still might be a need for a multiracial category. One cannot exhaust all the possible justifications. But certainly, resting justifications on blood and not considering the implication in terms of racism is problematic especially considering our history.[75] What would a socially constructed argument for multiracial categories be? There are obviously several, but one of the strongest is that the life experience of those designated mixed race in our society is qualitatively different than other groups designated as a single race.[76] This argument does not rest on the genetic or blood composition of those designated as mixed race. Nor is this argument weakened by the insight that we are virtually all mixed-raced, based on blood or genetic material. Rather, this argument relies on the socially constructed nature of the experience of people – individually and collectively – in our society.

The experience of those designated multiracial may be very different from those designated as uniracial. From an anti-racist perspective, one could argue that the experience of how multiracial people are treated by other people of color should be more important than how they are treated by whites. One reason for this is to avoid the house slave situation where whites can favor some pe[...] color over others, while maintaining their white privilege. Given our [...] history and practice, it is not surprising that the white community has been [...] accepting of designated multiracial people than the black community.[77]

While the black community has been more accepting than whites of both lighter skinned blacks and those designated as mixed race, this acceptance has not always been an easy one. The acceptance has often been provisional and with qualifications.[78] While the reasons for this are numerous and complicated, it is clear that if those designated as mixed race cannot find a home in the existing socially constructed categories, there will be a need to either reconstruct the existing categories or add to them.

The point of this article is not to defend our existing racial categories. I share in the sentiment that racial categories are not only incoherent and limiting, but often times oppressive and exclusive. The problem with the new right's position on race and power evasion is that it misappropriates the meaning of social construction. The problem with the multiracial position is that it fails to embrace the insight of social construction and instead falls back on the nineteenth-century meaning of biology. And yet the current categories need to be, and undoubtedly will be, reconstructed. One way of thinking about how the categories should be changed is to acknowledge that black does not mean all black blood or possibly any black blood; white does not mean all white blood or any white blood.

Conclusion

A more fruitful way of thinking about these issues is to both acknowledge the implications of the socially constructed nature of race, while simultaneously acknowledging that race operates differently in different spheres.[79] In the larger political sphere, race is not only socially constructed, the meaning and function of race is the site of intense social and political struggle.[80] When people are categorized in ways that disfavor them and favor others, there will be resistance and re-appropriation. The effort then to categorize people is not simply a question of getting it right. The process of racial categorizing is a power struggle implicating structural, cultural, economic, and identity politics.

Race being a social construction means that white and black has to be understood in relationship to each other. Social and political power, as well as the implications in social terms, must be identified. There is no black without white; there is no white without black. In this sense we are all multiracial. We are also fractured racially not because of blood, but because we are mutually and continuously defining and constituting our race by what we include and exclude of the racial other.[81] Black and white are not only co-dependent (though in different ways), but black is necessarily a part of white and white is necessarily a part of black in a fluid and destabilizing dance of consternation.

James Baldwin captures some of the subtlety of the inter and infra connection between different races:

But we are all androgynous, not only because we are all born of a woman impreg-
nated by the seed of a man but because each of us, helplessly and forever, contains
the other – male in female, female in male, white in black and black in white. We
are a part of each other. Many of my countrymen appear to find this fact exceed-
ingly inconvenient and even unfair, and so very often do I. But none of us can do
anything about it.[82]

The objections with how the new right and many multiracialists think about
race lie not in the categories they propose, but in their theoretical foundations
and assumptions. I have tried to suggest some alternative foundations that might
be useful in generating socially constructed racial categories.

We are all racially mixed, and there is probably no such thing as racial purity.
This is not to take away any special position that might be produced at the site
we call multiracial. Nor does it mean that there are no other uniracial categories.
What this does suggest is that we need to examine the political and power implications of reconsidering designated categories. Because politics and power
operate differently in different spheres, it may be appropriate to have multiple
approaches to this issue depending on the site. At the family level we may constitute and define race differently than at the public or group level. Although it is
clear that these spheres will continue to bleed into each other, we may want to
ask how race functions in a given sphere and how a change might impact racism
and power relationships.

While personal identification is and will remain important, for me the pivotal
issue is how the new racial project will impact the axis of racism in different sites.
At the family or personal level, there may be space for more personal involvement in racial identification. It is important for all people to be able to claim all
of their racial and ethnic heritage. This is even more true if collective structures
and practices treat people with parents of different races differently than people
with parents of the same race. But as we engage in these issues, it is important
that we guard against pigmentocracy and against exhausting our efforts on these
categories of race, while leaving racism intact and unexamined. It is also important that the white racial category and the privileges associated with being white
be part of the project.

The following are a few examples of how we might re-examine racial categories in light of being differently informed by the insight of race as a social
construction and an anti-racist project. In undertaking this effort we must
always ask how this particular effort impacts racial hierarchy? At the top of
that hierarchy is whiteness. David Roediger has stated that the term white
privilege is redundant.[83] This suggests that to destabilize racial hierarchy, we
start with whiteness. The race traitors [84] have responded to a similar understanding of whiteness as Roediger, in trying to develop a stance that rejects
whiteness. If one wanted to reconstitute blackness, brownness, or any other
anti-privileged racial category, one could consider how race is discussed in
England. All groups that are not categorized as white could be categorized as
black, brown, or some other inclusive term.[85] This non-white group could

include those who would have been formally designated as white but have rejected that "privilege."

Some claim that we are all racially mixed, not in terms of blood and genes, but at a deeper, more psychological level. If we are socially constituted, we are also constituted by multiple voices. In the blood sense and at a deeper level, there is no unitary race or even person. We carry many different racial and gendered voices inside of us. While we are not all the same or fungible, we are diverse with parts of each other inside us. From this perspective, diversity is both an internal and external issue. Our differences and similarities are relational, shifting, unstable, and constitutive. If we are willing to drop the claim of racial purity, we may be able to claim our different racial voices. We might be able to think and imagine together in concrete terms.

As we reconstruct racial categories – and this is not just a job for the multi-racialists but for all of us who care about a racial democracy – we must do so to dismantle racism, racial hierarchy, and white supremacy. Whites may want to consider the implication of abandoning the property interests associated with whiteness and explore becoming privileged traitors. We may want to seek out our different racial voices and see what structures call forth and repress these voices! The effort requires serious work and play. If our project to rethink racial categories is also about destabilizing racial hierarchy, we will reject the new right's colorblind position. The multiracial supporters need not wait until this effort is complete to seek a home. But it is important that they, and we, not unreflectively use the tools of the master's house or simply move closer to the master's house.[86] Our efforts may have implications beyond their immediate focus. Advocates of the new racial categories should think and feel very care-fully, historically, and pragmatically about how we proceed on a multiracial project.

Those who would maintain the existing categories need to subject the status quo to a similar examination. Perhaps the answer is to have only two categories, one supporting racial hierarchy, and the other supporting racial justice and democracy.

If we embark on this project of reconstituting racial categories and challenging racism, I hope we will follow the example of Trina Grillo and use our hearts, minds, and each other to be more expansive in our thinking than the old cate-gories and discredited methods might allow.

Acknowledgment

I would like to thank the University of Minnesota Law Library staff for their wonderful support and the *University of San Francisco Law Review* for doing this issue for Trina. I appreciate the research assistance of Bonnie Mookherjee. I would like to dedicate this article to Trina Grillo, her children Jeffrey and Luisa, and my children Fon and Saneta. Trina will always inhabit my heart and mind. I miss you.

Notes

1 *See* john a. powell, *The "Racing" of American Society: Race Functioning as a Verb Before Signifying as a Noun,* 15 LAW and INEQ. J. 99, 99–118 (1997) [hereafter powell, *"Racing"*]. I will focus on the United States' experience of race and racism in this article. I recognize that in other societies and even in the United States, how we discuss race changes both at different historical times and in different sites in our lives.

2 *See* Trina Grillo, *Anti-Essentialism and Intersectionality: Took to Dismantle the Master's House,* 10 BERKELEY WOMEN's L.J. 16, 16–19 (1995).

3 I will try to show in this paper that they in fact make similar mistakes and, more importantly, neither position seriously challenges racism.

4 *See* John O. Calmore, *Critical Race Theory, Archie Shepp, and Fire Music: Securing an Authentic Intellectual Life in a Multicultural World,* 65 S. CAL. L. REV. 2129, 2149–50 (1992). *See generally* Arthur M. Schlesinger, Jr., *The Disuniting of America* (1992) (asserting that identity politics is problematic and contributes to the disunity of America).

5 *See* Michael Omi and Howard Winant, *Racial Formation in the United States: From the 1960s to the 1990s,* 55 (1994). The new right's use of the colorblind and race neutral discourse has allowed them to co-op more of the center and liberal political spectrum. *See also* John O. Calmore, *Exploring Michael Omi's "Messy" Real World of Race: An Essay for "Naked People Longing to Swim Free"* 15 LAW and INEQ. J. 25, 79 (1997).

6 *See* Carol R. Goforth, *"What is She?" Now Race Matters and Why It Shouldn't,* 46 DEPAUL L. REV. 1, 9–11 (1996).

7 *See id.*

8 *See* Neil Gotanda, *A Critique of "Our Constitution is Color Blind,"* 44 STAN. L. REV. 1, 32 (1991).

9 *See* Shaw v. Reno, 509 US 630 (1993); Croson v. United States, 488 US 469 (1988); Arlington Heights v. Metropolitan Hous. Dev. Co., 429 US 252 (1977).

10 *See* Clarence Page, *Racial Consensus, Racial Confusion,* BALTIMORE SUN, July 29, 1997, at 9A.

11 *See* powell, *"Racing," supra* note 1, at 99–112; *see also* Richard J. Bernstein, *Beyond Objectivism and Relativism: Science, Hermeneutics, and Praxis* 18 (1983) (referring to dichotomous thinking as the "grand and seductive Either/Or").

12 *See* Michael Omi, *Racial Identity and the State: The Dilemmas of Classification,* 15 LAW and INEQ J. 7, 14–21 (1997).

13 *See* john a. powell, *Reflections on the Self: Exploring Between and Beyond Modernity and Postmodernity,* 81 MINN. L. REV. 1481, 1486–90 (1997) [hereinafter powell, *Reflections*]. *See generally* Anne Klein, *Meeting the Great Bliss Queen* (1995) (discussing the Buddhist concept of no self and stating that this position does not mean that the self does not exist but only that the permanent, unconditional self posited in Western thought does not exist).

14 This is not just a problem for late- and post-modernists. Hume's skepticism was based on the claim that we cannot know the world directly. That is, the world is always filtered through our senses. In his effort to construct a response to Hume, Kant accepted the basic principle that we do not have direct access to the world.

15 *See* Nelson Goodman, *Ways of Worldmaking,* 91–97 (1978).

16 *See* powell, *Reflections, supra* note 13, at 1486–90. *See generally* Kenneth J. Gergen, *The Saturated Self: Dilemmas of Identity in Contemporary Life* (1991). Gergen discusses the difficulty of choosing between competing voices or claims made upon oneself. He argues that there are multiple selves, each of which makes its own claims and demands. Implicit in this argument is the notion that the unitary self has been fractured. While there are some post-modernists that argue for the decentering of the self, there are still others that have suggested abandoning the self. Most, however, call for a rethinking and resituating of the self.

17 *See* powell, *Reflections, supra* note 13, at 1486–90. *See generally* Klein, *supra* note 13 (making a similar point in her discussion about the Buddhist concept of no self and stating that this position does not mean that the self does not exist but only that the permanent unconditional self posited in Western thought does not exist).

18 *See* Gotanda, *supra* note 8, at 32; *see also* Ruth Frankenberg, *White Women, Race Matters: The Social Construction of Whiteness* 142–9 (1993); powell, *Racing, supra* note 1, at 99–112.

19 *See generally* Bernstein *supra* note 11.

20 *See* Luther Wright, Jr., *Who's Black Who's White, and Who Cares: Reconceptualizing the United State's Definition of Race and Racial Classifications,* 48 VAND. L. REV. 513, 561–6 (1995).

21 Dr. King's colorblind language was often used by anti-affirmative action proponents in California. The King family express dismay that Dr. King's words are being misappropriated in this fashion.

22 *See* Calmore, *supra* note 4, at 2149–50; *see also* Frankenberg, *supra* note 18, at 142–9; Kimberley Williams Crenshaw, *Race, Reform, and Retrenchment: Transformation and Legitimation in Antidiscrimination Law,* 101 HARV L. REV. 1331, 1346(1988); john a. powell, *An Agenda for the Post-Civil Rights Era,* 29 USF. L. REV. 889, 892 (1995). *See generally* Omi and Winant, *supra* note 5.

23 *See generally* Frances Lee Ansley, *Stirring the Ashes: Race, Class and the Future of Civil Rights Scholarship,* 74 CORNELL L. REV. 993 (1989); Calmore, *supra* note 4, at 2149–50.

24 *See generally* Patricia J. Williams, *The Alchemy of Race and Rights* (1991).

25 *See* David Theo Goldberg, *Racist Culture: Philosophy and the Politics of Meaning 2* (1993). While this project tries to avoid specific reference to race, a new coded racial discourse has evolved that allows one to speak of race in apparently race neutral terms such as "welfare," "criminal," "crime victim," "silent majority," "good neighborhood and inner city," and "individual merit." *See id; see also* Thomas Byrne Edsall and Mary D. Edsall, *Chain Reaction: The Impact of Race, Rights, and Taxes on American Politics* 116–36 (1991) (discussing the achievements of the Civil Rights Movement and a growing conservatism among whites during 1964 through 1980).

26 *See* Omi, *supra* note 12, at 14–21 (discussing that there has been a substantial increase in the number of biracial children; currently there are over 2,000,000 children of biracial union). I will use the terms biracial and multiracial, recognizing that the terms are both imprecise and not free of problems. As Omi points out, the D mixed implies that there is a pure race and this has been called into question. Similarly multiracial implies that there is a unirace. This suffers from the same limitation as mixed raced.

27 *See id.* at 18.

28 *See id* at 14–21 (discussing the inconsistencies and incoherence of our current racial categories). *See generally* Wright, *supra* note 20 (suggesting that categories such as

black, white and Hispanic incorrectly imply that race is the distinguishing factor between these groups).

29 *See* Omi, *supra* note 12, at 14–21.

30 *Id* at 11(quoting Calvin Trillin, American Chronicles: Black or White, *New Yorker,* April 14, 1986, at 62).

31 *Id.*

32 *See id.*

33 *Id.*

34 *See id.* at 11.

35 *See id.*

36 *See id.* at 14–21; Wright, *supra* note 20, at 557.

37 *See* Grillo, *supra* note 2, at 16–19.

38 *See id.* Trina focused on the black/white multiracial experience in part because it is the one that she knew best. She was also careful not to conflate all minority and multiracial issues under the black/white experience.

39 *See id.*

40 *See id.* Trina focused on black and white because that was a part of her experience. She was also Latina. What she was not prepared to do was to assume that race and racism operate the same for all racial minorities. This article will focus primarily on the black and white multiracial experience.

41 *See id.* at 16–19; *see also* Howard Winant, *Racial Conditions Politics Theory, Comparisons* 22, 31 (1994). Trina was also concerned that the beneficiaries of multiracial categories are likely to have a very strong class dimension. Those of the middle and upper middle class are more likely be able to claim their multiracial status to make them something other than black. It is interesting to note that some of this tracks the Brazilian model of multiracial. And despite a popular misconception, Brazil is a society that is heavily racially stratified and strongly anti-black.

42 *See generally* Amy L. Chua, *Privatization-Nationalization Cycle: The Link Between Markets and Ethnicity in Developing Countries,* 95 COLUM. L. REV. 223 (1995); Grillo, *supra* note 2. Pigmentocracy is similar to colorism, only it extends across racial groups where the lighter the skin color, the more privilege is associated with one's whiteness. There was also a pigmentocracy in South Africa. It is not that multiracial categories would necessarily lead to pigmentocracy and colorism, but without challenging racial hierarchy and white supremacy the dangers increase. Trina was especially concerned about this because of the history of colorism and pigmentocracy in the United States.

43 I recognize that many people calling for a change in racial categories are not basing their appeal on the assumption that I consider in the text of this article.

44 *See* Wright, *supra* note 20, at 562–5.

45 *See* Powell, *Reflections, supra* note 13, at 1486–90. It is interesting to note for Star Trek fans that Spock in the original Star Trek and now Counselor Troi represent the mixed race subject. Because of their mixed status they are seen as having an internal conflict based on blood or genetics that other uniracial species are not supposed to have. I have argued that we are all internally fractured. That is the nature of the self and it is not dependent on biology, and it is important to reject the assumption that there is a pure race or gene pool.

46 *See generally* Goldberg, *supra* note 25.

47 Some anthropologists claim that most white Americans have at least 5 percent African blood and most African-Americans have at least 25 percent white blood.

48 The hypodescent rule asserts that white blood is pure, and therefore is contaminated by one drop of black blood.

49 *See* David W. Stowe, Uncolored People, *Lingua Franca*, Sept.–Oct. 1996, at 68, 74–5. Without relying on blood or genes, Toni Morrison asserts that all Americans are African-American. She is suggesting that the nature of America is a hybrid.

50 *See generally* Goldberg, *supra* note 25.

51 *See* Wright, supra note 20, at 513, 520–3; *see also* Ian F. Haney Lopez, *White By Law: TB Legal Construction of Race* 42–43 (1996).

52 *See generally* Goldberg, *supra* note 25.

53 *See* discussion *infra* Part m.

54 *See* Wright, *supra* note 20, at 557–9, 563.

55 *See id.*

56 *See generally* Jane Lazzare, *Beyond the Whiteness of Whiteness: Memoir of a White Mother of Black Sons* (1996); *see also* James Baldwin, *The Price of the Ticket* 690 (1985); Noelle Johnson, Race Traitor: The New Abolitionism, *N.Y. Beacon*, Jan. 29, 1997, *available in* 1997 WL 11706935. In *Race Traitor*, a white mother of black children talks about crossing over the racial divide in her multiracial family. Some have suggested that whiteness is chosen. I am not clear how or if this can be done, especially on an individual level, but it does suggest that there are other ways of thinking about these issues that might reinforce what we think about racial categories, at 799.

57 *See generally* Nancy A. Denton, *Racial Identity and Census Categories: Can Incorrect Categories Yield Correct Information?*, 15 LAW and INEQ. J. 83 (1997) (discussing how some advocates of multiracial categories support self-definition).

58 *See* powell, *Reflections, supra* note 13, at 1486–90.

59 *See* id. (discussing the false concept of individualism). *See generally* Goldberg, *supra* note 25; Michael J. Sandel, *Political Liberalism,* 107 HARV. L. REV. 1765 (1994) (reviewing John Rawls, *Political Liberalism* (1993)).

60 *See* powell, *"Racing, " supra* note 1, at 99–112.

61 *See* Loving v. Virginia, 388 US 1, 12 (1966).

62 *See generally* Wright, *supra* note 20.

63 *See* Goforth, *supra* note 6, at 9–11. Mulatto describes persons having from three-eighths to five-eighths black blood; Quadroon refers to those persons having one fourth black blood; and Octoroon defines those persons having one eighth or any trace of black blood.

64 *See id* at 14; *see also* Bijan Gilanshah, *Multiracial Minorities: Erasing the Color Line,* 12 LAW and INEQ. J. 183 (1993). The 1900 census dropped Octoroon, Mulatto, and Quadroon from the census. The 1940 census by contrast only had two racial categories white and non-white.

65 *See,* e.g., Plessy v. Ferguson, 163 US 537, 549 (1896), *overruled by* Brown v. Board of Educ., 347 US 483 (1954) (stating that "in any mixed community, the reputation of belonging to the dominant race, in this instance the white race, is property"); Cheryl I. Harris, *Whiteness as Property,* 106 HARV. L REV. 1709, 1758–59 (1993) (discussing the material significance of whiteness); *see also* Harvey M. Applebaum, *Miscegenation Statutes: A Constitutional and Social Problem,* 53 GEO. L.J. 49 (1965) (arguing that whites were only concerned with racial mixing that polluted the white race, and that only a few states applied anti-miscegenation laws to the mixing of non-whites); Harold L. Hodgkinson, *What Should We Call People? Race, Class, and the Census for 2000,* 77 PHI DELTA KAPPAN 173, 174

(1995) (discussing the restrictions on those classified as non-white in the 1890 Census).

66 *See* Gilanshah, *supra note* 64, at 183. Some have noted that the anti-miscegenation laws did not stop racial mixing but denied official status to racial mixing. This is clear even under slavery as there was no sanction against the slave owner for producing children with his slaves.

67 *See Plessy v.* Ferguson, 163 US 537, 549 (1896).

68 *See* Harris, *supra* note 65, at 1730–1 (1993). The article observed that:

> [P]roperty is a legal construct by which selected private interests are protected and upheld . . . When the law recognizes, either implicitly or explicitly, the settled expectations of whites built on the privileges and benefits produced by white supremacy, it acknowledges and reinforces a property interest in whiteness that reproduces black subordination.

> *Id.*

69 *See generally* Wright, *supra* note 20. The benefits of whiteness during the "separate but equal" era illuminate the actual and psychological disabilities attached to being black. For many being white automatically ensured higher economic returns in the short term, as well as greater economic, political, and social security in the long run. Being white meant gaining access to a set of public and private privileges that materially and permanently guaranteed basic subsistence needs and survival. Being white increased the possibility of controlling critical aspects of one's life rather than being the object of another's domination. These societal benefits connected to whiteness were the result of statutes and court holdings that determined who was, and who was not, white. The legislatures and courts were at the center of a system that routinely and purposefully distributed rights and opportunities along racial lines.

70 *See* john a. powell, *Transformative Action: A Strategy for Ending Racial Hierarchy and Achieving True Democracy in Brazil, South Africa and the United States* (1997) (article is forthcoming) [hereinafter powell, *Transformative Action*]. *See generally* I. K. Sundiata, *Late Twentieth Century Patterns of Race Relations in Brazil and the United States* 48 PHYLON 65 (1987).

71 *See* Loving v. Virginia, 388 US 1, 12 (1966).

72 *See* powell, *Transformative Actions supra* note 70.

73 *See generally* Winant, *supra* note 41.

74 *See generally* powell, *Transformative Action, supra* note 70 (discussing the negative aspects of a proliferation of race-based categories).

75 *See* Paul R. Spickard, *Mixed Blood: Intermarriage and Ethnic Identity in Twentieth-Century America* 329–31 (1989) (discussing how multiracialism might be used to destabilize racial hierarchy).

76 *See generally* Lazarre, *supra* note 56.

77 *See generally* Chua, *supra* note 42; powell, *Transformative Action, supra* note 70. Because our racial caste system is also based on pigmentocracy, there has been a history of whites, and even some blacks, favoring lighter color blacks over darker skinned blacks. There has also been preference for having mixed race blacks work in the master's house.

78 *See generally* David R. Roediger, *Towards the Abolition of Whiteness: Essays on Race, Politics, and Working Class History* (1994).
    The lack of full acceptance has been complicated. There has been a history of mistrust of mixed race blacks that is based on the fear that mixed race blacks have aligned

themselves with the white master. There has also been the claim that mixed race blacks look down on darker skinned blacks. But it is also clear that some of the approbation toward light skinned and mixed race blacks was not the internal ambivalence in the untraced blacks. There may be other reasons for blacks with different parents to want a designation that reflects their lineage. But any appropriation of whiteness without an examination of whiteness may easily slide back into our racist practices. What is clear is that if the existing racial categories do not provide for a real home for mixed race people, there will be a need for new categories. There is at least some suggestion that the push for mixed race categories is coming from the white parent of a mixed parentage after there has been a separation. white parents with mixed race children may have less interest in working at raising their children as black. Similar issues may come up in transracial and transnational adoptions.

79 *See* Gotanda, *supra* note 8, at 8. *See generally* Goldberg, *supra* note 25.
80 *See* Omi, *supra* note 12. *See generally* Goldberg, *supra* note 25.
81 See powell, *"Racing,"* *supra* note 1, at 99–118.
82 Baldwin, *supra* note 56, at 690.
83 *See generally* Roediger, *supra* note 78.
84 *See* Noel Ignatiev, *How to Be a Race Traitor: Six Ways to Fight Being White,* UTNE READER, Nov. – Dec. 1994, at 85.
85 *See id.*
86 *See* Audre Lorde, *An Open Letter to Mary Daly,* in *This Bridge Called My Back: Writings by Radical Women of Color* 94 – 97 (Cherríe Moraga and Gloria Anzaldúa eds, 1981) (suggesting that the master's tools will never dismantle the master's house).

10

Multiracial Asians: Models of Ethnic Identity

Maria P. P. Root

Nearly a decade ago Stephen Murphy-Shigematsu encouraged Asian-Americanists to reconsider the question "Who is an Asian American?"[1] Unfortunately, the fact that race has assumed a synonymity with ethnicity and culture in the US complicates the identity process and notion of group belonging for many multiracial Asians, domestically and internationally.[2] The rates of inter-marriage for Asian-Americans require that we redefine who is Asian-American. Rates of intermarriage in some groups in Los Angeles County are approximating 50 percent or higher. Kitano and others studying intermarriage have found that each succeeding generation of a group intermarries at a higher rate. One of the inevitable results of this racial mixing is an increased presence of multiracial children of Asian-American heritage. For example, the 1992 US Bureau of the Census documents that the number of children born of multiracial Japanese-American ancestry is approaching the numbers of these children of "monoracial" ancestry.[3] Eggebeen, Chew, and Uhlenberg note that a significant number of the multiracial households in the US comprise a person of some Asian ancestry through marriage, birth, and/or adoption.[4]

For US raised Asians of multiple heritages there is no evidence of psychopathology or maladjustment of their parents in Hawaii or their offspring in the related study in Hawaii.[5] Similar findings of community studies of multi-racial persons of Asian descent in Seattle and of a college student population on the east coast find no psychopathology in multiracial Asian heritage people. In contrast, the experiences of Amerasians from Vietnam, now in the US, offer a very different picture.[6] Poor adjustment is related to the traumatic experiences that arose at the intersection of living in a war-torn Vietnam. Individuals are often fatherless and persecuted because of this multiracial status, with mothers construed as bargirls and prostitutes. The level of social and political persecution often led to these children quitting school early, further compromising their social chances for work and status.

Multiracial Asian-Americans challenge current definitions and assumptions about culture and ethnicity in relationship to race.[7] Historically, hybridity has a negative valence and legacy both here and in various Asian countries. For example, many Vietnamese Amerasians suffered social and political persecution due to their racially mixed heritage which was often confounded with father-lessness and contact with an American.[8] Wagatsuma documented the emotional maltreatment of racially mixed Japanese people in Japan. Williams noted the evidence of racial hierarchicalization in Japan visited upon multi-heritage Asians. In the US a host of pejorative terms connote popular assumptions of the racially mixed person.[9]

Pearl S. Buck coined the term Amerasian in her novel, *East Wind, West Wind,* which originally referred to children of Asian mothers and American fathers, left fatherless in Asia. This term resurfaced when it was applied to the children of American fathers and Asian mothers left behind in Asia during and after the Vietnam War.[10] Whereas this term initially connoted binational parentage *and* multiracial heritage, its current use is the most inclusive for persons of mixed-race Asian heritage; it may or may not connote international parentage. Unfortunately, when used solely as an ethnic term in America, it connotes the marginalized status of Asian-Americans, i.e. the continued belief that Asians are not really Americans. In the racial politics of the US, it subtly reinforces black-white racial polarity.[11]

Even in Hawaii, a state with a high proportion of racially mixed people, and a pride in the racial melange, students at a community college on Oahu provided a multitude of pejorative terms to connote racially mixed persons.[12] When I ask students in my classes for nondenigrating terms for multi-heritage Asians, they have a difficult time coming up with terms such as Amerasian, Eurasian, AfroAsian, *hapa,* mestizo, or even Asian. Although a bit uncomfortable, the vocabulary that denigrates this experience is much more readily available. These labels often refer to animals or terms used to indicate that one is an inauthentic Asian.

Whereas there may be debate as to whether being multiracial constitutes a cultural experience, it clearly constitutes a phenomenological experience because of the meaning of race in this country.[13] Several variables mediate this experience, e.g., gender, generation, community, phenotype, sexual orientation, community acceptance, family socialization etc.[14] However, there are shared phenomeno-logical experiences that make it possible for persons of mixed heritage to assume some bond with one another – and with other multiracial people who do not have Asian ancestry. "What are you?" Questions, suspiciousness of loyalties, under-estimation of cultural competence, mistaken identities (Latino, Native American, Polynesian, etc.), ethnic legitimacy questions and tests, triangle stares (strangers trying to understand the child's phenotype from pointedly looking back and forth between the person and their parents' phenotypes), exotification (i.e. objectifi-cation – particularly of women), and not being counted as a "real Asian" are common, shared experiences. For many multi-heritage Asian-Americans, these experiences result in an acquired extra sense of vigilance to the environment, and an added sensitivity to one's physical appearance.[15] The complexity of estab-lishing a racial and ethnic self in relationship to a nation that is structured around race – and a monoracial model driven by assumptions that racial purity exists and is desirable and somehow necessary or sufficient for the retention of cultural heritage – can make the process difficult.[16]

Asian-Americans have probably subscribed to such concepts around racially mixed peoples, as have many other Americans. As used in the US, the definition of race assumes a notion that "pure race" exists. From a philosophical perspective, Zack argues that the difficulty we have in deconstructing race and improving its race relations is that the opposite of race is not racelessness, but impure race or acknowledged hybridity.[17] In a nation with a rigid mono-racial model for a template on interpreting race, notions of pure race are very entrenched, despite the increasing existence of racially mixed people.[18] The cognitive dissonance between the prevailing model and reality results in the ignorance, misperceptions, and mistrust of racially mixed persons. Ironically, Mass suggests that these attitudes towards mixed-race Asians that exclude them from communities or ethnic membership may cause some of the loss of members to the Asian-American community.[19] It may also result in colonial strategies such as authenticity tests posed to multi-heritage Asian-Americans by other multi-heritage Asian-Americans to establish legitimacy through oppressiveness. While Filipinos have considered themselves a mixed-race people, some of the younger Filipino-Americans raised in the US are internalizing the models of race which result in oppressive attitudes and behaviors towards Filipino-Americans of contemporary mixed parentage.[20]

Models of Identity Development

Much about the multiracial experience has changed because of historical factors.[21] The Civil Rights Movement, the repeal of anti-miscegenation laws, integration of neighborhoods, and a decrease in white opposition to interracial marriage constitute the climate in which multiracial people currently reach adulthood. For example, the common presence of mixed heritage children of Asian ancestry on the west coast, particularly, removes a feature of isolation that predominated in the experience of Amerasians a generation earlier.[22]

Consider the functions that multiracial identity serve at this point in time.[23] First, self-definition is empowerment. Second, asserting such an identity creates a different dialogue on the social, psychological, economic, and political construction and irrationality of race in this country as it strains the "five-race" framework formalized by the government in the 1970s.[24] Third, it provides a foundation for collective action to form a reference group and potential political coalitions to protect human rights of persons who do not fit neatly into the five-race framework.[25] It blurs the boundaries by introducing confusion about definitions of race, and thus, group membership. Lastly, it challenges us to re-define how central race has been to the definition of ethnicity in this country. Clearly these functions are necessary because the Asian-American community continues to subscribe to oppressive rules of race within a broader, racially-preoccupied society. The multiracial agenda challenges racial construction; often, as it is ironically pointed out, the historical oppressor and the oppressed are now using the same politics and definitions of race to attempt to silence multiracial people's attempt at new dialogues.

Rather than review the different models of racial identity, suffice it to say that the monoracial identity theories are largely stage models.[26] The majority of these models have been developed around the resolution of black identity in this country except for Atkinson et al. who offered a model to encompass the experience of all groups. These theories are remarkably similar in capturing the prevalent experience for persons of color. These researchers suggested an individual progresses through stages of existential conflict around the human need to belong and to be valued within their racialized existence. Without this value, the individual must struggle with the meaning of existence, the unfairness of life, and the delusional reality that surrounds them around racial politics. Responding to clinical data and observation, Parham introduced the notion of recycling through stages to explain the variance in identity lived by people of African heritage.[27] This change suggests resolution more complex than previously proposed. And more recently, Cross has offered additional interpretation of his model to account for variance in black identity.[28]

Kich observed that a normal part of the struggle of persons of multiracial heritage is to resolve the difference in perceptions of self and others' perception of self in a nation which offers delusional, incomplete models of racial existence.[29] The identity crisis around multiraciality has kinship with sexual orientation identity crises where one is expected to fit neatly into exclusively heterosexually – or homosexually – oriented social constructions.[30] Identity is a social construction in any society. What may differ are the dimensions around which belonging and acceptance are centered and the dimensions around which one is marginalized.[31] Thus, our identities are necessarily affected by the meaning of representation that individuals have of one another.[32]

Thornton noted that models of multiracial identity have moved from problematic ones to models suggesting a variant experience.[33] In order to understand the multi-heritage experience and the process and achievement of identities, complex models of identity and belonging must expand beyond a black-white polarized model of pure race. The human mind is able to synthesize and integrate experiences that have been deemed mutually exclusive. Hall showed that even before this contemporary generation of multiracial Asians, many participants in her study of black-Japanese were able to assume a duality or complexity, often misinterpreted as misguided notions of identity or inauthenticity.[34] Studies since then document the prevalence of multiple identities and fluid identities among multiracial people, though often perceived by the outsider as confusing. The outsider's confusion rests in their reality that resides upon a monoracial model of race relations. Kich suggests that the provision of a multiracial label by parents is helpful.[36] In order for many multiracial people to make peace with themselves, they must individually construct a reality that allows for duality and multiplicity, with an awareness that one may be perceived and categorized very differently than one perceives one's self. These challenges may increase awareness of the politicization of living not just around racial issues.[37]

The multiracial context challenges current models on at least six counts. First, the generic retreat into an ethnic community, common across monoracial models of racial identity, does not guarantee the multiracial Asian-American refuge. For example, the racism of different Asian-American groups may not regard a racially mixed Asian as a "real Asian." It may also discriminate against a multiracial who, is also African-American, a reflection on an oppressed group's internalization and subsequent projection of a hierarchically arranged racial system.[38] In some communities, the African-American community will be highly suspicious of the person who also insists on identifying simultaneously as Asian-American, interpreting the insistence on duality as a way of disavowing or diminishing one's African-American heritage.

Second, simultaneous aspects of other identities that inform the core of our existence are not considered in these models, e.g., sexual orientation, class, gender, or nationality. Race will not always be a person's primary identity, although it informs one's experience in the world.

Third, these previous models have not been able to address the shifting foreground and background of aspects of identity that are important and governed by changing contexts,[39] e.g., when is one's primary identity female rather than Asian – and can you truly separate the gendered experience of racial existence? When is it Asian rather than multiracial?

Fourth, the models have been implicily informed by a limited sample. Initially, the models were informed by a generation that came to maturity during the 1960s and 1970s. The later cohorts of participants informing theory have almost exclusively been college students which is often a circumscribed age and class cohort at the major universities in this country.

Fifth, physical appearance has not been directly addressed in these theories. The multiracial experience has a phenomenological aspect of physical appearance that is not yet well understood in how it informs or when it informs identity. Racialized identification by others utilizes physical markers as well as social markers: color, hair, and facial features. Explorations of the role of phenotype may need to explore each of these aspects: coloring of hair, skin, and eyes; hair color and texture; facial physiognomy in terms of eye, nose and lip shapes. The historical issues around colorism abound in all ethnic communities of color, though little work exists on this issue among Asian-Americans. The physical experience of being multiracial may even interact with gender, where physical appearance continues to be a significant social variable in women's social worth.

Sixth, for those persons who are also of European origins, differentiation from "whiteness" or even denigration from that which is European may not be a normal process for many multiracial persons. This would perpetuate a splitting of one's self or from some aspect of one's family. Simultaneously, given the racial politics of this country, Amerasians of European origin do not know the experience of living white. As Sartre notes, humans appear to be keen on spotting the "other."[40] Thus, while an Amerasian may look very white to a mono-racial

Asian, the majority of white people spot the "other" in them as evidenced by the frequently asked question, "what are you?" Given the belief of racial purity by many Asians, these people are also alert to the "other" features of someone who has non-Asian ancestry.

Whereas a few stage models have been proposed within the multiracial literature,[41] many of the contemporary studies actually move away from stage models. This change makes sense since contemporary conceptualizations of multiraciality emphasize the dynamicity, fluidity, and simultaneousness of identities. We might be more productive to accept the likelihood of increasing variability in the construction of identity for persons of multiple heritages since there are many possible identities that multiracial people might assume. Furthermore, these identities might change over a lifetime. The choices were influenced by social and environmental forces such as history, family, community, socioeconomic factors, geography, the period of history in which one grew up, and the possession of other oppressed statuses. In a previous article, I suggested four different ways in which a person might identify.[42] In summary: (a) people might identify as other people identify them, which carries implicit applications of rules of hypodescent (e.g., a person of Eurasian ancestry identifies as Asian-American, a person of Afroasian ancestry identifies as African-American); (b) people might carry a similar identity but derive it from feelings of kinship having been isolated or raised within a single community or in a particular family; (c) people identify as both or all (e.g., Chicano and Filipino-American); (d) people refuse to identify according to the established categories of race. An important part of this conceptual model was that no endpoint is necessarily better than the other. Contextual and historical experiences guide the formation of these identities which are malleable over one's lifetime.

In my attempts to understand commonalities and differences among models, I considered what broader aspects of human nature and socialization embedded in history might help us understand the complexity inherent in identity. The identity models, heretofore, have been oblique to other secondary statuses. For example, Bradshaw noted that one of the generic phases of monoracial identity is to seek refuge in the racial community that has been demeaned.[43] She observed, however, that such refuge does not always give support to women. How is the appreciation and resolution of gender identity accomplished if women cut off from the larger community of women? Recent conceptualization on sexual orientation would similarly suggest that to seek refuge in one's racially oppressed community may heighten one's feeling of difference and oppression along lines of sexual orientation. Thus, race may not always be the most salient identity; racial identity resolution likely interacts with the resolution of other secondary status since they become issues due to the consequences of oppression.[44] In summary, it seems that the reality for many people is that there is a fluid movement between real and symbolic communities implicitly important to aspects of one's identity. Consequently one needs to attend to aspects of one's roots differentially, depending on which ones need most nurturing in a given social, political, or geographic context and in a given developmental phase of one's life.

At least three general processes of identity exploration and integration may guide how we come to perceive and project ourselves. These processes, *exposure/absorption, competition/stratification,* and *reflective appraisal* mirror processes apparent in general life stages.[45] However, I do not propose these processes as sequential. In fact, they can be concurrent.

Exposure/absorption is the process of orienting and assigning meaning to new material. With input from others, one learns to interpret new information and absorb it into schemes through a schema of constructive differentiation or destructive differentiation. Constructive differentiation uses difference to add breadth and complexity to understanding difference. In contrast, destructive differentiation forecloses full exposure to the meaning of difference before a meaning is constructed.

Competition/Stratification allows us to categorize information and reformulate material. In an individualistic society, this process often has an orientation to positioning one's self in the most favorable light. This orientation sets up competition and judgement around superior and inferior for the sake of self-definition often without sensitivity to the collective's or group's goals. Thus, this process hierarchicalizes and advances one's schemes in a way that only one perspective can exist. In its most extreme form, one can use this process to destroy those who do not affirm one's existence or challenge one's priviliged position.

Reflective Appraisal is something that many people return to or engage in more as one acknowledges one's mortality or attempts to respond from a code of ethics. It fosters connection back to humanity and the needs of the whole. It uses hindsight for learning and questions what is important. In this process, there is a rearranging of priorities in which the good of the collective can stand before the priorities of the individual.

In line with what I am proposing, I do not suggest we throw out stage models. Rather, I suggest we must move towards more complex multiracial Asians models that help inform us about our interactive nature as people. Identity is no exception. Our status as women, as sexual minorities, as a Filipino rather than a Taiwanese or Japanese, as a fifty year old rather than a twenty-eight-year old all inform the identity process in a rich way.

I have proposed an ecological model that focuses on the intersection of perceived significant experiences through the lenses of gender, class, regional history of race relations and generation.[46] Within these larger frameworks are the inherited influences into which one is born such as language, parents' identities, nativity, presence of extended family, given names and nicknames, home values, sexual orientation, and phenotype. These interact with traits such as temperament, social skills, talents and coping skills. And these interact with our experiences in various communities such as home, school and work, community, friends, and being outside the community which knows you. All of these variables constitute lenses which further inform our experience. Any one of these lenses can be a main lens through which experience is informed. For example, sexual orientation may provide a salient lens through which other statuses and social locations in one's life are understood. Beginning ecological frameworks on multiracial identity have been previously offered by Miller and Stephan.[47] Such a framework allows for the dynamicity that we see with multiracial identity.[48]

Conclusion

Expanding the definition of Asian to include Amerasians of Latino, African, and Native American origins challenges the Asian-American community to deconstruct race and to challenge the racism inherent in our communities. The sins of our forerunners to the US remain much as an "original sin" around racism.[49] Asian-Americans, despite being an oppressed group in this country, are not exempt from being guilty in perpetuating this "original sin." Constructive differentiation (tolerance for ambiguity of meaning, resistance to hierarchicalizing difference) versus destructive differentiation (differentiation out of defensiveness and fear) will be essential for supporting and recognizing the voice of multiracial Asian-Americans. The construction of Asian-American identity has been dynamic over time. The multiracial experience extends, for the new millenneum, this dynamic process of identity.

Notes

1 Stephen Murphy-Shigematsu, "Addressing Issues of Biracial/Bicultural Asian Americans" in *Reflections on Shattered Windows: Promises and Prospects for Asian American Studies,* Gary Y. Okihiro et al., eds (Pullman: Washington State University Press, 1988), 111–16.
2 Teresa Kay Williams, "Prism Lives: Identity of Binational Amerasians," in *Racially Mixed People in America,* Maria P. P. Root, ed. (Thousand Oaks, CA: Sage Publications, 1992), 250–64.
3 US Census Bureau, 1992.
4 David Eggebeen, Kenneth Chew, and Peter Uhlenberg, "American Children in Multiracial Households," *Sociological Perspectives,* 32 (1989), 65–85.
5 Ronald Johnson and Craig Nagoshi, "The Adjustment of Offspring of Within-group and Interracial/Intercultural Marriages: A Comparison of Personality Factor Scores," *Journal of Marriage and the Family,* 48 (1986), 279–84.
6 J. Kirk Felsman, Mark C. Johnson, Frederick T. L. Leong, and Irene C. Felsman, *Vietnamese Amerasians: Practical Implications of Current Research,* Contract : 895 F463592 (Office of Refugee Resettlement, Family Support Administration, Department of Health and Human Services, 1989); P. LaBarbera, J. D. Nicassio Coburn, and R. Finley, "The Psychosocial Adjustment of the Amerasian Refugees: Findings from the Personality Inventory for Children," *Journal of Nervous and Mental Disease,* 174 (1986), 541–4.
7 Michael C. Thornton, "Hidden Agendas, Identity Theories, and Multiracial People" in *The Multiracial Experience: Racial Borders as the New Frontier,* Maria P. P. Root, ed. (Thousand Oaks, CA: Sage Publications, 1996), 101–20.
8 Caroline K. Valverde, "From Dust to Gold: The Vietnamese Amerasian Experience" in *Racially Mixed People in America,* 144, 161.

9   Teresa Kay Williams, "Prism Lives"; Teresa Kay Williams, "The Theater of Identity, (Multi-) Race and Representation of Eurasians and Afroasians" in *American Mixed Race: The Culture of Microdiversity* (Lanham, MD: Rowman and Littlefield Publishers Inc., 1995), 79–96. Also Jo Wagatsuma, "Mixed Blood Children in Japan: An Exploratory Study," *Journal of Asian Affairs*, 2 (1976), 9–16.

10 Pearl S. Buck, *East Wind, West Wind* (New York: John Day, 1930).

11 Christine C. I. Hall, "The Ethnic Identity of Racially Mixed People: A Study of Black-Japanese," Ph.D. dissertation, Los Angeles: University of California, 1980; Michael C. Thornton, "A Social History of a Multiethnic Identity: The Case of Black-Japanese Americans," Ph.D. dissertation, University of Michigan, 1983.

12 Maria P. P. Root, "Perceptions of Racially Mixed People in Honolulu, Hawaii," unpublished manuscript, 1991.

13 Michael C. Thornton, "Hidden Agendas, Identity Theories, and Multiracial People"; Cynthia L. Nakashima, "An Invisible Monster: The Creation and Denial of Mixed-Race People in America" in *Racially Mixed People in America*, 162–78; Teresa Kay Williams, *American Mixed Race*.

14 Robin L. Miller, "The Human Ecology of Multiracial Identity" in *Racially Mixed People in America*, 24–36; Cookie Stephan, "Mixed-heritage Individuals: Ethnic Identity Traits Characteristics" in *Racially Mixed People in America*, 50–63; Teresa Kay Williams, "Prism Lives"; Maria P. P. Root, "The Biracial Baby Boom: Understanding Ecological Constructions of Racial Identity in the Twenty-First Century," in *Racial, Ethnic, Cultural Identity and Human Development: Implications for Education*, R. H. Sheets and E. Hollins, eds (Mahwah, New Jersey: Erlbaum, in press).

15 Carla Bradshaw, "Beauty and the Beast: On Racial Ambiguity," in *Racially Mixed People in America*, 77–90; Cynthia L. Nakashima, "An Invisible Monster"; Maria P. P. Root, "Resolving the 'Other' Status: Identity Development of Biracial Individuals," in L. S. Brown and Maria P. P. Root, eds, *Diversity and Complexity in Feminist Therapy* (New York: Haworth Press, 1990), 185–206; Maria P. P. Root, "Mixed Race Women," in *Women of Color: Integrating Ethnic and Gender Identities in Psychotherapy*, Lillian Comas-Diaz and Beverly Greene, eds (New York: Guilford Press, 1994), 455–78; Teresa Kay Williams, "Prism Lives."

16 Cookie Stephan, "Mixed-heritage Individuals."

17 Naomi Zack, *American Mixed Race: The Culture of Microdiversity* (Lanham, MD: Rowman and Littlefield Publishers Inc., 1995).

18 Cynthia L. Nakashima, "An Invisible Monster"; Michael C. Thornton, "Hidden Agendas, Identity Theories, and Multiracial People."

19 Amy Iwasaki Mass, "Interracial Japanese Americans: The Best of Both Worlds or the End of the Japanese American Community?" in *Racially Mixed People in America*, 265–79.

20 Maria P. P. Root, "Contemporary Mixed Heritage Filipinos: Fighting Colonized Identities," in *Filipino Americans: Transformation and Identity* (Thousand Oaks, CA: Sage Publications, in press).

21 Cynthia L. Nakashima, "Voices from the Movement: Approaches to Multiraciality," in *The Multiracial Experience*, 79–97.

22 Maria P. P. Root, "Multiracial Asian Americans: Changing the Face of Asian America" in *Handbook of Asian American Psychology*, L. C. Lee and N. W. Zane, eds (Thousand Oaks, CA: Sage Publications, In Press).

23 Maria P. P. Root, "The Psychological Browning of America" in *American Mixed*

Race: The Culture of Microdiversity, Naomi Zack, ed. (Lanham, MD: Rowman and Littlefield Publishers Inc., 1995), 231–6.

24 Roger Sanjek, "Intermarriage and the Future of Races in the United States," in *Race,* Steven Gregory and Roger Sanjek, eds (New Brunswick, NJ: Rutgers University Press, 1994), 103–30.

25 Deborah A. Ramirez, "Multiracial Identity in a Color Conscious World," in *The Multiracial Experience,* 49–62; Carlos A. Fernandez, "Government Classification of Multiracial/Multiethnic People," in *The Multiracial Experience,* 15–36.

26 Donald R. Atkinson, George Morten, and Derald W. Sue, "A Minority Identity Development Model," in *Counseling American Minorities,* Donald R. Atkinson, George Morten, and Derald W. Sue, eds (Dubuque, IA: W. C. Brown, 1979), 35–52; William Cross, *Shades of Black: Diversity in African American Identity* (Philadelphia: Temple University Press, 1991); Janet E. Helms, *White Racial Identity: Theory, Research, and Practice* (New York: Greenwood Press, 1990); Thomas A. Parham, "Cycles of Nigrescence," *The Counseling Psychologist,* 17 (1989), 187–226.

27 Thomas A. Parham, "Cycles of Nigrescence."

28 William Cross, 1989; William Cross and P. Fhagen-Smith, "Nigresence and Ego Identity Development: Accounting for Differential Black Identity Patterns," *Counseling Across Cultures.* Pederson et al., eds (Thousand Oaks, CA: Sage Publications: 1996), 108–23.

29 George Kitahara Kich, "The Developmental Process of Asserting a Biracial, Bicultural Identity" in *Racially Mixed People in America,* 304–17.

30 Karen M. Allman, "(Un)Natural Boundaries: Mixed Race, Gender, and Sexuality," in *The Multiracial Experience,* 277–90; George Kich in "The Margins of Sex and Race: Difference, Marginality, and Flexibility" in *The Multiracial Experience,* 263–76; Teresa Kay Williams, *American Mixed Race.*

31 Helena J. Herschel, "Therapeutic Perspectives on Biracial Identity Formation and Internalized Oppression" in *American Mixed Race,* 169–81.

32 Henri Tajfel, "Human Groups and Social Categories: Studies" in *Social Psychology* (Cambridge: Cambridge University Press, 1981); Michael C. Thornton, "Hidden Agendas, Identity Theories, and Multiracial People."

33 Michael C. Thornton, "Hidden Agendas, Identity Theories, and Multiracial People."

34 Christine I. Hall, "The Ethnic Identity of Racially Mixed People: A Study of Black-Japanese"; Christine I. Hall, "Please Choose One: Ethnic Identity Choices for Biracial Individuals," in *Racially Mixed People in America,* 250–64.

35 Cookie Stephan, "Mixed-heritage Individuals"; Teresa Kay Williams, "Prism Lives."

36 George Kitahara Kich, "The Developmental Process of Asserting a Biracial, Bicultural Identity."

37 Stephan Murphy-Shigematsu, "Voices of Amerasians: Ethnicity, Identity, and Empowerment" in *Interracial Japanese Americans,* Ph.D. dissertation, Harvard University, 1987.

38 Christine I. Hall, "The Ethnic Identity of Racially Mixed People"; Michael C. Thornton, "A Social History of a Multiethnic Identity"; Teresa Kay Williams, "Prism Lives."

39 Maria P. P. Root, "The Biracial Baby Boom: Understanding Ecological Constructions of Racial Identity in the Twenty-First Century," in *Racial, Ethnic, Cultural Identity and Human Development: Implications for Education,* R H. Sheets and E. Hollins, eds (Mahwah, NJ: Erlbaum, in press).

40 Jean-Paul Sartre, *Critique of Dialectical Reasoning: Theory of Practical Ensembles*, trans., A. Sheridan-Smith (London: New Left Books, 1976).

41 Christine Kerwin, "Racial Identity Development in Biracial Children of Black/White Racial Heritage," Ph.D. dissertation, Forham University, 1991; George Kitahara Kich, "The Developmental Process of Asserting a Biracial, Bicultural Identity"; James H. Jacobs, "Black/White Interracial Families, Marital Process and Identity Development in Young Children," Ph.D. dissertation, Wright Institute, 1977; James H. Jacobs "Identity Development in Biracial Children," in *Racially Mixed People in America*, 109–206.

42 Maria P.P. Root, "Resolving the 'Other' Status."

43 Carla Bradshaw, 1994.

44 Karen Allman, "(Un)Natural Boundaries"; George Kitahara Kich, "The Margins of Sex and Race."

45 Maria P. P. Root, in press.

46 Ibid.

47 Robin Miller, "The Human Ecology of Multiracial Identity"; Cookie Stephan, "Mixed-heritage Individuals."

48 Christine I. Hall, "The Ethnic Identity of Racially Mixed People" and "Please Choose One"; Teresa Kay Williams, "Prism Lives."

49 Christine M. Chao, "A Bridge over Troubled Waters: Being Eurasian in the US of A." *Racism in the Lives of Women: Testimony, Theory, and Guides to Antiracist Practice* (New York: Harrington Park Press), 33–44.

11

Cipherspace: Latino Identity Past and Present

J. Jorge Klor de Alva

Al mestizo el Diablo lo hizo,
al indito el Dios bendito.
An old refrain still new.

The Empire's Need for Control

For over five centuries the social reality of the Americas has been primarily shaped by the ever evolving nature of what can be called "ethnoracial relations." Whether the aim has been winning battles or gaining status, the extent to which the participants have been defined as distinct, and their responses to the real or imposed differences, have profoundly affected the likelihood of their and their descendants' success or failure. Consequently, limiting or promoting the construction of ethnic groups and controlling their interactions has at all times been the critical task for nation builders and their enemies. However, given the amorphous but charged character of collective identities, the policing of ethnic boundaries has been both a futile exercise and the occasion for the resentment and isolation that continues to breed new social actors.[1]

Spanish colonial officials understood these truths from the beginning. Hoping to limit the turbulent effects of the proliferation of hybrids, in the course of the colonial period they penned a tangle of contradictory legislation. The often draconian rules – enacted in the hope that a place and role could be fixed for each emerging hybrid group – represent the myriad ways in which colonial leaders struggled against the increasing social disorder by attempting to restrict the rights and obligations associated with every major activity. No area of everyday life was meant to escape regulation, including the determination of who paid taxes, who could be educated, who could preach, who could rule, who could be free, and who could marry whom. Since social reality refused to cooperate, the crown's legal framework was constantly revised, forced to reflect both the hybrids' capacity to thwart the intentions of the legislators and the shifts in the dominant ideas concerning the nature and acceptable roles of non- or part-Spaniards. Significantly, it was the sweeping demographic changes that brought about the specific modes of resistance, the adaptive strategies, and the legal adjustments. First, the sharp drop in the native populations, devastated by epidemics and famines, left the colonial world with recurring labor shortages and immense tracts of seemingly underused land. Second, this phenomenon coincided with the arrival of large numbers of Europeans whose needs placed unprecedented pressure on the declining percentage of Indian workers. Third, the increasing demand for labor fueled the importation of large numbers of enslaved Africans, who now came in close and continuous contact with the indigenes. Fourth, widespread imbalances in sex ratios combined with the other demographic changes to hasten widespread miscegenation.

The Regulation of Reproduction

Knowing the success of the overseas enterprise rested on peaceful interactions between natives and Spaniards, as early as 1501 intermarriage was reluctantly permitted by the crown. But this pragmatic legislation was a stop-gap measure, meant to apply only until white females could be sent to the Indies. By 1539, after much mistreatment of Indian women by "encomenderos" (grant holders of native labor), the latter were given three years to marry, send for their wives, or risk losing their encomiendas (CDFS, 1953–62, I: 193). In effect, although intermarriage with American Indians was legalized almost two decades before the fall of the Aztecs, it was not officially promoted or easily tolerated unless the Indian nobility was involved, the assumption being that through this exception "all the caciques [local native leaders] would soon be Spaniards" (CDFS, 1953–62, I: 64).

Marriage with Africans or their descendants was a different matter. First, critical economic issues were involved if one of the partners was a slave. Marriage, for instance, could be used to gain freedom for the children or the spouse. Second, to the shame of a slave past was added the taint of a possible Moslem background, a serious threat to the status of all Spaniards seeking the privileges reserved for "old" Christians (i.e. those free of Jewish or Muslim ancestors). Because any status-seeking Spaniard sought to avoid this negative combination, only a miniscule number of Spanish-African marriages took place. In fact, relations with black Africans rarely surpassed concubinage, with rape a common alternative, and when relations were sanctified by the church, discriminatory regulations against Spaniards were likely to limit the family's fortunes. By 1805, the regulatory environment had become so restrictive that persons of "pure blood" now required the approval of the viceroy or the "audiencia" if they wanted to marry "elements of Negro and Mulatto origin" (CDFS, 1953–62, III: 794–6).

African-Indian unions were also discouraged and their prohibition was repeatedly sought. Local regulations went so far as to call for the castration of transgressors, although this brutality was explicitly forbidden by the crown

(Rumazo González, 1934: 386–8). The common opinion on the part of Indian and colonial leaders was that Africans, regardless of status, should be encouraged to marry only among themselves in order to avoid concubinage and the social disruption in the native communities that followed from involuntary or transient relations between the two groups. In fact, this form of miscegenation was assumed to represent so great a threat to social peace that, while serving as viceroy of New Spain, Martín Enríquez petitioned Philip II (in vain) to request from the Pope either a total prohibition against African-Indian marriages or a requirement that their children be considered slaves (Marshall, 1939: 173). Still, due to the small number of African women and the strong sanctions against inter-marriage, free and enslaved Africans had little choice but to seek partners primarily among Indian and, later, the poorer of the dark-skinned mixed women. Consequently, prior to 1650 Indian-African intermixtures were the most likely source of the free descendants of Africans. And the offspring of these mixtures most likely composed a significant portion of the so-called "Negro" slaves, es-pecially of those unscrupulous masters who refused to recognize the freedom of the mixed children of native women (Forbes, 1988: 189).

In the end, any attempt to regulate the number and quality of ethnic groups was doomed. Neither colonial prohibitions nor Indian opposition to miscegena-tion was successful in keeping Spaniards, Indians, and Africans out of each other's gene pools. Instead, the number and variety of "castas" (mixed peoples) expanded, unfettered by the many restrictions on intermarriage, the high volume of discriminatory legislation, and the social opprobrium aiming to restrict the ambitions of the unruly hybrids.

The Labeling of Difference

The near absence of European women in the Americas during the early decades led to the birth of a considerable number of genetically mixed offspring. But this biological fact did not in itself imply that a new, ethnically distinct community was being created. In order for an assortment of people to be socially or officially recognized as a "racially" or culturally different populace, when the only distin-guishing characteristic they share is a set of distinct physical features, there must exist a social need for them which is facilitated, or at least not stymied, by their physical or cultural differences. This need has historically appeared when changing material conditions (e.g., technological, financial, demographic) or governmental demands (e.g., military, policing, administrative) cannot be met by the prevailing social arrangements. During the period of earliest contacts in Spanish America there was no need for a separate community of hybrids because there was still an abundance of draftable native labor, only a few Europeans were present, and the percentage of the mixed population was small and easily assimilable.

In this regard, it is noteworthy that the term "mestizo" was absent from Antonio de Nebrija's dictionaries of c.1495 and 1520, but present in Hieronymus

Cardoso's Portuguese dictionary of 1560 (Forbes, 1988: 125, 327–8). Before the mid-century decline of the Indian population, and when the Portuguese had only minimal contact with sub-Saharan Africans, there were no ethnicizable categories to associate with the terms "mestizo" or "mulatto." Consequently, in everyday usage the words retained their traditional sense of "hybrid." In the case of "mestizo," the term referred to culturally mixed peoples, such as the "mozárabes" (Arabized Christians), or it meant the issue of a foreigner and a local, a tame and wild parent (as with semi-feral pigs), or of crossbred animals. But in the 1560s, with the number of mixed peoples rising and interactions with blacks in Africa more frequent, both terms took on the additional, usually disparaging, sense of peoples of mixed hues (i.e. having neither one specific color nor another).

By the seventeenth century, when a considerable population of hybrids began to form identifiable collections of tenacious urban laborers, the connotation of "mestizo" and "mulatto" shifted from primarily a mixture of *colors* to an emphasis on mixed *ancestry*. Prior to that time, most common classificatory words (e.g., "pardo" [brownish, reddish gray], "loro" [tawny, dark brown], "moreno" [dark brown], "negro," and so on) were more likely to have been used to describe physical appearance than to assign specific genealogies (i.e. "races") to individuals. But Nebrija's dictionaries between 1778 and 1790, reflecting actual usage over that century, defined "mulatto" solely as "hybrid Ethiopian," and "mestizo" as either an Indian-Spanish hybrid or an animal born of different species (Forbes, 1988: 101). This move from color to ancestry – explicitly celebrated by the eighteenth-century artists who embellished the "castas" paintings with textual annotations – extended the inequality in meaning that had always characterized the two terms. "Mestizo," identified with the impoverished Indians who nonetheless enjoyed the special protection of the crown, was a less negative word in common speech and seems always to have referred to a wider range of possible mixtures (including those of cultures, religions, and social practices) than "mulatto," which by the late colonial period came to be used almost exclusively and often pejoratively for mixed descendants of slaves and crossbred animals such as mules.

Nevertheless, the relative advantage of one term over the other should not be exaggerated. With the disappearance of most native nobilities, phenotype (physical appearance as determined genetically) became the single most important indicator of social and economic status. By the time the castas were ubiquitous, this color-coding of social differences exempted no one from its register. This meant that most relations between light-skinned males and darker-skinned women were likely to be both unequal and unstable. And this situation, constantly confirmed by the fact that most hybrids were the product of unmarried couples, closely associated both "mestizo" and "mulatto" with every kind of social transgression, especially adultery and illegitimacy. Thus, physical appearance was coded in socially demeaning and economically restrictive ways long before modern notions of scientific "racism" evolved.

But this code did not appear overnight. In the first two centuries, color and other descriptive terms multiplied as efforts were made to classify and fix unprecedented combinations of hues and physical types. The basic categories of *Indian* (or "natural"), *Spanish* (or "castizo" [Spanish-mestizo], "criollo" [Spaniard born in America]), and *Negro* (or "moreno" [dark-complexioned]) – always remaining the axes upon which all other types would be plotted – were first supplemented by widely used terms such as "mestizo," "mulatto," "ladino" (Spanish-speaking Indian or mestizo), "cholo" (urban Indian), "coyote," and "zambo" (African/mulatto-Indian). But official exigencies, then as today, favored simplification; in Mexico, for instance, parish priests frequently kept separate registers only for "Spaniards," "Indians," and "mixed castes." To these basic designations imaginative minds added a series of sometimes popular, often obscure descriptors reflecting the mystery that shrouded the genealogical tangles of colonial life. These subjective tags, such as "cambujo," "barcino," "calpamulo," "albarazado," "lobo," "zambaigo," or "tente en el aire," logically defied consistency in application or translation.

The Hierarchy and Subversion of Difference

By the 1700s the only social order to be found was an ethnic queue that organized all ethnoracial sectors into a hierarchy. This vertical structure reflected the most common nexus at which the reproduction of castas took place: Spaniards with light-skinned mestizos (especially castizos), Indians with part-Indians (mestizos or zambos), and Africans with part-Africans (mulattos or zambos). Many of the casta terms were temporary and regional, reflecting not only local caprice but the dissonance between stratification by legal condition and stratification by actual social practice. While the law recognized primarily four groups: "Spaniards," "Indians," "castas," and "slaves," in everyday life the hierarchy distinguished and ordered the sectors differently: first came "peninsular Spaniards," then "criollos," then "mestizos," followed by "zambos," "mulattos," and free "Negroes," then slaves, and lastly non-cacique "Indians" (Mörner, 1967: 60). This ordering, with the Indians at the bottom, is attested to by the occupations available to each, the wages paid, the ranks to which any of them could aspire, and the options available for mates.

Although a ubiquitous concern with ethnoracial status exploded the local taxonomies, it was not until official, intellectual, and artistic concerns with social and conceptual order intervened in the eighteenth century – in the guise of the administrative reforms of the Bourbons, in the wake of the fashionable theorizing following Linnaeus's 1735 edition of his *System of Nature*, and in the light of the newly developing Rococo sensibilities that playfully worked at systematizing Baroque exuberance – that an effort began to be made to rationalize the terminological outburst into logical nomenclatures.[2] Nevertheless, the competing interests between auto-description and official classification made all such attempts deceptive. After all, the end of any concern with categorization was likely to be focused on the identity of a petitioner claiming a reserved right, on an accused who had violated the restrictions on his or her ethnic community, or on a constituent seeking inclusion or exemption from some caste-specific privilege or duty.

Clearly, lighter-skinned castas had a strong interest in being identified as Spaniards, especially as "old" Christians, which meant they could dress in silk, carry and use arms, ride horses, reside in privileged areas, travel and trade freely, marry Spaniards, be appointed to ecclesiastic and government posts, and be exempt from tribute and forced labor. Similarly, Indians seeking to escape tribute payments, labor obligations, or any of the many sumptuary laws, often found themselves trying to convince skeptical officials, local priests, or other power-holders that they were mestizos, castizos, castas, or whatever other name was popular at the time. By the same token, mestizos seeking the legal privileges of Indians or hoping to have access to their commonly held lands or a post in the native governments found themselves pleading to be recognized as tribal members. Lastly, runaway slaves and lighter-skinned Africans with any hope of social or economic success, sought to be identified as mulattos or any other dark-skinned casta in order to escape their servitude or the legal restrictions that limited their chances in life.

Meanwhile, the marginalization of those with some visible African ancestry was increasing even as the distinction between mestizo and Indian was becoming primarily a social concept. By the eighteenth century "Indian" and its many cognates came to mean little more than that one still belonged and was subject to a native community. Those who abandoned their village, learned Spanish, and dressed like mestizos were generally considered mestizos. Nonetheless, the demeaning connotations of "Indian," "mestizo," "mulatto," and "casta" had reached such a nadir by the century's end that in 1810 the Mexican revolutionary leader José María Morelos, taking his cue from his fellow rebel priest Miguel de Hidalgo, forbade the use of the terms in favor of the more inclusive label "Americano" (González del Cossío, 1958: 23).

The situation in the nineteenth century, however, was not propitious for such a dismissal of ethnic categories. The strategies used to pass from one casta to another and the ways in which local powerholders manipulated the distribution of resources put a premium on interethnic competition. Thus, discrimination of those below one's caste was typical and made common cause nearly impossible across ethnoracial lines. Meanwhile, the disappearance of the special protections granted Indians by the crown and the loss of most of their land under the govern-ments that sought to emulate the free trade policies of the United States, all but destroyed the native communities. This made the indigenes all the more vulner-able to rapacious "mulattos," who were slowly passing into the "mestizo" category; "mestizos," who were growing in number – thanks to natural re-production and the passing of natives into their ranks – and "criollos," many of whom were former "mestizos." The genetic boundaries, then, continued to be highly flexible, but not so the anti-casta prejudices exacerbated by the dominant ideologies of the 1800s – from liberalism to positivism – that placed a high value on European practices, customs, and forms of social exclusion.

The replacement of Spaniards by nationalist criollos did little for the poor castas or Indians, but by the century's end the indigenist-oriented Revolution against the dictatorship of Porfirio Díaz ushered in the age of mestizaje and revisionism. Soon Mexicans on both sides of the border and Latin-Americans elsewhere busied themselves rewriting their respective histories as epic journeys where tragic beginnings became triumphant ends, as formerly warring "races" fused into a cultural and genetic mixture expressing a heretofore unknown and, to some, "cosmic" mestizaje. In short, mestizaje, especially as officially promoted, became the powerful nation-building myth that was to help link dark-skinned castas, Euro-Americans, and Indians into one nation-state.

However, once again social reality failed to cooperate. Rather than promote mutual tolerance and social synthesis, the ideology of mestizaje has been effectively used to salve the national conscience or promote collective amnesia in what concerns the dismal past and the still colonized condition of most native peoples in Latin America. It has failed to bring national unity and it has continued to be used to avoid addressing the hard fact that ethnic differences are primarily the effects of power and therefore usually serve the interests of the powerful. Given the challenge that ethnicity, racism, and nationalism continue to pose today, perhaps Morelos' call for a postethnic identification that focuses on inclusion rather than separatism is worth making once more (see Hollinger, 1995), even if, as I will now suggest, the likelihood of success is small.

Cipherspace: The Making of Latino Identities and Mestizaje Today

A cipher is a place holder denoting neither quantity nor magnitude. A cipher also stands both for a coded method of inscription and for the key that unlocks the encoded meaning. Given the adequacy of the fit, instead of using the popular term "border," with its emphasis on fixed and often false oppositional binaries, "cipherspace," – a space that can hide the secrets of identity while simultaneously providing the clues to its discovery – is my metaphor of choice for the conceptual and social space of mestizaje. As I have been suggesting, the cipher-like nature of mestizaje – because as an empty place holder it can be filled with almost any category of identity – has been paradoxically construed by many as the very essence of the Latin-American, particularly, the Mexican. "Mestizaje" in the Americas seems to refer to both a strategic social construct and a generic but ambiguous type of collective identity. Acting strategically, mestizaje can function as a register (e.g., a myth) through which a new people can be brought into existence, or as an elucidating metaphor that helps to make sense of the masking that goes on when fusion fails to take place as different peoples meet under asymmetrical conditions.[3]

Mestizaje, then, is an optional strategic maneuver. When mixing has been problematic to purists, mestizaje has been ignored as a distinct classification, as is the case in the US where hybrid Anglo-Americans bypassed mestizaje as a social category. Religious, social, and economic concerns with exclusivity, and the practical need to distinguish slaves physically and therefore to link civil status to "race," together gave birth to a rigorous social calculus based on the sociological law of the "excluded middle" (Klor de Alva, 1996a). This tragic principle, encoded in the "one-drop rule," meant that a woman considered white could give birth to a "black" infant, but a woman recognized as black could never beget a "white" child (Fields, 1982: 149). Under these conditions, no space was left in the popular or official imagination for "mixed" groups or cultures; instead, English colonists generally classified everyone as either white, black, or alien (Klor de Alva, 1995b).

Indians in the British colonies were among those marginalized as aliens; consequently, by the early nineteenth century, when extensive contact was made between Mexicans and Anglo-Americans, no cultural pattern of ethnic inclusion of non-Europeans existed to challenge the polar categories of white and black. Hispanics – a complex mixture of Indian, mulatto, and European hybrids – had to conform to known types or risk being conceived as foreigners. As Euro-American migration to the Southwest increased, especially in the last decades of the nineteenth century and the first-half of the twentieth, many Mexicans, painfully aware of the racial logic behind Anglo-American interethnic relations, struggled to be included as Caucasians.

Modern Latinos, in contrast, have had a variety of strategic ideas about who they are. Most Mexicans entered the US thinking of themselves as Mexican nationals and as mestizos. But most have understood mestizaje primarily in its official version, assuming both an absence of black Africans in their genetic and cultural past and the near disappearance of the indigenes and their world, not into a brew of Indian-Spanish composition, but into the cultural vortex of the West. Mestizaje, as learned from official and popular sources, is the collapse of distinct cultures into a Mexican way of being Spanish, as opposed to being identified as a dynamic and balanced fusion of formerly Indian and European ways. Not surprisingly, when the civil rights movement took hold in the US, many young Mexican-Americans, by then unschooled in the official ideology of mestizaje and eager to assert their difference from both the Mexicans and "Anglos" around them, sought to undermine official mestizaje's Westernizing assumptions through similarly reductive and equally strategic discourses.

For instance, hoping to facilitate a response to the Mexican-Americans' marginalized condition, in the late '60s the Mexican-American ethnic resurgence movement was set in motion as a collective "Chicano" identity began to be woven, among other things, out of the manipulation of primarily "Aztec" symbols (Klor de Alva, 1986a; 1986b; 1989). Creative Chicanos, searching for common roots to unite the disparate communities, identified Aztlán, the mythical homeland of the Aztecs, with the US Southwest and consequently – in the imagination of many – symbolically transformed all Chicanos (despite their differences) into the most authentic of Mexicans: the direct descendants of the original Aztecs! By leaping over the Europeanizing version of mestizaje all Mexican-Americans were thus linked to the *colonized* descendants of the precontact Aztecs. This Indianizing stance, inspiring a romantic return to the indigenous roots of "Mexicanidad" while rejecting both the Spanish and Anglo "colonizing" influences (Klor de Alva, 1992b), was not easily understood by Mexicans, many of whom are aware of the extremes to which millions of indo-mestizos have gone to deflect the negative consequences of being identified as "indios."

This dilemma underlines the extent to which the chameleonic or, better, cipher-like nature of mestizaje – Western in the presence of Europeans, indigenous in native villages, and Indian-like in contemporary US barrios – is its crucial characteristic (see Klor de Alva, n.d., a). At one time, this mimetic potency made it possible for an astonishing variety of impoverished castas to manipulate their identities as a survival strategy. The same is true today. The ideological privi-leging of mestizaje is primarily based on its ambiguity, one that has permitted past and present castas to negotiate their identities and make possible their progression to the centers of contemporary nationalist fantasies and to the core of popular imaginations where mestizos, like the ciphers they are, can be made to stand for anything anyone wants them to be. To conclude, I now turn to this mimetic role, which mestizaje has raised to an art form.

In the US a situation developed homologous to the colonial conditions that yielded mestizaje. At first, much like early New Spain, the country sought to keep every ethnic group in its separate place through the use of restrictive marriage laws and collective labels, which were ultimately reduced to three residual categories: white, black, and foreign. Beginning in the mid-1960s, how-ever, three critical changes occurred. First, the Civil Rights Act of 1964, although focused on African-Americans, set in motion a complex process of desegregation and integration that came to include progressively more cat-egories, such as women, Latinos, Native Americans, gays and lesbians, the disabled, and so on. Second, the 1965 reform of previously restrictive immi-gration laws had the unintended effect of opening the way to an immigration tide unlike any since the turn of the century; this time, however, composed primarily of non-Europeans. Third, to help enforce in an affirmative, proactive manner the provisions of the Civil Rights Act (and later the Voting Rights Act of 1965), a new and precise taxonomy of ethnoracial classification was estab-lished in 1977 by the Office of Management and Budget's Statistical Directive 15. In the spirit of the eighteenth-century reformers and artists who sought to fix the casta classifications, this bureaucratic initiative partitioned the US into a larger number of specific ethnoracial groups. In effect, after 1977 all "Americans" were understood to be white, black, red (Native American), yellow (Asian or Pacific Islander), or brown (Hispanic, i.e. a cultural category whose members can be "of any race").

All this set the political and legal stage for the cult of difference and the identity politics movements that prevail in the US today. In this context of heightened attention to race and collective identities, taking place at a time when many second and third generation descendants of Mexican immigrants have accultur-ated extensively, a growing number of Mexican-American youth, reacting against the powerful forces of assimilation that integrate them primarily into the lowest sectors of the mainstream of the new multicultural America, are transforming mestizaje in a totally novel fashion.

For example, reflecting the general tendency among contemporary students to focus their rebellion on cultural rather than socioeconomic or political issues (see Gitlin, 1995), over the last two decades a transformation has been taking place among some Chicanos who have taken the identification of the US Southwest with Aztlán to its logical conclusion. In keeping with the spirit of our time, these Chicanos, who are identifying themselves as direct descendants of the Nahuas, have changed their ethnic label to Xicanos. In their folk etymology, which they present (incorrectly) as grounded in the Nahuatl of the Aztecs, "xi" = "people," "ca" = "earth" or "peace," and "no" = "yes." "Xicano," then, depending on the source, can mean "people who live on this earth in peace" or "yes, we are the children of the earth." The shift from "Chicano" to "Xicano" implies a broadening of the Chicanos' ethnic identification to include not only the indigenous peoples of Mexico – as in the 1969 "Plan Espiritual de Aztlán," which set the ideological agenda of the Chicano Movement – but also *all* native peoples of the Americas, who, after all, are widely recognized as the traditional "children of the earth."

The Xicanos, who generally oppose the Westernized political vision of Chicano ethnic activists, are closely affiliated with the indigenist "conchero" dance, curing, and religious movement active in Mexico since the 1950s. Divided up into separate, highly disciplined and hierarchized Danza groups (dance and ceremonial collectives), the Xicanos, led by their respective officer corps of Capitanes, Generales, Jefes, Malinches, and so on, have organized themselves into closed (Chicano-only) communities of believers focused on spiritual renewal and cultural affirmation by way of prayerful performances of stylized "Aztec" dances and through a strong identification of themselves as, in my words, neo-Aztecs. This highly spiritualized and demanding avocation includes a commitment to three guiding principles: "Union, Conformidad, Conquista." "Union" implies a total devotion to a set of cultural values and goals that transcend individual personalities and divisions and which transform the group into a single "circle" or "home tribe." "Conformidad" means unquestioning acceptance of the hierarchy and rules of the group. "Conquista" alludes to the aim of the danzante as an "indigenous spiritual warrior" who with every dance enters into a "battle to conquer new souls for the armies of the Creator" (Aguilar, 1983: xxxii).

With Xicanismo, then, mestizaje has made a full circle. It is, after all, a complex contemporary (postmodern?) form of hybridity that mixes the traditional ceremonialism of the ancient Nahuas with the New Age concern with harmony and ecological balance articulated through Native Americanist ideologies (see Castañeda, 1996). It combines Catholic preoccupations with hierarchy and authority with a Protestant morality of opposition to drugs, drinking, and hedonism. And it links prayer to aerobics and both to rebellion (Shrader, 1996: 1) in an attempt to make a new place in the US for English-speaking, college-educated mestizos who, although willing to commit themselves to a form of spiritual renewal that harks back to a world that antedated the castas, must nonetheless address many of the same problems these colonial hybrids faced – using many of the same ruses.

In the end, we are forced to acknowledge that the cipherspace mestizaje may be capable of infinite variation, but today, as in the past, it continues to be both a dangerous site and a wellspring of creativity. It seems, then, that Morelos – the revolutionary priest who sought to identify all Mexicans as "Americanos" and nothing else – was ultimately both on target and off the mark.

Notes

1 For more detailed treatments of the critical issues raised in this essay, see Klor de Alva n.d., a, b; 1996b; 1995a, b; 1993a, b; 1992a, b, c; 1991; 1989; 1988.
2 It follows that the logic the famous "castas" paintings sought to capture visually was primarily the socially- and economically-based hierarchizing scheme that the society's prejudices and discriminatory practices superimposed upon the genealogical chaos. For all their classificatory richness, when categorizing beyond the second generation the castas paintings could not avoid being inconsistent. After all, as noted above, the policing of ethnic boundaries turned out to be an ineffectual effort and the castas paintings, when taken as a genre, evidence that fact.
3 Some of the ideas that follow rely on or modify what is explored in Klor de Alva 1995b.

References

Aguilar, M. E. (1983). *La Danza Azteca*. Unpublished manuscript.

Anaya, R. (1976). *Heart of Aztlán*. Berkeley: Editorial Justa.

CDFS (1953–1962). *Colección de documentos – para la formación social de Hispanoamérica. 1493–1810* (Vols 1 and 3). Madrid: Real Academia de la Historia.

Castañeda, Q. E. (1996). *In the Museum of Maya Culture: Touring Chichén Itzá*. Minneapolis: University of Minnesota.

Drinnon, R. (1980). *Facing West: The Metaphysics of Indian-Hating and EmpireBuilding*. New York: New American Library.

Fields, B. J. (1982). Ideology and Race in American History. In J. M. Kousser, J. M. McPherson, and C. V. Woodward (eds), *Region, Race, and Reconstruction*. New York: Oxford University Press.

Forbes, J. D. (1988). *Black Africans and Native Americans*. Boston: Basil Blackwell.

Gitlin, T. (1995). *The Twilight of Common Dreams: Why America is Wracked by Culture Wars*. New York: Metropolitan Books.

González del Cossío, F. (ed.) (1958). *Legislación indigenista de México: Recopilación* (no. 38). Mexico: Instituto Indigenista Interamericano.

Hollinger, D. A. (1995). *Postethnic America: Beyond Multiculturalism*. New York: Basic Books.

Klor de Alva, J. J. (n.d., a). Mestizaje as Myth and Metaphor in the New World and In Search of the American Chameleon: Mestizaje, Mimesis, and Mexican Identity. In J. J. Klor de Alva and A. Gonzales (eds), *American Identities: Traditional, Contested, and Imagined*. Washington, D.C.: Smithsonian Institution Press.

Klor de Alva, J. J. (n.d., b). Beyond Black, Brown, or White: Cultural Diversity, Strategic

Hybridity, and the Future of Democracy. In T. Keenan (ed.), *Cultural Diversities: On Democracy, Community,and Citizenship*.

Klor de Alva, J. J. (1986). California Chicano Literature and Pre-Columbian Motifs: Foil and Fetish. *Confluencia: Revista Hispanica de Cultura y Literatura*, 1, 18–26.

Klor de Alva, J. J. (1988). Telling Hispanics Apart: Latino Sociocultural Diversity in the United States. In E. Acosta-Belen and B. Sjostrom (eds), *The Hispanic Experience in the United States*. New York: Praeger Publishers.

Klor de Alva, J. J. (1989). Aztlán, Borinquen, and Hispanic Nationalism in the US. In R. Anaya and F. Lomeli (eds), *Aztlán: Essays on the Chicano Homeland*. Albuquerque: University of New Mexico.

Klor de Alva, J. J. (1991). The Hispanic World in the United States. In J. H. Elliott (ed.), *The Hispanic World: Civilization and Empire, Europe and the Americas, Past and Present*. London: Thames and Hudson.

Klor de Alva, J. J. (1992a). Indios y Criollos. In J. H. Elliott (ed.), *Europa/América 1492/1992. La Historia Revisada*. Madrid: Diario El País.

Klor de Alva, J. J. (1992b). La invención de los orígenes y la identidad latina en los Estados Unidos (1969–81). In J. J. Klor de Alva et al. (eds), *Encuentros interétnicos: De palabra y obra en el Nuevo Mundo* (vol. 2). Madrid: Ediciones Siglo XXI.

Klor de Alva, J. J. (1992c). La invención de los orígenes y la identidad latina en los Estados Unidos (1969–81). In J. J. Klor de Alva et al. (eds), *Encuentros interétnicos: De palabra y obra en el Nuevo Mundo* (vol. 2). Madrid: Ediciones Siglo XXI.

Klor de Alva, J. J. et al. (eds). (1993a). *La formación del otro: De palabra y obra en el Nuevo Mundo*. (vol. 3) Madrid: Ediciones Siglo XXI.

Klor de Alva, J. J. (1993b). Aztec Spirituality and Nahuatized Christianity. In G. H. Gossen and M. Leon-Portilla (eds), *South and Meso-American Native Spirituality* (vol. 4 of *World Spirituality: An Encyclopedic History of the Religious Quest*) New York: The Crossroad Publishing Co.

Klor de Alva, J. J. (1995a). Heteroglosia en el barrio: Cuando los nativos responden, las voces se multiplican. In J. J. Klor de Alva et al. (eds), *Tramas de la identidad: De palabra y obra en el Nuevo Mundo* (vol. 4). Madrid: Ediciones Siglo XXI.

Klor de Alva, J. J. (1995b). The Post-Colonization of the (Latin) American Experience: A Reconsideration of "Colonialism," "Postcolonialism," and "Mestizaje." In Gyan Prakash (ed.), *After Colonialism: Imperial Histories and Postcolonial Displacements*. Princeton: Princeton University Press.

Klor de Alva, J. J. (1996a). Is Affirmative Action a Christian Heresy? *Representations*, 55 (Summer).

Klor de Alva, J. J. (1996b). Nahua Colonial Discourse and the Appropriation of the (European) Other. In Bruce Ziff (ed.), *Studies in Cultural Appropriation*. New Brunswick: Rutgers University Press.

Marshall, C. E. (1939). The Birth of the Mestizo in New Spain. *The Hispanic American Historical Review*, XIX.

Mörner, M. (1967). *Race Mixture in the History of Latin America*. Boston: Little, Brown and Co.

Rosenblat, A. (1954). *La población indígena y el mestizaje en América* (vol. II). Buenos Aires: Editorial Nova.

Rumazo Gonzalez, J. (ed.) (1934). *Libro segundo de Cabildos de Quito* (vol. II). Quito: Publicación del Archivo Municipal.

Shrader, E. (1996). Native Dancers. *San José Mercury News*. January 17.

Part IV

The Color(s) of Whiteness

12

Establishing the Fact of Whiteness

John Hartigan, Jr.

Surveying the range of public discourses on race in the United States, one finds it hard to escape the conclusion that, as anthropologists and academics, we are struggling to keep pace with the innovations and obsessions this subject generates in popular culture. Granted, a certain mind-numbing redundancy characterizes most widely circulated representations of race: scenes of intergroup conflict predominate, to the exclusion of the array of social interactions between whites and peoples of color that are not conflictual; an "extreme gulf" generically summarizes the contours of interracial coexistence; and analytical views offered by commentators, newscasters, reporters, and politicians are woefully simplistic in comparison with the nuance and complexity manifest in many "racial" situations. Still, what stands out is the number of public forums given over to discussing or arguing about what race means and how it matters.

There is, however, one racial subject where an upsurge of interest by academics may precede and effectively recast public formulations of race problems: that is the matter of whiteness. Through the efforts of literary and film critics, historians, sociologists, and gradually, anthropologists, whiteness, as an analytical object, is being established as a powerful means of critiquing the reproduction and maintenance of systems of racial inequality, within the United States and around the globe.[1] Apart from the concept's usefulness to academics, discussions of how whiteness operates may provide a means of altering the terms of racial debates in the United States. As I listened to whites respond to the way racial inequality and the continued insidious effects of racism are highlighted in a range of public discussions – whether in relation to the O. J. Simpson trial, the spate of church burnings across the South, or more discrete tragedies such as the death of Cynthia Wiggins in Buffalo – one consistent lament I have heard voiced is that now racism is "everywhere" or that "race is an excuse for everything these days."[2] Rather than recognizing the pervasive effects of race, these white complaints dismiss the relevance of racism to current social conflicts, asserting that anything so omnipresent must be mythic. Perhaps whiteness offers a different purchase on the attention of whites. Whiteness specifies the cultural construction of what Ruth Frankenberg (1993) characterizes as a structural position of social privilege and power. Studies of whiteness are demonstrating that whites benefit from a host of apparently neutral social arrangements and institutional operations, all of which seem – to whites at least – to have no racial basis.

Whiteness has emerged as much from a series of distinct disciplinary developments as it has in response to the ongoing need for more effective analyses of how racial dominance is reproduced. The call to study whiteness is linked to long-simmering efforts to "decolonize anthropology" (Harrison, 1991), as well as to critiques of how the logic of Otherness perniciously informs ethnographic accounts of non-Western subjects and the push to include within the scope of anthropology studies of "nonexotic" people, such as whites in the West (Varenne, 1986). The convergence of these various disciplinary matters are evident in Helán Page's depiction of the turn to examining whiteness: "One of the most important things to be done is to encourage our students to seriously study white people. Here is a population that has achieved dominance. How did this happen and what are the lessons? . . . We shouldn't stop studying the 'Other,' but we need to study those who are reproducing themselves as dominant groups. We shouldn't study white ethnics, but how whiteness is constructed" (1995: 21).

Whiteness has been established as an object of study by scholars from an array of disciplines, each struggling with the task of making visible the operations of racial privilege and advantage that structure the lives, attitudes, and actions of white people. Out of these studies, several characterizations of whiteness have been established, all to some degree related but also often involving subtle disjunctures or contradictions. Film and literary critics fashioned a view of whiteness as a relational identity, constructed by whites defining themselves as unlike certain ethnic or racial Others.[3] In this view, blackness serves as the primary form of Otherness by which whiteness is constructed. Historians have followed a similar model in describing the century's long development of white identity. Their emphasis, though, has been on both the relational construction of whiteness in opposition to blackness and on the ever-changing content of this identity, stressing that whiteness has excluded certain ostensibly white European groups only to incorporate them at a later date.[4] The complicated matter of the cultural content of whiteness has also been examined as a repressed synthesis of many African or African-American styles and practices.[5] These diverse approaches underscore the novelty of whiteness as a subject of study; its coherence derives from the range of interests brought to bear on this topic, discerned and analyzed in numerous fields and mediums simultaneously.

In contemporary social settings, whiteness has been identified as a core set of racial interests often obscured by seemingly race-neutral words, actions, or policies.[6] From the terms or subjects of debate that comprise political campaigns to the placement and funding of freeway projects or the placement of waste dumps, limits determining access to home financing, and the varied practices that constitute and reproduce medical professions in the United States, a set of institutional routines and "white cultural practices" are evident in establishing and maintaining privileges generally associated with being white. Indeed, whites benefit from being white whether or not, as individuals, they hold supremacist notions, harbor racist sentiments, or are made anxious by the physical presence of people of color. The phrase *white culture is* proffered to convey the material relations and social structures that reproduce white privilege and racism in this country, quite apart from what individual whites may feel, think, and perceive (Frankenberg, 1993: 196–205, 228–34). As an analytical register, then, whiteness stands as a sweepingly broad, effective means to characterize the racial content of white peoples' cultural identity.

For these scholars, one central importance of whiteness as an analytical concept is that it identifies how the unmarked and normative position of whites is maintained by positing "race" as a category of difference.[7] "Racial" and "race" are typically used to characterize difference and deviance from social norms that have been seamlessly equated with what white people, generally speaking, do and think. Phrases such as *race relations* and *racial problems* have effectively focused on only one side of the equation, on the conditions of people of color and not upon the position of dominance that whites maintain. Whether in Frankenberg's definition of whiteness as a structural position conferring privilege and power or in historian George Lipsitz's (1995) characterization of it as an organizing principle in social and cultural relations, the common concern is in naming and factually objectifying the content of white peoples' character. Whiteness, thereby, stands as a concept that reveals and explains the racial interests of whites and links them collectively to a position of racial dominance. The concern that I want to raise here is that in this reformulation of the racial equation, the powerful description of whiteness as a position of dominance while opening up newly insightful analyses of how racial inequality is structured – will promulgate an assumption that whiteness simply exists and is real, thus undermining a potentially productive opportunity to reframe the long, contentious debate over what race is and how it matters. The contours of this assumption are apparent in the role that *culture* plays in these studies of whiteness.

Culture, in these definitions of whiteness, is used in a twofold manner. Primarily, it establishes a register apart from individual identity that affects and defines white people collectively while suggesting a broad range of means by which racial matters influence or inform the lives of white people, asserting that they, too, are "racial." Secondly, the notion of "white culture," developed and consistent through the long centuries of white global domination, reifies whiteness as a definable entity. This moves dangerously close to undermining the basis of social constructionist views of race because the conviction that there are no inherent affinities between people sharing a collective racial identity is destabilized by such a singular, unified definition of whiteness. There are already clearly emerging stresses in the position that race is a social construct, and they partially arise out of the effective demonstrations that racial systems of inequality are inscribed in the very infrastructure of societies, in a realm that, while not attaining the permanence of genetic and biological orders, reflects a durability that exceeds simple individual interventions or tinkering (Harrison, 1995; Smedley, 1993).[8] In place of race as an artificial category, we have accounts of whiteness and blackness as distinct historical traditions and identities; such is the consistency with which they can each be traced through the last 400 years of

global history. Determining the "fact" of whiteness – the durability of its dominance and the pernicious nature of its effects – may have the unintended effect of
undermining the concept of race as "constructed." This should not be surprising
since, after all, whiteness has been the core problem of race all along; if the
emphasis now shifts from the artificialness and plasticity of race onto the fairly
absolute forms through which whiteness is reproduced, this should not be too
troubling. But if the significance of race has reached a stage where it exceeds the
hierarchized, organizing principles of whiteness and blackness, then distinguishing between the "fact" and the "construction" of whiteness may be an
increasingly difficult matter for ethnographers to tackle.

Daniel Segal, in the course of describing the function of race and color in pre-
independence Trinidad and Tobago, points to the following conundrum in
approaches that analyze racial identities as social constructs: "Such groupings are
fundamentally contingent, though this is precisely what is obscured when they
are called 'races,' for these denominations represent historically contingent
groupings as facts given to us by objective reality" (1993: 81). When the fact of
whiteness is established with certainty and consistency, what becomes less easy
to grasp is the contingent basis of the significance of white racialness and the arbi-
trariness of racial categories and distinctions. This matter may be viewed more
clearly by highlighting the distinctiveness of Frankenberg's approach in contrast
to Lisa Douglass' study (1992) of white, upper-class families in Jamaica.
Frankenberg, in defining whiteness "as a set of normative cultural practices,"
asserts plainly that "white women are, by definition, practitioners of white
culture" (1993: 228). While there are structural similarities, in terms of dominance, between the whites in northern California whom Frankenberg interviewed
and the whites in Kingston, Jamaica, whom Douglass studied, Douglass views
racialness in a more strictly constructionist frame, as an arbitrary system. She
comments:

> I view gender, color, and class not as descriptions of particular groups or persons,
> but as categories that act as principles of distinction. . . . What these categories (or
> principles) mean, how they may combine in different ways, and how they affect a
> person at a given time vary; they are neither rigid, nor fixed, nor timeless. Above
> all, they are not "real," even though they often have concrete effects. Principles of
> distinction serve both as analytic and as commonsense categories that inform the
> way Jamaicans relate to one another and affect the way they explain and experience
> the world. (Douglass, 1992: 11–12)

In treating racial categories primarily as a means of organizing and interpreting
everyday life, Douglass draws upon the work of Jack Alexander (1977), whose
study of "the culture of race" among the middle class of Kingston examines racial
identities as interpretive categories rather than as a means to strictly define his
ethnographic subjects. This contrast is relevant to the factual status of whiteness;
it suggests that the difference between Douglass' and Frankenberg's studies is in
the shift from treating race as a generic subject to analyzing the perpetuation of

a historical, cultural tradition of white domination. The break between these two studies of white people arises in Frankenberg's deployment of "whiteness" to present a view of white privilege and dominance as a unified operation, implicating and influencing, to varying degrees, all white people, linking the racialness of whites to an inherent, motivational core. This shift does not necessarily limit the extent to which whiteness is seen as contemporarily constructed in distinct settings, but it raises the question of whether racial interpretive structures are best understood as strictly historically determined or as modes that are as mutable as the changeable, place specific contexts where they operate (Jackson and Penrose, 1993; Taussig, 1987: 179).

The fact of whiteness is based on its historical duration and its ideological coherence and effective power. In establishing the "social reality" of race, Audrey Smedley (1993) grounds the durability of this cultural construction in its historical determinants. Applied to whiteness, this view orients ethnographic investigations toward confirming the continuing effects of this historical order rather than toward assessing the permutations this construction may be undergoing. *"No amount of comparative definitions and synchronic explorations of modern race relations will lead us to more refined definitions and understandings of race.* On the contrary, it is a complex of elements whose significance and meanings lie in historical settings in which attitudes and values were formed" (Smedley, 1993: 16, emphasis added). While the durability of whiteness is confirmed from this view of race's social reality, this stance makes it difficult to grasp or learn from the settings where the significance of white racialness is currently in flux.[9]

The asserted ideological coherence of whiteness leads to a similar problem, as evidenced in David Roediger's oft-cited *Towards the Abolition of Whiteness* (1993). Finding that whiteness is "infinitely more false" than blackness, Roediger calls for "a sharp questioning of whiteness" that will lead to its eventual abolition (1993: 3, 12).[10] Aside from the question of how to validate an activist interest in abolishing an ethnographic subject of study – however clearly in the interests of humanity – this focus on whiteness apart from "the concept of race generally" is a mistake. Rendering whiteness as unique, a special ideological case apart from race, limits inquiries into the way changing racial terrains are discursively negotiated by whites in their daily lives, both in workplaces and at home. Out of confusions over race, new versions of white racialness are being articulated, oriented as much toward an unfolding present as they are bound to a determining past. The conditions through which racial identities are articulated will only become more complicated, not less so (Hartigan, 1997a). Unless whites are examined with this in mind, ethnographers will generate accounts that confidently link whiteness back to some originary impulse rather than recognizing that it is being continually restructured, revised, and disfigured in a host of discrete, local settings as something that draws its significance as much from diverse places as from an ideological unity.

Neither Frankenberg nor Harrison assert that the cultural coherence of whiteness derives from a simple, ontological condition. They each stress the relational construction of whiteness in opposition to blackness, and they both acknowledge that "race is always lived in class- and gender-specific ways" (Harrison, 1995: 63). But in the final analysis, their definitions of whiteness emphasize the unifying interest in, and reproduction of, dominance, diminishing the extent to which its meanings are contested or rearticulated through local "racial idioms" (Segal, 1993), inflected by place-specific contests over class and gender identity. I am not certain that their conceptualization of whiteness allows for a view of the plasticity of race in relation to white people. While it is unnerving to advocate a more nuanced view of whiteness when many whites still refuse to recognize the broad role of racism in this society, a more complex analysis is necessary if we are to understand the ways racialness conflates with other registers of meaning and modes of significance in white peoples' lives. White peoples' uses of identifying and differentiating terms also have to be analyzed in relation "to the larger problem of how informants use their ideas about race to make sense of their society" (Alexander, 1977: 413). We need to recognize the heterogeneity of whiteness that emerges from these interpretive uses in divergent, novel contexts, each featuring nuanced conflations of race with class and place-specific discourses. Race still eludes emphatic definition; though its association with forms of domination and subordination is consistent, there is a diffuse range of "racial" phenomena that are not all easily subsumed within this definition. Stressing emphatic links between whiteness and dominance has generated analyses that powerfully delineate the vast, diffuse scope of white privilege while unproblematically presenting white people as a collective order with a common cultural identity. The difficult question is whether white racialness can additionally be analyzed as contingent and articulated in registers that exceed the strict operation of domination.

While whiteness invites broadly devised analytics – both the sweeping scope of its reign of dominance and the insidious nature of its current effects make this clear (Harrison, 1995) – the uncertainty about what exactly constitutes race and the overriding importance of emphasizing the locales of culture requires further circumspection over how to analyze the racialness of white people.[11] Comparative studies of white supremacy in South Africa and the United States by George Fredrickson (1981) and John Cell (1982) offer a view of the complexities involved in treating whiteness as a unified subject of study. While the cultural similarities between whites in the two countries are striking, these historians differed in their assessment of white supremacy's historical origins and came to contrasting conclusions about whether or not white supremacy possesses an identifiable core.

Fredrickson seems to suggest that, rather than tracing whiteness as a consistent cultural order, constructions of white supremacy are best understood as resonant but distinctive structures. While his notion of whiteness as "a fluid, variable, and open-ended process" (1981: xviii) does not necessarily counter Harrison's depiction of it as "the key site of racial domination" (1995: 63), I think that Fredrickson's discounting of "common cultural influences" (1981: xviv) in explaining the distinct versions of white supremacy in these two countries suggests that white racialness must be analyzed as something more than a unified ideological order. Dominance is no doubt key to the processes that Fredrickson analyzes, but the interplay of "differing environmental circumstance and political contingencies" (1981: xviii) makes the matter of analyzing constructions of whiteness in the two countries tenuous because they constitute such distinct cultural, demographic, economic, and political domains. Fredrickson relates that this comparative effort "has strengthened my sense that race relations can best be understood in terms of the interaction of specific groups in particular historical situations and that attempts to generalize broadly about entire societies over long periods of time usually distort more than they illuminate" (1981: xx).

John Cell, in his comparative study of white supremacy, is not as hesitant to find a common core of beliefs and attitudes among whites. In deployments of the keyword *segregation,* he discerns a common "growing consciousness, synthesis and ideological crystallization" among whites of both countries. Even so, in defining *segregation,* he stresses attention to a matter that I think is easily overlooked in attempts to theorize whiteness, and that is ambiguity.[12] As it changed rapidly from a "*de facto* tendency or practice" into "both a *de jure* system and a coherent, articulate ideology," segregation produced a "state of ambiguity and contradiction [that] was skillfully and very deliberately created" (Cell, 1982: 3, 18–20). While a good deal of this structural ambiguity involved the "facade of constitutionality," a critical aspect of its operation was to obscure the conflicted and disjointed nature of the "white world." "The principal function of the segregationist ideology was to soften class and ethnic antagonisms among whites, subordinating internal conflicts to the unifying conception of race" (Cell, 1982: 234). The intraracial conflicts between whites in both countries suggest that coherence of this "unifying conception" is dependent on the stability of local conditions.

Vincent Crapanzano, in *Waiting: The Whites of South Africa* (1985), makes the case for studying dominant whites based on an acknowledgment of the specificity of their cultural identity. "Pathos, terror, guilt, the joy of power and acquisition, the weight of responsibility and the resentment of such responsibility, feelings of solitude, misunderstanding, and ununderstanding, to name only a few of the dispositions and predispositions of the dominant, have to be understood if any understanding of domination is to be achieved" (1985: 23). Such dispositions are not easily rendered in a generic sense of whiteness, especially when they are articulated through intense, intraracial contests animated by the severe distinction between English South Africans and Afrikanes. While qualifying his findings as drawn from specific field settings, Crapanzano suggests "that the blacks, coloureds, and Asians were not 'significant others' from whose standpoint the white could look reflectively at himself and discover, so to speak, his identity. They were too different – and too distant" (1985: 39). Crapanzano finds the "psycho-ontological dimensions of apartheid" well demonstrated in this structured white obliviousness to South African blacks. But this cultural dynamic indicates that the complex matter of how race remains significant will not be determined by exclusively keying on contests between the poles of whiteness and blackness.

While the consistency of white hegemony speaks to a unified definition of whiteness, the changing demographic and political circumstances unfolding in US cities suggest that we also maintain a view toward the changes underway in how racial identities are established and contested (Hartigan, 1997b). In the course of my own fieldwork on whites in Detroit, I found intraracial distinctions were crucial in how whites articulated their sense of the meaning of race in general and of the significance of being white. While my initial interest was in analyzing whiteness as a singular cultural identity, I found that the situations of whites in distinct class communities were not easily generalized or rendered in terms of a coherent identity such as whiteness. From July 1992 through February 1994, I worked in three sites in Detroit: two inner-city neighborhoods (Briggs, an "underclass" area, and the adjacent Corktown community, which is debatably "gentrifying") and a working-class neighborhood (Warrendale) on the city's far west side.[13] All three sites are predominantly white, though to varying degrees: Briggs, 54 percent white; Corktown, 63 percent; Warrendale, 80 percent. The demographics of Briggs are somewhat skewed by these figures, since the portion of Detroit in which it is located is predominantly black.

While these neighborhoods presented fairly homogeneous class circumstances, economic and social distinctions between whites in each of these sites were a primary means they deployed in talking about who belonged and who did not. In Briggs, which retained a large number of white Appalachian migrants (they had moved to Detroit between the years 1940 and 1960, and they remained behind in this increasingly decrepit neighborhood as "white flight" gutted the city), *hillbillies* was a term of contempt that native white Detroiters (born in the area in the 1920s and 1930s) used to denigrate poorer whites, whose shared regional characteristics with black migrants to the city undermined the clarity of racial division (Hartigan, 1996). For whites in Corktown, their position as whites who recently moved to the inner city and their professional skills caused a good deal of anxiety. In a conflation of racial and class identities, they used the term *gentrifier* to establish and contest who fit the "character" of the neighborhood: whites marked as gentrifiers (based on degrees of relative economic stability or employment opportunities) showed their whiteness too much to "properly" belong in this community. Warrendale was the site of an emotional conflict when the Detroit Board of Education decided to reopen a previously closed school – shut for lack of operating funds – as the Malcolm X Academy, with an Afrocentric curriculum. In this conflict, working-class whites faced off over whether or not to support the academy. The oppositional contours of the two positions were as much a matter of class distinctions as they were about racial attitudes or beliefs. In mutually exchanged accusations of racism, whites were in conflict over how to articulate class and community interests in relation to the obvious racial stakes of their debate with black professionals representing the city and the school board.

Racial matters in each of these sites were articulated through local idioms that whites and blacks used, with varying degrees of commonality, to position them-selves, neighbors, and strangers in relation to marked and unmarked identities. Whiteness was not readily apparent as either a unifying ideology or a shared sense of identity between these three neighborhoods. Partly, this is due to the fact that whiteness is not a normative identity in this city and, as whites, their racialness is rarely unmarked. But more importantly, in the most salient labels and cat-egories, race was rarely connotated in pure forms. Rather, it was conflated with class distinctions in a series of terms that negotiated the significance of being white without drawing uniformly on a historical notion of whiteness and without a clear opposition to blackness. The interpretive struggles these whites engaged in over the meaning of race in these communities were fiercely oriented toward the volatile present. In Detroit, white hegemony has been shattered, and in its wake whites assess, accentuate, or efface the significance of race through discourses complicated by class difference and relentlessly local in focus (Brackette Williams, 1991).[14] An attempt to read whiteness as uniformly at work in Detroit would obliterate the uniqueness of these settings and the heterogeneity of racial matters in these discourses.

My purpose here is neither to blithely insist that acknowledgments of the diver-sity of whites need always qualify analyses of whiteness nor to attempt to simply complicate the cultural critique of whiteness by stressing the conflation of racial and class identities according to place-specific dynamics. What I have tried to sketch is a certain ethnographic dilemma that the cultural critique of whiteness presents. The question that ethnographers face concerning this subject is whether to interrogate whiteness as a means of identifying the cultural core of white peoples' identity or to sketch the discursive predicaments in which whites are entangled as they operate, and are operated by, racial idioms of identity and difference. My concern is that efforts to establish the facticity of white culture may undermine recognition of the varied forms of racial significance in the disparate circumstances of whites in North America, South America, and the Caribbean (Hoetnik, 1985). While an analysis of domination and sub-ordination pertains to all these regions, the diversity of racial structures demonstrates that understanding whiteness remains contingent upon grasping how the heterogeneous functions of race alternate between stark definition, absolute positions, and swirling ambiguity.

This attention to the heterogeneous aspects of white racialness is one of the key contributions that cultural anthropology can make to studies of whiteness. If nothing else, efforts to theorize whiteness need to be informed by the long struggle to establish that blackness is a heterogeneous rather than homogeneous social order.[15] In his account of "the transformation of Creole culture into a black subculture centered on the aestheticization of blackness," Livio Sansone demon-strates that "their black culture and ethnicity is highly complex and eclectic – cacophonies rather than symphonic" (1994: 193). It is so because of the con-siderable degree of participation in white society that "the management of this new black ethnicity" requires; because "the leisure industry, music industry, and mass media play a key role in the marking of what is commonly considered black and white" and because the development of young people takes place amidst a host of new "facilitating conditions" where ethnic and racial identities are not simply preserved but actively refashion and "replace one ethnicity with another" (1994: 175, 192–3). Sansone insists that "a major barrier to constructing an anthropology of black people" has been the belief "that black culture is more 'genuine,' 'traditional,' and 'natural' than white culture, and that black ethnicity is given, static or scarcely manipulated" (1994: 175). These types of spurious distinctions are replicated when the racial complexity operating in the constitution of blackness is not seen as also at work in constructions of whiteness.

There are many ethnographic studies of whites that do not raise questions about race; such works largely confirm the basic critique of whiteness: that whites, especially those in racially homogeneous zones, are treated as normative rather than racial. But there are also a number of studies that deal with racialness and whites simultaneously. These works are, as of yet, untapped by theorists of whiteness. Principal among these are linguistic studies that track how language usage shapes social worlds. Shirley Brice Heath (1983), in her study of rural, working-class whites and blacks and their social distance from townspeople, black and white, in the Piedmont Carolinas, examines language as a medium driven by racial and class distinctions yet too fluid and mutable to be restricted in simple terms of "white" or "black" patterns. Teresa Labov (1990) examines reports "by liberal whites of conflicts with blacks" in a food cooperative in a racially mixed neighborhood in Philadelphia. Rather than abstracting out black or white "styles in conflict" (Kochman, 1981), Labov pursues the question of "when and how ideological themes, which do not appear relevant in one situation, can come to become defined as relevant" (1990: 155). This allows for a view of shifting definitions of "collections of people" that are only partially (and convolutedly) linked to matters of racial belonging and difference.

Interracial urban settings provide the most frequent depictions of whites negotiating racial matters.[16] In these situations, when whites and blacks from different regions and class backgrounds come to the city and clash, class and regional lines can blur stark racial divides, even to the point where the "unsocial bottom" is no longer assuredly linked to blackness.[17] Racially mixed urban neighborhoods range from volatile to benign, but usually the changeable and uncertain nature of urban terrains makes abstract notions of race tenuous. Surely, too, in these settings, racial identities are typically handy, blunt means for making blurred identities emphatic, but this tension shapes a cultural poetics patterned as much by the mutability of urban situations as it is by historically determined principles of racial distinctions. The forms of "street etiquette" that Elijah Anderson details are an interpretive set of rules that middle-class whites and blacks use in maneuvering through volatile public environments. While whiteness and blackness organize one level of perceptions, the unresponsiveness of these environments to "a formal set of rules rigidly applied to all problems" compels these middle-class city dwellers to develop additional, more sophisticated interpretive structures that draw on class distinctions as well (Anderson, 1990: 210).

White identity is transforming rapidly in relation to changes in the political landscape (Alba, 1990) and the demographic makeup of the United States, within and outside of whiteness (Lieberson, 1985). There are a number of efforts to conceptualize both this transformation and the shifting modes by which race continues to be culturally significant, and approaches to the problem of whiteness need to draw, in some manner, upon these as well. There is a developing interest in "deracialization" as an analytical construct in American urban politics (Perry, 1991). This concept is deployed to objectify the degrees of freedom and constraint black mayors face as they articulate campaign themes and strategies in a "postblack" register (Marable and Mullings, 1994). Another approach to the transformation of racial realities is found in the studies on "racelessness" or "acting white" by students of color in primary and secondary schools.[18] These strategies on the part of African-American and Latino students are formed through intricate engagements with the racializing practices of the schools and other bureaucratic institutions (Dominguez, 1994). Then, too, there are the studies of "white ethnics" that demonstrate the synthetic basis for any assumption of whiteness as a cultural construct.[19] Though whiteness may be a new subject of study, there is a tradition of anthropological research that is relevant to its examination.[20]

Attempts to objectify whiteness and establish its facticity have deep roots. Arguably, the first scientific attempt to analyze – rather than champion – whiteness was W. E. B. Du Bois's account of the white world in *Dusk of Dawn* (1980 [1940]). Du Bois rendered the white world as a sociological object and insisted that "it is impossible for the clear-headed student of human action in the United States and in the world, to avoid facing the fact of a white world which is today dominating human culture and working for the continued subordination of the colored races" (1980 [1940]: 145). This statement of the white world's facticity was demonstrated through a model of race in which whites constitute "The environing race" that "entombs" the "colored world" (1980 [1940]:138-9). He described the segregation that maintains these races as "some thick sheet of invisible – but horribly tangible plate glass" (1980 [1940]:137). A cursory glance at the United States confirms the continued relevance of Du Bois' model. Race still fundamentally determines the places, largely homogenous by race and class, where people live (Farley et al., 1993), and segregation is clearly influential in creating "intractable" problems such as the "underclass" (Massey and Denton, 1993). But interestingly, a city like Detroit, the most segregated metropolitan area in the United States (Farley et al. 1993), raises a discordant qualifier to Du Bois' objectification of the white world. Du Bois dismissed the idea of any whites "being possibly among the entombed or capable of sharing their inner thought and experience" (1980 [1940]:138). Today, at least structurally, such an emphatic stance is problematic; whites, too, are entombed in concentrated poverty areas such as Briggs. In this regard, Du Bois' sociological rendering depicts the central tension in this essay: although whiteness seems unchanging in its consistent position of dominance, racial orders are rapidly being contested and rearticulated.

Conceptually, whiteness is powerful and provocative, but it can also be an encumbrance. The power of whiteness lies in its ability to describe the coherence of privileges that white people, generically, have developed. Its encumbrance lies in this generic view, in rendering white people as a homogeneous cultural identity or order, which, as anthropologists, we know can only be a partial version. Homogenizing accounts stem from what has rightfully been established as a key function of whiteness: that it homogenizes whites from a range of ethnic and class positions in order to assert a normative social identity from which privileges can be secured and maintained. But it is important to maintain an awareness of the distinction between the process and the population to which it pertains: as Crapanzano suggests, "trying not to confuse dominance within a system with the domination of the system" (1985: 22). Indeed, Helán Page and Brooke Thomas (1994) describe "white public space" as a homogenizing process, specific to professionals, that includes, through coercion and manipulation, black participants as well. But homogenizing accounts are overwhelmingly common in analyses of race, and it will be hard for studies of whiteness to do otherwise.

If whiteness stands, definitionally, as equivalent with homogenizing processes in the workplace, at home, in neighborhoods, and in public debates, then we should additionally have a means of designating the heterogeneous aspects of white racial identity that are not effortlessly processed into whiteness, that, through ruptures of class decorums or other forms of social etiquette, undermine the unmarked status of some whites. Lest whiteness and blackness become static versions of the marxist superstructure/base paradigm – discrete, separate entities rather than constantly entangled registers – ethnographers must devise means to analyze how whites, as racial subjects, are embroiled in predicaments where the meanings of race are unclear and shifting, subjects of discourses or local idioms that are fashioned in fast-changing sites.

Acknowledgment

I am indebted to Helán Page and other reviewers for their critical comments on an earlier version of this essay.

Notes

1 The pioneering work by an anthropologist in this area is Virginia Dominguez's *White by Definition (1986)*. The current upsurge of interdisciplinary approaches to whiteness has been the subject of several reviews; see Brody 1996, Fishkin 1995, and Hyde 1995.
2 Quoted in ABC's *Nightline* segment "America in Black and White," which aired June 17, 1996.
3 Dyer 1988; Morrison 1992; Nelson 1992.
4 Allen 1994; Roediger 1991; Saxton 1990.
5 Holloway 1990; Lott 1993; Piersen 1993.
6 Frankenberg 1993; E. Jackson 1993; Jamieson 1992; Lipsitz 1995; Page and Thomas 1994.

7 The notion of marked and unmarked terms derives from linguistic theories (Waugh 1982).

8 The social construction of race is also under assault from a revived enthusiasm for objectifying race via genetics (Lieberman 1995; Rushton 1995).

9 I use the phrase *white racialness* to underscore this shift in analytical attention from a primary emphasis on the ideological unity of whiteness toward a more open-ended questioning of the continuing cultural significance of race via examinations of the racialness of whites (Hartigan, in press [b]).

10 Roediger asserts this position very strongly. He argues that "the central political implication arising from the insight that race is socially constructed is the specific need to attack whiteness as a destructive ideology rather than to attack the concept of race abstractly" (1993: 3). His purpose is to counter white claims to victimization by "reverse racism" and to undermine their interests in responding in kind to the overt politicization of blackness. While the political importance of this stance should be clear, it is exactly these confused efforts by whites to make sense of the changing significance of race that we need to analyze and understand.

11 Harrison allows that racial meanings and hierarchies are unstable, but this instability is constrained by poles of difference that have remained relatively constant; white supremacy and the black subordination that demarcates the social bottom. Although whiteness and blackness have not had fixed meanings and boundaries, the opposition between them has provided the stabilizing backbone for the United States' racialized social body (1995: 59).

12 An exception is Jane Hill's analysis of "the ambivalent project of Anglo domination, that attempts simultaneously to reduce Hispanics to economic dependence and marginality, yet adopts many of their practices and exploits their presence in the region as a source of 'color' and 'romance' that will attract tourists and investors" (1993: 150).

13 This fieldwork is recounted in *Cultural Constructions of Whiteness: Racial and Class Formations in Detroit* (Hartigan, in press [a]).

14 Whatever the state of race relations in Detroit, whiteness remains hegemonic nationally. The interplay of racial formations at the national, regional, city, and neighborhood level can be usefully figured through the model of "partial connections" that Marilyn Strathern (1991) has described (see Hartigan, in press [c]).

15 Collier-Thomas and Turner 1994; Green 1970; Harrison 1988; Wade 1993; Wilson 1985.

16 Anderson 1990; Foley 1990; Merry 1981; Schneider and Smith 1973; Brett Williams 1988; T. Williams 1992.

17 Alex-Assensoh 1995; Hartigan in press [b]; MacLeod 1987.

18 Fordham 1988, 1993; Page 1988; Urciuoli 1993.

19 Chock 1987; Di Leonardo 1984; Rieder 1985; Sacks 1994.

20 Foundational texts in this tradition include Davis et al. 1941, Dollard 1937, and Powdermaker 1993 [1939].

References

Alba, Richard (1990) *Ethnic Identity: The Transformation of White America.* New Haven, CT: Yale University Press.

Alexander, Jack (1977) The Culture of Race in Middle-Class Kingston, Jamaica. *American Ethnologist*, 4: 413–35.

Alex-Assensoh, Yvette (1995) Myths about Race and the Underclass: Concentrated Poverty and "Underclass" Behaviors. *Urban Affairs Review*, 31: 3–19.

Allen, Theodore (1994) *The Invention of the White Race*, vol. 1. New York: Verso.

Anderson, Elijah (1990) *Streetwise: Race, Class, and Change in an Urban Community*. Chicago: University of Chicago Press.

Brody, Jennifer (1996) Reading Race and Gender: When White Women Matter. *American Quarterly*, 48: 153–9.

Cell, John (1982) *The Highest Stage of White Supremacy: The Origins of Segregation in South Africa and the American South*. Cambridge: Cambridge University Press.

Chock, Phyllis (1987) The Irony of Stereotypes: Towards an Anthropology of Ethnicity. *Cultural Anthropology*, 2: 347–68.

Collier-Thomas, Bettye and James Turner (1994) Race, Class and Color: The African American Discourse on Identity. *Journal of American Ethnic History*, 14: 5–31.

Crapanzano, Vincent (1985) *Waiting: The Whites of South Africa*. New York: Random House.

Davis, Allison, Burleigh B. Gardner, and Mary R. Gardner (1941) *Deep South: A Social Anthropological Study of Caste and Class*. Chicago: University of Chicago Press.

Di Leonardo, Micaela (1984) *The Varieties of Ethnic Experience: Kinship, Class, and Gender among California Italian-Americans*. Ithaca, NY: Cornell University Press.

Dollard, John (1937) *Caste and Class in a Southern Town*. New Haven, CT: Yale University Press.

Dominguez, Virginia (1986) *White by Definition: Social Classification in Creole Louisiana*. New Brunswick, NJ: Rutgers University Press.

1994 A Taste for "the Other." *Current Anthropology*, 35: 333–48.

Douglass, Lisa (1992) *The Power of Sentiment: Love, Hierarchy, and the Jamaican Family Elite*. Boulder, CO: Westview Press.

Du Bois, W. E. B. (1980 [1940]) *Dusk of Dawn: An Essay towards an Autobiography of a Race Concept*. Franklin Center, PA: Franklin Library.

Dyer, Richard (1988) White. *Screen*, 29 (Fall): 44–64.

Farley, Reynolds, Charlotte Steeh, Tara Jackson, Maria Krysan, and Keith Reeves (1993) Continued Racial Residential Segregation in Detroit: "Chocolate City, Vanilla Suburbs" Revisited. *Journal of Housing Research*, 4: 1–38.

Fishkin, Shelly (1995) Interrogating "Whiteness," Complicating "Blackness": Remapping American Culture. *American Quarterly*, 47: 428–66.

Foley, Douglas (1990) *Learning Capitalist Culture: Deep in the Heart of Texas*. Philadelphia: University of Pennsylvania Press.

Fordham, Signithia (1988) Racelessness as a Factor in Black Students' Success: Pragmatic Strategy or Pyrrhic Victory. *Harvard Educational Review*, 58 (1):54–84.

1993 "Those Loud Black Girls": (Black) Women, Silence, and Gender "Passing" in the Academy. *Anthropology and Education Quarterly*, 24: 3–32.

Frankenberg, Ruth (1993) *White Women, Race Matters: The Social Construction of Whiteness*. Minneapolis: University of Minnesota Press.

Fredrickson, George (1981) *A Comparative Study of American and South African History*. New York: Oxford University Press.

Green, Vera (1970) The Confrontation of Diversity within the Black Community. *Human Organization*, 29: 267–72.

Harrison, Faye (1988) Introduction: An African Diaspora Perspective For Urban Anthropology. *Urban Anthropology*, 17 (2–3): 111–40.

Harrison, Faye (1995) The Persistent Power of "Race" in the Cultural and Political Economy of Racism. *Annual Review of Anthropology*, 24: 47–74.

Harrison, Faye, ed. (1991) *Decolonizing Anthropology: Moving Further Toward an Anthropology for Liberation*. Washington, D.C.: American Anthropological Association.

Hartigan, John, Jr. (1996) "Disgrace to the Race": "Hillbillies" and the Color Line in Detroit. In Philip Obermiller (ed.), *Downhome, Downtown: Urban Appalachians in the 1990s*. Dubuque, LA: Kendall and Hunt, pp. 55–71.

Hartigan, John, Jr. (1997a) When White Americans Are a Minority. In Larry Naylor (ed.), *Cultural Diversity in the United States*. Westport, CT: Bergin and Garvey, pp. 103–15.

Hartigan, John, Jr. (1997b) Name Calling: Objectifying "Poor Whites" and "White Trash." In Matt Wray and Annalee Newitz (eds), *White Trash: Class, Race and the Construction of American Identity*. New York: Routledge, pp. 41–56.

Hartigan, John, Jr. (In press [a]) *Cultural Constructions of Whiteness: Racial and Class Formations in Detroit*. Princeton, NJ: Princeton University Press.

Hartigan, John, Jr. (In press [b]) Green Ghettoes and the White Underclass. *Social Research*, 64 (2).

Hartigan, John, Jr. (In press [c]) Locating White Detroit. In Ruth Frankenberg (ed.), *Displacing Whiteness: Essays in Social and Cultural Criticism*. Durham, NC: Duke University Press.

Heath, Shirley Brice (1983) *Ways with Words: Language, Life, and Work in Communities and Classrooms*. Cambridge: Cambridge University Press.

Hill, Jane (1993) Hasta La Vista, Baby: Anglo Spanish in the American Southwest. *Critique of Anthropology*, 13: 145–76.

Hoetnik, H. (1985) "Race" and Color in the Caribbean. In Sidney Mintz and Sally Price (eds), *Caribbean Contours*. Baltimore: Johns Hopkins University Press, pp. 55–84.

Holloway, Joseph E., ed. (1990) *Africanisms in American Culture*. Bloomington: Indiana University Press.

Hyde, Cheryl (1995) The Meaning of Whiteness. *Qualitative Sociology*, 18: 87–95.

Jackson, Eileen (1993) Whiting-Out Difference: Why US Nursing Research Fails Black Families. *Medical Anthropology Quarterly*, 7: 363–85.

Jackson, Peter, and Jan Penrose (1993) *Constructions of Race, Place and Nation*. Minneapolis: University of Minnesota Press.

Jamieson, Kathleen Hall (1992) *Dirty Politics: Deception, Distraction, and Democracy*. New York: Oxford University Press.

Kochman, Thomas (1981) *Black and White Styles in Conflict*. Chicago: University of Chicago Press.

Labov, Teresa (1990) Ideological Themes in Reports of Interracial Conflict. In Allen Grimshaw (ed.), *Conflict Talk: Sociolinguistic Investigations of Arguments in Conversations*. Cambridge: Cambridge University Press, pp. 139–59.

Lieberman, Leonard (1995) An Attempted Revival of the Race Concept. The Evolution of Racism: Human Differences and the Use and Abuse of Science. *American Anthropologist*, 97: 590–2.

Lieberson, Stanley (1985) Unhyphenated Whites in the United States. *Ethnic and Racial Studies*, 8: 159–80.

Lipsitz, George (1995) The Possessive Investment in Whiteness: Racialized Social

Democracy and the "White" Problem in American Studies. *American Quarterly*, 47: 369–87.

Lott, Eric (1993) *Love and Theft: Blackface Minstrelsy and the American Working Class*. Oxford, England: Oxford University Press.

MacLeod, Jay (1987) *Ain't No Makin' It: Leveled Aspirations in a Low Income Neighborhood*. Boulder, CO: Westview Press.

Marable, Manning, and Leith Mullings (1994) The Divided Mind of Black America: Race, Ideology and Politics in the Post Civil Rights Era. *Race and Class*, 36: 61–72.

Massey, Douglas, and Nancy Denton (1993) *American Apartheid: Segregation and the Making of the Underclass*. Cambridge, MA: Harvard University Press.

Merry, Sally (1981) *Urban Danger. Life in a Neighborhood of Strangers*. Philadelphia: Temple University Press.

Morrison, Toni (1992) *Playing in the Dark: Whiteness and the Literary Imagination*. Cambridge, MA: Harvard University Press.

Nelson, Dana (1992) *The Word in Black and White: Reading "Race" in American Literature, 1638–1867*. New York: Oxford University Press.

Page, Helán E. (1988) Dialogic Principles of Interactive Learning in the Ethnographic Relationship. *Journal of Anthropological Research*, 44: 163–81.

Page, Helán E. (1995) North American Dialogue. Interview by Sam Beck. *Anthropology Newsletter*, 36 (1): 21–2.

Page, Helán E., and R. Brooke Thomas (1994) White Public Space and the Construction of White Privilege in US Health Care: Fresh Concepts and a New Model of Analysis. *Medical Anthropology Quarterly*, 8: 109–16.

Perry, Huey (1991) Deracialization as an Analytical Construct in American Urban Politics. *Urban Affairs Quarterly*, 27: 181–91.

Piersen, William (1993) *Black Legacy: America's Hidden Heritage*. Amherst: University of Massachusetts Press.

Powdermaker, Hortense (1993 [1939]) *After Freedom: A Cultural Study in the Deep South*. Madison: University of Wisconsin Press.

Rieder, Jonathan (1985) *Canarsie: The Jews and Italians of Brooklyn against Liberalism*. Cambridge, MA: Harvard University Press.

Roediger, David (1991) *The Wages of Whiteness: Race and the Making of the American Working Class*. London: Verso.

Roediger, David (1993) *Towards the Abolition of Whiteness: Essays on Race, Politics, and Working Class History*. London: Verso.

Rushton, J. Phillippe (1995) *Race, Evolution, and Behavior: A Life History Perspective*. New Brunswick, NJ: Transaction Press.

Sacks, Karen (1994) How Did Jews Become White Folks? In Steven Gregory and Roger Saruek (eds), *Race*. New Brunswick, NJ: Rutgers University Press, pp. 78–102.

Sansone, Livio (1994) The Making of Black Culture: The New Subculture of Lower-Class Young Black Males of Surinamese Origin in Amsterdam. *Critique of Anthropology*, 14: 173–98.

Saxton, Alexander (1990) *The Rise and Fall of the White Republic: Class Politics and Mass Culture in 19th-Century America*. London: Verso.

Schneider, David, and Raymond Smith (1973) *Class Differences and Sex Roles in American Kinship and Family Structure*. Englewood Cliffs, NJ: Prentice-Hall.

Segal, Daniel (1993) "Race" and "Color" in Pre-Independence Trinidad and Tobago. In Kevin Yelvington (ed.), *Trinidad Ethnicity*. Knoxville: University of Tennessee Press, pp. 81–115.

Smedley, Audrey (1993) *Race in North America: Origins and Evolution of a World View*. Boulder, CO: Westview Press.

Strathern, Marilyn (1991) *Partial Connections*. Savage, MD: Rowman and Littlefield.

Taussig, Michael (1987) *Shamanism, Colonialism, and the Wild Man: Study in Terror and Healing*. Chicago: University of Chicago Press.

Urciuoli, Bonnie (1993) Representing Class: Who Decides? *Anthropological Quarterly*, 66: 203–10.

Varenne, Herve (1986) *Symbolizing America*. Lincoln: University of Nebraska Press.

Wade, Peter (1993) *Blackness and Race Mixture: The Dynamics of Racial Identity in Colombia*. Baltimore: Johns Hopkin University Press.

Waugh, Linda (1982) Marked and Unmarked: A Choice between Unequals in Semiotic Structure. *Semiotica*, 38: 299–318.

Williams, Brackette (1991) *Stains on My Name, War in My Veins: Guyana and the Politics of Cultural Struggle*. Durham, NC: Duke University Press.

Williams, Brett (1988) *Upscaling Downtown: Stalled Gentrification in Washington, D.C.* Ithaca, NY: Cornell University Press.

Williams, Terry (1992) *Crackhouse: Notes from the End of the Line*. Reading, MA: Addison-Wesley Publishing.

Wilson, William Julius (1985) *The Declining Significance of Race*. Chicago: University of Chicago Press.

13

Constructions of Whiteness in European and American Anti-Racism

Alastair Bonnett

Introduction

It would be hard to imagine someone writing a book about what it means to be white. Most white people don't consider themselves to be part of a race that needs examining. They are the natural order of things.

(Saynor, 1995)

As James Saynor's remark implies, within white-dominated societies,[1] and among white people, whiteness remains a relatively underdiscussed and underresearched "racial" identity. Indeed, while the history and categorization of "non-whiteness" has frequently been subject to debate, it is only in the past few years that a comparable discussion has begun on the subject of whiteness. One of the most important consequences of this relative invisibility has been the naturalization of whiteness for white people; whiteness tends to be far more visible to non-whites – for example, to African-Americans (see hooks, 1992; Erikson, 1995; and on British Asians, see Puar, 1995). Within the vast majority of texts that draw on the notion of "racial" difference, whiteness is positioned as existing outside the political and economic forces that seem to shape other racialized identities. As Dyer (1988: 46) notes:

> It is the way black people are marked as black (are not just "people") in representation that has made it relatively easy to analyse their representation, whereas white people – not there as a category and everywhere as a fact – are difficult, if not impossible to analyse *qua* white.

The naturalization of whiteness has not been limited to racist discourses. In this chapter I will show that the reification of whiteness is also a central current within English language anti-racist thought and practice. I shall, in addition, be suggesting that this process has deleterious consequences for the anti-racist project. More specifically, I argue that the reification of whiteness has enabled people of European extraction to imagine that their identity is stable and immutable and, relatedly, to remain unengaged with the anti-racist historicization (and de-naturalization) of "racial" meaning.

As my title indicates, I shall be focusing on the European (more specifically, British) and North American anti-racist debate. The active and diverse anti-racist traditions within these societies are currently experiencing a series of intellectual and practical crises and opportunities. Traditional anti-racist paradigms are being challenged by a variety of forces, including a so-called "new ethnic assertiveness" (Modood, 1990a), conservative anti-anti-racism and postmodern critical interventions (for discussion, see Bonnett, 1993a; Rattansi, 1992). Ali Rattansi (1992: 52–3) has argued that "if anti-racism is to be effective" it will be "necessary to take a hard and perhaps painful look at the terms under which [it has] operated so far." More specifically, Rattansi calls attention to anti-racists' inadequate and simplistic modes of "racial" representation. Unprepared to acknowledge the "contradictions, inconsistencies and ambivalences" within white and non-white identities (ibid.: 73), orthodox anti-racism appears ill-equipped to engage creatively with the fluid and complex forces of the racialization process. This chapter represents an attempt to engage and move forward the debate around "racial" representations within European and American anti-racism.

My account begins with an assessment of the emergence of a white "racial" identity during the nineteenth and twentieth centuries. It is argued that the era witnessed the development of an increasingly fixed and narrow vision of the boundaries and meaning of the term "white." Second, I analyze some instances of the reified nature of whiteness implicit in contemporary British and North American anti-racism. These include "white" in anti-racist nomenclature; whiteness versus the "new ethnic assertiveness" and essentialist interpretations of the attributes of white identity. Having introduced the way anti-racism often erases and reifies whiteness, I turn to a review of recent anti-racist activism and writings that appear to offer an alternative approach. In particular, I address two forms of what I shall term "White Studies": first, the literature of "white confession"; and second, historical "geographies" of whiteness. As we shall see, although both discursive forms articulate problematic notions of whiteness, I want to suggest that the historical geography approach does point towards the possibility of more nuanced, and hence strategically and theoretically more useful, anti-racist reading of whiteness. The chapter concludes with an assessment of the practical and theoretical implications of anti-essentialist readings of whiteness.

The Creation of a White "Racial Identity"

Reference to a white "racial" identity is a relatively recent phenomenon. Indeed, as we shall see, the ubiquitous contemporary usage of the category "white," as referring only to "Europeans" and their descendants, does not appear to have been firmly established until the twentieth century. Before the emergence of the "race" concept in the late eighteenth and early nineteenth centuries (Banton, 1977; 1987), the notion that a group of people were "white" did not imply that they belonged to a discrete biological entity with a set of immutable "racial" attributes. Rather, the term's most common meaning referred simply to an individual's or group's skin color. The *Oxford English Dictionary* (1989) offers examples of the use of white (referring to "whiteness or fairness of complexion") in this sense from the early thirteenth century (see also Snowden, 1983 for earlier examples). This largely descriptive use of the term continued to be influential well into the period of European colonial expansion. Thus we find, as a recent study by Reid shows (1994: 274–5), that Portuguese "conquistadors routinely described their Gujerati or Arab antagonists as 'white,' as well as the Chinese and Ryukynans." The *OED* offers a similar example from a travel book published in 1604. Grimstone's *D'Acosta's History of the Indies* describes "a part of Peru, and of the new kingdom of Grenado, which . . . are very temperate Countries . . . and the inhabitants are white."

Other, more familiar uses of the category, which centred on notions of ethno-religious lines of descent, were also, however, developing as the West expanded its imperial dominion. Thus, for example, the first usage of white as an "ethnic type (chiefly European or of European extraction)" that the *OED* cites, and which is not specifically applied to a non-European group, is the distinction made by the English cleric, C. Nesse, in 1680, between "the White Line, (the Posterity of Seth)" and "the Black Line, (the Cursed brood of Cain)." Here whiteness is being associated with a moral lineage, an association that was inevitably strengthened by the intellectual conflation of "Europe" with "Christendom" that had developed from the late medieval period onwards (Hay, 1957; den Boer, 1995). Thus a triple conflation of "white," "Europe" and "Christian" arose that imparted moral, cultural and territorial content to whiteness.

The development of "racial" science at the end of the eighteenth century may be seen to have lent further authority to a number of the central categories employed within the ethno-religious tradition, and further subverted the development of "multiracial" uses of "white." However, the completion of this process is comparatively recent. Throughout the eighteenth and nineteenth centuries diverse readings of whiteness continued that transcended the narrowly "Eurocentric" vision of the category with which we have become so familiar in our own century. David Roediger's historical studies (1992; 1994) of the consolidation of white "racial" identity in the United States provide ample testimony to the instability of the term in nineteenth-century America. He explains how Irish and Italian immigrants were initially not deemed to be white, and had to struggle to establish themselves as a "natural" part of the white labor fraternity. Within the nineteenth and even early twentieth centuries, the mismatch between "European" and white may also be observed working in the other, more traditional direction: through the use of "white" to label groups associated with non-European areas of the world. This usage achieved a rather tense marriage with "racial" science in the English school textbook *A Geography of Africa* (Lyde, 1914: first published 1899). "The non-European population" of Africa, the book explains, "belongs mainly to one of two races, the white and the black" (Lyde, 1914: 2). Among the "whites" of Africa Lyde includes "Arabs and Abyssinians . . . Berbers and Tuaregs, Masi and Somalis" (ibid.).

Although, of course, whiteness is still subject to rearticulation and resignification, the twentieth century has seen the category become increasingly synonymous with "European." Indeed, the two words appear to be used interchangeably in the majority of English-language "race" commentaries. Clearly, this process makes the notion of "non-white Europeans" a problematic one (Bonnett, 1993b). It is interesting to note in this regard that – as Elba (1990) reports – in the United States the phrase "European American" is beginning to be used as a more ethnically resonant substitute for "white." Although this trend derives from an assumed equivalence of the two categories, it may eventually lead to white being seen as an archaic and offensive "racial" descriptor (like "yellow," "red," "brown" and, to a lesser extent, "black"). At the present time, however, this speculation merely serves to highlight the extraordinary resilience and ubiquity of the term.

Although a full explanation of the consolidation of a "European" meaning for white in the twentieth century lies beyond the scope of this chapter, the importance of one causal factor – the influence of the American "race relations" paradigm – appears relatively clear. In American "racial" discourse, a highly dualistic vision of "racial conflict" between "blacks" and "whites" has been a long and firmly established structuring dynamic of the "race" debate. As the cultural and economic power of America has spread across the world, these constructions have come to be diffused across the globe (adopted, but also sometimes adapted – for example, through British political uses of black; see Modood, 1990b).[2] Thus, although whiteness is far from being simply an American invention, its continuing ubiquity, restrictive interpretation and conceptual opposition to blackness may be understood to have been either introduced and/or consolidated in numerous different nations through the cultural and economic influence of the late twentieth century's principal hegemony.

We have seen that white is neither an eternal nor an immutable category. As this suggests, the contemporary meaning of whiteness is not necessarily stable or permanent but, rather, a site of change and struggle. What is particularly striking, however, is the failure of anti-racists to engage with this site of potential contestation.

Anti-Racism and the Reification of Whiteness

If a white "racial" identity has become both increasingly ubiquitous and narrowly defined, a similarly static and uncritical understanding of whiteness has permeated the anti-racist project.

I am not, of course, claiming here that the supposed attributes of white "racial" consciousness have not been examined by anti-racists (for they have at some length; see, for example, Katz, 1978; Wellman, 1977). Rather, I am seeking to show that whiteness has tended to be approached by anti-racists as a fixed, asocial category rather than a mutable social construction. In other words, anti-racists have, for the most part, yet to become aware of, and escape from, the practice of treating whiteness as a static, ahistorical, aspatial, objective "thing": something set outside social change, something central and permanent, something that defines the "other" but is not itself subject to others' definitions.

It is my contention that reifying myths of whiteness subvert the anti-racist struggle. They create an essentializing dynamic at the heart of a project that is necessarily critical not only of "racial" stereotypes, but of the "race" concept itself. They also lead towards the positioning (or self-positioning) of white people as fundamentally outside, and untouched by, the contemporary controversies of "racial" identity politics. For within much contemporary anti-racist debate, whiteness is addressed as an unproblematic category (albeit with negative attributes), a category which is not subject to the constant processes of challenge and change that have characterized the history of other "racial" names. This process enables white people to occupy a privileged location in anti-racist debate; they are allowed the luxury of being passive observers, of being altruistically motivated, of knowing that "their" "racial" identity might be reviled and lambasted but never actually made slippery, torn open, or, indeed, abolished.

To exemplify these points, I will offer three instances of the erasure and objectification of whiteness within anti-racism.

"White" in anti-racist terminology

Anti-racists have often sought to show that language matters. Writers as diverse as Gilroy (1987) and Modood (1988) have insisted that "racial" terms are neither politically neutral nor static; that they have contested histories. Not unrelatedly, anti-racists have tried to encourage the use of "racial" nomenclature that embodies political reflexivity and discourage expressions that appear imposed, outmoded, offensive and/or phenotypically reductive.

However, there is one exception to this linguistic sensitivity. "White" tends to be excluded from anti-racists' list of acceptable or debatable "racial" nouns (see, for example, ILEA, 1983; Gaine, 1987). Indeed, in the majority of anti-racist work the meaning of whiteness appears to be considered beyond dispute: its boundaries are obvious. Thus the reification of whiteness is enacted as an erasure: whiteness is simply left out.

For a typical example we may turn to the highly influential anti-racist policy documents published by the Inner London Education Authority (ILEA) in 1983. These documents made liberal use of the concept of whiteness. Thus, for example, in *A Policy for Equality: Race* (1983), references are made to the fact that "white people have very much to learn from the experiences of black people" (1983: 5) as well as to the way "racism gives white people a false view of their own identity and history." In all this the ILEA implies that there exists "a white community," a distinct and obvious group of people who have their "own identity and history." The reification inherent in such interpretations is cemented into unassailable common sense by this particular document's "Note on Terminology." The note begins with the somewhat cryptic clause "The following terms are used:." Beneath the authority's colon we find explanations of the meaning of three "racial" adjectives – "Afro-Caribbean," "Asian" and "black." There is no entry on "white." It is the only "racial" noun mentioned in the main text whose meaning is not explained. Thus white is allowed to "speak for itself." It is permitted the privilege of having an obvious meaning; of being a normal rather than an exceptional case; of being a defining, not a defined, category.

Destabilizing blackness/stabilizing whiteness

Much recent concern has been expressed in Britain about the meaning and boundaries of blackness. A number of writers, including Tariq Modood (1988; 1990b) and Ali Rattansi (1992), have made an important intervention into British anti-racism by arguing that the anti-racist practice of defining South Asian people as black denies the variety and multifaceted nature of the cultural identities of this group.

Yet these attempts to destabilize the homogenizing currents within anti-racism have been fragmentary and partial. It is only certain specific "communities," such as South Asians and Muslims, that are being disembedded from the monoliths of orthodox anti-racism. The corollary of blackness – whiteness – has been left entirely undisturbed. Thus we find that even within an article entitled "Beyond Racial Dualism" (in Modood, 1992), the mythologies of blackness are attacked, whilst those of whiteness are left undiscussed. Only one half of the dualism is surmounted: whiteness remains intact, while blackness is demolished.

This selectivity is, I would submit, a potentially disastrous facet of contemporary discourses that seek to reflect and/or reiterate the so-called "new ethnic assertiveness" (Modood, 1990a). It is important not to forget that, within Britain, anti-racists' constructions of blackness were designed to serve an important purpose: to establish and support a "community of resistance" within and against a white racist society. In other words, "black" was a politically self-conscious category necessitated by the existence of a naturalized and unselfconscious "whiteness." The close links established between blackness and a militant, relatively unethnicized, identity may be seen to have made the term incapable of incorporating, and sustaining, divergent ethnicities in the same way as whiteness appears to do. However, this vulnerability is rooted in the anti-essentialist tendencies inherent within any project that attempts to privilege political over "natural" solidarity. It is, then, a somewhat savage irony that it is "black," a relatively sophisticated and "self-knowing" construction, rather than "white," the unselfcomprehending identity that forced "black" into existence, that is on the receiving end of so many contemporary attempts to destabilize "racial monoliths."

"White racism" as an essentialist category

As I have implied, anti-racists have often implicitly, and even explicitly, placed a myth of whiteness at the center of their discourse. This myth views "being white" as an immutable condition with clear and distinct moral attributes. These attributes often include: being racist; not experiencing racism; being an oppressor; not experiencing oppression; silencing; not being silenced. People of color are defined via their relation to this myth. They are defined, then, as "non-whites": as people who are acted upon by whites; people whose identity is formed through their resistance to others' oppressive, silencing agency (this construction is discussed in Modood, 1990b).

To exemplify this point I will turn to a recent Canadian anti-racist text. In 1994, a Toronto-based private anti-racist consultancy called the Doris Marshall Institute produced an address on "Maintaining the Tensions of Anti-racist Education" in the journal *Orbit*. About a third of the piece is devoted to a commentary on the relationship between a white member of the group and the commissioning of the article. "The editors of *Orbit*," notes the Institute (DMI, 1994: 20), "approached Barb Thomas, one of the core members of the Doris Marshall Institute (DMI), to write an article on our approach to anti-racism education." However, this decision was in error, notes the Institute, because:

> Barb is a white woman who does not experience racism. There is a mounting, legitimate critique of white people getting the space, resources and recognition for anti-racism work. (1994: 20)

The Doris Marshall Institute goes on to explain that the role of anti-racism is to strengthen "the voices and leadership of persons of color" and to

> insist that white people take responsibility for confronting racism and assist white people in this when necessary, and challenge speakers and writers to make explicit their voices and locations and what their limits and possibilities are. (1994: 20–1)

It is being argued here that the "limits and possibilities" of a racialized subject's engagement with anti-racism are established by her or his experiences of racism. Although this proposition has a certain superficial straightforwardness (but see Miles, 1989; and Fuss, 1990), it relies on a number of essentialist demarcations and categorizations. More specifically, the experiences of "white people" are presented as manifest and unchanging. The characteristics of whiteness are removed from social context and set outside history and geography.

It is important to note that this process does not occur simply because racism is being associated by anti-racists, such as the Doris Marshall Institute, with "white" racism against "people of color." This conflation clearly removes from view many forms of racialized ethnic and religious antagonism and disadvantage. However, to recognize the diversity of racism and of white experience is not necessarily to deconstruct whiteness. The problem with the Doris Marshall Institute's interpretation is not merely their lack of sensitivity to the plurality of whitenesses but, more fundamentally, their faith in whiteness as a common-sense, obvious and discrete entity at the heart of "racial" history. Whiteness is thus employed as both the conceptual center and the "other" of anti-racism; the defining, normative term of anti-racist praxis and theory. As this implies, to define whiteness, to acknowledge its contingent, slippery constructions, would radically destabilize orthodox anti-racism. It is towards studies that appear to promise such a transformation that I now turn.

Challenges and Reaffirmations of Anti-Racist Orthodoxy Within "White Studies"

Some recent examples of anti-racist work seek explicitly to raise the issue of whiteness within anti-racist debate. This sensitivity to the existence of a white "racial" identity should not, however, be confused with an anti-essentialist agenda. A divergence between the two tendencies is particularly apparent in the form of white studies I discuss first, the literature of "white confession."

Confessions of a white anti-racist

The recent flurry of interest in whiteness in both Europe and America has generally been viewed as a new and original phenomenon. However, there are a number of pathways within this work, some of which are relatively well-worn. The most significant of these more traveled routes is the literature and practice of white confession.

This paradigm, which seeks to enable and provoke Euro-Americans to confront/realize/admit to their own whiteness, represents a reworking of the "consciousness-raising" or "awareness-training" forms of anti-racism that rose to prominence in the 1970s and early 1980s. These approaches were characterized by their interest in the way so-called white people develop "racial" prejudices (see, for example, Wellman, 1977; Katz, 1978). More specifically, they tended to suggest that "whites" need to "face up to" their own, and other "white" people's, racism in order successfully to expunge it from their psyche.

Over the past decade, a number of well-known critiques of the individualistic, moralistic character of "Racism Awareness Training" (RAT) have undermined its authority as a management and counselling resource (Sivanandan, 1985; Gurnah, 1984). However, its confessional dynamic remains a potent force within anti-racism, including white studies. At its crudest the confessional approach erases all questions relating to the contingent, slippery nature of whiteness. Instead, a moral narrative is offered based on the presumed value of "white" "self-disclosure" (see, for example, Chater, 1994; Camper, 1994). Thus in her article "Biting the Hand That Feeds Me: Notes on Privilege from a White Anti-Racist Feminist," Nancy Chater attempts to expose her own and other "white" feminists' "whiteness" to anti-racist critique. Drawing on that most reifying of reflexive devices, "speaking as a . . . ," followed by a keyword mini-autobiography, Chater explains that "as an anti-racist white feminist" she inevitably has to confront the ready potential of speaking or acting in ways that are based on or slide into arrogance, moralizing, self-congratulation, liberal politics, appropriation, careerism or rhetoric (Chater, 1994: 100).

Thus, whiteness is defined as referring to a "racial" group characterized by its moral failings; a community which is exhorted to be watchful of the reactionary tendencies apparently inherent in its anti-racist practice. Chater goes on prescriptively to sketch a number of ethical dilemmas faced by "white" anti-racist feminists. In particular, she suggests that such people need continually to monitor their seemingly innate capacity to silence non-whites, and to acknowledge their own embeddedness within a "racial" elite. "White" feminists should also avoid assuming "an edge of moral or intellectual superiority over and distance from other white people, especially those displaying a lack of politicized awareness of racism" (ibid.: 101). In other words, Chater is suggesting that so-called "whites" should not – indeed, cannot – escape being part of "their racial group," or its attendant political conservatism.

I am not suggesting here that Chater's prescriptive strategies are necessarily wrong, and that anti-racists should ignore or contradict her advice. What I wish to draw attention to is the process of category construction that structures her argument – more specifically, the process whereby whiteness assumes a fixed and pivotal role as both a "racial community" and a "site of confession." These locations establish whiteness as an arena not of engagement with anti-racism but of self-generated altruistic interest for "others" as well as for "white people's" own moral well-being. Indeed, it is tempting to argue that white confessional anti-racism establishes whiteness as the moral center of anti-racist discourse. For while non-white anti-racists are cast as taking part in an instrumental politics of "resistance" and "self-preservation," "white anti-racism" is continually elevated to a higher ethical terrain, removed from the realm of co-operation and participation to the more traditional (colonial, neo-colonial and anti-racist) role of paternalistic "concern."

The essentializing tendencies within Chater's text find echoes in other, more theoretically nuanced work. For although, as we shall see, the development of historical geographies of whiteness has enabled a decisive move away from the reifying traditions outlined above, even some of its most adept adherents sometimes slip into moralizing and confessional modes of analysis and address.

Thus, for example, Helen Charles writes of the importance of "Coming out as white." Explaining that "it is negatively exhausting teaching 'white women' what it is like to be black," she notes: "I feel it is now time for some verbal and textual 'outness'" amongst white women (Charles, 1992: 33). The implicit parallel Charles is making between gay activists' "outing" of closet homosexuals is an instructive one. It suggests that whiteness is being interpreted as a fixed disposition; a "trait" that needs to be admitted to and exposed. And once uncovered, whiteness may, presumably, be "lived openly." The association of whiteness with what is conceived to be a psychosocial proclivity (i.e. sexuality) undermines the anti-essentialist advances that have been made in recent "white" studies. More generally, I would conclude that the confessional approach forms a destabilizing and unhelpful tendency set against the more rigorously sociological trajectory being developed in other parts of the field.

Historical geographies of whiteness

Against the major tendency of anti-racists to reify whiteness, a genuinely new and original counter-tendency may be emerging. The writers and activists within this group offer an interpretation of whiteness characterized by three things:

(a) An analysis of the historical and geographical contingency of whiteness.
(b) A critique of the category white, as currently constructed and connoted, as racist (but not necessarily a belief that all those people commonsensically assumed to be, or labeled, "white" are, *ipso facto*, racist).
(c) A sensitivity to the hybrid nature of contemporary "racial" identities.

The critical focus of this group is upon the racialization process that produces whiteness. Their political problematic is how this process may be simultaneously recognized without being reproduced. Thus the existence of whiteness as a social fact is acknowledged, dissected and resisted.

However, there is considerable diversity within this school. Two broad tendencies may be discerned. The first attempts to subsume the analysis of whiteness within a class analysis of the racialization process. The second stresses the plural constitution, and multiple lived experiences, of those to whom whiteness has been ascribed.

Theodore Allen (1994), David Roediger (1992; 1994), Noel Ignatiev (1995) and the contributors to the journal *Race Traitor* (subtitle: *Treason to Whiteness is Loyalty to Humanity)* may be placed firmly within the former camp. Each traces whiteness as a project of American capitalism and labor organizations, and each explicitly calls for its "abolition."

These scholars and activists view white identity as the self-interested creation of racialized capitalism; an ideology that offers false rewards to one racialized fraction of the working class at the expense of others. Thus it is argued that the task of anti-racists is not to encourage so-called white people to confess to their "own identity" but to enable them politically and historically to contextualize, then resist and abandon, "whiteness." The editors of *Race Traitor* (1994a; 1994b) explain their project in the following terms:

> Two points define the position of *Race Traitor* first, that the "white race" is not a natural but an historical category; second, that what was historically constructed can be undone. (*Race Traitor*, 1994: 108)

Whiteness is presented here as an entirely oppressive identity. "We will never have true democracy," explains Rubio in the same journal "so long as we have a 'white community'" (1994: 125).

However, the political conclusions of these historical studies derive, in the main, from a relatively limited reading of the synchronic social context of whiteness. For although whiteness is seen as – to use Allen's words – "the overriding jetstream that has governed the flow of American history" (1994: 22), it is analyzed as if it were almost entirely a product of class, and particularly labor, relations. Thus, although a precise and useful account of the construction of whiteness emerges from these texts, it is not one that readily opens itself to dialogue with other histories or struggles.

Moreover, within this body of work there is an unhelpful romanticization of blackness. Indeed, *Race Traitor's* project is not merely to destroy whiteness but to enable whites to "assimilate" blackness. Of course, blackness, too, is seen as a social construction, but it is construed as a construction that needs to be supported and reproduced. The editors argue:

> When whites reject their racial identity, they take a big step towards becoming human. But may that step not entail, for many, some engagement with blackness, perhaps even an identification as "black?" Recent experience, in this country and elsewhere, would indicate that it does. (*Race Traitor*, 1994: 115)

This formulation is clearly based upon a series of assumptions concerning the meaning of blackness. It implies that the romantic stereotype of the eternally resisting, victimized "black community" needs to be further strengthened in order to create a suitable location for escapees from whiteness. Thus black people are condemned to reification as the price of white people's liberation from the racialization process.

The somewhat clumsy political strategies of the white abolitionists are, it seems to me, a disappointing conclusion to their work. However, this failure is less apparent in other historical geographies of whiteness. In particular, Ruth Frankenberg's study *The Social Construction of Whiteness* provides a number of insights into the slippery, incomplete and diverse nature of a white "racial" identity. Frankenberg draws from her interviews with thirty white Californian women a complex portrait of the

> articulations of whiteness, seeking to specify how each is marked by the interlocking effects of geographical origin, generation, ethnicity, political orientation, gender and present-day geographical location. (Frankenberg, 1993: 18)

Thus, for example, in a chapter entitled "Growing up White: The Social Geography of Race," Frankenberg explores her interviewees' childhood experiences of whiteness. For some, whiteness was always something explicit, and physically and morally separate from non-whiteness. "I grew up in a town," explains one respondent, where "everyone was aware of race all the time and the races were pretty much white people and black people" (1993: 51). However, for another women, as Frankenberg notes, "'white' or 'Anglo' merely described another ethnic group" (1993: 65). One interviewee, enculturated within a "mixed" Mexican and white community, explains that she

> never looked at it like it was two separate cultures. I just kind of looked at it like, our family and our friends, they're Mexicans and Chicanos, and that was just a part of our life. (1993: 66)

Unfortunately, Frankenberg does not engage with the ambiguities of "Hispanic" identity. Thus, for example, she ignores the surely pertinent fact that – as Henwood (1994: 14) notes – in "the 1990 Census half of all Hispanics reported themselves as white, a little under half as 'other,' and a few as black, native, or Asian." Despite this absence, however, Frankenberg's discussion of the multiple and shifting boundaries of whiteness is of immense value. It also provides a number of interesting points of contact with other studies of the hybrid nature of "racial" subjectivities. In particular her work invokes parallels with the creative appropriation and intermixing of ethnic identities observed by a number of commentators of contemporary youth cultures (for example, Hebdige, 1979; Ross and Rose, 1994; Jones, 1989).

Simon Jones, in his ethnographic study of white Rastafarians in Birmingham (Jones, 1989), looks at a "white community" that self-consciously splices its own whiteness with styles and ideologies associated with Rastafarianism. This escape, as Jones notes, draws on a correlation of whiteness with boredom and passivity and of blackness with rebellion and the exotic. It is an "escape," then, based on certain familiar clichés of whiteness and blackness. Despite this reliance, however, the process of becoming and socially interacting as a white Rastafarian inevitably opens up the fluidity of "racial" identity, creating incomplete, impermanent and explicitly constructed moments of appropriation and cultural "play."

Another moment of hybridity is addressed by Jeater in her account of the "multiracial" anti-racist politics of late 1970s inner London. At that time, recalls Jeater,

> We all began to celebrate the complexities and interdependencies of our cultural heritages. White people like myself . . . who grew up listening to reggae music and who perhaps took part in the urban uprisings against the state, were as much a part of this project as everyone else . . . the cosmopolitanism and the dynamic inter-actions of cultural traditions created a real sense that the world was there to be forged in new ways. (Jeater, 1992: 118–19)

Such moments of crisis and youth revolt provide, perhaps, the clearest in-dications of the possibility of the deconstruction of "racial" categories, of creative hybridity. As the work of the historical geographers of whiteness cited above implies, however, the "confusion," and intermixing, of "racial" signs and boundaries is not restricted to moments of youthful transgression. Disruptive and mutant forms of "white" identity have a long and varied lineage. Both such histories and contemporary analyses provide a useful resource for anti-racist engagements with white identity.

Conclusions: Engaging Whiteness

This chapter has focused on one of the most intractable and, I believe, counter-productive of anti-racism's traditional monoliths. It has argued that anti-racism has objectified whiteness, and that this process has been perpetuated within confessional approaches to anti-racism. As we have seen, however, the past few years have also witnessed signs of a new willingness to look at the historical and geographical contingency of whiteness. This latter body of work enables a re-conceptualization of whiteness as a diverse and mutable social construction. Clearly, this trajectory also implies a new level of sophistication in both the recognition of and resistance to whiteness.

I wish to conclude by engaging with the debate around the meaning, as well as the political and social implications, of an anti-racist and anti-essentialist perspective on white identity.

Within the academic field of "racial" studies, most of the English language debate about the merits and demerits of anti-essentialism has focused on black identity. More specifically, controversy has been aroused by the work of post-structuralist African-American writers (for example, Gates, 1986; 1988; Baker, 1986; Appiah, 1985; see also Fuss, 1990; Abel, 1993) who have seemed to under-mine the meaning and political coherence of blackness. To deconstruct blackness, it has been argued, is politically naive. "It is insidious," notes Joyce (1987a: 341; see also Joyce, 1987b), "for the black literary critic to adopt any kind of strategy that diminishes or . . . negates his blackness." As Fuss (1990: 77) points out, critics such as Joyce charge that "to deconstruct 'race' is to abdicate, negate, or destroy black identity." Identifying poststructuralism with white critics, Fuss argues:

> In American culture, "race" has been far more an acknowledged component of black identity than white; for good or bad, whites have always seen "race" as a minority attribute, and blacks have courageously and persistently agitated on behalf of "the race." It is easy enough for white poststructuralist critics to place under erasure something they *think* they never had to begin with. (Fuss, 1990: 93)

In the eyes of some critics the gulf between the deconstructive and essentialist positions has been bridged by the development of "a strategic use of positivist essentialism in a scrupulously visible political interest" (Spivak, quoted by Fuss, 1990: 31; see also Baker, 1986). Such a position enables minority groups to "preserve" identities that facilitate struggle, resistance and solidarity while main-taining a critique of reified notions of "race." Asked to expand upon the implications of strategic essentialism, the term's progenitor, Spivak, comments: "The only way to work with collective agency is to teach a persistent critique of collective agency at the same time. . . . It is the persistent critique of what one cannot not want" (1990: 93).

Spivak's allusion to "what one cannot not want" reinforces the impression that this is a debate formatted entirely around the perceived interests of oppressed groups (more specifically, African-Americans). As this implies, the question of when we should stick to blackness and when we should critique it cannot simply be transposed by analogy on to questions of whiteness. Given the exclusionary and normative nature of its development, any form of essentialist "sticking to" whiteness is not a viable anti-racist position. As we have seen, whiteness has developed, over the past two hundred years, into a taken-for-granted experience structured upon a varying set of supremacist assumptions (sometimes cultural, sometimes biological, sometimes moral, sometimes all three). Non-white identities, by contrast, have been denied the privileges of normativity, and are marked within the West as marginal and inferior.

Unfortunately, those seeking to develop arguments for – or counter arguments against – a politically engaged anti-essentialism have rarely considered the implications of these positions for white identity (though see Abel, 1993). Thus, some of the most important questions for an anti-foundationalist anti-racism have remained undiscussed. Perhaps the most pertinent of these is how whiteness can be made visible, exposed for critical inspection, while at the same time opened as a myth, either a racist or even a "black" construction that needs to be, if not abolished, permanently caged between inverted commas. In other words, we need to ask how the enormous power of Euro-American institutions and social dynamics can be acknowledged and confronted at the same time as the essentialist pretensions of whiteness are denied.

It is important to note that the central tension at work within these questions is not between essentialism and anti-essentialism. Acknowledging the social power, the social existence, of Euro-American hegemonies is not the same as claiming (however ironically or self-consciously) that whiteness – read as a possessive label of that power – is a fixed or natural category. As this implies, the position that bridges the tension outlined in the questions I ask above may more usefully be termed strategic deconstruction than strategic essentialism. The problematic of strategic deconstruction is not when and how to "stick to," "preserve" or "save" whiteness, but when and how whiteness should be opened up, torn apart, made slippery, and when and how it should be revealed and confronted.

One possible route out of this dilemma is to view whiteness as a political category. Ever since James Baldwin's provocative assertion "As long as you think you are white, there's no hope for you" (quoted in Roediger, 1994), a political reading of whiteness has remained a minor theme within the most incisive anti-racist work. In the mid-1980s Clark and Subhan suggested, but did not develop, the notion that "both in global terms and in the British context . . . white as a political term is a term for the oppressor" (n.d.: 33). The recent development of historical geographies of whiteness has provided this position with fresh potential. Thanks to the research of critics such as Roediger, the ideological contours of whiteness can be rigorously mapped and historically contextualized. This work offers a substantive empirical and theoretical base for anti-racist rearticulations of whiteness from a natural to a political category. Anti-racists may then assess how individuals, institutions and States embrace, overthrow or reflexively monitor their whiteness.

Political whiteness may most usefully be viewed as an intellectual resource, rather than a universal solution. In certain circumstances it may provide an appropriate way of approaching a "white" identity that is able to remain both theoretically and practically apt. In other contexts, however, political whiteness may distort the nature of anti-racist alliances, offering white people nothing but a sense of negation, expressed through indulgent guilt complexes that erase the multiple and fragmented ethnicities that overlap with whiteness. As many commentators have observed (e.g., Macdonald et al., 1989; Cohen, 1992), one of the most important tasks of contemporary anti-racism is to engage so-called "white" people to bring them "inside" the anti-racist project. This implies that the notion of political whiteness should be set within a wider and more sophisticated anti-racist project that enables the historical and personal experiences of Euro-Americans to be explored with people of all "races." Such a process could provide Euro-Americans with a stake in anti-racism, as a project that talks to and about them, while weakening the common-sense, normative nature of "white" identity.[3]

A central aspect of any such enterprise would be the opening up of both the mutative, contingent history of "racial" identities and the possibility of their creative collision and hybrid reconstitution in the future. Hybridity in this sense – as Bhabha (1990) explains – does not merely refer to a marriage of traditions (though see Young, 1995). Rather, it

> is the "third space" which enables other positions to emerge. This third space displaces the histories that constitute it . . . [and] gives rise to something different, something new and unrecognizable, a new area of negotiation of meaning and representation. (Bhabha, 1990: 211)

Anti-racists need simultaneously to recognize and resist whiteness while enabling and analyzing its hybrid supersession. Whiteness has traditionally been the invisible center of the "race" equality debate. It is now time to draw it into an explicit *engagement* with the anti-racist project.

Acknowledgment

This chapter incorporates sections previously published in *New Community*, 22, 1: 97–110 ("Anti-racism and the Critique of White Identities," 1996).

Notes

1 In this chapter the initial letter of "racial" terms is capitalized in order to signify that such expressions are being employed as sociopolitical rather than biological categories. Lower-case initial letters are used only in quotations or to signal the term's employment as a natural, as opposed to a social, construct.
2 The most distinctive usage of "black" in the United Kingdom is as a "pan-racial" label for those who seek to resist, and/or the victims of, white racism. This usage draws from established anti-colonial and anti-imperialist solidaristic discourses, as well as the practical benefits many black Britons have perceived within a political and broad-based anti-racist alliance (see Sivanandan, 1982).
3 This approach may also provide a way of engaging those so-called white people who have begun to construct a mythical history of themselves as belonging to an increasingly beleaguered ethnic minority. Charles Gallagher's recent interviews on American college campuses have indicated how the invisibility of whiteness is fading for many, only to be replaced by the desire to find "a legitimate, positive narrative of one's own whiteness . . . accomplished by constructing an identity that negated white oppressor charges and framed whiteness as a liability" (Gallagher 1995: 177). The irony of such narratives is that as they seek to connote an interest in whiteness, they expose their ignorance about and disinterest in the actual historical development of white identity. Perhaps, however, by challenging such "defensive whites" to make good their professed curiosity about whiteness – and drawing their particular experiences and anxieties into a wide-ranging and liberating history of the construction and mutual dependency of "racial" categories – they, too, may be drawn into the anti-racist and anti-essentialist project.

References

Abel, Elizabeth (1993) "Black Writing, White Reading: Race and the Politics of Feminist Interpretation." *Critical Inquiry*, 20, 3: 470–98.
Allen, Theodore (1994) *The Invention of the White Race: Volume One: Racial Oppression and Social Control*. London: Verso.
Appiah, Anthony (1985) "The Uncompleted Argument: DuBois and the illusion of race." *Critical Inquiry*, 12, 1: 21–37.
Baker, Houston Jr. (1986) "Caliban's Triple Play." *Critical Inquiry*, 13, 1: 182–96.
Banton, Michael (1977) *The Idea of Race*. London: Tavistock.
Banton, Michael (1987) *Racial Theories*. Cambridge: Cambridge University Press.
Bhabha, Homi (1990) "Interview with Homi Bhabha: The Third Space," in J. Rutherford (ed.) *Identity: Community, Culture and Difference*. London: Lawrence and Wishart: 207–21.
Bonnett, Alastair (1993a) *Radicalism, Anti-racism and Representation*. London: Routledge.
Bonnett, Alastair (1993b) "Forever White? Challenges and Alternatives to a 'Racial' Monolith." *New Community*, 20, 1: 173–80.
Camper, Carol (1994) "To White Feminists." *Canadian Woman Studies*, 14, 2: 40.
Charles, Helen (1992) "Whiteness – The Relevance of Politically Coloring the 'Non,'" in

A. Phoenix and J. Stacey (eds) *Working Out: New Directions for Women's Studies.* London: Falmer Press: 29–35.

Chater, Nancy (1994) "Biting the Hand That Feeds Me: Notes on Privilege from a White Anti-racist Feminist." *Canadian Woman Studies,* 14, 2: 100–4.

Clark, Gillian and Nazreen Subhan (n.d.) "Some Definitions," in K. Ebbutt and B. Pearce (eds) *Racism in School: Contributions to a Discussion.* London: Communist Party of Great Britain.

Cohen, Phil (1992) "'It's racism what dunnit': Hidden Narratives in Theories of Racism," in J. Donald and A. Rattansi (eds) *"Race," Culture and Difference.* London: Sage.

den Boer, Pim (1995) "Essay 1: Europe to 1914: The Making of an Idea," in K. Wilson and J. Dussen (eds) *The History of the Idea of Europe.* London: Routledge: 13–82.

Dyer, Richard (1988) "White." *Screen,* 29, 4: 44–64.

Doris Marshall Institute (1994) "Maintaining the Tensions of Anti-racist Education." *Orbit,* 25, 2: 20–1.

Elba, Richard (1990) *Ethnic Identity: The Transformation of White America.* New Haven, CT: Yale University Press.

Erikson, Peter (1995) "Seeing Whiteness." *Transition,* 67: 166–85.

Frankenberg, Ruth (1993) *The Social Construction of Whiteness: White Women, Race Matters.* Minneapolis, MN: University of Minnesota Press.

Fuss, Diana (1990) *Essentially Speaking: Feminism, Nature and Difference.* London and New York: Routledge.

Gaine, Chris (1987) *No Problem Here: A Practical Approach To Education and "Race" in White Schools.* London: Hutchinson.

Gallagher, Charles (1995) "White Reconstruction in the University." *Socialist Review,* 24, 1/2: 165–87.

Gates, Henry Jr. (ed.) (1986) *"Race," Writing and Difference.* Chicago: University of Chicago Press.

Gates, Henry Jr. (1988) *The Signifying Monkey.* Oxford: Oxford University Press.

Gilroy, Paul (1987) *There Ain't No Black in the Union Jack: The Cultural Politics of Race and Nation.* London: Macmillan.

Gurnah, Ahmed (1984) "The Politics of Racism Awareness Training." *Critical Social Policy,* 11: 6–20.

Hay, Denys (1957) *Europe: The Emergence of an Idea.* Edinburgh: Edinburgh University Press.

Hebdige, Dick (1979) *Subculture: The Meaning of Style.* London: Methuen.

Henwood, Doug (1994) *The State of the USA Atlas: The Changing Face of American Life in Maps and Graphics.* Harmondsworth: Penguin.

hooks, bell (1992) *Black Looks: Race and Representation.* Toronto: Between the Lines.

Ignatiev, Noel (1995) *How the Irish Became White.* New York: Routledge.

Inner London Education Authority (ILEA) (1983) *Race, Sex and Class: 3. A Policy for Equality: Race.* London: ILEA.

Jeater, Diane (1992) "Roast Beef and Reggae Music: The Passing of Whiteness." *New Formations,* 18: 107–21.

Jones, Simon (1989) *Black Culture, White Youth: The Reggae Tradition from JA to UK.* London: Macmillan.

Joyce, Joyce (1987a) "The Black Canon: Reconstructing Black American Literary Criticism." *New Literary History,* 18, 2: 335–44.

Joyce, Joyce (1987b) "'Who the cap fit': Unconsciousness and Unconscionableness, in the

Criticism of Houston A. Baker, Jr. and Henry Louis Gates, Jr." *New Literary History,* 18, 2: 371–84.

Katz, Judy (1978) *White Awareness: Handbook for Anti-racism Training.* Norman, OK: University of Oklahoma Press.

Levine, Judith (1994) "The Heart of Whiteness: Dismantling the Master's House." *Voice Literary Supplement,* 128: 11–16.

Lyde, Lionel (1914) *A Geography of Africa: Fifth Edition Containing Problems and Exercises.* London: Adam and Charles Black.

Macdonald, Ian et al. (1989) *Racism, Anti-racism and Schools: A Summary of the Burnage Report.* London: Runnymede Trust.

Mason, Peter (1990) *Deconstructing America: Representations of the Other.* London: Routledge.

Miles, Robert (1989) *Racism.* London: Routledge.

Modood, Tariq (1988) "'Black', Racial Equality and Asian Identity." *New Community,* 14, 3: 397–404.

Modood, Tariq (1990a) "British Asian Muslims and the Rushdie Affair." *Political Quarter,* 61, 2: 143–60.

Modood, Tariq (1990b) "Catching up with Jesse Jackson: Being Oppressed and Being Somebody." *New Community,* 17, 1: 85–96.

Modood, Tariq (1992) *Not Easy Being British: Color, Culture and Citizenship.* Stoke-on-Trent: Trentham Books for the Runnymede Trust.

Puar, Jasbir (1995) "Resituating Discourses of 'Whiteness' and 'Asianness' in Northern England." *Socialist Review,* 24, 1/2: 21–53.

Race Traitor (1994a) "Treason to Whiteness is Loyalty to Humanity." *Race Traitor,* 3. (Published at P.O. Box 603, Cambridge, MA, 02140, USA).

Race Traitor (1994b) "Editorial: When Does the Unreasonable Act Make Sense?" *Race Traitor,* 3: 108–10.

Rattansi, Ali (1992) "Changing the Subject? Racism, Culture and Education," in A. Rattansi and D. Reeder (eds) *Rethinking Radical Education: Essays in Honour of Brian Simon.* London: Lawrence and Wishart: 52–95.

Reid, Anthony (1994) "Early Southeast Asian Categorisations of Europeans," in S. Schwartz (ed.) *Implicit Understandings: Observing, Reporting, and Reflecting on the Encounters Between Europeans and Other Peoples in the Early Modern Era.* Cambridge: Cambridge University Press: 268–94.

Roediger, Dave (1992) *The Wages of Whiteness: Race and the Making of the American Working Class.* London: Verso.

Roediger, Dave (1994) *Towards the Abolition of Whiteness: Essays on Race, Politics, and Working Class History.* London: Verso.

Ross, Andre and Tricia Rose (eds) (1994) *Microphone Fiends: Youth Music and Youth Culture.* London: Routledge.

Rubio, Phil (1994) "Phil Rubio Replies." *Race Traitor,* 3: 124–5.

Saynor, James (1995) "Living in Precarious Times." *The Observer,* 27 August.

Sivanandan, A. (1982) *A Different Hunger: Writings on Black Resistance.* London: Pluto Press.

Sivanandan, A. (1985) "RAT and the Degradation of Black Struggle." *Race and Class,* 26, 4: 1–33.

Snowden, Frank (1983) *Before Color Prejudice: the Ancient View of Blacks.* Cambridge, MA: Harvard University Press.

Spivak, Gayatri Chakravorty (1990) "Gayatri Spivak on the Politics of the Subaltern." *Socialist Review*, 20, 3: 81–97.

Wellman, David (1977) *Portraits of White Racism*. Cambridge: Cambridge University Press.

Young, Robert (1995) *Colonial Desire: Hybridity in Theory, Culture and Race*. London: Routledge.

14

The Labor of Whiteness, the Whiteness of Labor, and the Perils of Whitewishing

Michael Eric Dyson

Bitter conflicts over the politics of identity are at the heart of contemporary debates about the labor movement, the political left, and the American academy. Such debates are often burdened by a truncated historical perspective that overlooks crucial features of the story of how identity politics, and the alleged special interests upon which such politics is said to rest, have come to dominate our intellectual and cultural landscape. This essay, then, has a modest ambition: to provide a small corrective to such stories by emphasizing how whiteness – which has reflexively, if unconsciously, been defined in universal terms – is composed of particular identities. These particular white identities have, until recently, been spared the sort of aggressive criticism that minority identities routinely receive. I will also argue that some critics of identity politics ignore these facts, and this ignorance smoothes the path for false accusations against blacks, women, and other minorities as the source of strife and disunity in the labor movement. Finally, I will suggest that, based on the uses of whiteness in the labor movement, the politics of identity was a problem long before the fuller participation of blacks and other minorities. Indeed, identity politics is most vicious when it is invisible, when it is simply part of the given, when it is what we take for granted.

One of the unforeseen, and certainly unintended, consequences of recent discussions of race is that we have come to question the identities, ideologies, and institutional expressions of whiteness.[1] For most of our national history, the term *race* has meant *black*. The collapse of the meanings of blackness into the term *race* has led to a myriad of intellectual blind spots, not only in the narrow conceptualization of black identity, but in the severe lack of attention paid to how whiteness serves as a source of racial identity. The result of this is a cruel irony: whiteness, the most dominant and visible of American racial identities, has been rendered intellectually invisible, an ideological black hole that negates its self-identification as one among many other racial identities. In the absence of viewing themselves as having a race, many whites latched onto citizenship as a vital means of self-definition. Whites were individuals and Americans; blacks, Latinos, Native Americans, and other minorities were collectively defined as members of racial and ethnic subgroups. Whiteness had a doubly negative effect: it denied its racial roots while denying racial minorities their American identities.

Prior to conceiving of whiteness as a social construct – as a historically mediated cultural value that challenges the biological basis of white identity – most blacks and whites viewed whiteness as a relatively fixed identity. For blacks, the meaning of whiteness was singularly oppressive. The varied expressions of whiteness were viewed as the elaboration of a single plot: to contain, control, and, at times, to destroy black identity. For whites, their racial identities were never as concretely evoked or sharply defined as when the meanings of blackness spilled beyond their assigned limitations to challenge white authority. In part, whiteness was called into existence by blackness; a particular variety of whiteness was marshaled as a defensive strategy against black transgression of sanctified racial borders. At the least, whiteness was tied to blackness, its hegemonic meanings symbolically linked to a culture it sought to dominate. As a result, blackness helped expose the dominant meanings of whiteness and helped reveal the meaning of whiteness as domination.

To be sure, whiteness as domination had many faces, though the body of belief they fronted shared profound similarities. White supremacist ideology united poor whites in the hoods of the Ku Klux Klan and sophisticated scholars in robes in the halls of academe. Still, if domination was the hub of the meaning of whiteness, there were many spokes radiating from its center. First, there was *whiteness as the positive universal versus blackness as the negative particular*. On this view, the invisibility of whiteness preserved both its epistemic and ethical value as the embodiment of norms against which blackness was measured. White styles of speech, behavior belief, and the like were defined as universal standards of human achievement; their origins in particular ethnic communities were successfully masked. Through this meaning of whiteness, whites were able to criticize blacks for their failure to be human, not explicitly for their failure to be white, although in principle the two were indistinguishable.

Then there was *whiteness as ethnic cohesion and instrument of nation-making*. This meaning of whiteness consolidated the fragmented cultures of white European ethnics and gave social utility to the ethnic solidarity that the myth of whiteness provided. The genius of unarticulated, invisible whiteness is that it was able to impose its particularist perspective as normative. Thus, the resistance of blacks, Latinos, and Native Americans to absorption into the white mainstream was viewed by whites as viciously nationalistic, while white racial nationalism managed to remain virtuously opaque.

Next, there was *whiteness as proxy for an absent blackness it helped to limit and distort*. The accent in this mode of whiteness is on its power to represent the ideals, interests, and especially the images of a blackness it has frozen through stereotype, hearsay, and conspiracy. In important ways, this use of whiteness parallels Renato Rosaldo's description of imperialist nostalgia, where a colonial power destroys a culture, only to lament its demise with colonialism's victims.[2]

In the present case, whiteness claims the authority to represent what it has ruined. The exemplars of this function of whiteness voice, instead of nostalgia, a presumptive right to speak for a minority it has silenced. Thus, there is a coercive representation by whiteness of the blackness it has contained. Needless to say, coercive representation often presents images that are feeble, distorted, or the idealizations of domesticated, colonized views of black life.

Finally, there was *whiteness as the false victim of black power*. This mode of whiteness is the ultimate strategy of preserving power by protesting its usurpation by the real victim. The process was driven as much by the psychic need of whites for unifying inclusion as it was by a need to find a force to combat the exaggerated threat of black power. Thus, whites were able to make themselves appear less powerful than they were by overstating the threat posed by blacks. D. W. Griffith's film, *Birth of a Nation,* exaggerated black male threats to white womanhood to justify the lynching of black men and to increase membership in white hate groups like the white Knights of Columbus. And in our own day, widely voiced complaints by "angry white males" about unfair minority access to social goods like education and employment often misrepresent the actual degree of minority success in these areas.

These strategies of dominant whiteness, as well as the orthodox views of race on which they are premised, held sway until the recent rise of constructivist views of race. One fallout from such constructivist views – challenging the racial stereotyping of minorities by dominant communities, as well as criticizing the romantic representations of minorities within their own communities – has been the wide denunciation of identity politics. It is not, I believe, coincidental that identity politics, and its alleged ideological cousins, political correctness and multiculturalism, has come under attack precisely at the moment that racial, sexual, and gender minorities have gained more prominence in our culture.

Although I favor forceful criticism of vicious varieties of identity politics – the sort where one's particular social identity is made a fetish, where one's group identification becomes an emblem of fascist insularity – the rush to indiscriminately renounce group solidarity without fully investigating the historical contexts, ideological justifications, and intellectual reasons for identity politics is irresponsible and destructive. If the labor movement, the left, the academy, and communities of color are to enjoy a renewed alliance, such investigations are crucial.

Still, taking history into account is no guarantee that the outcome will be just, or that it will profit the sort of balanced perspective for which I have called. Many critics have launched sharp attacks on identity politics as, among other things, the source of sin and suffering within the academy, the left, and the labor movement.[3] Many critics argue that the left – including civil rights groups, feminists, gays and lesbians, and elements of the labor movement – has, through its self-destructive identity politics, undermined the possibility of progressive consensus and community. The Hobbesian war of all against all, pitting minority groups against the majority – blacks against whites, gays against straights, and the handicapped against the able-bodied – results in each group talking (or, more likely, hollering) past the other, leading to a destructive politics of purity. Many critics suggest that the energy squandered on identity politics is nothing less than an American tragedy, because it negates a history of left universalism even as it supports a bitter battle over select identities. On this view, the larger tragedy is that right, long identified with privileged interests, increases its appeal by claiming to defend the common good.

Like these critics, I am certainly worried about the plague of the politics of identity when it is unleashed without concern for the common good.[4] I, too, lament the petty infighting and shameless competition for victim status among various groups. Still, such analyses inadequately explain how we got into the mess of identity politics to begin with. Such critics of identity politics fail to grapple with the historic meanings and functions of whiteness, especially the harsh stigma that whiteness brings to those identities and social ideals which fall outside its realm. Moreover, they do not account for the narrow definition of universality and commonality on which such a project of left solidarity often hinges. To paraphrase Alasdair MacIntyre, "Whose universality and which commonality?"

But if such critics' efforts at explicating our national malaise fall short, Michael Tomasky's similar story falls far shorter.[5] In trying to figure out where the left has gone wrong, Tomasky is even more unrelenting in assailing the left's "identity politics, and how those [intellectual] underpinnings fit and don't fit with notions about a civil society that most Americans can support." According to Tomasky, "the left has completely lost touch with the regular needs of regular Americans." He contends that the left "is best described as tribal, and we're engaged in what essentially has been reduced to a battle of interest-group tribalism." Further, Tomasky claims that "solidarity based on race or ethnicity or any other such category always produces war, factionalism, fundamentalism." He concludes that "[p]articularist, interest-group politics – politics where we don't show potential allies how they benefit from being on our side – is a sure loser." Tomasky warns that "will never do the left any good, for example, to remonstrate against angry white men." Tomasky says that this "is not to say angry white men don't exist. But what's the use in carrying on about them?"

Tomasky is certainly right to criticize the left for its failure to show possible fellow travelers how they might be helped by tossing in with our project. And he's within reason to decry the destructive tribalism of the left. But he fails to comprehend that creating a civil society that has the support of most Americans cannot be the goal of any plausible left in America. The role of a marginalized but morally energized American left is to occupy an ethical register that counters injustice, especially when such injustice passes for common sense. The welfare debate is only the most recent example of how the left should gird its loins to defend those who are unjustly stigmatized against the advocates of universal values and common sense. But nowhere is Tomasky's fatal lack of balanced historical judgment seen more clearly than in his dismissal of the political and social effect of "angry white men." Tomasky fails to understand that such anger often grows from the historical amnesia encouraged by the ideology of white supremacy and by the politics of neoliberal race avoidance as well.

Tomasky, and other critics of his ilk, are, to varying degrees, victims of what I term *whitewishing*. In my theory, whitewishing is the interpretation of social history through an explanatory framework in which truth functions as an ideo-logical projection of whiteness in the form of a universal identity. Whitewishing draws equally from Freud and Feuerbach: it is the fulfillment of a fantasy of whiteness as neutral and objective, the projection of a faith in whiteness as its own warrant against the error of anti-universalism because it denies its own particularity. Whitewishing is bathed, paradoxically enough, in a nostalgia for the future: too sophisticated simply to lament a past now gone (and in some ways never was), it chides the present from an eschatological whiteness, the safest vantage point from which to preserve and promote its own "identityless" iden-tity, Tomasky's and other critics' whitewishing permits them to play down and, at times, erase three crucial facts when it comes to the labor movement. First, identity politics has always been at the heart of the labor movement, both to deny black workers, for instance, their rightful place in unions and as wage earners in the workplace, and to consolidate the class, racial, and gender interests of working elites against the masses of workers. The identity politics now allegedly ripping apart the labor movement – as well as balkanizing the academy and the left in general – is a response to a predecessor politics of identity that was played out without being identified as such because of its power to rebuff challenges brought by racial, ethnic, and gender minorities. Even white proletarians enjoyed their second-hand brands of universalism. This shows how the move to decry "special interests" – that is, blacks, Latinos, Asian-Americans – within the labor movement denies a fundamental fact: all interests are special if they're yours.

Second, as the work of David Roediger has shown, race and class were in-tegrally related in shaping the (white) working class in America.[6] The class interests of white workers were based on their developing a sense of whiteness to help alleviate their inferior social status: they derived benefits from *not* being black. This simple fact is a reminder that, from the very beginning in the labor movement and in working-class organizations, race played a significant role in determining the distribution of social and economic goods. Such a fact flies in the face of arguments that the labor movement must reclaim its identity by retreating from identity politics to focus once again on class.

Finally, many debates about labor and identity politics are ahistorical in another way: they presume a functional equivalency between the experiences of all workers who are presently making claims about the weight certain features of identity should carry in a consideration of getting work, keeping work, and job advancement. The real history of racial and gender discrimination in the labor movement, and in the job sector, means that the affirmative action claims of blacks, Latinos, Asian-Americans, Native Americans, and women are not special-interest pleadings, but a recognition of their just due in arenas that were segregated by race and gender. To think and behave as if these differences are equal to the forms of disadvantage that white workers face is to engage in another form of whitewishing.

The only way beyond vicious identity politics is to go through it. As with race, we can get beyond the nefarious meanings of racism only by taking race into account. We cannot pretend in the labor movement that significant barriers have not been erected to prevent coalition and cooperation between minorities and the mainstream. Many of those barriers remain. Only when we engage in honest conversation, accompanied by constructive changes in our social practices, will we be able to forge connections between labor, the left, the academy, and communities of color that have the ability to empower and transform each partner in the struggle.

Notes

1 There is a growing literature on the socially constructed meanings of whiteness. For some of the best of this literature, see David Roediger, *The Wages of Whiteness: Race and the Making of the American Working Class* (New York: Verso Press, 1991); David Roediger, *Towards the Abolition of Whiteness: Essays on Race, Politics, and Working Class History* (New York: Verso Press, 1994); Theodore W. Allen, *The Invention of the White Race: Volume One: Racial Oppression and Social Control* (New York: Verso Press, 1994); Fred Pfeil, *White Guys: Studies in Postmodern Domination and Difference* (New York: Verso, 1995); Jessie Daniels, *White Lies: Race, Class, Gender, and Sexuality in White Supremacist Discourse* (New York: Routledge, 1997); Matt Wray and Annalee Newitz, eds, *White Trash: Race and Class in America* (New York: Routledge, 1997); Michelle Fine, Lois Weis, Linda C. Powell, and L. Mun Wong, eds, *Off White: Readings on Race, Power, and Society* (New York: Routledge, 1997).
2 Renato Rosaldo, *Culture and Truth: The Remaking of Social Analysis* (Beacon Press, 1989, 1993), pp. 68–87.
3 For a small sample of such criticism, see: Todd Gitlin, *The Twilight of Common Dreams: Why America is Wracked by Culture Wars* (New York: Metropolitan Books, 1995); Michael Tomasky, *Left For Dead: The Life, Death and Possible Resurrection of Progressive Politics in America* (New York: The Free Press, 1996); Arthur Schlesinger, Jr., *The Disuniting of America* (Whittle Direct Books, 1991); and Richard Bernstein, *The Dictatorship of Virtue: Multiculturalism and the Battle for America's Future* (New York: Knopf, 1994).
4 See Michael Eric Dyson, *Reflecting Black: African-American Cultural Criticism* (Minneapolis: University of Minnesota Press, 1993); *Making Malcolm: The Myth and Meaning of Malcolm X* (New York: Oxford University Press, 1994); *Between God and Gangsta Rap: Bearing Witness to Black Culture* (New York: Oxford University Press, 1996); and *Race Rules: Navigating the Color Line* (New York: Addison-Wesley, 1996).
5 Tomasky, *Left For Dead*, pp. 10, 15, 16, 17.
6 Roediger, *The Wages of Whiteness* and *Towards the Abolition of Whiteness*.

15

The Trickster's Play: Whiteness in the Subordination and Liberation Process

Aída Hurtado

My work requires me to think about how free I can be as an African-American woman writer in my genderized, sexualized, wholly racialized world . . . for me, imagining is not merely looking or looking at; nor is it taking oneself intact into the other. It is, for the purposes of the work, *becoming.*

Toni Morrison (1992: 4)

The Problem

Toni Morrison writes that, in reading literary works, the reader not only becomes engaged but also *watches* what is being read all at the same time. As a reader, she had been struck by how pervasive the use of black images are in expressive prose and "in the shorthand, the taken-for-granted assumptions that lie in their usage . . . the sources of the images and the effect they have on the literary imagination and its product." She goes on to explain that this matters to her because she, as an African-American woman, does not have the same access to these traditional constructs of blackness. She says:

> Neither blackness nor "people of color" stimulates in me notions of excessive, limit-less love, anarchy, or routine dread. I cannot rely on these metaphorical shortcuts because I am a black writer struggling with and through a language that can power-fully evoke and enforce hidden signs of racial superiority, cultural hegemony, and dismissive "othering" of people. . . . The kind of work I always wanted to do requires me to learn how to maneuver ways to free up the language from its some-times sinister, frequently lazy, almost always predictable employment of racially informed and determined chains. (Morrison, 1992: xi)

The intrinsic racism in our language is not completely conscious, and there-fore, it requires our watching what we read while simultaneously being engaged. The use of a language, which by its very nature racializes, is not the only thing that limits our imaginations in conceiving of non-racist worlds; how we write about race also restricts what may be possible in the world if we could redistribute power.

In this chapter I contend that we have not integrated privilege in the racializing process. We have explored and documented the effects of oppression on its victims and they have, in turn, borne powerful testimony to their injuries and resilience (Fine, Weiss, Powell, and Wong, 1997). We have yet to chronicle how those who oppress make sense of their power *in relationship* to those they have injured. We are all potentially oppressors given that having power over others varies from context to context and is primarily determined by race, class, gender, and sexuality. Yet, we lack an elaborate language to speak about those who oppress – how they feel about, think about, react to, make sense of, come to terms with, maintain privilege over, and ultimately renounce the power to oppress. Missing in the puzzle of domination is a reflexive mechanism for understanding how we are all involved in the dirty process of racializing and gendering others, limiting who they are and who they can become.

The Site for Theorizing

Toni Morrison describes the discomfort that many literary critics feel in integrating race into their analysis. In the social sciences the same discomfort exists when stepping outside the paradigms traditionally used to study race. Morrison attributes the lack of materials that integrate race into the reading of literary texts to the fact that,

> in matters of race, silence and evasion have historically ruled literary discourse. Evasion has fostered another, substitute language in which the issues are encoded, foreclosing open debate. . . . It is further complicated by the fact that the habit of ignoring race is understood to be a graceful, even generous, liberal gesture. According to this logic, every well-bred instinct argues *against noticing* and forecloses adult discourse. (1992: 10)

The ignoring of race results in the peculiar situation of whites assuming they are like people of color because they share significant characteristics (profession, gender, geographical residence, family structure, artistic interests). This is a false assumption in a racialized society. As Angela Davis states, "racism, like an ancient plague, it infects every joint, muscle and tissue of social life in this country" (1974: 37). Professor duCille calls this the "*Driving Miss Daisy* Syndrome," in which, through "an intellectual slight [*sic*] of hand that transforms power and race relations to make best friends out of driver and driven, master and slave, boss and servant, white boy and black man" (1994: 615). The assumption of similarity because a person ignores racism is not uncommon. Even those scholars who have dedicated their lives to the dismantling of race privilege feel a false commonality with those who live with the burden of their color. Racism is a burden that is not completely understood by those who do not share the stigma.

Ignoring race, however, does not erase it as a variable in social interactions. In fact, it is the polite ignoring of race in interethnic/interracial social interactions that is responsible for the assaultive feelings that many people of color feel when there is a lapse in racial etiquette. Even when there is no mention of race, there is racializing; even when there is no mention of gender, there is gendering. In Morrison's words:

> I assumed that since the author was not black, the appearance of Africanist characters or narrative or idiom in a work could never be *about* anything other than the "normal," unracialized, illusory white world that provided the fictional backdrop. . . . I came to realize the obvious: the subject of the dream is the dreamer. The fabrication of an Africanist persona is reflexive; an extraordinary meditation on the self; a powerful exploration of the fears and desires that reside in the writerly conscious. It is an astonishing revelation of longing, of terror, of perplexity, of shame, of magnanimity. It requires hard work *not* to see this. . . . What became transparent were the self-evident ways that Americans choose to talk about themselves through and within a sometimes allegorical, sometimes metaphorical, but always choked representation of an Africanist presence. (16–17)

Morrison, as well as other writers, recognizes that the degradation of individuals is a primary way of boosting one's self-esteem – a psychological process documented in social psychology – but there is something deeper than that. Self-aggrandizement may always exist, and we will always find ways to adorn ourselves physically and psychologically to feel superior to others. What is at stake, however, is no more and no less than the physical and psychological confinement of groups of people based on skin color, class, gender, and sexuality to regulate privilege. Most contemporary writings by white authors who try to dissect the mechanisms of privilege do so without ever *putting themselves, their group, and their history* into the analysis. Reflexive theories of subordination study the other not to find out who the other is but, rather, what we can learn about ourselves by studying the other (hooks and West, 1991: 33).

Ethnic studies and women's studies have made inroads in developing reflexive theories of subordination that will lead to liberation. These fields of study are at the forefront of inventing new methods to allow scholars the use of reflexive mechanisms in the study of subordination and privilege. Critical race studies is a new school of legal thought that developed within the auspices of African-American Studies that uses a method especially helpful in documenting the dynamics of power. As proposed by Derrick Bell and his followers, they use personal narratives and fictional stories in the form of fables to "examine the ways in which the law has been shaped by and shapes issues of race." Here I use a device used by critical race theorists of constructing my own fable to explore the unspoken rules of power.

I title my fable the "Trickster's Play" and its purpose is to articulate the unspoken rules of power. Through the use of this fable, I hope to bypass the pitfalls of our "genderized, sexualized, wholly racialized" language to submit the dynamics of power to closer scrutiny. I also use the most recent (and un-precedented) studies of whiteness[1] which deconstruct how unspoken "race" privilege is allocated. Other stigmatized characteristics, like being a woman, poor, or of color have been extensively scrutinized. Only recently have social scientists and essayists focused on the primary characteristic used to assign privilege through the study of whiteness (Fine, Weiss, Powell, and Wong, 1997: vii–viii).

The Trickster's Play: A Fable of Power

Trick number 1: The center of the universe – naturalizing whiteness

If I am not the center of the universe, you do not exist. If I am not the central actor in the drama, I will not listen to you, I will not acknowledge your presence, and I will remove myself from the situation. My absence will highlight my centrality to all actions. I will not acknowledge your presence; my ability not to see you is my power. If I do not see you, you do not exist. If you only exist at my will, you are nothing without my attention. I am, therefore, the one that controls who is real and who is not.

Whiteness is the "center of the universe" by being considered a "natural" and unmarked racial category (Fine, 1997). Indeed, the recurrent finding in the study of whiteness is that respondents do not consider their "whiteness" as an identity or a marker of group membership *per se*. As duCille writes:

> . . . practitioners continue to see whiteness as so natural, normative, and unprob-lematic that racial identity is a property only of the non-white. Unless the object of study happens to be the Other, race is placed under erasure as something outside immediate consideration, at once extratextual and extraterrestrial. (1994: 607)

Most respondents in these studies consider whiteness a "natural" identity because of its unproblematic nature and are hard-pressed to define it and the privileges that whiteness brings them. Whiteness only becomes definable when the privilege it accords is lost. Fine, Weis and Addelston (1994) document white-working class men's frustrations as they see their jobs "being taken" by people of color. They articulate what it means to be white only when their way of life is lost. That is, whiteness begins to matter when it is decentered and its privileges threatened (Fine, 1997: 63). Similarly, Tatum (1992) and Gallagher (1995) describe how students in multicultural college classrooms "discover" their white-ness when they are outnumbered by students of color. Although most respondents find it difficult to articulate what constitutes whiteness, they can, however, articulate the superiority they feel in comparison to people of color. For example, McIntosh (1992) lists the privileges that whiteness provides, exposing the superiority that many white people feel in most social contexts: "whites are taught to think of their lives as morally neutral, normative, and average, and also ideal, so that when we work to benefit others, this is seen as work that will allow 'them' to be more like 'us'" (1992: 73). "Normative," and "natural" also becomes superior. In other words, even though McIntosh does not see herself as personally oppressing anybody, the list of privileges she was socialized to expect have trained her to feel and act superior to non-white people.

Susan Ostrander (1984) also finds among upper-class women a feeling of unquestioned superiority. These women's "superiority" appears natural to them because they, personally, did not construct social inequality. At the same time that they acknowledge their superiority is based on access to material privilege, they do not see how it is related to whiteness. Their superiority is a legitimate birthright which allows these women not to question their class position. Many of these respondents proudly announced that "the door opens for position" and that access to every social sphere is "just a phone call away" (Ostrander, 1984: 29).

These women do not challenge their class and race positions because they feel they legitimately have a right to their privilege. According to Ostrander, they recognize that their husbands "know how to rule and are masters of the exercise of power" (ibid.: 151). Ostrander astutely observes that, in the unlikely event that they successfully challenged their husbands on their gender superiority, these women might endanger their class status. Therefore, they submit to their husbands: "They will do so perhaps in part because the gains of *gender* equality would not be enough to balance the losses of class equality" (ibid.: 151–2).

Trick number 2: Special needs population – defining white identity through domination and privilege

I will claim my right to be central to all action by claiming my special needs as a (white) child, a man with important work/ideas/artist/genius, a (white) woman with special demands that supersede the needs of anybody else involved in the situation. If you claim your own needs, I will proceed as if I did not hear you and reassert my initial claim. The more you push, the more I persist in my claims, with no reference to yours. Unless I want you to exist, you do not.

A "special needs population" is defined by social comparison with others that are considered not to have "special needs," claims within a specified context. Some populations, then, can assert their "special needs" deserve priority and should be privileged above others. The needs of others are either not articulated, become part of the background, or are subsumed under the privileged needs of the "special population." The "special needs" trick is described often in the ethnographies about women of color who work as maids. Romero (1992) documents the case of a sixteen-year-old maid in El Paso, Texas, who is perceived as a full adult in the service of the family, even though the employers have a sixteen-year-old child themselves. The "needs" of the employer's child are special and deserving of attention, whereas the sixteen-year-old maid actually is sexually harassed by the father of the sixteen-year-old in the household. The special needs of the sixteen-year-old daughter are legitimate and, of necessity, to be met; the needs of the sixteen-year-old maid are either non-existent, or she is categorized primarily as a maid and not as a sixteen-year-old.

Many of the studies on whiteness use social comparison between whites and non-whites to delineate white identity (Fine, 1997). McIntosh lists the non-conscious everyday "privileges" of her whiteness. The inventory is not based on what whites possess but rather on what people of color do not have. We also learn that many dominant individuals assume that their desires are the desires of all people. It is inconceivable that subordinates may have their own special needs independent of the dominant group (McIntosh, 1992: 73–4). As duCille queries: "Why are black women always already Other? . . . To myself, of course, I am not Other; to me it is the white women and men so intent on theorizing my difference who are the Other" (1994: 591–2). McIntosh is aware of this contradiction between how the other perceives herself in comparison to how many whites perceive her. Her essay deconstructs the privileges of whiteness and her honesty, which may be perceived as betrayal by some whites and offensive to some people of color, is a disruption of how we construct whiteness by problematizing the inferiority assigned to non-whites.

Both men and women use people of color to exalt whiteness but it is a process that is gendered. Whiteness and maleness are defined in opposition to "color" and "femaleness:" the other has to exist to exalt the centeredness of the subject. The absence of the other creates an identity crises for the dominant (Fine, Weis, and Addelston, 1994: 2; Fine, 1997). At the same time, the presence of non-whites creates a "humanity" scale in which white men represent the highest point of human development: they are rational, logical, unemotional, industrious, adventurous, in control, creators (Harris, 1993). These characteristics, or special (privileged) needs, are difficult to judge, unless people of color are present. Even the gender relations between whites are more "human" because of the presence of people of color. Morrison illustrates this when discussing Hemingway's novel *To Have and Have Not*. In the novel Harry and his wife, Marie, are making love. Marie asks her husband,

> "Listen, did you ever do it with a nigger wench?"
> "Sure."
> "What's it like?"
> "Like a nurse shark."

Morrison goes on to remark that for Hemingway the black woman is

> the furthest thing from human, so far away as to be not even mammal but fish. The figure evokes a predatory, devouring eroticism and signals the antithesis to femininity, to nurturing, to nursing, to replenishment. In short, Harry's words mark something so brutal, contrary, and alien in its figuration that it does not belong to its own species and cannot be spoken of in language, in metaphor or metonym, evocative of anything resembling the woman to whom Harry is speaking – his wife Marie. The kindness he has done Marie is palpable. His projection of black female

sexuality has provided her with solace, for which she is properly grateful. She responds to the kindness and giggles, "You're funny." (1992: 84–5)

It was in the owning of people of color, historically through slavery, not through their labor, that white men's manhood was transformed in the New World and that his special, privileged needs were created: "whatever his social status in London, in the New World he is a gentleman. More gentle, more man. The site of his transformation is within rawness: he is backgrounded by savagery" (Morrison, 1992: 44). Similarly, Gutiérrez (1991: 194) indicates that the Spanish colonizers in seventeenth-century New Mexico thought of society as composed of conquerors and conquered where "The Indians were vanquished heathens engulfed in satanic darkness" and they, in turn, were "Christians, Spaniards, 'civilized,' and white." The presence of people of color and their "savagery" open the gateways for white people to assume their color burden and to protect the "civilized world" through the use of brutality.

Morrison argues that people of color provide whiteness its identity largely because there was no "royalty" in the United States from which to draw a counterdistinction as there was in Europe:

> Americans did not have profligate, predatory nobility from which to wrest an identity of national virtue while continuing to covet aristocratic license and luxury. The American nation negotiated both its disdain and its envy . . . through the self-reflexive contemplation of fabricated, mythological Africanism. . . . [T]his Africanist other became the means of thinking about body, mind, chaos, kindness, and love; provided the occasion for exercises in the absence of restraint, the presence of restraint, the contemplation of freedom and of aggression; permitted opportunities for the exploration of ethics and morality, for meeting the obligations of the social contract, for bearing the cross of religion and following out the ramifications of power. (1992: 47)

Similarly, Gutiérrez notes that:

> The presence of Indian slaves in New Mexico society gave meaning to honor-status. Much of what was considered Spanish culture in this northern frontier of New Spain gained its meaning in opposition to and as an exaggeration of what it meant to be an Indian or *genízaro*.[2] What the Puebloans and *genízaros* were, the Spanish were not. What the Spanish were, the Puebloans and *genízaros* were not. Negative stereotypes of the other, that is, of the defeated and fallen Indian within Hispano society and outside of it, defined the boundaries between "them" and "us," between the dishonored and the honored. (1991: 180)

People of color are not entitled to special needs, because unlike whites, they are not fully human. Oppression is relational so therefore special needs are defined *in reference* to those present in the environment; however, there are fairly stable sets of rules about whose superiority takes precedence.

Trick number 3: Special games – teaching the dynamics of power

All rituals/games that involve me are life-affirming and enhancements for the soul, even if they are at the expense of your essential needs of food and clothing. I will build great stadiums and commit enormous resources for players to enact the rituals/games that glorify me and my group. I will make my rituals/games the center of our national identity and exclude you from the administration/ ownership of these rituals/games. Entire academic departments will be dedicated to the perfection of my rituals/games at the expense of finding ways to solve the most pressing social problems that will benefit your communities – homicide, drug abuse, child abuse, spousal battery. Instead, I will develop the perfect foot-ball, the most advanced athletic shoes, the most perfect regiment to play my rituals/games. All of this will only highlight my importance, including my leisure at the expense of your survival. This will show the world my importance and simultaneously diminish you to non-existence. I will also use these games to train my people to love and exercise power. I will teach the dynamics of power and domination under the guise of "having fun" by a lifetime of socialization through my games. My games are the boot camp of military training and teach the might of sheer physical domination.

For white men, the socialization into power happens primarily through the rituals of organized sports – either through viewing or playing them (Connell, 1995). Sports are identified as an important arena of informal decision making that has historically excluded women and men of color. Communal viewing of sports is also where working-class white men build camaraderie and bond in male solidarity (often excluding men of color and women). Ironically, although a significant number of men of color play professional sports, they are often barred from coaching or administering professional sports as well as from the rituals of watching them with those in power.

Sports are also played and viewed in exclusive private clubs. These venues have written and unwritten rules maintaining white racial (and some gender) ex-clusivity and are the sites for political and economic decision-making. Lawrence Graham interviewed professionals of color at more than six hundred corpora-tions all over the United States and found that they "were unable to build networks, find mentors, or even attract business opportunities because of their exclusion from private clubs that white peers were joining" (1995: xv). At a more personal level, Graham remarks that even though he grew-up in affluence, received a bachelor's degree from Princeton, and a law degree from Harvard, the color of his skin kept him from joining these exclusive clubs that would ultimately give him access to the inner circles of power:

> Today, I'm back where I started – on a street of five- and six-bedroom colonials with expensive cars and neighbors who all belong somewhere. Through my ex-periences as a young lawyer, I have come to realize that these clubs are where businesspeople network. . . . How many clients and deals am I going to line up on the asphalt parking lot of my local public tennis courts? . . . My black Ivy League

friends and I know of black company vice presidents who have to ask white sub-ordinates to invite them out for golf or tennis. . . . I wanted some answers. . . . But I figured I could get close enough to understand what these people were thinking and why country clubs were so set on excluding people like me. (ibid.: 2–3).

Graham goes underground as a busboy in one of these private clubs to figure out how privileged white people think in order to answer his question of why he is excluded – he finds no other answer except racism.

Trick number 4: The pleasing game – boosting and stroking

I will make it impossible to please me. I will make request upon request, in rapid succession, making it unrealistic for you to comply and barring you from thinking of anything else but me. I will rob you of time and energy to block the develop-ment of your subjectivity independent of my needs. I will not allow you to conceive of a world outside of pleasing me. I will not be belligerent when you fail to meet my standards. Instead, I will be dejected to increase your feelings of guilt and incompetence, which will increase my centrality to your life. You will feel empty without my presence. My centrality and my unwillingness to be pleased subvert your ability to exist outside of my presence. You are nothing when I am not around. I am the master and creator of the universe, and if I am not present, you do not exist.

Boosting. Ostrander indicates that the upper-class family has a well-established script, with the woman as the "booster," and the man as the provider. Wives in these families exist to show solidarity, give help, reward, agree, understand, and passively accept most of their husbands' actions. As one woman told Ostrander: "You have to be your husband's biggest booster. You have to make him feel good. He does not appreciate it if he comes home and I'm exhausted. I've got to be ready to find out what his week was like. He comes first, and I have to bend my life to fit his" (1984: 39). The husbands want a "sounding board" for their business strategies, *not* active participants (ibid.: 46). By boosting their husbands, these women are protected from the "mundane" chores assigned to them by gender. They have the economic resources to delegate their cleaning and other unpleasant responsibilities. In Ostrander's words, "Wives run the households for men who essentially run the nation's business" (ibid.: 42).

Stroking. These women are also responsible for maintaining a network of "congenial" people to meet their husbands' social needs (ibid.: 45). The creation and maintenance of social networks for the entire family is an important part of maintaining whiteness. In addition, they also smooth the social relationships between their group and subordinates. Lateral relationships are almost ex-clusively between whites, whereas relationships with subordinates exist both with whites and non-whites. These upper-class women entertain subordinates to express gratitude to their employees for a job well done. Their "entertainment function" makes them co-conspirators in the subordination of workers. The same is true of their charity work. These women speak of volunteer work as a way to give back to society for their wealth. Their charity work is also a way to appease subordinates and to diffuse structural opposition (129).

However, further probing reveals that even though these women enjoy tremendous privileges as a result of their race and class, they also pay a high cost. A structural paradox exists in which the higher the socioeconomic status of the husband, the more rigid the division of labor. Many of these upper-class white women regret not having "tested" their abilities to see if they could make it "on their own." They had restricted their own development in the service of their husbands. All of these women had inherited wealth independent of their husbands' considerable resources, yet they still submitted themselves to their husbands' will (Ostrander, 1984: 51). The need to please was independent of their economic survival.

The intimacy with their influential husbands did not result in personal empowerment. As sounding boards for their husbands, there was a potential for them to participate and learn the dynamics of the most influential circles of power. But this subversion of the "wife" role is only possible if someone has an independent subjectivity; someone who has an identity and an agenda *apart* from the husband. The subordinate can take these opportunities as valuable knowledge to learn about power. Tragically, many of these women were denied their subjectivity and, therefore, human agency in spite of their class and race privilege. Nevertheless, most of the women experienced their class position as desirable and their inherited privilege as a right they enjoyed fully. They dispensed their social responsibility through charity work and the raising of their families. They did not see much wrong with their class status and were oblivious to their active role in the construction of whiteness.

Trick number 5: Power solidarity – whiteness is a family affair

I will be a rabid individualist unless the power of my group (based on gender, superior social class, and white race) is threatened. If it is, I will use all my capacities to think of alternative, benevolent explanations for ruthless and abusive behavior for members of my group. If a member of my power group is attacked, we will close ranks without a single word. If pressed, I will turn my privileges into burdens: "You, as woman, don't understand what a burden it is to be a (white) man – the incredible responsibility and courage it takes to fight all these obstacles that society places before you."

Ultimately, white privilege depends on its members not betraying the unspoken power dynamics socialized in the intimacy of families. White solidarity on the surface may appear as an oxymoron. Yet many of the respondents and essayists in this review reveal a tacit understanding of white solidarity. Although whiteness to them is natural and although few can articulate the privileges, most can detect when whiteness is questioned and its privilege threatened (Fine, 1997). Solidarity on the basis of whiteness has to be understood before the deconstruction of race privilege can continue.

White race solidarity gets recreated within families, making them very important in the maintenance of whiteness. Women, in particular, are extremely important in reproducing white privilege and race solidarity because of their prominent roles in the socialization of children. Ostrander found that her respondents were very concerned that their children maintain power solidarity by *not* marrying outside their race and class. As one of her respondents stated: "I certainly wouldn't abandon them if they married someone I didn't approve of, a black person or whatever, but it would be difficult. It is easier to marry somebody near your own interests and background. It makes for compatibility" (1984: 88). Upper-class women considered it part of their role as mothers to maximize opportunities for their children to marry within their class. Frankenberg (1993: 95) also found that even among women professing belief in "common humanity stumble over the question of marriage and procreation." Moreover, even though the number of black-white interracial marriages has nearly quadrupled since 1970 when there were a total of sixty-five thousand black-white interracial couples, a large number of whites still remain strongly opposed to miscegenation (Graham, 1995: 34). For example, a 1992 Gallup Poll indicates that only 10 percent of whites would approve of a family member marrying outside the race. The approval for interracial unions only goes slightly up (15 percent) when the " survey participant was neither related to nor acquainted with the individuals being married" (ibid.: 34).

Roediger (1991) shows how working-class whites (such as Irish-American workers) elaborated anti-black ideologies – including a horror of miscegenation – gradually, as they found that this construction served complex economic, social and psychological purposes. Thus, he shows how different rationales were developed to support the claim of white superiority at different times and in different social class groups, but for my purposes the important point is that they always end up being developed in white families (see Wellman, 1993, for contemporary examples that cross social class lines). The particular rationales and dynamics that have been identified in upper-class white families provide an understanding of how families construct racial privilege when they are unconstrained by class subordination.

Race solidarity is maintained through biological ties inherited through marriage. Ostrander (1984) indicates that most of the respondents in her study readily acknowledged their class privilege, but did not recognize their race privilege and spoke instead of their lineage as the capital they brought to their marriage. In fact, when asked what made them upper class, they did not use their husband's income or education as evidence but, rather, their own family ancestry and the prestige that this accorded the marriage (ibid.: 34). If privilege is conferred through biological lineage, people of color will always be outside the confines of assigned privilege. The power of whiteness has not been explicitly documented (Harris, 1993); it is a birthright that is socialized from generation to generation in the largely racially segregated living arrangements that exist in the United States (McIntosh, 1992: 77). Like the construction of manhood through a lifetime of socialization in sports (Kimmel, 1993; Connell, 1995), the process is largely hidden, unless one has been admitted to this exclusive club.

Power solidarity is also socialized through feelings of belonging which can be communicated in a variety of ways. Susanna Sturgis (1988) discusses how the unmarked history she was taught in school provided a direct measure of her worth as a descendant of the "founding fathers" and as a member of those who *can* create history. The historical lessons she learned about the accomplishments of (mostly male) whites gave her a sense of her belonging to the American mainstream. Many white respondents immediately "see" how belonging is an integral part of their whiteness, when they are threatened by such things as "minorities" moving into their neighborhoods or by "minorities" demanding equal participation in the mainstream (Fine, Weis, and Addelston, 1994: 8–9). It is also clear how the sense of belonging is dependent on the processes of exclusion (Fine, 1997). For example, Gallagher quotes a white student whose sense of belonging was being threatened: "We can't have anything for ourselves anymore that says exclusively white or anything like that" (1995, 177).

Trick number 6: The pendejo[3] game – distancing and denial

When you, the outsider, come close to subverting my power through the sheer strength of your moral arguments or through organized mass protest, I will give you an audience. I will listen to you, sometimes for the first time, and will seem engaged. At critical points in your analysis I will claim I do not understand and will ask you to elaborate ad nauseam. I will consistently subvert your efforts at dialogue by "claiming we do not speak the same language." I will assert that many of our differences, if not all, are due to our different ways of communicating. I will ask you to educate me and to spend your energies in finding ways of saying things so that I can understand. I will not do the same for you. Instead of using your resources to advance your causes, I will see you like a rat in a cage running around trying to find ways to explain the cage to me, while I hold the key to open the door. At the same time, I will convince you that I have no ill intentions toward you or those like you. I am simply not informed. The claim of ignorance is one of my most powerful weapons because, while you spend your time trying to enlighten me, everything remains the same. The "Pendejo Game" will also allow me to gain intimate knowledge of your psyche, which will perfect my understanding of how to dominate you.

Distancing. The women interviewed by Ostrander consistently distanced themselves from the origins of their race/class privilege by claiming that it was an accident of birth even though they came from generations of wealth. They did not take responsibility for the consequences of their privilege because they claimed "not to know" how they were fortunate enough to receive their privileged position. They *distanced* themselves from the origins of their privilege as if it were a natural disaster that they had nothing to do with creating. Most of these women felt their privilege was the "natural arrangement" of things, and they did their personal best to help those less fortunate through their charity work.

Denial. Many researchers have documented the psychological strain involved in "passing" from a subordinate group to a dominant group, say fair-skinned blacks passing as whites (Harris, 1993). The same strain has been documented for those individuals who become conscious of racism and perceive the omnipresence of its effects in all areas of social life. This is one reason that individuals resist acquiring a "double" consciousness and thus avoid the psychological stress and pain of becoming aware of the consequences of their power (Du Bois, 1973; Harris, 1993: 1711; Tatum, 1992). It is not surprising, then, that many of the white respondents claim the privileges accorded to whiteness are earned through merit simply because whites perform better than people of color in many arenas. In fact, white privilege is only articulated once that privilege is threatened and it is in the process of dislocation that white respondents begin to acknowledge the privileges they previously denied (Fine, Weis, and Addelston, 1994; Gallagher, 1995).

Another form of denial is the assertion of ignorance of practices that exclude groups from certain privileges. Lawrence Graham documents how Princeton excluded blacks from admission until 1944:

> Founded in 1746 as the College of New Jersey, Princeton's antiblack policies very quickly began to stand out as an aberration among the top colleges in every segment of the United States except the South. . . . Princeton pursued a three tier strategy to ensure that blacks would not enroll, and was so successful that it accepted a black student exactly a hundred years after Harvard and eighty years after Yale. First, Princeton strictly enforced an unwritten rule of rejecting all black applicants; second, it denied having such a rule in the face of growing criticism; finally, it utilized "deflection" rejection letters directing high-profile black applicants to apply to other schools rather than explicitly denying admission; this was designed to deter those who might publicly protest their rejection by the school . . . these polite letters of deflection were written in a uniform format developed by Princeton's thirteenth president, Woodrow Wilson, just three years before he was elected president of the United States . . . [the] letter that begins, "Regret to say that is altogether inadvisable for a colored man to enter Princeton . . . ." Wilson never signed these letters, but instead had his secretary send them out with his own signature with the polite closing line, "I would strongly recommend you to secure your education in a Southern institution . . . (1995: 191)

Princeton University was not integrated until 1944 when the United States Navy began an ROTC program on campus and, unbeknownst to Princeton, four black students were part of the program (ibid.: 192). The unwritten practice of not admitting blacks continued for the next twenty years with virtually no blacks admitted in the classes of 1950 to 1959 "and only seven blacks were on the 3,500-student campus by 1962" (ibid.: 193). Princeton has to this day denied that such a policy ever existed and has refused any official comment on the outcome of its unwritten practices (ibid.).

Princeton University is not unique in maintaining its privilege through practices that are officially denied although practically applied to exclude those that should not be part of the Trickster's Play.

Casting the Play: Whiteness in the Maintenance of Structural Privilege and Promotion of Racism

I will develop elaborate pseudo-rules that will allocate how much power every person and child will have in my play, and I will call it "merit." Merit will be defined by me (or those like me) and will have the semblance of objective rules of achievement. When I am questioned about how the rules were developed, I will claim exclusive wisdom for their origins. I will develop mass testing techniques that will be skewed in favor of knowledge only available to those in my group. Everybody will have access to the tests, but few will have access to the knowledge in the test. When a sizable number of non-group members are successful, I will change the test and the rules of the game. If my people are failing and do not meet the standards, I will find exceptions to the rules that will leave our privilege untouched.

The casting of the play is inherited. Those most like me are determined through family ties of race and class. White women will have a special category because they are necessary for reproducing more people like me. They will be accessories to my power, but rarely will I allow them close to full participation. They are essential so I will treat them well if they obey but punish them if they do not.

The mechanisms of power described in the research on whiteness are designed to maintain its structural privilege. In a society that prides itself on being a race-blind democracy, how are the dynamics of whiteness used to maintain structural privilege? How can the trickster's play be cast without referring to race to avoid sabotaging its legitimacy? It is especially pressing to find answers when its possessors are apparently oblivious to its effects and some of its non-possessors seem to agree that it is not whiteness *per se* that confers privilege as they strive to climb into the (white) mainstream wagon (Chavez, 1991). The answer may lie in the different functions groups serve in the domination/subordination process as outlined by Erika Apfelbaum (1979). The formation of groups in industrialized societies is not independent of the process of enforcing power. The dominant group de-emphasizes its function as a group and portrays its existence as the "norm" to mystify how its members obtain power by their group membership. There appears to be a "universal rule" of achievement, that applies to *anybody* that "acts" according to prescribed standards that lead to societal and economic rewards. In theory, the universal rule applies to everybody and, in fact, applies primarily to those who possess whiteness and secondarily to those who act as white as possible. An unspoken double standard exists in which democracy and rules are exclusively for whites (or those who act as white as possible), while tyranny is justified for blacks and other people of color (Harris, 1993). This double standard is not dictated by the democratic state but, rather, by the "inherent" difference between blacks and whites. This inherent difference is biological race, which is codified into law through the one-drop rule – those individuals with at least one drop of "black blood" are legally cast as black. Belief in a biological basis for whiteness insures that it will take many generations of intermarriage with "pure" whites before individuals can *legally* possess the privileges of whiteness; meanwhile, they are without its privileges (ibid.).

On the other hand, the subordinate group is marked or stigmatized. The value attached to being white and the devaluation of being non-white makes group membership in a non-white ethnic/racial group problematic for its members. In effect, the non-white ethnic/racial group is (de)grouped and cannot serve the usual positive functions that groups serve – providing a basis for positive social identity, group solidarity, a sense of belonging and empowerment (Apfelbaum, 1979). At the same time, whiteness does serves those functions for its possessors (Sturgis, 1988; McIntosh, 1992). Degrouping also effectively sabotages resistance to domination. While ethnic/racial membership is not supposed to matter in the United States, all privilege and power is distributed according to race, class, gender, and sexuality: "In effect, the courts erected legal 'No trespassing signs' – passing, therefore, is largely a phenomenon from subordinate to dominant group rather than the other way around" (Harris, 1993: 1741, 1761). This is reminiscent of the movie *La Cage aux Folles II*, in which a gay man passes as a woman in Italy and, having to do grueling woman's work, he looks up from the floor he is scrubbing and states, "I want to be a man!"

Apfelbaum argues that a critical stage in overthrowing domination is when the subordinate group begins to use its own norms and standards for positive identity formation and political mobilization. When a previously degrouped group begins to actively resist, the dominant group increases its restrictive controls. Therefore, it is not surprising that when there are increasing numbers of people of color in the United States, as well as increasing awareness of how race is socially constructed – that is, at the very moment when race is about to take center stage in the analysis of oppression – all of a sudden we should be colorblind (Harris, 1993: 1768). In fact, the deconstruction of white privilege has brought a backlash of countercharges of reverse racism. From this perspective, whiteness is a legitimate criterion of resource allocation because merit is colorblind. It is a co-incidence (or inherent superiority) that most meritorious persons happen to be white and male. The unmentioned assumptions about the superiority of whiteness are nowhere clearer than in the legal battles on reverse discrimination. For example, in the famous Bakke case, where a white male student claimed and won a legal suit of reverse discrimination when he did not get admitted to medical school at the University of California, Davis. The defendant only claimed discrimination on one criterion, whiteness. Other selection criteria, such as that applicants were the children of wealthy donors, went unchallenged because these hierarchies are perceived as legitimate. Whiteness as property is possessed by all members of the defined group and lends itself to race solidarity. Wealth, on the other hand, is possessed in varying degrees and cannot be a criterion for solidarity. In fact, whiteness may be the only uniformly unifying characteristic of the dominant group. In Harris's words, "Bakke expected that he would never be disfavored when competing with minority candidates, although he might be disfavored with respect to more privileged whites" (ibid.: 1773). That is, competition among whites is *fair* because they are racial equals.

The inherent right for whiteness to serve as valuable property is based on biology; it is property that groups of color cannot possess immediately. This results in a priori structural privilege. When whiteness, because of its "natural" order and its elusive nature, remains unquestioned, we have racial *realism*, leaving no room to question whiteness or privilege (ibid.).

Beating the Trickster: Dismantling Privilege

The play is actually a pastorela[4] in which the skeleton is written, but the particulars have to be flexible to prevent the subversion of the play. I invite those like me to hone the skills of domination and invent new rhetoric that will leave our privilege intact and will insure our children's future reign. I also caution you against traitors who will divulge our tactics and impostors who will divulge knowledge gained about domination as they are allowed to rule in limited contexts. Traitors and impostors are the only way the play can be deconstructed to subvert our most perfect mechanisms of domination.

The study of whiteness is difficult because it is not viewed as problematic (we are more passionate about combating injustice, making us feel we are doing something worthwhile). Secondly, whiteness is natural and therefore difficult to describe. The semblance of naturalness in itself defends privilege from scrutiny. The struggle in the twentieth century has been to problematize "the natural." Progressive scholarship has produced a body of research questioning many forms of oppression. The challenge of the twentieth-first century will be to continue the work of the Enlightenment when the privilege of royal lineage was questioned to provide avenues for democracy to flourish. In our time, race privilege substituted for royal lineage. Race privilege, at times, countervails class, like "royal blood" did in the past. We believe in its goodness as former subjects believed in the direct connection to God through their kings.

Women's studies, men's studies, ethnic studies, and other progressive scholarship all subvert the play. New reactionary rhetorics, however, emerge to co-opt the advancements that scholarship can make on the trickster's play. It is like the Wizard of Oz manipulating those who choose to go down the yellow brick road toward finding the real Oz. At any point in time they can be diverted by the illusions of the trickster pulling levers behind the big screen.

The Solution

I began this chapter by stating the problematic nature of not integrating privilege in the analysis of domination and subordination. I hope it is clear that I am not speaking of moving the gaze from the oppressed to the oppressor, which results in the "exchange of dominations – dominant Eurocentric scholarship *replaced* by dominant Afro-centric scholarship . . . More interesting is what makes intellectual domination possible; how knowledge is transformed from invasion and conquest to revelation and choice" (Morrison, 1992: 8). What would power in a just society look like if we incorporate reflexivity in our theories of liberation?

First, most progressive scholarship concerned with reflexivity emphasizes participatory decision-making. It is hierarchical and elitist to separate leaders from their
constituencies to convince them to follow. Current forms of communication
make it possible for large-scale participatory forums (West, quoted in hooks and
West, 1991: 25). The emphasis in a reflexive theories of liberation is not on the
qualities of good leaders but on the types of leadership models that lead to
strategic action to accomplish particular goals:

> We need serious strategic and tactical thinking about how to create new models of
> leadership and forge the kind of persons to actualize these models. These models
> must not only question our silent assumptions about black leadership such as the
> notion that black leaders are always middle class but also force us to interrogate
> iconic figures of the past. This includes questioning King's sexism and homophobia
> and the relatively undemocratic character of his organization, and Malcolm's
> silence in the vicious role of priestly versions of Islam in the modern world.
> (Ibid.: 25)

Simultaneously, there is an emphasis on appreciating the strengths and struggles
of these "iconic black leaders . . . so that we learn from past struggles how to
strengthen and renew ourselves for the future" (ibid.: 25).

Reflexivity is happening with black writers especially in the area of critical race
studies. Many of these writers integrate their own privilege and bias in the quest
to give an accurate analysis about race. This reflexive scholarship also addresses
the diversity of constituencies within the black communities and how different
writers/leaders represent this diversity. For example, bell hooks, a feminist, interviews Ice Cube, a rapper, whose lyrics are not always on the "right side" of
feminist rhetoric and concerns. Hearing their conversation, the reader is witness
to how they make sense of their privilege to bond across their political differences
and provide responsible leadership for their constituencies. We still, however,
have not developed progressive scholarship that consistently integrates privilege
into its analysis. In other words, how is domination a puzzle that can be understood in order to dismantle it, and how are we players *in relationship* to one
another, with different access to power, much of it contextually based and some
of it ever present? Our social existence is intertwined, for better or worse, and,
whether we live next to one another or not, we influence one another's lives. To
be conscious of this *all* the time and to act in relationship to this *all* of the time
is what is required to conceive of, and construct a world in which race, sexual
orientation, and gender will not matter, and, in which we will not know the
meaning of class.

Notes

1 Much of the analysis presented here of the research of whiteness has appeared previously in Hurtado and Stewart, 1997.

2 Gutiérrez points out that the Kingdom of New Mexico's settled population in the eighteenth century consisted of four major groups: the nobility (the dominant class), below
   them, landed peasants, the indians (the middle group) and at the bottom were the
   genízaros. The *genízaros* were " . . . slaves, detribalized Indians, primarily of Apache
   and Navajo origin, who had been captured by the Spanish and pressed into domestic
   service" (1991, 148).
3 In Mexico there is a saying, *no te hagas pendejo,* meaning, "don't play dumb." It is
   used as a rhetorical device in conversation when individuals claim not to understand
   to avoid conceding the point. This expression is used mostly by working-class Mexicans
   to describe those in power who claim not to understand, especially when the factual
   evidence is overwhelming. It is also not used in the presence of dominant group
   members but used to refer to the mechanism when they are speaking to members of
   their group. For example, a worker may say about her boss, *sehace pendejo* (he plays
   dumb), when she requests her salary increased because of the extra duties he has
   assigned to her. The boss replies to her request "what extra duties?" to avoid her
   request.
4 A *pastorela* is a Catholic passion play brought to the Americas by colonizing Spaniards
   in the sixteenth century. The play, performed throughout the US Southwest and Latin
   America, consists of stock characters whose dialogue and specific plot twists get reinvented by those who perform it. The adaptability of the play includes substituting the
   dialogue with local slang to make it more accessible and enjoyable to working-class
   communities. Several scholars attribute the endurance of *la pastorela* to its flexibility.

References

Apfelbaum, Erika. 1979. "Relations of Domination and Movements for Liberation: An
   Analysis of Power between Groups." In *The Social Psychology of Intergroup Relations,*
   ed. William G. Austin and Stephen Worchel. Monterey, CA: Brooks / Cole Publishing,
   188–204.
Bell, Derrick. 1992. *Faces at the Bottom of the Well: The Permanence of Racism.* New
   York: Basic Books.
Chavez, Linda. 1991. *Out of the Barrio: Toward a New Politics of Hispanic Assimilation.*
   New York: Basic Books.
Connell, R. W. 1995. *Masculinities.* Berkeley: University of California Press.
Davis, Angela Y. 1974. *With My Mind on Freedom: An Autobiography.* New York:
   Bantam Books.
Domhoff, G. William. (1983). *Who Rules American Now?* Englewood Cliffs, NJ:
   Prentice-Hall.
Du Bois, W. E. B. 1973. *The Souls of Black Folk.* Millwood, NY: Kraus-Thomson
   Organization.
duCille, A. 1994. "The Occult of True Black Womanhood: Critical Demeanor and Black
   Feminist Studies." *Signs: Journal of Women in Culture and Society,* 19 (3): 591–629.
Fine, Michelle. 1997. Witnessing Whiteness. In *Off White. Readings on Race, Power, and
   Society,* ed. Michelle Fine, Lois Weis, Linda C. Powell, and Mun Wong. New York:
   Routledge, 57–65.
Fine, Michelle, Lois Weis, Linda C. Powell, and Mun Wong (eds). 1997. *Off White.
   Readings on Race, Power, and Society.* New York: Routledge.

Fine, Michelle, Lois Weis, and Judi Addelston. 1994. "(In)Secure Times: Constructing White Heteromasculinity in the 1980s and '90s." Ms, City University of New York, Graduate Center.

Frankenberg, Ruth. 1993. *White Women, Race Matters: The Social Construction of Whiteness*. Minneapolis: University of Minnesota Press.

Gallagher, C. A. 1995. "White Reconstruction in the University." *Socialist Review*, 24 (1–2): 165–85.

Graham, Lawrence O. 1995. *Member of the Club: Reflections on Life in a Racially Polarized World*. New York: HarperCollins Publishers.

Gutiérrez, Ramón A. 1991. *When Jesus Came, the Corn Mothers Went Away: Marriage, Sexuality, and Power in New Mexico, 1500–1846*. Stanford, CA: Stanford University Press.

Harris, Cheryl I. 1993. "Whiteness as Property." *Harvard Law Review*, 106 (8): 1709–91.

hooks, bell, and Cornel West. 1991. *Breaking Bread: Insurgent Black Intellectual Life*. Boston: South End Press.

Hurtado, Aida, and Abigail Stewart. 1997. "Through the Looking Glass: Implications of Studying Whiteness for Feminists Methods." In *Off White: Readings on Race, Power, and Society*, ed. Michelle Fine, Lois Weis, Linda C. Powell, and L. Mun Wong. New York: Routledge.

Kimmel, Michael S. 1993. "Invisible Masculinity." *Society*, 30(6): 28–35.

McIntosh, Peggy. 1992. "White Privilege and Male Privilege: A Personal Account of Coming to See Correspondences through Work in Women's Studies." In *Race, Class, and Gender*, ed. M. L. Andersen and P. Hill Collins. Belmont, CA: Wadsworth, 70–81.

Morrison, Toni. 1992. *Playing in the Dark: Whiteness and the Literary Imagination*. Cambridge, MA: Harvard University Press.

Ostrander, Susan. 1984. *Women of the Upper Class*. Philadelphia: Temple University Press.

Roediger, David R. 1991. *The Wages of Whiteness: Race and the Making of the American Working Class*. New York: Verso.

Romero, Mary. 1992. *Maid in the USA*. New York: Routledge.

Ryan, Jake, and Charles Sackrey. 1984. *Strangers in Paradise: Academics from the Working Class*. Boston: South End Press.

Sturgis, Susanna J. 1988. "Class/Act: Beginning a Translation from Privilege." In *Out the Other Side: Contemporary Lesbian Writing*, ed. C. McEwan and S. O'Sullivan. London: Virago, 7–13.

Tatum, Beverly D. 1992. "Talking about Race, Learning about Racism: The Application of Racial Identity Development Theory in the Classroom." *Harvard Educational Review*, 62 (1): 1–24.

Wellman, David T. 1993. *Portraits of White Racism*, 2nd edn. New York: Cambridge University Press.

Part V

Cultural Citizenship, Multiculturalism, and the State

16

Citizenship

Richard Delgado

Nativism, Then and How

History teaches that nativist movements tend to flourish when the country's social and economic situation is unsettled and then take one of two broad forms.[1] Society enacts restrictive immigration laws and policies to keep foreigners – usually ones of darker coloration – out.[2] And it enacts measures aimed at making things difficult for those who are already here.[3] In the late nineteenth and early twentieth centuries, for example, early immigration from southeastern Europe prompted proposals for the first literacy tests for immigrants.[4] It took nearly thirty years to get the tests enacted because successive presidents vetoed them on the grounds that they were contrary to the American tradition of open immigration. In 1917, a literacy requirement was finally enacted over President Wilson's veto.[5]

To the surprise of the test's proponents, many of the immigrants from southeastern Europe passed the new test. As a result, the proponents shifted ground, urging restrictive national-origins quotas. These quotas, which were aimed at maintaining America's ethnic makeup (namely, dominantly white) were enacted in 1924 and remained in place for over forty years.[6] During the height of hysteria over postwar communism, English literacy was made a condition of naturalized citizenship for the first time.[7]

Measures such as these, aimed at making immigration or naturalization difficult, have generally been coupled with round-ups, restrictive labor and business laws, and other repressive measures aimed at making life difficult for immigrant groups once they are here.[8] In our time, English-only laws extend the linguistic jingoism inherent in literacy requirements. In earlier times, labor laws were used to discourage Chinese laundries.[9] The campaign against affirmative action and in favor of eliminating social services for immigrants illustrates more contemporary forms of legal treatment designed to disadvantage the foreign born.[10]

Measures to Narrow the Constitutional Grant of Citizenship

One measure, new to our time, would narrow the constitutional grant of citizenship. Previous measures conditioned the grant of citizenship, or the right to immigrate, for example, denying it to foreigners who had committed a felony, were communists, or could not speak English.[11] The new measures are different – they would change the definition of citizenship itself. As such, they advance both types of nativist objective.[12] They send an emphatic message to would-be immigrants in other parts of the world. And they burden those who are already here by making acquisition of US citizenship more difficult for many who wish to do so.

One such measure is California's Joint Resolution 49. Introduced by Assembly members Mountjoy, Haynes, Morrow, and Rainey on August 23, 1993, the measure urged that the US Congress propose "appropriate amendments to the United States Constitution limiting United States citizenship to persons born in the United States of mothers who are citizens, legal residents of the United States, and of naturalized United States citizens." [13] The measure "would also propose that the constitutional amendments repeal the first sentence of Section I of the Fourteenth Amendment to the United States Constitution, among other things." [14] The text of the resolution declares that its purpose is to decrease the incentive for illegal immigration and thus reduce the demand for public services. A few days later, Governor Pete Wilson of California echoed the assembly proposal, calling for congressional action or a constitutional amendment to change the rule under which children born in the United States are automatically granted citizenship.[15]

Slightly less than one year later, four US congressmen introduced 1994 House Joint Resolution 396.[16] Echoing the language of the California version, the resolution proposed "an amendment to the Constitution of the United States to provide that no person born in the United States will be a United States citizen on account of birth in the United States unless a parent is a United States citizen at the time of the birth." The resolution builds on an earlier resolution put forward in March of the same year. The earlier resolution would have denied citizenship "on account of birth in the United States unless the mother or father of the person is a citizen . . . is lawfully in the United States, or has a lawful status under the immigration laws." [17] A third version (House Joint Resolution 129) likewise would limit citizenship by birth; at the time of writing it had attracted over forty cosponsors, including four Democrats.[18] All such proposals were pending at the time of writing.

How Should We See These Proposals?

The reader's first reaction may be to dismiss these proposals to change the constitutional grant of citizenship on the grounds that they are unlikely to be enacted into law. It is true that the Fourteenth Amendment, the Constitution's basic guarantee of equal citizenship, has never been amended in its entire history.[19] It is also true that the US Constitution makes the process of amendment relatively difficult.[20] Yet, most state constitutions also make their own amendment difficult; they make enactment of legislation by popular referendum costly and time-consuming as well. But this has not stopped a host of sponsors from enacting anti-gay or anti-immigrant measures in California and Colorado, or proposing similar ones in several other states.[21] Given the current climate, one cannot be certain that a national measure limiting the grant of citizenship does not lie ahead.

Such a measure would be consistent and continuous with numerous other nativist laws and policies that have been adopted or proposed. Moreover, the resolutions come at a propitious time. As was mentioned earlier, nativist sentiment increases during times of socioeconomic upheaval, like our own.[22] Changes in the job market, and the challenge from overseas competition for markets, mean that many Americans are today less secure of their jobs and status than in former years. At the same time, the conditions that produced the civil rights decade of the sixties are missing. Unlike then, we are not competing with the Soviet Union for the loyalties of the uncommitted Third World, most of which is black, brown, or yellow. Then, racism, lynching, and mean-spirited treatment of domestic minorities and foreign visitors were embarrassments which our competitors seized on as evidence of their system's superiority. Now there is less need to demonstrate that our system is better than godless communism. Derrick Bell's interest-convergence formula (which explains *Brown v. Board of Education* and other Cold War-era advances for blacks in terms of the interests of elite whites) would predict an era of rapid rollback in gains for ethnic minorities, foreigners, and other outsider groups.[23] Finally, we should recall that earlier nativist measures, like literacy tests, were first viewed with outrage but later enacted.[24] The same may happen with citizenship.

The Schuck–Smith Argument: Citizenship By Consent

In addition, today's efforts to limit immigration and citizenship are aided by an elegant and influential argument from national autonomy. First propounded by two moderate liberals, Peter Schuck and Rogers Smith,[25] the argument has been appropriated by conservative forces across the nation. In a nutshell, the Schuck–Smith position holds that a nation ought to have unlimited discretion in deciding whom it shall admit. Communities should be able to determine their own membership; this is an important aspect of national autonomy. If large numbers of outsiders were free to settle, bringing with them new values, languages, and patterns of behavior, they would in effect have the right to force the nation to become something it is not. This state of affairs is inconsistent with the idea of a community of self-defining citizens; any nation is free to resist it.

The argument draws on the premises of communitarianism, a moderate-liberal school of jurisprudence that sprang up in the 1980s, perhaps as an antidote to the unfettered individualism of the early Reagan–Bush years.[26] But the argument struck a chord as well with conservatives, offering them a principled argument for accomplishing what many of them wanted to achieve – the promotion of an America-first philosophy – but for a much less noble reason, namely a dislike of foreigners and immigrants.

How shall we see the Schuck–Smith argument? In an ideal world, it would deserve serious consideration. But we do not live in an ideal world. In the United States, the current community – the institution to which the argument would hand unfettered discretion regarding immigration policy – is deeply affected by racism and exclusionary practices.[27] For much of our history, a national-origin quota system and, before that, anti-Asian and anti-Mexican laws, kept the numbers of immigrants of color low. We denied immigration and travel visas to communists and others espousing ideologies deemed dangerous. Literacy and English-speaking requirements cut down the number of immigrants from areas other than northern Europe. And round-ups, *Bracero* programs, English-only laws, and the panoply of nativist measures detailed in other chapters of this book made things difficult for immigrants from disfavored countries once they were here. For much of our history, women and blacks were denied the right to vote or hold office. Higher education was virtually closed to both until about 1960, and in Southern states, Black Codes made it a crime to teach a black to read.

"The community," then, is deeply shaped by racism, sexism, and xenophobia. This is so not only in terms of its demography and makeup but also its preferences and values. Handing such a community the keys to determine immigration policy is a recipe for self-replication and stasis. The community would (perhaps without knowing it) opt for the familiar – itself. In similar fashion, but even more blatantly, limiting the grant of citizenship to those who can prove blood descent would simply perpetuate the racist past.

Back to *Dred Scott v. Sandford?*

In *Dred Scott v. Sandford,* [28] decided by the US Supreme Court in 1856, the US judicial system dealt with the question of runaway slaves. At the time *Dred Scott* was decided, the country was divided into two regions, the South, where slavery was legal and widely practiced, and the free North. The issue before the court was whether Dred Scott, previously a slave, had become free by virtue of a period of time spent in the free North. The Court rejected his plea, holding that African-Americans have "no rights which the white man was bound to respect."[29] The claim of such a person to citizenship was untenable, historically and legally: blacks could not be citizens because they had not been so from the beginning; and the Framers of the Constitution, "great men," never regarded them that way. Justice Taney's opinion regards blacks as subhumans, a status that was only little improved by enactment of the Civil Rights Amendments a decade later. If blacks had any doubts on that score, *Plessy v. Ferguson,*[30] the "separate but equal" case decided in 1896, should have dispelled them. *Plessy,* which remained the law of the land until *Brown v. Board of Education,* [31] did little to improve society's view of blacks as citizens deserving full equality. Separate facilities served as constant reminders that blacks were a separate, and lower, order of humanity from whites, deserving poorer treatment simply on the ground of who they were.

The argument, structure, and rhetoric of present-day nativism contain overtones of *Dred Scott*-type reasoning – particularly proposals to limit citizenship under the Fourteenth Amendment.[32] The Schuck-Smith national autonomy argument echoes Taney's by reasoning from preexisting attitudes and enshrining them in law. The rhetoric, like Taney's, has overtones of scorn and condescension – foreigners are treated as pollution, as threats to national values of thrift and hard work. The study of nativist movements, past and present, brings into focus these and other alarming parallels and alerts us to what we may expect in the future. Like Taney's opinion, efforts to limit citizenship are efforts to maintain a system of white supremacy and to give that system the veneer of fairness and principle.

Notes

1   See Thomas Muller, "Nativism in the Mid-1990s: Why Now?" discussing the economic causation of much nativism, chapter 6 in Juan F. Perea (ed.), *Immigrants Out! The new nativism and the anti-immigrant impulse in the United States* (pp. 318–23), New York: New York University Press.

2   The *Bracero* (temporary farmworker) program and national-origin quota system for allocating immigration permits are prominent examples. See introduction, *supra,* and Dorothy E. Roberts, "Who May Give Birth to Citizens? Reproduction, Eugenics and Immigration," chapter 11, and Gilbert Paul Carrasco, "Latinos in the United States: Invitation and Exile," chapter 10, both included in *Immigrants Out!*

3   See *id.*

4   See Juan F. Perea, "Demography and Distrust: An Essay on American Languages, Cultural Pluralism, and Official English," 77 *Minn. L. Rev.* 269, 332–6 (1992).

5   *Id.* at 333–5.

6   *Id.* at 335–6.

7   *Id.* at 337–9.

8   See Michael Olivas, "The Chronicles, My Grandfather's Stories, and Immigration Law: The Slave Traders Chronicle as Racial History," in *Critical Race Theory: The Cutting Edge*, 9 (R. Delgado ed., 1995).

9   *Id.* at 13–14.

10 See Leo R. Chavez, "Immigration Reform and Nativism: The Nationalist Response to the Transnationalist Challenge," chapter 4, and Jean Stefancic, "Funding the Nativist Agenda," chapter 7, both in *Immigrants Out!* See also Jean Stefancic, *No Mercy: How Conservative Think Tanks and Foundations Changed America's Social Agenda* (Temple University Press, 1996).

11 See, generally, T. Alexander Aleinikoff, *Immigration: Process and Policy,* (2nd edn 1991) (on the many grounds for denying immigration or naturalization).

12 See text and notes 2–10, immediately *supra.*

13 On file with author; see Alan C. Nelson, "Alien Immigration Tide: California Governor's Idea to Deny Benefits Logical," *Dallas Morning News,* August 29, 1993, at 5-J (discussing similar proposal).

14 Source cited *supra* note 13.

15 Nelson, "Tide," *supra* note 13.

16 On file with author.

17 On file with author.

18 On file with author.

19 The Fourteenth Amendment, which guarantees equal protection and due process of law, also provides for citizenship to "all persons born or naturalized in the United States and subject to the jurisdiction thereof."

20 See US Const. art. V, setting out the method for amendment (on application of two-thirds of the states, legislatures; two-thirds of both Houses; a Convention; further ratification, etc.).

21 Generally, the proponent must gather a large number of signatures within a relatively brief time and have them verified by a state official, such as the Secretary of State.

22 See editor's introduction, *Immigrants Out!*

23 Derrick Bell, *"Brown v. Board of Education* and the Interest-Convergence Dilemma," 93 *Harv. L. Rev.* 518 (1980).

24 Text and notes 4–5 *supra*.

25 Peter Schuck and Rogers Smith, *Citizenship without Consent* (Yale University Press, 1985).

26 On communitarianism, see, generally, Richard Delgado, "Rodrigo's Fifth Chronicle: *Civitas,* Civil Wrongs, and the Politics of Denial," 45 *Stan. L. Rev.* 1581 (1993).

27 See Dorothy E. Roberts, "Who May Give Birth to Citizens? Reproduction, Eugenics, and Immigration," chapter 11, and Daniel Kanstroom, "Dangerous Undertones of the New Nativism: Peter Brimelow and the Decline of the West," chapter 16, both in *Immigrants Out!*

28 60 US393 (1856).

29 *Id.* at 407.

30 163 US537 (1896).

31 347 US483 (1954).

32 See Gerald L. Neuman, "Back to Dred Scott," 24 *San Diego L. Rev.* 485 (1987).

17

Cultural Citizenship, Inequality, and Multiculturalism

Renato Rosaldo

The cultural citizenship project involves research teams that have worked in California, Texas, and New York. The project's central focus has been a set of social processes that we have chosen to call cultural citizenship. In defining cultural citizenship, a phrase that yokes together terms usually kept apart, I should like to begin with reflections on the component "citizenship" and then discuss the implications of "cultural."

Citizenship

Citizenship is often understood as a universal concept. In this view, all citizens of a particular nation state are equal before the law. A background assumption of our work, by contrast, is that that one needs to distinguish the formal level of theoretical universality from the substantive level of exclusionary and marginalizing practices. Even in its late-eighteenth-century Enlightenment origins, citizenship in the republic differentiated men of privilege from the rest, second-class citizens and non-citizens.

In France the people who gathered in public squares were putatively all equal. They were *les citoyens*, the citizens. Certain contemporary thinkers propose that we should return to the model of the public square, to the situation of the citoyens who were supposedly all equal. The public square, they argue, was the democratic space par excellence, and it should be adopted as the model for the late-twentieth-century civil society.

Such thinkers thus affirm that there were no distinctions among citizens who gathered in public squares. These gatherings were a significant step forward in the process of democratization, no doubt, particularly in comparison with the tyranny of excessive social distinctions that reigned during the regime dominated by the monarchy and the aristocracy. One cannot but agree, at least to a point, that the universal notion of citizen was a significant step toward democracy in relation to the *ancien régime* that preceded it. Nonetheless, at least from the present standpoint, the public square is not the final goal, but only a point of departure for democratization.

In this respect, I differ with commentaries that stress the central importance of developing urban spaces where people may form face-to-face civil societies in sites of public gathering. Such spaces appear to certain thinkers as a solution to problems of contemporary urban life where corporate takeovers and the Foucauldian disciplining of subject populations have replaced what was once relatively unregulated social life in parks and public squares. In this view, the very notion of the public in late-twentieth-century urban spaces begins to shrink as stadiums replace parks and shopping malls replace public squares.

Consider, however, the inequalities that operated in the public squares of the romanticized past. Begin with differences of gender. Can women disguise their gender in the public sphere? If they must appear as women, and not as universal unmarked citizens, then one can ask, who has the right to speak in public debates conducted in the square? Are men or women more likely to be interrupted with greater frequency? Are men or women more likely to be referred to as having had a good idea in these discussions? As much recent sociolinguistic and feminist research has shown, one must consider much more than whether or not certain categories of persons are present in the public square. One must consider categories that are visibly inscribed on the body, such as gender and race, and their consequences for full democratic participation. The moment a woman or a person of color enters the public square both difference and inequality come to the surface. It is difficult to conceal differences of gender and race, and given the prejudiced norms under which we still live, inequities will come to the surface.

Following Enlightenment ideals, the language of the US Constitution granted universal rights to its citizens. It declared that all citizens are equal (implicitly assuming, of course, that the condition of their equality is their sameness in relation to language and culture). In this sense the question of citizenship is bipolar and simple: either one is a citizen or one is not, and that is that.

In the beginning the US Constitution declared that citizens were white men of property. And indeed, as has often been remarked, the stipulation can be read the other way around: that is, the Constitution disenfranchised men without property, women, and people of color. These exclusions derive from discrimination based on class, gender, and race. In the long run, these forms of discrimination defined the parameters of dissident traditions that have endured into the present. The dissident traditions so engendered have involved struggles to be full citizens in ways that were set in motion by the Constitution's original exclusions.

The dissident traditions of struggle for first-class citizenship have achieved a great deal, even if much remains to be achieved. The struggle for women's suffrage (which did not succeed until 1920) was the first step in a historical process whose present phase is contemporary feminism. Issues of women's rights have moved beyond the vote to sets of practices where, in spite of formal equality, one notices such forms of marginalization as systemic differences in pay and subtle mechanisms for not attending to what women say. Similarly, the legacy of antislavery movements has moved through civil rights to the new social movements that encompass African-Americans, Asian-Americans, Native Americans, and Latinos.

The long history and the success of these dissident traditions of struggle grants a certain depth and legitimacy to their successors in the present. Slavery and formally disenfranchised women are obsolete as social institutions in the late-twentieth-century United States. Debates about race and gender today often invoke that history of abolition and suffrage.

While emphasizing the continuity of dissident traditions in the United States from the nineteenth century to the present, social analysts such as Stuart Hall and David Held (1990) have discussed the new politics of citizenship in the 1990s. They assert that "from the ancient world to the present day, citizenship has entailed a discussion, and a struggle over, the meaning and scope of membership of the community in which one lives" (1990: 175). For them, the key innovation has been an expansion of the definition of citizenship and the base upon which rights are demanded:

> A contemporary "politics of citizenship" must take into account the role which the social movements have played in expanding the claims to right and entitlements to new areas. It must address not only issues of class and inequality, but also questions of membership posed by feminism, the black and ethnic movements, ecology (including the moral claims of the animal species and of Nature itself) and vulnerable minorities, like children. (1990: 176)

The new social movements have expanded the emphasis on citizens' rights from questions of class to issues of gender, race, sexuality, ecology, and age. In effect, new citizens have come into being as new categories of persons who make claims on both their fellow citizens and the state. For Hall and Held, the rights of citizenship have expanded in a quantitative sense, but I should like to note that the shift is also qualitative.

In this qualitative shift one can identify two dimensions of change. First, one can think of the redistribution of resources. This dimension refers, above all, to class and the struggle for economic democracy. The second dimension of change could be called recognition and responsiveness. For example, one can consider gay and lesbian rights as an area where issues of the redistribution of resources may be less central than issues of recognition and unbiased treatment in the workplace and other institutional contexts. Such issues range from blatant to subtle matters of second class citizenship. If issues of class and the equitable distribution of resources were resolved, matters of recognition and fair treatment in the face of bias regarding sexuality, gender, and race would still remain.

A case in point for the politics of recognition would be the current situation of Latinos in the United States. A significant number of people in the United States, for example, have come to question the citizenship of Latinos by declaring undocumented workers to be "alien" or "illegal." By a psychological and cultural mechanism of association all Latinos are thus declared to have a blemish that brands us with the stigma of being outside the law. We always live with that mark indicating that whether or not we belong in this country is always in question. The distortions here are twofold.

First, the term "illegal" misleads because it suggests that undocumented workers are illegal in the sense of failing to obey and living outside the law. On the contrary, they obey the law more punctiliously than most citizens because they know that the punishment for the slightest infraction is deportation. In this respect, they tend to be more law-abiding than citizens with legal documents. Undocumented workers deserve to be treated in accord with universal human rights.

Second, the icon of the Latino illegal alien suggests, again obliquely but powerfully, that all Latinos in the United States are immigrants, most of whom came under questionable circumstances. A young Chicana poet expressed the real situation succinctly when she said, *"No cruce la frontera, la frontera me cruzo a mi"* (I did not cross the border, the border crossed me). After the War of 1848, Mexican territory became part of the United States and Mexican citizens in that territory found that the border crossed them as it moved from north to south. In other words, many Chicanos lived within the present territorial borders of the United States before the first northern European settlements were established in the New World, certainly well before Jamestown. These early settlements contained Spaniards, Indians, and Africans. Increasingly the mestizo and mulatto blends became evident. Far from being newcomers, Latinos are oldtimers in the New World. It is not difficult to document the continuous presence of Chicanos within the present territorial boundaries of the United States.

The mass media often present sensational views of Latinos as new immigrant communities with the consequence, intended or not, of questioning our citizenship and hardening racialized relations of dominance and subordination. Cynical politicians have used such ideological maneuvers to secure the approval of such legislation as Proposition 187. The tactic divides the Latino community against itself and separates Latinos from dominant white groups.

Culture

By way of moving on to the question of how culture intersects crucially with citizenship today, I now should like to make some themes concrete through a series of examples.

Public and private

In his memoir, *Hunger of Memory,* Richard Rodríguez asserts that Spanish is a domestic language; it is, he says, fine for expressing feelings, but it is no good for thinking. It's good for family life, but it has no place in school, politics, and the workplace. He thus opposes public bilingualism. In other words, he claims that racialized ethnic culture can thrive only within the domestic rather than the public sphere. Rodríguez is no doubt being true to his experience, but I would argue that he ignores the social and ideological factors that have structured his experience.

Rodríguez's perceptions do not, I think, belong to him alone. Thus is a case where ideology colors personal insights about culture. The segregationist ideology of white supremacy is speaking through Rodríguez, and one should not blame either the author or the Spanish language. A day in Mexico, elsewhere in Latin America, or Spain should suffice to make it clear that the linguistic limitations Rodríguez experiences are built into social arrangements, not the language. If the United States has placed a taboo on the use of Spanish in public life, it derives from prejudice manifest in legal and informal arrangements and not because of the language. In Mexico and Puerto Rico Spanish is the language of both the heart and the mind, domestic and public life.

Border theater, border violence

The US-Mexico border has become theater, and border theater has become social violence. Actual violence has become inseparable from symbolic ritual on the border – crossings, invasions, lines of defense, high-tech surveillance, and more. Social scientists often think of public rituals as events that resemble formal rituals separated from daily life in time and space and marked by repeated formal structures. In contrast the violence and high tech weaponry of border theater is at once symbolic and material. Social analysts need to recognize the centrality of actual violence and the symbols that shape that violence.

The new technologies of violence were tested in the Gulf War and in the staged television coverage of smart missiles and precision mayhem. These technologies are now directed at unarmed Mexicans as they enter the United States in search of work. The risk they run is real; the threat of death can readily be delivered. For North American politicians, however, the key element is theatrical, a cynical work of lethal art that they offer to their voters with an invocation of previous wars, not only the Gulf War but also the Vietnam War (thus the US-Mexico border becomes a DMZ, a Demilitarized Zone). They attempt to stage the vulnerability of North American citizens who are at risk because of the "illegals" (read: outlaws) invading their land. They of course add that the government is using all means at its disposal to protect citizens from the brown invaders from the south.

Voting

The vote is the citizen's most sacred right/rite. Yet in California statewide initiatives provide citizens with an occasion for voting their prejudices. Proposition 187 was arguably in large measure an expression of white supremacy. Proposition 209, the so-called California Civil Rights Initiative (CCRI) that appeared on the November 1996 ballot, actually dismantles affirmative action programs and thus opposes civil rights in a manner manipulated by self-serving politicians in order to deepen racial cleavages in the state. The

CCRI was explicitly designed to be a "wedge" issue that would divide Democrats and increase the chances of Republican presidential candidate Robert Dole. Indeed because of its popular referenda California has become a testing ground for hot-button conservative political issues at the national level.

The study of voter behavior requires analysis at the symbolic cultural level. Arguably, such referenda manifest legal juridical violence against Latinos, African-Americans, Asian-Americans, Native Americans, and women. The workings of such electoral violence cry out for an understanding of a voting subject who is quite unlike the rational choice-maker who is favored by political scientists who regard voter behavior as if it were the same as the consumer's market behavior. The people who voted for Proposition 187 and the CCRI are engaged less in a rational calculus than in expressing their inner prejudices and fears.

Quetzalcóatl in San José

My final example concerns the unveiling of a statue of Quetzalcóatl, the Aztec divinity of urban civilization, about a year ago in San José, California. The unveiling was marred by controversy and by protests from anti-abortion activist Evangelical Christians. The Evangelical groups inspired fear because they had been involved in militant actions at abortion clinics. For the eve of the unveiling I had been asked to give a talk at the San José Museum of Art on the cultural and historical significance of Quetzalcóatl. As I prepared to leave my house to go and give the talk, I felt anxious because I feared the worst, particularly from the Evangelical groups. Just before I left the house my daughter Olivia wrote and gave me the following poem, called "Remember," which she dedicated "To Dad and Quetzalcóatl":

> Remember
> who, how,
> Remember who you are.
> How did I get here?
> Remember your descendants.
> Remember your language.
> Remember who you are
> even where there's prejudice
> of who
> and what you are.
> Remember.

What I did not know as I left was that I would find, in addition to the Evangelicals I feared, an audience composed of public officials, militant Chicano brown berets, and Native American and Chicano costumed dancers from as far away as Mexico City, Texas, and New Mexico. Once I arrived and scanned the audience I felt secure and confident. I was present as a cultural interpreter at an event that had clear political as well as cultural meanings.

The examples just discussed – Rodríguez's view of Spanish as a domestic (not a public) language, border technology as cultural theater, referenda as expressions of prejudice, and the community event surrounding the unveiling of the Quetzalcóatl statue – are all instances of how we need to understand the way citizenship is informed by culture, the way that claims to citizenship are re-inforced or subverted by cultural assumptions and practices. In addition, each of the four cases contains a methodological principle critical to studies in cultural citizenship.

Rodríguez's example stands as a methodological caution against relying un-critically and exclusively on personal testimony, and as a reminder of the impact of larger structural factors on local situations. He sees English as the only language of citizenship in contrast with Spanish, which he sees as the language of the heart and of domestic life. He is true to his experience but, in a way made classic by the phrase internalized oppression, he studiously pays no heed to how his experience has been structured by larger forces of domination and white supremacy.

The US-Mexico border theater underscores the tenet that all human conduct is culturally mediated and that cultural citizenship studies, in everyday life, forms of exclusion, marginalization, and enfranchisement in modes that require joining together cultural meanings and material life. The way force is deployed at the border expresses dominant Anglo cultural views of limited Latino rights to full US citizenship. The physical border has become a line of demarcation enforced by stayed high-tech violence that is no less violent for being symbolic and vice versa – no less suffused with cultural meanings for being lethal and material.

The referenda of recent California politics underscore the way that cultural citizenship research seeks out cases that have become sites of contestation, negotiation, and struggle over cultural meaning and social violence. California referenda can productively be understood as ways of voting prejudices and fears. Unarmed Mexicans working in the United States have, for many voters, become objects of fear and hatred that require exceptional legislative action. This example emphasizes the psychological mechanism of projection, whereby people attribute their own feelings of hatred to somebody else and then in turn fear their own projected feelings.

For the Latino community of San José, the events surrounding the unveiling of the Quetzalcóatl statue were a classic act of cultural citizenship, using cultural expression to claim public rights and recognition, and highlighting the interaction between citizenship and culture. The artistic and cultural event of the unveiling was clearly seen as an important public statement both by the Evangelicals and by a number of distinct elements of the Latino community. In this struggle over the placement and meanings of public art, more was at stake than "culture" in a narrow sense. The Evangelical community clearly saw the cultural expression as a claim to rights in the public square.

My own reactions to the evening reflected the larger dynamic. I went as cultural interpreter, but initially felt disenfranchised as a citizen by the prospect of poten-tial violence. When I saw the remarkable and varied Chicano community presence at the rally – costumes and traditional dance reinforcing the group ties – my own sense of isolation evaporated. I found myself transformed from voice-less vulnerable individual to full-fledged citizen.

Cultural citizenship operates in an uneven field of structural inequalities where the dominant claims of universal citizenship assume a propertied white male subject and usually blind themselves to their exclusions and marginalizations of people who differ in gender, race, sexuality, and age. Cultural citizenship attends, not only to dominant exclusions and marginalizations, but also to subordinate aspirations for and definitions of enfranchisement. In her book on writing, Anne Lamott has eloquently described the hopes of cultural citizenship as virtually universal in the United States:

> Writing can be a pretty desperate endeavor, because it is about some of our deepest needs: our need to be visible, to be heard, our need to make sense of our lives, to wake up and grow and belong. (1994: 19)

The universality of cultural citizenship aspirations most probably reflects the historical experience of civil rights and suffrage struggles. In this vein, our research has found that Latinos are conscious and articulate about their needs to be visible, to be heard, and to belong.

The notion of cultural citizenship challenges social analysts to attend with care to the point of view from which they conduct their studies. Too often social thought anchors its research in the vantage point of the dominant social group and thus reproduces dominant ideology by studying subordinate groups as a "problem" rather than as people with agency – with goals, perceptions, and purposes of their own.

Inequality and social position are critical to studies of cultural citizenship. Social position is a reminder that people in different and often unequal subject positions have different understandings of a given situation and that as they make claims to proper first-class treatment they operate with distinct definitions of such treatment. Chicana poet Lorna Dee Cervantes (1981) sums this insight up in her poem entitled "Poem for the Young White Man Who Asked Me How I, an Intelligent, Well-Read Person, Could Believe in the War Between the Races." The young man sees peace and prosperity in his land; the poet sees a war being inflicted on her people in the "same" land. Cervantes derives this difference of perceptions from the stark fact that those conducting the race war are shooting at her, not him.

Cultural citizenship thus argues that analysts need to anchor their studies in the aspirations and perceptions of people who occupy subordinate social positions. This research demands studies of vernacular notions of citizenship. In this collection the term *respeto* (respect) has appeared frequently as a requirement of full citizenship for Latinos in the United States. Bridging the discourses of the state and everyday life, of citizenship and culture, the demand for *respecto* is a defining demand of cultural citizenship. As all the chapters in this book reveal, it is an ongoing, contested, and – for the participants – urgent process.

References

Cervantes, Lorna Dee. 1981. *Emplumada*. Pittsburg: University of Pittsburg Press.

Hall, Stuart, and David Held. 1990. "Citizens and Citizenship." In *New Times: The Changing Face of Politics in the 1990s,* ed. Stuart Hall and Martin Jacques. London: Verso, pp. 173–88.

Lamott, Anne. 1994. *Bird by Bird: Some Instructions on Writing and Life.* New York: Anchor.

18

Cultural Citizenship as Subject Making: Immigrants Negotiate Racial and Cultural Boundaries in the United States

Aihwa Ong

This chapter views cultural citizenship as a process of self-making and being-made in relation to nation-states and transnational processes. Whereas some scholars claim that racism has been replaced by "cultural fundamentalism" in defining who belongs or does not belong in Western democracies, this essay argues that hierarchical schemes of racial *and* cultural difference intersect in a complex, contingent way to locate minorities of color from different class backgrounds. Comparing the experiences of rich and poor Asian immigrants to the United States, I discuss institutional practices whereby non-white immigrants in the First World are simultaneously, though unevenly, subjected to two processes of normalization: an ideological whitening or blackening that reflects dominant racial oppositions and an assessment of cultural competence based on imputed human capital and consumer power in the minority subject. Immigrants from Asia or poorer countries must daily negotiate the lines of difference established by state agencies as well as groups in civil society. A subsidiary point is that, increasingly, such modalities of citizen-making are influenced by transnational capitalism. Depending on their locations in the global economy, some immigrants of color have greater access than others to key institutions in state and civil society. Global citizenship thus confers citizenship privileges in Western democracies to a degree that may help the immigrant to scale racial and cultural heights but not to circumvent status hierarchy based on racial difference.

In the fall of 1970, I left Malaysia and arrived as a freshman in New York City. I was immediately swept up in the antiwar movement. President Nixon had just begun his "secret" bombing of Cambodia. Joining crowds of angry students marching down Broadway, I participated in the "takeover" of the East Asian Institute building on the Columbia University campus. As I stood there confronting policemen in riot gear, I thought about what Southeast Asia meant to the United States. Were Southeast Asians simply an anonymous mass of people in black pajamas? Southeast Asia was a far-off place where America was conducting a savage war against "communism." American lives were being lost, and so were those of countless Vietnamese, Cambodians, Laotians, and others. This rite of passage into American society was to shape my attitude toward citizenship. As a foreign student I was at a disadvantage, ineligible for most loans, fellowships, and jobs. My sister, a naturalized American, could have sponsored me for a green card, but the bombing of Cambodia, symptomatic of wider disregard for my part of the world, made American citizenship a difficult moral issue for me.

Much writing on citizenship has ignored such subjective and contradictory experiences, focusing instead on its broad legal-political aspects. For instance, Thomas Marshall (1950) defines citizenship as a question of modernity, but he identifies it primarily in terms of the evolution of civil society and the working out of the tensions between the sovereign subject and solidarity in a nation-state. Other scholars have pointed to the contradiction between democratic citizenship and capitalism – the opposition between abstract, universalistic rights and the inequalities engendered by market competition, race, and immigration (Hall and Held, 1989; Portes and Rumbaut, 1990). But these approaches seldom examine how the universalistic criteria of democratic citizenship variously regulate different categories of subjects or how these subjects' location within the nation-state and within the global economy conditions the construction of their citizenship. Indeed, even studies of citizenship that take into account the effects on it of capital accumulation and consumption have been concerned with potential strategies for political change to remake civil society (Yudice, 1995). Seldom is attention focused on the everyday processes whereby people, especially immigrants, are made into subjects of a particular nation-state.

Citizenship as Subjectification

Taking an ethnographic approach, I consider citizenship a cultural process of "subject-ification," in the Foucaldian sense of self-making and being-made by power relations that produce consent through schemes of surveillance, discipline, control, and administration (Foucault, 1989; 1991) Thus formulated, my concept of cultural citizenship can be applied to various global contexts (see Ong, 1993; Ong and Nonini, 1996), but in this chapter I will discuss the making of cultural citizens in Western democracies like the United States. Philip Corrigan and Derek Sayer (1985) in their analysis of the state as a cultural formation, speak of "governmentality," by which they mean the state's project of moral regulation aimed at giving "unitary and unifying expression to what are in reality multifaceted and differential experiences of groups within society" (1985: 4–5). This role of the state in universalizing citizenship is paradoxically attained through a process of individuation whereby people are constructed in definitive and specific ways as citizens – taxpayers, workers, consumers, and welfare-dependents.

This notion of citizenship as dialectically determined by the state and its subjects is quite different from that employed by Renato Rosaldo (1994), who views cultural citizenship as the demand of disadvantaged subjects for full citizenship in spite of their cultural difference from mainstream society.[1] While I share Rosaldo's sentiments, his concept attends to only one side of a set of unequal relationships. It gives the erroneous impression that cultural citizenship can be unilaterally constructed and that immigrant or minority groups can escape the cultural inscription of state power and other forms of regulation that define the different modalities of belonging. Formulated in this manner, Rosaldo's concept of cultural citizenship indicates subscription to the very liberal principle of universal equality that he seeks to call into question.

In contrast, I use "cultural citizenship" to refer to the cultural practices and beliefs produced out of negotiating the often ambivalent and contested relations with the state and its hegemonic forms that establish the criteria of belonging within a national population and territory. Cultural citizenship is a dual process of self-making and being-made within webs of power linked to the nation-state and civil society. Becoming a citizen depends on how one is constituted as a subject who exercises or submits to power relations; one must develop what Foucault (cited by Rabinow, 1984: 49) calls "the modern attitude," an attitude of self-making in shifting fields of power that include the nation-state and the wider world.

Furthermore, in analyzing the pragmatic struggle towards an understanding of cultural citizenship, one must attend to the various regulatory regimes in state agencies and civil society. Michel Foucault (1991) notes that in modern Western democracies control of subjects is manifested in rituals and rules that produce consent; "governmentality" refers to those relations that regulate the conduct of subjects as a population and as individuals in the interests of ensuring the security and prosperity of the nation-state. A major problem with Corrigan and Sayer's (1985) approach is its restriction to the state sector, ignoring civil institutions and social groups as disciplinary forces in the making of cultural citizens. Indeed, it is precisely in liberal democracies like the United States that the governmentality of state agencies is often discontinuous, even fragmentary, and the work of instilling proper normative behavior and identity in newcomers must also be taken up by institutions in civil society. For instance, hegemonic ideas about belonging and not belonging in racial and cultural terms often converge in state and non-state institutional practices through which subjects are shaped in ways that are at once specific and diffused. These are the ideological fields within which different criteria of belonging on the basis of civilized conduct by categorically distinguishable (dominant) others become entangled with culture, race, and class (Williams, 1991: 2–29).

Race, Class, and Economic Liberalism

My approach constitutes an intervention into the conventional theorizing of American citizenship solely in terms of racial politics within the framework of the nation-state (Omi and Winant, 1986; Gregory and Sanjek, 1994). What is urgently needed is a broader conception of race and citizenship shaped by the history of European imperialism. African slavery and colonial empires were central to the making of modern Western Europe and the Americas. Encounters between colonizers and the colonized or enslaved gave rise to the view that white-black hierarchies are homologous with levels of civilization, a racist hegemony that pervades all areas of Western consciousness (Memmi, 1967; Fanon, 1967; Alatas, 1977; Said, 1978; Nandy, 1983; Gilman, 1985; Stoler, 1995). These historically specific ideologies, Western European in origin, order human groupings distinguished by real and alleged biological features into status hierarchies that become the bases of various forms of discrimination and exclusion in Western democracies (Dominguez, 1986; Miles, 1989; Gilroy, 1987; Williams, 1989; 1991; Hall, 1992; Gregory and Sanjek, 1994).

Recently, however, scholars claim that there has been a distinct shift in dominant Western European exclusionary practices whereby cultural rather than racial difference is used to justify calls for banning immigrants (Stolcke, 1995). Paul Gilroy, however, maintains that if we take race as a political rather than a biological category, newer discourses of marginalization in Britain focus on the "distinctive culture" of blacks without discarding racism (1987: 109, 149). He calls the discourse of cultural difference a new racism that is more diffused but still racist even though state policies, informed by sympathetic liberalism, combat the kind of crude, neofascist racism that characterized earlier forms of discrimination in Britain (1987: 148–50). What Gilroy fails to mention, from his British vantage point, is how US racial discourses, long interwoven with notions of cultural difference as in Patrick Moynihan's notion of "black pathology," may have influenced the biological cultural shift in discourses of marginal or ineligible citizenship on the other side of the Atlantic.

Thus this race-versus-culture construction of exclusionary discourses is, albeit unintentionally, a red herring. Nevertheless, leading US scholars such as Michael Omi and Howard Winant (1986) continue to study the shifting constructions of racial politics without reference to normative performance or schemes of cultural assessment. Gilroy cautions that "'race' is a political category that can accommodate various meanings which are in turn determined by struggle . . . racial differentiation has become a feature of institutional structures – legal subjectivity of citizenship – as well as individual action" (1987: 38). A fuller understanding of racism and its embeddedness in notions of citizenship requires an examination of racial concepts and their uses in liberal ideologies and cultural practices.

Another lacuna in theories of racism and citizenship is the effect of class attributes and property rights on citizenship status (see Harrison, 1991). As we shall see, the interweaving of ideologies of racial difference with liberal conceptions of citizenship is evident in popular notions about who deserves to belong in implicit terms of productivity and consumption. For instance, in the postwar United States, neoliberalism, with its celebration of freedom, progress, and individualism, has become a pervasive ideology that influences many domains of social life. It has become synonymous with being American, and more broadly these values are what the world associates with Western civilization. There is, however, a regulatory aspect to neoliberalism whereby economics is extended to cover all aspects of human behavior pertaining to citizenship. An important principle underlying liberal democracy emphasizes balancing the provision of security against the productivity of citizens. In other words, neoliberalism is an expression of the biopolitics of the American state as well as setting the nominative standards of good citizenship in practice. In the postwar era, such thinking has given rise to a human-capital assessment of citizens (Becker, 1965), weighing those who can pull themselves up by their bootstraps against those who make claims on the welfare state. Increasingly, citizenship is defined as the civic duty of individuals to reduce their burden on society and build up their own human capital – to be "entrepreneurs" of themselves (Gordon, 1991: 43–451). Indeed, by the 1960s liberal economics had come to evaluate non-white groups according to their claims on or independence of the state. Minorities who scaled the pinnacles of society often had to justify themselves in such entrepreneurial terms. A rather apt example was the 1990s nomination of Clarence Thomas to the Supreme Court of the United States, a move widely viewed as the token appointment of an African-American to the powerful white-dominated institution. In his confirmation hearings, Judge Thomas painted himself as a deserving citizen who struggled out of a hardscrabble past by "pulling himself up by his bootstraps." The can-do attitude is an inscription of ideal masculine citizenship; its legitimating power was more than sufficient to overcome the ugly stain of sexual harassment that plagued the judge's confirmation.

Attaining success through self-reliant struggle, while not inherently limited to any cultural group, is a process of self-development that in Western democracies becomes inseparable from the process of "whitening." This racializing effect of class and social mobility has evolved out of historical circumstances whereby white masculinity established qualities of manliness and civilization itself against the "Negro" and the "Indian" (Bederman, 1993). Inspired by W. E. B. Du Bois' work on race and class (1977), David R. Roediger (1991) argues that the nineteenth century was the formative period of "whiteness" among the working classes in a slave-owning republic. "Whiteness was a way in which workers responded to a fear of dependency on wage labor and to the necessities of capitalist work discipline" (1991: 13). The revolutionary ideal of masculine independence found in black slavery and "hireling" wage labor was a convenient other. The black population was viewed as embodying "the preindustrial, erotic, careless style of life the white worker hated and longed for" (1991: 13–14). "The Negro" as a "contrast conception" or "counter-race" is a legacy of white-black relations under slavery and Emancipation that "'naturalizes' the social order" (Copeland, 1939: 179).[2]

Although one need not imagine a contemporary synchrony of views on intrepid individualism, the white man, and deserving citizenship, the convergences and overlaps between hegemonies of race, civilization, and market behavior as claims to citizenship are too routine to be dismissed. Hegemonies of relative racial contributions often conflated race and class, as, for example, in the polarizing contrast between the "model minority" and the "underclass" (Myrdal, 1944), both economic terms standing for racial ones. As I will show, the different institutional contexts in which subjects learn about citizenship often assess newcomers from different parts of the world within given schemes of racial difference, civilization, and economic worth. Because human capital, self-discipline, and consumer power are associated with whiteness, these attributes are important criteria of non-white citizenship in Western democracies. Indeed, immigrant practices earlier in the century also subjected immigrants from Europe to differential racial and cultural judgments (see, e.g., Archdeacon, 1983). The racialization of class was particularly evident in the construction of Irish-American (and Southern European) immigrants whose whiteness was in dispute (Roediger, 1991: 14). This racializing logic of class attributes is applied even to current flows of immigrants from the South and East who seem obviously non-white; discriminatory modes of perception, reception, and treatment order Asian immigrants along a white-black continuum. Although immigrants come from a variety of class and national backgrounds, there is a tendency, in daily institutional practices, towards interweaving of perceived racial difference with economic and cultural criteria, with the result that long-term residents and newcomers are ideologically constructed as "the stereotypical embodiments" of ethnicized citizenship (Williams, 1989: 437).

Of course, these processes of implicit racial and cultural ranking do not exhaust the conditions that go into processes of subjectification as citizens. It is worth keeping in mind that when we attend to the pragmatic construction of belonging, we see that official racial categories are reproduced by everyday American activities of inclusion and exclusion, separating the civilized from the primitive. Constance Perin (1988) has described such attempts at maintaining symbolic coherence in the face of ambiguities and keeping fears at bay as "drawing" lines against the culturally deviant. Racial oppositions are not merely the work of discriminatory laws and outright racists but the everyday product of people's maintenance of their "comfort level" of permissible liberal norms against the socially deviant newcomers who disturb that sense of comfort. Again, such encoding of white-black oppositions in behavioral and discursive strategies also saturates everyday life in other liberal, white-dominated societies, such as Britain and New Zealand (Gilroy, 1987; Wetherell and Potter, 1993). I will present ethnographic accounts of interactions between key institutions and newcomers, the drawing of lines against Asian others, and the struggles over representations that are part of the ideological work of citizen-making in the different domains of American life.[3] While I will be dealing with the making of immigrants into American citizens, I maintain that the processes of explicit and implicit racial and cultural ranking pervading institutional and everyday practices are but a special case of similar constructions in Western democracies in general.

New Asian Immigrants in Metropolitan Countries

When I moved from Massachusetts to California in the early 1980s, I was struck by the range of peoples from the Asia-Pacific region at a time when the scholarly literature defined Asian-Americans as people largely of Chinese, Japanese, and Korean ancestry. (Filipinos were then viewed simply as Pacific Islanders.) Global conflicts and economic restructuring were important reasons that the 1980s were an especially turbulent era, bringing a renewed influx of refugees from Latin America, Africa, and Asia into metropolitan countries. It was not unusual to see Mayan Indians, still wrapped in their colorful clothes, working in English gardens or sarong-clad and turban-wearing Laotians shopping in the neighborhood market. The withdrawal of US troops from mainland Southeast Asia and the later invasion of Cambodia by Vietnam caused waves of refugees to flee, by way of refugee camps, to Australia, Western Europe, and the United States. Other waves of war refugees left Sri Lanka, Afghanistan, Ethiopia, and Central America for the same destinations. Concurrent diasporas of an economic nature introduced poor workers as well as wealthy investors from Africa and Asia into Europe and North America. These massive waves of immigrants from the metaphoric south radically challenged liberal conceptions of citizenship in Western Europe and the United States.

The San Francisco Bay area was one of the major sites of resettlement for refugees from all over the Third World, the majority of whom were Southeast Asians.[4] Most arrived in two waves: in the aftermath of the communist takeover of Saigon in 1975 and following the Vietnamese invasion of Cambodia in 1979. At about the same time, another flow of immigrants, mainly professionals and upper-middle-class people seeking investments in stable markets in the West, arrived from Southeast Asia and India. The combined impact of these flows greatly exceeded that of earlier arrivals from Asia, increasing the Asian population in America by 80 percent to 6.88 million by the end of the decade. Asians are "far and away the most rapidly growing minority in the country" (*New York Times,* February 4, 1991). They have fanned out across the country to establish sizable Asian-American communities outside the Chinatowns of the East and West coasts, spreading to the Southern states and the Midwest. Vietnamese fishing villages in Texas, Cambodian crab farmers in Alabama, and Asian professionals in fields such as electronics, medicine, and mathematics. The number of Chinese restaurants has increased in smaller towns all over the country. In major cities such as Queens, Houston, and Los Angeles, investments by Koreans and Chinese immigrants have raised real estate prices to stratospheric levels (see, e.g., *Wall Street Journal*, January 15, 1991).

The new Asian demographics are so striking that today Asians make up a third of the population of San Francisco and 30 percent of the student body at the

University of California, Berkeley. Overall, the Bay Area, with a population of over 6 million, has "emerged as the Western Hemisphere's first genuine Pacific metropolis," with one out of every five residents being of Asian background (*San Francisco Chronicle*, December 5, 1988). The increasing importance of the economic boom in Asia and the influx of Pacific Rim capital as well as boat people into the Western democracies make Asian immigration a highly charged issue that is framed differently from the issue of immigration from other parts of the world.

The changing demographics in California have changed the terms of debate on immigration and multiculturalism not just for the state but for the whole country. What will the United States as a Pacific country look like? Throughout the 1980s, the rising waves of Asian newcomers were exceeded by the influx of Central American refugees and migrant workers (Portes and Rumbaut, 1990: 44–6). Against the background of forecasts that whites will become just one more minority in California by the year 2000, there has been a backlash by political forces controlled or influenced by white voters. In 1986 an initiative was passed declaring English the state's official language; in 1994 another initiative called for the denial of health and educational services to illegal immigrants (mainly from Latin America). Both measures appeared to set limits to the increasing cultural and economic diversity of the state's population.

The measures reflect nationwide concerns about immigration from south of the border as well as from non-European countries. Nevertheless, there is discrimination among different categories of immigrants by national origin and by class. In a stunning move, the regents of the University of California system recently banned affirmative-action programs in admissions and hiring, setting off a national debate on official sponsorship of multiethnic representation in different areas of society. But what appear to be attempts to make all immigrants adhere to standardized, "color-blind" norms are in fact attempts to discriminate among them, separating out the desirable from the undesirable citizens according to some racial and cultural calculus. For instance, politicians such as House Speaker Newt Gingrich have declared affirmative action unfair to whites *and* Asians *(San Francisco Chronicle*, July 31, 1995). California's Governor Pete Wilson has been quoted as saying that affirmative action promotes "tribalism," a code word for colored minorities that presumably excludes Asian-Americans *(San Francisco Chronicle*, July 23, 1995). In the debate, Asian-Americans have been referred to as "victimized overachievers" – "victimized," that is, by other immigrants and minorities presumably not certified as "overachievers."[5] Such discourses "whiten" Asian-Americans while using them as a "racial wedge" between whites and minority "tribals." The fight over affirmative action is an excellent example of "whitening" and "blackening" processes at work, where racial difference or skin color is variously encrusted with the cultural values of a competitive society. As Thomas Archdeacon has observed, "ethnicity is a dynamic force that keeps America's national, racial, and religious groups in constant flux" (1983: 242). The continuing influx of immigrants keeps ethnic formation unstable, merging and diverging in ways that break up racial components (see Lowe, 1991), but ethnic identities are also inscribed by elite discourses as to where and how different populations are included in or excluded from mainstream society. Indeed, since explicit statements including Asian-Americans in the dominant sector of society have been so rare, very few Asian-Americans protest the image of them as victimized overachievers in the antiaffirmative-action discourses. Despite this silent acquiescence, the image of Asian overachievers is an ideological misrepresentation of the diversity among Asian populations in the country. Indeed, the Californian media have distinguished two categories of Asian-Americans: the "model minority" Chinese immigrants from Hong Kong, Taiwan, China, and Vietnam and the new underclass represented by Cambodians and Laotians. The bifurcated model follows the formula of academics and policymakers who use national origin as the basis of ethnic identity among immigrants (Portes and Rumbaut, 1990: 141–2). If, as I have suggested, we think of ethnicities as dynamic formations constructed out of the everyday processes of inclusion and exclusion, how do we account for the bifurcation of Asian immigrants into these two categories? How do different modalities of regulation use gender stereotypes in configuring race, nation, and citizenship privileges whereby differing groups are accorded cultural normativity or deviance in relation to white masculinity?[6]

I will examine institutional practices that differently receive and socialize Asian immigrants depending on their gender, position within racial hierarchies, and class and consumption. Drawing on ethnographic research, I will explore the ways in which Cambodian refugees, on the one hand, and affluent Chinese cosmopolitans, on the other, explore the meanings and possibilities of citizenship in California. By contrasting Asian groups from different class backgrounds I hope to show how despite and because of their racialization as Asian-Americans, they are variously socialized by and positioned to manipulate state institutions, religious organizations, civilian groups, and market forces inscribing them as citizens of differential worth.

Disciplining Refugees in an Age of Compassion Fatigue

The moral imperative to offer refugees shelter has been a hallmark of US policy since 1945, breaking from earlier policies that privileged race, language, and assimilation above concerns about human suffering (Loescher and Scanlan, 1986: 210). During the cold war, refugees from communist regimes were treated with special kindness because of the ideological perception that they had undergone great suffering as symbolic or literal "freedom fighters" (1986: xviii). This policy continued more or less even after the United States ended its intervention to prevent the spread of communism in Indochina, setting off waves of boat people fleeing Vietnam. In 1979, tens of thousands of Cambodians fled to the Thai border after the Vietnamese invasion of Kampuchea. President Carter, in the spirit of his human rights campaign, signed a refugee act to increase immigration quotas for them. Between 1975 and 1985, almost 125,000 Cambodians arrived in the United States. Anticommunist ideology and opportunities for making political capital in Congress dictated a system of "calculated kindness" whereby Southeast Asian and Cuban refugees were favored over those from Haiti, El Salvador, and Chile (1986: 213–15). But the shadow of the US defeat in the Indochina conflict hung over the reception of these war refugees. Furthermore, they arrived at a time when the country was suffering from an economic recession, and many Americans became worried about scarce housing, jobs, welfare needs, and competition from immigrants. Rioting by Mariel Cuban refugees contributed to the image of "difficult migrants" (1986: 217). Compassion fatigue quickly set in, and a climate of antagonism greeted the increasing influx of refugees of color from Asia, Latin America, and Africa.

From the beginning, a political ambiguity dogged Cambodian refugees because of the immigration authorities' suspicion that many Khmer Rouge communist-sympathizers managed to slip through screening by the Immigration and Naturalization Service (INS) and gain entry to the country (Golub, 1986; Ngor, 1987). This morally tainted image was accompanied by the perception of Cambodian refugees as mainly peasants, unlike the boat people, who were by and large unambiguously anticommunist Sino-Vietnamese and middle-class, despite significant numbers of fishermen and peasants among them. Cambodians in refugee-processing camps were quickly separated out as destined for lower-class status. At the Philippine Refugee Processing Center, classes trained US-bound Cambodians to be dependent on Americans, who dealt with refugees only from their positions as superiors, teachers, and bosses (Mortland, 1987: 391). One teacher charged that, from the very beginning, training programs were "ideologically motivated to provide survival English for entry-level jobs" in the United States (Tollefson, 1990: 546). Khmers were socialized to expect limited occupational options and taught subservient behavior, as well as a flexible attitude towards frequent changes of jobs which would help them adapt to cycles of employment and unemployment. Thus, the camp training of Cambodian refugees as dependent on Americans and as potential low-wage workers initiated the minoritization process even before they set foot in the country. This ideological construction of Khmers as a dependent minority channeled them into the same economic situations as other refugees from poor countries: "Policy and ideology underlying the [Overseas Refugees Training Program] ensure that refugees serve the same function as African-Americans and Latinos" (1990: 549).

Furthermore, once immigrants arrived in the country, whatever their national origin or race, they were ideologically positioned within the hegemonic bipolar white-black model of American society. The racialization of Southeast Asian refugees depended on differential economic and cultural assessment of their potential as good citizens. Although all relied on refugee aid for the first two years after their arrival, Cambodians together with Laotians and Hmongs found themselves, by acquiring an image of "welfare-dependent" immigrants, quickly differentiated from the Vietnamese, who had arrived in this country out of the same war. Cambodian and Laotian immigrants were ethnicized as a kind of liminal Asian-American group that had more in common with other poor refugees of color like Afghans and Ethiopians than with the Vietnamese. They were often compared to their inner-city African-American neighbors in terms of low-wage employment, high rates of teenage pregnancy, and welfare-dependent families.

As mentioned earlier, the transfer of racial otherness from one minority group to another in order to draw the lines of social and economic citizenship has a historical precedent in the differentiation between whites and blacks after Emancipation. The symbolic link between blackness and "preindustrial license" was even transferred to Irish immigrants, who were considered by some to be part of "a separate caste or 'dark' race" (Roediger, 1991: 107, 133–4). The ideological formation of whiteness as the symbol of ideal legal and moral citizenship today continues to depend upon the "blackening" of less desirable immigrants; Immigrants situated closer to the black pole are seen as at the bottom of the cultural and economic ranking. A Vietnamese social worker said to me:

> Most of the Khmers are not highly educated. They were farmers and their tendency is to be lazy. . . . So with the income they receive from welfare right now it is easy for them to be lazy. They are not motivated to go to work . . . they find some way to get out of [the training and language program] . . . They do not want to improve their skills here. . . . Maybe the young people will grow up here and become educated and want to change.

This man was partly expressing his frustration over the difficulty of getting the Cambodian refugees to sign up for job training in electronic assembly work, car mechanics, child care, and janitorial work but also revealing his own ethnic bias against Cambodians.

By 1987, well over half of the 800,000 Indochinese refugees in the country had settled down in California, and there was widespread fear that there would be "perpetual dependence on the welfare system for some refugees" (*New York Times,* April 27, 1987). This positioning of Cambodians as black Asians is in sharp contrast to the model-minority image of Chinese, Koreans, and Vietnamese (including Sino-Vietnamese), who are celebrated for their "Confucian values" and family businesses. Although there have been racist attacks on Vietnamese fishermen in Texas and California and exploitation of Vietnamese workers in chicken-processing plants in the South, the general perception of them is as possessed of "can-do" attitudes closer to the white ideal standards of American citizenship.[7] It is therefore not surprising that Cambodians are almost always referred to as "refugees" whereas Vietnamese refugees are viewed as immigrants. Regardless of the actual, lived cultures of the Khmers before they arrived in the United States, dominant ideologies clearly distinguish among various Asian nationalities, assigning them closer to the white or the black pole of American citizenship.

As I will show, the disciplining of the welfare state, combined with the feminist fervor of many social workers, actually works to weaken or reconstitute the Cambodian family. My own research on the welfare adjustments of Khmers, described below, may seem to reinforce the hegemonic picture of their dependency, but my goal is actually a critique of the effects of the welfare system as it operates now in an increasingly low-waged, service-oriented economy. Earlier generations of poor immigrants have managed to establish basic security for their families through blue-collar employment (Komorovsky, 1967). The welfare system continues to operate by withdrawing support from families with a single wage-earner, whereas for most poor immigrants like the Cambodians, part-time and unsteady low-wage employment are needed to supplement welfare aid. Like ghetto blacks and poor Puerto Rican immigrants, Cambodians are in a continual struggle to survive in a low-wage economy in which they cannot depend on earnings alone and, despite their organizational skills, everyday problems of survival and social interventions often adversely affect family relations and dynamics (Harrington, 1962; Valentine, 1971; Stack, 1974).

Within the refugee population, there are frequent reports of marital conflict, often attributed to the suffering and dislocation engendered by war and exile. However, I maintain that most of the tensions are exacerbated by the overwhelming effort to survive in the inner city, where most of the Cambodian refugees live. Many of the men, with their background in farming and inability to speak English, cannot make the leap into job training and employment in the United States. Their wives often lose respect for them because of their inability to make a living and their refusal to share "women's" household and child-care chores at home. Cambodian customs regarding family roles and gender norms have become if not irrelevant at least severely undermined as men fail to support their families, and wives become more assertive in seeking help. Relations between husband and wife, parents and children have come to be dictated to a significant degree not by Khmer culture as they remember it but by pressing daily concerns to gain access to state resources and to submit to the rules of the welfare state.

Male informants complain that "in America, men feel they have lost value because they are no longer masters in their own families." A *kru khmer* (shaman) who is often consulted by unhappy couples noted that "money is the root cause of marital problems in the United States." Welfare has become a system which provides families with material support and women with increased power and a bargaining position *vis-à-vis* their husbands and children. The shaman explained:

> For instance, most of us who came to the United States are recipients of welfare assistance; the majority of us are supported by the state. It is usually the wife who gets the welfare check but not the husband. She is the one who takes care of the kids. But when she receives the check, her husband wants to spend it. When she refuses, and wants to keep the money for the children, that's what leads to wife abuse.

Some Khmer men lash out at their wives, perhaps to restore the sense of male privilege and authority they possessed in Cambodia. In many instances, they beat their wives in struggles to gain control over particular material and emotional benefits. Besides fights over welfare checks, the beatings may be intended to compel wives to resume their former deferential behavior despite their newly autonomous role in supporting the children. Many women try to maintain the male-dominated family system despite the threats and abuse. A woman confided:

> There are many cases of wife abuse. Yes, everyone gets beaten, myself included. But sometimes we have to just keep quiet even after a disagreement. Like in my case, I don't want to call the police or anything. As the old saying goes, "It takes two hands to clap. One hand cannot sound itself." I just shed a few tears and let it go. If it gets out of hand, then you can call the police. But the men still think more of themselves than of women. They never lower themselves to be our equals.

This acknowledgment of a shift in the balance of domestic power, linked to dependency on state agencies, indicates that Khmer women do not think of themselves as passive victims but are aware of their own role in marital conflicts. The speaker seems to imply that she tolerates the occasional beating because men cannot adjust to their change in status and she always has the option of calling the police. Like their counterparts among European immigrants in the early-twentieth-century United States, Cambodian women are often caught in their "double position" as victims of wife abuse and guardians of their children (Gordon, 1988: 261); they stand up to their husbands in order to ensure their children's economic survival.

Some women who can manage on their own with welfare aid abandon their spouses. A social worker reported cases involving couples over 65 years old in which the wives kicked their husbands out and then applied for SSI (Supplementary Security Income). Informants told me that there were Cambodian women who, having fallen in love with American co-workers, left their husbands and even their children; this was something, they claimed, that happened in Florida and Long Beach, not in their own community. Speaking of her former neighbors, a woman noted that many Cambodian women had left their husbands because they "look down on them . . . for not working, for not being as clever as other men." They felt free to do so because Aid to Families with Dependent Children (AFDC) supported them and their children in any case. In an optimistic tone, she continued, "That's why Khmer women are very happy living in America, because they now have equal rights. . . . We can start up business more easily here. If we want to work, we can pay for day care."

One of the indirect effects of the welfare system is to promote rather complex strategies for manipulating and evading rules, thus affecting household composition. Cambodian households, often composed of mother-child units, routinely pool incomes from different sources, and many households depend on a combination of different welfare checks received by family members and both part- and full-time employment. Through the pooling of income from multiple sources, household heads hope to accumulate savings to buy a home outside the violent neighborhoods in which many live. As has been reported among inner-city blacks, such strategies for coping with the welfare system increase the networking among female kin and neighbors but contribute to the shifting membership of households (Stack, 1974: 122–3).

Many Khmers seek to prolong the time they can receive welfare support by disguising the age of children and by concealing their marital status and income-generating activities. In some cases, young girls who become pregnant are allowed to keep their babies so that the latter can receive financial aid that helps to support the entire family. Many girls who get pregnant marry the fathers of their babies but fail to register their change of status in order to avoid revealing that their husbands are working and thus forfeiting their chance to get AFDC for the babies. For instance, Madam Neou[8] lived with two sons, seven daughters, and a son-in-law in her one-bedroom apartment. Her eldest daughter was 18 and pregnant. She had married her boyfriend according to Khmer ceremonies but had not registered her marriage, and therefore she continued to receive her General Assistance (GA) check. Her husband, who worked in a fast-food restaurant, disguised the fact that they were living together by giving a false address. They hoped to have saved enough money by the time their GA stipends ended to move out and rent a home of their own. Thus, although parents try to discourage their daughters from having premarital sex, they also tolerate and support those who do become pregnant. Not all pregnant girls get married or receive their mothers' support. However, those who do marry are taken in to enable them to save on rent and perhaps continue to accumulate welfare benefits so that they can ultimately become an independent household.

Social workers are frustrated by the mixed motivations and strategies that, in their view, promote teenage pregnancy. A social worker complains about Cambodians "working the system" and says that young girls "become pregnant again and again and have no time to go to school." However, it appears that peer pressure and street culture are primarily responsible for the few pregnancies in girls younger than 16 (well below the average marriage age of 18 for women in Cambodia before the upheavals of war and diaspora). In one case, a social worker intervened and advised a Khmer mother to let her recently married daughter use contraceptives so that she could continue to go to school and have a career later on. However, the girl's husband, who was employed as a mechanic, refused to practice family planning and wanted her to get on welfare. They lived with her mother in exchange for a small monthly payment. The social worker threatened to expose the mother's strategy of combining welfare checks across households, thus exercising the disciplinary power of the state that threatens family formation among people at the mercy of the welfare system and a chronic low-wage market. The withdrawal of welfare support at a point in young people's lives when they are first breaking into the labor market thus compels poor families to scheme to prolong welfare dependency so that they can save towards economic independence. The dual structure of supporting poor mothers, on the one hand, while disciplining chronic underemployment, on the other, contributes to a particular minoritization process of Cambodian refugees that is not so very different from that experienced by other poor people of color (Valentine, 1971; Stack, 1974). Welfare policy promotes the "blackening" of the underprivileged by nurturing and then stigmatizing certain forms of coping strategies.

An academic cottage industry on refugee affairs, ignoring the disciplinary effects of the welfare state and the low-wage economy, has emerged to provide cultural explanations for the presumed differential economic and moral worth of different Asian immigrant groups. Cambodians (together with Hmongs and Laotians) are identified as culturally inferior to Vietnamese and Chinese and are thus a target for "civilizing" attention by state agents and church groups. In a report to the Office of Refugee Settlement, social scientists elaborated a "socio-cultural" portrait of Khmers (and Laotians) as more "Indian" than "Chinese" among the "Indochinese" (Rumbaut and Ima, 1988: 73) – a term that is itself the creation of French imperialism. This artifact drew upon the anthropological model of the "loosely structured" society (Embree, 1950), noting that Cambodians were more individualistic, prone to place feelings and emotions above obligations, and less likely to use Americans as role models than the Vietnamese (who were more Chinese) (1950: 76) – in other words, Cambodians were more deferential and susceptible to socialization by US institutions than groups that possessed Confucian culture. Cambodians were viewed as "affectively oriented"; their "love of children" and "nonaggressive" behavior seem in implicit contrast to the "more pragmatic" Vietnamese. This moral discrimination among Asian groups becomes a diffused philosophy that informs the work of agencies dealing with immigrants, thus demonstrating that in mechanisms of regulation, hierarchical cultural evaluations assign different populations places within the white-black polarities of citizenship.

The disciplinary approach to Cambodians often takes the form of teaching them their rights and needs as normative lower-class Americans. In the Bay Area, the refugee and social service agencies are driven by a feminist ethos that views immigrant women and children as especially vulnerable to patriarchal control at home. Implicit in social workers' training is the goal of fighting Asian patriarchy – "empowering" immigrant women and "teaching them their rights in this country," as one lawyer-activist explained. Perhaps influenced by essentializing statements that Khmers are "more prone to divorce and separation" than the Vietnamese (Rumbaut and Ima, 1988: 75–6), service workers tend to view the Khmer family as rife with patriarchal domination and violence. At the same time, service agents working with Cambodians frequently complain about their "primitive culture," especially as expressed in male control and a tendency to be swayed by emotions rather than by rationality and objectivity.

This ideological construction often puts Sam Ngor, a Cambodian social worker, in the uncomfortable position of being caught between his sympathy for the plight of Cambodian men and the social worker's implicit unfavorable comparison of them with white men. At a Cambodian self-help group meeting, Sam was trying to explain why a married couple gave contradictory accounts of their conflict. He noted that there was a difference between "oral and literate cultures"; in oral cultures, "people always change their minds about what happened" (presumably, in a literate society they do not).[9] Furthermore, in a literate society like the United States, men can be jailed for abusing their wives and children. Covert smiles lit up the faces of the women, while the men looked down. The man fighting with his wife crossed his arms and said, "I respect her, but it is she who controls me."

Indeed, Cambodian men complain that service workers are not only eager to interfere in their family affairs but favor women and children over men in domestic battles. Another social worker notes that "often, among refugees of all nationalities, men have lost their place in society. They don't like to ask for help, and it seems they've lost control over their families. Women tend to ask for help more." Sam added that both the welfare system and affirmative action favored women of color over men, so that the former had easier access to resources and jobs.

Some Khmer women, emboldened by service workers and the disciplining of refugee men, routinely call for outside intervention in settling domestic disputes. In one example, Mae, a woman in her thirties, called the police after claiming that her husband, an alcoholic, had hit her. A few days later she came to the self-help group and wanted assistance in getting him released from jail. She insisted that the policeman had misunderstood her and that she had never claimed that she was abused. Meanwhile, she called her husband in jail, boasting that she would try to "free" him if he promised, when he came out, to stop drinking and to attend the self-help group regularly. Mae's husband, it was reported, charged her with delusions of power: "I think that the judge is the one who will decide to release me, but she thinks she is the one who is controlling the situation. She thinks that by telling the police that I did not beat her she is securing my release." A couple of months later, Mae dropped the charges, and her husband was set free and prevailed upon by the group to join Alcoholics Anonymous. Although the marriage remained rocky, Mae apparently had manipulated the police, the self-help group, and the court system to discipline her husband. A neighbor reported that Mae's daughter said she wanted her mum to be in jail and her dad home. Public interventions in such domestic battles implicitly devalue men of color while upholding white masculinity, as presented by police and judge, as the embodiment of culturally correct citizenship and privilege.

Engendering Religious Modernity

Beyond the domain of the welfare state, institutions such as the church also construct commonsensical understandings of different ways and claims of belonging in Western democracies. Church groups are vital agents in converting immigrants into acceptable citizens, since they have always played a major role in sponsoring, helping, and socializing newcomers to Western culture, whether in the colonies or in the metropolitan centers.[10] In Northern California, the Church of the Latter-day Saints (LDS, or the Mormon church) shapes cultural citizenship by promoting white middle-class masculinity as the standard of civilization and class property to displaced Third World populations. In this civilizing mission, the LDS church has been perhaps more thorough and successful than other churches which also came to the aid of refugees and poor immigrants flowing north in the 1980s.

Harold Bloom refers to the LDS church as an "American original" in that it is homegrown, post-Christian, and, ultimately a religion of the manly self, one that seeks salvation and freedom through individual struggles rather than through the community (1992: 18–36).[11] Although ignored or feared by liberals, it is very much part of the religious mainstream and has pervasive influence throughout the United States and increasingly in Europe. Its basic goal is to establish the Kingdom of God in the world by the millennium. It is one of the fastest-growing religions in the world and by the year 2020 may dominate the western United States and large areas of the Asia-Pacific world through mass recruitments of both the living and (through postmortem baptism) the dead (Bloom, 1992: 122; see also Gordon, 1994).[12]

Mormonism promotes a modernity that makes middle-class respectability accessible to the displaced and the poor who are socially ambitious in new metropolitan contexts. Originally a church of outsiders in frontier conditions, the LDS church has become very adept at recruiting outsiders into the mainstream by ordering peoples of color into specific racial, gender, and class hierarchies with the hope of achieving social success as represented by white masculinity. This *modus operandi* depends on the rule of colonial difference, which represents the other as "inferior and radically different" (Chatterjee, 1993: 33) but with the hope of being socialized to dependency on Anglo-Saxon hegemony. Early Mormon doctrines linked depravity and sin with dark-skinned peoples; a history of denying black men ordination to priesthood (crucial to salvation) was ended only in the late 1970s, when the church vigorously expanded its missionizing activities overseas (Bringhurst, 1981). The church's initial hesitation over "African-like" Melanesians soon gave way to a greater flexibility towards peoples of color in Africa and the Asia-Pacific region when it became clear that their recruitment would be the most important part of the drive to become a worldwide, multiethnic religion (IP: 194). This new tolerance for multiracial and mixed-race recruits, however, operates as an alibi for the church's insistent invocation and mapping of barbaric others in relation to white Mormons (Gordon, 1994).

In the San Francisco Bay Area as elsewhere, the LDS church is divided into separate wards for different ethnic/racial groups such as Chinese, Vietnamese, Samoans, Cambodians, and blacks. This mapping of ethnic and racial difference is in relation to moral leadership by white men, who embody American goals of freedom, self-reliance, and individual responsibility. The Mormon masculine ideal is clean-cut, in conservative business suit and tie and often armed with a briefcase. For disadvantaged newcomers, the church must represent a ladder to the American dream, but first they have to learn the steps leading to economic success, moral superiority, and salvation by overcoming the stigma of racialized male inferiority. On Sunday mornings, little Cambodian boys and girls attend Sunday school at the Mormon temple. One teacher wrote "I MUST OBEY" on the blackboard right next to a poster of a kneeling Jesus Christ's "Agony in the Garden." Many children and their parents find the church a more effective institution for teaching English than the state-sponsored English as a Second Language classes. Such instruction, especially for the very young, provides the context wherein the church can prize the young away from their parents and culture and integrate them into the structure of white authority.

The church regularly engages in the symbolic violence that uses "primitive" difference as a way to appropriate the moral authority of parents and realign young Cambodians with the church hierarchy. White Anglo-American supremacy is defined in opposition to the pathologized sexuality of subaltern figures as represented by the patriarchal Asian families and unmasculine Asian men. Such native embodiments of deviant sexual norms make them ripe for salvation by the white church. The bishop told me that he had two specific goals regarding his Cambodian converts, both attempts to correct what he considered their dysfunctional heterosexuality. One was to help Khmer women who had had their marriages arranged for them by their parents when they were teenagers in Cambodia. Perhaps oblivious to the irony, he claimed that the church was a critical agent in fighting the patriarchy of Cambodian culture and teaching Asians about marriage as a partnership. His second goal was to promote an ideal nuclear family headed by a white man. A white supremacist ideology not only defines the Khmers as racially inferior and sexually deviant but also suggests their redemption through the conjoining of white (male) and non-white (female) bodies, a particular intertwining of race and sex that, while seemingly promoting multiracial diversity, reproduces white–non-white asymmetry in the Mormon order.

The LDS church appeals to young, displaced people because it sometimes becomes the key vehicle for their making the transition to white middle-class culture. Mormon missionaries not only teach American English but also instruct youngsters in the acquisition of other social and bodily skills that will win respect from Americans. For some young immigrant women, the path is through a white marriage. There is something enormously appealing to refugee girls seeking acceptance in the clean-cut young men in business suits who visit their homes and seek to convert them. Mormonism represents upward mobility into a white world where outsiders will be spiritually accepted, though still as racial others. Young Cambodian female converts report that they like the Mormon teachings of "young women's values," including chastity, modesty, and self-discipline. A young woman I will call Vanna confessed:

Being Mormon helps me to operate better in the US. When I was in high school, many Khmer girls married in the twelfth grade, about half of them to older Khmer guys whose jobs were not so good. They got pregnant or simply married to get away from strict parents who wouldn't let them out of the house, but they then found that it was worse in marriage. The husbands won't let them out; they are jealous about other guys, and worried about having no control.

The strict Mormon morality is appealing not only because it seems to echo Cambodian values for female virgins but also because it helps Cambodian girls to attain social mobility. By maintaining sexual purity, female converts avoid teenage pregnancy and early marriage to Khmer men, most of whom are working-class. Mormon lessons in balancing self-control with an affectionate personality socialize the young women to old-fashioned American values of emotion-work that prepare them for their future roles as loving wives and mothers. For instance, Vanna said that she was busy attending college and not dating. She wanted to wait and marry a returned missionary (a young Mormon man who has finished serving his two years as a missionary and is considered ready for marriage). "I really like the Mormon idea of being married for eternity. There is less divorce among Mormons. As far as sex is concerned, being Mormon and being Asian are the same – not to have sex before marriage. You have to be morally clean; it applies to the men too." The respectability, sexual allure, and moral purity attributed to white masculinity burnish the image of minority men who have comparable social and cultural capital. Says Vanna:

> It is more than likely that I'd marry a Caucasian. I want someone who is well-educated, doesn't smoke and drink, and who respects me for who I am. I find Caucasian and Chinese men more attractive than Khmer, for example, the tall Chinese guys who look Caucasian, who are light-skinned and more into American traditions like dating, whereas Khmer men hardly do that, like my brothers-in-law.

The latter also had working-class jobs such as glass manufacturing and packaging. In Vanna's eyes, the pursuit of middle-class status appears to be inseparable from marrying white men. Only through a marital relationship with white masculinity can she cross over the obstacles to the privileges of class and American citizenship.

The Mormon church, then, represents a disciplinary system providing an alternative modality of belonging which, more explicitly than state agencies, employs racialized masculinity in structuring class, gender, and citizenship ideals. Even as the church teaches recruits the self-discipline and entrepreneurship of American success, these attitudes are cast within the framework of white patronage or domination. Immigrant subjectivities, especially those of young girls seeking acceptance, are influenced by socializing processes that racialize gender and class through definitions of pathological (Khmer) and normalized (white) gender and sexuality. Thus Mormon Khmers are the latest in a historical process whereby the labor regimes of immigrants produce a conflation of race and class with the result that ambitious members of minorities often marry out of their community into the white community (see, e.g., Yanagisako, 1985). Do affluent Chinese immigrants to California, arriving with capital and credentials, experience other ways of "whitening" and its limits?

Chinese Cosmopolitans: Class Property and Cultural Taste

In Northern California, the so-called Hong Kong money elite resides in an exclusive community on the flank of the San Francisco Peninsula mountain range. All the homes in this suburb cost over a million dollars. The choicest are set into the hillsides, with mountains as a backdrop and a view of the bay. Mansions in an Asian-Mediterranean style stand amidst clearings where few trees remain unfelled. This was a sore point with locals, along with the fact that many of the houses were paid for in hard cash, sometimes before the arrival of their new occupants. The driveways are parked with Mercedes Benzes, BMWs, and even a Rolls Royce or two.

The *feng-shui* ("wind-water" propitious placement) of the place is excellent. Fleeing the impending return of Hong Kong to China's rule or merely seeking to tap into US markets, overseas Chinese crossed the Pacific to make this former white enclave their new home. Led initially by real estate agents and later by word of mouth, the influx of wealthy Chinese from Hong Kong, Taiwan, and Southeast Asia has spread to cities and upscale communities all over the state and the country. While many of the newcomers are well-educated professionals who work in the Silicon Valley, an increasing number are property developers, financiers, and industrialists who work on both sides of the Pacific.[13] Their presence has changed the social landscape of suburban California, increasing the number of shopping malls (called "Pacific Renaissance" and "Pacific Rim") and sophisticated restaurants that serve a predominantly Asian clientele (see also Fong, 1994). Thus, in addition to being the destination of Third World refugees and migrant workers, US cities are fast becoming the sites of overseas Asian investment and settlement.

What kinds of processes are making such cosmopolitan subjects into citizens? Although the affluent immigrant Chinese appear to be able to evade disciplining by the state, they are not entirely free of its citizenship requirements, on the one hand, and local mediations over what being part of the imagined American community (or the Northern Californian version of it) is all about. Unlike the vast majority of Cambodian refugees, the Chinese investor-immigrants and professionals are "transnational cosmopolitans" who strategically manage meaning as they negotiate and contest the shifting discursive terrains in the world economy (Hannerz, 1990; Ong, 1993; Ong and Nonini, 1996). However, these self-styled "astronauts" – so-called because they spend so much time shuttling back and forth across the Pacific (Ong, 1993) – are not always as attuned to the cultural norms of particular Californian locales as they are to the transnational opportunities opened up by globalization. Two examples will show that there are cultural limits to the ways in which they can negotiate the hegemonic production of Chineseness in California and the local values about what constitutes civilized conduct and appropriate citizenship.

Family biopolitics and parachute kids

The key motivation and predicament of the transnational strategies of affluent Chinese are their families. Although immigrant businessmen and investors are willing to shuttle back and forth across national borders themselves; locating their children in California is a major priority. These plans are the outgrowth of what, borrowing from Foucault, I have called "family biopolitics" (Ong, 1993). The heads of wealthy Chinese families manifest a biopolitical instrumentality in governing the conduct of family members in the interest of ensuring the security and prosperity of the family as a whole. Family biopolitics constitute members' sense of moral worth in terms of relations within the family. Parents instill in their children self-discipline in education, work, and consumption – habits that foster the steady accumulation of economic and symbolic capital – that contributes to the family's prosperity and honor. For instance, the term "utilitarian familialism" has been applied to the normative and practical tendencies whereby Hong Kong Chinese families place family interest above all other individual and social concerns (Lau, 1983: 73). As part of such family governmentality, the middle and upper-middle classes in Hong Kong and Taiwan deploy family members abroad to obtain universally certified educational degrees and eventually green cards for the entire family. By relocating some members in California the family maximizes opportunities for overseas business expansion while attempting to evade the governmentality of the home country. However, despite the flexibility afforded them by transnational capitalism, emigrant business families do not fully escape the disciplining of the host country.

At the moment, immigration law has changed to allow for an "investor category" whereby would-be immigrants can obtain a green card in return for a million dollar investment that creates at least ten jobs. On Wall Street there have been seminars on how to obtain US citizenship through real estate investment and acquisition. A sponsor urges Asian-Americans to "think of your relatives in Asia. If they invest $1 million in you, they get a green card and you get a new business" (*Wall Street Journal,* February 21, 1991). The new citizenship law thus constructs the affluent Chinese newcomer as a *homo economicus,* an economic agent who is a "manipulable man, a man who is perpetually responsive to modifications in his environment" (Gordon, 1991: 43). Perceived as economic agents of choice, overseas Chinese immigrants will nevertheless be disciplined by citizenship criteria and manipulated in their deployment of capital. However, even super-rich would-be immigrants refuse to be subjected to such controls on their investments, perhaps because they are ultimately more susceptible to capitalist instrumentality than to state biopolitics.

A more common strategy for gaining residence rights is to send children to US high schools and colleges. For instance, Alex Leong, a middle-aged executive from a Hong Kong-based finance company, confided that his father always told him, "Your future is really going to be outside Hong Kong. So you should be educated outside, as long as you maintain some Chinese customs and speak

Chinese." Since the 1960s an entire generation of middle-class and upper-middle-class Chinese students from Hong Kong and Taiwan have embarked upon overseas education in the United States, seeking educational certifications and residence rights that will eventually enable their families to settle in the US. Parents visit their children to buy homes, set up bank accounts, and assess the local real estate. Upon graduation the sons may open up a US branch of their family company. Thus, after graduating from Berkeley and the University of Wisconsin business school, Alex joined his father's business by setting up a San Francisco office. Because Alex is not yet a citizen, his parents plan to retire in Vancouver, where residential rights can be purchased with a smaller investment of C$300,000. He expects that eventually they will join him in the Bay Area.

The practice of sending young children to school in Califonia has given rise to another image of affluent Chinese immigrants. Taiwanese parents favor sending children to US high schools because they hope that they will give them a better chance (than in Taiwan) of gaining entry to college, while earning residence rights in the United States. Furthermore, children in the United States provide a chance to invest in property and establish a home base against political instability in Asia. However, sometimes the attempts to coordinate family biopolitics with the disciplining requirements of citizenship undermine carefully constructed plans of business travel, children's education, and managing a trans-Pacific lifestyle. Some 40,000 Taiwanese teenagers have been left to fend for themselves in California while their parents pursue business interests in Asia. Many of these youngsters live with their siblings in expensive homes, sometimes equipped with Asian servants. These so-called parachute kids have the run of the house and manage household finances like adults. One 17-year-old girl, who first arrived when she was 13, has been acting as parent to her younger sisters. Their parents drop by periodically from Taiwan. She is worried that her sisters will be quite lost when she goes to college. Other teenagers have developed a consumerist, laid-back attitude that both critiques and reinforces the *homo economicus* image of their parents. Some youngsters freely spend their parents' large allowances. Newspapers report a Taiwanese brother and sister, both high school students near Los Angeles, spending their free time shopping in malls and frequenting restaurants and karaoke bars. The girl, who dons the latest Valley Girl fashions, calls her father "the ATM machine" for issuing money but nothing else. The boy expresses his resentment more directly: "If they're going to dump me here and not take care of me, they owe me something. That is my right" (*Straits Times*, June 26, 1993). The effect of a transnational strategy of economic and cultural consumption has been to split up the much-vaunted Chinese family unit, with family biopolitics dictated in large part by accumulation concerns that oblige business couples to spend their time overseas while abandoning their children to develop a sense of individualistic rights and bravado. Some of the children have shoplifted, joined local Chinese gangs, or created problems in school, drawing the attention of the social services. By and large, however, it is the disciplining of accumulation strategies that produces a sense of global citizenship and contingent belonging for the business-immigrant family.

Affluent transnational Chinese in California are caught up in the dialectic of embedding and disembedding (Giddens, 1990) in the international economy, a process which enables them to escape to some extent the disciplining of the state because of their flexible deployment of capital but not within the locality where their families are based. The flexibility of Chinese professionals shifting back and forth across the Pacific thus contradicts local notions of belonging as nominative American citizens. Even compared with the proverbial restless Californians, the new Chinese immigrants are footloose cosmopolitans. As the following incident shows, the attenuated sense of a primary link to a particular society comes up against an American class ethos of moral liberalism.

Bad taste or the homeless in an affluent neighborhood?

Whereas poor Asians are primarily disciplined by state agencies, affluent Chinese immigrants, as home buyers and property developers, have encountered regulation by civic groups upset at the ways in which their city is being changed by transnational capital and taste. In wealthier San Franciscan neighborhoods, residents pride themselves on their conservation consciousness, and they jealously guard the hybrid European ambiance and character of particular neighborhoods. In their role as custodians of appropriate cultural taste governing buildings, architecture, parks, and other public spaces, civic groups routinely badger City Hall, scrutinize urban zoning laws, and patrol the boundaries between what is aesthetically permissible and what is intolerable in their districts. By linking race with habitus, taste, and cultural capital (Bourdieu, 1984), such civic groups set limits to the whitening of Asians, who, metaphorically speaking, still give off the whiff of sweat despite arriving with starter symbolic capital.

Public battles over race/taste have revolved around the transformation of middle-class neighborhoods by rich Asian newcomers. At issue are boxy houses with bland facades – "monster houses" – erected by Asian buyers to accommodate extended families in low-density, single-family residential districts known for their Victorian or Mediterranean charm. Protests have often taken on a racialist tone, registering both dismay at the changing cultural landscape and efforts to educate the new arrivals to white upper-class norms appropriate for the city. While the activists focus on the cultural elements – aesthetic norms, democratic process, and civic duty – that underpin the urban imagined community, they encode the strong class resentment against large-scale Asian investment in residential and commercial properties throughout the city (see Mitchell, 1996). A conflict over one of these monster houses illustrates the ways in which the state is caught between soothing indignant urbanites seeking to impose their notion of cultural citizenship on Asian *nouveax riches* while attempting to keep the door open for Pacific Rim capital.

In 1989 a Hong Kong multimillionaire, a Mrs. Chan, bought a house in the affluent Marina district. Chan lived in Hong Kong and rented out her Marina property. A few years later, she obtained the approval of the city to add a third story to her house but failed to notify her neighbors. When they learned of her plans, they complained that the third story would block views of the Palace of Fine Arts as well as cut off sunlight in an adjoining garden. The neighbors linked up with a citywide group to pressure City Hall. The mayor stepped in and called for a city zoning study, thus delaying the proposed renovation. At a neighborhood meeting, someone declared, "We don't want to see a second Chinatown here." Indeed, there is already a new "Chinatown" outside the old Chinatown, based in the middle-class Richmond district. This charge thus raised the specter of a spreading Chinese urbanscape encroaching on the heterogeneous European flavor of the city. The remark, with its implied racism, compelled the mayor to apologize to Chan, and the planning commission subsequently approved a smaller addition to her house.

However, stung by the racism and the loss on her investment and bewildered that neighbors could infringe upon her property rights, Chan, a transnational developer, used her wealth to mock the city's self-image as a bastion of liberalism. She pulled out all her investments in the United States and decided to donate her million dollar house to the homeless. To add insult to injury, she stipulated that her house was not to be used by any homeless of Chinese descent. Her architect, an American Chinese, told the press, "You can hardly find a homeless Chinese anyway" (*Asia Week*, May 6, 1995). Secure in her overseas location, Chan fought the Chinese stereotype by stereotyping American homeless as non-Chinese, while challenging her civic-minded neighbors to demonstrate the moral liberalism they professed. Mutual class and racial discrimination thus broke through the surface of what initially appeared to be a negotiation over normative cultural taste in the urban milieu. A representative of the major's office, appropriately contrite, remarked that Chan could still do whatever she wanted with her property; "We just would like for her not to be so angry." The need to keep overseas investments flowing into the city had to be balanced against neighborhood groups' demands for cultural standards. The power of the international real estate market, as represented by Mrs. Chan, thus disciplined both City Hall and the Marina neighbors, who may have to rethink local notions of what being enlightened urbanites may entail in the "era of Pacific Rim capital" (Mitchell, 1996).

Other Chinese investor-immigrants, unlike Mrs. Chan, try to negotiate the tensions between local and global forces and to adopt the cultural trappings of the white upper class so as to cushion long-term residents' shock at the status change of the racial other, until recently likely to be a laundry or garment worker. Chinese developers who live in San Francisco are trying harder to erase the image of themselves as "economic animals" who build monster houses, as well as the perception that they lack a sense of civic duty and responsibility. They try to maintain their Victorian homes and English gardens, collect Stradivari violins and attend the opera, play tennis in formerly white clubs, and dress up by dressing down their *nouveaux riches* appearances. I have elsewhere talked about the limits to cultural accumulation of Chinese gentrification in Western metropolitan circles (Ong, 1992). Perhaps realizing the limits to how they can be accepted through these whitening practices, some Chinese investors are for the first time making significant philanthropic contributions outside the old Chinatown. I interviewed a surgeon who was the first Chinese-American to sit on the board of the city symphony. When he complained about the lack of Chinese contributions to the symphony, I had to remind him that there were hardly music lessons in Chinatown or other poor urban schools.

But the effort to funnel Pacific Rim money upwards continues. Hong Kong-based companies are making generous donations to major public institutions such as universities and museums. Leslie Tang-Schilling, the daughter of a Hong Kong industrialist, married into a prominent San Franciscan family, and a commercial developer in her own right, leads the move to soften the hard-edged image of Chinese investor immigrants. The Tang family name is emblazoned on an imposing new health center on the Berkeley campus. Other overseas Chinese and Asian businesses have donated large sums to the construction of buildings devoted to chemistry, life sciences, computer science, and engineering. An East Coast example is the gift of $20 million to Princeton University by Gordon Wu, a Hong Kong tycoon whose money could perhaps better have benefited long-neglected universities on the Chinese mainland.

Whereas an earlier generation of overseas Chinese tycoons went home to build universities in China, today Asian investors wish to buy symbolic capital in Western democracies as a way to ease racial and cultural acceptance across the globe. Like earlier European immigrant elites looking for symbolic real estate, overseas Chinese donors show a preference for "hardware" (impressive buildings bearing their names) over "software" (scholarships and programs that are less visible to the public eye).[14] The difference is that subjects associated with Third World inferiority have scaled the bastions of white power.[15] Such show-case pieces have upgraded Asian masculinity, layered over the hardscrabble roots of the Asian *homo economicus,* and proclaimed their arrival on the international scene.

Nevertheless, there are limits to such strategies of symbolic accumulation, and white backlash has been expressed in a rise in random attacks on Asians. By placing an Asian stamp on prestigious "white" public space, the new immigrants register what for over a century – one thinks of the plantation workers and railroad men, maids and garment workers, gardeners and cooks, shopkeepers and nurses, undocumented workers laboring in indentured servitude, whether in the colonies or in cities like New York and Los Angeles – has been a space of Asia-Pacific cultural production within the West.[16]

Are the New Asians Asian-Americans?

Through an ethnographic examination of cultural citizenship as subjectification and cultural performance, I argue that the ideological entanglements of race and culture operate both to locate and to marginalize immigrants from the meta-phorical South and East. This approach thus suggests that while "cultural fundamentalism" may have replaced racism in rhetorics of exclusion (Stolcke, 1995), in practice racial hierarchies and polarities continue to inform Western notions of cultural difference and are therefore inseparable from the cultural features attributed to different groups. I maintain that the white-black polarities emerging out of the history of European-American imperialism continue to shape attitudes and encode discourses directed at immigrants from the rest of the world that are associated with racial and cultural inferiority. This dynamic of racial othering emerges in a range of mechanisms that variously subject non-white immigrants to whitening or blackening processes that indicate the degree of their closeness to or distance from ideal white standards.

The contrasting dynamics of the subjectification experienced by new immigrants demonstrate the critical significance of institutional forces, both domestic and international, in making different kinds of minorities. Cambodian refugees and Chinese business people did not arrive as ready-made ethnics. Through the different modes of disciplining – the primacy of state and church regulation in one and the primacy of consumption and capitalist instrumentality in the other – Cambodian refugees and Chinese immigrants are dialectically positioned at different ends of the black-white spectrum. The racialization of class, as well as the differential othering of immigrants, constitutes immigrants as the racialized embodiments of different kinds of social capital.

Thus, the category "Asian-American" must acknowledge the internal class, ethnic, and racial stratifications that are both the effect and the product of differential governmentalities working on different populations of newcomers. It must confront the contradictions and instabilities within the imposed solidarity and temporary alliances of what has been prematurely called an "Asian-American panethnicity" (Espiritu, 1992). The two new Asian groups represent different modalities of precarious belonging – one as ideologically blackened subjects manipulating state structures in order to gain better access to resources and the other expressing an ultramodern instrumentality that is ambivalently caught between whitening social practices and the consumer power that spells citizenship in the global economy. They are thus not merely new arrivals passively absorbed into an overarching Asian-American identity,[17] nor can they be easily subsumed within the inter-Asian coalitions that emerged among college students in the 1960s or united simply on the basis of having been treated "all alike" as biogenetic others sharing a history of exclusion (Chan, 1991: xiii). The entanglement of ideologies of race, culture, nation, and capitalism shapes a range of ethnicized citizenship in different fields of power. Given all these factors, the heterogeneity and instability of Asian-American identities (Lowe, 1991) suggest that a dramatic shift in coalitions may cut across racial lines – for example, Asian-Anglo partnerships in business or linkages between Cambodian and other refugees of color in dealing with the welfare state.

I end by resuming to the moral predicament of my own passage into American society. Twenty years later, and only after the birth of my first child (whose father is a fourth-generation Japanese and Spanish-speaking Chinese-American) did I feel ready to mark my long apprenticeship in cultural citizenship by becoming a legal citizen. I continue to view the term "Asian-American" with ambivalence, as much for its imposed racialized normativity as for what it elides about other-

Asians/other-Americans and for what it includes as well as excludes within the American scheme of belonging. One learns to be fast-footed, occasionally glancing over one's shoulder to avoid tripping over – while tripping up – those lines.

The unbearable lightness of being a non-white American means that the presumed stability and homogeneity of the Asian-American identity must, in this era of postcivil-rights politics (Takagi, 1994)[18] and globalization, be open to the highly particularized local reworkings of global forces. In California these forces have been dramatically played out in domestic, racial terms as well as in trans-national, class ones, foreshadowing the reconfiguration of citizenship in the West in the new global era.

Acknowledgment

I received a fellowship from the Rockefeller Gender Roles Program for research on Cambodian refugees and cultural citizenship. I thank Brackette Williams and Katharyn Poethig for their comments on earlier drafts of the paper and Kathleen Erwin for proof-reading the final version.

Notes

1 According to Rosaldo (1994: 57), cultural citizenship is "the right to be different (in terms of race, ethnicity, or native language) with respect to the norms of the dominant national community, without compromising one's right to belong, in the sense of participating in the nation-state's democratic processes. The enduring exclusions of the color line often deny full citizenship to Latinos and other people of color. From the point of view of subordinate communities, cultural citizenship offers the possibility of legitimizing demands made in the struggle to enfranchise themselves. These demands can range from legal, political and economic issues to matters of human dignity, well-being, and respect."

2 I thank Brackette Williams for discussing these points with me and supplying the references.

3 A recent volume, *Structuring Diversity* (Lamphere, 1991), provides ethnographic cases of encounters between newcomers and US urban institutions. The focus of these case studies is on the integration of immigrants into dominant American society. My approach views such encounters and practices as relations of power that constitute varied minoritization processes and foster different understandings of the cultural citizenship among different groups of newcomers.

4 In 1988, the Bay Area was the third-most-favored destination for legal immigrants, after New York and Los Angeles. Nearly 41,000 immigrants arrived in the Bay Area that year, 60 percent of them Asian (*San Francisco Chronicle*, July 6, 1989).

5 Some Asian-American professionals have protested being put into the position of a "racial bourgeoisie" – a buffer class between whites and other minorities (*San Francisco Chronicle*, August 22, 1995).

6   Cynthia Wong Sau-ling (1992: 111–21) employs the concept "ethnicizing gender," to describe a parallel racializing process whereby "white ideology assigns selected gender characteristics to various ethnic others," for example, in representations of effeminized Asian men and ultrafeminized Asian women.

7   See Kelly (1980), Nicholson (1989), Welaratna (1993), and Ong (1995a, b) for studies of how, after their arrival in the United States, Southeast Asian refugees are differently socialized in a range of institutional contexts to the requirements of the dominant white culture. Gail Kelly's (1980) concept of "internal colonialism" to describe the "schooling" of blacks, Native Americans, and immigrant communities as a generic colonized labor force is too general to capture the complex and contingent discriminations among different categories of immigrants.

8   All the names of informants are fictive to protect their privacy.

9   The notion of Khmer culture as "oral" – despite a literate history based on Sanskrit, Hinduism, and Buddhism stretching back to the 9th-century Khmer kingdom that built Angkor Wat and Angkor Thom, among other monuments (see Chandler, 1983) – is part of the misconception that Khmers are a "primitive" people.

10 For an example of churches socializing colonized populations to Western values, see Schieffelin (1981); for an example of churches socializing Asian immigrants, see Hirata (1979).

11 Harold Bloom, like others before him (see, e.g., Whalen, 1964), considers the LDS church a post-Christian "American religion" in that it is non-monotheistic, has no absolutely formal creeds, and rejects creationism, believing instead in a maternal and contingent God found within the believer. Its indigenous American roots are reflected in the romantic quest for oneself, freedom, progress, and even immortality (1992: 40–2, 113–15).

12 In the Mormon church, the family rather than the individual is the "unit of exaltation." The destiny of the Latter-day Saints is godhood. Baptism for the dead is a way to "save" ancestors, and spirit children are produced by Mormon couples so that these family members can join their living Mormon descendants in the "eternal progression" towards godness (Bloom, 1992: 121–3).

13 Of course, the influx into the United States of poor, working-class Chinese from the mainland and Southeast Asia, many in difficult and illegal conditions, continues. For a feminist perspective on Chinese emigration, see Ong (1995c). With the growing influx of affluent and professional Chinese, the image of the Pacific Rim male executive is eclipsing somewhat the image of the Chinese laundry worker and illegal alien (see Ong, 1993).

14 The Malaysian Chinese philanthropist Tan Kah Kee is famous for building Xiamen University and many other public works in Fujian, China, the land of his birth. Today his US-educated children are organizing a campaign to contribute to the chemistry building on the Berkeley campus.

15 Of course, in making donations to public buildings, Asian-American nouveaux riches are merely replicating a long immigrant tradition cultivated by Irish, Italian, and Jewish immigrants who made good. The Chinese newcomers to the Bay Area are following in the footsteps of the Hearsts, the Aliotos, and the Haases. However, for the first time we are seeing the non-white arrivals scaling the social heights with wealth gained in the international economy and causing reluctant, minimal adjustments in the domestic racial hierarchy. For an anthropological study of a major American family dynasty and the symbolic boundaries of wealth, see Marcus

(1992). For an account of the Chinese diaspora within the context of global flexible accumulation, see Ong and Nonini (1996). Finally. for an interesting comparison with another highly successful non-European immigrant community, Cubans in Florida, see Portes and Stepick (1993).

16 I am paraphrasing the title of a volume edited by Rob Wilson and Arik Dirlik (1996).

17 The construction of which, as Sylvia Yanagisako (1993) has noted, is ideologically dominated by the history of male Chinese railroad workers, thus marginalizing or excluding the experiences of women and of other Asian groups.

18 Takagi defines "post-civil-rights politics" as the struggle of multiethnic groups beyond the old black-white framework, marked by the tendency for racial interests to be disguised by social and economic language and for solutions to racial problems to be sought in class terms (1994: 237–9).

References

Alatas, Syed Hussein. (1977). *The Myth of the Lazy Native*. London: Cass.

Archdeacon, Thomas J. (1983). *Becoming American: An ethnic history*. New York: Free Press.

Becker, Gary C. (1965). A theory of the allocation of time. *Economic Journal*, 75: 493–517.

Bederman, Gail. (1993). Civilization, the decline of middle-class manliness, and Ida B. Wells's anti-lynching campaign (1892–94). In Barbara Melosh (ed.), *Gender in American History Since 1890* (pp. 207–39). New York: Routledge.

Bloom, Harold. (1992). *The American Religion: The emergence of the post-Christian nation*. New York: Simon and Schuster.

Bourdieu, Pierre. (1984). *Distinction: A social critique of the judgement of taste*. Cambridge, MA: Harvard University Press.

Bringhurst, Newell G. (1981). *Saints, Slaves, and Blacks: The changing place of black people within Mormonism*. Westport, CT: Greenwood Press.

Chan, Sucheng. (1991). *Asian Americans: An interpretive history*. Boston: Twayne.

Chandler, David P. (1983). *A History of Cambodia*. Boulder: Westview Press.

Chatterjee, Partha. (1993). *The Nation and its Fragments: Colonial and postcolonial histories*. Princeton: Princeton University Press.

Copeland, Lewis C. (1939). The Negro as a contrast conception. In Edgar T. Thompson (ed.), *Race Relations and the Race Problem: A definition and an analysis* (pp. 152–79). Durham: Duke University Press.

Corrigan, Philip and Sayer, Derek. (1985). *The Great Arch: English state formation as cultural revolution*. Oxford: Basil Blackwell.

Dominguez, Virginia. (1986). *White by Definition: Social classification in Creole Louisiana*. New Brunswick: Rutgers University Press.

Du Bois, W. E. B. (1977 [1935]). *Black Reconstruction in the United States, 1860–1880*. New York.

Embree, John F. (1950). Thailand – a loosely structured social system. *American Anthropologist*, 52: 181–93.

Espiritu, Yen Le. (1992). *Asian American Panethnicity: Bridging institutions and identities*. Philadelphia: Temple University Press.

Fanon, Frantz. (1967). *Black Skin, White Masks*. Translated by C. L. Markman. New York: Grove Press.

Fong, Timothy P. (1994). *The First Suburban Chinatown: The remaking of Monterey Park, California*. Philadelphia: Temple University Press.

Foucault, Michel. (1989). The subject and power. In H. L. Dreyfus and P. Rainbow (eds), *Michel Foucault: Beyond structuralism and hermeneutics* (pp. 208–28). Chicago: University of Chicago Press.

Foucault, Michel. (1991). On governmentality. In G. Burchell, C. Gordon, and P. Miller (eds), *The Foucault Effect* (pp. 87–104). Chicago: University of Chicago Press.

Giddens, Anthony. (1990). *Modernity and Self-Identity*. Stanford: Stanford University Press.

Gilman, Sander. (1985). *Difference and Pathology: Stereotypes of sexuality, race, and madness*. Ithaca: Cornell University Press.

Gilroy, Paul. (1987). *"There ain't no black in the Union Jack": The cultural politics of race and nation*. Chicago: University of Chicago Press.

Golub, Stephens. (1986). *Looking for Phantoms: Flaws in the Khmer Rouge health screening process*. Washington, D.C.: US Committee for Refugees.

Gordon, Colin. (1991). Governmental rationality: An introduction. In G. Burchell, C. Gordon, and P. Miller (eds), *The Foucault Effect* (pp. 1–51). Chicago: University of Chicago Press.

Gordon, Tamar. (1994). Constructing authenticities and modernities at the Polynesian Cultural Center. Paper presented at the American Anthropological Association meetings. Atlanta, November 30–December 3.

Gregory, Steven and Sanjek, Roger (eds). (1994). *Race*. New Brunswick: Rutgers University Press.

Hall, Catherine. (1992). *White, Male, and Middle-Class: Explorations in feminism and history*. London: Polity Press.

Hall, Stuart and Held, David. (1989). Citizens and citizenship. In S. Hall and M. Jacques (eds), *New Times: The changing face of politics in the 1990s* (pp. 173–88). New York: Verso.

Hannerz, Ulf. (1990). Cosmopolitans and locals in world culture. In Mike Featherstone (ed.), *Global Culture: Nationalism, globalization, and modernity* (pp. 237–52). London: Sage.

Harrington, Michael. (1962). *The Other America*. New York: Macmillan.

Harrison, M. L. (1991). Citizenship, consumption, and rights: A comment on B. S. Turner's theory of citizenship. *Sociology*, 25: 215–18.

Hirata, Lucie Cheng. (1979). Free, indentured, enslaved: Chinese prostitutes in nineteenth-century America. *Signs*, 5: 3–29.

Kelly, Gail P. (1980). The schooling of Vietnamese immigrants: Internal colonialism and its impact on women. In *Comparative Perspectives on Third World Women: The impact of race, sex, and class* (pp. 276–96). New York: Praeger.

Komorovsky, Mirra. (1967). *Blue-Collar Marriage*. New York: Vintage Books.

Lamphere, Louise (ed.). (1992). *Structuring Diversity: Ethnographic perspectives on the new immigration*. Chicago: University of Chicago Press.

Lau, Siu-Kai. (1983). *Society and Politics in Hong Kong*. New York: St. Martin's Press.

Loescher, Gil and Scanlan, John A. (1986). *Calculated Kindness: Refugees and America's half-open door: 1945 to the present*. New York: Free Press.

Lowe, Lisa. (1991). Heterogeneity, hybridity, and multiplicity: Masking Asian American differences. *Diaspora*, I: 24–44.

Marcus, George E. and Hall, Peter D. (1992). *Lives in Trust: The fortunes of dynastic families in late twentieth century America*. Boulder: Westview Press.

Marshall, Thomas H. (1950). *Citizenship and Social Class.* Cambridge: Cambridge University Press.

Memmi, Albert. (1967). *The Colonizer and the Colonized.* Translated by Howard Greenfield. New York: Beacon Press.

Miles, Robert. (1989). *Racism.* London: Routledge.

Mitchell, Katharyne. (1996). Transnational subjects: The constitution of the cultural citizen in the era of Pacific Rim capital. In A. Ong and D. Nonini (eds), *Ungrounded Empires: The cultural politics of modern Chinese transnationalism.* New York: Routledge.

Mortland, Carol. (1987). Transforming refugees in refugee camps. *Urban Anthropology,* 16: 375–404.

Myrdal, Gunnar. (1944). *An American Dilemma: The Negro problem and modern democracy.* New York: Harper and Row.

Nandy, Ashis. (1983). *The Intimate Enemy: Loss and the recovery of self under colonialism.* Delhi: Oxford University Press.

Ngor, Haing. (1987). *A Cambodian Odyssey.* New York: Macmillan.

Nicholson, Barbara. (1989). The influence of culture on teaching Southeast Asian paraprofessionals: A challenge to social work education. *Journal of Teaching in Social Work,* 3: 73–86.

Omi, Michael and Winant, Howard. (1986). *Racial Formation in the United States: From the 1960s to the 1990s.* New York: Routledge and Kegan Paul.

Ong, Aihwa. (1992). Limits to cultural accumulation: Chinese capitalists on the American Pacific Rim. *Annals of the New York Academy of Sciences, 645*: 125–45.

Ong, Aihwa. (1993). On the edges of empires: Flexible citizenship among cosmopolitan Chinese. *Positions,* 1: 745–78.

Ong, Aihwa. (1995a). Making the biopolitical subject: Khmer immigrants, refugee medicine, and cultural citizenship in California. *Social Science and Medicine,* 40: 1243–57.

Ong, Aihwa. (1995b). Mother's milk in war and diaspora. *Cultural Survival Quarterly,* 19: 61–4.

Ong, Aihwa. (1995c) Women out of China: Traveling theories and traveling tales in postmodern feminism. In R. Behar and D. Gordon (eds), *Women Writing Culture* (pp. 350–72). Berkeley: University of California Press.

Ong, Aihwa. (1996). Chinese modernities: Images of nation and capitalism in the Pacific era. In A. Ong and D. Nonini (eds), *Ungrounded Empires: The cultural politics of modern Chinese transnationalism.* New York: Routledge.

Ong, Aihwa and Nonni, Don (eds). (1996). *Ungrounded Empires: The cultural politics of modern Chinese transnationalism.* New York: Routledge.

Perin, Constance. (1988). *Belonging in America: Reading between the lines.* Madison: University of Wisconsin Press.

Portes, Alejandro and Rumbaut, Ruben G. (1990). *Immigrant America: A portrait.* Berkeley: University of California Press.

Portes, Alejandro and Stepick, Alex. (1993). *City on the Edge: The transformation of Miami.* Berkeley: University of California Press.

Rabinow, Paul (ed.). (1984). *The Foucault Reader.* New York: Pantheon.

Roediger, David R. (1991). *The Wages of Whiteness: Race and the making of the American working class.* London: Verso.

Rosaldo, Renato. (1994). Cultural citizenship in San José, California. *Polar,* 17: 57–63.

Rumbaut, Ruben G. and Ima Kenji. (1988). *The Adaptation of Southeast Asian Youth: A comparative study.* (Final report to the Office of Refugee Settlement, US Department of Health and Human Services, Family Support Administration) Washington, D.C.: Office of Refugee Settlement.

Said, Edward. (1978). *Orientalism*. New York: Pantheon.

Schieffelin, Edward. (1981). Evangelical rhetoric and the transformation of traditional culture in Papua New Guinea. *Comparative Studies in Society and History*, 23: 150–6.

Stack, Carol. (1974). *All Our Kin: Strategies for survival in a black community*. New York: Harper and Row.

Stolcke, Verena. (1995). Talking culture: New boundaries, new rhetorics of exclusion in Europe. *Current Anthropology*, 36: 1–24.

Stoler, Ann L. (1995). *Race and the Education of Desire*. Durham: Duke University Press.

Takagi, Dana Y. (1994). Post-civil rights politics and Asian-American identity: Admission and higher education. In Steven Gregory and Roger Sanjek (eds), *Race* (pp. 229–42). New Brunswick: Rutgers University Press.

Tollefson, J. W. (1990). Response to Ranard and Gilzow: The economics and ideology of overseas refugee education. *TESOL Quarterly*, 24: 543–55.

Valentine, Charles A. (1971). Deficit, difference, and bicultural models of Afro-American behavior. *Harvard Educational Review*, 41 (2).

Welaratna, Usha. (1993). *Beyond the Killing Fields: Voices of nine Cambodian survivors in America*. Stanford: Stanford University Press.

Whalen, William J. (1964). *The Latter-Day Saints in the Modern Day World*. New York: John Day.

Wetherell, Margaret and Potter, Jonathan. (1993). *Mapping the Language of Racism: Discourse and the legitimation of exploitation*. New York: Columbia University Press.

Williams, Brackette F. (1989). A class act: Anthropology and the race across ethnic terrain. *Annual Review of Anthropology*, 18: 401–44.

Williams, Brackette F. (1991). *Stains on My Name, War in My Veins: Guyana and the politics of cultural struggle*. Durham: Duke University Press.

R. Wilson and A. Dirlik (eds). (1996). *The Asia/Pacific as Space of Cultural Production*. Durham: Duke University Press.

Wong, Sau-Ling. (1992). Ethnicizing gender: An exploration of sexuality as sign in Chinese immigrant culture. In S. G. Lim and A. Ling (eds), *Reading the Literatures of Asian America* (pp. 111–29). Philadelphia: Temple University Press.

Yanagisako, Sylvia J. (1985). *Transforming the Past: Tradition and kinship among Japanese Americans*. Stanford: Stanford University Press.

Yanagisako, Sylvia J. (1993). Transforming Orientalism: Gender, nationality, and class in Asian American studies. In S. Yanagisako and C. Delaney (eds), *Naturalizing Power*. Stanford: Stanford University Press.

Yudice, George. (1995). Civil society, consumption, and governmentality in an age of global restructuring: An introduction. *Social Text*, 45 (Winter):1–26.

Part VI

Locating Class

19

The Site of Class

Edna Bonacich

Although lip service is often paid to the importance of class, for example, in university classes entitled "Race, Class and Gender," in practice class appears to have fallen into the background as a topic of central concern. Both feminism and multiculturalism have placed great emphasis on the politics of "identity." They focus upon "difference" based on race, ethnicity, and gender. Within this framework, class gets treated as another form of identity, another basis of difference. Class comes to refer to class ground: does a person have a working class or a middle class background as part of their identity? Each individual can then be categorized in terms of their race, their gender, and their class: for example, one is a working class, African-American woman, or one is a middle class, white man. These clusters of difference then determine identity, which in turn affects both experience and consciousness. Multiculturalism urges that institutions take account of all these varied identities, and make sure that they are represented both in the people who participate in the institution, and in the ideas and concerns with which the institution deals. For example, the university should include a more diverse faculty and student body, in terms of race, class, and gender, and the curriculum should reflect this diversity.

In my view, this approach to class strips it of its most important features. Class is not an identity, but a system of economic power and domination. Class relations are not relations of identity, but relations of dominance and resistance.

To show the contrast, consider the meaning of the idea that the university should be composed of people with class-based diversity. This is a contradiction in terms. The university occupies a position within the class system. It is an institution that is closely linked to the ruling, capitalist class in this society, and to the state. One of its important missions is to train the professional and managerial stratum. All the faculty are already a part of the professional elite, and students are in the process of preparing to enter that elite.

To speak of class diversity in the university is thus to speak of diversity solely in terms of sources of recruitment. Students may originate from working class families, but their sojourn in the university is aimed at transforming them from working class to middle class individuals. Unlike race and gender, their "class" is not a fixed identity, but a changing one.

Now certainly a case can be made that class background affects one's consciousness. Students who come from working class backgrounds are much more likely to be conscious of social inequality and injustice. And they are possibly more likely to use their professional and managerial training to try to work on behalf of social change (though there is no guarantee that they will). Furthermore, recruiting university students from diverse class backgrounds is obviously a good thing in itself. The university should not be the private property of the wealthy and powerful. But we should avoid confusing the class from which one has come with the class into which one is moving. The university obviously does employ working class people – as secretaries, custodians, and groundskeepers – but its students and faculty share a certain current and potential class homogeneity. The faculty and students are middle class now and in the near future. While one may strive to make the institution more diverse in terms of racial and gender composition and orientation, the requirement that it change in class composition and orientation has much more revolutionary implications. In practice, our claims that multiculturalism increases the class diversity of the university are false. When the university recruits more women and people of color, it may not recruit only *from* the middle class, but it certainly recruits only *to* the middle class.

I use this illustration to show how the concept of class has been distorted within "multiculturalism." As a background characteristic, or element of identity, the concept of class has had its teeth pulled. It becomes a relatively non-threatening idea. After all, who in mainstream US society can object to the recruitment of people from diverse backgrounds into the middle class? This is exactly what is meant by "equality of opportunity" within the dominant ideology. Everyone, regardless of class background, should have an equal opportunity for upward mobility within the system. If the university, and other institutions, are able successfully to incorporate people from working class backgrounds is this not a clear sign that the system is working as it is supposed to?

The basic issue, as I see it, is how capitalism works to produce economic and political inequality, and how we can fight against these tendencies. I do not believe we can talk about class in the United States without talking about race, since the class system of the US is highly racialized. By this I mean that the exploitation of labor, upon which the capitalist system rests, depends upon racial disability and a racial division of labor. Thus we have a race-class or a class-race system, neither of which can be discussed separately.

I do recognize that gender also plays a part in the class-race system, but it does not operate on the same level. While women, as a category, do share some common disabilities, women in each race-class group face very different circumstances, and their race-class position is more determinative of their overall position in the social system than is their gender. Thus white, upper class women participate in, and benefit from, the social order that extracts surplus from people of color even if they have lower status in relation to their husbands. Efforts to homogenize race, class, and gender as equivalent types of oppression are, I believe, misplaced.

The fundamental class issue in capitalism is the issue of private property. Private property allows for the expropriation by a small elite of the socially generated surplus. Put another way, everyone in the society participates in the generation of the wealth of our society, but only a few people are able to lay claim to the bulk of it. This they do, not on the basis of how hard they have worked, but on the basis of having made investments, or by taking a risk with their capital. The returns to property have absolutely nothing to do with work. They only have to do with gambling, and only those with a big stake can play.

One can, of course, raise the question of how they got the big stake in the first place. Did they not work hard for it? Sometimes they did, but all too often the origins of the major fortunes of this country are rooted in some form of theft. There was, of course, the initial theft of land from the American Indian and Mexican population that enabled some people to amass huge estates. Then there was the theft of African people from their homeland and the creation of a class of workers who received no returns for their labor. The labor of slaves allowed the illegitimate accumulation of fortunes by their owners, through a form of daily theft, in which the products of their labor were expropriated simply on the basis of ownership. Similarly, waged workers, too, were robbed by the fact that owners did not pay workers the value of what they produced, but only paid them sufficient to cover their subsistence. This kind of theft continues to this day. In other words, property owners are able to steal the social surplus from the rest of the society because the latter lack the power to claim it.

Not only does the capitalist class expropriate most of the wealth that is generated, by taking out profits, interest, and rent, but they also make all of the major decisions of the society. Formal democracy is very limited in what it actually can control. In fact, most of the important decisions that affect our daily lives and livelihoods are made by a group of people whose sole criterion for making them is whether or not they, or the property holders they represent, will make money. They decide what the society will build, what goods it will produce, and who will produce them under what conditions. They also spend billions of dollars trying to shape and manipulate the demand for products. They control most of the communications media, thereby exercising a kind of stranglehold over ideology. And they control state institutions.

Capitalism has developed an ideology that says that the owners of property deserve this kind of power and these kinds of rewards, that the social allocation we have is just. The system is rationalized by the argument that owners are the creators of wealth, and that everyone else is dependent upon them. This ideology, of course, turns reality on its head. People are only dependent on capitalists for their livelihood because they have been robbed of any property themselves and have no means of survival other than to sell themselves, their time, and their ability to work to those who control all the property. In reality, workers do not need owners who take out profits. They may need a management team and they may need to have a group that makes investment decisions, but there is no social need for a group of property owners who simply take out profits.

However, the ideology of the system argues that capitalists, rather than workers, are the great creators of wealth. They are great benefactors who create jobs for the rest of us, and we should be eternally grateful for the gift they provide us. This mythical rendering of the way the system works masks the fact that these relationships are purely a social-political construction. The system does not permit public entities to engage in productive enterprise; only private production is permitted, and therefore only private entities can create wealth. This is not inherent in production, but in a particular legal-political set of institutions.

Because private production is the only legitimate form, both workers and communities are placed in a dependent relationship on the owners of private property. Cities, for example, must bend over backwards to woo businesses to come to their area, and provide jobs for their residents and a tax base for their social services. Property owners have all the power in this relationship and can threaten to leave if they are not given what they want: a cheap, controllable labor supply, the absence of intrusive regulations, and low taxes. Because they control production, they control wealth, so everyone else is at their mercy.

In late capitalism another important class has emerged, namely the managerial and professional stratum. This group also expropriates the socially-generated surplus, but in the form of bloated salaries as opposed to profits. The huge size and growth of US CEO salaries, for example, has recently received some negative publicity, as the gap between the earnings of production workers and executives has sky-rocketed. These high earnings are usually justified by the claim that managers and professionals have scarce human capital; their salaries are bid up by companies competing in the market for their much-needed skills. In fact, at least to a certain extent they act more like a club that has the power to reward its own members exorbitantly.

Both the owners of capital and the managerial-professional stratum tend to be heavily white. They have the real power in this society, and they often collude and overlap. For example, high level managers are often granted stock options that bring them into the ownership class, while many higher level professionals are able to use their large salaries for investment purposes. Moreover, managers and professionals play a critical role in providing institutional support of all kinds for private property. They are the implementers of capital's rule.

Another important class in US capitalism is the petite bourgeoisie, or small business sector, a class of special relevance to Asian-Americans. Like managers and professionals, small business owners serve as an intermediary class that also can perform a controlling role. While there are obviously small business people of all ethnicities, there is a tendency for Asian immigrants to be over represented in this class.

I would like to illustrate how the class system works by briefly describing my current work, namely a study of the garment industry in Los Angeles. The garment industry is hierarchically, as well as racially organized. Manufacturers, who design and market clothing, and who are mainly white, contract out the sewing, mainly to Asian contractors, especially Koreans. The contractors, in turn, employ workers, who are mainly immigrant Latinos, although Asian immigrants also comprise a significant minority of the working population. The contracting shops often violate labor and safety standards, and workers are poor, abused, and live under harsh conditions.

Despite the poverty of workers, considerable wealth is generated by this industry. I have tried to figure out where this "surplus" goes. My tentative conclusion is that it goes to two broad categories of people: owners of property, and high-paid managers and professionals. Let us consider the owners first. Three types of owners are relevant:

1 Owners of businesses. These include the contractors, the manufacturers, and also the retailers of apparel, who exercise considerable power over the manufacturers. These people, who are sometimes stockholders, make profits.

2 Owners of financial institutions. Apparel manufacturing uses standard banking, but also has a special form of financing, namely factoring. Factors are intermediaries between manufacturers and retailers, who pay the former what the retailers owe them before it is due, thereby providing the manufacturers with operating capital. They later collect these debts from the retailers themselves. Financial agents make money in the form of interest. Some make it indirectly, particularly through interest owed on leveraged buyouts, which were prominent in the apparel retailing sector.

3 Owners of real estate. This group takes out surplus in the form of rent. They include the owners of the downtown buildings where sweatshops are located, the owners of the California Mart, where manufacturers rent showrooms, and the owners of malls where retailers are located. To give one example, Jack Needleman, owner of several downtown buildings where garment contracting shops are located, is estimated to be worth $250 million.

Apart from owners, upper-end managers and professionals take a chunk of the surplus in the form of bloated salaries. This is especially clear with the top executives of manufacturing and retailing firms. These executives sometimes overlap with owners when they take advantage of stock options. For example, an article in the *Los Angeles Times* reported the earnings of the 100 California CEOs with the highest earnings in 1992. Topping the list was the president of the Gap, a garment specialty store. He made $41.9 million in that year, $40 million of which was in stock awards, and most of the remaining $1.9 million in salary.

Professionals include garment lawyers, CPAs, designers, advertisers, teachers in industry related schools, and journalists. While their earnings are variable, the higher end usually makes six-digit salaries, and can work in relatively luxurious surroundings.

There is a widening divide in Los Angeles between rich and poor, which is heavily correlated with race. The garment industry illustrates the dynamics of capitalism that produce this effect. The extraction of surplus is sanctioned by the state in its endorsement of these property relations. In addition, in this case (as in many Los Angeles industries), workers are frequently undocumented, a product of immigration law that creates, in practice if not in overt intention, a group of especially rightless, disenfranchised workers. These workers are not racially defined according to the law, as in the old Jim Crow South, but in reality they suffer from a combination of racial and class oppression. They are typically indigenous Americans, though not from the United States, who are still being ripped off by the conquering Europeans.

The implication of a class-race analysis is that there is a need to struggle against the fundamental economic and political institutions of our society. In order to achieve justice and equality, and an end to racism, it is necessary for us to fight against the existing property relations of this society. This would require a massive redistribution of all the ill-gotten gains that have depended on the theft from, and exploitation of others. And it would require the construction of a new social order, based on principles of non-exploitation, of sharing the socially generated surplus, and providing for the well-being of every society member.

Needless to say, our society is a million miles from such a vision, let alone program. The discussion of such issues is completely drowned out from the public discourse, since the owners of capital and wealthy managers and professionals control the government and virtually all means of communication. They control the media and the schools. They control the military and police. As an aside, police relations are an especially vivid instance of class relations in that one of the main purposes of the police is to protect private property from the typically racially defined dispossessed, whose anger at their dispossession might be expected to arouse efforts to effect their own low-level efforts at redistribution. A non-capitalist police force might aim its efforts at punishing the theft inherent in private property. A capitalist police force does not recognize this theft and only punishes the victims' efforts to regain what has been stolen.

The task of those who want to engage in class struggle against the system of domination under which we live must keep in mind this larger picture, and must try to have their political work move towards the goal of revolutionizing property relations, however remote that goal might seem. There are numerous struggles to pursue along these lines, including working with the labor movement, working in communities to gain more control of capital, experimenting with alternative organizations of production, fighting for greater political representation for the disenfranchised, creating alternative media, working against police abuse, fighting for changes in numerous state regulations, and on and on.

I started with the university and want to end there. Part of my purpose has been to show the limitations of treating class as an identity. If we really want to change the class-race system, as it is manifested in the university, we must do much more than change the identity composition of its faculty and students. We must also go beyond changing the curriculum to reflect the diverse histories and cultures of the various class-race-gender groups in the United States (and in the world). These are admirable goals, and I do not want to minimize their importance in themselves, but they do not really challenge the class-character of the university, and the role it plays in perpetuating the class system.

To revolutionize the university from a class perspective would require that we fight to change the role that the university plays within the society. This includes research that is done primarily on behalf of the propertied classes and the state. (Even critical research often has a reformist cast, aimed at finding ways to ameliorate the worst aspects of the system and getting it to function more smoothly.) It includes fighting against the creation and propagation of ideology in support of dominant property relations. And it involves fighting against the teaching role played by the university in constructing the next generation of managers and professionals. We need to develop a concept of the university that moves our society beyond its current exploitative class-race relations.

I do not by any means expect the easy achievement of these goals. What I am calling for is greater clarity about what we mean by the class struggle, and what its political implications are. Somewhere along the line, our concerns over gender and race have led us to lose sight of property relations, or to treat them as an old issue, whose time has passed. Marxist ideas are denounced as male and Eurocentric. While there are certainly some shortcomings along these lines in Marx's original writings, I believe that he started a school of thought that is still of vital relevance to understanding our society today, and to understanding both what needs to be changed and how to struggle to change it.

20

Between Nationality and Class

Stanley Aronowitz

You can get it if you really want
But you must try, try, try, try
You"ll succeed at last
                    Jimmy Cliff [1]

On the eve of the first anniversary of the astounding Million Man March, the journal Black Renaissance commemorated the event with a special section that contained, among other articles, reporter David J. Dent's account and reflection on the significance of the March. As do many black intellectuals and liberals, Dent admits his own skepticism. But as he travels from Hempstead, New York, on a bus filled with marchers, his doubts about participating in an event organized by the cultural nationalist Louis Farrakhan begin to dissolve. The march was by no means a repeat of the great 1941 and 1963 marches; instead of focusing on discrimination and political freedom, the talk on the bus concentrated on self-help, black economic development, and education. Dent concludes:

> In many ways the March was a large-scale protraction of the tendency of African-Americans in the nineties to create new cultural spaces where freedom and individuality can thrive independently of the baggage of race and racism. In this respect the March inadvertently created a new sense of redefining black maleness in popular and broad enough terms to reflect the reality and diversity of black America.[2]

But the burden of the report itself is that the bulk of the participants – who drove, according to Dent, "Lexuses, Hondas, Mercedes, Tauruses," as well as those who rode buses and the trains – were part of the growing middle class and the better-paid workers. Dent's own use of the term "African-American" is an indicator that many in the African-American community are eager to overcome the "otherness" that has plagued blacks for centuries. They want cultural affirmation in distinctly American terms, a validate can be purchased only by enunciations such as "self-help," "individuality," and "education." Indeed, the incredible response to Farrakhan's call for a convocation towards a new definition of black manhood may be understood as a movement among a considerable section of blacks from race to ethnicity. Its key words are "diversity" rather than "difference," "individual" and "collective struggle," "self-help" not "rights." The massive response march, and especially to these key words, indicates that many blacks are eager to adopt identities that mark them, for example, like Polish-Americans and Jewish-Americans rather than with the single terms "Latino," "black," "Haitian," and other diasporic significations.

Far from the confrontational style for which Farrakhan and black Muslims are famous, the March ratified the cardinal achievement of the black freedom movement in the twentieth century: the black freedom movement forced government and large corporations to provide jobs and, equally important, to provide the opportunity for millions of blacks to achieve one of the crucial components of the American Dream, climbing out of poverty into the (mainly) salaried middle class. His voice dripping with irony, Reggae singer Jimmy Cliff makes fun of this possibility and even the desire that underlies it in the quote that began this article. But there was no irony in the lovefest that was the Million Man March. Even as conservative politicians adopt a slash-and-burn policy towards the public sector – a bastion of black achievement – and the corporate sector abolishes hundreds of well-paid factory jobs held by blacks, the nineties are still a time when the gap between the black poor and the black middle class approaches canyon-like proportions. While annual incomes for the black poor have declined by 25 percent in the last decade, the black middle class has grown in the same period from 12 percent to 15 percent of the total black population. For most black women and men, the last decade has been an unmitigated disaster; for the ambitious and otherwise fortunate 15 percent, times have never been better. Such are the ambiguities of American life.

Ethnicity and American Culture

American ideology contains two elements: first, the United States is believed to confer equality of opportunity on each individual citizen, even as it punishes many, such as immigrants of all descriptions who have not (yet) attained citizenship in either the economic or the political meaning of the term. The second is that, unlike other advanced industrial societies, the United States is considered, in its more refined phrase, an "Open Society." While some politicians and social scientists acknowledge the persistence of the color line in American life, the United States has no distinct social class lines. A leading presidential contender even blurted out during the 1996 campaign that the United States was "classless." That conditions of birth do not determine the economic and social fate for many whites and some racialized minorities is offered as proof that the United States is the great exception to the general rule that social class is destiny. In this paradigm of virtually unlimited opportunity, the person who keeps her/his nose to the grindstone by working, especially to earn educational credentials, will eventually "make it" into the (salaried) middle class. In this paradigm, the task of affording racial minorities and women the same chances to escape the working class as those enjoyed by white men defines a political goal that, since the Civil Rights Act of 1964, is well on the way to fulfillment.

In achieving social mobility, no institution plays a more important role than higher education. Since the emergence of the "new" middle class – salaried professional, technical, and managerial employees rather than self-employed entrepreneurs – colleges and universities provide the crucial rites of passage to the salariat in US society. But the centrality of post-secondary credentials for erecting the architectonic of mobility is not a force of nature. Although many advanced capitalist societies in Europe and Japan have extensive higher education systems, the proportion of their adult populations attending these institutions is far less than in the United States, where 62 percent of high school graduates enter college. With nearly fifteen million students, one out of nine Americans under age sixty-five attends some kind of post-secondary school; of those who enter college, half attend four-year colleges and universities, and half attend community colleges. In contrast, European and Japanese higher education systems are far more restrictive. In France, Germany, and the United Kingdom, fewer than a quarter of high school graduates are in universities, and less than 5 percent of the total adult population is in higher education. In 1995, the United States had more than 3,200 schools of higher education (70 percent in the public sector), more than double the pre-World War II number. Europe and Japan have had parallel growth, but have not achieved nearly the same level as the United States.

The college or university degree may not guarantee a job, let alone a career, but it has become the premier sign that informs employers and other educational institutions that the candidate has endured a regimen that, on balance, assures their reliability. One may not acquire a set of job-ready skills in any educational institution, except those, such as schools of medicine and social work, whose curriculum includes as much on-the-job training as classroom instruction. But the credential signifies the student's mobility aspiration, in particular their ability to endure a long journey toward an indefinite conclusion and their capacity to tolerate boredom. These, more than any specific content, are crucial job and educational skills, for the "hidden" curriculum of schooling is that the student is willing to jump through hoops without being assured of a definite employment outcome.

Since we have no antagonistic classes and competing political ideologies corresponding to a fundamental divide in society, the polity is said to act on the basis of consensus, which amounts to the statement that people make decisions on the basis of generally agreed upon national interests. While Americans may differ with one another concerning economic and social policy and may form distinct political parties, on the whole they agree on the underlying free-market, capitalist framework of social arrangements. Among other things, this agreement presupposes the historic success of assimilation of immigrant groups into a common ground of values and beliefs. For while America is a land of immigrants and thus technically plural, it is said, in the felicitous phrase of the early-twentieth-century Jewish poet and novelist Israel Zangwill, to be a great "melting pot." Whatever one's background in the old country, by the second generation the scions of immigrants are fully American in culture, politics, and religion. According to this litany, individualism and consensus are so pervasive that whether the immigrant generation spoke German, Polish, or Greek, their children will speak English. Folk culture may be displayed during holidays, but is routinely ignored for the rest of the year. Grandad may have been a flaming socialist or anarchist but, whatever their private sentiments, his grandchildren are persuaded by the dominant US ideology that free-market capitalism and the American system of liberal democracy is the best of all possible worlds.

Whether you are black or white or any complexion in between, America is a deeply religious country whose people and their morality are firmly planted in the Judeo-Christian tradition of the ten commandments and of One God. Others may practice their non-Western forms of worship, but these religions are, after all, leftovers of a bygone age. While, for instance, practitioners of Muslim or Buddhist faiths are not required to convert to the dominant religion(s), they are usually obliged to observe the tenets of the dominant ideology in nearly every other respect – especially in business and education.

A corollary of the American consensus is the conception of public life as essentially white and male. The consensual society may, indeed, engage in the nefarious practice of exclusion, but such practices are contrary to its precepts of integration and of equal opportunity. Even among those who discriminate on the basis of race or gender, many admit that law and custom must be changed to permit the excluded to enter into public life. Perhaps the most vivid example of this contradictory behavior is affirmative action. Acknowledging discrimination, institutions such as corporations and government agencies have instituted set-asides, quotas, and other programs to admit some minorities and women. But the conditions for entrance are that one accept a definite series of preconditions, the violation of which disqualifies the candidate from participation. Of those preconditions, none ranks higher than civility. American ideology disdains rancor and other indications of social division. Strikes, demonstrations, and other forms of "in-your-face" political protest violate the precept that, in the United States, we have orderly ways to resolve the temporary conflicts arising (mostly) from misunderstandings. Genuine interest conflicts are subject to democratic processes, such as legal remedies, legislation, and electoral resolution, all of which preclude direct action.

Consensually, Americans believe blacks and women should be nominated and elected to public office, gain access to the leading professions – law, the professoriate, medicine, and the sciences – and that their interests and complaints should be granted a hearing in the corridors of power and under law. But there is no question of recognizing the validity of counter or oppositional discursive practices and rules, which not only differ from but also contradict those of the dominant group. Thus, the debate about Ebonics turns crucially on whether blacks accept Standard English as normative. Educational leaders and politicians have tolerance for the "other" as long as she/he recognizes the practices of the dominant group as those to which all others must strive, regardless of the path they may take to achieve them. The task for society remains that of assimilating potential or actual dissent into a prescribed public sphere, whose values remain unchanged even as it makes room for new groups to join the American celebration in culture, as well as politics and economics.

Hence, for example, jazz may be classified as America's "classical" music, a designation that qualifies it to be performed at New York's Lincoln Center. This and other classical venues may display its virtues, which plants it firmly in the Western, high cultural tradition. In this framework, Charlie Parker, Theolonius Monk, and John Coltrane are doing no more, but also no less, than what we might expect of any twentieth-century composer, say, Stravinsky or Schoenberg. The novels of Richard Wright and Toni Morrison may be coded as "literature" and receive high awards. We can recognize some of the outpouring of women's fiction as among the legitimate heirs to the traditional canon. But their work must be measured by the degree to which it corresponds to what is recognized as high art. What has been coded as popular culture – rock 'n' roll, hip-hop, heavy metal, alternative, and all genres of television (except the products of public television) – are distinctly low forms and have no place in the legitimate public sphere. In fact, they are subject in some circles to proscription if conventional morality deems them unfit for minors, or even for adults. Finally, as "art critic" Senator Jesse Helms has remarked, every artist has the right to paint or write what she/he pleases, but the "American people" have no obligation to fund smut or radical ideas.

A "New" Concept of Ethnicity

What I want to call the "new" ethnicity arises on the ruins of nationhood. Recall the term "Americanism," which for a century has been invoked to remind the millions of immigrants who have arrived on US shores since 1880 that they may retain their cultural Old World identities, but must shed their political and social allegiances to the past. While such reminders retain their power among some, our collective sense of nationality is, to say the least, in crisis. Since the 1960s revealed the depth of differences among the American people, "ethnicity" is one of the names invoked to describe and explain what American ideology has denied: that difference may signify more than benign diversity, that it may signal conflict, especially with the ideal of assimilation. Ethnicity has become ubiquitous in public conversation, but its boundaries have proven elusive to most investigators. For example, W. Lloyd Warner attempted, in his 1949 book, *Social Class in America*, to introduce ethnicity alongside class as an important designation of individual and group identity.[3] However, and perhaps more to the point of interest, his work was largely ignored in the shadow of the Great Depression when the class divide was very hard to overlook. But ethnicity re-emerged in the wake of the postwar boom when Americans discovered both the possibilities of social and class mobility and its limitations. By the 1970s, when in pursuit of opportunity an unprecedented half of high school graduates enrolled in some (public) institution of post-secondary education, many found that a degree, while necessary, was not sufficient to achieve genuine social mobility – that is, the ability to move between classes and strata. Since in the conventional account there cannot be structural job shortages, many Americans began to ascribe their unexpected fate to the stigma of ethnic identity rather than to the end of economic expansion. Perceiving an alarming market glut of qualified labor, newly minted recipients of advanced degrees cast about for additional weapons to break open barriers to employment. For example, the difficulty a woman with a Ph.D. in physics might experience getting a job may be ascribed to job shortages as much as to sexism. Some social scientists and civil rights activists grasped the significance of the degree hierarchy: we have equal opportunity, but some opportunity is more equal. They sought to reach beyond the third-tier colleges and universities to gain admission to elite schools. In turn, ethnicity became a weapon of criticism of the prevailing state of affairs and was eagerly grasped by employers – public and private – as well as university and college administrators, as a new criterion for inclusion.

The *Oxford English Dictionary*'s definition of ethnicity, "a people or a nation," seems to have been transmuted in the literature.[4] In the main, social scientists such as Nathan Glazer and Daniel Patrick Moynihan have identified ethnicity with almost any subculture. It stands between the nation and the individual as the embodiment of group identity, but has no necessary implication that membership has more than cultural consequences. That is, it has implications for explaining political and social behavior. The emergence of ethnicity as a social category may be ascribed to the vicissitudes of assimilation under conditions where, differentially by national origin, a fair number of white males appeared to have transcended their collective conditions of birth, while many blacks, Latinos, and women were left behind. In the 1960s, some white "ethnics" began to emulate their ancestors by reforming job networks; Italians and Poles discovered that their civil rights had been abrogated by educational and employment discrimination and formed associations to remedy their condition of deprivation.

Except for turn-of-the-century labor turmoil and the Great Depression of the 1930s, class discourse has never enjoyed much currency in the United States. And, during the long wave of US economic expansion, ethnicity has been generally viewed as a temporary condition on the way to assimilation. I contend that its reappearance may be explained by a shift in the labor movement away from class to interest group or associational discourse in the post-World War II era. After the war, while riding the quarter-century wave of American prosperity, organized labor abandoned its brief period when unions identified labor's interests with the national or general interests and with its leadership of the entire working class. As labor retreated from its short-lived bid for cultural and political hegemony, it left space for new discursive practices that could embody discontent.

The 1950s were the years in which trade unions seemed to shift from their Depression-bred perspective of speaking for all working people to return to the job conscious, membership-based orientation of the older craft or business unionism against which industrial unions had rebelled. Industrial workers, once the epitome of an insurgent working class, were rapidly retreating from the public sphere to the quasi-corporatist security of the labor agreement. As plants moved from the city centers to the suburbs, and federally funded highway programs littered the geography, many war veterans were the beneficiaries of federal loan programs that assisted them in moving with the plants into single-family suburban homes. To outward appearances, these workers, many of whom were highly paid, never looked back at the cities where black and Latino majorities were left to work in low-paid service industries and small factories, or were becoming permanently unemployed in growing numbers. Under these circumstances, to speak the vocabularies of class appeared anachronistic. From the perspective of this consumer-driven society, industrial workers, most of whom had few educational credentials, seemed to have joined the middle class. The workers in leading industrial corporations, such as General Motors, General Electric, and Boeing, were bringing home pay equivalent to or higher than most teachers, nurses, and social workers, and equivalent to that of engineers and many professors. Race and gender appeared to have permanently displaced class as a negative signifier in political and economic terms. Twenty years later, many of these industrial workers were facing unemployment and underemployment due to technological displacement or due to employers closing older industrial plants and moving to the American South or overseas. Unions that had established the private welfare state through the union contract negotiated away many of these benefits, such as fully paid health care and ever more paid holidays and paid vacations, in hopes of hanging onto workers' jobs. During the 1980s, according to Barry Bluestone and Bennet Harrison's calculations in *The Deindustrialization of America*, half of the best industrial jobs disappeared.[5] Many white male workers rediscovered their ethnic ties and, instead of turning toward the politics of class solidarity, they turned on blacks and women, whom they perceived were the real culprits causing their pain. During this period, once militant-industrial unions were conceding hard-won gains to employers and, in their tribute to the rule of law, at almost every turn opposing rank-and-file resistance. Responding invidiously to the apparent successes of the black freedom movement of the late 1960s, white ethnicity displaced the politics and culture of class during the 1970s, when many groups of white male workers experienced an erosion of their standard of living and social power. At the same time, the appearance of ethnic discourse among blacks and other racialized minorities signaled the emergence of a new subaltern middle class for which "black" racial identity had become too confrontational with a social system within which it wanted to rise.

Accordingly, although the American ideology seems unshaken – most still believe they can "make it" if they really try – political scientists and sociologists claim people have increasingly discovered that their economic and political interests, as well as their cultural sentiments, may be expressed through the formation of ethnic blocs rather than through class affiliation. In the first half of the twentieth century, ethnicity was regarded as a cultural identity, which, nevertheless, did not disturb the progress of assimilation. By the 1960s, it \ increasingly evident that ethnicity had become the designation that express discontent as well as hope, and its emergence spurred a new debate.

Ethnicity and Class

Whether, as some have argued, ethnicity is a "myth" or merely "symbolic," or whether its emergence has genuine practical effects on politics, especially cultural politics, there is no doubt that for the last thirty years there has been a new ethnic "question" that occupies both journalism and scholarship. The lines are drawn in two ways. In *Ethnicity*, Nathan Glazer, Daniel Patrick Moynihan, and Daniel Bell have argued that ethnicity displaces class because, in Bell's terms, ethnicity combines interest with the "affective tie," while class as the repository of interest remains locked into the instrumental rationality of interest.[6] In a society where class lines are progressively blurred by the capacity of American capitalism to respond to demands on it from the margins and by education, class seems to have declined, together with Bell's celebrated "end of ideology." Others writing in the same anthology, such as Herbert Gans, for example, grant symbolic significance to ethnicity but find little or no evidence that ethnicity has retained the powerful political and social influence it possessed among first generation immigrants. Perhaps with the exception of Chicago and a few smaller cities, the urban political machines once dominated by white ethnic groups have, in the main, broken down. Even when blacks have captured City Hall, they have been unable to consolidate power, as the experiences of New York, Cleveland, and Los Angeles demonstrate.

In the wake of the partial breakdown of nationality's ability to sustain consensus and class's inability to offer an alternative basis for solidarity, ethnicity refers instead to a subjective feeling of pride. Yet, Gans and Steven Steinberg find that assimilation remains the dominant mode of integration of the US population.[7] For Steinberg, the vagaries of assimilation may be ascribed to the persistence of the class system, of which racial oppression is an important part, rather than ethnicity. In his systematic refutation of the salience of ethnicity to such established modes of assimilation as education and work, Steinberg argues against "culturalist" explanations of why some groups attain disproportionate levels of educational and occupational achievement to their representation in the general population. For example, to the widely accepted belief that the reason Jews are stunningly successful in the professions and in education is their traditional "love of learning," Steinberg shows that most immigrant groups have similar sentiments that have deep roots in their cultures. But while these immigrant groups recognize the importance of education for social mobility, most lack the means to achieve it and some, especially those groups that were able to achieve secure berths in machine and construction trades, may not want it.

Steinberg attributes the difference between Jews and others to the Jews' experience in the cities of Eastern Europe, where they were business people and industrial workers, unlike Poles and southern Italians, who were chiefly peasants before their migration to the United States. Arriving in the United States with these skills and some capital, Jews were able to secure better economic niches in the emerging industrial system, which provided more opportunities for their children to attend colleges and universities. Thus education *follows* attainment of economic niches rather than causing it. Armed with degrees, the Jews took advantage of the best mobility opportunity available at the turn of the twentieth century: school teaching. But, contrary to expectations that credentials are all that is needed to gain access to the best and most lucrative professions, until World War II, Jews were, in the main, excluded from the professions, such as medicine and academia. During the 1920s and 1930s, most reading Jewish intellectuals were unable to find academic jobs and, when they did, were excluded from tenure by racial criteria.

The burden of Steinberg's argument is that economic rather than cultural advantages account for the differential gains among some ethnic groups in the United States. In his analysis, the race/class nexus is a far more reliable index of opportunity than ethnicity. In opposition to the profoundly essentialist explanations according to which culture – either of poverty or of learning – account for black failure or Jewish success, the articulation of blacks, Jews, and other groups with the class system may be a more reliable mobility indicator.

Thus, as William Julius Wilson reports in *When Work Disappears*, there are fewer black men working than are unemployed in the cities – black male unemployment in the cities had reached 58 percent by 1996. It is not primarily a function of the deficits of black culture, such as the absence of a two-parent household, lack of skills, or the absence of cultural values such as adherence to family and work as desirable states of being;[8] the "lack" is one of jobs. Blacks are barred from the trades for reasons of race, from industrial employment because factories have left the cities in droves, and from many retail establishments in the cities because of rank discrimination. While in the 1960s and 1970s black student enrollment in institutions of higher education rose rapidly, their numbers are currently in a freefall due to the decline of student aid and the widening gap within black communities between a rising middle-class salariat and an increasingly proletarianized and unemployed working class.

Abandoned in the 1980s and 1990s by the government's renunciation of its own policies, and also by the labor movement and by middle-class-led civil rights organizations, many black men have become attracted to "ethnicity." The famous Million Man March organized by Muslim leader Louis Farrakhan and the designation "African-American" adopted by many intellectuals to replace "black" (which, in the wake of the Black Power movement replaced "Negro") signify a definite cultural turn. Mass, primarily male, black pride, rather than the struggle against discrimination and other forms of economic and political exclusion, has taken front rank in black communities. Here the specificity of ethnicity may be a marker of despair and disbelief in the capacity of government and traditional civil rights organizations to wage a determined fight for jobs and income.

Despair was in evidence during the bleak summer of 1996 when, with a stroke of the pen, a Democratic US President achieved what no Republican could have done: signing away income guarantees for the jobless poor. To be sure, members of the Congressional Black Caucus, joined by a shrunken corporal's guard of remaining white liberals, voted against the "welfare reform" proposal. But neither labor nor the black civil rights groups were able, or even willing, to oppose Bill Clinton's capitulation in the midst of his re-election bid. Consensus, in the form of closed-mouth inaction, overwhelmed the waning tradition of distributive justice.

The rise of ethnic discourse corresponds not only to the disaggregation of the consensual basis of nationality in the face of the emergence of stark inequalities as a visible feature of American economic and political life. It may be traced, in part, to the emergence of a minority, but sufficiently numerous, middle class among groups who have historically been excluded from the professions and from other segments of the salariat. Under pressure from the black freedom movement, whose most militant detachment during the 1960s and 1970s was urban youth, government policy was directed less to addressing blatant economic inequality than to assisting in the formation of a new black and Latino middle class. Among policymakers and corporate leaders in the 1960s, there was a general consensus that the mass radicalization among black, Latino, and white student youth, many of whom were allied to the black freedom movement, and women had to be redirected to acceptable American outcomes, especially mobility. The urban uprisings, anti-war demonstrations, and civil rights and feminist marches of those decades could be stemmed best not by police repression, although this method was frequently used, but by a systematic effort to promote, through ethnic identification, a series of measures the sum of which would generate a new class of managers, including politicians, whose main assignments would be to run the now decimated "inner-city" welfare agencies, schools, and the criminal justice system. Under the panoply of legislation under the rubrics "anti-poverty" and "anti-discrimination," gender, race, income, and ethnicity became the crucial criteria for opportunities in education, job training, public housing, and public job creation programs. The most successful of these were the programs directed at increasing minority admissions in colleges and universities and affirmative action employment programs, the most visible of which were directed to staff and supervisory positions, which, with government prodding, were adopted by a large segment of major corporations. Both open admissions in many state colleges and universities, according to which a student need only attain a high school diploma in order to gain admission, and stepped-up student loan programs underwritten by federal and state government were the chief staging grounds for the formation of the new middle-class salariat. In short, as social movements grounded in generational and class discourse waned, ethnicity waxed – but not spontaneously. Ethnic identities became markers of state-sponsored opportunity.

President Richard Nixon's inauguration, in 1971, of an affirmative action program pegged educational, training, and job opportunities to various ethni-cities. On the one hand, it continued certain economic criteria, namely the poverty line for school and training admission, but shifted emphasis to race and ethnicity, especially Chicanos, Puerto Ricans, and some Asian categories. The guidelines even specified which Latinos were eligible for affirmative action. For example, Colombians were in, but Argentinians and Salvadorans were out, a blatant exclusion based not on need but on US foreign policy.

Needless to say, the adoption of ethnic identity by some racialized minorities had a distinct class flavor. This adoption was oriented largely to those who sought to achieve specific modes of class mobility, especially from manual labor to the professions and to management. For immigrant and first-generation white ethnic working-class groups, ethnicity was a mechanism for establishing a unique form of *working-class* identity – whiteness – and had a specific economic goal: establishing monopolies over a particular segment of the blue-collar occupations or industries. Until the 1960s, black, Latino, and Asian working-class groups had only limited success in deploying ethnicity for the purpose of forging their own economic niches. And, when they were able to establish hegemony over some occupations, it was primarily in the services and in the second- and third-tier construction trades. Until the 1960s, most black professionals were trained for the clergy, medicine, and law in negro colleges and universities. Their represen-tation in engineering and the sciences was limited to biology and chemistry, and their presence in mostly white universities was negligible.

This pattern contrasts rather sharply with the experience of turn-of-the-century white working-class groups for whom ethnic identities were, to a large extent, vehicles for the expression of economic interest even as they were increasingly culturally assimilated into American society. Labor monopolies were formed under the sign of ethnicity, rather than of the white race in general; but "white-ness" defined the social and cultural position of these ethnic groups. Even in mass production industries such as steel and coal mining, "white" ethnicity played an important role in determining who was hired: Poles and other Eastern Europeans formed hiring networks, as did Italians, through their social clubs and church organizations. During the successful effort to organize the Chicago stockyards and packing plants and again in the preparation for the failed post-World War I steel-organizing drive and consequent strike, labor organizers were obliged to print union material in Italian, Spanish, Portuguese, and nearly all of the Eastern European languages because "language" groups did not communicate in English and frequently did not understand each other. Or, as in the case of coal mining, they worked in different parts of the mine.

Perhaps the most undisputed black organizing success was in the sleeping car porter trade. Once a poorly paid form of servitude in which the Pullman Corporation enjoyed unchallenged sway over wages and working conditions for some 10,000 black men, in the late 1920s, the porters organized into a national union, the Brotherhood of Sleeping Car Porters. These workers became among the best paid and most respected members of many black communities. Their union and its long-time president, A. Philip Randolph, were, until the late 1960s, among the most fervent supporters of the civil rights upsurges. In early 1941, Randolph threatened a march on Washington unless President Roosevelt issued an executive order banning employment discrimination. During the freedom rides, sit-ins, and civil rights marches of the 1960s, regional leaders of the union often provided access to important elements in the black community, including the black churches, where many served as deacons or lay preachers.

The Sleeping Car Porters organized in the tradition of social movement unionism. Acutely aware of their racial identity, they nevertheless saw themselves as participants in the widest sense in a struggle for class justice. They affiliated with the American Federation of Labor, and Randolph became the first black member of its executive council. Many of its leaders, including Randolph, were socialists, and they committed the union to the general labor struggle. By the late 1930s, Randolph was widely regarded as America's leading civil rights figure and its most prominent black trade unionist. His career embodied the fusion of class and race.

But unlike the Sleeping Car Porters, domestic workers and residential construction workers did not achieve anything like the power and wage standards that unionism could provide. These jobs were coded as semi-skilled work, even though they required considerable ability and training. Skilled black carpenters and bricklayers were only able to get rehabilitation and renovation jobs in the largely non-union residential sector of the construction industry because white-dominated unions refused to organize black workers for fear that they might successfully compete in the more lucrative commercial sector of the industry. Even during World War II, when severe labor shortages afflicted construction, like many other industries, opportunities for black building craftspersons such as black carpenters were limited to ship repair and other vital but marginal work in the industry. And with few exceptions, notably the short-lived New York-based Domestic Workers Union of the war years, domestic workers remained unorganized.

When, today, these domestic skills are transposed to union-organized office cleaning, black women often do not get the jobs. They are occupied by largely immigrant, Eastern European women who enjoy union wages and benefits abetted in many large cities by employment networks reminiscent of earlier periods. Black and Latino workers in these occupations and industries are part of the large and growing race/class of the working poor, including Latino and Asian garment workers, who are increasingly choosing to identify with unions and neighborhood quasi-union organizations, which fight for immigrant rights, against employer abuses of wage-hour standards, and against unsafe working conditions. Their ethnic identity does not disappear; but to the extent that unions of the working poor, like the Union of Needle Trades and Textile Employees, the United Farm Workers, and the Service Employees International Unions, have organized among blacks and Latinos, their success may be attributed to their adroit fusion of class and ethnicity.

Many first- and second-generation Asians and Latinos identify with their respective national cultures and often experience the United States as a diaspora.[9]

They live in communities separated from those of the mainstream, occupy limited economic niches, and continue to speak their native languages. Moreover, their links to their countries of origin are still quite close and, even when they become citizens, they do not feel at home. Like the Indian untouchables in some cases, they have formed strong networks to assure their positions close to the bottom of the job scale – in low-wage factory jobs, as taxi-cab drivers, and in restaurants. For example, Dominicans have an elaborate system of labor contracting, especially in the Northeast and in industrial plants. Similarly, Indians are the largest group among newsstand workers, and Pakistanis and Indians are represented in large numbers in Washington's and New York's taxi industries.

But succeeding generations have typically been culturally and sometimes economically assimilated. During the era of ethnic social policy, many recovered what might be termed "strategic" ethnicity because this path was the only one available for those who sought class mobility. Among the entailments of this strategic ethnicity was the reintroduction of the hyphen into cultural identity. For there was little question that what some sought was as much integration into mainstream American society as educational credentials could bring. By the self-designation "African-American," "Mexican-American," or "Chinese-American," rather than the more radical terms black, Latino, or Asian, which were distinctly diasporic terms, this fraction of racialized communities announced its primary identification with the nation in which ethnicity was situated as a plural modifier. In which case, the claim is that the fundamental individualist and consensual premise of American ideology is fulfilled by higher education or, in a relatively small number of instances, by entrepreneurship.

New Directions Beyond Ethnicity

The second feature of American ideology is the doctrine of the open society, best enunciated by philosopher Karl Popper, who spent most of his career in Great Britain.[10] H. T. Wilson has argued persuasively on this theory, that in contrast to Europe, America is "open," rendering class theory entirely obsolete.[11] If on the strength of individual achievement anyone can climb the economic and social ladder, *structural* inequalities may be explained by reference to culture. If the overwhelming majority of blacks, Asians, and Latinos remained class-locked, this unfortunate circumstance could be ascribed to a culture of poverty, social disorganization, or any explanation that avoids naming the class structure as the chief barrier to economic well-being. And that the social structure proved capable of providing paths of mobility for some was sufficient proof of its openness.

Of course, the concepts of mobility and equality of opportunity imply inequality. Open societies must facilitate those with ambition to make of themselves anything their talents will permit. In open societies, limits are deemed entirely individual; societies must remove only those barriers that inhibit the individual from realizing her/his potential but should not put value on economic and social equality lest it degenerate by dull leveling. Inequality is an entailment of freedom that is preferable to an egalitarian society, such as the former Soviet Union. Freedom – that is, market capitalism – is preferable to a society governed by the principles of central government and planning, both for the ethical reason that it provides more liberty to the individual and because the historical record demonstrates that the Soviet Union and its satellites were unable to provide high living standards for most of its professionals, let alone manual workers.

Proponents of the open society thesis never deny that some injustice still exists in democratic countries. Some, such as Samuel Brittan, are aware of the inherent inequalities of the market, do not countenance or ignore discrimination, and are sympathetic to reform.[12] What they disdain are claims that market capitalism can be convicted of structural inequality that cannot be rooted out by piecemeal reform. Rather, according to Popper, open societies are capable of reforming themselves because they are democratic.[13] Rejecting grand programs and comprehensive state planning, they are always subject to the pressures exerted by advocates or by aggrieved interest groups. And because liberal democracy rests on the consent of the governed, when the governed speak, the representatives must listen. If change is too slow, this is the price we pay for freedom; the alternative, convulsive revolutionary transformations frequently and perhaps inevitably lead to totalitarian rule.

Since radical change has not been on the agenda of American political life and seems to oppose the most fundamental precepts of its political culture, piecemeal reform rather than radical social change has been assiduously observed by social movements during the course of the twentieth century. This program has been reinforced by the impressive expansion of American capitalism after the two World Wars. Among other features, piecemeal reform was marked by the emergence on a large scale of scientifically based production labor forces and administrative staffs in major corporations, the growth of public and private bureaucracies, and the expansion of health and educational services after World War II. Single-issue movements based on ethnicity, race, and gender were able to make substantial gains for a minority of their constituencies when they were militant, but also because their demands did not entail the question of a zero-sum game. During periods of economic expansion, blacks have demanded entrance into professions and skilled trades dominated by whites. Under these circumstances the demand for access can be accommodated. Since power never concedes without a struggle (there was little room at the top), the middle seemed more hospitable to pressure. While existing power is threatened, economic privilege is not, except indirectly.

Globalization, downsizing, technological displacement, the emergence of temporary, part-time, and contingent jobs as the characteristic product of the Great American Job Machine, and, equally to the point, the palpable overproduction of qualified educated labor are straining the credibility of American ideology. As the labor movement attempts to rouse itself from its half-century of slumber and to reassert class discourse, and as the political embodiment of the open society (the Democratic Party and liberal Republicanism) adapts to a rightwing version of the Consensus, the open society seems to have been relegated to

Utopian hope. But if the open society was merely a product of the specific historical period of a lapsed American global hegemony, what are the elements for its
rebirth? Can American capitalism renew its breakneck pace of economic growth?
If not, what is the fate of ethnicity?

Clearly, regardless of the short-term economic forecast, ethnicity has positioned itself and has been positioned by elements of the political and economic
power groups to remain a major, if not *the* major, identity of those struggling
against exploitation of workers and other oppressed groups. As I have already
argued, class appeals among the working poor have already coalesced with
ethnic, racial, and gender identities, not only because "pure" class identities are
rarely adopted by American workers or managers, but also because such barriers
as the color line and the glass ceiling remain at all levels of the social structure,
even at the bottom. The question that remains in doubt is whether "identity"
politics will adopt a class dimension despite the overwhelming ideological
campaign against class discourse.

Finally, we are in the midst of a massive re-evaluation by government and
university administrations of the postwar program of expanded educational
opportunity for traditionally excluded groups. To be sure, even in the halcyon
days of the 1960s and early 1970s, colleges and universities were open only to
the deserving poor and minorities, that is, those who made the grades and the
test scores. Now, as legislatures slash higher education budgets in the Northeast,
California, and some midwestern states, and federal student aid withers, state as
well as private school tuition climbs everywhere. Even as high-level politicians
such as President Bill Clinton, who, in his 1997 State of the Union Address,
proclaimed the centrality of education and training for America's economic
future, the market, that term for the materialization of capitalist social policy, is
beginning to take care of the educational surplus. In some universities, admissions criteria have climbed beyond the reach of well-prepared middle-class
students. In others, the deserving others may still gain admission, but discover
that they are offered little more than vocational training, even at four-year
colleges. The liberal arts institutions are in crisis: except for the elite institutions,
second- and third-tier private school enrollments are declining due to tuition
hikes. Some Catholic universities especially, but not exclusively, are reducing
their admission standards to a high school diploma plus a regular heartbeat.
Except for community colleges, which many state systems use to fulfill the opportunity for social mobility promise and to keep a segment of the work force off
the job market, state schools have raised admissions criteria even as they increase
tuition, a virtual move towards privatization, because state legislatures have
caught the parsimony bug. In other cases, the colleges sell curriculum power to
private corporations wishing to train its work force and, at the same time, provide
credentials to its employees. Of course, most famously, just as many research
universities sold their wares to the defense department during the Cold War, now
they are rapidly shifting to becoming supplicants of the major pharmaceutical
and electronics companies, which provide research funds in return for patent
rights.

Vocationalization and downsizing correspond to the scarcity of good salaried jobs. Administrators and many students are moving toward a regime of schooling in which education and training are once more conflated, and families are asking whether the expenditure in lost income as well as fees is worth the five to eight years the average working-class student needs to complete degree requirements. Under these circumstances, the fight for higher education *as a right* takes on class rather than primarily ethnic significance, and no longer corresponds to the experience of the 1960s through the early 1980s when educational credentials were reasonably certain rites of passage out of manual or low-waged service labor and a working life of frequent unemployment.

The remaining question is whether, as we approach the millennium, Americans will revise their ideology of individual opportunity, consensus, and the open society, and recognize the limits of piecemeal reform of which ethnicity and other forms of identity politics were symptoms. Needless to say, doctrine frequently maintains its effective power over experience long after the material conditions for its efficacy have passed. But we can ask new questions because there are new circumstances to be faced. One is whether we are at the beginning of a new class discourse in this most classless of advanced industrial societies. Is it time to ask whether the best preparation for what Ulrich Beck has called "The Risk Society" is a critical education, rather than career or vocational training.[14] I admit these questions are posed against the grain of contemporary discourse, which is moving in exactly the opposite direction. Public universities are scurrying to vocationalize and privatize as fast as they can in the hopes of minimizing the effects of state-mandated budget cuts. Even in states where budgets are stagnant, public universities are convinced that the private sector holds the key to the future of education. Yet, it must be apparent to all but the most blinkered observer that we are in the midst of a climatric in the terms and conditions of our economic and political history.[15] The outcome of these changes depends, in the last instance, on whether civility, a concomitant of consensus, yields to confrontation and difference from those who counsel complacency.

In this article, I have argued that, as in its past, the future of ethnicity as a politics as much as a form of personal identity is inextricably linked to whether and how classes and social strata define themselves. Further, I have tried to show that, in the United States as well as other countries, the categories of identity are always displaced and emerge in their own terms only for short periods. In essence, how people define themselves varies according to collective practices and the discursive terms that accompany them – whether identities are adopted by groups in political and cultural motion or whether the specificity of the economic is addressed or is institutionally displaced, for example, to education. Moreover, I have insisted on the concept of the social individual; when people adopt certain ethnic identities rather than identities of race, gender, and class, it is often because social movements and social ideas have led them to make these choices. Some of these decisions are based on interests such as whether concrete gains can be made by selecting one identity over another. Other decisions are based on much longer range ideological formations. For example, one can see this progress in the history of self-adopted racial identities: black, negro, African-American; black slaves, negro workers, black workers, and so forth.

We are in the midst of a sharp turn back towards conceptions of educational opportunity in which higher training replaces higher education, and the liberal arts are reserved for the few. In the emerging regime, the promise of mobility slowly fades as working-class, racialized students are offered the chance to enter highly specialized technical occupations. Under these conditions, ethnicity acquires a new meaning: we discover that people are "hardwired"; that is, intelligence is no longer described in sociohistorical terms, but becomes a function of the DNA molecule and its codes, which for some may be linked to ethnicity and race. In this case, individuals fail, not societies. Under these conditions, the new terms of educational opportunity can be more frankly retrograde, as in Richard Hernnstein and Charles Murray's social Darwinist tract, *The Bell Curve*.[16]

These "new" theoretical and ideological formulations may justify new social and fiscal policies that close the doors to educational opportunity or, equally, to reconfigure the idea of democratic access to mean occupational education in a frankly stratified system of post-secondary education in which "culture" is reserved for the few. This is reflected in the pressure to accelerate the transformation of public colleges and universities into trade schools, thereby reserving what remains of the intellectual pursuits to a few elite private schools.

The remaining question is whether, in these circumstances, the thirty years of black middle-class growth will continue and whether other racialized minorities will reproduce the historic assimilationist trajection of Eastern and Southern Europeans at the turn of the twenty-first century. My conjecture is that the new situation of post-Cold War America militates against history, repeating itself, for young blacks and the new immigrants face a radical shortage of jobs, especially in the major cities where they are concentrated. To be sure, the shortage is unevenly distributed across the occupational structure, but for the first time since the Great Depression it has affected the professional and technical occupations as well as those in manual categories. And, if the scientific and technological revolution, globalization, and economic stagnation remain characteristic features of the labor market, we may expect current trends towards "disappearing" work to continue.

How, then, can the open society with its preference for piecemeal reform address these issues? As I have suggested, the main mechanism has been through a discursive shift from the language of democratic access to justification of closing doors to higher education and other institutions on the basis of the new eugenic and social Darwinism. As the discourse shifts back to racialized explanations for class hierarchies, liberal opinion is increasingly indistinguishable from conservatism, as those who favored the compassionate state discover its limitations in a time of austerity.

Perhaps it is unrealistic to hope that, finally, American intellectuals will realize that the time for civility and consensus is past, and those who have placed their hopes in ethnicity and race to nudge the conscience of the leading power groups will have to turn to social movements to achieve the goals of equality, even equality of opportunity. Yet, every day brings additional evidence that corporations and the liberal state have all but abandoned the open society. Perhaps the time has come for those who defend it in the name of justice to smell the coffee.

Notes

1 Jimmy Cliff, "You Can Get It If You Really Want," from the movie, *The Harder They Come*, 1973. Soundtrack from Mango Compact Disks, an Island Records Incorporated Company.
2 David Dent, "A Million: Whose Reality?" *Black Renaissance*, 1, no. 1 (1996), 61.
3 W. Lloyd Warner, *Social Class in America* (1949; rpt. New York: Harper Torch Books, 1960).
4 *Oxford English Dictionary* (London: Oxford University Press, 1978): 368.
5 Barry Bluestone and Bennet Harrison, *The Deindustrialization of America: Plant Closings, Community Abandonment, and the Dismantling of Basic Industry* (NewYork: Basic Books, 1982).
6 Daniel Bell, "Ethnicity and Social Change," in *Ethnicity*, ed. Nathan Glazer and Daniel Patrick Moynihan (New York: Free Press, 1970), pp. 136–55.
7 Steven Steinberg, *The Ethnic Myth*, 2nd edn (Boston: Beacon Press, 1989).
8 William Julius Wilson, *When Work Disappears* (Cambridge, MA: Harvard University Press, 1996).
9 Paul Gilroy, *The Black Atlantic* (London: Verso Books, 1995).
10 Karl Popper, *The Open Society and its Enemies* (London: Routledge and Kegan Paul, 1951).
11 H. T. Wilson, *The American Ideology* (London: Routledge and Kegan Paul, 1977).
12 Y. Samuel Brittan, *The Role and Limits of Government* (Minneapolis: University of Minnesota Press 1983).
13 Popper, *The Open Society*.
14 Ulrich Beck, *The Risk Society* (Los Angeles: Sage, 1992).
15 Climatric is a term of recent origin, meaning a major shift in the economic, political, and cultural environment.
16 Richard Hernnstein and Charles Murray, *The Bell Curve: Intelligence and Class Structure in American Life* (New York: Basic Books, 1994).

21

Class Racism

Étienne Balibar

Academic analyses of racism, though according chief importance to the study of racist theories, none the less argue that "sociological" racism is a popular phenomenon. Given this supposition, the development of racism within the working class (which, to committed socialists and communists, seems counter to the natural order of things) comes to be seen as the effect of a tendency allegedly inherent in the masses. Institutional racism finds itself projected into the very construction of that psycho-sociological category that is "the masses." We must therefore attempt to analyze the process of displacement which, moving from classes to masses, presents these latter both as the privileged *subjects* of racism and its favoured *objects*.

Can one say that a social class, by its situation and its ideology (not to mention its identity), is predisposed to racist attitudes and behavior? This question has mainly been debated in connection with the rise of Nazism, first speculatively and then later by taking various empirical indicators (Aycoberry, 1981). The result is quite paradoxical since there is hardly a social class on which suspicion has not fallen, though a marked predilection has been shown for the "petty bourgeoisie." But this is a notoriously ambiguous concept, which is more an expression of the aporias of a class analysis conceived as a dividing up of the population into mutually exclusive slices. As with every question of origin in which a political charge is concealed, it makes sense to turn the question around: not to look for the foundations of the racism which invades everyday life (or the movement which provides the vehicle for it) in the nature of the petty bourgeoisie, but to attempt to understand how the development of racism causes a "petty bourgeois" mass to emerge out of a diversity of material situations. For the misconceived question of the class bases of racism, we shall thus substitute a more crucial and complex question, which that former question is in part intended to mask: that of the relations between racism, as a supplement to nationalism, and the irreducibility of class conflict in society. We shall find it necessary to ask how the development of racism displaces class conflict or, rather, in what way class conflict is always already transformed by a social relation in which there is an inbuilt tendency to racism; and also, conversely, how the fact that the nationalist alternative to the class struggle specifically takes the form of racism may be considered as the index of the irreconcilable character of that struggle. This does not of course mean that it is not crucial to examine how, in a given conjuncture, the class conditions [*la condition de classe*] made up of the material conditions of existence and labor, (though also of ideological traditions and practical relationships to politics) determine the effects of racism in society: the frequency and forms of the "acting out" of racism, the discourse which expresses it and the membership of organized racist movements.

The traces of a constant overdetermination of racism by the class struggle are as universally detectable in its history as the nationalist determination, and everywhere they are connected with the core of meaning of its phantasies and practices. This suffices to demonstrate that we are dealing here with a determination that is much more concrete and decisive than the generalities dear to the sociologists of "modernity." It is wholly inadequate to see racism (or the nationalism-racism dyad) either as one of the paradoxical expressions of the individualism or egalitarianism which are supposed to characterize modern societies (following the old dichotomy of "closed," "hierarchical" societies and "open," "mobile" societies) or a defensive reaction against that individualism, seen as expressing nostalgia for a social order based on the existence of a "community" (Popper, 1966; Dumont, 1986). Individualism only exists in the concrete forms of market competition (including the competition between labor powers) in unstable equilibrium with association between individuals under the constraints of the class struggle. Egalitarianism only exists in the contradictory forms of political democracy (where that democracy exists), the "welfare state" (where that exists), the polarization of conditions of existence, cultural segregation and reformist or revolutionary, Utopias. It is these determinations, and not mere anthropological figures, which confer an "economic" dimension upon racism.

Nevertheless, the *heterogeneity* of the historical forms of the relationship between racism and the class struggle poses a problem. This ranges from the way in which anti-Semitism developed into a bogus "anti-capitalism," around the theme of "Jewish money," to the way in which racial stigma and class hatred are combined today in the category of immigration. Each of these configurations is irreducible (as are the corresponding conjunctures), which make it impossible to define any simple relationship of "expression" (or, equally, of substitution) between racism and class struggle.

In the manipulation of anti-Semitism as an anti-capitalist delusion, which chiefly occurred between 1870 and 1945 (which is, we should note, the key period of confrontation between the European bourgeois states and organized proletarian internationalism), we find not only the designation of a scapegoat as an object of proletarian revolt, the exploitation of divisions within the proletariat and the projective representation of the ills of an abstract social system through the imaginary personification of those who control it (even though this mechanism is essential to the functioning of racism).[1] We also find the "fusion" of the two historical narratives which are capable of acting as metaphors for each other: on the one hand, the narrative of the formation of nations at the expense of the lost unity of "Christian Europe" and, on the other, that of the conflict between national independence and the internationalization of capitalist economic relations, which brought with it the attendant threat of an internationalization of the class struggle. This is why the Jew, as an internally excluded element common to all nations but also, negatively, by virtue of the theological hatred to which he is subject, as witness to the love that is supposed to unite the "Christian peoples," may, in the imaginary, be identified with the "cosmopolitanism of capital" which threatens the national independence of every country while at the same time re-activating the trace of the lost unity.[2]

The figure is quite different when anti-immigrant racism achieves a maximum of identification between class situation and ethnic origin (the real bases for which have always existed in the inter-regional, international or intercontinental mobility of the working class; this has at times been a mass phenomenon, at times residual, but it has never been eliminated and is one of the specifically proletarian characteristics of its condition). Racism combines this identification with a deliberate confusion of antagonistic social functions: thus the themes of the "invasion" of French society by North Africans or of immigration being responsible for unemployment are connected with that of the money of the oil sheikhs who are buying up "our" businesses, "our" housing stock or "our" seaside resorts. And this partly explains why the Algerians, Tunisians or Moroccans have to be referred to generically as "Arab" (not to mention the fact that this signifier, which functions as a veritable "switch word," also connects together these themes and those of terrorism, Islam and so on). Other configurations should not, however, be forgotten, including those which are the product of an inversion of terms: for example, the theme of the "proletarian nation," which was perhaps invented in the 1920s by Japanese nationalism (Anderson, 1983: 92–3) and was destined to play a crucial role in the crystallization of Nazism, which cannot be left out of consideration when one looks at the ways in which it has recently reappeared.

The complexity of these configurations also explains why it is impossible to hold purely and simply to the idea of racism *being used* against "class consciousness" (as though this latter would necessarily emerge naturally from the class condition, *unless* it were blocked, misappropriated or de-natured by racism), whereas we accept as an indispensable working hypothesis that "class" and "race" constitute the two antinomic poles of a permanent dialectic, which is at the heart of modern representations of history. Moreover, we suspect that the instrumentalist, conspiracy-theory visions of racism within the labor movement or among its theorists (we know what high price was to be paid for these: it is tremendously to the credit of Wilhelm Reich that he was one of the first to foresee this), along with the mechanistic visions which see in racism the "reflection" of a particular class condition, have also largely the function of denying the presence of nationalism in the working class and its organizations or, in other words, denying the internal conflict between nationalism and class ideology on which the mass struggle against racism (as well as the revolutionary struggle against capitalism) depends. It is the evolution of this internal conflict I should like to illustrate by discussing here some historical aspects of "class racism."

Several historians of racism (e.g., Poliakov, 1974; Duchet and Rebérioux,

1969; Guillaumin, 1972; Williams, 1944 on modern slavery) have laid emphasis upon the fact that the modern notion of race, in so far as it is invested in a discourse of contempt and discrimination and serves to split humanity up into a "super-humanity" and a "sub-humanity," did not initially have a national (or ethnic), but a class signification or rather (since the point is to represent the inequality of social classes as inequalities of nature) a caste signification. From this point of view, it has a twofold origin: first, in the aristocratic representation of the hereditary nobility as a superior "race" (that is, in fact, the mythic narrative by which an aristocracy, whose domination is already coming under threat, assures itself of the legitimacy of its political privileges and idealizes the dubious continuity of its genealogy); and second, in the slave owners' representation of those populations subject to the slave trade as inferior "races," ever predestined for servitude and incapable of producing an autonomous civilization. Hence the discourse of blood, skin color and cross-breeding. It is only retrospectively that the notion of race was "ethnicized," so that it could be integrated into the nationalist complex, the jumping-off point for its successive subsequent metamorphoses. Thus it is clear that, from the very outset, racist representations of history stand in relation to the class struggle. But this fact only takes on its full significance if we examine the way in which the notion of race has evolved, and the impact of nationalism upon it from the earliest figures of "class racism" onwards – in other words, if we examine its political determination.

The aristocracy did not initially conceive and present itself in terms of the category of "race": this is a discourse which developed at a late stage,[3] the function of which is clearly defensive (as can be seen from the example of France with the myth of "blue blood" and the "Frankish" or "Germanic" origin of the hereditary nobility), and which developed when the absolute monarchy centralized the state at the expense of the feudal lords and began to "create" within its bosom a new administrative and financial aristocracy which was bourgeois in origin, thus marking a decisive step in the formation of the nation-state. Even more interesting is the case of Spain in the Classical Age, as analyzed by Poliakov: the persecution of the Jews after the *Reconquista,* one of the indispensable mechanisms in the establishment of Catholicism as state religion, is also the trace of the "multinational" culture against which Hispanization (or rather Castilianization) was carried out. It is therefore intimately linked to the formation of this prototype of European nationalism. Yet it took on an even more ambivalent meaning when it gave rise to the "statutes of the purity of the blood" *(limpieza de sangre)* which the whole discourse of European and American racism was to inherit: a product of the disavowal of the original interbreeding with the Moors and the Jews, the hereditary definition of the *raza* (and the corresponding procedures for establishing who could be accorded a certificate of purity) serves in effect both to isolate an internal aristocracy and to confer upon the whole of the "Spanish people" a fictive nobility, to make it a "people of masters" at the point when, by terror, genocide, slavery and enforced Christianization, it was conquering and dominating the largest of the colonial empires. In this exemplary line of development, class racism was already transformed into nationalist racism, though it did not, in the process, disappear (Poliakov, 1974, 2: 222–32).

What is, however, much more decisive for the matter in hand is the overturning of values we see occurring from the first half of the nineteenth century onwards. Aristocratic racism (the prototype of what analysts today call "self-referential racism," which begins by elevating the group which controls the discourse to the status of a "race" – hence the importance of its imperialist legacy in the colonial context: however lowly their origins and no matter how vulgar their interests or their manners, the British in India and the French in Africa would all see themselves as members of a modern nobility) is already indirectly related to the primitive accumulation of capital, if only by its function in the colonizing nations. The industrial revolution, at the same time as it creates specifically capitalist relations of production, gives rise to the *new racism* of the bourgeois era (historically speaking, the first "neoracism"): the one which has as its target the *proletariat* in its dual status as exploited population (one might even say superexploited, before the beginnings of the social state) and politically threatening population.

Louis Chevalier (1973) has described the relevant network of significations in detail. It is at this point, with regard to the "race of labourers" that the notion of race becomes detached from its historico-theological connotations to enter the field of equivalences between sociology, psychology, imaginary biology and the pathology of the "social body." The reader will recognize here the obsessive themes of police/detective, medical and philanthropic literature, and hence of literature in general (of which it is one of the fundamental dramatic mechanisms and one of the political keys of social "realism"). For the first time those aspects typical of every procedure of racialization of a social group right down to our own day are condensed in a single discourse: material and spiritual poverty, criminality, congenital vice (alcoholism, drugs), physical and moral defects, dirtiness, sexual promiscuity and the specific diseases which threaten humanity with "degeneracy." And there is a characteristic oscillation in the presentation of these themes: either the workers themselves constitute a degenerate race or it is their presence and contact with them or indeed their condition itself which constitute a crucible of degeneracy for the "race" of citizens and nationals. Through these themes, there forms the phantasmatic equation of "labouring classes" with "dangerous classes," the fusion of a socioeconomic category with an anthropological and moral category, which will serve to underpin all the variants of sociobiological (and also psychiatric) determinism, by taking psuedoscientific credentials from the Darwinian theory of evolution, comparative anatomy and crowd psychology, but particularly by becoming invested in a tightly knit network of institutions of social surveillance and control (Netchine, 1978; Murard and Zylberman, 1976).

Now this class racism is indissociable from fundamental historical processes which have developed unequally right down to the present day. I can only mention these briefly here. First, class racism is connected with a political problem that is crucial for the constitution of the nation-state. The "bourgeois revolutions" – and in particular the French Revolution, by its radical juridical egalitarianism – had raised the question of the political rights of the masses in an irreversible manner. This was to be the object of one and a half centuries of social struggles. The idea of a *difference in nature* between individuals had become juridically and morally contradictory, if not inconceivable. It was, however, politically indispensable, so long as the "dangerous classes" (who posed a threat to the established social order, property and the power of the "elites") had to be excluded by force and by legal means from political "competence" and confined to the margins of the polity – as long, that is, as it was important to *deny them citizenship* by showing, and by being oneself persuaded, that they constitutionally "lacked" the qualities of fully fledged or normal humanity. Two anthropologies clashed here: that of equality of birth and that of a hereditary inequality which made it possible to re-naturalize social antagonisms.

Now, this operation was overdetermined from the start by national ideology. Disraeli, who showed himself, elsewhere, to be a surprising imperialist theorist of the "superiority of the Jews" over the Anglo-Saxon "superior race" itself (Arendt, 1986: 68; Polanyi, 1957: 290ff.), admirably summed this up when he explained that the problem of contemporary states was the tendency for a single social formation to split into "two nations." In so doing, he indicated the path which might be taken by the dominant classes when confronted with the progressive organization of the class struggle: first divide the mass of the "poor" (in particular by according the qualities of national authenticity, sound health, morality and racial integrity, which were precisely the opposite of the industrial pathology, to the peasants and the "traditional" artisans); then progressively displace the markers of dangerousness and heredity from the "laboring classes" as a whole on to foreigners, and in particular immigrants and colonial subjects, at the same time as the introduction of universal suffrage is moving the boundary line between "citizens" and "subjects" to the frontiers of nationality. In this process, however, there was always a characteristic lag between what was supposed to happen and the actual situation (even in countries like France, where the national population was not institutionally segregated and was subject to no original apartheid, except if one extends one's purview to take in the whole of the imperial territory): class racism against the popular classes continued to exist (and, at the same time, these classes remained particularly susceptible to racial stigmatization, and remained extremely ambivalent in their attitude towards racism). Which brings us to another permanent aspect of class racism.

I am referring to what must properly be called the *institutional racialization of manual labor*. It would be easy to find distant origins for this, origins as old as class society itself. In this regard, there is no significant difference between the way contempt for work and the manual worker was expressed among the philosophical elites of slave-owning Greece and the way a man like Taylor could, in 1909, describe the natural predisposition of certain individuals for the exhausting, dirty, repetitive tasks which required physical strength, but no intelligence or initiative. The "man of the type of the ox" of the *Principles of Scientific Management:* paradoxically, an inveterate propensity for "systematic soldiering" is also attributed to this same man: this is why he needs a "man to stand over him" before he can work in conformity with his nature (Linhart, 1976; Coriat, 1979; Balibar, 1983). However, the industrial revolution and capitalist wage labor here effect a displacement. What is now the object of contempt – and in turn fuels fears – is no longer manual labor pure and simple (we shall, by contrast, see this theoretically idealized – in the context of paternalistic, archaizing ideologies – in the form of "craft work"), but *mechanized* physical work, which has become "the appendage of the machine" and therefore subject to a violence that is both physical and symbolic without immediate precedent (which we know, moreover, does not disappear with the new phases of the industrial revolution, but is rather perpetuated both in "modernized" and "intellectualized" forms – as well as in "archaic" forms in a great many sectors of production).

This process modifies the status of the human body (the human status of the body): it creates *body-men,* men whose body is a machine-body, that is fragmented and dominated, and used to perform one isolable function or gesture, being both destroyed in its integrity *and* fetishized, atrophied *and* hypertrophied in its "useful" organs. Like all violence, this is inseparable from a resistance and also from a sense of guilt. The quantity of "normal" work can only be recognized and extracted from the worker's body retrospectively, once its limits have been fixed by struggle: the rule is overexploitation, the tendential destruction of the organism (which will be metaphorized as "degeneracy") and, at the very least, excess in the repression of the intellectual functions involved in work. This is an unbearable process for the worker, but one which is no more "acceptable," without ideological and phantasmatic elaboration, for the worker's masters: the fact that there are body-men means that there are *men without bodies.* That the body-men are men with fragmented and mutilated bodies (if only by their "separation" from intelligence) means that the individuals of each of these types have to be equipped with a *superbody,* and that sport and ostentatious virility have to be developed, if the threat hanging over the human race is to be fended off.[4]

Only this historical situation, these specific social relations make it possible fully to understand the process of aestheticization (and therefore of sexualization, in fetishist mode) of the body which characterizes all the variants of modern racism, by giving rise either to the stigmatization of the "physical marks" of racial inferiority or to the idealization of the "human type" of the superior race. They cast light upon the true meaning of the recourse to biology in the history of racist theories, which has nothing whatsoever to do with the influence of scientific discoveries, but is, rather, a metaphor for – and an idealization of – the somatic phantasm. Academic biology, and many other theoretical discourses, can fulfill this function, provided they are articulated to the visibility of the body, its ways of being and behaving, its limbs and its emblematic organs. We should here, in accordance with the hypotheses formulated elsewhere regarding neo-racism and its link with the recent ways in which intellectual labor has been broken down into isolated operations, extend the investigation by describing the "somatization" of intellectual capacities, and hence their racialization, a process visible everywhere – from the instrumentalization of IQ to the aestheticization of the executive as decision maker, intellectual and athlete.

But there is yet another determining aspect in the constitution of class racism. The working class is a population that is both heterogeneous and fluctuating, its "boundaries" being by definition imprecise, since they depend on ceaseless transformations of the labor process and movements of capital. Unlike aristocratic castes, or even the leading fractions of the bourgeoisie, it is not a social caste. What class racism (and, *a fortiori*, nationalist class racism, as in the case of immigrants) tends to produce is, however, the equivalent of a caste closure at least for one part of the working class. More precisely, it is maximum possible closure where social mobility is concerned, combined with maximum possible openness as regards the flows of proletarianization.

Let us put things another way. The logic of capitalist accumulation involves *two* contradictory aspects here: on the one hand, mobilizing or permanently destabilizing the conditions of life and work, in such a way as to ensure competition on the labor market, draw new labor power continually from the "industrial reserve army" and maintain a relative over-population; on the other hand, stabilizing collectivities of workers over long periods (over several generations), to "educate" them for work and "bond them to companies (and also to bring into play the mechanism of correspondence between a "paternalist" political hegemony and a worker "familialism"). On the one hand, class condition, which relates purely to the wage relation, has nothing to do with antecedents or descendants; ultimately, even the notion of "class belonging" is devoid of any practical meaning; all that counts is class situation, *hic et nunc*. On the other hand, at least a section of the workers have to be the sons of workers, a *social heredity* has to be created.[5] But with this, in practice, the capacities for resistance and organization also increase.

It was in response to these contradictory demands that the demographic and immigration policies and policies of urban segregation, which were set in place both by employers and the state from the middle of the nineteenth century onwards – policies which D. Bertaux (1977) has termed "anthroponomic" practices – were born. These have two sides to them: a paternalistic aspect (itself closely connected to nationalist propaganda) and a disciplinary aspect, an aspect of "social warfare" against the savage masses and an aspect of "civilizing" (in all senses of the term) these same masses. This dual nature we can still see perfectly illustrated today in the combined social and police approach to the "suburbs" and "ghettos." It is not by chance that the current racist complex grafts itself on to the "population problem" (with its series of connotations: birth rate, depopulation and over-population, "interbreeding," urbanization, social housing, public health, unemployment) and focuses preferentially on the question of the *second generation* of what are here improperly called "immigrants" with the object of finding out whether they will carry on as the previous generation (the "immigrant workers" properly so-called) – the danger being that they will develop a much greater degree of social combativeness, combining class demands with cultural demands; or whether they will add to the number of "declassed" individuals, occupying an unstable position between subproletarianization and "exit" from the working class. This is the main issue for class racism, both for the dominant class and for the popular classes themselves: to mark with generic signs populations which are collectively destined for capitalist exploitation – or which have to be held in reserve for it – at the very moment when the economic process is tearing them away from the direct control of the system (or, quite simply, by mass unemployment, is rendering the previous controls inoperative). The problem is to keep "in their place," from generation to generation, those who have no fixed place; and for this, it is necessary that they have a genealogy. And also to unify in the imaginary the contradictory imperatives of nomadism and social heredity, the domestication of generations and the disqualification of resistances.

If these remarks are well founded, then they may throw some light on what are themselves the contradictory aspects of what I shall not hesitate to call the "self-racialization" of the working class. There is here a whole spectrum of social experiences and ideological forms we might mention: from the organization of collectivities of workers around symbols of ethnic or national origin to the way in which a certain workerism, centred on criteria of class origins (and, consequently, on the institution of the working-class family, on the bond which only the family establishes between the "individual" and "his class") and the over-valorization of work (and, consequently, the virility which it alone confers), reproduces, within the ambit of "class consciousness," some part of the set of representations of the "race of workers" (Noiriel, 1985; Duroux, 1982; Fremontier, 1980).

Admittedly, the radical forms of workerism, at least in France, were produced more by intellectuals and political apparatuses aiming to "represent" the working class (from Proudhon down to the Communist Party) than by the workers themselves. The fact remains that they correspond to a tendency on the part of the working class to form itself into a closed "body," to preserve gains that have been made and traditions of struggle and to turn back against bourgeois society the signifiers of class racism. It is from this reactive origin that the ambivalence characterizing workerism derives: the desire to escape from the condition of exploitation and the rejection of the contempt to which it is subject. Absolutely nowhere is this ambivalence more evident than in its relation to nationalism and to xenophobia. To the extent that in practice they reject official nationalism (when they do reject it), the workers produce in outline a political alternative to the perversion of class struggles. To the extent, however, that they project on to foreigners their fears and resentment, despair and defiance, it is not only that they are *fighting competition*; in addition, and much more profoundly, they are trying to escape their own exploitation. It is a hatred of *themselves*, as proletarians – in so far as they are in danger of being drawn back into the mill of proletarianization – that they are showing.

To sum up, just as there is a constant relation of reciprocal determination between nationalism and racism, there is a relation of reciprocal determination between "class racism" and "ethnic racism" and *these two determinations are not independent*. Each produces its effects, to some extent, in the field of the other and under constraints imposed by the other. Have we, in retracing this overdetermination in its broad outline (and in trying to show how it illuminates the concrete manifestations of racism and the constitution of its theoretical disclosure), answered the questions we posed at the beginning of this chapter? It would be more accurate to say that we have reformulated them. What has elsewhere been called the excess which, by comparison with nationalism, is constitutive of racism turns out at the same time to be a shortfall as far as the class struggle is concerned. But, though that excess is linked to the fact that nationalism is formed in opposition to the class struggle (even though it utilizes its dynamic), and that shortfall is linked to the fact that the class struggle finds itself repressed by nationalism, *the two do not compensate one another*; their effects tend, rather, to be combined. The important thing is not to decide whether nationalism is first and foremost a means of imagining and pursuing the unity of state and society, which then runs up against the contradictions of the class struggle, or whether it is primarily a reaction to the obstacles which the class struggle puts in the way of national unity. By contrast, it is crucially important to note that, in the historical field where *both* an unbridgeable gap between state and nation and endlessly re-emerging class antagonisms are to be found, national-ism necessarily takes the form of racism, at times in competition with other forms (linguistic nationalism, for example) and at times in combination with them, and that it thus becomes engaged in a perpetual headlong flight forward. Even when racism remains latent, or present only in a minority of individual consciousnesses, it is already that internal excess of nationalism which betrays, in both senses of the word, its articulation to the class struggle. Hence the ever recurring paradox of nationalism: the regressive imagining of a nation-state where the individuals would by their nature be "at home," because they would be "among their own" (their own kind), and the rendering of that state uninhabitable; the endeavor to produce a unified community in the face of "external" enemies and the endless rediscovery that the enemy is "within," identifiable by signs which are merely the phantasmatic elaboration of *its* divisions. Such a society is in a real sense a politi-cally alienated society. But are not all contemporary societies, to some degree, grappling with their own political alienation?

Acknowledgment

Editions La Devouverte for material from "Class Racism" in Étienne Balibar and Immanuel Wallerstein, *Race, nation, class, les identities ambigues*. La Decouverte 1988.

Notes

1 The personification of capital, a social relation, begins with the very figure of the *capi-talist*. But this is never sufficient in itself for arousing an emotional reaction. This is

why, following the logic of "excess," other real-imaginary traits accumulate: life-style, lineage (the "200 families"), foreign origins, secret strategies, racial plots (the Jewish plan for "world domination"), etc. The fact that, specifically in the case of the Jews, this personification is worked up in combination with a process of fetishization of money is clearly not accidental.

2 Matters are further complicated by the fact that the lost unity of "Christian" Europe, a mythic figuration of the "origins of its civilization," is thus represented in the register of race at the point when that same Europe is embarking upon its mission of "civilizing the world," i.e. submitting the world to its domination, by way of fierce competition between nations.

3 And one which substitutes itself, in the French case, for the "ideology of the three orders," a basically theological and juridical ideology, which is, by contrast, expressive of the organic place occupied by the nobility in the building of the state ("feudalism" properly so-called).

4 Clearly, the "bestiality" of the slave has been a continual problem, from Aristotle and his contemporaries down to the modern slave trade (the hypersexualization to which it is subject is a sufficient indication of this); but the industrial revolution brought about a new paradox: the "bestial" body of the worker is decreasingly *animal* and increasingly technicized and therefore humanized. It is the panic fear of a *super-humanization* of man (in his body and his intelligence which is "objectivized" by cognitive sciences and the corresponding techniques of selection and training), rather than his *sub-humanization* – or, in any case, the reversibility of these two – which discharges itself in phantasies of animality and these are projected for preference on to the worker whose status as an "outsider" [*etranger*] confers upon him at the same time the attributes of an "other male," a "rival."

5 Not only in the sense of individual filiation, but in the sense of a "population" tending towards the practice of endogamy; not only in the sense of a transmission of skills (mediated by schooling, apprenticeship and industrial discipline) but in the sense of a "collective ethic," constructed in institutions and through subjective identification.

References

Anderson, B. (1983), *Imagined Communities,* Verso, London.

Arendt, H. (1986), *The Origins of Totalitarianism*, Part One, "Antisemitism," André Deutsch, London.

Aycoberry P. (1981), *The Nazi Question; An Essay on the Interpretation of National Socialism,* translated by R. Hurley, Routledge and Kegan Paul, London.

Balibar, É. (1983), "Sur le concept de la division du travail manuel et intellectuel," in J. Belkhir et al. (ed.), *L'intellectuel, l'intelligentsia et les manuels*, Anthropos, Paris.

Bertaux, D. (1977), *Destins Personnels et Structure de Class*, PUF, Paris.

Chevalier, L. (1973), *Labouring Classes and Dangerous Classes in Paris During the First Half of the Nineteenth Century,* translated by F. Jellinek, Routledge and Kegan Paul, London.

Coriat, B. (1979), *L'Atelier et le Chronomètre*, Christian Bourgeois, Paris.

Duchet, M. and Rebérioux, M. (1969), "Prehistoire et histoire du racisme," in P. de Commarond and C. Duchet (eds), *Racism et Societe*, Maspero, Paris.

Dumont, L. (1986), *Essays on Individualism: Modern Ideology in Anthropological Perspective*, University of Chicago Press, Chicago.

Duroux, F. (1982), La Famille des ouvriers: Mythe ou politique?, unpublished thesis, University of Paris VII.

Fremontier, J. (1980), *La Vie en bleu: Voyage en culture ouvriere*, Fayard, Paris.

Guillaumin, C. (1972), *L'Idéologie Raciste: Genese et langage actuel*, Mouton, Paris and The Hague.

Linhart, R. (1976), *Lenine, les paysans, Taylor*, Seuil, Paris.

Murard, L. and Zylberman (1976), *Le Petit Travailleur Infatigable ou le Proletaire Regenere: Villes-usines, habitat et imtimites au XIXe siècle,* Editions Recherches, Fonteny-sous-Bois.

Netchine, G. (1978), "L'individuel et le collectif dans les representations psychologiques de la diversité des êtres humains au XIX siècle," in L. Poliakov (ed.), *Ni juif ni grec: Entretiens sur le racisme* (11), Mouton, Paris-The Hague.

Noiriel, C. (1985), *Longwy: Immigres et proletaires 1880–1890*, PUF, Paris.

Polanyi, K. (1957), "Appendix II: Disraeli's 'Two Nations' and the Problem of colored races," in *The Great Transformation*, Beacon Press, Boston, pp. 290–4.

Poliakov, L. (1974), *The History of Anti-Semitism,* translated by R. Howard, 4 vols, Routledge and Kegan Paul, London.

Popper, K. (1966), *The Open Society and its Enemies*, 5th edn, 2 vols, Routledge and Kegan Paul, London.

Taylor, F. Winslow ([1911] 1993), *Principles of Scientific Management,* Routledge, London.

Williams, E. (1944), *Capitalism and Slavery*, University of North Carolina Press, Chapel Hill, NC.

Part VII

Globalized Futures and Racialized Identities

22

Multiculturalism and Flexibility: Some New Directions in Global Capitalism

Richard P. Appelbaum

Marx is dead, buried, all but forgotten. The headlong global rush to embrace capitalism, with (as Marx might have said) all its warts and pimples, has left only Cuba and North Korea as the standard-bearers of state-sponsored versions of socialism. Perhaps, if we stretch the definition of socialism a bit, we might include Myanmar. Vietnam? No way. With the Clinton administration ready to finally inter the last traces of MIA remains, Vietnam is poised to become a vast factory of low-wage, highly-skilled labor for American firms. China has already moved well down the capitalist road, and its southern Guangdong province is the fastest-growing economic region in the world – perhaps in world history. In China, in fact, both local and foreign capitalists have the best (or worst) of both worlds: the heavily subsidized and virtually captive workforce characteristic of what used to be called socialism, combined with a cowboy capitalist labor regime based on piecework, zero job security, and prohibitions against anti-management organization.

But wait! Is Marx really to be relegated to the scrap heap of modernist history, displaced by a decentered postmodern global economy in which the seductions of capitalism and the global assembly line have rendered class struggle all but moot? Have science, technology, and information replaced labor-intensive factory production as the basis of global wealth? Are we truly entering a post-industrial world in which the labor theory of value has been superseded, with ordinary workers increasingly replaced by what US labor secretary Robert Reich calls "symbolic analysts," people who work with their heads rather than their hands?

I think the news of Marx's death is premature. I say this not only as a realist who suspects that the Russian people may be having second thoughts about the virtues of unbridled capitalism, but also as a scholar who remains convinced that Marxist theory continues to have relevance for understanding the nature and limits of global capitalism. Moreover, these observations have implications for the future of multiculturalism; for as capitalism reasserts itself on a global scale, race, ethnicity, and gender are occupying a central role in the restructuring of capitalist relations.

The following theoretical observations grow out of a long-term study of changes in global capitalism. Alongside the explosion of low-wage factory jobs in what were once peripheral countries has come the reperipheralization of the core – the coming home of sweatshops to take advantage of the home market and cheap immigrant labor. Consider the fact that the only manufacturing industry in the United States that experienced a growth in employment in 1991 was the apparel industry, one that depends increasingly on a subminimum wage workforce from Mexico, Central America, and Southeast Asia. What does it mean that Los Angeles alone employs some 120,000 workers in five thousand sweatshops that are for the most part owned by ethnic minorities?[1]

Global capitalism has meant the feminization of labor worldwide, and the ethnicizing of labor on the home front. Class differences are overlaid with differences based on race and ethnicity in a highly volatile multiculturalism predicated on exploitation rather than mutual understanding. This essay is an attempt to reinsert a bit of forgotten Marxist materialism into the discourse of multiculturalism. It is organized into three theoretical moments, divided by two historical interludes, and followed by some reflections on capitalism and multi-culturalism in both Los Angeles and the world capitalist economy.

Theory 1: Marx's Theory of Industrial Capitalism

In volume 1 of *Capital*, Marx elaborates on his theory of capitalist production.[2] Drawing on the labor theory of value, Marx distinguishes between constant capital, variable capital, and surplus value as constitutive of the value of individual commodities as well as commodities in the aggregate (the wealth of nations). To briefly summarize his distinction, constant capital represents sunk investment in machinery and equipment, a fruit of past or congealed labor that comprises the principal means of producing wealth in capitalist society. Marx terms this form of capital "constant" because its value is given once in use; it can create no additional value on its own. Constant capital represents a fixed cost that must be paid off whether or not it is actually productively employed. To introduce a distinction that will become of central importance in the ensuing discussion, capital costs are essentially inflexible, once machines are bought they must be paid for whether they are running twenty-four hours a day or idled by labor strife or a sluggish economy.

Variable capital represents the cost of living labor, as indicated by the wage bill. In Marx's view, this is a form of "capital" because, under the capitalist mode of production, workers are equivalent to machines, objects to be used up in production in the most efficient ways possible. By this Marx means that workers are treated as appendages to the machines they operate, their labor power to be scientifically reorganized and managed until all conscious and self-controlling aspects have been rationalized away. Marx regards this quasi-human form of capital as "variable" because unlike constant capital, its value can vary according to the degree of exploitation: variable capital is capable of creating new value, in the form of variable amounts of surplus value, which are then appropriated by the capitalist. Furthermore, it is useful to see variable capital as varying in yet another way, which Marx elaborates in his analysis of the dynamics of capitalist production: workers, unlike machines, can be hired and fired to suit the momentary needs of production. Living labor can be broken down into nearly infinitesimal increments, enhancing the capitalist's flexibility in responding to changing market conditions. Workers can be hired or fired; they can be paid by the piece or the hour, according to the needs of the moment.

Surplus value is, of course, the difference between the value produced and the value of the capital (both constant and variable) required to produce it. Drawing on the labor theory of value, Marx argues that since only productive labor can make machinery, provide the raw materials required to quench its hunger, and then set it in motion to produce commodities, surplus value represents the unpaid labor extracted by the capitalist. Surplus value results from inequitable social relationships, which permit one class of people to exploit the labor of another. Among other things, it is the source of the capitalist's profit, which is what keeps the capitalist in business. When surplus value is threatened, by pressures from either rising capital costs or declining sales, the capitalist goes out of business. The story of the development of capitalism is the story of the struggle between labor and capital over the allocation of these costs of production.

Labor, then, provides capitalists with infinite flexibility, although of course labor's part in class struggle is to seek to reduce that flexibility by speaking with one voice, thereby taking on the "lumpy" character of constant capital. If all workers are treated as one, they are then equivalent to a single machine, a constant cost that must be incurred regardless of the needs of the capitalist. Marx predicts that capitalists will resist these efforts on the part of variable capital to simulate the power of constant capital through technological innovations that render such simulations moot: replacing them with actual machines. In Marx's terms, over time constant capital replaces variable capital, leading to a long-term rise in the ratio between the two (what Marx termed capital's "organic composition.") Marx recognized that built-in structural pressures for automation would result from both price competition between capitalists, which dictates a strategy of reducing unit costs through raising productivity, and class struggle, which dictates a parallel need to control living labor by substituting more tractable machinery.

Although Marx couldn't fully anticipate the end point of this process, it is clear that he foresaw the possibility of the fully robotic factory with continuously running machinery operated by a relative handful of highly trained engineers and technicians. The mixed consequences of this long-term tendency toward automation were also anticipated by Marx. On the one hand, automation would reduce costs and increase the amount of surplus that could be extracted from a diminishing workforce, while disciplining the remaining workers by threatening to render them superfluous. On the other hand, automation would lead to an increasing concentration of capital as enterprises became ever larger, fewer, and more capital-intensive. While this concentration would increase the power of gigantic monopolies, it would also increase their vulnerability, since vast amounts of capital would be tied up in machinery that must be kept running constantly in order to turn a profit. Labor actions could prove increasingly strategic in this regard, since a well-placed strike could send shock waves through the entire economy. Furthermore, the growing army of workers displaced by machines are a poor market for the goods those machines were churning out, leading to chronic and growing problems of overproduction and underconsumption. Devastating labor stoppages and economic stagnation were two of the prices capital would eventually pay for automation.

Interlude 1: The transition to postindustrial capitalism

In the past twenty years, since Intel's 1971 invention of the microchip, capitalism has gone truly global. Communication and information technology has made it possible to coordinate most activities with a virtual disregard for time and space. The global assembly line has emerged, on which no country can leave its exclusive stamp. From cars to clothing to electronics, the hands that produce our goods and services reveal the exploitative side of multiculturalism: they are hands of color, of women, of impoverished Third World peoples driven by hardship and hunger to labor in the global factory.

The theories of the transition to a postindustrial world order have recognized the emerging global nature of capitalism. These theories, which have emerged in response to the rapidly shifting conditions of global production, have successively emphasized dependency,[3] the possibility of dependent development,[4] the new international division of labor,[5] and the world capitalist system.[6] Common to all of these theories is the recognition that capital is increasingly footloose on a global scale that in their search for profits, transnational businesses have emerged that have a truly global reach.

Yet in different ways all of these theories share a number of assumptions that reflect the paradigm of industrial society out of which they grow, rather than a new framework based on a postindustrial world order. First, in varying degrees they all assume that the nation-state remains sovereign. One consequence of this assumption, for example, is an analysis of the class system reproduced at the global level, resulting in a world system of upper(core), lower- (peripheral), and middle-class (semiperipheral) nations, with surplus flowing up and exploitation flowing down. Second, they all assume that physical labor remains the principal source of the wealth of nations. What drives the global economy, in the view of most of these theorists, is the search for cheap labor to run the global assembly line.

Theory 2: The Theory of Postindustrial Capitalism: Karl Marx Meets Robert Reich

In the *Grundrisse*, his 1857–58 notebooks that were to become the foundation of volume 1 of *Capital*, Marx advanced the notion that in the final stages of capitalism, science and knowledge would replace labor as the source of value in production:

> The tendency of capital is thus to give a scientific character to production, reducing direct labor to a simple element in this process. . . . The production process has ceased to be a labor process in the sense that labor is no longer the unity dominating and transcending it. Direct labor and its quantity cease to be the determining element in production and thus in the creation of use value. It is reduced quantitatively to a smaller proportion, just as qualitatively it is reduced to an indispensable but subordinate role as compared with scientific labor in general. . . . Labor does not seem anymore to be an essential part of the process of production. The human factor is reduced to watching and supervising the production process. Invention then becomes a branch of business.[7]

Thus, in what must rate as one of the most prescient passages on the future of industrial society written at the time of its birth, Marx anticipates the post-industrial theorists. From Secretary of Labor Robert Reich to Harvard business economist Michael Porter,[8] from the post-Fordist Marxist geographers to Daniel Bell,[9] all seem agreed: we are entering a period in which information itself, rather than the physical production of goods, holds the key to wealth.

Using the terminology, if not the assumptions of the original labor theory of value, economists, sociologists, and social geographers from left to right agree that "value-added" results come increasingly from the application of knowledge, and not from the hands that make the goods. Reich, for example, in his postmodern rereading of Adam Smith, argues that the wealth of the twenty-first-century nation will be found in the work of its citizens, with work redefined in purely symbolic terms. This is the labor theory of value turned on its head: intellectual rather than physical labor holds the key to success in the global economy. Invention, design, marketing, retailing, networking, and other forms of "symbolic analysis" are the true source of value in the postindustrial world.

Needless to say, Marx and Reich drew opposite conclusions from these anticipated futures. In Marx's view in the *Grundrisse*, to the extent that the logic of capitalist development rendered labor superfluous, capitalism's ideological nature would be revealed for all to see: why should workers continue to slave away at meaningless, poorly paid, and increasingly unnecessary jobs, enriching a small group of capitalists and their professional-managerial entourage?[10] If machines could do the work, so be it; all that remained was to shatter the system of oppressive social relations that kept one class perpetually in thrall to another.

Reich, on the other hand, envisions a postindustrial Utopia populated entirely by capitalists and members of the professional-managerial class, symbolic analysts all. In Reich's "can-do" world of people who use their minds to make things happen, there are no workers to be found – at least not in those nations that invest sufficiently in their most valuable resource, their people. Woe be unto the nation that fails to so invest, however, since that nation's semiskilled and unskilled workers are competing with an infinitely substitutable global workforce, one that will drag its wages down to a global level. Reich never makes it entirely clear whether or not he believes that the United States, to take one national example, could in fact develop a workforce of one hundred million or so symbolic analysts who would be effectively insulated from the potential loss of their jobs through global competition. But it does seem clear that he is not overly concerned about the hands that will eventually wind up doing the detail labor, particularly if they are found half a world away.

Let us take one set of such hands – an actual case study of a woman who labors in one of Nike's six Korean-run Indonesian shoe factories. Sadisah (the pseudonym provided by *Harper's* Magazine, which first told the tale) earns about fourteen cents an hour, raking in just under forty dollars each month by laboring sixty-plus-hour workweeks manufacturing athletic shoes.[11] The shoes she makes sell for about eighty dollars a pair, of which her value-added contribution is a full eleven cents. There are various types of arithmetic that can be performed on these data. For example, it is easy to compute that it would take Sadisah two months to earn enough money to buy back the shoes she makes, although it is unclear where she would find the time for crosstraining at the local athletic club. An even more interesting calculation is that Sadisah would only have to work an estimated 44,492 years to earn the $20 million multiyear endorsement fee Michael Jordan commanded before his short-lived retirement from professional basketball. It should be pointed out in this regard that Nike's 1991 profits reached $287 million on $3 billion in sales, a figure that is of course calculated after Michael Jordan and all of Nike's designers, advertising agencies, marketing services, managers, and owners have taken their cut.

This is a handsome rate of return, and reveals the "rational kernel" underlying Reich's reasoning: Michael Jordon's value-added alone is estimated at 10 percent of Nike's sales, roughly equivalent to the company's total annual profit. From a strictly capitalist viewpoint, his $20 million fee was a bargain, perhaps even more so than Sadisah's eleven cents. After all, there is only one Michael Jordan, and there are probably a billion or so Sadisahs around the globe, all hungry and available for work. Although it is unclear whether or not Michael Jordan truly qualifies as a symbolic analyst, there can be no question that he is a potent symbol to millions of consumers. Nike's highly paid in-house ad agency, which constructed one of the most effective ad campaigns in history around this particular symbol, performs the very sort of symbolic analysis that Reich believes will fuel the global economy of the future.

Interlude 2: Globalizing and localizing forces in global capitalism

As capitalism embarks on its information-driven postindustrial phase, its contours are shaped by forces that simultaneously result in the spatial disaggregation of production on a global scale as well as the localization of production in tightly integrated economic regions. The former, centrifugal forces are driven by the search for cheap and controllable labor and are abetted by modern information technology. Bar scanners, electronic mail, telephones, fax machines – all permit a global coordination of just-in-time production and delivery systems.

The latter, centripetal forces are driven by the advantages that continue to accrue to spatial concentration of production in dense metropolitan industrial districts. Even in this high-technology age of information, there is no substitute for a hands-on approach to integrated design, marketing, retailing, buying, financing, and even production. It is hard to put several heads together to come up with a new design or advertising campaign or marketing plan if the heads are spread out around the globe. At the manufacturing level, the printed circuit must be inspected to determine if it meets company standards; the fabric must be felt to know if the garment will hang properly. Other things being equal, it is still better to have the company headquarters, research and development teams, factories, and principal customers close to one another. Labor costs are only one consideration among many in the changing geography of global capitalism.

Perhaps virtual reality simulations will eventually do away with time and space altogether, finally enabling quality-control officers or designers or company presidents to beam themselves abroad wherever they think they are really needed. But for the present time, face-to-face relations still confer quick turnaround and flexibility. When the presence of low-cost Third World labor is found in core country metropolitan areas, capital finds the best of both worlds: it needn't go too far from home to find cheap labor, such "global cities" as Los Angeles, New York, London, and Tokyo combine core and periphery in a single centrally located region, constituting a form of black hole that swallows up the otherwise globalizing networks of postindustrial capitalism.[12]

Theory 3: Flexibility, Subcontracting, and Contradictions

Let us try to bring some of these ideas together by drawing on several theoretical frameworks that seem to be grappling with a common set of issues.

First, an increasingly globalized economic dispersion has occurred through the creation of global commodity chains, "network[s] of labor and production processes whose end result is a finished commodity."[13] These commodity chains consist of such pivotal points in the production process as raw materials extraction and processing, production and manufacturing, export, retailing, financing, marketing, and design – the entire spectrum of activities required to make a commodity.[14] While commodity chains are conceptualized as being dispersed over time and space, they must eventually "touch down" at different times and in different places, with different impacts on different locales. Commodity chain analysis shifts the framework for analyzing production; manufacturing is conceptualized as a dynamic process among interconnected firms, rather than as a static property of nations or nation-based corporations.

Commodity chains are particularly likely to be highly dispersed in such labor-intensive, cost-sensitive, retailer-driven production as apparel, athletic shoes, electronic assembly, toys, dolls, and so forth.[15] The companies that fabricate such commodities are truly manufacturers without factories, who source production through globally distributed subcontracting arrangements. Production is typically done in low-wage areas, from Indonesia to Los Angeles. In commodity chain analysis, core, periphery, and surplus value extraction are not conceptualized as attributes of nations, but as aspects of the commodity chain itself. There are core and peripheral activities; where each touches down, it will leave its stamp on the economic region. In the Reichian world of the information-based economy, core activities are those that require symbolic analysis, while peripheral activities are those that require physical labor. Often, contrary to Reich's Utopian vision, they occur side by side in the same industrial district. Factory production may have been key to surplus value extraction and hence capitalist development during the phase of industrial capitalism, but in the postindustrial world this is no longer necessarily the case. Sadisah's factory may never induct her into the aristocracy of labor, nor will Indonesia's export processing zones necessarily ever elevate that country into core or even semiperipheral global status.

Second, it is clear that economic concentration in industrial districts continues to benefit capitalist production, as has been recognized since Alfred Marshall.[16] Industrial districts consist of dense concentrations of economic actors, who rely on one another to get the job done. They consist of elaborate subcontracting arrangements, often based on a handshake, and are characterized by speed, trust, and quick lines of communication. "Networks of trust" are typically mediated by intense familistic and ethnic ties; as one of the leading figures in the Los Angeles apparel industry explains it, "We're an information business."[17] Such "transaction-intensive networks" confer the flexibility required for effficiency and competitive advantage in a global economy.

It will be useful at this point to distinguish two meanings of "flexibility." The first meaning takes us back to our original discussion of Marx: flexibility entails the creation of truly variable capital through global subcontracting.[18] Labor can be taken on and cast off according to the momentary requirements of the marketplace. Surplus can be realized in one place, such as a Los Angeles design studio or marketing firm, while labor exploitation can occur in another – in the factory down the street or across the Pacific Ocean.

Since manufacturers subcontract labor rather than own their own factories, they are no longer legally responsible for wages, factory conditions, or the exploitation of labor; as the production manager for a major US apparel manufacturer put it, "I'm not the sheriff."[19] Thus, costs and risks can be externalized: there is no danger of strikes closing down one's factory or idling one's machines, since one can always switch to more hospitable contractors elsewhere.

Manufacturers no longer need worry about local or national health, safety, or labor regulations; they can always find a new subcontractor in a different state or a different country. Worries about health insurance, lawsuits, workers' compensation, and the other evils of class struggle can similarly be externalized. There is not even any serious danger of rising wages: somewhere in the world there is a factory where the price is right. Flexibility thus defines a contemporary moment in the class struggle, a means acquired by capitalists to once again render labor a truly variable form of capital just as it seemed to be gaining some measure of constancy.

This first, organizational form of flexibility is made possible by a second, more technological form: flexibility as the ability to respond instantly to changes in market conditions. During the industrial phase of capitalism, businesses relied on vertical integration to achieve quick response. Organizationally, it typically made sense for large firms to own or otherwise directly control as many forward and backward linkages as possible, from raw materials extraction to final sales. Because communications technology was rudimentary, only such internalized control and coordination seemed to afford the possibility of avoiding bottlenecks as well as intermediate layers of surplus value extraction.

In the postindustrial phase, however, a high degree of coordination can be achieved through advanced information technology without the need for vertical ownership or management. One American clothing giant, the Gap, can deploy more than five hundred factories around the globe, none of which it owns. When a shopper buys a Gap shirt at the local mall outlet, information about the purchase is scanned into a computer at the point of sale, where it joins a stream of thousands of other sales in a centralized computer in Hong Kong. There, the Gap's overseas buying office analyzes the pattern of sales, placing its orders with factories from Egypt to Hong Kong, from the Philippines to Mauritius. In the words of James Cunningham, the Gap Far East's Vice President for Offshore Sourcing, "the best retailers will be the ones who respond the quickest, the best . . . the time between cash register and factory shipment is shorter."[20] The Gap is an example of a buyer-centered commodity chain, a firm that is organized around retailing and sales rather than internalized sources of supply.[21] It is typical of many labor-intensive industries, from clothing to electronic assembly. I believe it is the organizational form of the future, one that will increasingly come to characterize all forms of production.

The growth of subcontracting is abetted by the recent acceleration of information technology, which has made possible just-in-time delivery, long-distance coordination and control, and a radical disaggregation of the commodity chain. The firm of the future will avoid investing in large amounts of constant capital and the workers to set it in motion. In the postindustrial world, "lean and mean" are the watchwords.[22] In the words of management guru Tom Peters associate Jim Kouzes, "contract out everything but your soul – what you do better than everybody else."[23] For many businesses it is better to have a small in-house design office, advertising agency, and perhaps retail outlet, and subcontract for everything else.

If modern information technology provides the means, subcontracting provides the organizational vehicle for a truly postmodern form of lean, mean capitalism in which only the profit centers remain in-house. Depending on the size of the firm, its organizational resources, and the nature of its business, subcontracting networks can extend down the street, throughout the metropolitan area, or around the world. An estimated thirty million Americans today work at subcontracted jobs, including temporary workers, part-timers, independent subcontractors, and other forms of contingent workers. One out of five nonmilitary workers put in fewer than thirty-five hours a week. It is estimated that as many as a third of US workers fall into this category today, a number that may reach half by the end of the century, approaching the percentage in Japan.[24] Manpower, Inc., the world's largest temporary employment agency, handles more workers each day than General Motors or IBM. Manpower and similar agencies now handle 1.5 million workers, three times as many as a decade ago.[25]

Thus, thanks to modern technology, capitalism has the best of both worlds – it can globalize and/or localize to maximize its flexibility in both senses of the word. It can obtain organizational flexibility from subcontracting, reducing labor to truly variable capital, maximizing surplus extraction while minimizing costs and risks. And it can attain the technological flexibility needed to respond quickly to market changes, while retaining complete control over the labor process.

As with all structural contradictions of capitalism, this postindustrial resolution of the problems of labor's growing power during the industrial phase carries with it its own complications. I will mention two in passing, before turning in greater detail to a third that bears directly on the question of multiculturalism.

First, while subcontracting solves capital's growing problem of internalized labor costs, it also multiplies layers of profit centers. Every layer of subcontracting must have its cut in order to stay in business. During global expansionary times this may not pose a problem for capital, but during global recessionary times such as the present there is a severe profit squeeze. Kouzes' "soul of the business" may find itself acting in a very unsoulful manner, mercilessly cutting the prices it pays to its vendors, who in turn do the same to their own subcontractors, and so on down the line. Smaller subcontractors may be severely hurt, and workers will ultimately bear the brunt of the cost cutting. With each layer marching to the orders of the layer above it, and each layer taking its own cut, there is less and less left over for the people whose labor ultimately makes the goods. The only difference between exploitation in the industrial and postindustrial age is that during the latter the soulful managers at the head of the line are spared the sight of the workers, who are now somebody else's problem.

Second, it should be obvious that the purpose of subcontracting (like all capitalist relations) is to cut costs to the capitalist. As I have indicated, sub-contracting is specifically intended to chasten labor, destroying the once proud "aristocracy of labor" in core countries by rendering it competitive with a low-paid global workforce. To the extent that this strategy is successful, Marx's problem of underconsumption once again rears its head although now on a global scale. The so-called global economic recession, which currently plagues Japan and Germany as well as the United States, is in fact largely the result of this organizational restructuring of capitalism. The long boom in the global economy of the 1960s through to the mid-1980s, during which time the four Asian dragons and other newly industrializing countries came of age, actually marked the undermining of the very global economic order that had made such "economic miracles" possible.[26] The Pacific shift was based in large part on the growing buying power of European and American workers, which it eventually undermined. Indonesian women workers, earning thirty-five dollars a month from Nike, are hardly a viable market for Air Jordans nor are garment workers in Los Angeles, whose subminimum wages are in part repatriated to their families in Mexico or El Salvador or Guatemala.

The New Multiculture of Capitalism: The Case of Los Angeles

The third contradiction of postindustrial capitalism, which I will illustrate with the example of the Los Angeles apparel industry, is that it has promoted the ethnicization of capitalism on a global scale. As capitalism becomes a multitiered machine of many subcontracting arrangements, the faces and hands at the different levels differ in color from one another.

Beginning a generation ago, high and rising costs in the unionized apparel industry of the northeastern United States began to drive factories out of the region, first to the south, then to Mexico and the Caribbean, to Asia, to the world – and today back home to Los Angeles, where an abundance of impoverished immigrants from Mexico and Central America render long-distance subcontracting in search of cheap labor less necessary. This is not the place to explain the reasons for this reperipheralization of the core, which has to do with the failed economies in Mexico and Central America, as well as civil warfare and repressive governments in Guatemala and El Salvador. (Our own involvement in these causes is less well understood, particularly our support – through international lending organizations – of austerity programs that have driven wages down and contributed to the enormous cross-border wage disparities.)[27]

In Los Angeles county there are an estimated 125,000 garment workers laboring in some five thousand factories.[28] As many as a quarter of the workers are undocumented immigrants, and an unknown (but probably larger) percentage of the factories are unlicensed. Los Angeles today accounts for nearly a tenth of total US employment in apparel.[29] The city's spatially concentrated downtown garment district – as well as numerous other similar concentrations spread throughout Los Angeles, Orange, and San Bernardino counties – confers multiple synergies for garment manufacturing.

Downtown Los Angeles provides a combination of working conditions associated with peripheral country status and postindustrial core country opulence, one that affords a disturbing vision of the emerging "global city" of the twenty-first century. On one side of the downtown divide – flanked by man-made barriers (the Harbor and Hollywood Freeways) that reinforce the existing hilly topography – lies the business, financial, governmental, and cultural heart of Los Angeles. Here one finds the city's centers of culture – the Music Center, the Dorothy Chandler Pavilion, the Mark Taper Forum. Just south of the Hollywood Freeway lie the principal federal, state, and local government agencies, including city hall, the central police station, and the courthouse. The corporate headquarters of the *Los Angeles Times* are found here, as are the towering spires of the major banks and financial institutions of the Pacific Rim economy: First Interstate World, ARCO Plaza (now Bank of America), Union Bank Square, Wells-Fargo, Home Savings, Citicorp, the World Trade Center, and the Pacific Stock Exchange. For the small part of the Pacific Rim economy that constitutes the garment industry, many of these institutions help provide capital, accounting, and other financial services. Nearby are the hotels, malls, and plazas of the Bunker Hill redevelopment project, "one of the largest postwar urban designs in North America."[30] "Little Tokyo" is found on the eastern fringe of this upscale portion of downtown; Chinatown is just across the Hollywood Freeway. All in all, one can locate some two dozen government buildings, an even greater number of banks, cultural institutions, and trade centers of various sorts, and nearly as many first-class hotels catering to the business traveler. The visual image is one of towering steel and glass, gerbil-like pedestrian walkways set several floors above street level, and integrated parking plazas that remove any need for ground-level pedestrian traffic. This anti-pedestrian downtown design was far from accidental, but rather was intentionally constructed so as to prevent any danger of human spillover from the surrounding impoverished slums and factory districts into the citadels of global capitalism.

As one moves south and east of Bunker Hill, this small area of capital and the symbolic analysts who serve it quickly gives way to the teem and dirt of the garment district, where one finds the hands that make the goods. The modern California Apparel Mart, at the corner of Los Angeles and Ninth, Streets, symbolizes the transition. In a neighborhood filled with factories, discount clothing stores, and the enormous open-air "knock off" apparel bazaar at Santee Alley, this thirteen-story structure, which claims its own zipcode, houses the showrooms of some fifteen hundred manufacturers, including some of the most celebrated labels in the fashion business. A few blocks east of the California Mart lies the Fashion Institute of Design and Merchandising, training the future designers and marketers of the "California Look," while providing interns for the local apparel manufacturers.

The garment district for the most part is characterized by low, eight- to twelve-storey buildings, mainly constructed during the 1930s, and many in need of repair. These buildings house the small factories (average size: sixteen workers) that produce the "California Look."[31] A contractor may occupy an entire floor, or share the floor with others; a building may house as many as a dozen or more different sewing factories, all using the same bathroom. Not far from the sewing factories are a handful of buying offices that shop wholesale for the country's principal retailers. Here also are found yarn factories, fabric providers, and related fabric services; the flower, produce, and jewelry marts; sewing schools; immigration services, lawyers, and others serving or living off of the largely immigrant workforce.

The apparel industry in Los Angeles is spatially concentrated and ethnically stratified in a way that reveals the push-pull forces at work in the global economy. The industry has grown in Los Angeles because the concentration of industry-related professional, managerial, financial, and technical services, design and manufacturing capability, and a low-wage immigrant workforce in the heart of the world's largest apparel market has for many manufacturers overcome the attractiveness of yet cheaper labor at a greater distance. Local production also enables manufacturers to avoid quotas and tariffs, which add especially to production costs outside the Mexico Central America-Caribbean Basin region. (This region benefits from special programs designed to pay duties only on the value added in production, which, because of the low labor costs, is typically minimal.) Finally, local production enjoys the flexibility that results from subcontracting, in a system of labor control that divides the industry along ethnic lines.

The principal profits in the industry are realized by those who design the clothing, the firms that provide necessary financial and legal services, and those engaged in its sales. These include the manufacturers (more correctly designers, since they seldom engage in actual manufacturing of final products); bankers and accountants who specialize in apparel-related financing; the factors who buy up the retail accounts receivable from the manufacturers, freeing up money for fabric purchases; and retailers and retail buying offices. This upper stratum of the industry is almost entirely white, largely but not exclusively male, and disproportionately Jewish. It goes back to the turn of the century, when shepherding and apparel manufacturing began in Los Angeles. Union Bank, which continues to finance apparel manufacturers, was founded at that time as a repository for funds generated by the fledgling industry. Wealth generated in large part by the industry's founders gave rise to two of Los Angeles's principal hospitals, City of Hope and Cedars-Sinai. Family, friendship, and religious community ties that originated at that time continue into the present.

But the original founders of the industry have been largely supplanted by immigrants, first from New York City, then from the Middle East, and most recently from Asia. The apparel manufacturing community still remains relatively small and largely known to one another. Its core members – those longtime Angelinos, as well as East Coast transplants from one or two generations ago – honor one another at charitable fund-raisers, sit on the same boards, and belong to the same civic organizations and commissions. The interlopers – Middle Eastern Jews and Koreans are less well integrated into the community. Such dense networks contribute to a Marshallian industrial district where apparel is "in the air." Here a deal is easily made over lunch at the outside patio of the California Mart, a design is readily imitated from among the thousands of wholesale lines on display within a few city blocks. Competition and personal rivalries complement a strongly shared culture, fostering an unending spin-off of fashion ideas and marketing strategies.

The other half of the local industry is concerned with the fabrication of clothing. The thousands of small factories are run mainly by small immigrant entrepreneurs, many of whom are barely a rung on the ladder above the workers they exploit. Turnover is estimated at 50 percent or more a year, as immigrants from Mexico, Guatemala, El Salvador, Korea, Taiwan, Hong Kong, and South Korea scramble for a toehold in the apparel economy. The factory owners constitute a layer between manufacturer and worker, often a layer of yellow skin between white and brown. The workers are almost entirely immigrants, predominantly female (although increasingly male), and, to an unknown extent, undocumented. Because manufacturers subcontract to factory owners they have until recently been treated as legally exempt from factory violations, so long as they employ licensed contractors; because contractors are small, economically unstable, and can easily procure fictitious licenses, they are virtually impossible to hold accountable.

The result is an industry where no one is likely to be held responsible for labor abuses – where there are no sheriffs. It is an industry ready-made for exploitation along lines of race and ethnicity, in which a white manufacturer might place an order to a struggling Korean contractor, who employs a Latino workforce that can neither understand his language nor fathom his culture. Such a situation is ripe for racial and ethnic resentment, an explosive situation in an already explosive city.

Conclusion: Race, Ethnicity, and Gender in Global Capitalism

Capitalism has always reinforced class divisions with divisions based on race, ethnicity, gender, and other forms of ascription. In any system based to a large degree on the exploitation of one group of people by another, such distinctions provide a useful basis for justifying inequality. Not only does this foster a "divide-and-conquer" ideology among those who otherwise might find common cause, but it also helps to foster a standard of exploitation based on what is accorded the least common denominator – whichever group finds itself at the bottom of the economic heap.

Since modern industrial capitalism originated in northern Europe, its racialization until recently has tended to divide along white and non-white lines. Today, with Japan a global capitalist player and the emerging Asian dragons (including China) in hot pursuit, we can expect this historically fundamental racialization to be overlaid by new and innovative forms. The Japanese are well known for their racial attitudes and corresponding practices toward Japanese-born Koreans, for example, while Koreans have themselves acquired a well-deserved reputation for their own brand of racialized economic exploitation in Central America and Los Angeles.[32] No racial or ethnic group is exempt from the possibility of developing its own brand of racism as a rationalization for its class practices. Racism preceded capitalism, and will likely survive it. But capitalism benefits from racism, and so gives it a particular focus and direction depending on the circumstances.

Capitalism may often appear to be colorblind. If African-American superstar athletes can sell athletic shoes, they will be elevated into the upper tier of the class structure by shoe companies. If Latinos constitute a growing market for goods, then goods will be produced and sold for Latinos. Yet capitalism continues to reinforce racial and ethnic divisions, albeit in different ways and on a global scale. What has occurred is a scrambling of the racial topography. The black-white made-in-America model of racialization is supplanted by a rainbow constellation of exploitative race relations, reinforcing class divisions with often virulent differences across racial and ethnic lines.

In the United States, where several decades of legislation and judicial decisions have outlawed most forms of overt discrimination, only those truly at the margins remain completely unprotected: newly arrived (and undocumented) immigrants, and inner-city African-American males. The former provide the local battalions of the reserve army of the global proletariat, while the latter are simply sacrificed, the frontline casualties of global economic restructuring joined with a national policy of economic triage. In both cases, racism and sexism play key justificatory roles; but the causes are, at root, economic. Within the American production system, race, ethnicity, and gender continue to serve class divisions. As I have sought to show in the example of the Los Angeles garment industry, one encounters a rainbow coalition of conflicting interests: Asians against Latinos, whites against people of color, documented against undocumented workers.

Globally, the lowest stratum of the class structure is comprised disproportionately of women, rural immigrants to urban areas and export processing zones, and racial and ethnic minorities as defined in a particular country. Although exploitation of these groups undoubtedly preceded their incorporation into the global economy, it has now taken on new forms, designed to keep their wage demands low and their interests divided. It is perhaps a telling irony that while the most egregious types of exploitation are formally illegal in the United States, American businesses continue to profit from such exploitation elsewhere in the world, where even the effort to struggle against exploitation is often ruthlessly suppressed.

Flexibilization and subcontracting facilitate these global patterns of exploitation, since not even paternalistic loyalties or corporatist leanings are permitted to detract from the hard-nosed pursuit of profit in the fast-moving information age. If businesses today are counseled to retain only their soul, will that soul include people whose color or gender differs from that of the few remaining soulful managers? It seems that as capitalism moves into its information-driven stage, it will find new and creative ways to reproduce its old racial, ethnic, and gender differences on a global scale.

Notes

1 Richard P. Appelbaum and Edna Bonacich, *A Tale of Two Cities: The Garment Industry in Los Angeles* (Los Angeles: Report to the Haynes Foundation, 1993).

2 Karl Marx, *Capital,* vol. 1: *A Critique of Political Economy* (New York: International Publishers, 1967 [1867]).

3 Samir Amin, *Accumulation on a World Scale* (New York: Monthly Review Press, 1974); A. Emmanuel, *Unequal Exchange: A Study of the Imperialism of Trade* (New York: Monthly Review Press, 1972); and André Gunder Frank, *Latin America: Underdevelopment or Revolution?* (New York Monthly Review Press, 1969), *World Accumulation: 1492–1789* (New York: Monthly Review Press, 1978), and *Dependent Accumulation and Underdevelopment* (London: Macmillan, 1979).

4 Fernando H. Cardoso and Enzo Faletto, *Dependency and Development in Latin America* (Berkeley: University of California Press, 1979); Peter Evans, *Dependent Development* (Princeton, NJ: Princeton University Press, 1979); Tom Gold, "Dependent Development in Taiwan" (Ph.D. dissertation, Harvard University, 1981); Hyun-Chin Lim, *Dependent Development in Korea, 1963–1979* (Seoul, South Korea: Seoul National University Press, 1985).

5 Folker Frobel, Jurgen Heinrichs, and O. Krege, *The New International Division of Labor: Structural Unemployment in Industrialized Countries and Industrialization in Developing Countries* (Cambridge: Cambridge University Press, 1980), and "The Current Development of the World Economy: Reproduction of Labour and Accumulation of Capital on a World Scale," *Review* 5: 4 (1982): 507–55; Dieter Ernst, *Innovation, Industrial Structure and Global Competition: The Changing Economics of Internationalization* (New York: Campus Verlag, 1987), and *The New International Division of Labour, Technology and Underdevelopment: Consequences for the Third World* (New York: Campus Verlag, 1980); and A. Lipietz, "New Tendencies in the International Division of Labor: Regimes of Capital Accumulation and Modes of Regulation," in *International Capitalism and Industrial Restructuring,* ed. R. Peet (Boston: Allen and Unwin, 1986).

6 Immanuel Wallerstein, *The Modern World-System* (New York: Academic Press, 1974), *The Capitalist World Economy* (Cambridge: Cambridge University Press, 1979), and *The Modern World-System II* (New York: Academic Press, 1980); and Terence K. Hopkins and Immanud Wallerstein, "Commodity Chains in the World Economy Prior to 1800," *Review* 10: 1 (1986): 157–70.

7 Karl Marx, *Grundrisse,* trans. Martin Nicolaus (New York: Vintage Books, 1978 [1857–8]), 375–80.

8 Robert Reich, *The Work of Nations* (New York: Alfred A. Knopf, 1991); Michael E. Porter, "The Competitive Advantage of Nations," *Harvard Business Review* (March – April 1990): 73–93, and *The Competitive advantage of Nations* (New York: Free Press, 1990).

9 Allen J. Scott, "Flexible Production Systems and Regional Development," *International Journal of Urban and Regional Research* 12 (1988): 171–86; Allen J. Scott and Michael Storper, eds, *Production, Work, and Territory: The Geographical Anatomy of Industrial Capitalism* (Boston: Allen and Unwin, 1986); Michael Storper and Richard Walker, *The Capitalist Imperative: Territory, Technology, and Industrial Growth* (New York: Basil Blackwell, 1989); Michael Storper and S. Christopherson, "A Flexible Specialization and Regional Industrial Agglomeration: The Case of the US Motion Picture Industry," *Annals of the Association of American Geographers* 77 (1987):

104–17; Daniel Bell, *The Coming Crisis of Post-industrial Society: A Venture in Social Forecasting* (New York: Basic Books, 1973), and "The Third Technological Revolution and its Possible Socioeconomic Consequences," *Dissent* (spring 1989): 164–76.

10 Barbara Ehrenreich and John Ehrenreich, "The Professional Managerial Class," in *Between Labor and Capital*, ed. Pat Walker (Boston: South End Press, 1979).

11 Jeffrey Ballinger, "The New Free Trade Hell: Nike's Profits Lump on the Back of Asian Workers," *Harper's Magazine* (August 1992): 40–7.

12 Saskia Sassen, *The Global City: New York, London, Tokyo* (Princeton, NJ: Princeton University Press, 1991).

13 Hopkins and Wallerstein, "Commodity Chains in the World Economy Prior to 1800," 159.

14 See the essays in Gary Gereffi and Miguel Korzeniewicz, *Commodity Chains and Global Capitalism* (Westport, CT: Greenwood Press, 1994).

15 Gary Gereffi, "The Organization of Buyer-Driven Global Commodity Chains: How US Retailers Shape Overseas Production Networks," in ibid.: 95–122.

16 Scott, "Flexible Production Systems and Regional Development"; Scott and Storper, *Production, Work, and Territory*, Storper and Walker, *The Capitalist Imperative*, Storper and Christopherson, "Flexible Specialization and Regional Industrial Agglomeration"; Porter, "The Competitive Advantage of Nations"; Michael J. Piore and Charles Sabel, *The Second Industrial Divide: Possibilities for Prosperity* (New York: Basic Books, 1984).

17 Sidney Morse, personal interview, October 28, 1992. Morse was the largest owner and director (in 1992) of the California Mart. (Two years later the mart was foreclosed and is currently under new ownership.)

18 Jeffrey Pfeffer and James M. Baron, "Taking the Workers Back Out: Recent Trends in the Structuring of Employment," *Research in Organizational Behavior* 10 (1988): 257–303.

19 Mitch Glass, personal interview, August 14, 1991. Glass was the vice president of production, Cherokee Corporation.

20 James Cunningham, personal interview, November 28, 1991. Cunningham was the Vice President for Offshore Sourcing, the Gap Far East, Hong Kong.

21 Gereffi, "The Organization of Buyer-Driven Global Commodity Chains."

22 Tom Peters, *Liberation Management: Necessary Disorganization for the Nanosecond Nineties* (New York: Alfred A. Knopf, 1992).

23 James M. Kouzes, *The Challenge of Leadership: How to Get Extraordinary Things Done in Organizations* (San Francisco: Jossey-Bass Publishers, 1987).

24 Robert Rosenblatt, "Benefits Studied for Part-Time Workers," *Los Angeles Times*, June 16, 1993: D14; Lance Morrow, "The Temping of America," *Time*, March 29, 1993: 40–1; Marco Orru, Gary G. Hamilton, and Mariko Suzuki, "Patterns of Inter-Firm Control in Japanese Business," *Organization Studies* 10 (1989): 549–74; and Michael Gerlach, *Alliance Capitalism: The Strategic Organization of Japanese Business* (Berkeley: University of California Press, 1992).

25 Janice Castro, "Disposable Workers," *Time*, March 29, 1993: 43–7.

26 Jeffrey Henderson and Richard Appelbaum, "Situating the State in the Asian Development Process," in *States and Development in the Asian Pacific Rim,* ed. Richard Appelbaum and Jeffrey Henderson (Newbury Park, CA: Sage Publications, 1992).

27 See Richard Rothstein, "Continental Drift: NAFTA and Its Aftershocks," *American Prospect* 12 (winter 1993): 68–84.

28 For a more detailed elaboration of these points, see Appelbaum and Bonacich, *A Tale of Two Cities,* and Bonacich in this volume.

29 Edna Bonacich and Patricia Hanneman, "UA Statistical Portrait of the Los Angeles Garment Industry," unpublished manuscript (1991).

30 Mike Davis, *City of Quartz: Excavating the Future of Los Angeles* (London and New York: Verso, 1990), 229.

31 See Bonacich and Hanneman, "A Statistical Portrait of the Los Angeles Garment Industry."

32 Kurt Peterson, *The Maquiladora Revolution in Guatemala* (New Haven: Yale Law School, Orville H. Schell Jr. Center for International Human Rights, Occasional Paper Series 2, 1992); Appelbaum and Bonacich, *A Tale of Two Cities;* Gregg Scott, "Achieving Dignity and Embracing Hope: Daily Battles for Justice in the Los Angeles Garment Industry" (Santa Barbara, CA: UCSB Department of Sociology, Report to the Haynes Foundation, 1993).

23

Analytic Borderlands: Race, Gender and Representation in the New City

Saskia Sassen

I speak here as a political economist in the hope of establishing an intellectual dialogue on the subject of race, gender and representation in the city. I begin with the facts and narratives about the economy of the city and move towards an attempt at theorizing the presences that are not represented in these accounts. In this attempt at theorizing I make use of elements from critical theory in feminism, art and architecture. I take liberties, because my intention is to use these elements to illuminate subjects and arenas which they have not addressed and are not meant to; the multiple presences and articulations of race and gender in the urban economy and their multiple absences in the dominant representations of that economy.

First a few clarifications and remarks to situate what I am trying to do. Feminist and other critical theories have contributed to a decentering of the subject and a valorizing of that decentering. I want to use this language to describe a basic transformation in the organization of the urban economy over the last twenty years, including a sharp distortion in the valorization dynamic of the economy, and to re-narrate what is now eviction as decentering. In so doing, I seek to valorize what has been evicted from the center.

In the last twenty years we have seen the expulsion and continuing exclusion from the center of significant components of the economy and a sharp increase in earnings inequality. Yet many of these components are actually servicing the center. Exclusion from the center makes economic survival precarious both for firms and workers. It also tends to make them either invisible or appear as backward, unnecessary, anachronistic. These devalorized components/subjects need to be recovered, and the center therewith transformed, brought down. This eviction and devaluing are embedded in a sharp demographic transformation as well; the growing presence of women, immigrants, and people of color generally in the urban economy. One important question is whether this demographic embeddedness has facilitated eviction and devalorization.

How do we valorize the evicted components of the economy in a system that values the center? There are here parallels with some issues in feminist theory, such as for example, the question of valorizing forms of knowledge associated with the female experience in a context where positivism and its variants are valued above all other forms of knowledge. Or, the debate on the positioned viewer and its assumption of one correct perspective. In economic analysis and in the narratives it produces there is one form of knowledge that is valued as the only correct one and one account that is considered to be a full rendering of the crucial elements in the economy. There is then, also, what one could think of as a positioned viewer behind the dominant narrative in economics.

What I have sought to do in much of my politico-economic work on cities is to valorize components of the economy that have been devalorized through their being evicted from the center or because they were never installed in the center. I have sought to show that they are articulated with sectors considered central, but are articulated in ways that present them as marginal, backward, unnecessary. Thus it is the form of this articulation which produces their representation as marginal. By revealing the facts of this articulation and the multiplicity of forms it assumes, I hope to begin the process of valorizing these various types of sectors, firms and workers that constitute the devalorized part of the urban economy.

It is also through a detailed examination of these devalued sectors that I hope to contribute to the specification of a multiplicity of femininities and racial identities, and to go beyond some of the dominant economic stereotypes, such as the white professional woman vs. the black welfare mother. There is a multiplicity of identities being formed and reproduced in these decentered spaces of the economy. Recognizing the representations being shaped by the constituents themselves is, clearly, a central task if we are to develop a political programmatics, in this particular case for revalorizing these spaces and presences of the economy.

How do we construct a narrative about the city, and particularly the economy of the city, that includes rather than evicts? For me as a political economist it has meant working in several systems of representation. Critical theory in feminism, art and architecture, each is a system of representation, with its own definitions, rules, boundaries, narratives. And so is economics. You may thus ask how one can use several of these systems, let alone have a dialogue across them. I recognize, further, that many would reject this possibility as not only unfeasible, but also undesirable.

Let me make three observations as to why I am interested in this kind of intellectual exploration. First, I think the time is ripe. To a much greater extent than in the past we have recognized the existence of multiple systems of representation, and there have been profound advances in their elaboration. The new politics of identity and the new cultural politics, especially evident in large cities, have brought this recognition into the everyday lives of people, onto the streets and out of theoretical texts.

A second observation is methodological. There are analytical moments when two systems of representation intersect. Such analytical moments are easily experienced as spaces of silence, of absence. One challenge, work that needs to be done, is to see what happens in those spaces; what operations (analytic, of power, of meaning) take place there. These operations may not be easy to recognize, either because they coexist in two different systems of representation, or because the intersection itself engenders a distinct third presence. It may require constructing a narrative about the operations that take place in these spaces of intersection. At a less theorized level, much of my own work on urban economies has consisted of exploring what I call analytic borderlands – the sharp discontinuities in the economy that lead me to posit that there is a multiplicity of economies. The narrative I have constructed about these analytic borderlands pivots on the question of circuits for the circulation and installation of economic operations. More on this later.

Third, the theoretical work on the body as a site of inscription opens up new possibilities for analyses of the sort I am exploring here. I would like to emphasize an aspect not usually developed in cultural analyses of the body and one that would serve the task of exploring the spaces of intersection I referred to above. This is the notion that the body is also inscribed by the workplace and specific work cultures. Beyond the variety of workplaces and cultures found in the "western" tradition, there is the multiculturalism of large cities such as New York and Los Angeles today. It is not only a question of the corporate versus the factory workplace, but also of the different ways in which a particular workplace can be inscribed by specific cultural environments, for example, an all-Latino shopfloor in a garment factory. It seems to me that a focus on the body, culturally inscribed and inhabiting many different spaces in the city, may well be one of the elements facilitating the exploration of analytic borderlands.

These are the terrains and the instruments through which I want to reread the city's economy in a way that recovers organizational, spatial and cultural dimensions that are now lost in representations of that economy. I do this in four sections. The first section briefly presents some of the key elements in the dominant narrative about the economy and argues that cities are useful arenas within which to explore the limitations of this narrative. The second section discusses how recovering place, particularly cities, in analyses of the economy allows us to see the multiplicity of economies and work cultures through which it is constituted. It also allows us to recover the concrete, localized processes through which globalization exists and argues that much of the multi-culturalism in large cities is no less a part of globalization than is international finance. The third section examines how space is inscribed in the urban economy, and particularly how the spaces of corporate culture, which are a representation of the space of power in today's cities, are actually contested spaces – they contain multiple presences even though their representation is exclusively corporate. The final section brings these various elements together in an effort to move from an economic narrative of eviction to one of inclusion. Conflicts of a profound nature become visible in this movement.

The Dominant Economic Narrative

The dominant narrative about the economy has several key elements through which the system is constructed and explained. I will focus on three of them. Probably fundamental to it is the notion of continuous flow, also referred to as the trickle down: the idea that there are no structural barriers to the circulation of economic growth, or no discontinuities to be negotiated in this circulation and installation of economic growth. Thus growth emanates from the leading sectors and flows down to the rest of the economy via a series of mechanisms and inter-mediaries. Politically this establishes the superiority of the leading sectors; these are the ones that should receive support from the larger polity and the government when necessary. Sectors that lack technological development and have a preponderance of low-wage workers and small, low-profit firms, are considered as backward and not really belonging to an advanced economy. Hence the location of each component, whether at the top or at the bottom, reflects its value. In some sense one could say that the leading sector occupies the privileged location of the positioned viewer in theories of visuality. This account of the economy creates a "white knight" theory of economic growth: one sector is privileged as the one that will rescue the economy. Again, you can see the resonances with accounts in other disciplines. In the US you can see this white knight version of economic growth in the hope and fanfare put onto high-tech industries in the 1970s and on finance in the 1980s as the sectors that would pull the economy ahead, make us strong, beautiful and happy.

There have been times when the center incorporated a majority of workers and firms under its regulatory umbrella and therewith empowered workers and their families – for example in the 1950s and 1960s, through well-paying unionized jobs and subsidized housing for the suburban middle class. When this protected center shrinks and begins to expel a growing number of workers and firms, then we are dealing with another situation. And this distinction clearly is important within the conventional account and policy debate.[1] But it does not begin to touch on two issues central to this talk; that much of that expanded protected center in the economy – epitomized by the two decades after World War II – privileged men over women, and whites over blacks. And second, that exclusion and de-valorization are embedded in a sharp demographic transformation in the urban workforce – women, immigrants and African-Americans now constitute a numerical majority in our large cities. But this is not the place to go into the policy issues.

A second aspect of importance here is economic internationalization. The account of the economy which takes off from the internationalization of trans-actions and firms is in many ways a more concrete account, one with lower scientific aspirations. It privileges certain elements and has only silences about others. The discussion about the internationalization of the economy privileges the reconstitution of capital as an internationalized presence; it emphasizes the vanguard character of this reconstitution.

At the same time it remains absolutely silent about another crucial element of this internationalization, one that some, like myself, see as the counterpart of the internationalization of capital: which is the internationalization of labor. We are still using the language of immigration to describe this process. Elsewhere I have argued at length that this language constructs immigration as a devalued process in so far as it describes the entry of people from generally poorer, disadvantaged countries, in search of the better lives that the receiving country can offer. It contains an implicit valorization of the receiving country and a devalorization of the sending country.[2] It is furthermore a language derived from an earlier historical period which proceeds as if the world economic system were the same today as it was one hundred years ago. What would happen to the representation of that process which we call immigration if we were to cast it in terms akin to those we use to describe the internationalization of capital, a process represented as imbued with economic rationality, technological advances and other attributes privileged in the mainstream narrative about the economy? What would happen if we did not privilege wealth over poverty, wealthy countries over poor countries? If we saw immigrants as using bridges built by the internationalization of capital or the internationalization of the military activities of dominant countries? If we saw immigrants as moving within an internationalized labor market?

A third aspect of the economic system and its representation has to do with the tendency towards concentration – concentration of power, of control, of appropriation of profits. This tendency, produced and reproduced through different historical periods under different specific forms and contents, clearly feeds the valorizing of the center of the economy. That is, it constitutes a center and then valorizes it. Elsewhere I have written in great detail about how this formation and reproduction of a center in the economy takes place through a variety of mechanisms and intermediaries.[3, 4] A general question we need to address is whether an economic system with strong tendencies towards concentration in ownership and control can have a space economy that lacks points of intense agglomeration.[5]

This dominant narrative of the economy can be usefully explored in large cities such as New York and Los Angeles, or any of the major West European cities. There are at least two reasons for this. First, cities are the site for concrete operations of the economy and we can distinguish two forms of this. One is about economic globalization and place. Cities are strategic places which concentrate command functions, global markets, and, I add, production sites for the new advanced information industries. The other form through which this concreteness can be captured is by an examination of the day-to-day work in the leading industrial complex, finance and specialized services. Such an examination makes it clear that a large share of the jobs involved in finance, for example, are lowly paid clerical and manual jobs, many held by women and immigrants. These types of workers and jobs do not fit the dominant representation of what the premier industry of this period is about.

Second, the city concentrates diversity.[6, 7] Its spaces are inscribed with the dominant corporate culture but also with a multiplicity of other cultures and identities. The slippage is evident: the dominant culture can encompass only part of the city. And while corporate power inscribes these cultures and identities with "otherness" thereby devaluing them, they are present everywhere. This presence is especially strong in our major cities which also have the largest concentrations of corporate power. We see here an interesting correspondence between great concentrations of corporate power and large concentrations of an amalgamated "other." It invites us to see that globalization is not only constituted in terms of capital (international finance, telecommunications, information flows) but also in terms of people and cultures.

The Global City

Changes in the geography, composition and institutional framework of economic globalization over the last two decades have led to sharp concentration of economic functions in major cities.[8, 9, 10] Some of this concentration reflects the reinvigoration of old functions but much of it consists of new functions. Major cities have emerged as strategic places in the world economy. In the past cities were centers for imperial administration and international trade.[11] Today they are transnational spaces for business and finance where firms and governments from many different countries can transact with each other, increasingly bypassing the firms of the "host" country.

I note two other economic operations, not sufficiently recognized in the literature on economic globalization. One is that global cities are a new kind of production site. They contain the combination of industries, suppliers and markets, including labor markets, necessary for the production of highly specialized services: from financial innovations to international accounting models, international legal expertise, management and the coordination functions for just about any transborder flow. Emphasizing production brings to the fore a broad range of presences that are usually lost in discussions of globalization and the information economy. These presences range from the material conditions underlying global telecommunications to the various types of workers and firms we do not usually associate with globalization and the information economy: secretaries, manual workers, the truckers who deliver the state of the art software (and that old-fashioned xerox paper). It is particularly important, it seems to me, to effect these analytical operations in the case of the leading sectors of the information economy because the mainstream account of this economy is so radically distorting in its privileging of information flows over the material and concrete conditions through which it operates, in its privileging of the advanced professional workforce, in its exclusion of non-professional workers and firms.[12]

The third aspect that matters in the discussion is that global cities are also internationalized spaces in terms of people. The emphasis on production discussed above brings to the fore place-bound aspects of globalization. [13, 14, 15] And a recovery of place in a discussion of globalization brings forth the fact that it is not only firms from many different countries that can meet to do business. It is also the terrain where peoples from many different Third World countries are most likely to meet and a multiplicity of cultures come together. It's not only the material infrastructure, the jobs and firms, it is also the many different cultural environments in which these workers exist. One can no longer think of centers for international business and finance simply in terms of the corporate towers and corporate culture at its center.

From the perspective of the dominant narrative of the economy, there has been growing recognition of the formation of an international professional class of workers and of highly internationalized environments due to the presence of foreign firms and personnel, the formation of global markets in the arts, and the international circulation of high culture. What has not been recognized is the possibility that we are seeing an internationalized labor market for low-wage manual and service workers. This process continues to be couched in terms of immigration, a narrative rooted in an earlier historical period.

I think that there are representations of globality which have not been recognized as such or are "contested representations of globality."[16] Among these is the question of immigration, as well as the multiplicity of cultural environments to which it contributes in large cities, often subsumed under the notion of ethnicity. What we still narrate in the language of immigration and ethnicity I would argue is actually a series of processes having to do with the globalization of economic activity, of cultural activity, of identity formation.[17, 18] Immigration and ethnicity are constituted as otherness. Understanding them as a set of processes whereby global elements are *localized*, international labor markets are constituted, and cultures from all over the world are de- and re-territorialized, puts them right there at the center along with the internationalization of capital as a fundamental aspect of globalization.[19] This way of narrating the migration events of the postwar era captures the ongoing weight of colonialism and post-colonial forms of empire on major processes of globalization today, and specifically those binding countries of emigration and immigration. The major immigration countries are not innocent bystanders; the specific genesis and contents of their responsibility will vary from case to case and period to period. Today's global cities are in part the spaces of postcolonialism and indeed contain conditions for the formation of a postcolonialist discourse.[20, 21] An interesting question concerns the nature of internationalization today in ex-colonial cities. King's analysis about the distinctive historical and unequal conditions in which the notion of the "international" was constructed[22] is extremely important. It brings up, in part, the types of questions raised by Hall[23] in his observation that contemporary postcolonial and postimperialist critiques have emerged in the former centers of empires, and that they are silent about a range of conditions evident today in ex-colonial cities or countries. In many ways during the time of empire, the old colonies were far more internationalized than the metropolitan centers; yet the notion of internationalization as used today is rooted in the experience of the center. The idea that the international migrations, now directed largely to the center from the former colonial territories, and neo-colonial versions in the case of the US and Japan,[24] might be the correlate of the internationalization of capital that began with colonialism is simply not part of the mainstream interpretation of that past and the present.

Methodologically speaking, this conception of the global city contains one way of addressing the question of the unit of analysis. The national society is a problematic category but so is the "world economy."[25] Highly internationalized cities such as New York or London offer the possibility of examining globalization processes in great detail, within a bounded setting, and with all their multiple, often contradictory aspects. It would begin to address some of the questions raised by King about the need not only of a differentiated notion of culture, but also of the international and the global.[26]

We need to recognize the specific historical conditions for different conceptions of the international. There is a tendency to see the internationalization of the economy as a process operating at the center, embedded in the power of the multinational corporations today and colonial enterprises in the past.[27, 28] One could note that the economies of many peripheral countries are thoroughly internationalized due to high levels of foreign investment in all economic sectors, and of heavy dependence on world markets for "hard" currency. What center countries have is strategic concentrations of firms and markets that operate globally, the capability for global control and coordination, and power. This is a very different form of the international from that which we find in peripheral countries.

Globalization is a contradictory space; it is characterized by contestation, internal differentiation, and continuous border crossings.[29] The global city is emblematic of this condition.

Contested Spaces in the City

Space in the city is inscribed with the dominant corporate culture. Sennett[30] observes that "the space of authority in western culture has evolved as a space of precision." And Giddens notes the centrality of "expertise" in today's society, with the corresponding transfer of authority and trust to expert systems.[31]

Corporate culture is one representation of precision and expertise. Its space has become one of the main spaces of authority in today's cities. The dense concentrations of tall buildings in major downtowns or in the new edge cities are the site for corporate culture – though as I will argue later it is also the site for other forms of inhabitation, but they have been made invisible. The vertical grid of the corporate tower is imbued with the same neutrality and rationality attributed to the horizontal grid of American cities.

Much has been said about the protestant ethic as the culture through which the economic operations of capitalism are constituted in the daily life of people. Sennett opens up a whole new dimension both on the protestant ethic and on the American city by suggesting that what is experienced as a form of rational urban organization, the grid, is actually a far more charged event. It is "the representation in urban design of a protestant language of self and space becoming a modern form of power."[32] We can recognize that the neutralization of place brought about by the modern grid contains an aspiration to a modern space of precision. This same aspiration is evident in the self-inscription of corporate culture as neutral, as ordered by technology, economic efficiency, rationality. This is put in contrast to what is thought of as the culture of small businesses, or even more so, ethnic enterprises. Each of these is a partial representation, in one case of the city, in the other of the economy.

The dominant narrative presents the economy as ordered by technical and scientific efficiency principles, and in that sense as neutral. The emergence and consolidation of corporate power appears, then, as an inevitable form that economic growth takes under these ordering principles. The impressive engineering and architectural output evident in the tall corporate towers that dominate our downtowns are a physical embodiment of these principles. And the corporate culture that inhabits these towers and inscribes them is the organizational and behavioral correlate to these ordering principles.

Authority is thereby "divorced from community. . . The visual forms of legibility in urban designs or space no longer suggest much about subjective life. . . ."[33] Subjective life is installed in a multiplicity of subjectivities, and this undermines the representation of the advanced modern economy as a space of neutrality, the neutrality that comes from technology and efficiency; the ordering principles of a modern economy.

We can easily recognize that both the neutralization of place through the grid in its aspiration to a modern space of precision, and the self-inscription of corporate culture as neutral, as ordered by technology and efficiency, are partial representations of the city and of the economy. This inscription needs to be produced and reproduced, and it can never be complete because of all the other presences in the city which are inscribed in urban space. The representation of the city contained in the dominant economic narrative can exclude large portions of the lived city and reconstitute them as some amalgamated "other."

The lived city contains a multiplicity of spatialities and identities, many indeed articulated and very much a part of the economy, but represented as superfluous, anachronistic or marginal. Through immigration, a proliferation of originally highly localized cultures have now become presences in many large cities; cities whose elites think of themselves as cosmopolitan, that is transcending any locality.[34] An immense array of cultures from around the world, each rooted in a particular country or village, now are reterritorialized in a few single places, places such as New York, Los Angeles, Paris, London, and most recently Tokyo.[35]

The space of the amalgamated "other" created by corporate culture is constituted as a devalued, downgraded space in the dominant economic narrative; social and physical decay, a burden. In today's New York or Los Angeles, this is the space of the immigrant community, of the black ghetto, and increasingly of the old manufacturing district. In its most extreme version it is the space of the "underclass, full of welfare mothers and drug addicts." Corporate culture collapses differences, some minute, some sharp, among the different socio-cultural contexts into one amorphous otherness; an otherness that has no place in the economy; the other who holds the low-wage jobs that are supposedly only marginally attached to the economy. It therewith reproduces the devaluing of those jobs and of those who hold the jobs. The dominant economic narrative, by leaving out these articulations, can present the economy as containing a higher-order unity by restricting it only to the centrally placed sectors of the economy.

The corporate economy evicts these other economies and workers from economic representation, and the corporate culture represents them as the other. It evicts other ways of being in the city and in the economy. What is not installed in a corporate center is devalued; will tend to be devalued. And what occupies the corporate building in non-corporate ways is made invisible. The fact that most of the people working in the corporate city during the day are low-paid secretaries, mostly women, many immigrant or African-American women, is not included in the representation of the corporate economy or corporate culture. And the fact that at night a whole other work force installs itself in these spaces, including the offices of the chief executives, and inscribes the space with a wholly different culture (manual labor, often music, lunch breaks at midnight) is an invisible event. (I have shown elsewhere the whole infrastructure of low-wage, non-professional jobs and activities that constitute a crucial part of the so-called corporate economy).

In this sense, corporate architecture assumes a whole new meaning beyond the question of the economy of offices and real estate development. The built forms of the corporate economy are representative of its "neutrality" – the fact that it is driven by technological development and efficiency, which are seen as neutral (there is a good literature, by the way, showing how this is not the case). Corporate architectural spatiality is one specific form assumed by the circulation of power in the economy, and specifically in the corporate economy. Wigley[36] notes that the house is not innocent of the violence inside it. And we now have an excellent literature showing how the design of different types of buildings – homes, factories, "public" lobbies – is shaped by cultural values and social norms. This "rational" organization of office space illustrates certain aspects of Foucault's microtechnologies of power.[37]

But the changes in the details of habitation – institutional practices, the types and contents of buildings – indicate there is no univocal relation between these and built form. I agree with Rakatansky's observation that the play of ideologies in architectural form is complex. And I would add that this concept is essential if we are to allow for politics and agency in the built environment. Yes, in some sense buildings are frozen in time. But they can be re-inscribed. The only way we can think of these towers now is as corporate, located downtown (and as failed public housing projects if they are in poor ghettos). Another dimension along which to explore some of these issues is the question of the body ". . . as the site of inscription for specific modes of subjectivity." [38] The body is citified, urbanized as a distinctively metropolitan body.

The particular geographical, architectural, municipal arrangements constituting a city are one particular ingredient in the social constitution of the body. Grosz adds that they are by no means the most important one. She argues that the structure and particularity of the family and neighborhoods is more influential, though the structure of the city is also contained therein.[39] I would add to this that the structure, spatiality and concrete localization of the economy are also influential. In these many ways the city is an active force that "leaves its traces on the subject's corporeality."

But it is citified in diverse ways; it is inscribed by the many socio-cultural environments present in the city, and it in turn inscribes these. There are two forms in which this weaves itself into the space of the economy. One is that these diverse ways in which the body is inscribed in the many socio-cultural contexts that exist in the city, works as a mechanism for segmenting and, in the end for devaluing, and it does so in very concrete ways. For example research by the anthropologist Philippe Bourgeois[40] shows us the case of an eighteen-year-old Puerto Rican from East Harlem who gets a job as a clerical attendant in an office in downtown Manhattan. He tells us that walking over to the xerox machine past all the secretaries is humiliating. The way he walks, the way he is dressed, the way he moves presents him to the office staff, secretaries and managers as someone from the ghetto; someone who "doesn't know the proper ways." This particular young man eventually fled the downtown world and entered the ghetto economy where at least his gait, speech and dress were the norm.

The other way in which this diversity weaves itself into the space of the economy is that it re-enters the space of the dominant economic sector as merchandise and as marketing. Of interest here is the fact that contemporary forms of globalization are different from earlier ones: the new global culture is absorptive, a continuously changing terrain that incorporates the new cultural elements whenever it can. In the earlier period, the culture of the empire epitomized by Englishness was exclusionary, seeking always to reproduce its difference.[41] At the same time, today's global culture cannot absorb everything, it is always a terrain for contestation, and its edges are certainly always in flux. The process of absorption can never be complete.

One question is whether the argument developed above regarding the neutralization of space brought about by the grid and the system of values it entails or seeks to produce in space, also occurs with cultural globalization. As with the grid, culture never fully succeeds in this neutralization, yet absorption does alter the absorbed. An interesting issue here that emerges out of my work on the urban economy is whether at some point all the "others" (at its most extreme, the informal economy) carry enough weight to transform the center. In the case of culture one can see that the absorption of multiple cultural elements along with the cultural politics so evident in large cities, have transformed global culture. Yet, as Hall argues, it is still centered in the West, its technologies and its images. Thus absorbed, the other cultures are neutralized. And yet they are also present.

We can perhaps see this most clearly in urban space, where a multiplicity of other work cultures, cultural environments, and culturally inscribed bodies increasingly inhabit a built terrain that has its origins visibly in another culture; the culture lying behind the grid.[42] Here again, I ask, at what point does the "curve effect," as social scientists would put it, take hold and bring the center down?

Conclusion: The New Frontier

There are three important developments over the last twenty years which I believe set the stage for the re-reading of the city I am proposing here. One of them is the decentering of a growing share of economic activity with the ensuing shrinking of the center, as I discussed earlier. The second is what I describe as a dynamic of valorization which has sharply increased the distance between the devalorized and the valorized, indeed overvalorized, sectors of the economy. The third is the growing presence of women, immigrants and African-Americans in the urban economy of large cities, and their disproportionate concentration in the devalued sectors.

Large cities have emerged as strategic territories for these developments. On the one hand, they are crucial cogs in the new global economic system: they function as command points, global marketplaces for capital, and production sites for the information economy. On the other hand, they contain the multiplicity of economic activities and types of workers and cultural environments that are never represented as part of the global economy but are in fact as much a part of globalization as is international finance. These joint presences have made cities a contested terrain.

In the preceding sections I have tried to show that cities are of great importance to the dominant economic sectors; that these sectors represent themselves through narratives and spaces that are partial representations of what the economy and urban space are; that devalorized economic sectors are servicing the corporate center of the economy and hence are necessary to that center even though presented as marginal; that this devalorization of growing sectors of the economy has been embedded in a massive demographic transition towards a growing presence of women, African-Americans and third world immigrants in the urban workforce; and that the new politics of identity and the new cultural politics have brought many of these devalorized or marginal sectors into representation.

Secondly I have sought to argue that globalization needs to be thought of as a series of processes that are constituted by people as much as capital; for instance, it seems crucial to recognize that what we continue to think of as immigration is, today, an instance of globalization. There are consequences to this way of representing immigration. Our large cities, and increasingly the large cities in western Europe, are the terrain where a multiplicity of globalization processes assume concrete, localized forms. These localized forms are, in good part, what globalization is about. We can then think of cities also as the place where the contradictions of the internationalization of capital come to rest, or fight. If we consider, further, that large US cities especially also concentrate a growing share of African-Americans and Latinos, two populations that have suffered massive disadvantage in the economic system, then we can see that cities have become a strategic terrain for a whole series of conflicts and contradictions.

On the one hand they concentrate a disproportionate share of corporate power and are one of the key sites for the overvalorization of the corporate economy; on the other, they concentrate a disproportionate share of the disadvantaged and are one of the key sites for their devalorization. This joint presence happens in a context where the internationalization of the economy has grown sharply and cities have become increasingly strategic for global capital; and marginalized people have come into representation and are making claims on the city as well. This joint presence is further brought into focus by the sharpening of the distance between the two. White flight to the suburbs and the pronounced transformation in income distribution have reduced the mostly white middle class residing in the city, creating a series of intermediate spaces. Now the overvalorized center is smaller and its edges are sharper, and the devalorized others are far larger in number and inhabit a growing area of the city.

These conditions make it less and less likely that the hierarchical ordering that has up until now created the semblance of a unitary economic system, can be maintained. The center now concentrates immense power, a power that rests on the capability for global control and the nakedness of unencumbered greed. And marginality, notwithstanding weak economic and political power, has become in Hall's words a "powerful space."

If cities were irrelevant to the globalization of economic activity, the center could simply abandon them and not be bothered by all of this. Indeed this is what some politicians are arguing – that cities have become hopeless reservoirs for all kinds of social despair. It is interesting to note again how the dominant economic narrative argues that place no longer matters, that firms can move anywhere now thanks to telematics; that the dominant industries are information-based and hence not place-bound. This line of argument devalorizes cities at a time when they are a strategic terrain for the new cultural politics. And it makes it possible for the corporate economy to extract major concessions from city governments under the notion that firms can simply leave – which is not quite the case for a whole complex of firms.

In seeking to show that cities are strategic to economic globalization because they are command points, global marketplaces and production sites for the information economy and also that many of the devalued sectors of the urban economy actually fulfill crucial functions for the center, I try to recover the importance of cities precisely in a globalized economic system and of those devalued sectors which rest largely on the labor of women, African-Americans and immigrants. It is all the intermediary sectors of the economy (routine office work, headquarters that are not geared to the world markets, the variety of services demanded by the largely suburbanized middle class) and of the urban population (the "middle class") that can and have left cities. The two sectors that have remained, the center and the "other," find in the city the strategic terrain for their operations. Because they find in the city such a terrain and because they matter to each other, we can think of cities as a new frontier charged with conflict between two opposites; charged with the possibility of fundamental transformation in the West. The global city is, perhaps, the premier arena for these battles – it is the new territory where the contemporary version of the colonial wars of independence are being fought. But today's battles lack clear boundaries and fields: there are many sites, many fronts, many forms, many politics. There are battles being fought in neighborhoods, schools, court rooms, public squares. They are fought around curriculums, rights, identity. Their sites of resistance are streets, parks, culture, the body.

Notes

1 The shrinking of the protected center has engendered considerable debate and caused much impoverishment. It is an important subject into itself, and there is a whole policy discussion that could become of interest eventually in the more theoretically oriented examination I am seeking to develop here.
2 S. Sassen, *The Mobility of Labor and Capital: A Study in International Investment and Labor Flow* (Cambridge University Press, New York, 1988).
3 Ibid.
4 S. Sassen, *The Global City: New York, London, Tokyo* (Princeton University Press, 1993).
5 Ibid., parts 1 and 2.
6 A. D. King, *Global Cities: Post-Imperialism and the Internationalization of London* (Routledge, London and New York, 1990).
7 An important point made by King (ibid.) is that during European colonization, it was in the colonial cities where different cultures and races met. The cities of Europe and North America have only recently become places where such diversity is concentrated.
8 The term globalization requires some clarification. Robertson (see note 9) posits that concepts of globalism are not economically fixed; I agree with this. Tagg agrees and adds that such concepts have "no status outside the fields of discourse and practice that constitute them" (see note 10: 156). But he argues further that such concepts of representations of globality are not the expression of some "real" process of globalization. In this discussion Tagg sees "global" as having come to mean the world is "systematic or one place" (ibid.: 157). But this is merely one, albeit a very typical way of reading globalization. Such a world would indeed "not be present to itself." But authors as diverse as Hall on culture (see note 20) and me on the economy do not work with this version of the global. Detailed research on globalization makes it clear that it is a highly diversified and contested process, with a multiplicity of geographies and events, narratives and self-reflexive mechanisms (see Giddens, note 31, on the self-reflexivity of modernism). It seems to me that it is not simply a question of choosing between two extremes: either a singular, non-reflexive narrative of globalization, or a series of concepts that only exist in terms of the discourses that contain them and that can never be the clay of that multiplicity of geographies, events and contradictions that constitute globalization, one can indeed see the gravitation of discourses (see the discourse on the global information economy which I have sought to critique in much of my work), but also the concrete specifics of lived experience. I would certainly agree with Tagg's observation that "the meaning and value of photographic practices cannot be adjudicated outside specific language games." But what I call for is a differentiating of what the object being narrated is, rather than a universalizing. Photographic

practices, yes, I can see that; manual work in a plantation or sweatshop, no: they leave their own inscription regardless of what discourse they are contained in. The question for me is how globalization is constituted, not just as a narrative but in terms of concrete specific, often place-bound, operations. Thus the narrative about globalization that is centered on the information economy and telematics is, in my analysis, a very partial and distorted representation because it leaves out a variety of elements that are part of globalization; and secondly, what it leaves out tends to be overwhelmingly that which lacks power.

9 R. Robertson, "Social Theory, Cultural Relativity and the Problem of Globality," in A. D. King (ed.), *Culture, Globalization and the World-System. Current Debates in Art History 3* (Department of Art and Art History, State University of New York at Binghamton, 1991), pp. 69–90.

10 John Tagg, "Globalization, Totalization and the Discursive Field," in A. D. King (ed.), *Culture, Globalization, and the World-system. Current Debates on Art History 3* (Department of Art and Art History, State University of New York at Binghamton, 1991), pp. 155–60.

11 King (see note 6) notes that a major instrument of European colonization was the colonial city. It played a different role from that of the imperial capital cities.

12 In accounts of other sectors such as manufacturing or transportation, these "other" types of workers, firms and places are less likely to be excluded, indeed they are often put at the center of the account and used to devalorize much of manufacturing. The exception is high-tech and here again we see a privileging of the research and professional staff and a veiling of the production workforce which is mostly low-wage, female and immigrant. Technology and the different classes of workers that embody, enact or use its components – whether technicians, professionals, clericals, manual workers – are not a preexisting condition in the organization of the economy but are constituted by that economic organization.

13 Cf. Robertson's notion of the world as a single place (see note 9), or the global human condition. I would say that globalization is also a process that produces differentiation, only the alignment of differences is of a very different kind from that associated with such differentiating notions as national character, national culture, national society. For example the corporate world today has a global geography, but it isn't everywhere in the world: in fact it has highly defined and structured spaces, and secondly it also is increasingly sharply differentiated from non-corporate segments in the economies of the particular locations (a city such as New York) or countries where it operates. There is homogenization along certain lines that cross national boundaries and sharp differentiation inside these boundaries. We can also see this in the geography of certain built forms; from the bungalow (King, see note 14) to the corporate complex (Sassen, note 4) or the landscapes of American theme parks (Zukin, note 15). We can see that these various built forms are both global yet highly localized in certain places. Globalized forms and processes tend to have a distinct geography.

14 A. D. King, *The Bungalow: The Production of a Global Culture* (Routledge and Kegan Paul, London and New York, 1984).

15 S. Zukin, *Landscapes of Power* (California University Press, Berkeley, 1991).

16 U. Hannerz, "Scenarios for Peripheral Cultures," in A. D. King (ed.), *Culture, Globalization and the World-System. Current Debates in Art History 3* (Department of Art and Art History, State University of New York at Binghamton, 1991), pp. 107–28.

17 Elsewhere I have tried to argue that the current post-1945 period has distinct con-
    ditions for the formation and continuation of international flows of immigrants and
    refugees. I have sought to show that the specific forms of internationalization of
    capital we see over this period have contributed to mobilize people into migration
    streams and build bridges between countries of origin and the US. The first took place
    through the implantation of western development strategies, from the replacement
    of smallholder agriculture with export-oriented commercial agriculture to the west-
    ernization of educational systems. At the same time the administrative, commercial
    and development networks of the former European empires and the newer forms
    these networks assumed under the Pax Americana (international direct foreign
    investment, export processing zones, wars for democracy) have not only created
    bridges for the flow of capital, information and high level personnel from the center
    to the periphery but, I argue, also for the flow of migrants (Sassen, notes 2 and 18).
    On this last point, see also Hall's account of the postwar influx of people from the
    Commonwealth into Britain and his description of how England and Englishness
    were so present in his native Jamaica as to make people feel that London was the
    capital where they were all headed sooner or later (see note 20).
18 S. Sassen (see note 4).
19 That is why in a book mostly on immigration, I refused to use the concept immi-
    gration in the title and sought to link the internationalization of capital and labor.
20 S. Hall, "The Local and the Global: Globalization and Ethnicity," in Anthony D.
    King (ed.), *Culture, Globalization and the World-System: Contemporary Conditions
    for the Representation of Identity. Current Debates in Art History 3* (Department of
    Art and Art History, State University of New York at Binghamton, 1991).
21 A. D. King (see note 6).
22 A.D. King, *Urbanism, Colonialism, and the World Economy. Culture and Spatial
    Foundations of the World Urban System* (Routledge, London and New York, 1990):
    78.
23 S. Hall (see note 20).
24 S. Sassen (see note 4).
25 I would tend to agree with Robertson's comment (see note 9) that the proliferation
    of the ideas of nation, nationalism and national culture, especially in the twentieth
    century, is connected to globalization processes. Various forms of nationalism and
    sub-nationalism are speaking with increasingly loud voices today precisely because
    the nation-state and national society are eroding from within *and* without. This
    erosion assumes distinct modalities and degrees of intensity in different countries. It
    is by no means a uniform and universal process. The new nationalisms range from
    reemergence of older nationalisms in extreme forms, as is evident in the former terri-
    tories of Yugoslavia, to the renewed intensity of statements about the American
    people, the American character, and English as the official language in the last two
    decades in the US.
26 A. D. King, "The Global, the Urban, and the World," in A. D. King (ed.), *Culture,
    Globalization and the World-System. Current Debates in Art History 3* (Department
    of Art and Art History, State University of New York at Binghamton, 1991), pp. 4,
    149–54.
27 Similarly, in the social sciences the most common way to proceed is to study such
    categories as economic power, leading industries, or economic globalization, from
    the top down. I agree with Barabara Abou-El-Haj (see note 28) that we also need to
    proceed from the bottom up. The central assumption in much of my work has been

that we learn something about power through its absence and by moving through or negotiating the borders and terrains that connect powerlessness to power. Power is not a silence at the bottom; its absence is present and has consequences. The terms and language of the debate force particular positions and pre-empt others.

28   Barbara Abou-El-Haj, "Languages and Models for Cultural Exchange," in A. D. King (ed.), *Culture, Globalization and the World-System. Current Debates in Art History 3* (Department of Art and Art History, State University of New York at Binghamton, 1991), pp. 139–40.

29   There are many examples. Global mass culture homogenizes and is capable of absorbing an immense variety of local cultural elements. But this process is never complete. My analysis of data on electronic manufacturing shows that employment in leading sectors no longer inevitably constitutes membership in a labor aristocracy. Thus Third World women working in Export Processing Zones are not empowered: capitalism can work through difference. Yet another case is that of "illegal" immigrants; here we see that national boundaries have the effect of creating and criminalizing difference. These kinds of differentiations are central to the formation of a world economic system. See, for example, I. Wallerstein, "Culture as the Ideological Battleground of the Modern World-System," in Mike Featherstone (ed.), *Global Culture: Nationalism, Globalization and Modernity* (Sage, London, Newbury Park, and Delhi, 1990).

30   R. Sennett, *The Conscience of the Eye: The Design and Social Life of Cities,* paperback edition (Norton, New York, 1992).

31   A. Giddens, *The Consequences of Modernity* (Polity Press, Oxford, 1990), pp. 88–91.

32   R. Sennett (see note 30).

33   Ibid.: 37.

34   Hall (see note 20), makes an important observation when he uses the term ethnicity to describe that which is grounded and rooted, and notes two aspects: one, the inevitability of this if a group is to recover its own hidden history to enter into representation; and second that ethnicity, while necessary, is also about exclusion of all others. Politics should not be reduced to the politics of ethnicity as it risks becoming yet another form of fundamentalism. The discussion about culture as increasingly deterritorialized offers additional narratives to encompass certain aspects of the immigrant experience.

35   Tokyo now has several, mostly working-class concentrations of legal and illegal immigrants coming from China, Bangladesh, Pakistan and the Philippines. This is quite remarkable in view of Japan's legal and cultural closure to immigrants. Is this simply a function of poverty in those countries? By itself it is not enough of an explanation, since they have long had poverty. I posit that the internationalization of the Japanese economy, including specific forms of investment in those countries and Japan's growing cultural influence there, have created bridges between those countries and Japan and reduced the subjective distance from Japan (see Sassen, note 4, chapter 9).

36   M. Wigley, "Untitled: The Housing of Gender," in Beatriz Colomina (ed.), *Sexuality and Space.* Princeton Papers on Architecture (Princeton Architectural Press, 1992), pp. 327–90.

37   M. Rakatansky, "Spatial Narratives," in J. Whiteman, J. Kipnis and R. Burdett, *Strategies in Architectural Thinking* (The MIT Press, Cambridge, MA, Chicago Institute for Architecture and Urbanism, 1992).

38 E. Grosz, "Bodies-Cities," in Beatriz Colomina (ed.), *Sexuality and Space,* Princeton Papers on Architecture (Princeton Architectural Press, 1992), pp. 241–53.
39 Grosz (ibid.) suggests a model of the relation between bodies and cities that sees them not as distinct megalithic total entities but as assembles or collections of parts, capable of crossing the thresholds between substances to create new linkages. She does not stress the unity and integration of body and city, or posit their ecological balance. Rather, she posits a fundamentally disunified series of systems and inter-connections, disparate flows, events, entities and spaces, brought together or drawn apart in more or less temporary alignments.
40 P. Bourgeois, *In Search of Respect: Selling Crack in El Barrio.* Structural Analysis in the Social Sciences Series (Cambridge University Press, New York, forthcoming).
41 S. Hall (see note 20).
42 Similarly the informal economy when acknowledged, which is rare, is conceived of as a distortion, an import from the Third World. Elsewhere I have documented the diverse ways in which goods and services produced in the informal economy circulate in the mainstream economy and can be shown to meet the needs of a broad variety of firms and households in that economy. Thus I posit that informalization is one way of organizing a range of activities that on the one hand produce goods and services in demand in the overall economy, and on the other hand have been devalorized and are hence under immense competitive pressure.

Further reading

M. Castells, *The Informational City* (Blackwell, London, 1989).
Beatriz Colomina (ed.), *Sexuality and Space.* Princeton Papers on Architecture (Princeton Architectural Press, 1992).
B. Colomina, "The Split Wall: Domestic Voyeurism," in Beatriz Colomina (ed.), *Sexuality and Space.* Princeton Papers on Architecture (Princeton Architectural Press, 1992), pp. 73–128.
M. Morris, "Great Moments in Social Climbing: King Kong and the Human Fly," in Beatriz Colomina (ed.), *Sexuality and Space.* Princeton Papers on Architecture (Princeton Architectural Press, 1992).
J. Whiteman, J. Kipnis and R. Burdett, *Strategies in Architectural Thinking* (The MIT Press, Cambridge, MA, Chicago Institute for Architecture and Urbanism, 1992).
S. Zukin, "The Postmodern Debate over Urban Form," *Theory, Culture and Society,* 5 (2–3) 1988, pp. 431–46.

24

Globalization, the Racial Divide, and a New Citizenship

Michael C. Dawson

Large numbers of Americans believe that they are further from achieving the American dream than they were a decade ago, and the resulting economic anxiety is responsible for a good deal of the unease that people feel about their future. The globalization of the American economy has spurred new political conflicts and alliances, many of which are profoundly racialized. Globalization makes inequality worse, exacerbating the deprivation of many African-Americans, Latinos, and other less privileged Americans who have been in difficult circumstances all along. Immigration pressures also increase in a more globally integrated economy, and this can spark new or renewed tensions among groups already in the country.

A progressive politics will have to recognize that the globalization of the American economy is remaking the racial and ethnic map of the United States. If progressives ignore or minimize the racial realities and fail to further an inclusive kind of American citizenship, they doom any chance of achieving a broad alliance and risk stoking the fires of racial conflicts that could dominate politics well into the next century. On the other hand, if popularly oriented progressives can respond creatively to the economic anxiety that is gripping millions of people in the US, we have a chance to rebuild a strong multiracial alliance for a better America for all, an alliance of the sort that has not existed during the past several decades.

Globalization and Racial Politics

Globalization is creating economic anxiety among all Americans, but for many its impact is filtered the lens of racial group interests and the racial order. Globalization has produced a racial effect and encouraged racialized political responses.

Global changes are undercutting the state and manufacturing sectors of the American economy and crushing the American labor movement. The economic devastation that has hit both the manufacturing and government sectors of the economy affects whites and people of color very differently. The latter are heavily concentrated in these sectors, which have historically provided relatively high-paying jobs to relatively low-skilled workers. The cities have been particularly hard hit by both white flight and the severe contraction of the urban tax base. Much of the nation's economic growth during the past ten years has occurred in suburban regions, like Oakland and Macomb counties in Michigan, while leaving neighboring jurisdictions, like Detroit, facing economic, social, and civil disaster. One-sided economic growth has shattered the organizational and institutional base of the inner-city black community.

Economic devastation has produced social and political isolation, with everyone inside the devastated urban communities becoming mistrustful of everyone outside (Cohen and Dawson, 1993). The residents of the poorest black communities are even suspicious of labor unions, the black middle class, and other working people – those who might seem like natural allies. The partial collapse of the black left and the co-optation of black activists into electoral politics and the corporate world have led to a growing political vacuum in inner-city black communities.

Globalization, or what Sassen (1988) characterizes as the "international-ization" of production, has spurred immigration into the United States, producing new forms of racial conflict and intensifying the perceived threat to American workers at all wage levels. During the past couple of decades, those at the bottom of the economic ladder, particularly blacks, have come to believe that they are increasingly the victims of high rates of displacement due to immigrant labor. Many African-Americans think that immigrants, including black Haitian immigrants, should not be allowed to take American jobs until "real" Americans have their opportunity (Dawson, 1996). One-fifth of whites think that increased Latino immigration is bad for the nation, and nearly one-fifth of blacks believe the same about increased Asian immigration (Brodie, 1995). The large impact that globalization has had on black attitudes can be seen in the fact that 60 percent of blacks are worried about their economic future as opposed to "only" 38 percent of whites, 31 percent of Asian-Americans, and 43 percent of Latinos. While econometric studies suggest that more immigration has caused little or no displacement of low-skilled workers among blacks or other ethnic groups, the media and political rhetoric have fueled the politics of resentment to the point where many Americans believe that society is threatened by increased immigration (Card, 1996).

The process of globalization and intensified international competitiveness has led to widespread downsizing by corporations. As employment becomes less secure, tensions increase among actual and would-be workers of different groups. Accompanying all of this have been massive attacks on taxes and the scope of state activities. Budget-slashing has produced endless fights over the redistribution of scarce governmental resources, with direct racial implications. The budget debates represent significant conflicts between urban and suburban groups who hold very different views on the size and scope of government.

At first blush these debates appear to be about dry budgetary issues but more is at stake. Budgetary debates are also about the nature of the state and the nature of citizenship. If smaller and smaller groups of citizens are deemed worthy of citizenship, then there is less and less of a need for a strong central government. This is particularly the case if one believes that the domestic role of government is primarily centered on delivering benefits or services to morally undeserving members of society. An ever spiraling increase in the level of distrust toward government among the majority leads to the dismantling of the central state and the privatization of large swathes of governmental functions. Devolution of public functions proceeds until governmental institutions serve populations that are overwhelmingly homogeneous. As one Wisconsin doctor put it, "I want to make sure my tax money goes to people like me."

One, Two, Many Worlds

Because people experience the economic transformations of our era in different ways, to varying degrees, and from divergent vantage points, particular racial and ethnic groups of Americans are coming to see different worlds. Americans certainly share many values and concerns, as we shall consider later, but more striking now are the forces pushing blacks and whites in particular, but also Asian-Americans and Latinos, to call for radically different solutions to the nation's problems. America's racial groups sharply differ in their assessments of each other's social position, and they offer sharply different assessments of why racially disadvantaged groups remain in deprived circumstances. All these differences in turn encourage sharply contrasting views about the role of government – about what government has already done to help or hurt, and what it might do in the future.

Differing worldviews, then, are at the root of the corrosive silences that are poisoning American politics and the possibility of building a progressive new majority; blacks and whites hold different views on a broad range of issues, from crime to macroeconomic policy, which are traceable to the two groups' distinct social realities. Basic perceptions of social reality are in fact so different that political debates between blacks and whites often leave participants from both sides completely baffled.

Blacks and whites by and large speak the same language (the controversy over Ebonics notwithstanding). But public opinion researchers constantly overestimate how much blacks and whites share the same media and information sources. Blacks and whites usually attend different, segregated churches, and churches are a critical source of political information for blacks; blacks tend to listen to talk shows whose politics are quite distinct from those of talk shows favored by whites. Black citizens are also exposed to a multitude of alternative but influential black news sources which are virtually invisible to white Americans (Dawson, forthcoming). Further, while blacks and white espouse a shared set of values, they differ in their value priorities. Blacks tend to value equality more than liberty, whereas for whites, liberty has priority.

Blacks, whites, and Latinos are in different socioeconomic situations and offer very different economic assessments. Because they were forcibly brought to this country, many African-Americans believe the nation's racial order and their own subjugation are rooted in economic hierarchy. African-Americans believe that they are doing considerably less well than whites, and this belief structures much of black public opinion (Dawson, 1994a). Many whites, in contrast, believe that blacks are doing pretty well – and that where they are not, blacks themselves bear a great deal of the responsibility. Whites doubt that government can do much more to help, and even if it could, they are not sure that doing so is a proper role for government. Blacks disagree strenuously on every point.

Blacks and whites also disagree about the basic facts of economic status, as was evident in a national survey conducted in 1995 by the *Washington Post*, the Kaiser Family Foundation, and Harvard University. Although people in all groups understand that blacks and Latinos have high poverty rates, more than 30 percent of whites believed that black incomes are greater than or the same as white incomes. The reality is much closer to black perceptions: in 1992, median incomes for whites were over $32,000, whereas median incomes for blacks were below $19,000 (Brodie, 1995). Even more amazingly, when it comes to jobs, 58 percent of whites (as opposed to 23 percent of blacks) believe that blacks are as well off as whites. In a land where blacks continue to be the last hired and the first fired, it should come as no surprise that in 1993, as in the past four decades, black unemployment rates continued to be twice as high as white unemployment levels. Frequent white misperceptions about black well-being are the norm across numerous other domains as well, ranging from health care to housing.

Such misperceptions of one another's status carry over into dramatically different black and white assessments of prospects for the future. While fewer than 45 percent of non-racial and ethnic groups are "very concerned" about their family and personal economic prospects over the next ten years, fully 60 percent of blacks are very worried. The disagreements extend to assessments of group economic attainment as well. Only 27 percent of blacks believe that blacks have achieved middle-class status, but a majority of all other groups think that most blacks belong to the middle class. Indeed, two-thirds of whites believe that blacks have achieved middle-class status.

The vast majority of blacks, who perceive their own economic circumstances relatively accurately, see racism as a major and continuing problem in American society. Meanwhile, substantial segments of other groups reject this proposition. In a survey conducted during the summer of 1995, individuals were asked whether they thought that racism in America was a big problem, somewhat of a problem, a small problem, or no problem at all: whereas only 33 percent of Asians, 38 percent of whites, and 49 percent of Hispanics thought that racism was a big problem, 70 percent of blacks did. The best predictors of a person's stance on whether racism is a major problem for society are therefore race (black or not) along with beliefs about whether blacks fare worse than whites when it comes to jobs. These remain the over-riding predictors, even when controls are introduced for such factors as Latin or Asian ethnicity, age, income, gender, and ideology. Racial identities and interests, in short, powerfully shape Americans' views of society and its problems – including the problem of racism.

Government as Problem or Solution

Not surprisingly, sharply divergent views of problems are associated with equally divergent views about possible solutions to problems of racial disadvantage. Here the differences span matters ranging from how aggressively the federal government should pursue anti-discrimination efforts to issues of tax policy and government spending. Still, there are some new complexities and new twists in the responses of various racial groups to public policy questions. Whereas Latinos and Asian-Americans were closer to whites on assessments of economic position and racial disadvantages, on anti-discrimination policies they are closer to blacks. Even before one broaches the matter of affirmative action, massive group differ-ences are evident in attitudes toward conventional anti-discrimination measures. Although fewer than one half of whites agree that the federal government should enact "tougher anti-discrimination laws to reduce racial discrimination in the workplace" (Brodie, 1995: 91), overwhelming majorities of other groups agree with this statement, ranging from 74 percent of Asian-Americans to 90 percent of blacks.

Whites are still less willing to help minorities if it means higher taxes. Asians are divided, but a small majority of Latinos and more than 75 percent of blacks are willing to pay higher taxes to help low-income minorities. White and Asian-American aversion to taxes extends generally to such trade-offs as more taxes for greater services, while Latinos are divided, and a substantial majority of blacks are willing to pay higher taxes in return for greater services.

Racial disagreements about the role of government are not confined to issues of taxation and spending. Blacks differ from every other racial and ethnic group in their conviction that, in areas of racial policy-making, devolving public authority to the states will hurt rather than help them. Most African-Americans, but only a minority of whites, think that only the federal government is capable of helping blacks. Blacks remain the group most skeptical of subnational govern-ment and the strongest supporters of a strong federal government.

White resistance to government efforts to improve the position of minorities in society seems attributable to the perception of many whites that they are the real losers under government racial policies. Although no racial group has a majority believing that fewer jobs or promotions for whites is a "bigger national problem" than discrimination against minorities, 40 percent of whites do think this, compared to 21 percent of Asian-Americans, 16 percent of Hispanics, and only 4 percent of blacks. Contrasting group perceptions on this issue hold up even after controlling for income, age, gender, and education.

In turn, people's perceptions about which group loses more – the majority or minorities – pattern attitudes toward such remedial racial policies as affirmative action. Even when controlling for ideology, party identification, and the degree to which one thinks racism a serious problem (in addition to the standard racial and demographic variables), a perception that whites lose turns people even more strongly against affirmative action. While Kinder and Sanders (1996) have shown that personal interests do not shape white preferences on racial policy, it is very much the case that perceptions of racial winners and losers influence the policy preferences of all Americans, not only blacks (see Dawson, 1994a for more details).

Of course, there are important historical reasons for African-Americans' tendency to look toward a strong central state for remedies to social problems while other Americans may rely more on subnational governments or market openings. Historically, blacks have faced immense official and unofficial hostility from local authorities and white private citizens. The notion of states' rights is hardly politically innocent; it has been associated with the political disenfranchisement and economic dispossession of African-Americans.

Black skepticism about relying on market forces to correct social inequalities likewise has deep roots. African-Americans can remember at least a century's worth of instances where people were set back after clawing their way to a modicum of economic opportunity. Blacks amassed some land and started farming, only to be dispossessed; black laborers found themselves excluded from jobs in labor markets where they were prepared to compete. And there have also been very visible recent instances, such as the contemptuous actions toward black employees by the managers of Texaco Corporation. Experiences such as these have led blacks since the Civil War to believe that opportunities for them must be bolstered by federal regulations and initiatives.

Groups are in conflict about how to pursue the American dream. Progressives will have to wrestle with sharp differences about the relative importance of liberty and equality; the nature, rights, and obligations of citizenship; and the role of the state in the economy. For long-standing historical reasons, only blacks are strong supporters of a strong national government across all spheres, although Asians and Latinos believe that the state should play a role in redressing discrimination aimed at minorities. These days, many whites suspect that they have a lot to lose from government intervention in the economy on behalf of minorities and are therefore skeptical of any strong government measures. These are perplexing ambiguities for progressives today, because times of economic uncertainty create openings for building broad coalitions yet at the same time exacerbate the types of value conflicts that have historically destroyed progressive coalitions in this country.

Although all non-white groups are more supportive of government intervention than whites, then, only African-Americans champion strong governmental intervention across a variety of domains. Many other Americans believe that a strong state is of dubious value in winning the American dream, and some think that certain kinds of government action may hinder the access of some Americans to a better life. But the black experience has been that the national government must be on your side if you are to have a chance at the American dream. Generalizing from this experience, blacks favor government interventions in both the economy and race relations. Progressives, in short, will need to find ways to speak about government both to groups of Americans who are skeptical of strong public actions and to groups who feel a vital stake in such actions.

Black Anger and the Democratic Party

The economic and racial processes that I have described have led to very high levels of black dissatisfaction with all aspects of American society. This dissatisfaction has been growing steadily since 1988 (Dawson, 1996) and has now reached the point where many blacks may no longer be reliable members of the Democratic Party base. Unless a convincing progressive counterweight is established in black communities and appeals effectively to black voters, nationalist or even demagogic appeals to African-Americans may be successful to a degree that we have not seen before in the twentieth century. Although the chance that blacks would defect to the Republicans is slight, many blacks might very well join an independent third party or withdraw from electoral politics altogether. These possibilities, all of which are certain to undercut popular progressive prospects in the Democratic Party, are strong and growing.

Black dissatisfaction is pushing African-Americans toward black nationalism (Dawson, 1996; forthcoming). Nearby two-thirds of all blacks believe that racial equality will be achieved neither in their lifetime nor at any point in the history of the United States. These doubts about achieving racial equality are producing dramatic increases in support for independent politics. One half of blacks now support the formation of an independent political party, a doubling of such supporters since 1988. A majority of blacks now believe that blacks should belong exclusively to black organizations – a belief that obviously poses an enormous challenge for those who seek to build multiracial coalitions.

The root of the problem is a corrosive dissatisfaction with American society as blacks experience it. Blacks continue to believe that they live in a country that is fundamentally racially unjust; 83 percent of blacks say that the legal system is not fair to blacks, 82 percent say the same about American society in general, and 74 percent say this about American corporations. An overwhelming 86 percent of blacks say that the American economic system is unfair to poor people. Significantly, large majorities see no prospect of an improving racial climate in the foreseeable future; indeed, a majority believe that the racial situation will get worse. This deep dissatisfaction and sense of exclusion challenge the ideal of an "American community." Over one half of blacks believe that blacks constitute a nation within a nation, not just another ethnic group.

Doubts about participation in the American community go hand in hand with discontent about the Democratic Party in all sectors of the black community. The Democratic Party has had a historic contract with blacks though its inclusive strategies were not always intended and were never fully effective. Blacks entered a Democratic Party that remained segregationist because the New Deal nevertheless expanded economic relief and recovery programs and made desperately needed aid somewhat open to African-Americans. New Deal programs were far from universal and were often administered by racists, but they still benefited large, impoverished sectors of the black community. Since the New Deal, all groups in the black community have supported the Democratic Party because it seemed committed to building a national state strong enough to advance a relatively egalitarian economic program.

But even as they have become intensely angry with and alarmed about Republicans, blacks have become increasingly discontented with Democrats since 1988. By 1994, the percentage of blacks believing that the Democrats work very hard on issues of concern to the black community had declined by 10 percent. During the same period, a growing percentage of blacks came to think that the Republicans are totally uninterested in supporting issues of importance to African-Americans. On economic as well as social issues, blacks oppose moves to the right by both parties. They are worried about the growth in both parties of anti-urban sentiments, attacks on welfare programs, and highly punitive measures against criminals. Vociferous debates around affirmative action and immigration alarm many blacks. And blacks suspect that the Democratic Party in particular may be backing off from promoting racial equality as it seeks to win greater support from whites.

Rising black discontent with the two parties has led to growing volatility in black political opinion and politics. For example, over the course of one year, black assessments of George Bush went from the highest approval level for a modern Republican (61 percent) to the lowest such rating, as approval of Bush dipped lower than even the low approval rates for Ronald Reagan during a recession and for Nixon during Watergate (Dawson, 1997). Black voter turnout has declined since the mid-1980s; and more blacks, according to time series data, are identifying as independents. This volatility reminds us of the 1950s and earlier in the twentieth century, when the perceived unfriendliness of both major parties also brought greater black electoral volatility.

During the 1980s, the racialized nature of the American political system was mirrored by Ronald Reagan and Jesse Jackson, each of whom anchored one end of the political spectrum and was viewed with approval by his racial group and with repugnance by the other. Again in the 1990s we see a similar racial duo helping to define the political spectrum. While neither Patrick Buchanan nor Louis Farrakhan are embraced as wholeheartedly by whites or blacks, respectively, as Reagan and Jackson were, both enjoy significant support in their racial group. In short, the racial politics of the 1990s is defined not only by group (mis)perceptions of exclusion and advantage but also by racial angers and recriminations so high among blacks and whites that a significant portion of each community is attracted to a truly extremist leader who rejects conventional talk of racial comity.

Wanted: A Convincing Progressive Strategy

In this globalized and racialized environment blacks who are given the choice support politicians who call for public intervention in the economy, more government control over corporate decision making in areas ranging from plant location to employment policies, and an increase in spending for a wide range of domestic programs from urban initiatives to education. In the current environment of budget cutting and balancing, many black voters do not hear meaningful proposals from politicians. Blacks face a national politics full of silences. Political calculus encourages politicians to ignore the vast racial divisions in the country. Just as the Democrats want to attract white suburban votes while retaining their black base, Republicans need to hold on to a share of the Latino vote while strengthening white suburban support. Public silences about matters of concern to blacks are often the result – except when they are replaced by shrill calls for the political exclusion of one unpopular group or another.

What is missing is a serious national debate about full citizenship, the good society, and the proper role of active democratic government. These are at the heart of concerns about inclusion and the direction of the country that presently divide groups in American society. Popular progressives face a challenge and opportunity to promote government efforts to address particular and shared concerns as well as a more robust vision of the good society and a common citizenship.

The critical question, of course, is what progressives can do about festering racial divisions. Surely the starting point must be an open conversation among all citizens about the economy, the role of government, and our mutual obligations to one another. We must begin with an honest recognition that blacks and whites, as well as Latinos, come to these challenges and questions from very different social realities, with different perceptions of the world and different value priorities. But members of all groups also share a common citizenship, even if that ideal often seems under attack. Americans of all groups also worry about realizing the American dream for themselves and their children during an era of globally driven economic transformations.

Table 24.1 Causes Cited as Roadblocks to the American Dream

	Whites (%)	Blacks (%)	Asians (%)	Latinos (%)
Discrimination	54			
Crime		57	55	58
Lack of Jobs	54	72	53	67
High Taxes	56	62	56	
Rising cost of living	74	78	56	78

Source Poll: conducted by Harvard University, Kaiser Foundation, and the *Washington Post,* summer 1995. Only cells with 50 percent or greater support are displayed.

Widespread belief in the desirability of the American dream continues across racial and ethnic groups. Blacks are the most skeptical, with 30 percent professing that they do not believe in the American dream at all. But two-thirds of all blacks still do believe in the dream, and the percentages of believers are even higher among the other racial and ethnic groups. Except for Asian-Americans, however, majorities in every other group believe that people like themselves are further from achieving the dream than they were a decade ago: 55 percent of Hispanics, 58 percent of blacks, and 60 percent of whites all say that they have lost ground in the last ten years. Globalization and threats to wages and employment have increased worries about economic security and the future while sparking new (albeit racially differentiated) frustrations about what government has or has not done.

Blacks remain the most intensely dissatisfied, however. Blacks believe that they are being kept back by a big range of factors, above all by such economic ones as lack of jobs and a rising cost of living (table 24.1). Dissatisfaction is higher across the board for blacks than for any other racial and ethnic group. Not only are blacks the only group that has large numbers worried about discrimination and jobs, but blacks are also the group most dissatisfied with high taxes and the rising cost of living. Blacks are caught in the paradoxical situation of supporting the American dream but believing that virtually all of the key components of American life are seriously flawed.

Progressives will not be able to ignore the depth and scope of African-American discontent if they are to build an inclusive politics. Blacks have been crucial participants in progressive coalitions since the Civil War whenever they have been allowed to participate. African-Americans cannot be left out today if a new majority progressive coalition is to form. Not understanding, let alone addressing, the roots of black discontent can lead only to racially fractured, weak coalitions that are progressive in name only and incapable of defeating the right.

Jobs and Decent Communities for All

As popular progressives consider how to build bridges across the racial divide, it is important to highlight the importance of economic problems to blacks and whites alike in this period of global change. Economic hardships are the main obstacles that they face, say blacks. And whites, too, often focus on economic issues. As noted in table 24.1, nearly three-quarters of whites cite living standards as an impediment to realizing the American dream, and a comparable number of blacks agree. Problems with jobs are cited by 54 percent of whites; this is considerably below the percentage of blacks who express concerns about jobs, but it is a majority nonetheless. The overlapping economic worries of whites and blacks suggests possibilities for a broader progressive discourse relevant to people of both races.

Concern about group economic status underlies many of the concerns that blacks have about their racial status (Dawson, 1994a). Throughout the 1980s and in survey after survey, large majorities of African-Americans listed jobs as the number one problem facing the nation. Even in the 1990s, despite growing concern with crime and drug problems in black communities, jobs and the economy remain the problems most often cited by blacks. In fact, black concern with the economy has been connected to a strong and stable majority view among blacks that the government should act to guarantee jobs to all Americans who want to work.

A frankly pragmatic view of US politics has often led African-Americans to support political efforts featuring a progressive economic agenda, even if their racial agenda was either ignored or openly opposed. The original movement of blacks into the Democratic Party was not based on the New Deal's racial policies, which were in no way progressive. It was in response to the New Deal's progressive economic initiatives (Dawson, 1994b; Lewis, 1991). The modern relationship between black Americans and the Democratic Party is a pragmatic one, with blacks voting for Democrats on the understanding that Democrats would work for a strong federal government able and willing to shape a growing and inclusive national economy.

In this period of economic change, progressives must seriously agitate for an inclusive, job-centered economic program; a vigorous education program to re-vitalize the public education system throughout the country and the type of strong health care and child care systems that allow adults to work while children thrive. This core economic program can be similar to the one that was beginning to garner a significant number of non-black votes for Jesse Jackson, even in the face of widespread distrust of Jackson in non-black communities.

A progressive program should be centered around job security and protection of the rights of unions to organize and strike. The programs should rally those who are fighting governors and national leaders intent on jeopardizing the eight-hour work day. At the center should be a guarantee of work for all those who desire to work. And the moral core of the new progressivism should be these twin principles: all able-bodied citizens are expected to work, and in return all are assured decent wages and benefits for honest work. The program must feature educational and health care reforms to ensure that American adults can both secure work and earn decent incomes.

A progressive program also needs to include rebuilding the quality of life in this country. Progressives must argue that the country cannot afford to write off the cities or entire groups of cities. It is not only dangerous to do so but immoral. Only in an environment where *all* residents of civil society have decent opportunities to earn a living and safe and happy lives for their families can we have the type of mutual trust that is vital for a good America. People in all areas of this nation – cities, suburbs, and rural areas – can, after all, find common cause in providing decent environments for our children and grandchildren. Many of the most sinister environmental problems occur in the cities, but there are problems everywhere that need to be addressed through shared or similar measures. As with concerns about jobs and economic opportunity, concerns about family and community can, if tackled cooperatively, build mutual trust and strengthen intergroup alliances.

A New Citizenship

To build real trust, progressives must defend the rights of every group to prosper within the shared social contract and within national boundaries. Progressives must defend legal immigrants and attack anti-immigration appeals often based on racial chauvinism, while supporting trade and foreign policies that make it more possible for workers in other countries also to earn a safe and decent living.

In these troubled times, shared citizenship is a fundamental mechanism for making and enforcing claims and acknowledging mutual obligations. Will we, at this point in history, continue along the difficult path forged by W. E. B. Du Bois and Martin Luther King Jr., fighting for an inclusive polity that embraces active citizens with equal rights and dignity? Or will we embrace the dark and retrograde notions of Peter Brimelow (1995) and Richard J. Hernnstein and Charles Murray (1994), who propose a retreat from egalitarianism on the grounds that some groups will never be fit for democratic citizenship? Our choice will determine the shape of American politics for much of the next century.

Any progressive movement that remains silent in the face of division over who should belong to America, that does not discuss what shape the nation needs to take in order to include everyone, is bound to fail, as so many progressive movements have already failed in America's past. Today, the challenges posed by racial division are not exactly the same as those faced by earlier generations of progressives, and there are new potentials for building a multiracial progressive movement as well, but the need to face up to racial divisions and inequities remains as pressing as ever, and progressives will be measured by how well they promote the causes of a common citizenship and justice for all in our time.

References

Brimelow, Peter. 1995. *Alien Nation*. New York: Random House.

Brodie, Mollyann. 1995. The Four Americas: Government and Social Policy Through the Eyes of America's Multiracial and Multiethnic Society: A Report of the *Washington Post*-Kaiser Foundation–Harvard Survey Project.

Card, David. 1996. Immigration Inflows, Native Outflows, and the Local Labor Market: Impacts of Higher Immigration. Working Paper no. 368. Industrial Relations Section, Princeton University

Cohen, Cathy J., and Michael C. Dawson. 1993. "Neighborhood Politics and African-American Politics." *American Political Science Review*, 87: 286–302.

Dawson, Michael C. 1994a. *Behind the Mule: Race and Class in African-American Politics*. Princeton: Princeton University Press.

Dawson, Michael C. 1994b. "A Black Counterpublic? Economic Earthquakes, Racial Agenda(s), and Black Politics. *Public Culture*, 71: 195–223.

Dawson, Michael C. 1996. "Structure and Ideology: The Shaping of African-American Public Opinion." Unpublished manuscript.

Dawson, Michael C. Forthcoming. *Black Visions: the Roots of Contemporary African-American Political Ideologies.* Chicago: University of Chicago Press.

Dawson, Michael C. 1997. "African American Political Opinion: Volatility in the Reagan-Bush Era." In *African American Power and Politics*, ed. Hades Walton, Jr. New York: Columbia University Press.

Hernnstein, Richard J., and Charles Murray. 1994. *The Bell Curve: Intelligence and Class Structure in American Life.* New York: Free Press.

Kinder, Donald R. and Lynn M. Sanders. 1996. *Divided by Color: Racial Politics and Democratic Ideals.* Chicago: University of Chicago Press.

Lewis, Earl. 1991. *In Their Own Interests: Race, Class, and Power in Twentieth-Century Norfolk Virginia.* Berkeley: University of California Press.

Sassen, Saskia. 1988. *The Mobility of Labor and Capital: A Study in International Investment and Labor Flow.* New York: Cambridge University Press.

Part VIII

Critical Engagements

25

Interview with Stuart Hall: Culture and Power

Peter Osbourne and Lynne Segal

A leading figure of the New Left in the 1960s, Stuart Hall is one of the founders of cultural studies in Britain and its most influential representative, internationally. The first editor of New Left Review, *1960–61, and author (with P. Whannel) of* The Popular Arts, *1964, Hall was Director of the Centre for Contemporary Cultural Studies at Birmingham University from 1967 until 1979. During this period, he oversaw the collective production of a wide range of work, through which many of the central ideas of European sociology, semiotics and the theory of ideology were introduced into the study of culture for the first time in Britain (see, for example, S. Hall et al., eds,* Culture, Media, Language: Working Papers in Cultural Studies, 1972–79, *1980; and S. Hall and T. Jefferson, eds,* Resistance through Ritual: Youth Subcultures in Post-war Britain, *1976). At the same time, the Centre was at the forefront of analysis of the increasing importance of race within British politics (see S. Hall et al., eds,* Policing the Crisis: Mugging, the State, and Law and Order, *1979 – a work which prefigured aspects of Hall's own subsequent analysis of Thatcherism). Following his move to the Chair of Sociology at the Open University, and his participation in the debates at the Communist University of London in the late 1970s, Hall's essays on Thatcherism made him the dominant intellectual figure in a group of writers associated with the heretical Communist Party monthly,* Marxism Today, *and its project for a new kind of Left politics: "New Times" (see S. Hall,* The Hard Road to Renewal: Thatcherism and the Crisis of the Left, *1988). More recently, Hall has written extensively on questions of identity and ethnicity – essays which are collected, along with interviews and critical essays by other writers, in David Morley and Kuan-Hsing Chen, eds,* Stuart Hall: Critical Dialogues in Cultural Studies, *Routledge, 1996. Stuart Hall retired from his position as Professor of Sociology at the Open University earlier this year. He is an editor of the journal* Soundings.

PO and LS: How would you describe the current state of cultural studies in Britain in relation to its past?

Hall: It's a question of how far back you want to go, because everybody has a narrative about this and everybody's narrative is different. There was certainly something distinctive about the founding moment in the 1960s, but even during that period, when it was mainly Birmingham, the field was transformed several times by some pretty major reconfigurations; and in any case, there was never simply one thing going on at any one time. This was partly because of the structure of the Birmingham Centre, each study group had its own trajectory so there wasn't a uniform field. Since then, each appropriation, each widening, has brought in new things. Nonetheless, it's pretty extraordinary to compare the founding moment with what cultural studies is today. Increasingly varied practices go under the heading of cultural studies. If you include the US, that's another bag of tricks, and global dispersion is happening very rapidly. Australians have gone in for cultural studies in a very big way and the Asian development is massive: in Taiwan, Saigon . . . So the most distinctive thing about the present is its situational appropriation. There must be some core which allows people to identify this as opposed to that as cultural studies, and not something else, but in each case there is a tendency for it to take on the intellectual coloration of the place where it's operating. The questions that people are asking cultural studies to answer in Japan are very different from those in Australia or the UK.

PO and LS: What makes up the core?

Hall: It's quite difficult to define. You could say something very general – that culture is the dimension of meaning and the symbolic – but cultural studies has always looked at this in the context of the social relations in which it occurs, and asked questions about the organization of power. So it's cultural power, I think, that is the crux of what distinguishes cultural studies from, say, classical studies, which is after all the study of the culture of Roman times. There are all kinds of cultural studies going on, but this interest in combining the study of symbolic forms and meanings with the study of power has always been at the centre. However varied the appropriation becomes, I would hesitate to call it cultural studies if that element was not there. So I would distinguish between cultural studies and certain versions of deconstruction, for instance. A lot of deconstructionists do work which they consider to be a kind of cultural studies. But a formal deconstructionism which isn't asking questions about the insertion of symbolic processes into societal contexts and their imbrication with power is not interested in the cultural studies problematic, as I see it, although it may be a perfectly appropriate practice. It doesn't mean that deconstruction is ruled out. But around the circumference of cultural studies there has always been this link with something else: cultural studies and psychoanalysis, cultural studies and feminism, cultural studies and race.

PO and LS: It's interesting that you haven't referred to your well-known periodization of this history in terms of changes in a core regulating notion of culture – in that, in Britain, cultural studies began with an anthropological notion of

culture, and then shifted towards a more semiotic conception, at a particular point in the early 1970s. Is there no new notion of culture regulating the field today, in the way that these two paradigms did in the past? Or has the field become more piecemeal, lost its theoretical core?

Hall: I am not sure that there is, or ever was, one regulative notion of culture, although the shift you are talking about is a very substantial one. The Williams appropriation, "a whole way of life" as opposed to "the best that has been thought or said" or high ideas, raised questions from the very beginning. He'd hardly written the sentence before a critique of the organicist character of that definition emerged. It was an important move, the sociological, anthropological move, but it was cast in terms of a humanist notion of social and symbolic practices. The really big shift was the coming of semiotics and structuralism; not because the definition of culture stopped there, but that remains the defining paradigm shift, nonetheless – signifying practices, rather than a whole way of life. There had to be some relative autonomy introduced into the study of signifying practices. If you want to study their relation to a whole way of life, that must be thought of as an articulation, rather than the position which Williams had, which was that "everything is expressive of everything else," the practices and the signification, they're all one; the family and ideas about the family are all the same thing. For Williams, everything is dissolved into practice. Of course, the new model was very linguistic, very Saussurean, but nevertheless, that was the definitive break. Everything after that goes back to that moment. Post-structuralism goes back to the structuralist break. Psychoanalytic models are very influenced by the Lévi-Straussian moment, or the Althusserian moment. If I were writing for students, those are still the two definitions I'd pick out, and I wouldn't say there is a third one. I suppose you might say that there was a postmodern one, a Deleuzian one, which says that signification is not meaning, it's a question of affect, but I don't see a break in the regulative idea of culture there as fundamental as the earlier one.

PO and LS: How does Marxism fit in here? In terms of the two paradigms, something rather ironic would appear to happen, which is that Marxism comes in with the linguistic turn, the turn to signification, through structuralism. So the very thing that people might have thought was distinctive about Marxism – its emphasis on practice over and against some self-sufficiency of meaning – was one of the things it was used to attack.

Hall: The late 1960s and early 1970s was such a big moment. A big moment in terms of cultural studies, to be sure, but also a big moment for everything else, politically. So people see cultural studies in terms of its Marxian development. The moment of its flowering was also that moment. But to understand that moment, you have to go back to an earlier point. Cultural studies was already developing on the presumption that classical Marxism alone cannot explain the cultural; that there are weaknesses there. You can read Williams' early work as an attempt to speak a kind of cultural Marxism without ever mentioning Marx. If you know how to translate Raymond, you can write in "mode of production" in *The Long Revolution,* but he would never use the term. It goes back to the 1930s. It goes back to Leavis. It goes back to the fact that the Marxism that was available then was a very economistic Marxism. It wasn't European Marxism, it wasn't Lukács – that was unknown. What was available was Ralph Fox or *Left Review*; the best of the literary Marxists. And Leavis said: this is inadequate to a conception of culture. Everything begins there. Some people never asked the question about that connection ever again, but a lot of people went on worrying about it, including a lot of Leavisites; L. C. Knights, critics like that, kept wanting to know "What is the relationship between language, literature, and society?" If you can't do it in a Marxist way, you still have to answer that question, or rephrase it, or reformulate it. That was the formation that Raymond addressed. The relation to Marxism was *already inside* the argument prior to 1968. We knew we couldn't simply go by that route. Then, after 1968, something happened; *New Left Review* translated all those writings. Suddenly there was an available European Marxism. There was Adorno, there was Lukács, and so on. There was a moment when the possibility arose that cultural studies might have grounded itself in a Hegelian tradition, rather than a Saussurean one.

PO and LS: This was the moment of the sociology of literature?

Hall: Yes, that's right, but remember, at this point the Birmingham Centre was reading practically everything: reading Mannheim, reading Parsons, reading Weber, reading Goldmann – anything which would help us to ask the question of the relation between culture and society in a way which wouldn't be subject to an economistic reduction, but which would avoid formalist criticism. That's when we first heard about Gramsci. Everything was read as a possible model. It wasn't until the 1970s that things became more grounded in a theoretical under-standing of Marxism – but critically, a Marxism which was distinctive in that it tried to get around the problem of reductionism. That's why Gramsci and Althusser became important: they offered ways through these questions without reductionism.

PO and LS: One thing the Birmingham Centre wasn't reading much of was philosophy. Cultural studies developed in Britain almost wholly without recourse to the theoretical resources of the philosophical tradition – "analytical" or "continental." On the other hand, as people became increasingly interested in theory – theory in the generic sense, the unqualified sense, Theory with a capital "T" – some of the bad things about philosophical abstraction get reinstituted as theory. Cultural studies often seems to have lacked the conceptual resources to deal with this. Do you regret the lack of a philosophical dimension to the formation of cultural studies in Britain?

Hall: I have two possibly contradictory thoughts about this. One is that we were in various ways inheritors of the critique of philosophical abstraction as such; not in a Wittgensteinian way, but as part of the Marxist and sociological critiques of philosophy. We did shift very powerfully towards theory, but we resisted Althusser's notion of theoretical practice, in the name of that earlier critique. We never accepted the notion that theory was an autonomous instance which produced its own internal validation. On the other hand, equally important was the pragmatic absence of anybody interested in or trained in philosophy. Cultural studies came out of history and literature, partly because those were the people who were there. Later, something huge happens with the appropriation of philosophy through literary theory. Homi Bhabha is a product of that moment, when all that had been excluded by British analytical philosophy was taken up by literary people, including psychoanalysis, of course.

It's already there in Anderson's "Components of the National Culture" essay. Literature became a repository of psychoanalysis in Britain, and also of a kind of sociology, because there were no powerful indigenous traditions. Similarly, British philosophy excluded so much that seemed to be relevant if you wanted to read Hegel – no chance, if you wanted to read Saussure – nothing, if you wanted to read Kant – not much, not much that was intelligible to a broader readership anyway. What was there as philosophy wasn't of any help to us in a pragmatic sense. You could see this as disabling, since there are rich traditions in philosophy and a disciplined mode of thinking, which would have made us much more rigorous.

The Relevance of Gramsci

PO and LS: Nonetheless, you continue to be suspicious of general theory. In your recent piece "The Relevance of Gramsci to the Study of Ethnicity," I was struck by your insistence that Gramsci is not a general theorist. It seems that Gramsci continues to be a point of orientation for you *because* he is not a general theorist. This raises an interesting question about the role of Gramsci's thought in the rethinking of Marxism, especially in relation to Althusser. What has Gramsci's role been for you?

Hall: That's a big question. First of all, I am perfectly well aware of making Gramsci up, of producing my own Gramsci. When I read Perry Anderson's classic piece on Gramsci, "The Antinomies of Antonio Gramsci," – Gramsci, the true Leninist – I recognize that there are many aspects of Gramsci's life and work that my Gramsci doesn't take on. It's an appropriation at a particular moment for a particular purpose. I don't think I'm doing violence to Gramsci, but I do know that I am reading him in a certain way, for my own purposes. I'm not a Gramsci scholar, trying to re-occupy his moment. The legitimacy or illegitimacy of this as a practice is neither here nor there. One thinks as one can. Now, one of the most important things about Gramsci for me is precisely his insertion in the specificity of the historical moment. That operates for me as a kind of protocol. Since this isn't Italy, you can't take him literally. You've got to do your own work to make Gramsci work for England. What is good about him is precisely the specificity; the intricate interweaving of religious, regional, cultural, historical, political and rural elements in the Italian context.

But there is also a second aspect, which I find most powerful about Gramsci: the analysis of conjunctures. Conjunctures are precisely an overdetermination. That is to say, the level of analysis at which the conjuncture operates is the level of analysis at which various different elements that you can analytically separate out are no longer separated out, because they're in an overdetermined relation. You can go back and isolate out, analytically, the economy, or the political, but at that level Gramsci doesn't do very much for me. What he offers me is a way of understanding the condensation of all of these elements at a moment which is not repeatable, in a condition which is not repeatable. This focus on the conjuncture is theoretical, in a way, because it defines the level at which the analysis operates, but it is also specific, historically specific. In addition to the question of economism, the aspects of Marxism about which I've always been most hesitant are the ones which are often most attractive theoretically; the ones which allow you to break into the messiness of the historical conjuncture and show that really, if you understand things in much longer terms, in terms of aggregates and tendencies, then it *will* all work out in the end. It's not that I deny that level of the analysis, but what interests me is the next, more determinate, stage (to use Marx's own terms).

It's about privileging a certain level of analysis, a certain object of analysis. I am not interested in capitalism as such, I am interested in why capitalism was like that in the 1960s – or is like this in the 1990s – and why these moments have to be understood as an overdetermination of cultural and political, and other factors: "the concrete analysis of a concrete situation" as Lenin said about 1917, and Althusser reminded us. Of course, there is a sense in which, for Marx, it all has to make sense in terms of the logic of capital, but you couldn't have predicted the moment of 1917 without taking a variety of other determinations into account. This is the level at which Gramsci operates. When he is writing about the analysis of situations he is much better than when he is telling you about what's happening to capital. He doesn't tell you anything new about that. It's a practical-theoretical interest. What is interesting about Althusser is that he was also trying to theorize many determinations. "Contradiction and Overdetermination" is a reworking in another language, a structuralist language, of the Gramscian method. However it seems to me that Althusser is actually better at the opposite moment. He's better at the *longue durée*, analytically separating out the instances. So I use Gramsci as a check on Althusser.

PO and LS: This sounds very empirical, this opening up of the order of determinations to history, but isn't there also a theoretical focus to Gramsci's interest in overdetermination? Isn't overdetermination in Gramsci always something to do with the way that class forces are mediated in their relations to the state? Gramsci may want to avoid class reductionism, but his is still a politics of class, in the

sense that the political function of other social forces is to rearticulate the relationship between classes via their relations to the state. Doesn't this cast doubt on the idea that Gramsci is the route to a political pluralization of social forces, in which class becomes just one social force among others, without any inherent theoretical privilege?

Hall: That is my difference from the people who write about Gramsci who don't take my road. I'm interested in what enabled Gramsci to be so good at elaborating the *other* actors on stage. Take the movement from class to the national-popular, for instance. This movement between the class and the national-popular, which has class inscribed in it but is never reducible to it, is an intriguing movement for me.

PO and LS: Is there a connection here for you between Gramsci's notion of the popular and the emphasis on the ordinary in Williams? Is the former a way of continuing the political work of the latter? Indeed, could one say that the popular is the key political concept of cultural studies?

Hall: Well, the idea recurs in slightly different forms in a continuing thread. In my own case I have made no proper attempt to be consistent between the various versions. Williams was interested in moving down from high theory to thinking about world-class organizations as a part of culture, rendering culture ordinary. I was interested in the popular arts. This was the first thing I ever wrote about: the breakdown between high cultural forms and popular forms, and the idea that popular forms give one, not an unmediated access, but some access to forms of consciousness which are not inscribed in the great books or in the serious high-level philosophies. Then you come to Gramsci and you get the meditation between philosophy and common sense – the popular. Common sense is what ideologies transform, the relationships between common sense and good sense. Then there's the national-popular. Each of these is somewhere along the continuing thread of interest, but I wouldn't say that Williams' culture of the ordinary is the same as my popular culture, is the same as common sense, is the same as the national-popular.

The national-popular has some powerful elements in it, but it also has some worrying ones too. The nation is inscribed there in a slightly different way from other notions of the popular. Common sense doesn't have that notion of the national in it: it is often articulated against the national. Williams is not interested in inscribing his "Culture is Ordinary" into a particularly national framework; although when you reread it later, you realize that in his world it does have all kinds of national peculiarities inscribed in it. But it's not conceived as *English* popular culture, *English* common sense. By the time you get to the national-popular though, you have a more political approach to the question of the popular, because the national-popular becomes an object of national political strategy. So you can use it to think about the terrain of operation of the state. Nonetheless, it also inserts us into a curious argument where we suddenly find ourselves at the edge of socialism in one country, the idea that you could create a national-popular conception of the UK which wouldn't have anything to do with anywhere else. It's a very tricky moment. We're only saved from that by the fact that I move out of the Birmingham Centre and Paul Gilroy moves in! If you go down that path too far, thinking that the privileged object of politics must be the nation – the national-popular rather than the popular – what a bag that puts you in.

PO and LS: This is because Gramsci develops his concepts out of an analysis of fascism?

Hall: Sure. First, out of the Italian context and then out of the appropriation of that context in fascism. Absolutely. It works for him because the problem of the nation is so critical in Italy. The issue of the nation was a focus of popular politics and agitation in Italy and still is, in a way it wasn't in Britain where the contours of the nation were already resolved. Here, the problem of the nation is only too well destined with its borders – its signifying borders – very clearly delineated. This is one of the areas in which the transfer of ideas from Gramsci doesn't work well, the fit isn't good, and it lands you in problems that you didn't foresee.

The Ideological Instance

PO and LS: These problems appear to be connected to the descriptive character of the Gramscian analysis or what has been called the "neutrality" of its concept of ideology. Your use of the concept of ideology has been criticized, by Jorge Lorrain for example, for remaining neutral, for rejecting the element of epistemological critique associated, for some, with its classical Marxist variant. How do you respond to this criticism? It's important because one of its upshots is that people are going to accuse you of complicity in Thatcherism as a consequence of the neutrality of your analysis of its success.

Hall: The problem arises from the Althusserian framework of three different "instances" of the social (the economic, the political, and the ideological) because there is no cultural instance. Where do you put culture, especially after culture has been redefined in terms of signification? Well, one solution is to absorb what is going on in cultural studies into the place of the ideological instance. There is in Althusser's "Ideological State Apparatuses" essay a broad definition of ideological apparatuses which is very close to what Gramsci would have called a hegemonic institution – despite its functionalism, which destroys that essay. "Church, state, family, and school" presents a much broader definition of the ideological apparatuses than the media. So that's one issue: the interface between the Althusserian schema and the more Hegelian question of theorizing the place of culture. The Althusserian schema accepts that each instance is constitutive rather than reflexive. One is looking for what is constitutive about each of them, and then at the articulation between them. That's where the notion of articulation comes in. It's very important. One has already escaped from the notion that if this is the ideological instance it is because it reflects economic and political practice, or because it is dependent on them.

Second, there is the Althusserian argument about the impossibility of getting outside of ideology. I accept it. If you have substituted culture for ideology, the notion that getting outside of ideology is possible, because you can get into science, no longer holds. You can't get outside of culture, because you can't understand what a human being would be like outside of a cultural frame. You can't get outside of the economy either – you can't get outside of the repro-duction of material life – but also, you can never get outside of the reproduction of symbolic life. Culture is forever. Thus, for me, the difference between one cultural formation and another cannot be conceptualized in terms of the dis-tinction between ideology and science where the latter stands for "truth"; it cannot be thought in terms of mystification in the straightforward sense of "mystification versus enlightenment." It may be thought in terms of relative degrees of mystification or misunderstanding, but all culture is misunderstand-ing, in the sense that all culture imposes particular maps on everything. Everybody is not constantly mystified in the same way or to the same degree. There are differences between a better and a worse explanation of something. But there is no truth versus mystification which we can write into the very *a priori* definition of ideology.

PO and LS: So you would say that the charge that you fall prey to a certain "ideologism" misunderstands the concept of ideology that you are working with?

Hall: Yes, it does. Ideology is "neutral" in the sense that ideology and culture are inscribed in language and language is the infinite semiosis of meaning. Now, particular ideologies intervene in language to secure a particular configuration. Language always goes out having many meanings and ideology says: "This is the particular linguistic thing that explains the world. The meaning must stop here, because this is the truth." Ideology intervenes to stop language, to stop culture producing new meanings, and that, of course, is the opening through which interest operates. Why do you want to stop the slide of meaning? You want to halt it because you want to do something, you want to control society in some way. That is the moment of the articulation of power in language. The moment of power is not in ideology or culture as an instance. The moment of power is in the historically situated intervention of ideology in practices of signification. That is the moment of overdetermination. That is the moment of suturing. As Voloshinov says, that's when the powerful want to bring history to an end. They want one set of meanings to last for ever and of course it doesn't, it can't: hege-mony is never forever. It's always unwoven by culture going on meaning more things. There are always new realities to explain, new configurations of forces. So a neutral definition of ideology and culture does not require me to leave the critical question aside. But I place it elsewhere, in the contingent articulation between social forces and signifying practices, not definitionally in the signifying practices themselves.

PO and LS: But doesn't that leave you with a kind of pragmatism?

Hall: Of course it does. I would say it leaves me with a much more contingent notion of history, because ideology is never the *necessary expression* of a class interest. It is the way certain class interests and other social forces attempt to intervene in the sphere of signification, to articulate or harness it to a particular project, to hegemonize.

PO and LS: Something else happens at this point, which is the reception of Foucault. The discursive becomes ever more powerful as a way of understanding subjectivity. Yet in the move from the Althusserian moment to the Foucauldian moment the social forces that you mention seem to disappear. The discursive becomes the total social interest. If Williams dissolved everything into practice, Foucauldians dissolve everything into language. Isn't this what happened in the mid-1980s?

Hall: It happens in a lot of Foucault, but I don't think it's necessary. The reason one doesn't swallow Foucault whole is because Foucault does not recognize the importance of the state, or the importance of social forces in securing a configuration of discourse. Nonetheless, I buy the Foucauldian critique of the science/ideology couplet; I buy the Foucauldian notion that it's not only classes that intervene and I buy the notion that one has to rethink an expressive relationship between class and ideas. A discursive definition is close to the way in which I've been using the terms "ideology" and "culture," but I want to ask residual ideological questions about the Foucauldian notion of the discursive. This is why I wouldn't call myself a paid-up Foucauldian.

The notion of discourse is ambiguous in Foucault. A thinking of discourse as *both* what is said and what is done, which breaks down the distinction between language (discourse in the narrow sense) and practice, is much closer to what I think he intends than just language, but this is not always how he uses the term himself. Unfortunately, most people who use the word discourse think he is talking about what people say. For me, the only function of discourse is to end the action/language distinction. Here I am closest to Laclau – a weak Laclauian or Wittgensteinian position: building a wall includes the things you say, a model in the head, and the things which you do with your body. You can't reduce it to the things you do with your body and you can't reduce it to the things you say. So why say "discursive?" To resist the notion that there is a materialism which is outside of meaning. Everything is within the discursive, but nothing is only discourse or only discursive. It's a convenience, really. Rather than battle on with "ideology," always adding, although not in the classical Marxist sense, in a world saturated by the question of discourse, I find it more convenient to conduct that argument in polemical relation to the linguistic appropriation of

Foucault, instead of going on doing it within the Gramscian-Althusserian-Marxist frame, which is not how people are talking about it any longer. It's a strategy of theorizing – to insist on the constitutive nature of the symbolic-cultural level.

Loosening the moorings

PO and LS: It's a strategy, yes; but surely it has theoretical effects of its own. One of which is an intensification of the pragmatism of the position, a further embrace of contingency. One thing I find problematic about this is that one of the great strengths of Marxism – its status as a historical discourse, a discourse which allows you to think historically about the present – seems to get lost once the present acquires a certain theoretical self-sufficiency. The notion of conjuncture shifts from describing a condensation of forces about which you can also tell a broader story, to a temporally self-sufficient complex of events. Narrative is reduced to the serial sum of conjunctural moments. In Laclau, for example, the idea of discourse is tied up with the notion of contingency in such a way that there's very little credibility given to broader historical and political narratives, which allow one to look *beyond* the conjuncture.

Hall: There is clearly a link between the interest in the conjuncture, the interest in overdetermination, the interest in the infinite semiosis of meaning, and the interest in contingency. All of them are about structuration without structure, or structure without closure. They are all open-ended structures. This is why I like the notion of discursive formation too. I am interested in all of these contingent concepts. However, I do believe that at a certain point, in thinking the appropriation and expropriation, the reappropriation or reconfiguration of Gramsci, Laclau was in danger of moving to a point where anything could be articulated with anything – where any story is as good as any other story – where any narrative can be told. What I resist saying is that there's only one story to be told, whose "truth" one knows from another level. But I do insist that some stories have a much longer structuration, a *longue durée*, almost a historical inertia. Some stories are just bigger than others. Certain social forces have been attached to them historically, and they are likely to go on being attached to them. Unless you do something fairly radical, in Britain, the notion of nation will connect you with particular social forces and a particular, imperial definition of Britain. It's not inevitable – you could decouple it, but a huge struggle has to go on to do so. Why? Because that is how a formation has developed, has become embedded in its subjects, embedded in its institutions, embedded in public narratives. At a certain point in the argument, discursive reconfiguration became a loose, free-floating thing. But the way to tie it down is in terms of historical specificity. That limits my notion of contingency, but it doesn't get rid of it. I agree with Laclau that, without contingency, there is no history. If there's an inertia in historical systems, it's the result of a historical, not theoretical materialism.

PO and LS: Yet it was an ahistorical idealism, which dominated the reception of these ideas. For people coming out of the social movements of the 1970s, what was so strange about the take-up of Laclau by *Marxism Today* in the mid-1980s was that the historical theorizing which those movements had done – of the entrenched nature of gender hierarchy, and the entrenched nature of race, for example – was ignored in favour of a general theoretical principle of equivalence between different social forms of subjectivity. There was a clearing away of political-historical narratives at the very moment when the forms of power they narrated were reasserting their centrality to political life. And all in the name of supporting a politics of movements!

Hall: Well, I agree that is largely what happened. But I would say that it wasn't necessary from the theorizing that it should have been so. It was more to do with the Communist tradition which these people came from. Coming from a very fixed position, they embraced its opposite with a kind of heady openness. They jumped over the intermediary space, which is historically defined. In looking at the actual conjuncture, they should have asked: what are the actual social forces opening this up, on the real terrain in front of us? But they didn't ask that question. It wasn't grounded in that way. In spite of the fact that the Laclau and Mouffe book is about hegemony – *Hegemony and Socialist Strategy* – hegemony wasn't thought in a Gramscian way. What I like about Gramsci is that there is always some concrete instance there, and there is always power. This doesn't prevent you from generalizing, but you can always see some forces on the ground. Whereas what happened in Britain was that the theorizing went up a notch. I agree.

PO and LS: It went up another notch when Lacan was thrown into the brew, because on top of this linguistically based equivalence of subject positions we suddenly had overlaid an account of sexual difference as something which over-rides all other differences. We were presented with a version of feminism which you have described very well, I think, as "reductionism upwards," in which the only issue is positionality in relation to sexual difference in language. All the other work which was done by feminists in the 1970s was let go – in relation to the state, social structure, even gender regimes. All that became unimportant and we were back to fixity again. Once Foucault's concept of discourse is conflated with Lacan's notion of the symbolic – and Laclau does this explicitly – it's hard to see how to make a politics out of it. All this happened in the late 1980s of course, when politics was not a very desirable terrain to be occupying.

Hall: At that moment, the psychoanalytic reduction upwards was very seductive. It reminded one of the valid critique: that so many of the other theories are in-adequate to subjectivity, inadequate to sexuality, inadequate to the psychic. It validated that critique. It also has some common origins with cultural studies in terms of Lacan's relationships to Saussure and Lévi-Strauss. It seemed to come from the same stable: it's about gender, which people need to talk about, since it's been neglected in most of the other central strands of theorizing; but it does land you in an apolitical space in the end. I agree, it leaves you with what I continue to see as the central problem: the more difficult question of the relationship between the symbolic and the social; the psychic and the social. It's a puzzling terrain.

PO and LS: The way you address it in your recent work is through the idea of identity. In particular, you have been trying to give the notion of positionality a cultural turn. In your essay "What's Black about Black Popular Culture?" for example, you talk about moving away from the essentialism debate towards "a new kind of cultural positionality, a different logic of difference." What is it, this "new kind of cultural positionality?"

Hall: It's the notion that identity is position, that identities are not fixed. I make exactly the same moves that I make in relation to Laclau: I loosen the moorings, but I won't float. Identity is not fixed, but it's not nothing either. The task is how to think the fact that identities are important to us, and register some continuities along a spectrum, but we're never just what we were. I think of identity in terms of positionality. Identity is, for me, the point of suture between the social and the psychic. Identity is the sum of the (temporary) positions offered by a social discourse in which you are willing for the moment to invest. It is where the psyche is able to invest in a public space, to locate itself in a public discourse, and from there, act and speak. It's both a point of enunciation and a point of agency, but it won't be repeated, it won't be the same position that you will take up later on; or at least, it won't be the same position that you have in relation to another discourse. The question of whether you identify with black causes is different if it's in relation to white, from when the question of black men or black women is at issue. These are two positionalities. What you might call your "self" is composed of the different positionalities or identities that you are willing to subject yourself to be "subjected" to. The only model that I have for thinking this in a broader way is the Derridean model of *différance*. As you know, this is a model which thinks difference, but not in a binary way. Any particular meaning stakes a positionality on a spectrum which is given by its binary extremes, but you cannot occupy either end. You just need the ends theoretically to think of the spectrum. That's what I call a cultural logical of difference. Difference is important, but I don't think of difference in binary terms. It is positional.

Diasporic Identities

PO and LS: In this work on identity there is one notion which has grown in prominence as a way of giving determinacy to the kind of distributive difference of cultural positionalities that you have been talking about. This is the notion of diaspora. Diaspora has become increasingly generalized: from the Jewish context, to the black context, to ethnicity in general. Do you see it as offering a theoretical model for cultural identity *tout court*?

Hall: Well, it is certainly doing a lot of work. It's connected with the Derridean notion of dissemination, so it's connected with the idea of movement – there is no single origin – and the movement outwards, from narrower to wider, is never reversed. It's connected with the notion of hybridity, so it's connected with the critique of essentialism. But the notion of diaspora suggests that the outcome of the critique of an essentialist reading of cultural transmission is not that anything goes, is not that you lose all sense of identity; it is the consequential inscription of the particular positionalities that have been taken up. The history depends on the routes. It's the replacement of "roots" with "routes." There are no routes which are unified. The further back you go, something else is always present, historically, and the movement is always towards dissemination.

So I certainly don't mean diaspora in the Jewish sense – some umbilical connection to the holy land – quite definitely not! Quite the opposite. That is the most dangerous notion of all. I prefer to use the word adjectivally – diasporic – and I think of ethnicity in the same way. I don't mean by ethnicity some kind of collective home, which you then police. I use ethnicity to signal something specific in the positionality, the particular histories inscribed in the position: what makes your difference different from my difference? That is our ethnicity. And because it is disseminated, it is constantly open to repositioning. That's the logic of *différance* which I am using to think the question of positionality, the question of ethnicity, and the question of diaspora. Theoretically there is a kind of low-flying use of erasure, in the Derridean sense. Ethnicity is the only terminology we have to describe cultural specificity, so one has to go back to it, if one doesn't want to land up with an empty cosmopolitanism – "citizens of the world" – as the only identity. But I don't go back to the concept in its original form. I use it with a line drawn through it. The diaspora has a line through it too: in the era of globalization, we are all *becoming* diasporic.

PO and LS: Is this a historical phenomenon, then?

Hall: That's a big issue which I haven't yet resolved in my mind: whether you can look at earlier periods – pre-conquest, say – when cultures were more self-sufficient and had been over a long period of time, and apply the notion of diaspora there. Whoever lived in Latin America pre–1494 lived in seclusion from Europeans. I'm interested in globalization because it describes our increasing interdependence. It is not that everywhere is the same, but nowhere is any longer outside the play of influence of somewhere else. That is, increasingly, a historical phenomenon. These terms are urgent now because more of the world looks like this. But it isn't that once things were fixed and now they are diasporic. They always were diasporic, at least in the sense that they were always open to difference, always had a bit of the other inside them. So these are relative questions. Those societies were relatively closed, compared with now; just as the old ideologies were relatively stable, compared with now. In the age of the media and the global, ideologies are transformed much more rapidly.

PO and LS: How does this relate to multiculturalism? One of the consequences of Homi Bhabha's use of the term "hybridity" would appear to be a rejection of the established notion of multiculturalism, on the grounds that if culture is produced through difference, *all* culture is multicultural.

Hall: This is an instance of taking an insight one step too far. I'm critical of American multiculturalism, which is inscribed pluralism, because it is grounded in an essentialist notion: each group to its own culture. As in the case of "ethnic" and "diasporic." I prefer to use the word "multicultural" adjectivally. Ours is a multicultural society because of the different cultural registers, but it is not closed. You can see the impact when you walk through London, the impact of difference: differences which are hybridized but not erased. It doesn't enclose any one group to the exclusion of another. There isn't a strong boundary. However, in Bhabha's work, there is a movement towards a radical cosmopolitanism. The notion of cosmopolitanism has some interesting things going for it, but it doesn't ask the questions "Who has the power to become cosmopolitan?" and "What kind of cosmopolitanism is this?" Is the cosmopolitanism of the Humanities Institute at Chicago University the same as the cosmopolitanism of the Pakistani taxi driver in New York who goes back to Pakistan to look after his wife and family every year? These differences have not been inscribed in the idea. That's one difference of emphasis between us.

Having refused the binarism which is intrinsic to essentialism, you have to remind yourself that binaries persist. You've questioned them theoretically, but you haven't removed their historical efficacy. Just because you say there is no absolute distinction between black and white doesn't mean that there aren't situations in which everything is being mobilized to make an intractable difference between black and white. So in that sense, conceptually, I want the binary reintroduced under "erasure." The binary's relation to power is like meaning in language; it is an attempt to close what, theoretically, you know is open. So you have to reintroduce the question of power. The binary is the form of the operation of power, the attempt at closure: power suturing language. It draws the frontiers: you are inside, but you are out. There is a certain theoreticism from the standpoint of which, having made a critique of essentialism, that is enough. It isn't enough. It isn't enough in the world. Apartheid tried to mirror the fantasy of binary closure. It wants to produce exactly what it thinks should be the case. I can't be cavalier about the Nation of Islam if, in an LA project, they are the only people capable of protecting black kids against the LA police. Under these circumstances, let us have a little "strategic essentialism."

PO and LS: I can see how your account of positionalities works at the level of the histories of individuals, the level of existential biography, but I am less sure how it relates to the construction of explicitly political identities.

Hall: Positionalities may begin individually, in the sense that there is a psychic investment in them, but they become positions of enunciation and agency. If the agency includes the building and developing of a common programme around some collective political identity, then they acquire exactly the institutional historical inertia that I described earlier. It doesn't mean you can never leave them: it just means that it's much more difficult. You don't exchange them, like dealing the cards, every time you come back to them. You come to situations with a history and the enunciation is always in the light of an existing terrain. You've already said something like this before and to a degree you're bound by what you said before. Even if you're not wanting to say that again, the new thing you say has to make sense in terms of the thing that you said before, although it also moves it on a bit, of course. The past narrows the field of contingency. There are collective projects and there are therefore collective identities. Those identities are not given for ever, but they're hard to shift. The longer you live them, the more historical weight they have.

PO and LS: But in what sense are these collective identities "political" rather than just "social?" There are different ways of thinking about politics in a society like Britain today. One would be to say politics is about the distribution of social identities; everyone is involved in the constant rearticulation of the elements of the signifying chains which suture people's identities, so all social identity is political. Another, more restrictive approach would be to say political identities require identifications with collective projects for the constitution of the social, but there are relatively few people who have such identifications, because we don't live in a particularly politicized society; there's not a lot of political identity around. How would you respond to that?

Hall: I would tend towards distinguishing the political from the social, but not quite as much as you do. You are talking about the institutionalization of political practice. I think of politics as the mobilization of social identities for particular purposes, rather than in terms of political identities as things in their own right. This is a shift I made during my analysis of Thatcherism. To begin with, I was interested in the political identities that were being staked out, the political project, the seizure of power in the state, and I saw society and culture as the terrain on which this was happening. Today, I would view it the other way round. I think of Thatcherism as a mobilization of shifts that were already going on in the socio-cultural field. It built a political programme by recruiting political agents out of that wider field. So I have inverted the relative weight of the two perspectives. It comes from a suspicion of people who write about politics in a very narrow way, who said about my work on Thatcherism that when political surveys are taken, it turns out that everybody *is* willing to pay their taxes after all. Of course, if you stop people in the street, they will tell you that. But behind that lies the definition of the taxpayer as a socio-cultural figure. Once that discursive figure gets a grip, it doesn't matter what anyone tells the British Social Attitudes survey, because when they get into the polling booth, that is not how they are going to behave. It's another Gramscian notion: what's happening in civil society is where the real political articulations are made.

The Infernal Mix: Marxism Today and the Left in Britain

PO and LS: Perhaps this is a good moment to move on to some questions about your political views, and in particular, your role during the 1980s in helping to define the political project of that group within the Communist Party of Great Britain associated with the journal *Marxism Today,* through your analysis of Thatcherism. That project was enormously influential, far beyond the parochial circles of the CPGB out of which it emerged. Yet it was also highly contentious. In particular, many people, ourselves included, felt that the way it conducted its criticism of the rest of the Left, at its weakest moment for several decades, contributed significantly to its demoralization. At times, *Marxism Today* seemed to want not so much to transform the Left as to destroy it. There was no solidarity. Indeed, it hardly seemed to consider itself part of the *actual* Left. If one looks at the mode of address of most of those pieces, there is no "we" in them. You have spoken elsewhere, biographically, about your difficulty in adopting any of the available positions marked out by the "we" in British politics – speaking about race. *Marxism Today* could never bring itself to adopt the "we" of the British Left. How do you view these matters today?

Hall: I agree about the "we," but I think that there were two different aspects to it. In the first place, *Marxism Today* had a problem with the "we" because of the historic relationship of the Communist Party to the Labour Party, which was always an antagonistic one. Once the *MT* people left the moorings of the Communist Party tradition, they did not want to stop at social democracy. There was an anti-Labour element in their formation and they couldn't give up the reflex habit. The tradition of the New Left which I came from, was different. The New Left had a long history of being both inside and outside, with and not-with, Labour. It recognized Labour as the only viable instrument – not just tactically, but out of a commitment to respect the broadly democratic institutions of the labour movement, with all its faults. But it had a profound critique of "Labourism" as a political culture.

PO and LS: But it wasn't just, or even primarily, the Labour Party that *Marxism Today* attacked, It was "the Left" – something much broader than Labour. The Left included many people who weren't necessarily in the Labour Party, or even in any of the various Trotskyist groups. There was a non-aligned, broadly Marxist and libertarian Left and *Marxism Today* attacked that too.

Hall: That is the second aspect. You may think this is apologetics, but I believe the non-aligned Left disappeared from *Marxism Today* for different reasons. It disappeared because it had never been part of the culture of the CP. My position was that some people, at least, on the non-aligned Left should be our natural allies. I argued that we should have more people writing about the women's movement, about race. There was no actual resistance to the idea, but with a few exceptions they didn't then take the social movements very seriously. This was different from their relationship to the Left of the Labour Party or the Trotskyist Left, whom I think they genuinely believed – on good evidence – weren't convinced that anything fundamental had changed, and didn't see the need to question in any radical way traditional Left ideas.

PO and LS: What prospects do you see for the revival of a broad Left politics today, beyond the mainstream of the Labour Party?

Hall: Having the Labour Party in government presents problems of tactics and organization. When it's in power the Labour Party has a rather different, *modus operandi* from when it's in opposition. When it's in opposition, it's formulating policy and is still open to certain grassroots pressures. When it's in power, the doors close, so you have to push from the outside. But the project is no different. The project remains getting people to recognize how radically the context of power has shifted, and to find ways of intervening on the strategic questions that mark out a real difference between Right and Left.

PO and LS: This would be some kind of transformed social-democratic politics? Would it retain the horizon of an anti-capitalist project, or do you think that has disappeared for the foreseeable future?

Hall: In the present circumstances, social democracy is the only field we have on which to play. It contains anti-capitalist elements, but nothing so automatic or comprehensive as to be labelled "anti-capitalism," because social democracy also means acceptance of the market, to some extent, though never without qualification. Where the stopping point to the market is in each instance is what the politics is now all about. It is also about advancing the public, the collective, the social interest, in opposition to the market, while nevertheless recognizing that a society without markets is a society seriously in danger of authoritarianism. That's what I call "the terrain of social democracy." (I don't use the term in its more historically delimited sense.) It is the infernal mix. It is anti-capitalist in the sense that it's committed to the notion that markets alone cannot deliver the social good, but markets can be regulated, markets can be more or less competitive, and markets can operate alongside the public and the cooperative.

PO and LS: So it's not anti-capitalist in the sense of projecting another, qualitatively different kind of society?

Hall: Exactly. It's not anti-capitalist in the sense of gathering together a whole other alternative solution. It's about setting limits to capitalism, setting limits to possessive individualism, and setting the limit separating the private from the public. That's why it's inevitably a messy kind of politics and a dangerous kind of politics. It can always be appropriated to a softer version of itself. It requires "sleeping with the enemy," which is why today, in the Labour Party, John Prescott remains one of its great hopes. It's more important to have an element of publicity sponsored transport in a public/private system than to have a fully nationalized transportation system, for example.

PO and LS: Prescott is the symbol of a new kind of social-democratic politics?

Hall: He could be. Where he stops, where he can be pushed to, where someone like him is positioned along the spectrum is very important. He is somebody who is willing to play.

PO and LS: He's a rather old-fashioned symbol for the much heralded "new times!"

Hall: I know, but that's interesting. You don't take me seriously enough when I say that ideology is contradictory. What excites one is exactly somebody with the older instincts like Prescott, formed in the old traditions, addressing the new issues: because none of this is about repudiating the past. It is not about saying you were wrong in the past, it's about the fact that the past is past, it's not that period now. One needs more bridging features, who were formed in the adult education movement, who lived their lives in Labour, but who are able to take on the question of public space, to take on the new, modern issues. This was the hope of the GLC [Greater London Council]; an old type of politics becoming a new one. This is what is exciting – not Prescott himself, as such, but figures like him. Blair has never had much connection with these older things. They aren't a real presence for him, in his culture, his formation. He's never been part of even the male-dominated son of democratic structures where at least in principle you have to be accountable for what you do to anybody. That's why Prescott's very ambiguity is exciting. He stands for where most folks out there are, in relation to modernity.

If Prescott can become aware of environmental questions, gender questions, questions of public safety for women, and if he can battle through to a new kind of solution which wins private money and makes it regulated by social ideals, it's a path that thousands of others could take. He's an old trade unionist who's become a new kind of person in the 1990s. These continuities are exciting. *Marxism Today*'s attack on Labourism was not a destruction or a repudiation of these forces. It was a critique of the idea that they could provide the basis for a new politics in a new situation. They are not adequate as such, but they're not inadequate as historical resources. The trade union movement is a resource that one has, but the resource has to think itself anew in new conditions, where you are not going to have the collective ownership of the means of production, distribution and exchange; where you can't nationalize everything. What then does that ideal mean now, in the context of a globalized market and an unregulated capitalism? What would it be like to want those old things in these new conditions? The politics of *Marxism Today* was risky because it aimed to shock the Labour movement out of its security. Our hunch was that they wouldn't face up to the novelty of the new unless they were really shaken. They'll make a small concession here and there and then go back to thinking what they always did. That's why we felt we had to polemicize against the old Left – the radical challenge posed by modernity.

Education, Democracy, New Labour

PO and LS: You referred to Prescott coming out of adult education – he studied at Ruskin College, with Raphael Samuel, among others. This takes us back to an idea which was central to the politics of both the New Left and cultural studies in its original form, the democratization of education. We have seen a rather different version of this idea realized over the last few years in the massification of higher education in the new universities, under conditions of radically reduced resources per student, and in a quite different political climate from what was originally envisaged. How do you view these developments, and the institutionalization of cultural studies within the academy which has accompanied them?

Hall: I'm in favour of the democratization of the university system and opposed to its elitism and narrowness, but of course I have mixed feelings about what has actually happened. It's been done in a very instrumental and contradictory way, at the expense of teaching. The change in the balance between the number of students and the teaching staff has been no benefit to students. We are upping the numbers at the serious expense of the quality of the education we offer. That may sound conservative, but it's true. I can't look my Open University students in the face and tell them that I think they're getting the best education that they could get in our system at present. The Research Assessment Exercise is structured to favour the already established older universities, to validate their position at the top of the tree, and to create differences between teaching universities and research universities, and between teaching staff and research staff. So it's very divisive.

Regarding the institutionalization of cultural studies, I have been criticized for romanticizing the marginality of the Birmingham Centre, and for remarks I've made about the problems that I see affecting cultural studies in its academic institutionalization, particularly in the US – problems about the kinds of questions cultural studies now asks itself. I can see that there may be a romance of the margins in this, but there *was* a connection between the intellectual productivity of the Centre and its attempt to transform its own ways of working. And both were connected with, on the one hand, its relative marginality in relation to the university, and, on the other, the political context in which it was operating, 1968 and after. We were very involved in the sit-in in 1968 in Birmingham, for example, and in student politics generally. In relation to the democratization of knowledge, this was a very creative moment. We had a genuinely collective way of producing knowledge, based on a critique of the established disciplines, a critique of the university as a structural power, and a critique of the institutionalization of knowledge as an ideological operation.

It was not massively successful, but it was very exemplary, very instructive. If you look at the books we produced, they are in a sense unfinished. They lack the tightness of argument that you can get out of a singly authored book. They don't have the coherence of conception. But we were making up the field as we went along. Positions of authority were not open to us. We were deciding what went into next week's MA seminar this week. The circumstances made the field open to the pressure of students, as much as to staff, across those traditional barriers. The most significant act that I performed in the democratization of knowledge was to buy a second photocopier to which everybody in the Centre had access, so that everybody could duplicate, everybody could circulate. It was a literal collectivization of the means of dissemination. We operated by means of internal bulletins and papers, and anybody could put any position into circulation. Of course, there were rows as a result of what appeared, but other people could say "I don't agree" and distribute that. It was very heady. Then there was trying to write collectively, which has its perils. There's nothing quite like having your own sentence rewritten by a student whom you are convinced does not understand and is not going to put it as well as you can! You can get over it, but the experience is certainly salutary.

Now, this is not the only position from which questions about culture and power can be asked, but one does have to struggle with the practice of cultural studies in order to keep on asking such questions when it is situated differently in relation to academically institutionalized knowledge. Institutionalization is not necessarily depoliticization, but you have to work very hard for it not to be. The present situation of cultural studies is not unlike that of feminism, where the permeation of feminist ideas is much wider than those who are consciously in touch in a sustained way with feminist politics, but its moment may already be passing. The backlash against feminism is there, and I can see it coming against cultural studies and media studies. It could be that cultural studies is being taken up by large numbers of institutions at the very moment it has actually crested. One sign of this is the extent to which it is unaware of the way in which the intellectual milieu is being ideologically transformed by a preoccupation with certain kinds of science: genetics and evolutionary theory, especially. It doesn't understand how massive this new line is.

PO and LS: What about its relationship to cultural production; specifically, alternative forms of cultural production? This is clearly something that preoccupied Raymond Williams, although his thoughts on the matter were closely tied up with his hopes for a transformation of the Labour Party. Has the academicization of cultural studies broken that connection, insofar as it was there previously?

Hall: I'm not sure that it was there, in practice, in the 1960s and 1970s, although it was there in the head, in the sense that people involved in one sector were influenced by people involved in the other. There wasn't a very direct relationship, it was more a flow of ideas. There are more developments now, actually, given the institutional expansion, if you include media studies; although that's not always the same thing as cultural studies, by any means. But this is less a relationship to *alternative* cultural production than to the cultural *industries*. In part, it's a question of survival, because you get funded more generously if you teach practice in the media. At no time has there been an adequate connection between the two spheres. At one stage, we imagined that the Centre might take people for a short period, six months or so – the editor of *Spare Rib* could come and work with us, and then go back to the magazine – but it never happened.

There is one exception, though, and that is in the black community. This is one area where alternative production is theoretically informed by what happened in the 1980s – in photography, film, video, painting, and installation. It's an area where cultural politics has very deep roots and resonances, where a lot of the political issues are also issues about identity and representation. This was the first generation which entered higher education, art schools and the polytechnic colleges, where they encountered a lot of new ideas. It's been extremely valuable for me, because my own work on ethnicity and race has been as much informed by the work of people who are actually producing creative work as by those who are theorizing about it. I'm excited about the forms in which a lot of that theorizing now takes in artistic practice.

With respect to Raymond, I must say that this is the area where I have always believed that it was least worth thinking strategically in relation to the Labour Party. Cultural politics is the one thing Labour seemed destined not to understand (Blair may actually represent a shift here). The GLC was the last moment when urban politics, alternative cultures, and the idea of a popular politics came together. Since then, for all its talk about modernization, the Labour Party has, until recently, been rather deaf to cultural change.

PO and LS: Is this connected to its apparent indifference to questions about race?

Hall: In part. It's stuck in a minority equal opportunities strategy, and if it can keep that ticking over it thinks it's done its duty as far as race is concerned. It has no idea about the cultural diversification that has taken place in Britain, of how important cultural politics and identity questions have become to the politics of race. It has no sense of the infiltration of black street culture into mainstream British popular culture, or of the transformation of popular language by the black vernacular. It is deaf to the wider cultural terrain. The Labour Party could not have occupied so complacently that dead appeal to "Middle England" in the way it did in the last election, if it had any inkling of the importance of cultural diversity. So it's not only about race, it's about all the different cultures that make up the mosaic of culture in Britain today.

PO and LS: Presumably, this will cause them trouble over Europe. Further unification doesn't seem likely without some transformation in people's cultural identities. Unless people can be persuaded to think of themselves as in some sense European citizens, Euroscepticism will never go away. How do you view this?

Hall: I'm gloomy. I've always been dubious about the way in which Labour became converted to Europe on narrowly economic grounds. It never asked itself how it's going to govern people who don't think of themselves as sharing the European inheritance in any large cultural sense. Again, the cultural dimension has been missing. They don't have a strategy for it. They don't have a language for it. It could put a brake on other things they want to do. Euroscepticism, as a cultural phenomenon, may just keep repeating itself and limiting how far it's possible for them to go.

PO and LS: Is this the sort of thing you had in mind when you wrote about the "lost opportunities" of New Labour in *Soundings* recently?

Hall: It was one of them. The lost opportunity I had in mind was the opportunity to develop a truly transformative reformist politics: a politics which explicitly sets out to mark its difference from Thatcherism in carefully defined ways. New Labour are right about the profoundly changed conditions in which they are operating. Thatcherism was very effective in mobilizing a political project out of the confusions of socio-economic and socio-cultural change. It almost succeeded in making it appear as if there was only one project, only one politics that could flow from these changes. It has always seemed to me that the only way in which any kind of Left could be rescued from that situation is by saying: "Yes, we will address the change, in the Gramscian sense, and direct our minds violently towards the reality of the changed circumstances in which we find ourselves. But at every point we will try to mark out the difference of our philosophical-political response to these circumstances."

Labourism was rooted in a historical moment which has gone. The Labour Party had to go through a process of asking itself: "What is this society really like? What are the forces at work, leading in what direction? What are the changed global conditions in which we take power? And what would be a Left political project which could be developed out of that?" Then it had to undertake a second, tactical assessment, at the popular level: "How far can we go?" It needed both things: a strategic assessment and a tactical adaptation. These things would have changed the reflexes of Labourism. But I'm afraid Blair settled for something more cosmetic.

PO and LS: You said earlier that if they'd had a cultural politics, they could never have made the kind of appeal to Middle England that they did. Yet some would say that was the basis of their electoral success. So if they'd had a cultural politics, would they still have got elected?

Hall: That's why I separated the two things out. Strategically, one thinks: "This is a much more culturally diverse society and this is a good thing." Tactically one thinks: "After eighteen years of Thatcherism, this is not a message we can quite put out at the moment." One needs a minimum programme. You don't simply announce that cultural diversity is wonderful. You do things each of which has something attached to it which says: "What is important about this is that it is for a more culturally diverse population, which can't any longer be harnessed to one identity, in one place. What is important about this is that people also think like this in France and Denmark." You don't just plonk cultural diversity down, because then nobody votes for you.

Take privatization. You can't find the money to take everything back from privatization, and in any case you probably don't want to, but you do need an alternative to privatization as an exemplary resolution. You don't say, "This is a programme designed to roll back privatization." You pick the most unpopular privatization and make an example of it. You pick rail privatization, which nobody wanted. You get as many Middle England people on to your side as possible. You say: "Rail happens to be one of the things which we cannot run properly through privatization and the market. Draw your deductions from that." That's what I mean by a minimal but paradigmatic programme. The difference isn't what you organize on politically, to get the vote, but you always look for the wider, philosophical deduction which can be drawn from what you do, which can be generalized: "If that is so, what else is like that? Water is like that." This is like that, that is like that . . . In ten years of the educative function of the state, people will be saying: "Some things have to be run by the state, because you can't get what you want by the market alone." Thinking about tactics in terms of a broad strategic, long-term historical alternative perspective, this is what "learning from Thatcherism" always meant.

Interviewed by Peter Osbourne and Lynne Segal
London, June 1997

26

Angela Y. Davis:
Reflections on Race, Class,
and Gender in the USA

Lisa Lowe

LL: Please begin by considering the social, political, and economic shifts that have taken place in the United States during the period of the 1960s to the 1990s. I would like to invite you to characterize what, in your opinion, has shifted and what has not. In other words, we no longer have the FBI and police assaults on Black Panther chapters all over the country; but we do have Mumia Abu-Jamal on death row in Pennsylvania. We no longer have Jim Crow segregation, but we have another kind of segregation: we have a Supreme Court ruling that it is unconstitutional to have "racial preferences" for affirmative action. I wonder if you could put this current moment in the 1990s into a dialectical relation with the 1960s.

AD: There are many ways to talk about the relationship between the '60s and the '90s. The social movements of the '60s – the civil rights movement, various movements of Native Americans, Chicanos/Latinos, Asian-Americans, the women's movement, the student movement – did bring about significant, if not radical, transformations. Much of what we can call progressive change, particularly in the area of race, can be attributed to struggles waged by those movements. However, at the same time, a new terrain was established, which at times appears to contradict the meaning of the movements of the '60s. Did we work so hard in order to guarantee entrance of a conservative black man, who opposes affirmation action and women's reproductive rights, into the Supreme Court? Rather than simply despair that things are taking a reactionary turn, I think it is important to acknowledge the extent to which the black movement allowed for the emergence of a much more powerful black middle class and the breakup of an apparent political consensus. There are similar middle-class formations among other racial ethnic groups. So the question today is not so much how to reverse these developments to re-find ourselves, based on a kind of nostalgic longing for what used to be, but rather, to think about the extent to which movements for racial and gender equality can no longer be *simply* based on questions of desegregation. A different kind of "political," a different kind of politics, really, has to inform this movement. I don't know. Does that make any sense?

LL: It makes a great deal of sense. When Stuart Hall talks about the convergence of the different contradictions of race, class, and gender, he suggests that the material conditions of a given historical moment make a certain contradiction rise to the surface. Could you speak about the conditions of our current moment in relation to these contradictions, addressing the ways that capitalism utilizes racism and sexism? Has the conjunction of race, class, and gender shifted in our contemporary period?

AD: Well, one of the strongest factors that has brought about the current set of transformations is deindustrialization. And the increased mobility of capital. And what I would say initially is that the collapse of an international socialist community – for good reasons, one can point out – which has led to the assumption that capitalism is the only future alternative makes it increasingly difficult to draw connections between the deteriorating conditions in communities of color and the restructuring of global capitalism, for example, the focus on crime as the most serious social problem, and the rise of the punishment industry. Another example is the related criminalization of single mothers of color through the ideological representation of the "welfare queen" as the reproducer of poverty. So the connection between the globalization of capital and these developments – which began with the Reagan–Bush administration, but have reached their peak recently – aren't generally made.

LL: Are you saying that because of global restructuring, the proletarianization of women of color in the United States is simultaneous with the exploitation of women in the so-called third world? In other words, that both exploitations are specific to the global restructuring of capitalism?

AD: Absolutely. But at the same time, what I'm trying to get at is the way in which these developments are actually represented within social movements, for example, within the black community, the increased focus on young black males, which is important, but dangerous at the same time. Important because of the fact that black youth, young black men, certainly are very much at risk since a quarter of them are under the direct jurisidiction of the criminal justice system, either in prison, on parole, or on probation. But at the same time, the demonization and criminalization of young black women is often totally neglected. What is also neglected is the fact that the increase in the incarcerated population of women is about twice that of the increase in the rate of incarceration of men.

Consider the recent movement spearheaded by Reverend Ben Chavis and Minister Farrakhan of the Nation of Islam, which calls upon black men to reassert their primacy within black families and communities. A Washington demonstration of "a million black men" in the fall of 1995 is predicated on the fact that women will stay at home in support of "their men." Certainly, in this period of increased mobility of capital, there is a gendered assault on young black men – jobs that used to be available have migrated to other parts of the world. However, to assume that saving black communities is equivalent to saving black men harks back to a dangerous, unreflective masculinist nationalism that informed black movements earlier on. There are productive ways in which a gender analysis can specifically identify ways in which men are disproportionately affected by deindustrialization. Moreover, during this period, if black men choose to organize as men, questions such as male support of women's reproductive rights and of lesbians' right to adopt and male opposition to violence against women should be emphasized. Rather than male primacy in families and communities, gender equality in private as well as public spheres needs to be foregrounded.

LL: From your vantage point now, when you think about the breakup and the transformations of black liberation struggles in the '60s, what is your understanding of the relationship between the external assault from the FBI, the police, and the state and the internal difference and conflict about priorities, about methods?

AD: In a sense, the external assaults worked hand in hand with the internal contradictions. We know that J. Edgar Hoover identified the Black Panther Party as the greatest threat to the internal security of the country, and that the FBI orchestrated assaults from one end of the country to the other, in collaboration with local police departments. This has been documented. What has not been taken as seriously are the internal struggles within radical black and Latino organizations. It was the inability to address questions of gender and sexuality that also led inevitably to the demise of many organizations. Many elder activists, as well as people who had not yet been born during the era, mourn the passing of the Black Panther Party, and nostalgically look back to that period as one in which questions of who and what constituted the enemy were crystal clear. The recent film by Melvyn Van Peebles represents the Black Panther Party in that kind of nostalgic and romantic way. If you look at Elaine Brown's book, which has been abundantly criticized – for good reasons, in part – she does reveal the extent to which the BPP and many of its fraternal organizations were very much informed by masculinist notions of what it meant to engage in struggle. These notions of struggle depended on the subordination of women, both ideologically and in practice. The women were responsible for a vastly disproportionate amount of work in a struggle constructed as one for the freedom of "the black man." This kind of critique has to continue. A number of recent Ph.D. dissertations look at women's roles in organizations like the Young Lords, the Black Panther Party, the Brown Berets, and the American Indian movement. Tracy Matthews, who was in the history department at the University of Michigan, has written her dissertation on women in the Black Panther Party. Hopefully there will be a nice collection of books coming out in the next few years, which will begin to demystify the images of radical organizations of people of color in the late '60s and early '70s, for the sake of young people who desire to do activist work in the contemporary period.

LL: Can I ask a little more about a different kind of contradiction? In *Racial Formation in the United States*, Michael Omi and Howard Winant argue that during the period of civil rights struggles, civil rights legislation was in a way the state's attempt to appropriate and co-opt certain parts of the broader, wider variety of social movements pressuring for more change on race.[1] Would you agree with this analysis?

AD: During the civil rights era, the primary struggles were for legal transformation. It was important at the time to break down the legal barriers, to change the laws, to challenge the juridical status of people of color. Parenthetically, one of the real weaknesses of the civil rights movement was its paradigmatic black-white focus on race. But Omi and Winant point out correctly that social movements addressed issues that went beyond the legal construction of race. Beyond voting rights and desegregation, issues of education, health care, police repression, issues of jobs, etc. were raised. Organizations like SNCC [Student Nonviolent Coordinating Committee] that were rooted in voter registration and desegregation struggles initially focused on those issues, but then went on to address questions that emerged from the urban northern black communities as well.

LL: They don't argue, of course, that there was total co-optation. But rather that civil rights legislation was the response of the state to activist social movements, some of which could have called for much more radical change.

AD: Absolutely.

LL: In a way, it goes along with what you were pointing out earlier, that Clarence Thomas is where he is because of affirmative action and the contradictions of liberalism. Yet, despite such contradictions, we must still insist on the concept of rights, and humanity, and fight to keep in place the legislation that is now under attack.

AD: Yes, but the assumption that the state is the primary guardian of the victories that were won by the civil rights movement has led to a great deal of chaos, and an inability to conceptualize where social movements can go from here. At the same time, many of the leaders of the civil rights movement now occupy putative positions of power within the state structure. Look, for example, at Ron Dellums, who was initially associated with the Black Panther Party in Oakland, California. As a matter of fact, he was elected to Congress based on his militant and radical positions. For the past twenty-five years, he's had to negotiate very different kinds of positions. His work within Congress has been very important.

But the constituencies which were activist constituencies became electoral constituencies. With the election of Clinton, which ended the Republican Reagan–Bush era, there was the assumption that now, yes, the state will fulfill the goal that was set for it during the transformative period of the civil rights struggle. And that, as a matter of fact, the reliance on the new administration led to the absorption of oppositional organizations – and sometimes almost entire movements – into state structures.

LL: With the priority, would you say, on enfranchisement and assimilation into the state, as opposed to working for a larger transformation?

AD: That is true, and it is a rather complicated process. In many instances people truly believe that they will be able to bring about radical transformations from and within new positions of state power. The work that I am doing on prisons is a case in point. Many people whose connection with prison issues comes from their earlier involvement in oppositional struggles – who were involved in, and in some instances were initiators of, the prisoner rights movement – are now working within correctional bureaucracies. Here in San Francisco, the current sheriff and assistant sheriff have a long history of involvement in progressive movements. The assistant sheriff spent many years in prison during the '60s and early '70s and was associated with George Jackson and the internal prisoner movement. He was one of the founders of the California Prisoners Union. Now he inhabits the very positions which were once occupied by his adversaries. Under his leadership people have been hired to work within the jail structures who are former prisoners (such as myself and Johnny Spain, once of the San Quentin Six) and who were once visible as militant activists (such as Harry Edwards, who organized the protests at the 1968 Mexico City Olympics). The assumption, of course, is that these individuals will press for transformation. However, under such conditions transformation is conceptualized very differently. The formulation of radical prison work as leading toward the reduction of prison populations and the abolition of jails and prisons as the primary means of addressing social problems such as crime, unemployment, undereducation, etc. recedes and is replaced with the goal of creating better, more progressive jails and prisons. I am not suggesting that we should not use whatever political arenas are available to us. However, once one becomes integrated into state structures, it becomes increasingly difficult to think about ways of developing radical oppositional practices.

LL: You have always been a voice for feminist concerns within black liberation struggles, yet it has been difficult for Marxist anti-racist work to find a "home" in feminism as it has existed in the US women's movement. In *Women, Race, and Class*, but also in your lectures "Facing Our Common Foe" and "We Do Not Consent," you argue that racism and classism affect the construction of political agendas even and especially in the white women's movement regarding race and reproductive rights.[2] I wonder if you could discuss the struggles

within US feminism in the last decade. You argue eloquently that historically rape has been defined as rape of the white woman's body, who is the property of elite white men, which obscures the possibility of thinking of black women's bodies as victims of rape, or victims of assault, and subordinates the issue of black women's health. Has the anti-racist critique successfully changed white feminism?

AD: From one vantage point, those critiques have been very successful. Which isn't to say that hegemonic white feminism, in the sense in which Chela Sandoval uses the term, has really substantively changed. But it is no longer possible to ignore issues of race. Even those who only pay lip service to race analysis understand this. Twenty-five years ago, dominant feminism began to evolve as if women of color did not exist. As a result, vast numbers of women of color who were interested in women's issues did not associate themselves with early feminist approaches. Toni Morrison, who is very much associated with black feminists today, wrote an article in the early 1970s in the *New York Times Magazine* in which she argued that feminism belonged to white women and had no relevance for black women. The most interesting developments in feminism, I think, over the past couple of decades have occurred within the theories and practices of women of color. US feminism would not be what it is today, US feminisms would not be what they are today, if it hadn't been for the interventions by women of color. So I think that's a very positive sign. At the same time, within communities of color, feminism has become a much more powerful force and has had an impact on all kinds of issues, on the way issues are constructed, the way campaigns are developed. The critique has to continue, though I'm not suggesting that the work has been done. It's a lot more complicated today. Women of color who refer to themselves as feminists still find that it is not easy to identify as a feminist. For one, feminism is often considered obsolete. There are a number of new works that have been published by young feminists, both feminists of color and white feminists, that, in order to dissociate themselves from traditional feminism, tend to revert to pre-feminist ideas.

LL: I would like to ask you to situate yourself in women of color discourse. Many people would locate women of color critique in the anti-racist critique of white feminism: Cherríe Moraga, Gloria Anzaldúa, or Audre Lorde would be key figures in this nexus. Or alternatively, others would locate it in the black feminist critique of male-dominated cultural nationalism. But I understand the genealogy of your work and practice as articulating a feminist anti-racist critique within the Marxist critique of capitalism. Yours is a most important synthesis that really advances women of color critique. Please share your thoughts about women of color as a political project and as a research project.

AD: Well, I don't know if we can talk about women of color politics in a monolithic way.

LL: It's perhaps even difficult to understand it as a social movement. In a way it's a critique that has various locations.

AD: There have been really interesting developments over the past fifteen years or so, since most people date the development of women of color as a new political subject from 1981, when *This Bridge Called My Back* was published.[3] Women of color conceptualized as a political project, to borrow Chandra Mohanty's notion, is extremely important. You might also use Omi and Winant's notion and argue that it is possible to think about women of color as a different kind of racial formation. And the work that you, Lisa, have done on women of color emphasizes the fact that it is a provisional identity that allows the move beyond identity politics articulated in the traditional way. The fact that race is placed at the forefront of women of color politics is important, because it also challenges the influence of nationalism on identity politics. Women of color formations are compelled to address intersectionality and the mutual and complex interactions of race, class, gender, and sexuality. That is what is so exciting about the possibilities of women of color research and organizing strategies. For the last four years or so I have been working with the Research Cluster for the Study of Women of Color in Collaboration and Conflict. Many students and faculty involved locate their work within a progressive scholarly and activist tradition that seeks to bring about structural and ideological change. The Women of Color Resource Center here in the San Francisco Bay Area attempts to forge stronger ties between researchers and grassroots organizers. Asian Immigrant Women's Advocates (AIWA) is one of the groups associated with the Women of Color Resource Center. This organization traces its genealogy back to the Third World Women's Alliance founded in 1970. This means that what we call women of color work predates 1981, the year in which *This Bridge Called My Back* was published, which is usually evoked as the originating moment of women of color consciousness. During the earlier era, the anti-imperialist character of third world women's work inflected it with a strong anti-capitalist kind of critique. The influence of Marxism is still very much visible in, for example, the Combahee River Collective manifesto. While it is important to affirm the momentous cultural work initiated with the publication of *This Bridge*, the earlier, more explicitly anti-capitalist traditions should not be erased.

LL: And those connections are like a history that needs still to be written.

AD: Yes. What we call women of color work or US third world women's work can be traced back to the civil rights era. During the 1964 campaign spearheaded by SNCC in Mississippi, Georgia, and Alabama, there was an emergent anti-masculinist critique, directed against the obstinately male leadership. This critique crystallized in an internal organization of black women which later established itself as an autonomous organization, the Black Women's Alliance. While cross-racial coalitions were not as self-consious as they tend to be today, the political projects to which Puerto Rican women (antisterilization work, for example) and Asian-American women (Vietnam solidarity work, for example) were drawn, were also embraced by the Black Women's Alliance, which later reconceptualized itself as a Third World Women's Alliance. Some of the same women associated with those efforts in the late '60s – like Elizabeth Martinez, Linda Burnham, Fran Beal – continue to be active through organizations like the Women of Color Resource Center. Around the same time, numerous lesbians of color organizations emerged. In fact, the term *lesbian of color* acquired currency before *women of color* entered into our political vocabulary. In other words, although we refer to "women of color" as a new political subject, there is a rich, unexplored history of women of color political projects. We shouldn't assume that women of color work has been going on for only a decade or so.

LL: Or that it's a reaction against . . .

AD: . . . what we used to call white middle feminism. NOW was founded in 1964. We can also trace the emergence of a radical women of color feminism back to the same year.

LL: Would you speak a bit about your recent book project on women and the blues? I'm wondering if you could comment on the question of cultural forms as alternative species, or popular culture as an informal site for the transmission of oppositional strategies and popular wisdom about survival.

AD: The fact that historical modes of transmitting culture are not mechanically determined by economic relations does not mean that all modes are equally possible regardless of a group's class position. I have been interested in the history of gender consciousness in black communities since the research I did around *Women, Race and Class*. Much of the material I utilized in that work – even that which specifically addressed issues of working-class women's consciousness – was produced by women and men who can be defined as members of the black intelligentsia. My own interest in popular culture is related to an attempt to expand that original project on gender consciousness in black communities, focusing on the blues as a site for reflecting on black working-class feminist consciousness and on the transmission of that consciousness. In this book, which is called *Blues Legacies and Black Feminisms*, I try to present blues performances as an alternative site for recovering historical forms of working-class women's consciousness.

LL: In your autobiography you wrote, "the forces that have made my life what it is are the very same forces that have shaped and misshaped the lives of millions of my people. I'm convinced that my response to these forces has been unexceptional as well, that my political involvement, ultimately as a member of the Communist Party, has been a natural logical way to defend our embattled humanity."[4] I wonder if you could talk about your formation in Marxism and what Marxism has meant to you.

AD: From where I stood – which was a very different location from that of the vast numbers of people who followed my trial – I did not feel that my life experiences were exceptional enough to merit inscription in an autobiography. Besides, I was very young, so I had to think about that project as a "political" autobiography. At the time I didn't realize that I had conceptualized it in the tradition of the black autobiographical genre that could be said to go back to the slave narrative. That didn't occur to me until long after I had written it. It's difficult to identify a single development that led me to Marxism. I grew up in a family which had numerous ties to individuals in the Communist Party. Although my mother never joined the Communist Party, she worked in organizations with black communists who were organizing in Birmingham, Alabama, which, because of the steel mills, had become an industrial center in the '30s. She was an officer in the NAACP and in the Southern Negro Youth Congress, which had been established by communists. Because of my mother's connection with communists, we were often followed by the FBI during the McCarthy era. By the age of six, I was already aware of the extent to which the government would pursue people who had different ideas of what kind of social order should prevail in this country. While I was attending a progressive high school in New York, I read the *Communist Manifesto* for the first time. I was fortunate enough to have a history teacher who openly espoused Marxism and encouraged us to think critically about the class interests represented by dominant historiography. At the same time I was active in a communist youth organization and for many months picketed Woolworth's every Saturday because of their policies of segregation in the South. I guess you might say that I learned very early to take for granted the insightfulness of Marxist literature and also to draw connections between theory and practice.

As an undergraduate, my interest in Marxism was further stimulated by professors like Herbert Marcuse. As a French major, I became very interested in the way Marxism was integrated into existentialist philosophy – and by Sartre's political activism. Working with Marcuse, I began to study the philosophical history of Marxism and read Kant, Hegel, as well as Marx. As a young activist in high school, I already considered myself a Marxist. By the time I finished college, I was even more convinced that Marxist analyses could help me make sense of a world which seemed to be so saturated with racism and class exploitation. I guess I had the good fortune to sort of grow into Marxism or grow up with Marxism, rather than having to later work to replace dominant modes of thought with a critical Marxist approach. I should probably point out that the high school I attended, Elizabeth Irwin High School, was rather exceptional. It was actually cooperatively owned by teachers, many of whom had been blacklisted as a result of their political involvements during the McCarthy era.

LL: How important is it, do you think, for students and young people who want to be activists to read Marx and to have a rich education in Marxist theory?

AD: I think it's extremely important. However, many students today encounter

Marx's ideas not so much by reading the original works, but rather through their reception in contemporary theoretical literature and in popular culture. Many students might be familiar with Marx the political economist, but are entirely unfamiliar with the early philosophical writings. While I would not make the kind of argument that conservatives present regarding the need to return to the basic – to the "classical" texts in the Western intellectual tradition – I do think that a closer familiarity with Marx's writings might help students to assess critically our contemporary conditions.

LL: Moving into a discussion of the university, pedagogy, and the role of intellectuals of color, I wonder if I could ask you about how you think of your role as an educator and your role in the formation of intellectuals of color.

AD: I grew up in a household of teachers. Both my mother and father were teachers. Although my own decision to go into education came much later, I learned very early to value education and its liberatory potential. In the black community in which I was reared, teachers were among the most respected members of the community and were expected to provide leadership – perhaps in even more fundamental ways than ministers, who are often considered the community's natural leaders. Education and liberation were always bound together. I was persuaded very early in my life that liberation was not possible without education. This is one of the reasons I always felt drawn to the radical potential of education and why I am particularly interested in working not only with students of color, but with white students as well who make this connection.

LL: Who and what were your influences in this regard?

AD: Studying with both Adorno and Marcuse allowed me to think early on about the relationship between theory and practice, between intellectual work and activist work. Adorno tended to dismiss intellectual work that was connected with political activism. He argued that the revolution had failed, not so much because of problems presenting themselves in the practical implementation of revolutionary theory, but rather because the theory itself was flawed, perhaps even fundamentally flawed. He therefore insisted that the only sure way to move along a revolutionary continuum was to effect, for the present, a retreat into theory. No revolutionary transformation was possible, he said, until we could figure out what went wrong in the theory. At the time student activism was on the rise in Germany. I studied in Frankfurt from 1965 to 1967, which was a period during which the German Socialist Student Organization gained in membership and influence. Because many of the student leaders were directly inspired by the history of the Frankfurt School – and some young professors affiliated with the Frankfurt School like Oscar Negt were actively involved in the SDS (Sozialitische Deutsche Studentenverbund) – we were able to critically engage with Adorno's ideas. Interestingly enough, many of Horkheimer's and Adorno's ideas were mobilized in challenging this advocacy of theory as the only possible mode of practice. I was involved, in fact, in the production of a pirate edition of *Dialectic of Enlightenment*, which Adorno and Horkheimer were not yet willing to republish. We typed the text on stencils, mimeographed it, and sold it for the cost of its production. A similar edition of Lukács' *History and Class Consciousness* was also produced.

Marcuse, of course, called for a very different relationship between intellectual work and political practice. There is a story I like to tell about Marcuse's involvement in UCSD campus politics, which certainly informed my ideas on the role of the teacher and on the need to maintain always a creative tension between theory and praxis. Back in the late '60s, the emergent Black student organization, in alliance with the Chicano student organization, decided to campaign to create a new college at UCSD, which we wanted to name the Lumumba-Zapata College. We envisioned it as a college which would admit one-third Chicano students, one-third Black students, and one-third working-class white students. We had it all worked out! Or at least we thought we did. At one point in a rather protracted campaign, we decided to occupy the registrar's office. I said I would ask Herbert about his possible participation in the takeover. I explained to him that we would have to break a window in order to gain entrance. In other words, we risked being charged with breaking and entering and trespassing. If he were the first person to enter the building, we were less likely to be arrested and/or expelled from the university. Without a moment's hesitation, Herbert agreed: "Of course I'll do it." There was no question in his mind. At that time he was about seventy-five years old. He was the first person to walk into the registrar's office. Our work acquired a legitimacy that would have been impossible without his participation. In the classroom and through his writings and lectures, Marcuse defended the radical activism of the late '60s. The emergence of an international student movement, the social movements of people of color, the rise of feminist activism brought a new, more optimistic dimension to Marcuse's ideas. The seduction of the "one-dimensional society" could be resisted. He not only theorized these developments, but actively participated in mobilizations both in the United States and Europe. Working so closely with him during that period, I learned that while teaching and agitation were very different practices, students need to be assured that politics and intellectual life are not two entirely separate modes of existence. I learned that I did not have to leave political activism behind in order to be an effective teacher. Of course, this insight got me fired from my first job at UCLA and during my first year there spies recorded every comment I made in class which might have political undertones. I was first fired for my membership in the Communist Party. The second time I was fired it was becasue of my off-campus activities in support of political prisoners.

LL: Please speak about your teaching, how you encourage students to do projects that are both activist and intellectual. What sort of role do you take in shaping these projects? Perhaps you could describe the Women of Color Research Cluster at UC-Santa Cruz.

AD: Many of the students who work with me are involved in very interesting projects on social movement history, cultures of resistance, applying new historiographical approaches. One student is attempting to rethink black women's involvement in the labor movement. Another is attempting to develop new ways of theorizing Puerto Rican migration, foregrounding questions of gender and sexuality. My students are doing very interesting work, work that can potentially make a difference.

The Women of Color Research Cluster at UC-Santa Cruz was formed four years ago. It was the brainchild of Margaret Daniels, a History of Consciousness graduate student who is doing her dissertation on women of color film festivals. She examines these film and video festivals as an important site for the construction of women of color as a political subject. Maria Ochoa, also a History of Consciousness student, worked closely with her. Thanks to their leadership, an impressive number of graduate students, faculty, staff, and some undergraduates came together under the auspices of the cluster, funded by the Center for Cultural Studies. A major project undertaken by the Cluster was the editing of a special issue of *Inscriptions*, the journal of the Center for Cultural Studies.[5] I should point out that the full name of the group is the Research Cluster for the Study of Women of Color in Collaboration and Conflict. Its emergence represented a desire to explore not only the possibilities of cross-racial coalition and alliance, but also to think about the inevitable tensions and conflicts among women of color. We took note of the important role black and Korean women were playing in the effort to negotiate a relationship between these communities that had become especially difficult in the aftermath of the 1992 Los Angeles uprising.

Other projects we have developed include writing groups for students, a lecture series involving cross-radical conversations, colloquia, meetings with the Women of Color Resource Center in Oakland. When I was chosen to hold the UC Presidential Chair, it meant that the Women of Color Cluster would receive more substantial funding. A significant aspect of my proposal – which was the basis for my selection – was a curriculum development project that would be directed by the Cluster. Over the next period we will develop a number of courses to satisfy the Ethnic Studies requirement at UC-Santa Cruz. These courses will be collaboratively taught by graduate students and tenured faculty. The Cluster will not only collaboratively develop these courses, but there will also be focused deliberations on pedagogical questions.

LL: You mention the focus on women of color "in collaboration and conflict." Moving outside of the university in order to think more broadly about the forging of the alliances across groups, what are the difficulties and the opportunities for black, Chicana-Latina, and Native and Asian-American women working together? What are the specific issues for each group that need to be addressed in order for coalition to take place? What sorts of things keep coming up?

AD: This work is very difficult. Coalition building has never been easy. But I think it might be more productive to move away from constructions of women of color as a coalition. The assumption behind coalition building is that disparate groups of individuals come together with their own separate – and often racially based – agendas, which have to be negotiated and compromised in order for the group to come together. Coalitions also have an ephemeral and *ad hoc* character. I am not suggesting that the concept *women of color* is not here to stay, but I do think that it might be a very difficult political project. First of all, not all "women of color" choose to embrace this identity. In fact, an Asian-American woman who might prefer to call herself Chinese-American might be equally reluctant to identify as a woman of color. But that's all right. There is no hard and fast requirement in the sense that a woman of African descent has little choice but to identify as black. However, those who do involve themselves in women of color projects need to make strong commitments – to borrow Jacqui Alexander's formulation – "to become fluent in each other's stories."

This is not to say that significant women of color work has not taken place within coalition formations. There is, for example, the Women of Color Coalition on Reproductive Health that has brought together representatives from four different health organizations: the Asian Women's Health Organization, the Latina Women's Health Project, the Black Women's Health Project, and the Native American Women's Health Organization. This coalition played an important role at the UN Conference on Reproductive Rights which took place in Cairo the year before the women's conference and NGO forum in Beijing. However, it has been beset with serious problems that afflict many coalitional forms which emanate from the difficulties of compromise and agenda negotiation. Women of color work also takes place within caucus and task force formations that often develop within predominantly white organizations such as the National Women's Studies Association and the National Coalition Against Domestic Violence. It is interesting that women of color formations emerged within both of these organizations in 1981 – a pivotal year for women of color. Early on, women of color groups also organized within a number of lesbian groups.

The groups I find most interesting, however, are those that consider "women of color" a point of departure rather than a level of organizing which arises out of and breaks down into a series of racially specific agendas: in other words, those organizations that challenge the census-category approach to "women of color." Which means that women of color work can foreground race at a time when dominant discourse attempts to erase it, yet at the same time avoid the pitfalls of essentialism. I referred earlier to the Women of Color Resource Center. This organization develops projects which bring grassroots organizers and scholars together. It also sponsors projects like AIWA – Asian Immigrant Women's Advocates – which in turn appeals to all women of color (and white women as well) to support campaigns like the Jessica McClintock boycott. I have also referred to the Women of Color Research Cluster, which does not establish its agenda by considering so-called priority issues.

A woman of color formation might decide to work around immigration issues. This political commitment is not based on the specific histories of racialized communities or its constituent members, but rather constructs an agenda agreed upon by all who are a part of it. In my opinion, the most exciting potential of women of color formations resides in the possibility of politicizing this identity – basing the identity on politics rather than the politics on identity.

LL: You have written about visiting Egypt, and the complications of being both a black woman activist and yet also a "representative" from the United States, a dominant first world power.[6] Taking up these complications, I wonder if you could comment about the importance, the possibilities, and the difficulties of work between radical US women and women in the third world.

AD: Women's organizations have been engaged in international solidarity work at least since the previous century, since the beginning of this century. I think it's important to acknowledge this internationalism. Some of this work was supported by the former socialist countries – the former Soviet Union, the German Democratic Republic, where the NGO Women's International Democratic Federation was located. Women for Racial and Economic Equality, a US-based organization, has ties with women's organizations all over the third world. I am suggesting that there are precedents for the kind of organizing across borders that women are presently attempting to do. However, during the earlier period, women's organizations tended to be rather confined to specific agendas: peace, for example, which was certainly important. But now the possibilities are vaster, considering the globalization of capital and the circuits that have been opened up by migrating corporations. In other words, it is even more important today to do transnational organizing – around labor issues, sexual trafficking, and violence against women. While there is not enough time to make specific reference to all the current international struggles US women are and need to be connected with, I would like to mention the need to strengthen women of color work in opposition to the economic embargo of Cuba. Cuban women are hurt most by the blockade and are on the front lines of opposition. Alice Walker and I are presently trying to organize a campaign to "Boycott the Blockade." In general, considering the impact of NAFTA, the need for networking and inter-national organizing among women trade unionists in Canada, the United States, and Mexico is especially great. Considering the global assembly line – and the extent to which immigrant women working within the United States may work for the same corporations that are exploiting women in Asia, in Canada, in Mexico – organizing possibilities are vast.

LL: Yes. Can I ask you about immigration, since we touched on that? How do you think the influx of Asians and Latin Americans into the United States, particularly since 1965, has changed communities of color and race relations in the United States? Is the current policing of immigration and immigrant communities an index of similar, yet different, contradictions than those that operated in the 1960s?

AD: Well, it's no longer possible to talk about issues of race in exclusively black and white terms. While larger communities of color that are not black – Native American, Asian, Latina/o – have parallel histories of racism, oppression, and militant resistance, civil rights discourse established terms that were largely based on a certain construction of black history that excluded women, gays and lesbians, and other marginalized groups. Especially since questions of immigration are moving to the fore, it is no longer possible to confine race discourse and anti-racist activism to a simple black-white binary. New issues, new problems, new contradictions have emerged and old ones have been uncovered. Many veteran activists bemoan the fact that there are so many tensions and contradictions within and among communities of color and that it can no longer be assumed that a person who is not white will necessarily assume progressive positions on racial issues – on affirmative action, for example. They bemoan the fact that you cannot expect a person of color by virtue of her/his racial location to speak out against racism, regardless of the group targeted. This has become especially apparent in the failure of significant numbers of black organizations to actively mobilize against Proposition 187 in California and similar measures in other states. I am afraid that the impact of anti-immigrant rhetoric on black communities is inhibiting the development of a political awareness of the radical potential of Latin American and Asian immigrant workers. It used to be the case that within the more progressive sectors of the trade union movement black workers were acknowledged as a radical and militant force. Today, if there is any hope for the labor movement, it will come, in my opinion, from the new forms of organizing immigrant workers that are developing.

LL: Asian women and Latinas in the garment and electronics industries.

AD: Yes. Absolutely. What is really exciting are the new forms of organizing that aren't contained within single trade unions, nor are they focused on narrow trade union issues. It's been virtually impossible within the labor movement over the decades to address issues that aren't traditional union issues. Like wages, benefits, workplace – these are extremely important. But there are also issues that go beyond the workplace that affect workers as well.

LL: Child care, language.

AD: Yes. Environmental issues, as well. I'm thinking about the work that's being done in Los Angeles immigrant communities, a project that is a multiunion effort with a community base. Considering these new forms of resistance, there are ways to think about these changes in an optimistic way.

LL: Yes. I really agree. Even though there's been an intensification of the exploitation of women of color and third world women, it has also generated new methods and strategies for addressing that exploitation.
Regarding different organizing strategies for the new kinds of populations of workers and the specificities of labor exploitation under new capitalist modes

like "mixed production" and "flexible accumulation," perhaps we can get back to the initial discussion of the shifts over the past thirty years. We know that conditions have worsened particularly for the women in communities of color. What kinds of activist projects are possible now? In these times, how do we measure what significant change means?

The Southwest Network for Environmental and Economic Justice is really interesting to me, the group under which AIWA along with La Fuerza Unida organized the Lévi-Strauss boycott. It seems that the issues of the environment, health, and toxic waste dumping are places where labor concerns and racialized community concerns come together.

AD: Exactly. The environmental justice movement is a relatively new and very promising organizing strategy in communities of color. New strategies are also suggested by the workers' centers in Chinatown that link work against exploitative sweatshop conditions with campaigns against domestic violence and simultaneously make appeals for multi-racial solidarity. We will have come a long way if we succeed in convincing a significant number of black women's organizations, for example, to support Asian immigrant women's labor and community struggles. This would be yet another form of women of color consciousness that is politically rather than racially grounded and at the same time anchored in a more complex anti-racist consciousness.

LL: There's a project in San Diego called Beyond Borders that has a support committee for *maquiladora* workers in Baja, California, Mexico, and Central America. They document working conditions and occupational health and safety violations in the *maquilas*, publicize the attacks on workers' rights to organize, and promote cross-border worker organizing by connecting US trade unionists with their counterparts in Mexico. Interestingly enough, a number of the women who work in this group are Asian-American.

AD: This kind of cross-racial, cross-border organizing needs to be encouraged in many different contexts.

LL: You've done considerable work with women in prisons, political prisoners, and prisoners' rights. Could you say a bit about your different projects with prisoners?

AD: My work with prisoners – both research and organizing work – has been one of the most consistent themes of my political life. It seems that the struggle to free political prisoners is unending. The campaign to free Mumia Abu-Jamal is a case in point. With respect to women prisoners, I am presently working on a project with Kumkum Bhavnani, who teaches sociology at UC-Santa Barbara and has a similar political history. We have interviewed women prisoners in an attempt to add new voices to the debate around prisons and to suggest that abolitionist strategies need to be taken seriously. In general, we need more activist projects against the proliferation of prisons, against what Mike Davis calls the "prison-industrial complex."[7] Our earlier discussion of labor is relevant here, too. There is a dangerous privatization trend within the correctional industry, which not only involves the privatization of entire state correctional systems and some sectors of the federal system, but the increasing reliance on prison labor by private corporations as well. The state of California can boast of the largest prison system in the country – and one of the largest in the world. The Department of Corrections in California has established a joint venture system, which invites corporations to establish their shops on prison grounds. The advertising scheme represents prisoners as a cheap labor force that does not require employers to respect minimum wage provisions or provide health benefits. The advertisement points out that prison workers never ask for paid vacations or have transportation or baby-sitting problems. This means that prisoners are considered cheap labor in the same sense that immigrants within the United States and third world workers abroad are treated as the most profitable labor pools. Rather than crossing national borders, corporations simply go behind prison walls.

LL: Perhaps that's the "Made in the USA" label.

AD: Yes, that's the "Made in the USA" label at no cents an hour with no benefits. Prisoners have been unsuccessfully trying to organize labor unions for decades. Perhaps we need to think about organizing that will bring together prisoners, prisoners' rights groups, immigrant worker organizations, and some of the traditional labor unions. In other words, there *is* a place for coalitions. While I find identity-based coalitions problematic, I do concur with Bernice Reagon when she says that coalition work must be central in late-twentieth-century political organizing. However, I think that we should focus on the creation of unpredictable or unlikely coalitions grounded in political projects. Not only prisoners, immigrant workers, and labor unions, but also prisoners and students, for example. This might be the most effective way to contest the shifting of the funding base for education into prison construction and maintenance. One of the other coalitions that should be encouraged is between welfare rights and gay and lesbian organizations. Both welfare mothers and gays and lesbians are directly targeted by conservative emphasis on "family values."

LL: Such a coalition could include legal and undocumented immigrants, too, if it were organized around the proposed Personal Responsibility Act, which bars not only undocumented immigrants but legal permanent residents from receiving federal benefits.

AD: That's right. We might also think about coalition work that would bring together legal and undocumented immigrant youth, on the one hand, and young African-American and Latino American youth, on the other, who are all targeted by a devious criminalization process that replaces a legitimate need for jobs, education, and health care with a very effective demonization of these groups.

And it is certainly time to revive the demand for a reconsideration of the eight-hour workday. A shorter workday could help provide jobs for undocumented immigrants as well as the vast unemployed sectors among youth in communities of color. If the new cultural arenas that have developed over the past decade are utilized, young activists might be able to create a powerful campaign.

Notes

1 Michael Omi and Howard Winant, *Racial Formation in the United States, from the 1960s to the 1990s* (New York: Routledge, 1994).
2 Angela Y. Davis, *Women, Race and Class* (New York: Random House, 1981), chs 11 and 12. "Facing Our Common Foe: Women and the Struggle against Racism" and "We Do Not Consent: Violence against Women in a Racist Society" in Angela Y. Davis, *Women, Culture, and Politics* (New York: Random House, 1989).
3 Cherrie Moraga and Gloria Anzaldúa, eds, *This Bridge Called My Back: Writings by Radical Women of Color* (New York: Kitchen Table Press, 1981).
4 Angela Y. Davis, *An Autobiography* (New York: Random House, 1974).
5 Maria Ochoa and Teresia Teaiwa, eds, "Enunciating Our Terms: Women of Color in Collaboration and Conflict," *Inscriptions*, 7 (1994).
6 Angela Y Davis, "Women in Egypt: A Personal View," in *Women, Culture, and Politics*.
7 Mike Davis, "A Prison-Industrial Complex: Hell-Factories in the Field," *The Nation*, 260, no. 7 (1995): 229.

Index

Abel, Elizabeth, 213
Aboriginals, 117
abortion politics, 113
absorption processes, 164
Abu-Jamal, Mumia, 413, 428
academic performance, 25–6
Accelerated Schools Process (ASP), 96
Addelston, Judi, 228, 230, 236, 237
Adorno, Theodor, 392, 422–3
affirmative action, 49, 54, 58, 223, 307,
    313–14
  campaigns against, 52, 53, 247, 257
  color blindness, 56
  Supreme Court ruling, 142, 413
  University of California, 57, 269
  white views on, 61, 378
Afghan immigrants, 272
African-Americans
  acceptance of multiracial people, 148–9
  American dream, 381–2
  anti-Semitism, 28
  and Asian-Americans, 162
  black conservative movement, 27, 54
  black nationalism, 27–8, 128, 129, 131–2,
    134, 305, 313
  citizenship, 250–1
  Civil Rights Movement, 23, 56, 413, 416
  community organizations, 58
  concern over immigrant labor, 374, 427
  construction industry, 314–15
  criminal justice system, 51, 58, 414
  Democratic Party, 379–80, 383
  discipline in schools, 96
  disparities between family types, 51
  disparities with whites, 50–1
  dissatisfaction with American society, 379,
    382
  diversity of constituencies, 241
  economic status, 376
  employment patterns, 51, 52
  ethnicity, 304–5, 312–13
  family role, 58
  gender relations, 414–15
  global capitalism, 351
  globalization, 373–4
  goals and strategies, 58
  heterogeneity of, 191–2
  higher education, 312
  images and representations of, 53–5, 60–1
  integration strategies, 58, 128, 129
  intelligence measurement, 2–3
  job concerns, 382–3
  and Korean community, 424
  leadership, 59, 240–1
  levels of earnings, 50–1, 305, 376
  Los Angeles riots, 1, 35, 424
  masculinist-nationalism, 414–15
  middle-class, 50, 60, 94–5, 192, 304, 305,
    313, 376, 413
  migration to northern states, 23
  multiracial feminism, 105, 108–9
  primacy of men in families and
  communities, 414–15
  professional classes, 314
  public policy issues, 377–9, 381
  racelessness strategies, 193
  racial and cultural
  distinctiveness, 106
  racial solidarity, 132, 134
  racialization, 10, 47
  racialized barriers and hostility, 47, 49–52,
    55–7, 60
  racialized identities, 50, 59, 80, 81, 82
  religious traditions, 133
  resistance strategies, 57–60
  resistance to white mainstream, 220
  sleeping car porter trade, 314–15
  unemployment, 312, 376
  urban politics, 311
  urban workforce, 358, 363, 366, 367
  US government racial
  classifications, 144
  variance in identity, 161
  visibility of whiteness, 200
  working class, 314
  worldviews of, 375–7
  see also women, black
African Episcopalian Churches, 58

Africans, Spanish America, 170–1, 173, 174
Afrocentrism, 27
agency, 91, 92, 108
Aguilar, M. E., 178
Aid to Families with Dependent
    Children(AFDC), 274
AIWA, 419, 425, 428
Akbar, Na'im, 61
Alarçon, Norma, 108
Alatas, Syed Hussein, 265
Alba, Richard, 193
Alexander, Jack, 186, 188
Alexander, Jacqui, 425
Allen, Theodore, 209, 210
Althusser, L., 391, 392, 393, 394, 396–7
Amerasians, 159
American Anthropological Association, 4
American Apartheid, 51
American Association for the
    Advancement of Science, 20
American Federation of Labor, 315
American Indian movement, 415
American Psychological Association, 42
Americanism concept, 308
Anderson, B., 10, 324
Anderson, Elijah, 192
Anderson, G., 80, 81, 88, 91, 95, 97
Anderson, J., 88
Anderson, Perry, 393
anglomorphy, 116
Anthias, Floya, 71, 112, 114, 115, 116
anti-capitalism, 323–4, 406
Anti Defamation League, 85
anti-miscegenation laws, 147, 155–6n
anti-racism
    antibias pedagogy, 92–5
    biological race categories, 26
    ideologies, 57
    modes of racial representations, 201
    multiculturalism, 118
    notion of difference, 43
    transversal politics, 121–3
    white confession literature, 207–9
    whiteness, 200–1, 203–14
anti-Semitism, 28, 323–4
antibias pedagogy, 92–5
Anzaldúa, Gloria, 418
apartheid, 66
Apfelbaum, Erika, 238, 239
apparel industry see garment industry
Appiah, K. A., 30, 212
Arabs, 324
Archdeacon, Thomas J., 267, 269
architecture, 364

Arendt, H., 327
Argentinean immigrants, 314
aristocracy, 325–6
Armstrong, J., 114
Aronowitz, S., 79
art
    personal and ethnic identities, 96
    racialized discourses, 71
Asia Week, 285
Asian Immigrant Women's Advocates
    (AIWA), 419, 425, 428
Asian immigrants, 262, 267, 268–88
Asian Women's Health Organization, 425
Asian Women's Refuge, 119
Asian-Americans
    affirmative action, 314
    American dream, 381–2
    distinctive place in racial hierarchy, 106
    ethnicity, 315–16
    garment industry, 300, 315, 350
    growth and significance of, 52
    multiracial, 158–65
    multiracial feminism, 105, 108–9
    public policy issues, 377, 378
    racial and cultural
        distinctiveness, 106
    racialization, 10
    racism of, 162, 165
    small business sector, 300
    social movements, 413
    as victimized overachievers, 269–70
    working class, 314
Asians, in Britain, 205
Atkinson, Donald R., 161
Atlanta, 82
Atlantic Monthly, 34
Australia, multiculturalism, 115, 116, 119
authenticity, 118, 160
authoritarianism, 88, 118–19
automation, 339–40
Awkward, Michael, 135
Aycoberry, P., 322
Aztecs, 176, 178
Aztlán, 176, 178

Baca, L., 79
Back, Les, 73, 74, 75, 76
Baker, Houston, Jr., 212
Bakhtin, M. M., 88
Bakke, case, 239
Baldwin, James, 149–50, 213
Balibar, Étienne, 8, 9, 33, 34, 328
Ball, A., 96
Ball, S., 81

Balzac, Honoré de, 43
Bambara, Toni Cade, 126
banking industry, 52
Banton, Michael, 3, 22, 48, 49, 72, 202
Baptist Churches, 58, 59
Barkan, E., 21
Barker, M., 72
Bassett, Angela, 53
BBC Radio, 75
Beal, Fran, 420
Beck, Ulrich, 319
Becker, Gary C., 266
Bederman, Gail, 266
*The Bell Curve: Intelligence and Class
    Structure in American Life*, 2–3, 4, 7, 8,
    25, 320
Bell, Daniel, 311, 341
Bell, Derrick, 227, 249
belonging, feelings of, 236
Benjamin, Lois, 61
Bertaux, D., 329
Beyond Borders, 428
Bhabha, Homi, 74, 119–20, 214, 393, 402–3
Bhabha, Jacqui, 119
Bhachu, P., 71
Bhavnani, Kumkum, 428
Biesta, G., 80, 83, 88
bilingual education, 90, 256
Billingsley, Andrew, 58
binary oppositions, 5, 7–8, 403
biracial children, 144, 153n
Birmingham, 73
Birmingham Centre, 69–70, 390, 392, 408–9
Birth of a Nation, 221
Black Codes, 250
black community
    Britain, 74, 410
    Mormon church, 278
    see also African-Americans
black conservative movement, 27, 54
Black Leadership Forum, 59
Black Marxism, 67
black nationalism, 27–8, 128, 129, 131–2,
    134, 305, 313
Black Panther Party, 415
black pathology, 265
Black Renaissance, 304
Black Womanist Ethics, 129
black-Japanese, 161
Black Women's Alliance, 419–20
Black Women's Health Project, 425
blackness
    association with term "race", 219
    deconstruction of, 212
    destabilization of, 205

image in literary texts, 225
as the negative particular, 220
representation by whiteness, 220–1
romanticization of, 210
ties with whiteness, 220
Blair, Tony, 407, 410, 411
Blauner, B., 28, 29
Bloom, Harold, 278, 289n
Blues Legacies and Black Feminisms, 420
blues music, 420
Bluestone, Barry, 310
Boas, Franz, 3–4, 39
Boeing, 310
Bologna Women's Resource Centre, 121
Bondi, L., 80
Bonnett, Alastair, 201, 203
boosting role, 233
border crossings, 84
*Border Crossings: Cultural Workers and the
    Politics of Education*, 84
border pedagogy, 82, 84–9
    and politics of difference, 89–92
Bordo, Susan, 104
Bosnia, 53, 114–15
Boston, Stuart case, 52, 61
Boston, Thomas, 54
Bottomley, Gill, 113
Bourdieu, Pierre, 284
Bourgeois, Philippe, 365
bourgeois revolutions, 326–7
Bourne, Jenny, 118
Bowers, C. A., 84
Bowles, S., 85
Bradshaw, Carla, 163
Brah, Avtar, 113
Brazil, 6, 93, 148, 154
Brimelow, Peter, 384
Bringhurst, Newell G., 278
Britain
    aristocratic racism, 326
    black culture, 74, 410
    cultural difference, 265
    cultural diversity, 410, 411–12
    cultural studies, 389–93
    higher education, 306
    identity construction, 31
    immigrants, 21–2, 23
    meaning of blackness, 205
    multiculturalism, 116
    race as an analytical category, 2, 21–5
    racial oppositions, 267
    racism, 25, 70, 71–2, 265
    Rastafarianism, 211
    South Asian community, 205
    usage of term "black," 215n

Brittan, Samuel, 317
Britzman, D., 81, 82
Brodie, Mollyann, 374, 376, 377
Brooks, C., 93
Brotherhood of Sleeping Car Porters, 314–15
Brown Berets, 415
Brown, Elaine, 415
Brown, Elsa Barkley, 123
Brown v. Board of Education, 86, 249, 250
Buchanan, Pat, 56, 380
Buck, Pearl S., 159
Buddhism, 152n, 153n
Bundists, 113
Buriel, R., 80
Burnham, Linda, 420
Bush, George, 48, 56, 380
Busia, Abena, 131

La Cage aux Folles II, 239
Cain, Harriet, 118
California, 36
    affirmative action, 57, 269
    Asian immigrants, 268–9, 272, 281–6
    Joint Resolution 49, 248
    prison labor, 429
    Proposition 187, 52, 256, 257, 258, 427
    referenda, 249, 257–8, 259
    withdrawal of bus routes, 57
California Civil Rights Initiative (CCRI), 57, 257–8
California Prisoners Union, 417
Cambodian immigrants, 268, 270–80, 287
Camper, Carol, 207
Canada, 116
Cannon, Katie Geneva, 129
Capital, 338, 341
capital, internationalization of, 358–9, 370n
capitalism, 34, 36, 317
    aristocratic racism, 326
    black women, 126
    citizenship, 262, 263
    class, 298–303
    constant capital, 338
    ethnicization of, 347–51
    global, 337–51, 414
    ideologies, 55
    industrial, 338–40, 345
    postindustrial, 340–50
    racism, 414
    sexism, 414
    surplus value, 339
    variable capital, 338–9
    white identity, 209
capitalist patriarchy, 106
Caraway, Nancie, 131

Carby, Hazel, 70, 126
Card, David, 374
Cardoso, Hieronymus, 171–2
Cardoza, D., 80
Caribbean, black/colored designations 15n
Carter, B., 22
Carter, Jimmy, 270
Castañeda, Q.E., 178
castas, 171, 172, 173–5, 177, 179n
Castells, M., 71
castizos, 173
Castles, Stephen, 67
CDFS, 170
Cell, John, 188, 189
Centre for Contemporary Cultural Studies
    (CCCS), Birmingham, 69–70, 390, 392, 408–9
Cervantes, H., 79
Cervantes, Lorna Dee, 260
Chan, Sucheng, 287
Chang, Edward T., 52
charity work, 233–4
Charles, Helen, 208
Chater, Nancy, 207–8
Chatterjee, Partha, 278
Chavez, Linda, 238
Chavis, Ben, 414
Chevalier, Louis, 326
Chew, Kenneth, 158
Chicago
    black employment patterns, 52
    urban politics, 311
Chicago School, 23
Chicanos, 256, 258, 259–60
    affirmative action, 314
    identity formation, 176–7, 178
    social movements, 413
Children's Defense League, 58
Chile, 271
China, 337, 350
Chinese immigrants, 268, 276, 281–6, 287
    garment industry, 350
    as model minority, 270, 272
Chinese laundries, 247
Christian, Barbara, 59, 60, 134
Chronicle of Higher Education, 20
Church of the Latter-day Saints, 277–80, 289n
churches, 58, 59, 277–80
cinema see film media
cipherspace, 175–9
cities see urban economy; urban
    pedagogy
citizenship, 247–51, 253–6, 384
    boundaries of, 117
    budgetary debates, 375

capitalism, 262, 263
class, 255, 265–7
cultural, 253–60, 262–88
inequality, 253–4, 260
language, 256–7, 259
of the masses, 327
race, 107, 254–5, 265
as subjectification, 263–4
whites, 219–20, 272
women, 254–5
Civil Rights Initiative, 52, 57
Civil Rights legislation, 49, 177
Civil Rights Movement, 23, 56, 413, 416
Clara's Heart, 55
Clark, Gillian, 213
class, 297–303
citizenship, 255, 265–7
ethnicity, 311–16
identity politics, 297, 302
multiracial feminism, 104, 107–8
race, 298, 301–2
racialization, 33–4, 68–9
racism, 66–7, 322–31
United States, 297–303, 305, 309–10,
311–16, 318
whiteness, 209–10, 223
see also middle-class; underclass;
upper-class; working class
class reductionism, 69, 392, 394–5
Cleage, Pearl, 130–2
Cleveland, 311
Cliff, Jimmy, 304, 305
Clinton, Bill, 1, 4, 313, 318, 417
clubs, 232–3
coalition politics, 121–3, 424–5, 429
Cohen, Cathy J., 374
Cohen, Phil, 214
collectivities
ethnicity, 112–13
women's role, 114–15
Collins, Patricia Hill, 59–60, 107, 121, 126,
132
Collins, Sheila D., 58
Colombian immigrants, 314
colonialism, 21, 31, 74, 265
globalization, 361–2
Spanish America, 169–71
color blind policies, 48, 56, 57, 59, 61, 141–3,
239
Color Line, 50
Colorado, 249
The Colour Problem, 22
Coltrane, John, 308
Combahee River Collective manifesto, 419
commodity chains, 343–5

common sense, 395
communications, 53
control of, 299, 302
communicative action, 81, 88
communism, collapse of, 33
The Communist Manifesto, 33, 421
Communist Party of Great Britain, 405
Communist Party USA, 420, 421, 423
communitarianism, 249
communities, possibility of, 86
competition/stratification processes, 164
computer technology, 53
Congressional Black Caucus, 59, 313
conjunctures, notion of, 394, 399
Connell, R. W., 232, 235
consciousness-raising, 120
conservatism
black movement, 27, 54
colorblindness, 142
concept of difference, 89–90
construction industry, 314–15
constructive differentiation, 164, 165
Conti, J., 27
contingency, 33, 399
contingent identities, 121
continuous flow notion, 358
Copeland, Lewis C., 266
Coriat, B., 328
corporate cultures, 359–60, 362–4
Corrigan, Philip, 263, 264
Cosby show, 53
cosmopolitanism, 403
counter-narratives, 119–20
Cox, Oliver, 66
Crapanzano, Vincent, 189, 194
Creole culture, 191–2
Crichlow, W., 82
crime, 54, 61
criminal justice system, 51, 58, 414
criollos, 173, 174–5
critical race studies, 27, 227, 241
critical theory, 355, 356
Crooklyn, 59
Cross, William, 161
Cuba, 337, 426
Cuban-Americans, 35, 271
cultural assimilation, 90–1, 306–7, 311, 316
cultural citizenship, 253–60
as subject making, 262–88
cultural conflicts, 9, 82
cultural difference, 265
cultural diversity
Britain, 410, 411–12
in cities, 359–60
see also multiculturalism

cultural diversity initiatives, 81–2, 90
cultural fundamentalism, 8, 262, 286
cultural harmony, 81
cultural needs, 117
cultural politics, 410, 411–12
    antibias pedagogy as, 92–5
cultural power, 390
cultural production, 409–10
cultural racism, 8–10, 71–2, 73
cultural resources, 113
cultural studies, 389–93, 408–9
cultural switching, 79
cultural traits, 41
culture
    citizenship, 256–60
    corporate, 359–60, 362–4
    ethnicity, 113, 305–8
    Hall interview, 389–412
    race, 158
    whiteness, 185
    women, 113–15
Culture and Learning, 94–5
Cummins, J., 79
Cunningham, James, 345
Curcio, J., 88
Cyprus, 114

D'Acosta's History of the Indies, 202
Daniels, Margaret, 424
Danza groups, 178
Dark Strangers, 22
Dash, Julie, 59
Dashner, D., 79
Daughters of the Dust, 59
Davis, Angela, Y., 59, 126, 131, 226, 413–30
Davis, Mike, 429
Dawson, Michael C., 374, 375, 376, 378, 380,
    383
De Vancy, A., 86
deconstructionism, 390
deindustrialization, 414, 415
The Deindustrialization of America, 310
Delany, S., 82
Deleuze, G., 391
Delgado, R., 27
Dellums, Ron, 416
democracy
    citizenship, 253–4
    in the classroom, 83–9, 92–6, 408–9
    limits of control, 299
    and multiculturalism, 117
democratic equivalence, 85, 87
Democratic Party, 379–80, 381, 383
den Boer, Pim, 202
Dent, David J., 304

Denton, Nancy, 51, 52, 127, 193
deracialization, 193
Derrida, Jacques, 8, 401, 402
destructive differentiation, 164, 165
Detroit, 193, 374
    black employment patterns, 52
    racial identities, 82, 190–1
deviance, 89–90
Devil in a Blue Dress, 52, 59
Dialectic of Enlightenment, 423
dialects, 91
diaspora, 401–4
Diawara, Manthia, 59
Díaz, Porfirio, 175
différance, 401, 402
difference
    border pedagogy, 89–92
    celebration of, 81
    as central concern of feminism, 104–5
    conservative conception of, 89–90
    cultural, 265
    feminist emphasis on, 103–5, 297
    Hall on, 401
    liberal conception of, 90–1
    multiculturalist emphasis on, 297
    multiracial feminism, 103–9
    race, 43–4, 185
    radical conception of, 91–2
    see also multiculturalism discourse
    Foucault, 398, 400
    Laclau, 399
    as praxis of border pedagogy, 88
    shaping of identities, 91
Disraeli, Benjamin, 327
Dole, Robert, 258
domestic workers, 315
Domestic Workers Union, 315
domination
    class relations, 297
    multiracial feminism, 103, 105, 106, 107–8
    racial, 184–5, 188–9, 220–1, 225–41
Dominguez, Virginia, 193, 265
Dominican immigrants, 316
Doris Marshall Institute, 206–7
Douglas, M., 5
Douglass, Lisa, 186
Dred Scott v. Sandford, 250
Driving Miss Daisy, 55
Driving Miss Daisy Syndrome, 226
drug crimes, 54
Du Bois, W. E. B., 193, 237, 266, 384
Duchet, M., 324
duCille, Ann, 126, 226, 228, 230
Dumont, L., 323
Duroux, F., 330

Dusk of Dawn, 193
Duster, Troy, 54
Dyer, Richard, 75, 200
Dyson, Michael, 132

East Wind, West Wind, 159
Ebony, 52
economic concentration, 359
economic growth theories, 358
economic internationalization, 358–9, 362
economic liberalism, 266
economics, 49, 50, 60
education, 50, 51, 58
  achievement of social mobility, 297–8,
    302–3, 306, 308–9, 311–12
  antibias pedagogy, 92–5
  authorizing student voices, 88–9
  bilingual, 90, 256
  black women, 126
  boundaries of the urban school, 95–7
  democratization of, 83–9, 92–6, 408–9
  liberatory potential of, 422
  meaning in classrooms, 86
  political subjectivity, 83–4
  politics of difference, 89–92
  power/knowledge in classrooms, 84–6, 88–9
  Princeton University admissions
  policy, 237
  production of texts, 86
  student identities, 79–84, 85, 86, 91–2,
    94–5, 96–7
  theory of urban pedagogy, 84–9
  United States, 306, 308–9, 318–19, 320
Edwards, Harry, 417
egalitarianism, 323
Eggebeen, David, 158
Egypt, 113, 426
Eitzen, D. Stanley, 54
El Salvador, 271, 314, 347, 350
Elba, Richard, 203
Elizabeth Irwin High School, 421
Elliott, R., 83, 85
Ellsworth, E., 88
Embree, John F., 276
The Empire Strikes Back, 69–70
employment inequalities, 50, 51
encomenderos, 170
Engels, Friedrich, 65
England, black/colored designations 15n
Enlightenment, 83
Enloe, Cynthia, 115
Enríquez, Martin, 171
Entrepreneurial Coalition, 86
environmental justice movement, 428
equality of opportunity, 298, 305–16

Erikson, Peter, 200
Espiritu, Yen Le, 287
Essed, P., 26
Ethiopian immigrants, 272
ethnic assertiveness, 201, 205
ethnic dialects, 91
ethnic groups, social definition of, 14–15n
ethnic projects, 112–13
ethnic studies, 227
Ethnicity, 311
ethnicity
  African-Americans, 304–5, 312–13
  American culture, 305–8
  analytical status of, 1–2
  Asian-Americans, 315–16
  class, 311–16
  conceptualization of, 80
  culture, 113, 305–8
  definition, 112–13
  embracing of, 81–3, 85
  global capitalism, 347–51
  globalization, 361
  Hall on, 371n, 402
  identity, 308
  Latinos, 315–16
  Marxism, 65–77
  new concept of, 308–11
  race, 28, 158
  white, 82, 193, 309, 310, 314
Eurocentrism, 67, 70
Europe
  collapse of communism, 33
  immigration policies, 68
  race relations, 24
European Americans, 203
European Union, 53
Europeans, hierarchical classifications, 3
Euroscepticism, 410–11
Evangelical groups, 258, 259
Everhart, R., 85, 97
exposure/absorption processes, 164

factoring, 301
family
  African-Americans, 51, 58
  Chinese immigrants, 282–3
  race, 107
  white solidarity, 234–6
Family Affairs, 55
family units, 114
Fanon, Frantz, 71, 265
Farley, Reynolds, 193
Farrakhan, Louis, 54, 58, 304, 305, 312, 380,
    414
Faryna, S., 27

fascism, 24, 28, 396
FBI, 415, 421
Feagin, Joe R., 52, 61
Federal Reserve, 52
feminism
    Angela Y. Davis on, 417–18
    black women's participation, 131
    central concern of difference, 103–5, 297
    challenge from women of color, 103–4,
        418–20
    definition, 130–1
    global agenda, 131
    Hall on, 400, 409
    identity politics, 92, 297
    multiculturalism, 120–1
    urban economy, 355–6
    US social workers, 276
    white confessional literature, 207–8
    white women, 131, 132
    womanism, 128–9
    see also gender; women
feminism, black, 27, 127, 130–6, 418
feminism, indigenous, 105
feminism, multicultural, 105
feminism, multiracial, and difference, 103–9
feminism, postmodern, 104
feminism, socialist, 106
feminism, US Third World, 105
Feuerbach, Ludwig, 223
Fields, B. J., 30, 31, 176
Filipino-Americans, 160
film media, 53, 55, 59, 74
    white ethnicity, 75
finance sector, 359
Fine, Michelle, 226, 228, 230, 234, 236, 237
First, P., 88
Fishman, J., 79, 90
flexibility, 344–6, 351
Fong, Timothy P., 281
Forbes, J. D., 171, 172
Fordham, S., 82
Foster, M., 82
Foster, W., 84, 85, 88
Foucault, Michel
    citizenship, 263, 264
    disciplinary power, 96
    discourse, 398, 400
    family, 282
    power, 85, 364
Fox, Ralph, 392
France
    aristocracy, 325
    citizenship, 253
    class racism, 326, 327
    higher education, 306

immigration, 324
    migrant political rights, 67
    race relations, 25
    racism, 46
    women as national symbol, 114
    workerism, 330
Frankenberg, Ruth, 108, 109, 183, 185, 186,
    187–8, 210–11, 235
Frankfurt School, 422
Frazier, L., 91
Fredrickson, George, 28, 188–9
free-market policies, 55, 57, 59
Freire, Paulo, 88, 93
Fremontier, J., 330
French Revolution, 327
The Fresh Prince of Bel Air, 55
Freud, Sigmund, 223
La Fuerza Unida, 428
fundamentalism, 121–2
    cultural, 8, 262, 286
Fuss, Diana, 5, 121, 206, 212

Gaine, Chris, 204
Gallagher, C. A., 215n, 228, 236, 237
Gans, Herbert, 311
Gap garment stores, 301, 345
garment industry, 300–2, 315, 338, 347–50
Garvin, J., 95
Gates, Henry, Jr., 71, 74, 212
gay rights, 255, 429
gender
    Angela Y. Davis on, 413–30
    challenge to unitary theories of, 103–5, 108
    efforts to contextualize, 104
    The Empire Strikes Back, 69
    ethnicizing gender concept, 289n
    global capitalism, 350–1
    multiracial feminism, 107–8
    in the urban economy, 355–68
    see also feminism; women
gender relations
    African-Americans, 414–15
    Cambodians, 273–4, 276–7
    whites, 229, 230–1, 233–4
gender skepticism, 104
General Electric, 310
General Motors, 310
genetics, and intelligence, 2–3
Geneva Convention, 114
genízaros, 231, 242n
A Geography of Africa, 202–3
Georgia, 57
Gergen, Kenneth J., 153n
Gerima, Haile, 59
German Democratic Republic, 426

German Socialist Student Organization, 422
Germany
  economic recession, 347
  fascism, 28
  higher education, 306
  migrant political rights, 67
  race relations, 25
  unification, 53
Giddens, Anthony, 81, 83, 90, 91, 93, 284, 362
Gilligan, C., 97
Gilman, Sander, 265
Gilroy, P., 30, 69, 71, 72, 265, 396
  collective identities, 70
  cultural politics, 74
  cultural racism, 8
  multiculturalism, 121
  racial oppositions, 267
  use of racial terms, 204
Gingrich, Newt, 269
Gintis, H., 85
Giroux, Henry, 4
  border pedagogy, 82, 84–92
  concept of difference, 89–92
  cultural racism, 8
  democratization, 81, 83–9, 92, 93, 94, 95–6
  racial narratives, 93
  reading of texts, 93
Gitlin, T., 178
Glazer, Nathan, 309, 311
GLC, 407, 410
Glenn, Evelyn Nakano, 54, 59
global competition, 53
globalization
  capitalism, 337–51, 414
  cities, 359, 360–2, 365, 366–8
  definition, 368–9n
  postmodern theory, 33
  racial politics, 373–5
Gobineau, Joseph Arthur, 44
Goldberg, David Theo, 29, 30
  class exploitation, 69
  conceptualization of race, 72, 74
  multiple racisms, 71
  postmodernism, 71
  power of race, 5
  resistance to racism, 19
Goldner, V., 84
Golub, Stephens, 271
González del Cossio, F., 174
Gordon, Colin, 266, 282
Gordon, Linda, 108
Gordon, Tamar, 278
governmentality, 263, 264
Graham, Lawrence, 232–3, 235, 237

Gramsci, Antonio, 1, 392, 393–6, 399, 400
Greater London Council (GLC), 407, 410
Greece, 327
Gregory, Steven, 265
Grewal, Inderpal, 122
Griffith, D. W., 221
Grillo, Trina, 141, 145, 151, 154n
Grossberg, L., 79
Grosz, E., 364–5, 372n
Grundrisse, 341
Guangdong province, 337
Guatemalan immigrants, 347, 350
Guerrero, Ed, 54, 55
Guillaumin, C., 25, 325
Gulf War, 53, 257
Gumbel, Bryant, 53
Gunew, Sneja, 121
Gurnah, Ahmed, 207
Gutiérrez, Ramôn A., 231, 241–2n
Guy-Sheftall, Beverly, 27, 59

Habermas, J., 88
Haiti, 53, 271
Hall, Arsenio, 53
Hall, Catherine, 265
Hall, Christine I., 161
Hall, Stuart, 69, 74, 367, 389–412, 414
  binary oppositions, 5, 8
  citizenship, 255, 263
  cultural globalization, 365
  ethnic identity, 81
  ethnicity, 371n
  globalization, 368n
  immigration 370n
  New Times thesis, 76
  postcolonialism, 361
  whiteness, 75
The Hand that Rocks the Cradle, 55
Hannerz, Ulf, 281
Harding, Sandra, 104
Harper's Magazine, 342
Harrington, Michael, 273
Harris, Cheryl I., 230, 235, 237, 238, 239
Harris, Marvin, 6
Harrison, Benet, 310
Harrison, Faye, 184, 185, 187–8, 195n
Harrison, M.L., 265
Hartigan, John, Jr., 187, 190
Harvard University, 376
Hatcher, R., 88
Hawaii, 158, 159
Hay, Denys, 202
health, 50, 51, 58, 131, 425
Heath, Shirley Brice, 96, 192
Hebdige, Dick, 211

Hebrew language, 113
Hegel, G. W. F., 392, 393, 396, 421
hegemonic institutions, 396
Hegemony and Socialist Strategy, 400
Held, David, 255, 263
Helms, Jesse, 308
Hemingway, Ernest, 130
Henwood, Doug, 211
Herr, K., 80, 81, 88, 91, 95, 97
Hernnstein, Richard J., 384
    The Bell Curve, 2–3, 4, 7, 8, 25, 320
Hewitt, R., 71, 74
Hidalgo, Miguel de, 174
Hiernaux, Jean, 40
high-tech sector, 369n
Higher Learning, 59
Hill, Anita, 29, 132
Hill, Jane, 195n
Hine, Darlene Clark, 59
Hispanics *see* Latinos
History and Class Consciousness, 423
Hmong refugees, 271, 276
Hoetnik, H., 191
Hollinger, D. A., 175
Holocaust, 24
homophobia, 130
honor, women as symbol of, 114–15
hooks, bell, 27, 59, 126, 135
    collective identity, 82
    commodification of difference, 104
    interview with Ice Cube, 241
    participatory decision-making, 241
    reflexive theories of
        subordination, 227
    whiteness, 75, 200
Hoover, J. Edgar, 415
Horkheimer, Max, 422–3
housing, 49, 50, 51, 52, 58
Houston, Whitney, 53
human agency, 91, 92, 108
Hume, David, 152n
Hunger of Memory, 256
hyphenated feminisms, 121
hypo-descent rule, 6, 146, 155n, 163, 176, 238

Ice Cube, 241
identities, ambiguous, 33
identities, collective, 70, 79–82, 403–4
identities, diasporic, 401–4
identities, plural, 33
identities, political, 70, 403–4
identities, racialized, 73, 79–97, 308–11, 318,
    319–20
    African-Americans, 50, 59, 80, 81, 82

British bourgeoisie and working class, 31
    consciousness of other ethnic
        groups, 81–3
    instability of, 91, 92
    Latinos/Hispanics, 91–2, 169–79, 211
    monoracial identity theories, 161–3
    multiracial Asians, 158–65
    as social process, 80–1
    students, 79–84, 85, 86, 91–2, 94–5, 96–7
    urban economy, 82, 190–1, 192, 356
    whites, 109, 184, 190–3, 201–3, 209–12,
        219–24, 228, 229–31, 314
identity politics
    class, 297, 302
    conflicts over, 219
    denunciation of, 221–2
    feminist emphasis on, 92, 297
    feminist version of
        multiculturalism, 120–1
    Hall on, 401
    labor movement, 223–4
    multiculturalist emphasis on, 297
    students, 79
    women of color, 419
ideological apparatuses, 396
ideologies
    racialized, 55–7, 60–1
    student, 86
ideology, 396–8
Ignatiev, Noel, 209
ILEA, 204–5
Illich, I., 88
illiteracy, 93
Ima, Kenji, 276
imaginary unities, 81
immigrants
    African-American concern over, 374, 427
    Angela Y. Davis on, 426–7
    anti-immigrant racism, 10–11, 23, 324, 351
    Asian, 262, 267, 268–88
    assimilation, 90–1, 306–7, 311, 316
    California, 36, 268–9, 272, 281–6
    Cambodian, 268, 270–80, 287
    Chinese, 268, 270, 272, 276, 281–6, 287,
        350
    European policies, 68
    garment industry, 347, 349–50
    globalization, 361, 366, 373, 374
    importance of education, 311
    internationalization of labour
        thesis, 359, 361, 370n
    as the other, 9
    political action, 69
    to Britain, 21–2, 23
    to Japan, 371n

urban workforce, 358, 363, 366, 367
US reforms (1965), 177
In Search of Our Mothers' Gardens, 127
income inequalities, 51, 376
India, 114
Indian immigrants, 316
individualism, 55, 59, 147, 316–17, 323
individuation process, 263–4
Indonesia, 344
industrial districts, 344
industrial revolution, 326, 328
inequality
    capitalism, 298–303
    citizenship, 253–4, 260
    open society doctrine, 316–17
    racialized, 50–3, 376
informal economy, 372n
information, as source of value, 341
information economy, 360
information technology, 343, 345–6
Inner London Education Authority, 204–5
Inscriptions, 424
institutional racism, 27, 49, 50–3, 60, 66, 135
integration strategies, 58
    black nationalist opposition to, 128
    and pluralism, 129
Intel, 340
intellectuals of color, 422
intelligence, 2–3
intermarriages
    anti-miscegenation laws, 147, 155–6n
    Asian-Americans, 158
    black-white, 147, 235
    Spanish America, 170–1
internal colonialism, 289n
Iran, 119, 123
Ireland, 114
Irish Abortion Support Group, 122
Irish community
    identification with Celtic race, 21
    migrants to Britain, 65
    migrants to US, 202, 267, 272
Israeli feminists, 122
Italian immigrants, 28, 202, 309, 312, 314

Jackson, George, 417
Jackson, Jesse, 54, 58, 380, 383
Jackson, Peter, 187
Jacques, M., 76
Jagger, Alison M., 105
Jakubowicz, Andrew, 115
Jamaica, 186
James, Stanlie, 131
Japan, 10, 53
    economic recession, 347

higher education, 306
immigration, 371n
proletarian nation, 324
racial attitudes, 159, 350
subcontracted jobs, 346
Japanese-Americans, 158
Jayasuriya, L., 117
jazz, 308
Jeater, Diane, 211
Jennings, James, 52
Jet, 52
Jewell, K. Sue, 54
Jewish community
    anti-black racism, 28
    anti-Semitism, 28, 323–4
    exclusion from US in the 1920s, 28
    garment industry, 349
    genocide, 24, 28
    identity, 109
    migration to Britain, 21
    persecution by Spanish, 325
    professional success, 311–12
    use of language, 113
Jewish Socialist Group, 122
Jones, Simon, 74, 75, 211
Jordan, June, 59, 126
Jordan, Michael, 53, 342
Joseph, Gloria I., 131
Joshi, S., 22
Journal of Black Higher Education, 142
Joyce, Joyce, 212

Kaiser Family Foundation, 376
Kandiyoti, Deniz, 113–14
Kant, Immanuel, 152n, 393, 421
Kaplan, Caren, 122
Karenga, M., 27
Katz, Judy, 203, 207
Katznelson, I., 28
Kelly, Gail, 289n
Keyes, Alan, 54
Khmer Rouge, 271
Khmers *see* Cambodian immigrants
Kich, George Kitahara, 161
Kids of Survival, 87
Kimmel, Michael S., 235
Kinder, Donald R., 378
King, A.D., 361, 362
King, Jr., Martin Luther, 143, 153n, 241, 384
King, Rodney, 35, 52
kinship, 161, 163
Kitano, Harry H. L., 158
Klein, Anne, 152n, 153n
Klor de Alva, J. J., 176, 177
Knights of Columbus, 221

Knights, L. C., 392
Knopfelmacher, Professor, 116
knowledge
    in classrooms, 84–6
    feminist theory, 356
    as source of value, 341
    student production of, 88–9
Knox, Robert, 3, 7, 8
Kochman, Thomas, 192
Komorovsky, Mirra, 273
Korean-Americans, 268
    and African-Americans, 424
    garment industry, 300, 349, 350
    Los Angeles riots, 35
    model minority image, 272
KOS (Kids of Survival), 87
Kouzes, Jim, 345, 346
Ku Klux Klan, 56, 220

labor
    exploitation of, 299
    internationalization of, 359, 361, 370n
    in prison system, 429
    race, 107
    as source of value, 338–9, 340–1
labor laws, 247
labor market, 34
labor movement, 219, 223–4
Labour Party, 405–7, 410–11
Labov, Teresa, 192
Lacan, J., 400
Laclau, E., 6, 398, 399, 400, 401
Lamott, Anne, 260
Lamphere, Louise, 288n
Lang, Fritz, 40
language
    anti-racist views on, 204–5
    citizenship, 256–7, 259
    as cultural resource, 113
    Foucault, 398
    ideology, 397
    intrinsic racism of, 225
    shaping of identities, 91
    theory of border pedagogy, 87–8
language-forms, 41
Laotian immigrants, 270, 271–2, 276
Larner, Wendy, 121
Larry King Live, 4
Laszlo, Ervin, 118
Latina Women's Health Project, 425
Latinos
    affirmative action, 314
    and African-Americans, 34
    American dream, 381–2
    arrests for drug crimes, 54

citizenship, 255–6, 260
    distinctive place in racial
        hierarchy, 106
    domestic workers, 315
    ethnic categories of, 91
    ethnicity, 315–16
    garment industry, 300, 315, 347
    globalization, 373
    growth and significance of, 52
    identity, 91–2, 169–79, 211
    Los Angeles riots, 35
    middle-class, 313
    multiracial feminism, 105, 108–9
    public policy issues, 377, 378
    racelessness strategies, 193
    racial and cultural
        distinctiveness, 106
    racialization, 10
    resistance to white mainstream, 220
    social movements, 413
    US government racial
        classifications, 144
    working class, 314
Lau, Siu-Kai, 282
Lauria, M., 79
Lawrence, E., 70, 71
Layton-Henry, Z., 22
leadership, 59, 240–1
Lee, Spike, 59
Left Review, 392
left wing groups, 221–2, 405–8
legal system, racialization process, 49
Lenin, V. I., 394
Leong, Russell C., 52
Lerner, M., 28
lesbian of color organizations, 420
lesbian feminism, 103–4
lesbian rights, 255
lesbianism, 130, 133, 429
Lévi-Strauss boycott, 428
Lévi-Strauss, C., 391, 400
Lewis, Earl, 383
liberalism, 266
    ambivalence with race, 90–1
    colorblind position, 141
Lieberman, L., 29–30
Lieberson, Stanley, 193
linguistic switching, 79
linguistics, 43, 192, 391
Linhart, R., 328
Linnaeus, 43, 173
Lipsitz, George, 185
literacy, 93
literacy tests, 247, 249
literature, 71, 74, 393

Liverpool, 21
Lloyd Warner, W., 308
Loescher, Gil, 270
The Long Revolution, 392
Lorde, Audre, 126, 133, 418
Lorrain, Jorge, 396
Los Angeles
    black employment patterns, 52
    garment industry, 300–2, 338, 347–50
    intermarriage rates, 158
    multiculturalism, 357
    urban politics, 311
Los Angeles riots, 1, 34–6, 56, 424
Los Angeles Times, 19, 34, 301
Louisiana, 148
Lowe, Lisa, 15n, 270, 287
Loyola University, 94–5
Lugones, Maria C., 104
Lukács, George, 392, 423
Lumumba-Zapata College, 423
Lusane, Clarence, 53, 56, 58, 59
Lyde, Lionel, 202–3

McCarthy, C., 82
McClintock, Jessica, 425
Macdonald, Ian, 214
McIntosh, Peggy, 228–9, 230, 235, 239
MacIntyre, Alasdair, 222
McLaren, P., 87
Malcolm X, 241
managerial stratum, 297, 300–1
Mani, Lata, 108
Manpower, Inc., 346
manufacturing sector, 369n
maquiladora, 428
Marable, Manning, 58, 135, 193
Marcuse, Herbert, 421, 422, 423
Marshall, Alfred, 344
Marshall, C. E., 171
Marshall, Thomas, 263
Martin, 55
Martin, Jane Rowland, 104
Martin, Jeannie, 119
Martinez, Elizabeth, 420
Marx, A. W., 28
Marx, Karl, 33, 65, 303, 337, 346–7, 421–2
    industrial capitalism, 338–40
    postindustrial capitalism, 341–2
Marxism, 65–70, 391–2, 394, 419, 420–2
Marxism Today, 399, 405–8
Mass, Amy Iwasaki, 160
Massey, Douglas, 51, 52, 127, 193
Matthews, Tracy, 415
meaning
    assigning of, 164

in classrooms, 86
media
    African-American images, 53, 60
    racialized discourses, 71
Memmi, Albert, 265
Mercer, Kobena, 81
mestizaje, 175–9
mestizos, 171–2, 173, 174, 177, 256
Methodist Churches, 58
metonymic elaborations, 73
Mexican-Americans, 56, 176–8
    garment industry, 347, 350
    Los Angeles riots, 35
Mexicans, mestizaje, 175–9
Mexico
    border with US, 257, 259
    ethnoracial categories, 173
    pendejo, 242n
Miami, 92
Michigan, 374
microchip, 340
middle-class
    African-Americans, 50, 60, 94–5, 192, 304,
        305, 313, 376, 413
    Latinos, 313
    universities, 297–8
    whites, 192, 310
Miles, Jack, 34
Miles, Robert, 206, 265
    concept of race relations, 48
    concept of racism, 30
    criticism of race as an analytical
        category, 22, 25, 29, 30, 31, 33, 68–9
    Marxist analysis of racism, 67–9
    race in Britain, 22
    racial violence, 10
    racialization, 7, 15n, 33, 49, 68–9
    semantics of race, 76
Miller, Mark, 67
Miller, Robin, 165
Million Man March, 52, 58, 59, 304–5, 312,
    414–15
Minh-ha, Trinh T., 115, 120
Mirón, L., 79, 83, 85, 86, 87, 93, 96
Mitchell, Katharyne, 284, 285
model minority, 267, 270, 272
Modood, Tariq, 113, 201, 203, 204, 205, 206
Mohanty, Chandra, 108, 419
Mokhiber, Russell, 54
Monk, Theolonius, 308
Montagu, A., 23
Moraga, Cherríe, 418
Morelos, José María, 174, 175, 179
Mormon Church, 277–80, 289n
Mörner, M., 173

Morrison, Toni, 126, 308
    Americans as hybrids, 155n
    criticism of Hemingway, 230–1
    feminism, 418
    integration of race in literary
        texts, 225, 226, 227
    intellectual domination, 240
    white identity, 231
Mortland, Carol, 271
Moses, Y. T., 4
Mosley, Walter, 59
Mouffe, C., 85, 87, 400
Mouzelis, N., 93
Moynihan, Daniel Patrick, 265, 309, 311
mozárabes, 172
Mukhopadhyay, C. C., 4
mulattos
    147, 155n
    Spanish America, 172, 173, 174, 256
Mullard, Chris, 118
Mullings, Leith, 193
The Multi-Cultural Planet, 118
multicultural curricula initiatives, 81–2
multiculturalism, 59, 115–20
    concept of class, 298
    denunciation of, 221
    feminism, 120–1
    global capitalism, 337–51
    Hall on, 402–3
    politics of identity, 297
multiracialism, 144–51
    Asian-Americans, 158–65
    feminism, 103–9
    Latino identity, 169–79
Murard, L., 326
Murphey-Shigematsu, Stephen, 158
Murray, Charles, 384
    The Bell Curve, 2–3, 4, 7, 8, 25, 320
Murray, Pauli, 131
Muslims, 117, 119
Myanmar, 337
Myrdal, Gunnar, 267

NAACP, 54, 58, 421
NAFTA, 426
Nahuas, 178
Nandy, Ashis, 265
Nation of Islam, 54, 58, 403, 414
nation-states, 9, 33
National Advisory Commission on Civil
    Disorders, 35
National Association for the
    Advancement of Colored People
    (NAACP), 54, 58, 421
national autonomy, 249–50, 251

National Baptist Convention, 59
National Coalition Against Domestic
    Violence, 425
National Conference of Black Mayors, 59
national-popular, 395–6
National Women's Studies Association, 425
nationalism, 31, 59, 71
    class racism, 324–6, 330–1
    globalization, 370n
    see also black nationalism
Native American Women's Health
    Organization, 425
Native Americans
    American Indian movement, 415
    British colonies, 176
    multiracial feminism, 105, 108–9
    racial and cultural
        distinctiveness, 106
    racialization, 10
    resistance to white mainstream, 220
    social movements, 413
    Spanish America, 170–1, 173, 174–5, 231
    US government racial
        classifications, 144
nativism, 247, 249, 251
Nazism, 40, 42, 322, 324
Nebrija, Antonio de, 171, 172
Needleman, Jack, 301
Negt, Oscar, 422
neo-Marxism, 65–77
neo-racism, 8
neoliberalism, 266
Nesse, C., 202
Netchine, G., 326
New Deal programs, 380, 383
New Left Review, 392
New Orleans, 82
    Loyola University, 94–5
New Right, 89
New Times thesis, 76
New York, 61
    black employment patterns, 52
    drug crimes, 54
    multiculturalism, 357
    urban politics, 311
New York Times, 268, 272
New York Times Magazine, 418
New Zealand, 267
Ngor, Haing, 271
Nicholson, Linda J., 121
Nightline, 4
Nike, 342
Nixon, Richard, 56, 262, 313–14, 380
no self concept, 152n, 153n
nobility, 325–6

Noddings, N., 84
Noiriel, C., 330
Nonini, Don, 263, 281
North Korea, 337

Ochoa, Maria, 424
octoroons, 147, 148, 155n
Office of Refugee Settlement, 276
Ogbu, J., 82
O'Hare, William P., 51
Oliver, Melvin L., 50–1, 52, 53
Olsen, L., 81
Omi, Michael, 29, 30–3, 67, 142, 419
   biracial children, 153n
   black images, 54
   citizenship, 265
   civil rights legislation, 416
   hypo-descent rule, 6
   racial hierarchies, 3
   racialization process, 49
   racialized ideologies, 56, 57
   US government racial classifications, 144
Omolade, Barbara, 127
"One America in the 21st Century: The
   President's Initiative on Race," 1, 4–5
one-drop rule see hypo-descent rule
Ong, Aihwa, 263, 281, 282, 285
Orbit, 206
Ostrander, Susan, 229, 233, 234, 235, 236
other, 9, 112, 162–3, 184, 230
overdetermination, 394, 399
Overseas Refugees Training Program, 271
Oxford English Dictionary, 202, 309

Page, Helán, 184, 194
Pakistani immigrants, 316
Palestinian feminists, 122
parachute kids, 283
Parham, Thomas A., 161
Parker, Charlie, 308
Parmar, Pratibha, 70
Parsons, T., 392
pastorela, 240, 242n
patriarchal bargaining, 113–14
patriarchy, 106, 276
La Patrie, 114
patriotism, 71
Paulston, C., 79, 96
Pedagogy of the Oppressed, 93
pendejo, 236–7, 242n
Penrose, Jan, 187
Perin, Constance, 267
Perry, Huey, 193
Peters, Tom, 345
petite bourgeoisie, 300, 322

phenomenological experiences, 159
phenotype, 162, 172
Philadelphia, 192
Philip II, 171
Philippine Refugee Processing Center, 271
philosophy, 392–3
Phizacklea, Annie, 10
physical anthropology, 40
Piedmont Carolinas, 192
pigmentocracy, 145, 148, 154n
Pinar, W. F., 84
Pinkney, Alphonso, 128
Plessy, Homer, 148
Plessy v. Ferguson, 148, 250–1
pluralism, 129
Polanyi, K., 327
Poliakov, L., 324, 325, 326
police, 302
A Policy for Equality: Race, 204–5
Polish-Americans, 309, 312, 314
political coalitions, 87
political correctness, 221
political power, 50
political subjectivity, 83–4, 85
politics, 50, 60, 66–7
popbead metaphysics, 107
Popper, Karl, 316, 317, 323
popular, 395
population genetics, 40
Porter, Michael, 341
Portes, Alejandro, 263, 269, 270
post-civil-rights politics, 288, 290n
post-Fordism, 35
postcolonialism, 74, 361
postindustrialism, 337, 340–50
postmodern feminism, 104
postmodernism
   class, 33
   conceptualizing racism, 71, 74
   politics of racialized identities, 79–97
   race as social construct, 142
   self, 142–3, 153n
poststructuralism, 71, 74, 212, 391
Potter, Jonathan, 267
Powell, Enoch, 24
Powell, Linda C., 226, 228
power
   in classrooms, 84–6, 88–9
   Foucault, 85, 364
   globalization, 367, 370–1n
   see also domination
power, cultural, 390
power, political, 50
power relations, multiculturalism, 118
power solidarity, among whites, 234–6

Prescott, John, 406–7, 408
Princeton University, 237, 286
Principles of Scientific Management, 327
print media, 53
prison system, 417, 428–9
private clubs, 232–3
private sphere, 256–7
privatization, 412
privilege *see* domination
production relations, racialization, 33–4
professional stratum, 297, 300–1
Project RACE (Reclassify All Children
        Equally), 144
proletariat, 326–7
property, 299–303
Protestant ethic, 362–3
Proudhon, P. J., 330
psychoanalysis, 391, 393
psychopathology, 158
Puar, Jasbir, 200
public sphere, 256–7
public square model, 253–4
Puerto Rican immigrants, 314
Pullman Corporation, 314–15

quadroons, 147, 155n
Quayle, Dan, 56
Quetzalcóatl, 258, 259–60
Qur'an surahs, 113

Rabinow, Paul, 264
race
    and academic performance, 25–6
    as an analytical category, 1–2, 21–7, 30–3
    Angela Y. Davis on, 413–30
    as biological/natural category, 3–4, 5–6, 8,
        19–20, 22–3, 26, 31, 41–2, 48, 142, 146
    and blackness, 219
    British Labour Party, 410
    caste signification of, 325
    citizenship, 107, 254–5, 265
    class, 298, 301–2
    contemporary position, 44–6
    contested meanings of, 47, 48
    cultural politics of, 74
    culture, 158
    as difference, 43–4, 185
    differentiation from racism, 30
    ethnicity, 28, 158
    evolution of, 41
    existence of, 5–7, 20–1, 40–1, 45–6
    fixing of, 7–11
    globalization, 373–5
    hierarchical classifications, 3–4, 7, 150–1,
        265

    ignoring of, 226–7
    lack of neutrality, 39–40
    as a legal notion, 42, 46
    liberal's ambivalent attitude, 90–1
    in literary texts, 225, 226
    mainland northwest Europe, 24
    multiple meanings, 7
    multiracial feminism, 103, 104, 105–9
    notion of purity, 160
    original sense of, 41
    as a political construct, 73
    shifting meanings of, 107
    significance of, 4
    as site of power struggle, 149
    as social category of exclusion
        and murder, 45–6
    as a social construct, 5–7, 30–3, 141, 142,
        143, 149, 185–6, 221
    social reality of, 187
    social science need for concept of, 20
    in the urban economy, 355–68
    US government classifications, 6, 15n,
        144–5, 177
    West on significance of, 20, 26, 29
Race Matters, 19, 29, 34
Race Relations, 22
race relations
    analytical status of, 1–2, 21–7, 30–3
    Britain, 22–5
    contested meanings of, 48
    Los Angeles riots, 1, 34–6
    one-sided view of, 185
    United States, 47–61
Race Relations in Sociological Theory, 22
Race Traitor, 209–10
racelessness strategies, 193
racial, contested meanings of, 48
racial categories, 68–9, 141–57
    colorblind position, 48, 56, 57, 59, 61,
        141–3, 239
    multiracial position, 144–9
    possibilities of deconstruction, 211
racial classifications, 6–7, 15n, 144–5, 177
Racial Formation in the United States, 67, 416
racial segregation, 189, 193
    Loyola University, 94–5
racial symbols, 74
racialization
    class, 33–4, 68–9
    Miles on, 7, 15n, 33, 49, 68–9
    racism, 8, 10, 15n, 27–33
    United States, 10, 27–33, 47–61
racialized barriers, 47, 49–50
racialized discrimination, 52, 61

racialized groups, 49
racialized hostility, 47, 49–52, 55–7, 60
racialized ideologies, 55–7, 60–1
racialized inequality, 50–3, 376
racialized relations, 49, 60
racialized structures, 50–3, 60–1
racism, 7–11, 26–7
  academic performance, 25–6
  Angela Y. Davis on, 226
  anti-immigrant, 10–11, 23, 324, 351
  of Asian-American groups, 162, 165
  Banton on, 22
  benefits to some racial groups, 93
  Britain, 25, 70, 71–2, 265, 326
  capitalism, 414
  class, 66–7, 322–31
  in classrooms, 85, 94
  contemporary conceptualization of, 71–7
  contested meanings of, 47–8
  cultural, 8–10, 71–2, 73
  differentiation from race, 30
  as an essentialist category, 206–7
  feminist organizations, 131, 132
  global capitalism, 347–51
  ideologies, 55–7, 60–1
  as ideology of domination and
  exclusion, 2
  institutionalized, 27, 49, 50–3, 60, 66, 135
  in language, 225
  liberal's ambivalent attitude, 90–1
  Los Angeles riots, 36
  Loyola University, 94–5
  mainland northwest Europe, 24
  Marxism, 65–77
  nationalism, 31, 71
  notion of difference, 43–4
  political context, 50, 60, 66–7
  Princeton University admissions
  policy, 237
  racial categories, 150–1
  racialization, 8, 10, 15n, 27–33
  replacement by cultural
  fundamentalism, 8, 262, 286
  reverse, 54, 57, 195n, 239
  role of the state, 66–7
  scope of concept of, 27–8
  as source of division within
  working class, 66–7
  student social identities, 86
  United States, 27–33, 36, 47–60, 250, 351,
  376–7
  West on, 27–8
  white comments on, 183
  working class, 235, 322

Racism Awareness Training, 207
Racism and Migrant Labour, 68
racist, contested meanings of, 48
racist discourse, 112
rail privatization, 412
Rainbow coalition strategy, 58
Rakatansky, M., 364
Randolph, A. Philip, 314–15
rape, 114–15, 418
Rastafarianism, 211
Rattansi, Ali, 53, 118, 201, 205
Reagan, Ronald, 56, 380
Reagon, Bernice, 429
real estate, 301
  see also housing
Rebérioux, M., 324
reductionism, 69, 392, 394–5
reflective appraisal, 164
reflexivity, 227, 240–1
refugees, Cambodian, 268, 270–80, 287
Reich, Robert, 337, 341–2
Reich, Wilhelm, 324
Reid, Anthony, 202
religion, 277–80
Republican Party, 380, 381
residential segregation, 51
resource distribution, 50, 60
reverse racism, 54, 57, 195n, 239
Rex, John, 22–3, 117
Reynolds, L. T., 30
Rice, Jerry, 53
right-wing movements, colorblind position,
  141–2, 143
riots, Los Angeles, 1, 34–6, 56, 424
rituals, 232–3
Robertson, R., 368n, 370n
Robinson, Cedric, 67
Roc, 55
Rodríguez, Richard, 256–7, 259
Roediger, David, 30, 213
  shaping of white working class, 223, 235,
  266
  white privilege, 150
  white racial identity, 202, 267, 272
  whiteness, 187, 195n, 209, 214
Romero, Mary, 229
Roosevelt, Franklin D., 315
rooting, 121, 123
Rosaldo, Olivia, 258
Rosaldo, Renato, 220, 264, 288n
Rose, Tricia, 52, 54, 211
Rosenberg, Alfred, 44
Ross, Andrew, 211

Rothenberg, Paula M., 90, 105
Rubio, Phil, 210
Ruffié, Jacques, 40, 42
Rumazo Gonzalez, J., 171
Rumbaut, Ruben G., 263, 269, 270, 276
Rushdie, Salman, 76, 117, 123
Russia, 114

Sahgal, Gita, 118
Said, Edward, 265
St. John, E., 87, 96
Salvadoran immigrants, 271, 314, 347, 350
Samuel, Raphael, 408
San Francisco Bay, 268–9, 284–6, 288n
San Francisco Chronicle, 269, 288n
San José, 258, 259–60
San Quentin Six, 417
Sanders, Lynn M., 378
Sandoval, Chela, 105, 418
Sanjek, Roger, 265
Sankofa, 59
Sansone, Livio, 191–2
Sartre, Jean Paul, 162, 421
Sassen, Saskia, 374
The Satanic Verses, 76
Saussure, F., 391, 392, 393, 400
Sayer, Derek, 263, 264
Saynor, James, 200
Scanlan, John A., 270
Scheper-Hughes, N., 7
Schierup, Carl-Ulrik, 115–16
Schlechty, P., 87
Schlesinger, Arthur M., 116
Schooling and Capitalist America, 85
schools *see* education
Schuck, Peter, 249–50, 251
science, as source of value, 341
Scott, Dred, 250
SDS, 422
Seattle, 158
Segal, Daniel, 186, 188
self
    Buddhism, 152n, 153n
    multiracialism, 161
    postmodernism, 142–3, 153n
self-aggrandizement, 227
self-concept, 82
self-esteem, 82, 227
semiotics, 391
Sennett, R., 362–3
separatist strategies, 58
    and womanism, 128
Service Employees International Unions, 315
sexism, 59, 70, 131, 135, 250, 414

sexuality
    monoracial identity theories, 163
    multiracial Asians, 161
    multiracial feminism, 107–8
    womanism, 130
Shange, Ntozake, 126
Shapiro, Thomas M., 50–1, 52, 53
Shaw, Bernard, 53
shifting, 121, 123
Shrader, E., 178
Simon, David R., 54
Simpson, O. J., 52, 53, 54, 61, 183
Singleton, John, 59
Sivanandan, A., 76, 113, 118, 207
skin color, 32, 82
slavery, 250, 265
    anti-miscegenation laws, 147
    binary oppositions, 8
    economic origins, 48
    as form of theft, 299
    Marxism, 65
    representation as inferior races, 325
    Spanish America, 170, 171, 174, 231
    white men's manhood, 231
Small, Stephen
    affirmative action, 61
    black images, 54
    black resistance strategies, 58
    color blind policies, 48
    Color Line, 50
    European Union, 53
    language of race relations, 48
    racialization, 28, 49
    racialized hostility, 50, 52
Smedley, Audrey, 185, 187
Smith, Adam, 341
Smith, Barbara, 130
Smith, M. P., 79, 80, 83, 86
Smith, Rogers, 249–50
Smith, Susan, 10
SNCC, 416, 419
Snipes, Wesley, 53
Snowden, Frank, 202
Social Class in America, 308
The Social Construction of Whiteness, 210–11
social democracy, 406–7
social deviance, 89–90
social processes, ethnic identity, 80–1
social structure, 108
social traits, 41
socialism, state, 337
socialist feminism, 106
Socrates, 84
Solomos, John, 22, 53, 66, 69, 73
Somalia, 53

South Africa, 21, 66
  pigmentocracy, 154n
  racial categories, 6–7, 40, 42
  white supremacy studies, 188–9
Southall Black Sisters (SBS), 119, 122
Southern Negro Youth Congress, 421
Southwest Network for Environmental
  and Economic Justice, 428
Soviet Union, 53, 119, 317, 426
Sowell, Thomas, 27, 28, 54
Sozialitische Deutsche
  Studentenverbund, 422
Spain, aristocracy, 325
Spain, Johnny, 417
Spanish language, 256–7, 259
special needs population, 229–31
Spelman, Elizabeth, 107
Spindler, G., 79
Spindler, L., 79
Spivak, Gayatri, 74, 121, 212, 213
sports, 232–3
Squires, Gregory D., 127
Stack, Carol, 273, 275
Stalinism, 33
Star Trek, 154n
Stasiulis, Daiva, 120–1
state
  racial domination, 66
  role in universalizing citizenship, 263–4
state institutions, control of, 299, 302
Steele, Shelby, 54
Steinberg, Steven, 311–12
Stephan, Cookie, 165
Stetson, B., 27
Stolcke, Verena, 8, 9, 265, 286
Stoler, Ann L., 265
Straits Times, 283
strategic deconstruction, 213
strategic essentialism, 121, 212–13, 403
stratification processes, 164
street etiquette, 192
stroking role, 233–4
structuralism, 391
Structuring Diversity, 288n
Stuart case, 52, 61
student identities, 79–84, 85, 86, 91–2, 94–5,
  96–7
student movement, 413
Student Nonviolent Coordinating Committee
  (SNCC), 416, 419
students, production of knowledge, 88–9
Sturgis, Susanna, 236, 239
subaltern identity, 79
subcontracting, 344–7, 351
Subhan, Nazreen, 213

subordination
  multiracial feminism, 106, 108
  see also domination
Supreme Court, 142, 413
System of Nature, 173

Tagg, John, 368n
Takagi, Dana Y., 288
Tan Kah Kee, 289n
Taney, Justice, 250, 251
Tang-Schilling, Leslie, 286
Tatum, Beverly D., 228, 237
Taussig, Michael, 187
tax system, 50
Taylor, F. Winslow, 327
technology sector, 369n
teenage pregnancies, 275
television, 53, 55
terrorism, 53
Texaco Corporation, 378
Thatcherism, 404, 411
Third World Women's Alliance, 419, 420
This Bridge Called My Back, 419
Thomas, Barb, 206
Thomas, Brooke, 194
Thomas, Clarence, 29, 132, 266, 416
Thornton, Michael C., 161
Time, 52
To Have and Have Not, 230
Tobago, 186
Tocqueville, Alexis Charles Henri
  Clérel de, 34, 39
Tokyo, 371n
Tollefson, J. W., 271
Tomasky, Michael, 222–3
Torres, R., 35
trade unions, 309–10, 314–15, 427
transnational corporations, 53, 340, 362
transportation sector, 369n
transversal politics, 121–3
trickle down notion, 358
Trinidad, 186
Troyna, B., 88
Truth, Sojourner, 131
T'Shaka, Oba, 50, 58, 59
Tsing, Anna Lowenhaupt, 120
Turner, Bryan, 117
Tyack, D., 87

Uhlenberg, Peter, 158
underclass, 193, 267, 270, 363
UNESCO, 23, 24, 42–3, 118
Union Bank, 349
Union of Needle Trades and Textile
  Employees, 315

United Farm Workers, 315
United States
  anti-immigrant behaviors, 10–11
  Asian immigrants, 262, 267, 268–88, 350
  black versus white varying
    perceptions, 375–9
  border with Mexico, 257, 259
  budgetary debates, 374–5
  Cambodian immigrants, 268, 270–80, 287
  Chinese immigrants, 268, 270, 272, 276,
    281–6, 287, 350
  citizenship, 247–51, 254, 384
  Civil Rights legislation, 49, 177
  class, 297–303, 305, 309–10, 311–16, 318
  collective sense of nationality, 308
  concept of whiteness, 203
  consensual politics, 306–7
  culture and ethnicity, 305–8
  dissident traditions, 254–5
  economic growth, 358, 374
  economic recession, 347
  equality of opportunity, 298, 305–16
  ethnicity, 305–21
  exclusion of Italians and Jews in
    1920s, 28
  executive salaries, 300, 301
  garment industry, 300–2, 315, 338, 347–50
  globalization, 373–5
  higher education, 306, 308–9, 318–19, 320
  immigrant assimilation, 90–1, 306–7, 311,
    316
  immigration laws, 177, 247, 250, 282
  impact on "race relations" problem
    in Britain, 23–4
  lack of royalty, 231
  left wing groups, 221–2
  multiculturalism, 116
  national-origins quotas, 247, 250
  nationalism, 370n
  open society doctrine, 305, 316–21
  racial classifications, 6, 15n, 144–5, 177
  racial divisions, 373–84
  racialization, 10, 27–33, 47–61
  racism, 27–33, 36, 47–60, 250, 351, 376–7
  religion, 307
  residential segregation, 51
  subcontracted jobs, 346
  urban racial identities, 82, 190–1, 192
  welfare system, 274–5
  white supremacy studies, 188–9
  see also African-Americans; Asian-
    Americans; Latinos
universities, 306, 318–19
  class diversity, 297–8, 302–3
  democratization process, 408–9

University of California, 57, 269
University of New Orleans, 85
upper-class, white women, 229, 233–4, 235,
  236, 298
urban economy, 355–68
  contested spaces, 362–6
  cultural diversity, 359–60
  dominant economic narrative, 358–60, 366
  globalization, 359, 360–2, 365, 366–8
Urban League, 58
urban pedagogy, 84–9
  antibias pedagogy, 92–5
  boundaries of, 95–7
  politics of difference, 89–92
utilitarian familialism, 282

Valentine, Charles A., 273, 275
Valle, V., 35
value, labor theory of, 338–9, 340–1
Van Deburg, William L., 128, 129
Van den Berghe, P. L., 6, 14–15n, 28
Van Peebles, Melvyn, 415
Varenne, Herve, 184
Vera, Hernan, 52, 61
vertical integration, 345
Vietnam, 337
Vietnam War, 257
Vietnamese-Americans, 158, 159, 268, 270,
  271–2, 276
violence, 10–11, 257, 259
virtual reality, 343
voting rights, 49, 257–8

Wagatsuma, Jo, 159
Waiting: The Whites of South Africa, 189
Waiting to Exhale, 52
Walker, Alice, 126, 127–30, 135–6, 426
Wall Street Journal, 268, 282
Wallerstein, I., 33
Walvin, James, 58
Ware, V., 74, 76
warfare, 114–15
Washington D.C., 52
Washington, Denzil, 53
Washington Post, 376
Watts riots, 36
wealth inequalities, 50–1, 376
Weber, M., 392
Weis, Lois, 226, 228, 230, 236, 237
Wellman, David, 27, 29, 203, 207, 235
West, Cornel, 135, 241
  black nationalism, 27–8
  Los Angeles riots, 34, 35–6
  participatory decision-making, 241
  politics of difference, 90

Race Matters, 19, 20, 26, 29, 34
racialized identities, 81, 82
reflexive theories of
subordination, 227
Westwood, Sallie, 53
Wetherell, Margaret, 267
Wexler, Philip, 80–1, 97
When Work Disappears, 312
White American Resistance (WAR), 56
white confessional literature, 207–9
white culture, 185
White, E. Frances, 134
white ethnicity, 82, 193, 309, 310, 314
white racialness, 187–9, 195n
whiteness
  anti-essentialism, 205, 209, 212–14
  anti-racism, 200–1, 203–14
  benefits of, 148, 150, 156n, 183–5
  as center of the universe, 228–9
  characterizations of, 184
  citizenship, 219–20, 272
  cultural content, 184
  denial technique, 236–7
  distancing technique, 236
  domination and privilege, 184–5, 188–9,
    220–1, 225–41
  establishment of facts of, 183–94
  as ethnic cohesion, 220
  as false victim of black power, 221
  family role, 234–6
  heterogeneity of, 188, 191
  historical duration, 187
  historical geographies of, 209–12
  homogenizing accounts, 194
  ideological coherence, 187–8
  labor of, 219–24
  multiracial Asians, 162–3
  multiracial feminism, 109
  pleasing roles, 233–4
  as a political category, 213–14
  politics of, 75–6
  as the positive universal, 220
  power solidarity, 234–6
  racial identity, 109, 184, 190–3, 201–3,
    209–12, 219–24, 228, 229–31, 314
  reification of, 200–1, 203–7, 228–9
  representation of blackness, 220–1
  rituals/games, 232–3
  sense of belonging, 236
  as special needs population, 229–31
  structural privilege, 238–40
  superiority feelings, 228–9
  ties with blackness, 220
whites
  acceptance of multiracial people, 148–9

American dream, 381–2
economic status, 376
gender relations, 229, 230–1, 233–4
job concerns, 382
middle-class, 192, 310
public policy issues, 377–9
working class, 223, 228, 232, 235, 266, 314
worldviews of, 375–7
Wieviorka, Michel, 1
Wiggins, Cynthia, 183
Wigley, M., 364
Williams, Brackette, 191, 264, 265, 267
Williams, Eric, 48, 325
Williams, Patricia, 143
Williams, Raymond, 391–2, 395, 398, 409
Williams, Sherley Ann, 129, 134
Williams, Teresa Kay, 159
Wilson, H.T., 316
Wilson, Pete, 248, 269
Wilson, William Julius, 27, 56, 95, 312
Wilson, Woodrow, 237, 247
Winant, Howard, 29, 30–3, 67, 142, 419
  citizenship, 265
  civil rights legislation, 416
  hypo-descent rule, 6
  international factors, 53
  race relations, 48
  racial hierarchies, 3
  racialization process, 49
  racialized ideologies, 56, 57
Winfrey, Oprah, 53
Wing, A. K., 27
Wittgenstein, L., 398
womanism, 127–30, 133–6
women
  class-race system, 298
  coalition politics, 121–3, 424–5
  culture, 113–15
  economic status, 131
  health issues, 131, 425
  international solidarity work, 426
  marital and family issues, 131
  monoracial identity theories, 163
  multiculturalism, 119
  as national symbol, 114
  political rights, 131
  in the public sphere, 254
  rape, 114–15, 418
  rights, 254
  social movements, 413
  symbolization of collectivities, 114–15
  transversal politics, 121–3
  unequal citizenship, 254–5
  urban workforce, 358, 366, 367

women *(continued)*
  wife abuse, 273–4
  see also feminism; gender
Women Against Fundamentalism (WAF), 114,
  121–2
Women in Black, 122
women, black, 126–36
  in the academy, 134–5
  black feminism, 27, 127, 130–6, 418
  criminalization of, 414
  diversity among, 126–7
  domestic workers, 315
  resistance strategies, 57–8, 59–60
  role in activist organizations, 415
  womanism, 127–30, 133–6
  writings, 126
women, Cambodian, 273–4, 276–7
Women of Color Coalition on
  Reproductive Health, 425
Women of Color Research Cluster, 419,
  423–4, 425
Women of Color Resource Center, 419, 420,
  424, 425
Women, Race, and Class, 417, 420
Women for Racial and Economic Equality,
  426
women, white
  black feminism, 133
  booster role, 233
  distancing technique, 236
  feminism, 131, 132
  stroking role, 233–4
  upper-class, 229, 233–4, 235, 236, 298
  white solidarity, 235
  womanism, 128–9
women's agency, 108
Women's International Democratic
  Federation, 426
women's studies, 227
Wong, Mun, 226, 228

Wong, Sau-ling C., 55, 289n
Wood, E.M., 33
work cultures, 357
working class, 66–7, 74
  institutional racialization of, 327–30
  racism of, 235, 322
  university students, 297–8
  white, 223, 228, 232, 235, 266, 314
workplaces, 357
A World of Difference, 85
Wrench, John, 53
Wright, Richard, 308
Wu, Gordon, 286

xenophobia, 250, 330
Xiamen University, 289n
Xicanos, 178–9

Yanagisako, Sylvia J., 280
Yeatman, Anna, 118, 121
Yiddish language, 113
Young Lords, 415
Young, R., 74
Young, Robert, 214
Yudice, George, 263
Yugoslavia, 119, 370n
Yuval-Davis, Nira
  ethnicity, 112
  multiculturalism, 116, 117, 118, 121
  racist discourse, 112
  transversal politics, 121
  woman as national symbol, 114
  women as transmitters of culture, 115
  women and warfare, 115

Zack, Naomi, 160
zambos, 173
Zangwill, Israel, 307
Zionists, 113
Zylberman, P., 326